ALLIES AGAINST THE

RISING SUN

Allies against THE Rising Sun

THE UNITED STATES, THE BRITISH NATIONS, AND THE DEFEAT OF IMPERIAL JAPAN

Nicholas Evan Sarantakes

University Press of Kansas

Published by the University Press of Kansas (Lawrence, Kansas
66045), which was organized by the Kansas Board of Regents and is
operated and funded by Emporia State University, Fort Hays State
University, Kansas State University, Pittsburg State University,
the University of Kansas, and Wichita State University

Library of Congress Cataloging-in-Publication Data

Sarantakes, Nicholas Evan, 1966–
Allies against the rising sun : the United States, the British nations,
and the defeat of imperial Japan / Nicholas Evan Sarantakes.
p. cm. — (Modern war studies)
Includes bibliographical references and index.
ISBN 978-0-7006-1669-5 (cloth : alk. paper)

1. World War, 1939–1945—Diplomatic history. 2. United States—
Foreign relations—Great Britain. 3. Great Britain—Foreign relations—United States.
4. World War, 1939–1945—United States. 5. World War, 1939–1945—Great Britain.
6. United States—Military relations—Great Britain. 7. Great Britain—
Military relations—United States. 8. World War, 1939–1945—Campaigns—
Pacific Area. 9. Alliances—History—20th century. I. Title.
D748.S26 2009
940.54'26--dc22
2009027968

British Library Cataloguing-in-Publication Data is available.

Printed in the United States of America

10 9 8 7 6 5 4 3 2 1

The paper used in this publication is recycled and contains 30
percent postconsumer waste. It is acid free and meets the minimum
requirements of the American National Standard for Permanence of
Paper for Printed Library Materials Z39.48-1992.

This book is dedicated to:

Lt. Col. Nick Sarantakes, USA (Ret.)
Lt. Col. John Sarantakes, USA (Ret.)
Maj. Andrew T. Sarantakes, USAR

Col. David E. Thompson, USA (Ret.)
Col. David E. Thompson II, USA
Capt. Jeffery B. Thompson, USA (Ret.)

The Coordinator and Fellows of the 1999
West Point Summer Seminar in Military History

Stanley Adamiak
John Beeler
Thomas Berg
Michael Creswell
Everett Dague
Mark H. Danley
Jeffrey A. Engel
Claude Hargrove
John Harvey
James Isemann
Daniel Kowalsky
John Lavalle
James P. Levy
Thomas D. Mays
Jacqueline McGlade

Salvatore R. Mercogliano
Van Mobley
Sarandis Papadopoulos
Jean Paquette
Galen R. Perras
Jonathan Phillips
Ethan S. Rafuse
Jennifer L. Speelman
Charles Steel
Barry M. Stentiford
Hal Sweet
Larry A. Valero
George N. Vourlojianis
John Weinzierl
Robert P. Wettemann, Jr.

The Students of Seminar 3,
U.S. Air War College, Class of 2005

Col. John "Elwood" Amidon, USAF
Col. Kevin Booth, USAF
CDR Christopher Burkett, USN
Lt. Col. Mark "Last" Chance, USAF
Col. Dennis Crimiel, USAF
Col. Douglas Fehrman, USAF
Col. Michael Kirsch, USA
Lt. Col. Jeff Jackson, USAF

Col. Milan Marek, CAF
Col. Odirile Mashinyana, BDF
Lt. Col. Jonathan "Scott" Phillips, USAFR
Lt. Col. Consuella "Connie" Pockett,
   USAF
Lt. Col. Dave Sutton, USAF
Col. Liu Tung-Hai, ROCAF
Col. Christopher Valle, USAF

and to the memory of

Cpl. Pat Tillman, USA
(1976–2004)

Contents

Acknowledgments

One of my favorite parts of any book is the section where authors thank those who helped them produce their work. My interest in these sections has something to do with my interest in my own professional development as a writer. Although the author is the only person with his or her name on the book, writing is far more of a collective exercise than most people think. Publishers, editors, graphic design artists, and copyeditors all significantly influence the final product on matters ranging from the font used in the book to the design of the dust jacket.

Before a book ever gets to those stages, an author needs to produce a manuscript, a task that is easier said than done. The origins of this particular project go back to 1999. Two important events took place during that summer that played an enormous role in the development of this book. As far as the chronology goes, the second event was my participation in the British Studies program run by the University of Southern Mississippi. My then home institution, Texas A&M University–Commerce, under the leadership of Kenneth "Rock" Clinton, was part of a USM consortium that offered and continues to offer undergraduate courses in London. The Faculty Development Committee of A&M University–Commerce, mainly due to the efforts of "Rock," awarded me one of their International Studies Grants to observe a course. I audited the class that Andy Wiest of USM taught on World War II. This course introduced me to the British Public

Record Office, now the British National Archives. With someone else paying for a month in London, I decided I should make use of the opportunity and do some research for an article about British participation in the planned invasion of Japan. I found a gold mine of material and realized that I could get two, and then three, articles out of this topic. When I got to four, I decided that I should write a book.

Andy ran his course in a very creative and innovative manner. He brought in a number of British scholars to give guest lectures on various topics about the war. One of them was Gary Sheffield, then at the Royal Military Academy, Sandhurst, and now at the University of Birmingham. While we were both doing research at the Liddell Hart Centre for Military Archives, he suggested that I look at the papers of The Earl Mountbatten of Burma at the University of Southampton. (Several years later, he mentioned an article about the British Pacific Fleet that proved useful in the relevant chapters.) Andy wrote a letter of introduction to the archivists at the university. One of my most frustrating travel experiences in the United Kingdom was trying to get from the train station in Southampton to the grounds of the university, but it was worth the effort, and an effort it was. I quickly found an exceptionally important memo that Mountbatten wrote about his meeting with Douglas MacArthur in 1945. Without their support, I would have never found this document and am profoundly grateful for their assistance.

The month before I went to London, I spent four weeks as a Fellow at the West Point Summer Seminar in Military History. That time in New York was probably the most important event in my academic career. The seminar combined a distinguished speaker series, a graduate school readings course, and a teaching workshop with a series of staff rides. I learned a lot; those four weeks were like taking another field of study in graduate school. The scheduled events of the seminar were informative and useful and made one think about the issues that scholars must confront. More important than the formal events in the program was the social bonding experience of the seminar. The thirty Fellows assembled nightly in the parking lot of the hotel where we shared drinks and ideas, getting to know one better. We continued on with our discussions from earlier in the day in an informal setting that was often more informative and rewarding than the formal sessions. We also slowly became a close network of peers with shared professional interests.

Fellow alumni of the 1999 West Point Summer Seminar have supported me in numerous ways in this project. Galen Perras, now of the University of Ottawa, shared documents, advice, and information. He is working on a study of Canadian participation in the Pacific theater, and it is my hope that this account steals nothing from his argument. Sal Mercogliano was one of the sharpest individuals in our seminar (he had just passed his qualifying exams before arriving at West Point). Some comments he made in passing at the 2000 Society for Military History conference were important in helping me understand the strengths and weaknesses of the British Pacific Fleet. He also shared his knowledge about the role of logistics in World War II and pointed me to relevant works on the topic. Randy Papadopoulos, now of the Naval Historical Center, was very supportive. He twice (in 2002 and 2003) offered me a place to stay while I was on research trips to Washington, D.C. This support was significant because A&M–Commerce has little funding to provide to its faculty for research and travel. The second stay was particularly generous because he was away on a trip to California and trusted me with free run of his home.

A huge thanks must go to another veteran of the West Point summer. Larry Valero, now of the University of Texas at El Paso—previously of the University of Salford in the greater Manchester metropolitan area—was responsible for getting me a CAMPUS (Campaign to Promote the University of Salford) Fellowship in the spring of 2004. The European Research Studies Institute and the School of English, Sociology, Politics and Contemporary History at Salford provided an intellectual home that facilitated further research and writing. At the time, I worked at a school with a heavy teaching load, and I am profoundly grateful for the release that this fellowship offered. Toward the end of my stay, Salford sponsored a research symposium on this study. A number of people traveled across the United Kingdom to attend: Richard Aldrich of the University of Nottingham, Saki Dockrill of Kings College London, Martin Alexander and Douglas Ford of the University of Wales (Aberswyth), Jeremy Crang of the University of Edinburgh, Antony Best of the London School of Economics, Max Jones of the University of Manchester, and Eric Grove of the University of Hull. Gerry Wyant, Paddy Griffith, Armin Krishnan, Chris Garwood, Matthew Hughes, Nikolas Gardner, and John Keiger, all from Salford, were also present. I have no idea if the symposium was a profitable experience for them, but I found it an exceptionally useful meeting. Scholars are usually asked to give talks about studies they have already published. In many cases, they have already moved on to other projects.

The people at this gathering offered exceptionally good advice and suggestions that I was able to incorporate into my ongoing research efforts. The net result is that this study is much, much stronger thanks to their comments.

Mark Stoler of the University of Vermont was one of the distinguished guest speakers at the West Point Summer Seminar. He was the commentator on a panel at the 2000 Society for Historians of American Foreign Relations annual meeting when I presented an early version of one chapter. He made several comments about questions that I needed to answer and where I could find the papers of several members of the U.S. Joint Chiefs of Staff. His remarks were some of the most useful I have ever received at an academic conference.

I met my intellectual grandfather, Ernest May (he was my dissertation advisor's advisor), at another conference, and he suggested that I take a look at the MacEachin study on signal intelligence. Roger Dingman, my dissertation advisor, has been a constant source of advice. He also suggested the Willmott study on British naval planning.

In the history department at A&M–Commerce, my colleagues were particularly supportive. The head of the department, Judy Ford, wrote several letters of recommendation—often at the last minute—for grants and some modest release time from our fairly heavy teaching responsibilities. Peter Messer made a number of comments on early drafts of articles that became chapters.

Meredith Hindley of the National Endowment for the Humanities put together the panel that brought Stoler and me together. She also offered me some good advice on doing research in the United Kingdom, which despite the shared language, is a foreign environment for an American researcher.

In 2001, I traveled to New Zealand to do some research and then some snow skiing. Leo Clayton of the New Zealand National Archives generously allowed me to make photocopies of some very important files, saving me a good deal of time, which was all the more precious given the distance and expense required to travel to Wellington. In Christchurch, Campbell Craig arranged for me to give a talk at the University of Canterbury. This study involves five nations, and although all are English-speaking, each enjoys its own history and culture. The opportunity to converse with students and scholars interested in international affairs was particularly important in getting different perspectives that have helped inform this study.

As this study grew from an article to several articles to a book, I have had to return to London four additional times. London is extremely expensive and the currency exchange rate makes it even more so for an American. My sister's good friend, Kelly McCourt, helped reduce my expenses during two of these trips with a free place to stay in her small apartment. Like Randy Papadopoulos, she was exceptionally kind in letting me stay at her place while she was on a business trip of her own. Despite such assistance, I still managed to spend over £200 in incidental expenses in three days. It is a pricey city.

Randy Papadopoulos, Galen Perras, Mike Creswell of Florida State, Group-Captain Nigel Huckins of the Royal Air Force, H. W. Brands of the University of Texas, and Robert J. Rabel of Victoria University of Wellington in New Zealand read earlier versions of this study. Robert Coram of the *Atlanta Journal-Constitution* and biographer of the legendary Col. John Boyd read an early proposal for this book and made several useful comments that were on the mark and arrived at the right moment.

I never met the legendary Barbara Tuchman, but her book *The Guns of August* has had a profound influence on me. I first read this book when I was in the sixth grade. It was beyond me then, but I have often reread it in the years since. I constantly read the book while I was writing this one, studying her elegant style and structure. If I have produced something half as good as what she wrote, I will be most satisfied. Roger Dingman and Richard Frank deserve special thanks. Both read this manuscript when the marketing department of this press asked them to write an endorsement quote. They did so, but then went the extra mile and alerted me to errors in the manuscript. Frank provided a five-page evaluation of the manuscript and places where I needed to do revisions, some minor, others more than minor. Some of the mistakes he found were quite embarrassing, and I am deeply grateful they came to my notice before rather than after this book went to print.

I kept notes on the assistance extended to me on this project, but if I have forgotten someone I apologize for the slight. It was not intended, really. I would never have gotten to this point without the kindness of others and they have in many ways made this project stronger. Any weaknesses that remain are despite rather than because of this assistance for which I am truly grateful. These types of remarks seem standard in works of nonfiction, but having written now five books or unpublished manuscripts, I can tell you that they are accurate.

Laptop computers are wonderful inventions. They have allowed me to continue writing this account even when I was traveling. I find that this book is truly a transnational history, having been written not only all over North America, but in various parts of the United Kingdom and Europe. I referenced a number of books while I was writing on both sides of the Atlantic. Those checking my footnotes or wishing to pursue their own research should be aware that there are often differences between British and American editions, mainly in page numbering.

This book is dedicated to fifty-two people. That might seem like a lot of people, but I have learned from all of them and want to honor each for such. With these comments, I hope you enjoy this read.

NEΣ

Summer 2008

Atlanta, Georgia
Augusta, Georgia
Commerce, Texas
Houston, Texas
College Station, Texas
Arlington, Virginia
Virginia Beach, Virginia
College Park, Maryland
Manchester, England
Glasgow, Scotland
Edinburgh, Scotland
London, England
Stuttgart, Germany
Montgomery, Alabama
Newport, Rhode Island

■

A Note on British Titles, Spelling, and Japanese Names

A word or two is in order about how British titles and Japanese names are rendered in this book. The system and styles of British titles can be confusing even to people who live in the United Kingdom. Below the royal family are five separate hereditary titles of nobility. In descending order they are as follows: duke, marquess, earl, viscount, and baron. Titles are usually, but not always, inherited through the male line, and the wife of a nobleman receives the appropriate female title as a courtesy. An individual can often become a baron on a nonhereditary basis. People so honored are called life peers, and the title becomes extinct when they die. Dukes, marquesses, and most earls usually have a title that represents a geographic location; for example: the Earl of Halifax. Louis Mountbatten was an exception to this pattern, keeping his name when he became The Earl Mountbatten of Burma. Viscounts and barons in the British system follow this pattern of having a title before the geographic region that their title represents; for example: Viscount Portal of Hungerford. Most of the people involved in this account took the family names as their titles in a fashion similar to Portal. Some of these individuals, however, chose to take titles other than their family name. Sir Alan Brooke became Viscount Alanbrooke of Brookeborough and Sir Anthony Eden became the Earl of Avon.

The British designation "Lord" is used in two ways. In many cases,

Lord is a general title that applies to peers below the level of duke. So, instead of using the long title of Viscount Portal of Hungerford, one can simply call him Lord Portal, and the Earl of Avon becomes Lord Avon. Lord is also a courtesy title awarded to the children of high-ranking nobility, usually dukes, marquesses, and earls. As the son of a marquess, Mountbatten was Lord Louis Mountbatten, but not Lord Mountbatten. He became Lord Mountbatten only when he became a peer in his own right.

Many individuals have several titles over the course of their lifetime. For example, the Earl of Halifax was Lord Irwin before he became Lord Halifax. In this case, he was awarded a title in his own right before he inherited the title Viscount Halifax of Monk Bretton from his father, and then later became an earl. In most cases, though, the reason that peers have several different titles and names throughout their lives is that these titles go to the heirs to a higher title much as the Prince of Wales is the title that goes to the heir to the throne. For example, Churchill's cousin and close friend, Charles Spencer-Churchill, was the Earl of Sunderland, then the Marquess of Blandford, before he became the Duke of Marlborough.

Knight is the lowest rank in the British nobility and is nonhereditary in nature. The title of "Sir" accompanies a knighthood, and the proper way of referring to a knight is as Sir Andrew Cunningham or Sir Andrew, not Mr. Cunningham or Sir Cunningham. Military ranks precede all titles of nobility, for example, Admiral Sir Andrew Cunningham.

In this book, an individual's full title is given at the first appearance in the narrative, and thereafter, "Lord" is used; for example: the Earl of Halifax, with subsequent references to him as Lord Halifax. The notes and bibliography had the potential to become quite complicated because several individuals wrote memoirs after receiving their titles and some, like Cunningham, used their full titles, while others, like Ismay, simply wrote using the general prefix of Lord. In order to have some uniformity that the reader will understand, all authors with a title of nobility are cited by their full title the first time they appear in the notes. In the notes that follow this first reference, they receive the simple title of Lord. In the bibliography, individuals appear under the name of their title. As a result, Brooke and Eden will be found under Alanbrooke and Avon, respectively.

Japanese names are also confusing to a Western audience. In Japan, the family name precedes the personal name, and it is in that order that they are rendered in the text; for example: Admiral Yamamoto Isoroku and then after, simply Admiral Yamamoto. Since many publishers used the Western order of personal name first, family name second, for their Japanese authors, an exactly opposite system appears in the notes mainly for the sake of clarity and uniformity.

Acronyms

ABC	Andrew Browne Cunningham
a/c	aircraft carrier
AEF	American Expeditionary Forces
AIF	Australian Imperial Force
BBC	British Broadcasting Corporation
BDF	Botswana Defence Force
BEF	Bonus Expeditionary Force
BPF	British Pacific Fleet
CAF	Czech Air Force
CAS	Chief of the Air Staff
CIGS	Chief of the Imperial General Staff
C in C	Commander-in-Chief
CINCAFPAC	Commander-in-Chief, U.S. Army Forces Pacific
CINCPAC	Commander-in-Chief, U.S. Pacific Fleet
CINCUS	Commander-in-Chief, U.S. Fleet
COMINCH	Commander-in-Chief, U.S. Fleet
COS	Chiefs of Staff (British)
CTF	Carrier Task Force
D.C.	District of Columbia
ETO	European Theater of Operations
FDR	Franklin Delano Roosevelt

F.O.	Foreign Office
GCM	George C. Marshall
GHQ	General Headquarters
HB	Heavy Bombers
HIJMS	His Imperial Japanese Majesty's Ship
HM	His Majesty
HMCS	His Majesty's Canadian Ship
HMNZS	His Majesty's New Zealand Ship
HMS	His Majesty's Ship
HSH	His Serene Highness
MP	Member of Parliament
NCO	Non-Commissioned Officers
NZ	New Zealand
NZEF	New Zealand Expeditionary Force
PM	Prime Minister
RAAF	Royal Australian Air Force
RAF	Royal Air Force
RAN	Royal Australian Navy
RCAF	Royal Canadian Air Force
RCN	Royal Canadian Navy
RMS	Royal Mail Ship
RN	Royal Navy
RNZS	Royal New Zealand Ship
ROCAF	Republic of China Air Force
ROTC	Reserve Officer Training Corps
SEAC	South-East Asia Command
SMS	Seiner Majestät Schiff (German: His Majesty's Ship)
SWPA	Southwest Pacific Area
TF	Task Force
UK	United Kingdom
U.S.	United States
USA	United States Army
USAAF	United States Army Air Forces
USAF	United States Air Force
USAFR	United States Air Force Reserves
USCOS	United States Chiefs of Staff (Joint Chiefs of Staff)
USN	United States Navy
USS	United States Ship

VC	Victoria Cross
VLR	Very Long Range
VMI	Virginia Military Institute
W	Winston (Churchill)
WD	War Department

Introduction:
Truman's Funeral

The weather was right for a funeral. The gray winter sky was growing dark and the temperature was keeping pace with the sun as it dropped. It would soon be raining. Workers were lowering a light-colored mahogany coffin covered in a blanket of red carnations into the ground. At the head of the grave was a wreath of red, white, and blue flowers that Richard Nixon, the president of the United States, had placed next to the coffin. The man in the casket was one of his predecessors, Harry S. Truman, a failed haberdasher and small-town Missouri farmer before entering politics.[1]

Truman was also the last of the great British and American leaders of World War II. Two U.S. presidents and two British prime ministers, along with their Chiefs of Staff, had met in places like Malta, Quebec, Cairo, and Casablanca. Now, all of them were gone. Franklin D. Roosevelt even before the war ended. Winston Churchill in 1965, at 90 years of age, a hollow and feeble remnant of the great man he had once been. Clement Attlee, Churchill's wartime deputy and political rival, who replaced him as prime minister, died in 1967 as The Earl Attlee of Walthamstow. At all these meetings, the Chiefs of Staff had accompanied Roosevelt and Churchill, Truman and Attlee. These generals, admirals, and marshals had been some of the most powerful, influential, and well-known men of the war. Admiral of the Fleet Sir Dudley Pound and Field-Marshal Sir John Dill died before victory. Dill's successor as head of the British Army, Sir Alan Brooke, lasted

1

until 1963. Admiral of the Fleet Sir Andrew Browne Cunningham, known to the Royal Navy simply as ABC, went that same year and like any good sailor was buried at sea. Marshal of the Royal Air Force Sir Charles Portal, the Chief of the Air Staff, remained until 1971. All three of the British Chiefs were viscounts at the time of their deaths. Portal and Cunningham had taken their family names as their titles, but Brooke had merged his names into one and was known as Lord Alanbrooke.

Their American counterparts departed even sooner. General of the Air Force Henry H. Arnold, plagued with heart attacks during the conflict, lasted less than five years after the war, dying in January 1950. Fleet Admiral Ernest J. King lived longer, at least on paper. A stroke in 1947 decimated his health, and he spent the rest of his life in hospitals before his death in 1956. Unlike the other wartime Chiefs, Fleet Admiral William D. Leahy continued to serve Truman in the same post well after the end of the war. The oldest of all the Chiefs, American or British, he died in 1959. General of the Army George C. Marshall, the only Chief to attend all the wartime summit meetings, went three months later. His body simply collapsed from age and heavy use.

Truman had been one of these men. During his first five months in office, he had been one of the leaders of the great coalition of English-speaking powers that fought and won World War II. His health had been bad for the past few years, but it declined rapidly in early December 1972 and he went into the hospital one last time. He held out until December 26, and then he was gone. He was 88 years old. His body lay in state at his presidential library for a day. The first person to pay his respects was another former president, Lyndon Baines Johnson. He arrived with his wife, Lady Bird, and their two daughters and their husbands, but they stayed for only half a minute. Nixon and his wife, Pat, arrived half an hour later and presented their wreath. The crowd outside broke into cheers and applause when they saw the president. The reception clearly put Nixon at unease. It was a funeral, a somber occasion. His trademark awkward smile and wave were, for once, appropriate. The Nixons stayed for a minute and then went to the Truman residence a few blocks away to express their condolences to the family. Half an hour after they departed, the Johnsons arrived. Both parties stayed for roughly fifteen minutes.[2]

After the two presidents left, the library opened up, allowing average citizens to pay their respects. A line formed shortly after Nixon's departure that eventually became a mile long. A spokesman for the Fifth U.S. Army,

Funeral of a President. Harry S. Truman was buried in a simple, short ceremony in the courtyard of his presidential library. He was the last of the great British and American leaders of World War II. Courtesy of the Truman Presidential Library

the organization handling the arrangements for the state funeral, later estimated that 75,000 people passed by the coffin during the hours the library was open. Each person had no more than sixty seconds in front of the casket. Some waited as long as six hours in the cold.[3] "We were admirers of President Truman's years and years back," a 78-year-old woman said, explaining her wait until 3:30 A.M. "I think it's a privilege just to be able to come." James J. Hoffman of Kansas City had gotten Truman's autograph at a barbershop. "I didn't really pay much attention to the guy in the next chair. Then he gets up and puts on his glasses and it's the man," he told a reporter from the *Kansas City Star*. He had to wait into the early morning hours as well. "I'd stand in line for about three days," he said. Dan Newby, a 19-year-old resident of Independence, like many Americans, had little interest in history, but that attitude changed after listening to a radio special on his town's most famous resident. The Truman story impressed him. "You might say I'm paying my first and last respects." People from the entire Kansas City area trekked to the Truman Library. "We wanted to be here," Gwendolyn Neas of Overland Park, a suburb on the other side of the Kansas-Missouri state line, remarked. "He's one of our own."[4]

Editorial praise for Truman rolled in from across the country. Given the circumstances, it is hardly surprising that most of the comments were positive. "Harry Truman was quintessential middle America," an editorial in the *Christian Science Monitor* stated. The editors of the *Philadelphia Inquirer* wrote, "What he lacked in charisma he made up for in courage." Similar views appeared in the South. "President Truman had the old virtues that made this country great. He was straightforward. He was determined. He was tough minded," the editorial board of the *Atlanta Journal* declared. The editors of the *Sun* in Baltimore proclaimed: "Harry S Truman had the touch of greatness as President, and one of the qualities that made him great was the way in which he kept the common touch." In California a headline in the *San Francisco Chronicle* called him "A Mighty Man from Missouri." Another one in the *Boston Globe* read: "A Good and Courageous Man."[5]

Some of the highest praise came from publications that had voiced negative views about him during his residence in the White House. The editors of the *Wall Street Journal* noted that the paper had been quite critical of him in earlier years. "Yet now, these 20 years later it grows increasingly hard to remember what Harry Truman did wrong, and increasingly hard to dispute that he did most of the big things right."[6] Perhaps the most famous image of Truman's presidency came the night he won the 1948 presidential election and he held up a copy of the *Chicago Daily Tribune* that declared: "DEWEY DEFEATS TRUMAN." The editorial board later stated, "It was not one of our proudest moments." In 1972 the chairman and publisher of the paper, Harold Grumhaus, had planned to make amends to Truman. He had a plaque made with a replica of that front page and the photograph, and an engraved message that declared his "admiration and affection" for the former president. Grumhaus had hoped to give the plaque to Truman as part of the paper's 125th anniversary, but the decline in Truman's health prevented this gesture. Grumhaus said it was his hope "to have this famous incident closed on a note of candor and respect."[7]

The *Washington Post* is never a friend of any president or administration, and Truman was no exception. He, however, tarnished his own reputation in 1950 when he wrote a letter in which he threatened the music critic of the paper with bodily violence after a harsh and negative review of an operatic performance that First Daughter Margaret Truman gave at

Constitution Hall: "Someday I hope to meet you. When that happens you'll need a new nose, a lot of beefsteak for black eyes, and perhaps a supporter below!" His rage and frustration had boiled over. The war in Korea was going badly and his press secretary, Charlie Ross, a friend from his youth, had died the day before. Truman's opponents exploited the outburst. The editors of the *Chicago Daily Tribune*, in the days before their "admiration and affection" for Truman, questioned his "mental competence and emotional stability." The letter was more a matter of sound and fury than an issue of long-term significance, and the editorial tribute to the late president that appeared in the *Post* noted his strengths and weakness in a way that made him appear all the more human: "Diffidence and doughtiness, humility and self-confidence, vulgarity and grandeur were mingled in this solid, unpretentious man, a seemingly typical product of small-town politics in middle America." While noting that he was "able and conscientious" in the Senate, these journalists remarked that he had been no star during his tenure in the upper chamber. Others had been more significant and influential. "Yet when immeasurable responsibility was suddenly thrust upon him against his honest wish and will, he found within himself the resources to meet the task honorably and, indeed, greatly." Still, Harry S. Truman was hardly a saint. He was a working politician. "And he understood with unblurred realism that specific gains in American political affairs are achieved by leadership which embraces not only an imaginative appeal to the aspirations of a free people but also the crasser arts of political influence, pressure and manipulation." He had excelled in life without losing himself to fame, glory, or power, and on the whole, "Harry Truman showed his countrymen what they were made of and what they could become."[8]

The service was short and, according to one reporter covering the event, "simple nearly to the point of being spare." A small crowd of roughly 250 gathered in the auditorium of the library. The event, however, was televised live on national television. The Truman family sat on the stage near the casket, but behind a green screen to shield them from the cameras. The Rev. John H. Lembecke, Jr., pastor of the Episcopalian church where the Trumans had married years before, officiated using the Book of Common Prayer. He then made way for W. Hugh McLaughlin, grand master of the Masons of Missouri—a post Truman once held—who started, "Our brother by adoption. He was our companion by choice." The Rev. Harold Hunt, pastor of the First Baptist Church, followed, offering a brief prayer.

Truman had wanted his funeral to be simple and had helped plan the service. He got his wish. The function was over in thirty-four minutes.[9]

The graveside service was an altogether different matter. The burial of a president of the United States is never a private, little affair. The courtyard of the library was full of people. Military pallbearers slowly escorted the flag-covered casket to the grave. The Fifth U.S. Army band stood in formation and played "Ruffles and Flourishes" as Lieutenant General Patrick Cassidy, the commander of the Fifth U.S. Army, escorted the family to their places. The gusty, cold wind had the U.S. and presidential flags near the coffin snapping on their poles. Guests slowly assembled along the sides of the courtyard. Truman's old unit from World War I, Battery D, 1st Battalion, 129th Field Artillery, Missouri Army National Guard, its howitzers arrayed on the south lawn of the library, fired off a 21-gun salute. The smoke from the guns rolled over the lawns and mixed in with the gray sky. The reverberations startled Truman's grandsons. Bess Truman began to tear up, but kept her composure. Three volleys of musket fire followed and a trumpeter played the sorrow-laden notes of "Taps." After the pallbearers finished folding the flag, Cassidy gave it to Mrs. Truman: "This flag is presented to you on behalf of a grateful nation." She accepted the flag and handed it to her daughter, who was standing next to her. The sorrow etched on their faces reflected their stages in life. Bess Truman was sadly resigned to her loss, Margaret Truman Daniel's grief was painful and emotional, and the former president's grandchildren were confused and terrified. After the benediction, family and guests filed out. Within an hour of the service, the grave was closed and a fine but cold rain had started to fall.[10] Harry S. Truman was gone.

Truman's life now belongs to the annals of history. His presidency is well studied and for good reason. The use of the atomic bomb, the occupations of Germany and Japan, the onset of the Cold War, a failed health care program, the Fair Deal, the Marshall Plan, the Truman Doctrine, the Berlin blockade, the creation of the Central Intelligence Agency, the institution of a peacetime draft, the desegregation of the military, the creation of the North Atlantic Treaty Organization, the Korean War, and the conformation with Douglas MacArthur were some of the issues he wrestled with while in office. His event-laden presidency makes him a rich topic for historical investigation. His actions and decisions had enormous influence on American society in the decades that followed his stay in the White House. Indeed, Truman and Ronald Reagan are the two most significant occupants of the executive mansion in the second half of the twentieth century, because of the strong and enduring nature of their legacies.

One of the biggest of these controversies, and in fact one of the biggest in American history, is how World War II ended in the Pacific. For decades most attention focused on the use of the atomic bombs over Hiroshima and Nagasaki. This understandable focus has made it easy to ignore many other factors at work in bringing this conflict to a conclusion. Bringing the fighting to an end was an exceptionally complex business.

Alliance politics were an important factor in this story, and one topic that has seen little investigation from historians is Truman's success at preserving the wartime coalition Americans enjoyed with other world powers. The most important relationship the Americans had was with the United Kingdom and the British nations of the Commonwealth. Coalition warfare has been an important part of the U.S. presence in world affairs. Throughout the twentieth century, Americans have gone to war allied with other nations. There is every reason to believe that this trend will continue as the twenty-first century progresses. Prior to the 1940s, though, the American experience with coalition warfare was not a particularly happy one. Americans and Filipinos were in deadly combat with each other when the United States replaced the Spanish in the Philippines rather than giving the islands their independence as the rebels wanted. The alliance between the Americans and British did not come to such a brutal end after World War I, but come to an end it did despite common interests in preserving the peace settlement. One of the first issues that Truman confronted when he came into office had enormous repercussions on the larger issue of U.S. relations with its allies in the postwar period: the role that the United Kingdom and the other British nations would play in the defeat of Imperial Japan.

This account attempts to answer three major questions related to British participation in the closing stages of the Pacific war: Why did the United Kingdom wish to take part in the invasion of Japan and other operations in and around the home islands? Why did the Commonwealth nations wish to contribute, given that political sentiment among their people favored starting the demobilization process and that many of their leaders believed that their countries had made a contribution to victory that was proportionally far in excess of the major powers? Why did the United States agree to British and Commonwealth participation in these operations, when these foreign units displaced American ones that had greater firepower?

The answers to these questions form the central argument of this book.

Worried about a future in which history might repeat itself, high-placed individuals in both the United Kingdom and the United States believed that if there were to be any hope of postwar cooperation between their two countries, then His Majesty's Government had to contribute to the decisive operations in Japan itself for the good of both countries. If the British spent their time trying to reclaim colonies lost to the Japanese early in the war, or if they focused their attention and energy on demobilization, the general expectation in both Washington and London was that the American people would turn against Great Britain as they had done in the 1920s. The leadership in the various Commonwealth Dominions decided to support the mother country in service of their own ambitions, but also to bolster the power and prestige of the United Kingdom, which was still a major force in the lives of these nations. Policy makers and strategists in both Washington and London, particularly those in uniform, realized that the war was a cooperative effort that had to service many interests, not just those found in their own capital. The British proposed and the United States agreed to their participation largely for political reasons. The considerations involved in these decisions were substantial and involved long-term interests rather than being petty or selfish, as the term "political" implies on occasion.

Another key mission is to present the historical actors in this drama as what they were—human beings with real lives and emotions, living and working under some of the most trying of conditions imaginable. There is all too often a tendency in the historical profession to present individuals in the past as plaster figures devoid of their humanity and who know or should know the outcome of the events they faced. While people reading and writing history usually know how the story ends, those living it rarely do. The political and military leaders who led the war effort in Washington and London were amazingly talented and able men. There is much we can learn from their managerial and leadership techniques in response to trying conditions in which they worked that only enriches the story. Theater and battlefield commanders like Dwight D. Eisenhower and Sir Bernard Montgomery have received a good deal more attention than their superiors—Marshall and Brooke—men who clearly had greater responsibilities. This presentation should bear witness to what these two Chiefs and many others did in their national capitals and give them the public attention that is their due.

It is crucial to note that the British struck several blows at the Japanese as the war came to a conclusion. The British Pacific Fleet saw combat in Japanese waters and, as we will see, gave a good account of itself. More significantly, few people in Washington or London foresaw the war ending as soon as it did. Negotiations between the armed services of the two Atlantic powers took place. Arrangements and plans went forward. The talks are important because they tell us much about the nature of U.S. relations with the British world at this time and how the war ended.

A more reasonable question might be why we need another book on the end of the Pacific war. Ronald H. Spector, the first civilian historian to serve as the Director of Naval History for the U.S. Navy, observed that the atomic bombs have "inspired a mountain of writing so immense as to dwarf the total literature devoted to all other aspects of the conflict."[11] He is right. The amount of work done on this matter is extensive.[12] This state of affairs has changed a bit since the end of the Cold War. In preparation for, as well as in response to, the fiftieth anniversary of World War II, individuals began to examine other aspects of the final days in the Pacific theater. Free from the ever-present concern of global thermonuclear war that shaped much thinking on this matter up to 1989, writers have moved beyond the atomic bomb and examined strategic planning,[13] public opinion,[14] intelligence operations,[15] the consequences of unrestricted submarine warfare,[16] the conventional strategic bombing of Japan,[17] and various aspects of the planned invasion of the home islands.[18]

The surrender terms the Allies offered the Japanese are another topic that many have explored even if most of the work is older in nature.[19] There have been several significant works presenting the Japanese perspective to an English-language audience.[20] We have even seen novelists enter into the debate with several "what if" novels that have the invasion actually taking place.[21] This book is different from all these works in that it places the end of the conflict into an international context, but one in which Washington was the main pivot point.

This account seeks to also add to the study of U.S.-British relations. Works in this field since the 1970s have, in varying degree, focused on the conflict between the two English-speaking allies and have questioned the uniqueness of their "special relationship," with the film *Patton* perhaps being the best-known manifestation of this trend.[22] Studies of the English-speaking coalition in Asia have been few in number and these books have continued to emphasize the disputes in the partnership.[23] While all of these individual studies have been accurate on an individual basis, their collective emphasis has produced a misleading picture. The disputes between the Americans and the British were often minor echoes of the confrontations that took place within His Majesty's Government. Much more importantly, one might wonder how the Americans and British were ever able to defeat their enemies given all the time they spent squabbling with one another. Historians have exaggerated the importance of many differences that were nothing more than honest disagreements about the best policy option. The Americans and the British both realized their fates were tied together. In the end, we should remember that their partnership worked much better than the one among the Germans, Italians, and Japanese.

This story starts twenty-eight years before the funeral in Missouri and fifteen months before Truman came into office. As the fourth year of the war ended, Winston Churchill, First Minister to His Majesty King George VI, and the Chiefs of Staff Committee began one of the most intense arguments on strategy that took place in the war. The dispute had for a time the potential to bring down Churchill's government, and before it was all over would involve Roosevelt, Truman, the U.S. Joint Chiefs of Staff, while far-off battles like Okinawa would alter the course of debate. The issue: what effort should the British make to the final defeat of Imperial Japan?

ONE

∎

ABC Comes to Whitehall

In 1943 Admiral of the Fleet Sir Dudley Pound, First Sea Lord of the Royal Navy, died. He worked almost until the end, as a brain tumor slowly did its work, and resigned a few days before his death. His demise was significant because it brought Admiral of the Fleet Sir Andrew Browne Cunningham, or ABC as he was known in the navy, to Whitehall. Cunningham's presence on the Chiefs of Staff Committee changed the personal dynamics between the Chiefs and their political master, Winston Churchill, and led to a major clash over the war in the Pacific.

Cunningham was a good sailor and preferred duty at sea to the staff work he found in London as head of his service. "I felt a great joy in being at sea again," he reflected on his trip to assume command of the Mediterranean Fleet at the start of the war, "steaming at high speed in perfect weather to what I have always considered is the finest appointment the Royal Navy has to offer."[1]

Cunningham was a short man with bright blue eyes, a ruddy complexion, and badly discolored teeth that kept him from smiling. His father was a Scottish physician and professor of anatomy at the Royal College of Surgeons of Ireland and then Trinity College, Dublin. Cunningham, as a result, was born in Dublin in 1883.[2]

There was no military or seafaring tradition in his family, but in 1897 Cunningham joined the Royal Navy as a naval cadet following a suggestion from his father. In the testing to determine those that the service accepted that year, he placed fourteenth out of sixty-five. He had just turned 14 years old, and the navy would be the main focus of his adult life. He earned the nickname "Meat Face" as a naval cadet, indicating he settled many differences with his fists. He had almost no social life as a young officer. While his peers would use their leaves drinking and whoring, he would spend his time sailing, or like a true Scotsman, playing golf. He had few possessions, lived aboard ship, and had a family life only indirectly through his nieces and nephews. His main hobby outside the service was fishing. He also liked dogs, dirty stories, and—much later in life—gardening.[3]

Cunningham did well in the navy. When war broke out in 1914 he was a lieutenant-commander in command of the *Scorpion*. Cunningham and his ship were part of the British force that hunted SMS *Goeben* and SMS *Breslau*, trying and failing to keep them from reaching refuge in a port of the Ottoman Empire. The two German ships helped bring the Turks into the war. The *Scorpion* also took part in the naval effort to force open the Dardanelles Straits. Cunningham had little faith in the operation: "It sounded just too easy." When that effort failed, Cunningham's ship was part of the naval force that supported an amphibious assault on the Gallipoli peninsula. Cunningham was there at the end, providing naval gunfire that helped thwart a Turkish advance, saving the lives of many soldiers as the British Army withdrew. "So ended the Dardanelles campaign, a failure but a very gallant one," he observed later.[4]

Despite this setback, Cunningham had a good war. He ended the conflict with the rank of Commander and was shortly thereafter promoted to Captain. Many people wanted to avoid serving under him, though. He could be quite abusive toward his subordinates, addressing his junior officers as "Oh *miserable* Sub, what *are* you doing!" or "You young devil!" It was not uncommon for him to have his officers sent to their quarters under arrest. He was a shrewd judge of character, though, and many officers thrived under his harsh reign. "I knew that ABC was a friend who trusted me and who, if need be, would stick by me through thick and thin," one sublieutenant placed under arrest recalled. "I loved serving under him." After the war, another junior officer on the ship noted: "Cunningham had three favourite phrases, frequently repeated, which have remained ingrained in my mind down the years. 'Duty is the first business of a sea officer,' 'NDBGZ (No Difficulty Battles Great Zeal),' and 'Intelligent anticipation must be your watchword'—not bad principles for any walk of life."[5]

His last command of a ship was the battleship *Rodney*, and a week after taking the helm, he married Nona Byatt. Both were marrying for the first time, but he was 47 and she was 40, and their efforts to start a family failed.[6]

After leaving this sea duty, he became Commodore of the Royal Naval Barracks, Chatham, and in 1932 became a rear-admiral in the Mediterranean Fleet. Despite his rank, Cunningham was still in the marrow of his bones a sailor. He was truly in his element leading ships at sea. "I watched this absolute wizard handle 36 ships entirely by himself," Lord Louis Mountbatten, a naval officer serving in the fleet, remarked. "In spite of his rather red and watery eyes he always saw everything first." Mountbatten knew he had seen a master at work: "It was the greatest one-man performance I have seen on the bridge of a ship." When the war started in 1939, Cunningham was a Knight Commander of the Order of the Bath, held the rank of Admiral, and was the new Commander-in-Chief of the Mediterranean Fleet. He was the only one of the Chiefs to earn wide acclaim as a combat commander. The admiral was twice the feature of *Time* magazine cover stories. Cunningham's attitude toward recognition and fame was complex. He required and wanted little public attention, but he could become quite sensitive about the honors of others when he thought they were unjustly rewarded or their acknowledgments slighted him in some fashion.[7]

Early in the war in an effort to weaken the British in North Africa, the Italian and the German air forces attempted to sink supply convoys at sea and destroy the British garrison at Malta. Cunningham's response came in November 1940. Planes flying from the aircraft carrier HMS *Illustrious* attacked the Italian fleet at the naval base of Taranto, dropping bombs and torpedoes on them. The raid incapacitated three of the five battleships in the harbor. The British planes also did extensive damage to a cruiser, destroyers, and oil storage facilities on land. In response, the Italians moved their fleet further north to Naples. This action conceded a good deal of power in the southern Mediterranean to the Royal Navy. Since Cunningham tended to underestimate the value of airpower and was not one to clamor after acclaim, he failed to appreciate the actions of his pilots and recognize them with appropriate combat decorations. The awards the navy gave to personnel in this operation were limited. Cunningham later admitted he made a mistake.[8]

In March 1941 in an effort to wrest control of the Mediterranean from the British, the Italian Navy sailed out to sea. The Germans were planning to launch an offensive against the British, and the Italians initiated maritime operations in an effort to support their allies. The Italians wanted to attack British convoys, but they were also giving the Mediterranean Fleet another opportunity to hit them. Cunningham took advantage of this opportunity between March 27 and 29 in what became the Battle of Matapan. In a surface engagement between two fleets, Cunningham used aircraft and radar to spot the Italians and then catch them unprepared. The British sank three Italian cruisers and two destroyers and heavily damaged a battleship. The biggest result of the battle, though, was that the Italians were reluctant to fight the Royal Navy again. The British needed such intimidation. Following German attacks on Greece and then Crete, the navy had to extract the army from the beaches. The Germans enjoyed air superiority, and their land-based aircraft were pushing the Mediterranean Fleet to its limits. Ships were operating for two months straight without any stay in port for repair or maintenance. Crews were exhausted, and deaths from minor enemy actions were undermining combat effectiveness. At one point, the fleet amounted to all of two battleships, one cruiser, two antiaircraft cruisers, one minelayer, and nine destroyers. Cunningham called these evacuations "a period of great tension and anxiety such as I have never experienced before or since." When Mountbatten, who captained a ship in the fleet, asked him about this period, Cunningham replied: "I felt like going out on a destroyer into the thickest of the bombings and getting killed."[9]

Cunningham spent 1942 in Washington, D.C., as the head of the British Admiralty Delegation. It was not a happy experience. He had to deal regularly with Admiral Ernest J. King, the Chief of Naval Operations for the U.S. Navy. "He was abominably rude," Cunningham reported.[10]

At the beginning of 1943, he was promoted to the highest rank in the navy, Admiral of the Fleet, and shortly thereafter returned for another stint as Commander-in-Chief, Mediterranean. It was only the second time in the long history of the Royal Navy that a man had held this command twice. He also served as naval deputy to General Dwight D. Eisenhower during the allied assault on North Africa and in the invasions of Sicily and Italy. The British, concerned about Eisenhower's lack of experience, had insisted on a committee system that delegated a good deal of authority to deputy air, ground, and sea commanders. "The American papers said it looked as if Eisenhower was to be the stooge and that the Tunisian campaign was to be run by Alexander, Tedder and Cunningham," the admiral noted. "Which is what happened." Cunningham, however, kept such condescending views private. In the interests of allied unity, he proved a loyal and cooperative partner. When Italy capitulated, though, he insisted that the Italians surrender their fleet to the Royal Navy. He sent a cable to the Admiralty that invoked the lineage of Nelson: "Be pleased to inform Their Lordships that the Italian Battle fleet now lies at anchor under the guns of the fortress of Malta."[11]

When Cunningham arrived in Whitehall, he joined two other men on the Chiefs of Staff Committee. The chairman and leader of the Chiefs was General Sir Alan Brooke in his role as Chief of the Imperial General Staff. The head of the British Army was extremely intelligent, highly perceptive, and analytical but also high-strung and almost neurotic. He masked his feelings well. After reading Brooke's published diaries, Baron Moran of Manton, Churchill's personal physician, wrote that he had no "inkling until now that that the highly strung, sensitive, apprehensive creature we meet in the diaries was most days pulling long faces behind the iron mask he presented to the world." The general moved and talked at a fast pace, which reflected his personality as much as it did the demands of war. "Hurry, man, hurry," he would tell generals as he encountered them in hallways of the War Office. He had amazing talent for a profession that he loathed, and religion offered him comfort from the evil that he oversaw.

I am not a highly religious individual according to many people's outlook. I am however convinced that there is a God all powerful looking after the destiny of this world. I had little doubt about this before the war started, but this war has convinced me more than ever of this truth. Again and again during the last 6 years I have seen His guiding hand controlling and guiding the destiny of this world toward that final definite destiny which He has ordained.[12]

Brooke came from an English family that had settled in the Irish province of Ulster and first made its name defending the crown's authority during the great Irish rising of 1641. Alan Brooke was the youngest child of Sir Victor Brooke, the third Baronet of Colebrooke, who died when his son was eight. Although a knight of Ireland, Alan Brooke was a son of France as well. He was born in 1883 in Bagnères-de-Bigorre, a small town in the Pyrenees mountains, and he spent much of his youth in France. As an adult, he was bilingual in French and English.[13]

Despite his continental upbringing, Brooke followed family tradition and joined the army in 1902. In 1908, he proposed to Jane Richardson, a neighbor. Since he had few financial resources of his own, the engagement stayed unofficial for six years. They married in July 1914, and six days later the army cancelled his leave and honeymoon as Europe marched to war.[14]

World War I allowed Brooke to thrive in a professional sense. He started the war as a Lieutenant, ended it as a Lieutenant-Colonel, and won the Distinguished Service Order. An artilleryman, Brooke developed his professional skills during the conflict. "We had made great progress in the coordinated control of artillery," he commented later. "We were, however, still obsessed with the idea that the total destruction of all enemy defences must be achieved before the attack." He thought the real offensive role of the artillery was the suppression of the machine gun and artillery fire that the enemy used to defend against offensives designed to breach their trench lines.[15]

The 1920s were to be a time of great professional advancement, private sorrow, and then personal joy for Brooke. He was a Brigadier by the end of the decade. In 1925, though, the worst incident in his life occurred, when he and his wife were out driving on a wet road. A bicycle rider turned across the road, forcing Brooke to hit the brakes. The car skidded and then overturned. He broke several ribs and a leg, but his wife was paralyzed and eventually died from pneumonia following surgery. "I very much wish I could have been finished off myself at the same time," he stated two years later. His son and daughter, neither more than eight years old, needed him, but they only reminded him of their mother. "I feel ashamed of myself for not having done more for them at a time when they quite unknowingly made life much more difficult." Brooke tried to find some comfort in his job, but it was only in 1928 when he met and fell in love with Lady Benita Lees that he escaped the pain. Lees was a widow, and both found in the other something that they had lost. "I am continually marvelling at my completely transformed outlook on life generally due to your existence, the increased interest in everything and the complete *joie de vivre* which I had entirely lost." They married before the end of the year.[16]

When war came in 1939, Brooke was a general and the army gave him command of II Corps, and under him that unit managed to escape at Dunkirk.[17] Shortly after his return to England, he became Commander-in-Chief, Home Forces. In this position, he was responsible for thwarting the expected German invasion of the United Kingdom. "The idea of failure at this stage of the war is too ghastly to contemplate," he observed.[18]

In November 1941, Brooke receive an invitation to visit the prime minister at Chequers, his official country estate. After dinner, Churchill offered him the job of leading the British Army. "It took me some time to reply as I was torn by many feelings." Churchill, wondering about Brooke's silence, asked, "Do you not think you will be able to work with me? We have so far got on well together." Brooke quickly replied, explaining his hesitation. The prime minister left the study, giving the general some time to think. He kneeled down and prayed for guidance. "There is no doubt I was temporarily staggered by the magnitude of the task I was undertaking." Great Britain was alone without any true allies, facing a foe that controlled all of the European continent. He accepted, but was up well past 4 A.M. tossing and turning as he thought about the demands and responsibilities of his new position.[19]

Three months after becoming the Chief of the Imperial General Staff, Brooke also assumed the position of chairman of the Chiefs of Staff Committee when Pound stepped down to focus on his job of leading the Royal Navy. On V-E Day, Brooke recorded in his diary the role that he and the other Chiefs had played in the war: "The whole world has now become one large theatre of war, and the Chiefs of Staff represent the Supreme Commanders, running the war in all its many theatres, regulating the allocation of forces, shipping, munitions, relating plans to resources available, approving or rejecting plans, issuing directives to the various theatres." This work involved a good deal of diplomacy, as he explained. "And most difficult of all handling the political aspects of this military action, and co-ordinating with our American allies. It is all far less spectacular than the winning of battles by commanders in the field, and yet if the COS makes any errors the commanders in the field will never be in a position to win battles."[20]

Once he had selected his commanders, he would support them without reservation until they proved themselves inadequate to the task at hand. He also tolerated no questioning of his authority, making it clear to the commanders in the field who had seniority in the chain of command. He could be extremely harsh to subordinate generals. On the other hand, he was approachable to junior officers. "I'm new to this," he told one of the Joint Planning Staff before his first meeting of the Chiefs of Staff Committee. "If you see me making a fool of myself, say so!" He rarely attended the social events that accompanied the various allied conferences. He was also not one to wallow in ambiguity. He was clear in the military advice he gave to Churchill even when it conflicted with the prime minister's creative ideas. Churchill appreciated his input: "Brooke was the right man—the only man."[21]

The other member of the committee that Cunningham joined was Marshal of the Royal Air Force Sir Charles Portal. The marshal had a dark complexion, a large nose that many called "beak-like," and thinning hair that he parted to the side. He came from a family of prominent French Huguenots that could trace its history back to the year 1094. After arriving in England, the Portals adapted well to their new homeland and spent the 180 years until Charles Portal's birth in 1893 as comfortable members of the middle class. Throughout his life, Portal was called Peter despite the fact that it was never one of his given names. He attended private school (or what the British refer to as public school) and then went on to the University of Oxford. His academic education came to an end in 1914 with the outbreak of World War I. He enlisted in the British Army as a motorcycle courier with the rank of Corporal. Assigned to the headquarters of I Corps, the work of a motorcycle courier was grueling during the early, fluid days of the conflict. Portal got stuck behind enemy lines once, was in an artillery barrage that knocked him back through the doorway of a house that he had just left, and never got more than four hours of sleep at a time. While he was assigned to drive behind the staff car of General Sir Douglas Haig, General Officer Commanding of I Corps, he fell asleep and rear-ended the general's vehicle when it stopped. Despite this incident, Haig recommended Portal for an officer's commission, which he received. When the war moved to its static stage, the work of a motorcycle courier became rather boring and Portal asked to be seconded to the Royal Flying Corps. He started off as an observer, helping the artillery of the British Army find their targets. Later, as the technology of British planes improved and the air service acquired new missions, Portal became a pilot. An essay he wrote while a student at the Royal Air Force's Staff College during the interwar period says much about his approach toward command and his view of himself as an officer during World War I: "The element which is most strikingly common to Cromwell, Nelson and Garibaldi, is physical

Churchill and the Chiefs. This photo was taken in the garden at 10 Downing Street on V-E Day, May 7, 1945. Front row from left to right: Marshal of the Royal Air Force Sir Charles Portal, Chief of the Air Staff; Field-Marshal Sir Alan Brooke, Chief of the Imperial General Staff; Winston Churchill, Prime Minister of the United Kingdom of Great Britain and Northern Ireland; Fleet Admiral Sir Andrew Cunningham, First Sea Lord and Chief of the Naval Staff. Second row: Major General Leslie Hollis, Secretary to the Chiefs of Staff Committee, and General Sir Hastings Ismay, Chief of Staff to the Minister of Defence. Courtesy the Imperial War Museum

courage. Great moral virtues are, no less than vices, contagious, and there can be no doubt that the bravery of these men inspired their followers with that contempt of personal danger which is the first attribute of the fighting man."[22]

Toward the end of the war, Portal met Joan Welby, a wealthy and stunningly attractive young woman from a well-connected family. It is no surprise that she had the highly fortuitous dilemma of having a number of suitors. After she met Portal, she told her sister: "I think my problems are solved." Portal proposed the day the war ended after taking her up in his biplane. Eight months later, the two wed in Denton just outside Manchester. The ceremony was a major social event sprinkled with nobility. Of all the Chiefs on either side of the Atlantic, Portal married the best. Not only was the marriage to Joan Welby a good career move on Portal's part, the two were by all accounts honestly in love with one another. The Portals had two daughters. Joan Portal kept her looks as she aged, and Portal—never a handsome man—grew older with distinction. The only mar to this happy home life was that one of their daughters had cerebral palsy, which would be a source of concern and worry for the Portals for the rest of their days.[23]

Portal's military career advanced nicely in a fashion that clearly marked him for high command. After his wedding, he received a permanent commission in the new Royal Air Force. He attended the new service's Staff College and was the commanding officer of No. 7 Squadron. After turning over command of this unit, he turned himself into a legend. On a return visit on the squadron's sports day, he won the officers' footrace running in his socks. He was also one of the first officers of the air force to attend the Imperial Defence College, where he and Cunningham were classmates. He was the pilot on ABC's first plane trip, but it made little impact on the operational thinking of the future admiral.[24]

Although he was the youngest of the Chiefs, Portal had seniority over Brooke and Cunningham as a member of the Chiefs of Staff Committee. A number of people who worked with him during this period used the words "calm," "cool and detached," or "charming" to describe him. Every member of the Combined Chiefs of Staff (the U.S. Joint Chiefs of Staff and the British Chiefs of Staff meeting as a collective group) considered Portal the smartest of them all. After the war, a friend asked Sir Hastings Ismay, Churchill's chief of staff, to name the greatest commander the Allies had during the war. "It isn't a difficult question to answer at all," Hastings responded. "The answer is Peter Portal—*quite easily.*" Ismay's lieutenant, Sir Leslie Hollis, thought along similar lines. Portal, he said, was a "calm character with a brain like a rapier." One British staff member noted that Portal had the personality that was "best understood by the Americans." Brigadier Ian Jacob, military assistant secretary to the War Cabinet, noted in a diary he kept at the Casablanca Conference that "his greatest asset is his unshakeable honesty of thought and deed. They know he knows his stuff and they trust him one hundred per cent." He had other talents, as Jacob noted: "He also gave you the impression of being exceedingly honest and unprejudiced—fair-minded. And this is where the Americans thought so much of him—He was a very good influence in the Combined Chiefs of Staff."[25]

Testimony from the other side of the Atlantic confirms these views. General Henry "Hap" Arnold, Portal's American counterpart, noted in his diary during a visit to England where they met for the first time: "Portal is a brilliant man who does things, is capable and knows his job." General George C. Marshall, chief of staff of the U.S. Army, observed that Portal had "the best mind of the lot."[26]

Even Churchill thought along these lines. "Portal has everything," he told Lord Moran.[27] Sir Noel Hall, an official of the Ministry of Economic Warfare, attended a number of meetings with the Chiefs of Staff in 1940 and 1941 and noticed that the quality of the discussion improved noticeably after Portal arrived.[28]

Portal had only a few recreational outlets. Perhaps it was appropriate for the head of the British Royal Air Force that he liked to go hawking. He also liked to fish. During the war, like other soldiers, he would muse about his life after his service ended as a way to escape from the troubles of the moment. He thought about living in a cottage in Scotland on £300 a year and spending his time fishing. Like many of the Chiefs, American and British, Portal was a chain smoker. Photograph after photograph shows him holding some type of tobacco product, but he was generally partial to the pipe.[29]

These three men, extremely distinctive in personality and representing armed services with significantly different interests, bonded as professional colleagues and even as friends in the truest sense of that word. Portal and Brooke had a shared interest in birds, and all three fished. One staff officer recalled finding the three chiefs studying a small object. "The object which they found so engrossing was a particularly repulsive looking bait called the 'Bleeder,' which looked to me like an imitation prawn. The 'Bleeder's' special merit was that when immersed, it gave off a red fluid which presumably attracted its intended victims." In fact, the Chiefs of Staff talked about their hobby so much that their secretariat jokingly referred to fishing as "Item No. 1 on the Agenda."[30]

The Chiefs understood that they had to work together not only in the face of their German enemies and their American allies, but their civilian master. "I take away with me," Portal told Brooke, what I know will be an enduring memory of your friendship and of what I learned from you. I can honestly say that I have an unbounded admiration for the way you handled our COS affairs and for the forcefulness and complete sincerity and the clearsightedness and soundness with which you always dealt with Ministers on our behalf—no one could ever hold a candle to your record in that respect and it was about the biggest factor in getting results.[31]

Brooke thought the same way. "I had the greatest admiration for Peter's ability," he observed after the war, "not only in connection with the air where he was superb, but in all other matters we had to deal with."[32] He had similar views about Cunningham. "I found him first and foremost one of the most attractive of friends, secondly a charming associate to work with, and finally the staunchest of campaigners when it came to supporting a policy agreed to amongst ourselves, no matter what inclement winds might be brought to bear on it."[33]

Cunningham's opinions of his colleagues were no less positive. He thought Brooke one of the best soldiers Great Britain had ever produced. In his memoirs he stated: "Straight, absolutely honest and outspoken, he was outstandingly able in his difficult and most responsible position. Though impulsive at times, he always spoke out fearlessly and fluently against what he knew to be wrong." He also had kind words for the head of the air force.

> Charles Portal is an exceptional man, eminently able, calm and not easily to be roused. When I first met him as a fellow student at the Imperial Defence College, years before, I realized he was destined to rise to the top of his Service. He and I had many a difference of opinion; but it never engendered any hard feelings. I shall always treasure his friendship and admire his great qualities.[34]

The "inclement winds" that bore down on the Chiefs in their struggle to define strategy for the war against Japan came from Winston Spencer Churchill. The prime minister was born in 1874, two months premature—an accident induced early labor—at Blenheim Palace, the estate of his grandfather, the Duke of Marlborough. Churchill's schoolboy days were rather unhappy. He called them "a somber grey patch on the chart of my journey." He could joke about it in later days, though: "I am all for the Public schools, but I do not want to go there again."[35]

His academic preparation was such that it took Churchill three tries to pass the entrance exam for the Royal Military College, Sandhurst, and then only after taking an intensive preparatory class. He entered the college in September 1893 and received a commission in the 4th Hussars in February 1895. His first military assignment sent him to India. In 1898 he joined the 21st Lancers after much lobbying to join its expedition into the Sudan. There he participated in the cavalry charge at the Battle of Omdurman.[36]

Churchill soon decided that the best way he could make a name for himself would be in the political arena. "If I had two lives I would be a soldier and a politician," he told his mother's sister. "But as there will be no war in my time I shall have to be a politician." He saw the path of a politician as a reputable way for a man of good breeding to make his mark on society, but his political career started with a setback. It took him two tries before he entered the House of Commons on February 14, 1901. With a few notable breaks, he would spend the rest of his life in Parliament, and the reason was simple: he was in his element. "Asking me not to make a speech," he remarked after nearly thirty years in the Commons, "is like asking a centipede to get along and not put a foot on the ground."[37]

When Sir Henry Campbell-Bannerman became prime minister, he offered Churchill a junior cabinet post as Financial Secretary to the Treasury. He turned this position down, asking instead for assignment as Under-Secretary of State at the Colonial Office, even though this position ranked lower than the one he had been offered. He wanted this position, because the Colonial Secretary, the Earl of Elgin, was a member of the House of Lords and as a result, the Under-Secretary would answer for the department during questioning in the House of Commons. Campbell-Bannerman agreed, and Churchill became a member of the government. When Herbert Asquith replaced Campbell-Bannerman he made Churchill President of the Board of Trade. He was 33 and in the Cabinet.[38]

Churchill's greatest political asset was his wife, Clementine. She offered him political advice that was sound and that he ignored at his own risk on several occasions. They first met at a ball. "Winston just stared," she later said. "He never uttered one word and was very gauche—he never asked me to dance, he never asked me to have supper with him." Nearly four years later, he got another opportunity and this time he got things right.

The two spent the weekend chatting and strolling about the countryside. The emotion between them was genuine, as Churchill explained to Clementine's mother: "I am not rich nor powerfully established, but your daughter loves me & with that love I feel strong enough to assume this great & sacred responsibility; & I think I can make her happy & give her a station & career worthy of her beauty & her virtues." The courtship lasted only five months, and the wedding took place in St. Margaret's, Westminster, the parish church of the House of Commons.[39]

After the election of 1910, Asquith thought Churchill deserved a promotion and offered him the Irish Office. Churchill declined this position, asking instead for either the Admiralty or the Home Office. He got both jobs. Asquith had him replace Herbert Gladstone, son of the legendary nineteenth-century prime minister William Gladstone, at the Home Office. Then in 1911, Asquith made him First Lord of the Admiralty, the civilian Cabinet officer overseeing the Royal Navy. He would hold this position for four years, giving it up only after the disastrous Gallipoli campaign of World War I.[40]

In 1914 Churchill took a strong stand that Great Britain had vital interests at stake even before German troops invaded Belgium. "Afterwards by participating in the peace we can regulate the settlement and prevent a renewal of the 1870 conditions," he told David Lloyd George in a Cabinet meeting. A letter he wrote to Clementine captures his mood at the time: "Everything tends towards catastrophe & collapse. I am interested, geared up & happy. Is it horrible to be built like that? The preparations have a hideous fascination for me. I pray to God to forgive me for such fearful moods of levity. Yet I would do my best for peace, & nothing would induce me wrongfully to strike the blow."[41]

Churchill was no warmonger, but he never flinched from the demands of his job, knowing that hesitation and uncertainty were deadly now that the fight had arrived. He was equal to the challenge that faced him and his nation. "I claimed and exercised an unlimited power of suggestion and initiative over the whole field, subject only to the approval and agreement of the First Sea Lord on all operative orders," he explained after the war. His hard work impressed many. The *Times* declared that of the members of the Cabinet he was the one "whose grasp of the situation and whose efforts to meet it have been above all praise." Admiral of the Fleet Baron Fisher of Kilverstone, who served as First Sea Lord during the war, declared, "His power of work is absolutely amazing."[42]

Yet it was a bold and innovative move that nearly destroyed his political career. With the trench war in northeastern France deadlocked, British leaders looked for strategic venues other than northwestern France where the United Kingdom could strike at Germany. An idea that gained popularity in the War Cabinet was to force the Dardanelles Straits, seize control of the Gallipoli peninsula, and capture Istanbul, the capital of the Ottoman Empire. This move would knock the Turks out of the war, allow the British to get supplies to the Russian Army more easily, and make southeastern Europe a threat to the security of the Central Powers. The problem with this plan was that Churchill wanted the Royal Navy to try to knock out the Ottomans on its own. He was not alone in thinking this plan would work. The Earl Kitchner of Khartoum, the Secretary of State for War, had a low opinion of Ottoman soldiers and thought they would run in terror once they came under naval bombardment. Such was not to be. On March 18, a force of ten battleships, six British and four French, entered the straits, but six either sank or suffered heavy damage after running afoul of Ottoman mines. The British Army then tried to take the peninsula with an amphibious assault. Despite picking some of the worst terrain imaginable for such an operation, British, Australian, and New Zealand troops came close to breaking out of the beachheads. It was the valiant effort of the Ottoman defenders and the incompetence of British commanders that turned Gallipoli into one of the worst military disasters in World War I.[43]

The Dardanelles campaign had repercussions back in London when Admiral Lord Fisher resigned as First Sea Lord. He was upset about the possibility that the navy might lose more ships in another effort to force the straits. He wrote a letter of resignation addressed to Churchill without ever discussing the matter with him and then disappeared. Churchill and Asquith found it hard to believe that the senior uniformed leader of the navy had simply walked off the job, but that was exactly what he had done. Fisher made sure that the political opposition knew about his move, which made parliamentary investigation of either the conduct of the war or the Gallipoli campaign a possibility. Such a development would cost people their positions in the Cabinet and perhaps even their political careers. The most vulnerable was Churchill. Depressed that his longtime affair with a cousin of Clementine Churchill's was coming to an end, Asquith flinched and decided to ask the Conservatives to join the Cabinet in a national coalition government. He had to give the newcomers some good offices, and since the First Lord was in an exposed position, the prime minister decided that the head of the navy had to go. "I am finished," Churchill remarked at the time. His wife later said, "I thought he would die of grief."[44]

Taking political hits on his right and left, Asquith resigned as prime minister in 1916. After a month of maneuvering, Lloyd George formed a new government. The new prime minister was an old friend and a political ally of Churchill's, but he was unable to include him in his new Cabinet. He had to wait until July 1917 before he could offer to make Churchill the Minister of Munitions. Churchill would hold this position for the rest of the war. A month after the war, Lloyd George's coalition won the election and the prime minister asked Churchill to take over the War Office. In 1921 he went to the Colonial Office.[45]

The election of 1922, though, was a disaster for Churchill. Recovering from surgery, he was unable to travel or do any campaigning until just before election day. Churchill went down to defeat. "In the twinkling of an eye I found myself without an office, without a seat, without a party, and without an appendix," he noted with a certain perverse humor. He eventually regained a seat in Parliament, representing a constituency in Epping. Then, Stanley Baldwin, the new prime minister, asked him if he would join the Cabinet as Chancellor of the Exchequer. Churchill thought to himself, "Will the bloody duck swim?"[46]

Churchill held this office for five years until Labour gained control of the government in 1929. Churchill kept his seat in the House of Commons but was out of the Cabinet. It would be ten years before another prime minister asked him to serve as a Minister of the Crown. What is best remembered about Churchill's wilderness years is not his antidemocratic stand on India or his moral blind eye to King Edward VIII's affair with a married woman, but his early and uncompromising stand against Nazi Germany. As early as 1933, he stated in public, "There is grave reason to believe that Germany is arming herself, or seeking to arm herself, contrary to the solemn treaties extracted from her in her hour of defeat." Churchill's views were out of step with those of most British subjects at the time. The public was looking not to the future but to the past and wanted to avoid seeing bloodshed and suffering on the scale of World War I.[47]

It was only after World War II started that the public began to appreciate the wisdom of Churchill's early stand against the Nazis, and Prime Minister Neville Chamberlain asked him to join the government. "It's the Admiralty," he told Clementine after the meeting. "That's a lot better than I thought." He was 64 years old at the time. After Churchill returned to the Cabinet, an old political foe wrote him a letter apologizing for opposing him on the German issue. Churchill's response was generous: "As far as I am concerned the past is dead." Sir Samuel Hoare, the Lord Privy Seal, remarked to a supporter about Churchill, "I should say that at the moment he is the one popular figure in the Cabinet."[48]

Given Chamberlain's strong identification with the policy of appeasement, it was highly likely that he would leave office now that war had come to pass. It was the military and naval failures in Norway, though, that finally brought down his government. In the eyes of many, Chamberlain was responsible for the current state of affairs, having been prime minister during the immediate prewar years. This perception boded ill for him when the House of Commons debate, or the "inquest on Norway," as many people called it, began on May 7. Clement Attlee, leader of the Labour Party, stated, "Norway comes as the culmination of many other discontents. People are saying that those mainly responsible for the conduct of affairs are men who have had an almost uninterrupted career of failure. Norway followed Czechoslovakia and Poland. Everywhere the story is 'too late.'" The most devastating statement came from L. S. Amery, a longtime political ally of the Chamberlain family. Toward the end he found himself "going on to an increasing crescendo of applause"; he turned toward the prime minister and quoted the words Oliver Cromwell delivered to the Long Parliament 300 years earlier: "You have sat too long for any good you have been doing. Depart, I say, and let us have done with you. In the name of God, go!" On the second day Labour called for a division of the House of Commons. The Conservative majority of 213 had fallen to 81, but Chamberlain had survived, at least on paper. As the results were announced members of Parliament began singing "Rule Britannia" and others began shouting "Go! Go! Go! Go!" at the prime minister as he left the chamber.[49]

With many in his own party turning against him, Chamberlain knew his days at 10 Downing Street were over. He resigned, and on May 10, Churchill became prime minister. In his first speech to Parliament in this new post, he projected the confidence and realism that would be characteristic of his wartime statements: "I would say to the House, as I said to those who have joined this government, that I have nothing to offer but blood, toil, tears and sweat." He also made it clear that this war was one that was much starker than those that had come before it: "You ask, what is our aim? I can answer in one word: It is victory, victory at all costs, victory in spite of all terror, victory, however long and hard the road may be; for without victory, there is no survival." These comments hit the right mark for a public wanting strong, commanding leadership.[50]

Three years later it became clear that Sir Dudley Pound was nearing his end. He suffered a stroke and told Churchill that he needed to find a replacement for him. He then died on October 21, Trafalgar Day, which had appropriate symbolism. When First Lord of the Admiralty A. V. Alexander pushed Cunningham as Pound's successor, Churchill refused. Alexander continued advancing the admiral's cause, but detected what he perceived as "Churchill's fear of the Board of Admiralty" and another Fisher. He made this view clear when he accepted ABC. "All right," the prime minister rumbled. "You can have your Cunningham, but if the Admiralty don't do as they are told I will bring down the Board in ruins even if it means my coming down with it." On October 3, he reluctantly offered Cunningham the job, which the admiral quickly accepted. Cunningham soon regretted this decision. He found the pace at Whitehall slow. The admiral also found that he had "an inherent difficulty in expressing myself in verbal discussion." Since he was out of his element as an administrator and since allied naval supremacy was no longer an issue at this point in the war, Cunningham found himself supporting the more intellectually gifted Portal and the more vocal Brooke in Chiefs of Staff meetings rather than offering his own ideas. Still, his presence did change the personal dynamics of the Chiefs. With him on the committee instead of the fading Pound, Brooke had the backing he needed to challenge the exceptionally strong personality of their political master, much as Churchill feared. Portal was usually not one to challenge the prime minister, but even that changed.[51]

It was the alteration in the personal relationship among these four men that came close to destroying Churchill. The Chiefs of Staff would consider using the same tool that Lord Fisher used to bring down Churchill one war before: resignation. How an issue that paled in comparison to most of the matters over which the Chiefs had disagreements with Churchill during the war is the next part of this story.

T W O

■

Churchill versus the Chiefs

Brooke, Portal, Cunningham, and Churchill faced a number of serious issues throughout the war. The fact that the policies they developed resulted in the deaths of their own soldiers, even if in a successful operation, is powerful testimony to the weight of the matters they confronted. The job of deciding who lives and who dies made for exceptionally stressful circumstances. The most contentious matter that these men handled turned out to be the formulation of what role the United Kingdom should play in the Pacific war after the defeat of Germany. This dispute over strategy came close to costing the Chiefs their jobs and bringing down Churchill's government. With the power of hindsight, these arguments might seem trivial; but the participants had no way of knowing the outcome. Both sides took strong, uncompromising positions because they thought the future of Great Britain was at stake and that the strategy the other was advocating put the future of the realm at risk.

The origins of this confrontation started at the 1943 conference that Churchill had with Roosevelt in Cairo, Egypt. At that summit, the Combined Chiefs of Staff developed a strategy for defeating Japan. This group decided that "the main effort against Japan should be made in the Pacific." Operations in all other regions should have the ultimate mission of helping the allied forces "obtain objectives from which we can conduct intensive air bombardment and establish a sea and air blockade against Japan, and from which to invade Japan proper if this should prove necessary." Planning officers working for the Combined Chiefs believed that nine months after the defeat of Germany, the British could contribute a force of four divisions to what would ultimately become the invasion of Japan. The Royal Navy had the ability to play a bigger role with a force that included a battleship, nine or ten aircraft carriers, six cruisers, sixteen fleet destroyers, twelve frigates, and numerous support ships. The British Pacific Fleet would operate alongside the Third and Fifth Fleets, the main forces of the U.S. Navy. Both Roosevelt and Churchill initialed the final report of the Combined Chiefs of Staff.[1]

The Chiefs began work on informing the Dominions about this decision. After the war, Brooke explained that British participation would serve the interests of the United Kingdom in several ways.

> I felt that at this stage of the war it was vital that British forces should participate in direct action against Japan in the Pacific. First of all, from a Commonwealth point of view, to prove to Australia our willingness and desire to fight with them for the defence of Australia as soon as the defeat of Germany rendered such action possible. Secondly, I felt it was important that we should cooperate with all three services alongside of the Americans in the Pacific against Japan in the final stages of this war.

Bringing the war to a rapid conclusion would also help Great Britain avoid a manpower shortage crisis that appeared likely to develop if the war continued on into 1946.[2]

Churchill, however, had different ideas. He wanted British soldiers to rebuild the British Empire, and an important task in doing that was retaking Singapore and avenging the humiliation of that defeat. "I have not become the King's First Minister in order to preside over the liquidation of the British Empire," he stated in 1942. As a first step in the process of reclaiming Singapore, the South-East Asia Command had to retake the island of Sumatra. "This I am determined to press to the very utmost, day in and day out," he told Admiral The Lord Louis Mountbatten. He had no problem with the ideas of the Chiefs as long as they had no negative impact on a Sumatra operation "on which I am increasingly resolved after the monsoon."[3]

When the Chiefs informed him that Operation: FIRST CULVERIN—which was the codename for an attack on Sumatra—was inappropriate given the

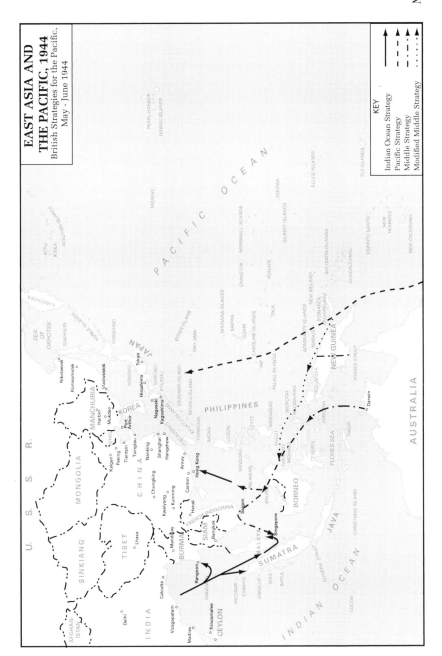

EAST ASIA AND THE PACIFIC, 1944
British Strategies for the Pacific,
May - June 1944

KEY
Indian Ocean Strategy
Pacific Strategy
Middle Strategy
Modified Middle Strategy

Map 1

allied focus on hitting Japan itself, Churchill became rather unhappy. He instructed the Chiefs to hold off on contacting the Dominion governments until after they had discussed the situation with him. Staff officers dutifully scheduled a meeting on January 19, 1944, to discuss the matter. During that conference it became clear that the prime minister was largely ignorant about the details of FIRST CULVERIN. Brooke was infuriated.

> We accomplished nothing!! I don't think I can stand much more of it. We waffled about with all the usual criticisms, all the usual optimist's plans, no long term vision, and we settled nothing. In all his plans he lives from hand to mouth. He can never grasp a whole plan, either in its width (ie all fronts) or its depth (long term projects). His method is entirely opportunist, gathering one flower here another there! My God how tired I am of working for him![4]

Under normal circumstances, the prime minister was good about tracking the arguments the Chiefs made. Clementine Churchill once advised Major-General Sir Edward Spears, himself a member of Parliament, on how to work with her husband. Unlike most politicians, talking to him was not the most effective form of communication. According to Spears, Clementine advised, "Put what you have to say in writing. He often does not listen or does not hear if he is thinking of something else. But he will always consider a paper carefully and take in all its implications. He never forgets what he sees in writing."[5]

The problem that Churchill faced and what made the confrontation with the Chiefs so serious was that the early months of 1944 were anything but normal. In the middle of December 1943, the prime minister contracted pneumonia and then had an atrial fibrillation, which is something like a minor heart attack. He spent two weeks in bed, resting some of the time. Each of the health issues he faced normally requires much time devoted to recuperation, but Churchill had suffered all of them on top of one another and simply could not and would not focus on regaining his health. The demands of his position simply would not allow him to do so, which complicated his recovery. For the next six months, many individuals would comment on a recurring basis that he lacked his once formidable presence. "Somehow today he looks 10 years older," one of his dictating secretaries noted in her diary. Sir Alexander Cadogan of the Foreign Office observed: "P.M. this morning confessed he was tired—he's almost done in." Henry Channon, a member of Parliament who had been a supporter of Chamberlain, declared, "he looked tired, wounded and barely audible." Churchill's health problems also had an impact on his job performance. "P.M., I fear, is breaking down," Cadogan wrote in a diary entry. "He rambles without a pause, and we really got nowhere." He also added: "He is *not* the man he was 12 months ago, and I really don't know whether he can carry on." Perhaps most damning is the observation that Lord Moran made about his patient: "As, year after year, I watched the P.M. doing the work of three men, I kept saying to myself that this could not go on forever." Then what he feared came to pass. "He never seemed the same man again."[6]

Despite his health problems, Churchill raised four complaints with the Chiefs about strategy for the Pacific war. A broad one was that Russian entry into the contest with Japan would change the nature of that conflict. How the prime minister expressed that view changed significantly with the ebb and flow of the war. On some occasions, he thought it might be possible to use Russian territory as a staging area for an attack on Japan, and at other times, he thought the might of the Soviet Union in and of itself would compel Japan to surrender or at least offer terms. Another problem he had with the strategy was that the United States still had not determined the nature of the final operations against Japan. The prime minister had a good point. The divided command structure in the Pacific between the headquarters of General Douglas MacArthur and Admiral Chester Nimitz, and the army-navy rivalry that it produced, made planning the endgame of the Pacific war highly contentious. The American attitude was to put off deciding the matter. At this date, no one knew if the United States could or would initiate a naval blockade of the home islands, a sustained strategic bombing campaign, or an invasion of Japan. Churchill also pointed out that the U.S. Navy had more than enough resources at hand to defeat the Imperial Japanese Navy and had no need of assistance from the Royal Navy. Again, Churchill was correct on this matter. Admiral Ernest J. King, Chief of Naval Operations and Commander-in-Chief, U.S. Fleet, made the same point in a conversation he had with the head of the British Admiralty Delegation in Washington. Finally, Churchill said contributing resources to a drive through the Central Pacific would make no use of the British forces assembling in Southeast Asia. As a result of these views, staff officers would spend the next three months studying various possible operations that could be based in Southeast Asia or Australia.[7]

There were three critical meetings on Far East strategy in February and March. The individuals attending these meetings varied, but Brooke, Portal, Cunningham, and Churchill were present at all of them. As far as the Chiefs were concerned, the purpose of these meetings was to convert the prime minister to their point of view. Brooke makes this position bluntly clear in a diary entry he made in between these sessions with Churchill: "Long COS with Planners, discussing Pacific strategy and deciding on plan of action to tackle the PM with, to convince him that we cannot take the tip of Sumatra for him. We shall have very serious trouble with him over this. But we have definitely decided that our strategy should be to operate from Australia with the Americans and not from India through Malacaa Straits."[8] The first meeting came on February 14. The conversation centered on the strengths and weaknesses of an operation designed to take Sumatra. After the meeting, Brooke returned home and logged his views into his diary:

> I had long and difficult arguments with the PM. He was again set on carrying out an attack of north tip of Sumatra and refusing to look at any long term projects or concrete plans for the defeat of Japan. Again showing his terrible failing of lack of width or depth in his strategic vision. He lives for the impulse and for the present, and refuses to look at lateral implications or future commitments. Now that I know him well episodes such as Antwerp and the Dardanelles no longer puzzle me![9]

For the next week and a half, the Chiefs as a group devoted most of their attention to the Mediterranean and preparing for the coming invasion of Normandy. On February 25, 1944, the three returned to the topic of strategy for the Far East. They spent seven and a half hours that day in three meetings with the prime minister arguing about Sumatra and the Pacific theater. The first confrontation started at noon after a routine Chiefs meeting. When Brooke, Portal, and Cunningham arrived at 10 Downing Street, Churchill was livid. He had only just received notice that a sizable Japanese fleet was stationed at Singapore. The Chiefs had thought nothing of the deployment, recognizing that the Japanese had made the move mainly as a way to avoid the Americans and to stay close to oil fields under their control. The meeting went on for two hours and never escaped the sour tone of the initial exchange. A heated discussion followed on the nature of sea power with Churchill on the one hand and the Chiefs on the other seeing the presence of the Japanese fleet as a development that ratified their views while exposing those of the other side as unsound.[10]

After breaking for a little over an hour, the Chiefs had another meeting with Churchill that focused mainly on Sumatra. "He was still insisting on doing the North Sumatra operation, would not discuss any other operation and was in a thoroughly disgruntled and bad temper. I had a series of heated discussions with him," Brooke scribbled into his diary. "Thank God I have got Andrew Cunningham to support me! It makes all the difference from the days of poor Dudley Pound."[11]

Foreign Minister Anthony Eden was present at the meeting and argued that the interest of the various British nations and colonies in the South Pacific required an attack on Sumatra. In a paper he had provided Churchill four days earlier, he declared, "A strategy which until a later date leaves the Japanese virtually unassailed in those regions which mean most to the peoples of Asia and to the Japanese themselves, will cast a considerable strain upon the already stretched endurance of the occupied territories and will materially retard their rehabilitation upon recovery." If the British were simply an adjunct in an American crusade in the Central Pacific, it would be "no exaggeration to say that the solidarity of the British Commonwealth and its influences in the maintenance of peace in the Far East will be irretrievably damaged." Comments along these lines infuriated Brooke. "I got very heated at times, especially when Anthony Eden chipped in knowing nothing about Pacific strategy!" The comments of Major-General Richard Dewing were too much for the head of the British Army to endure, though. "Dewing chipped in and talked unadulterated nonsense, and I lost my temper with him. It was a desperate meeting, with no opportunity of discussing strategy on its merits." In the battle of diaries, Eden gave as good as he took. "The height of absurdity was reached when CIGS—who was in bad temper triumphant—insisted that Americans wanted our forces in the Pacific as to which I had expressed my doubts."[12]

Later that evening, Churchill asked Brooke to dine alone with him. "I thought it was to tell me that he couldn't stick my disagreements any longer and proposed to sack me!" Instead, he found Churchill "quite charming, as if he meant to make up for some of the rough passages of the day." Their conversation focused on family matters, their concerns about their children, and just a little about strategy. "He has astonishing sides to his character," Brooke observed. He thought the conversation during their meal was much more reasonable in nature, and a Chiefs of Staff meeting later that evening went smoothly compared to the events earlier in the day. The general thought "that a great deal of what we have been doing has soaked in."[13]

After the war and after reading this diary entry, Brooke wrote that his hope had been foolish since he had many subsequent conflicts with Churchill. "It was as well that I did not know all that lay ahead of me connected with the tip of Sumatra! It was indeed a pious hope to think that anything we had done up to date had 'soaked in'! We were just at the very beginning of the most difficult period I had with Winston during the whole of the war."[14]

Their differences in strategic outlook flared up only a week later at a moment that should have been one of unreserved honor for Brooke. On March 1, King George VI made Brooke a Field-Marshal and presented him with the baton of that rank. The King had heard that there was a proposal to use Australia as a base for combat operations in the Pacific and wondered if his newest field-marshal had any maps or documents that he could examine. Brooke found himself in a difficult position. He could hardly say no, but if he briefed his sovereign, it might seem like he was trying to circumvent the authority of the Cabinet. He avoided giving a firm answer, even though His Majesty asked for the material a second time as Brooke was leaving. The next day, after a Chiefs of Staff meeting with Churchill, he tried to discuss the issue of informing the King. The prime minister, however, kept avoiding the subject. In a rather immature effort to avoid addressing the issue at hand, he started reading out loud a paper he had written on British participation in the Pacific. Even after Brooke interjected that the Chiefs would consider his paper in full, the prime minister continued reading the document. Frustrated, Brooke suggested that he inform the palace that the government had not had enough time to review the paper and that the military should hold off on its briefing of the King until Churchill had an opportunity to prepare some remarks. The prime minister quickly agreed to this settlement of an embarrassing problem.[15]

Five days before his third meeting with the Chiefs, Churchill produced a memorandum that from the first line stated the seriousness of the debate. "A question of major policy and strategy has now opened on which it may be necessary to obtain a decision by the War Cabinet." In this lengthy document, he summarized fairly the position of the Chiefs of Staff Committee and contrasted it to his own. Citing sunk costs in base facilities in Egypt and India and port facilities available on the subcontinent, he proceeded to argue for an operation in Southeast Asia. He also pointed out a legitimate logistical problem with what the Chiefs were proposing: "What diminution of our striking power against the enemy is involved in the enormous lengthening of our lines of communication entailed by passing them south of Australia round in the south-west Pacific as compared with operating across the Bay of Bengal." He suggested that he contact Roosevelt to see if the Americans required any assistance in their advance through the Pacific. He probably already knew the answer he would get from the president, but he warned that there were hazards to letting the Americans think that they had won the battles against the Japanese on their own.

> A decision to act as a subsidiary force under the Americans in the Pacific raises difficult political questions about the future of our Malayan possessions. If the Japanese should withdraw from them or make peace as the result of the main American thrust, the United States Government after the victory feels greatly strengthened in its view that all possessions in the East Indian Archipelago should be placed under some international body upon which the United States would exercise a decisive control.[16]

The Chiefs responded five days later with a paper of their own that was combative from the start. "Your definition of the Pacific Strategy omits its first object, namely to obtain a footing in Japan's inner zone at the earliest possible moment." Their proposal would have the United Kingdom involved in "the main advances against the Philippines, Formosa and ultimately Japan." They also noted that CULVERIN—with a different plan, the operation received a modified codename—required resources then being used in the European war. The Chiefs argued that their proposal would allow British forces to start playing a role in the Pacific almost immediately.[17]

Brooke, Portal, and Cunningham admitted that political calculations had to be considered, but insisted other factors, like resources and geography, were at work. "Whatever strategy we follow the major credit for the defeat of Japan is likely to go to the Americans." Yet the decisive arena would be the one that contributed most to the defeat of Japan. "The first mortal thrust will be the Pacific thrust, upon which the Americans have already embarked. We should not be excluded for a part in this thrust."

They did not believe that Churchill should consult Roosevelt asking what resources the United States required from the United Kingdom, as the prime minister was proposing. It was unlikely that the president would reply affirming any need. "We submit that the right approach is to consider what strategy is best calculated to bring about the early overthrow of Japan and what contribution we can make to that strategy, and then to go to the Americans and put forward our case."[18]

On the matter of sunk costs, they reported that bases in the Middle East and Ceylon would still prove useful in a Pacific strategy, because they lay along the line of direct communication between London and the Southwest Pacific. "Their usefulness would, therefore, be continuous." India, however, simply lacked the industrial and transportation resources to provide support for military bases. "The Australian base will be established in a white country, free from the vagaries of climate. The Indian base is always subject to monsoon conditions and to the other disruptive climatic, economic and political factors inherent in India." They also responded to Churchill's proposal for basing operations out of the Soviet Union, never contesting the fairly dubious assumption that Stalin would allow the British to do such a thing. If the Soviet Union entered the war against Japan, the Maritime Provinces sitting on the North Pacific would require much development in transportation infrastructure before any armed service could use them as staging areas. Churchill, though, had one exceptionally strong argument for which the Chiefs had no answer—strategic consumption. The King's forces would become weaker and weaker as they operated further and further from their bases. In a limp response, the Chiefs noted, "The distance is certainly greater, but our part in the operations could begin earlier and involves the use of fewer land forces, though the navy and air commitments would eventually be much the same." Pacific operations would, they conceded, require more shipping, but with Germany's defeat, convoy operations would no longer be necessary, making it easier to supply the armed forces.[19]

The Chiefs knew Churchill wanted to rebuild the empire and agreed that this objective was a legitimate one. "The Pacific strategy does not mean casting away facilities we now enjoy in the Bay of Bengal. The hard fact is that there are no practical steps we can usefully take in that theatre until six months after Germany is defeated." British forces in Southeast Asia would remain idle for the next eighteen months regardless of what Churchill wanted.[20]

Although polite in tone, the Chiefs' paper was combative. Brooke, Portal, and Cunningham had complicated feelings toward their political master. All three, like many others in the War Cabinet, resented the rambling, inconclusive meetings Churchill imposed on them. If one line can summarize their relationship over the entire course of the war, it was a sentence Brooke entered into his diary early in his stay at the War Office: "God knows where we would be without him, but God knows where we shall go with him!"[21]

Relations between the Chiefs and Churchill had started to deteriorate during that spring. Brooke, Portal, and, to a lesser extent, Cunningham had received little recognition for their exceptionally important work. "It is a strange thing what a vast part the COS takes in the running of the war and how little it is known or its functions appreciated," Brooke reflected as he wrote in his diary. "The average man in the street has never heard of it. Any lime light for it could not fail to slightly diminish the PM's halo!"[22] Churchill had any number of ways of recognizing the three, including having the King award them titles of peerage, higher ranks of knighthood than they already possessed, or bestowing upon them a little public recognition. As it was, Cunningham was the only one of the three who had anything of a public reputation, mainly because of Matapan. As the admiral would attest, command in a time of war is the ultimate mission for any military officer, and Brooke had passed up opportunities to serve as the commander-in-chief of a theater in order to continue developing British strategy. Churchill had three times promised to give him command of the cross-channel invasion. Such a position of responsibility would have been the peak of his professional career and would have allowed him to make a direct contribution to the outcome of the war rather than through his indirect role as the administrative head of the British Army. Instead, in 1943 Churchill casually informed Brooke that the position would go to an American officer.

It was a crashing blow to hear from him that he was now handing over this appointment to the Americans, and had in exchange received the agreement of the President to Mountbatten's appointment as Supreme Commander for South East Asia! Not for one moment did he realize what this meant to me. He offered no sympathy, no regrets at having had to change his mind, and dealt with the matter as if it were one of minor importance!

Brooke admitted that it took him several months to recover from his disappointment.[23]

Because of the disillusion that accompanied this rejection, Brooke saw more and more defects in the prime minister's character and had less tolerance for them. Although he indulged in good cigars and strong drink, his reputation for consuming large quantities of alcohol is overdone. Yet, Churchill refused to compromise in these areas, even in 1944 when he was weak and ill. His body had less ability to handle the alcohol and the results were predictable. There are entries in both the Brooke and Cunningham diaries that make reference to the prime minister's intoxication. Brooke recorded arriving at the prime minister's underground map room on one night: "I found him very much the worse for wear having evidently consumed several glasses of brandy at lunch. It was not very easy to ensure that he was absorbing the seriousness of the situation. We had many references to Marlborough and other irrelevant matters." Years later, after reading his own diaries, Brooke wrote: "I remember that ghastly evening as if it were yesterday."[24] Becoming intoxicated on an occasion or two in no way makes Churchill a problem drinker, much less an alcoholic, but his behavior was massively irresponsible. Brooke was offended and his reaction was entirely justified. For a chief of any government at war to end up drunk is a profound abdication of responsibility.

What appears to have made this situation all the worse for Brooke was that he realized that Churchill was a great man and he liked him. "There had been very difficult times, and times when I felt I could not stand a single more day with him, but running through all our difficulties a bond of steel had been formed uniting us together," he wrote after the war. "It would have been impossible for us to go on striving together unless a deep bond of friendship had existed." Such respect and admiration made it possible for their relationship to survive despite their intense disagreements. "I shall always look back on the years I worked with him as some of the most difficult and trying ones in my life. For all that I thank God that I was given an opportunity of working alongside of such a man, and of having my eyes opened to the fact that occasionally such supermen exist on this earth."[25]

Portal was the only one of the Chiefs who kept no diary, and his views are more difficult to determine. He seems, however, to have had the same complicated view of Churchill as Brooke. In 1958 he told the BBC that several of Churchill's "brainwaves on strategy" had created numerous problems for the military. In Portal's opinion, the prime minister's positive

CHAPTER TWO

traits, including his "matchless courage and energy, his tremendous strength and stamina, and, above all, . . . the wonderful support he gave us when everything was going wrong" more than made up for these defects.[26]

Cunningham's views on Churchill were much more negative than those of his two friends. When he wrote his memoirs, the admiral was fortunate to have a talented but uncredited coauthor who helped him strike a polite tone while not altering the spirit of the original manuscript when discussing the prime minister: "We had not always seen eye to eye, and had had our occasional disagreements and arguments. But never for a moment could I lose my profound admiration and respect for that most remarkable and courageous Englishman who by his energy, obstinacy and sheer force of character led Britain and her people through the greatest perils the country ever experienced."[27] While there is no reason to doubt Lord Cunningham's sincerity on this matter, he is much less reserved in the pages of his diary: "He really is a most selfish + impossible man to work with."[28] Other entries have a similar tone and show little qualification. After the war he made a comment to Lord Moran about Churchill's contribution to British strategy: "Well, anyway, it did not amount to much."[29]

Churchill gave as good as he got, or even better. He found the Chiefs a frustrating group that, in his opinion, needed much prompting. "I am certainly not one of those that need to be prodded," he explained in 1942 to fellow members of the House of Commons. "In fact, if anything, I am a prod. My difficulties rather lie in finding the patience and self-restraint to wait through many anxious weeks for the results to be achieved." When Lord Moran asked him what he thought of Brooke's job performance, Churchill grunted after a long pause: "He has a flair for the business." Moran added, "That was all he would concede." The prime minister was willing to give the First Sea Lord more due: "I like Cunningham very much," he told his physician. "I'm very lucky to get such a successor to dear old Pound." He made similar comments about the Chief of the Air Staff: "Portal has everything." Despite this praise, he thought little of the three as a group. During a trip to the Mediterranean, an individual remarked that the Chiefs of Staff Committee organization was a good system. "No not at all," Churchill retorted. "It leads to weak and faltering decisions—or rather indecisions. Why, you may take the most gallant sailor, the most intrepid airman, or the most audacious soldier, put them at a table together—what do you get? The sum of their fears!" Unlike the Chiefs, he made his comments in public.[30]

There were others in the government who had similar views. John Colville, a professional civil servant in the Foreign Office who served at various times in the war as junior private secretary to Chamberlain and Churchill, noted in his diary: "Whatever the P. M.'s shortcomings may be, there is no doubt that he does provide guidance and purpose for the Chiefs of Staff and the F. O. on matters which, without him, would often be lost in the maze of inter-departmentalism or frittered away by caution and compromise."[31]

Neither the Chiefs nor Churchill were willing to concede on an issue that they thought was of vital importance to the very existence of the United Kingdom as a world power. The stakes were high, and the three Chiefs were prepared to bring about the mutual professional destruction of themselves and the prime minister. On March 3, two days after receiving his field-marshal's baton, Brooke wrote in his diary: "It is all about the future Pacific Strategy, it looks very serious and may well lead to the resignation of the Chiefs of Staff Committee." The resignation of any one Chief would have been rather insignificant. At least one other individual had held each position during the war. The mass resignation of all three of the Chiefs of Staff was a different matter. In World War I, Fisher's departure had forced a coalition Cabinet on Asquith and nearly destroyed Churchill's political career. The collective departure of Brooke, Portal, and Cunningham would have invoked memories of the past and could have quite easily eroded much support for the prime minister in Parliament. For his part, Brooke was prepared to make this move. "I am shattered by the present condition of the PM. He has lost all balance and is in a very dangerous mood."[32]

No one can know what would have happened had the Chiefs resigned en masse, but the result would most likely have been negative. General Sir Hastings Ismay, Churchill's military chief of staff, called the dispute "protracted and vehement" and decided to try to avert a showdown. "I therefore conceived it my duty to try to mediate in a manner which I had never done before and never did again." The day after the Chiefs began contemplating professional Armageddon, Ismay wrote a memo to the prime minister warning him that Brooke, Portal, and Cunningham "are extremely unlikely to retract the military opinions that they have expressed." He warned Churchill that their collective resignation was a real possibility. "A breach of this kind, undesirable at any time, would be little short of catastrophic at the present juncture." Ismay was no politician and he made no effort to tackle such issues; rather his concern focused on military matters, specifically the pending invasion of Normandy. "'Overlord' is, in all conscience, a sufficiently hazardous operation. It should be given every chance." This statement invoked the disaster of the Dardanelles campaign, the failed Gallipoli landings, and Fisher's resignation without having to cross overtly into the arena of politics. Ismay suggested that Churchill hold a series of meetings on Pacific strategy. These might result in an agreement on strategy, and if so, all the better. If not, then he could declare that political factors outweighed military operational concerns.

> I cannot but think that the Chiefs of Staff would accept this decision with complete loyalty and would set to work at once to make the best possible plans for implementing it. Their position vis-à-vis their United States colleagues would then be perfectly clear. They could say—"We are not authorised to discuss any plans for moving British land, sea and air forces into the Pacific. We should like to concert with you how best to implement the Indian Ocean strategy."[33]

Ismay wrote his memo on March 4, a Saturday. After a weekend break, the Chiefs of Staff Committee met on Monday, Tuesday, and Wednesday, focusing most of their discussion on Churchill and the Far East. Churchill had scheduled a meeting for the evening of Wednesday, March 8. As the invasion of France neared, an operation that Brooke had wanted to command, his frustration at Churchill grew and he poured his feelings onto the pages of his diary. The pending conference was the source of his anger. Two days before the event, he directed his rage at Eden, Attlee, Oliver Lyttelton—the production minister—and Baron Leathers of Purfleet—the transportation minister. Of these men, Brooke wrote, "He is to bring his chorus of 'Yes' men (Eden, Attlee, Oliver Lyttelton and Leathers) with him. It will be a gloomy evening and one during which it will be hard to keep one's temper." The day before the meeting he decided a memo Churchill had written on the topic they would discuss was "the worst paper I have seen him write yet." He expected a "royal row" on Wednesday evening. After the war, when Brooke read his diary, he realized his statements, private though they were, had been too harsh and negative.

> In classifying these four statesmen as "Yes" men I was considering them from the point of view of Pacific strategy. None of them had

given any deep thought to the matter, had, in fact, only scratched the surface of the problem, as was palpable from their remarks, and as for Leathers; from what I had seen of him no matter what he might have found in scratching the surface he would have continued to trim his sails to whatever wind Winston blew.[34]

The meeting came and their differences remained. "Our party consisted of Chiefs of Staff," Brooke noted.

Portal as usual not too anxious to argue against PM, and dear old Cunningham so wild with rage that he hardly dared let himself speak!! I therefore had to do most of the arguing and for 2 1/2 hours, from 10 pm to 12:30 am I went at it hard arguing with the PM and 4 Cabinet Ministers. The arguments of the latter were so puerile that it made me ashamed to think they were Cabinet Ministers! I had little difficulty in dealing with any of the arguments they put forward.

It became clear to both sides that the details of each proposal needed more staff study, in particular, the amount of shipping tonnage each plan would require. The Admiralty and the Ministry of War Transport had numbers that were different. One of the decisions that came out of the meeting was that the British should solicit information on these matters from Australia. Brooke thought he had scored a victory. "Finally we had succeeded in getting the PM to agree to reconnaissances of Australia being carried out as a possible base for future action and we had got him to realize that his plans for the defeat of Japan must go beyond the mere capture of the tip of Sumatra."[35]

The principal figures at that meeting also agreed that Churchill should send a cable to Roosevelt on this matter. Churchill used this correspondence as an opportunity to weaken the position of the Chiefs of Staff. It says something about the strength of the American-British alliance that the prime minister was willing to seek assistance from Roosevelt in thwarting his officers even though concern about American anticolonialism was one of the factors behind his strategic ideas. He informed Roosevelt that he had gotten the impression from Admiral King that British forces were not needed in the Pacific, and if they did make an appearance that they must provide their own supplies. "I am in the upshot, left in doubt about whether we are really needed this year. Accordingly I should be very grateful if you could let me know whether there is any specific American operation in the Pacific (a) before the end of 1944 or (b) before the summer of 1945 which would be hindered or prevented by the absence of a British Fleet detachment." He made it clear in subtle fashion what his personal preference was in the matter. "Would your Pacific operations be hindered if, for the present at any rate and while the Japanese Fleet is at Singapore, we kept our centre of gravity in the Indian Ocean and the Bay of Bengal and planned amphibious operations there as resources come to hand."[36]

That same day, Churchill sent another cable to Field-Marshal Sir John Dill. An Ulsterman like his good friend Brooke, Dill had entered the British Army in 1901 after compiling a mediocre record at the Royal Military College, Sandhurst. It was World War I that made his career much more than it did Brooke's. He started the war a Captain and ended it as both a Brigadier-General and one of the most important planning officers in the headquarters of the British Expeditionary Force. When war came a second time, he was the Commander-in-Chief, Home Forces, which many in the army considered a stepping-stone for command of any contingent sent to the continent. Instead, he took command of I Corps. In the midst of the disaster in France, Churchill made Dill Chief of the Imperial General Staff. The association between the two men was never good. "He is full of ideas," Dill wrote about the new prime minister, "many brilliant, but most of them impracticable." He offered Churchill cautionary advice when the prime minister wanted and needed action. Churchill called him "the dead hand inanition" to his face, and gave him the nickname "Dilly-Dally." These comments were unfair. It was Dill's misfortune to hold high office during the darkest days of a war Britain had never been fully ready to fight. "I am sure that you, better than anyone else, must realize how difficult it is for a soldier to advise against a bold and offensive plan," he informed Churchill. "It takes a lot of moral courage not to be afraid of being thought afraid." It was during his tenure at the War Office that his wife died. It had not been a happy marriage, a series of strokes had destroyed her health, and Dill spent little time mourning her loss. Less than a year later, he married Nancy Furlong, the widow of one of his staff officers, who was more than twenty years his junior. Despite the age difference, the Dills' marriage flourished. "She makes a great difference to my life and keeps me young." A month later, Churchill relieved him of his post, replacing him with Brooke.

Churchill had had Dill promoted to Field-Marshal as a consolation and intended to make him Governor of Bombay, but then Japan attacked Pearl Harbor. Since he was still the head of the army, Dill accompanied Churchill to an emergency summit meeting in Washington, D.C. The Americans and the British agreed to establish the Combined Chiefs of Staff, which would coordinate the allied war effort. The Combined Chiefs would meet regularly in Washington, and British service delegates would represent the Chiefs of Staff Committee except during summit meetings when all the Chiefs would be present. Churchill needed an officer to head the British Joint Staff Mission in Washington and had an extra field-marshal to spare. "It is odd that Winston should want me to represent him here when he clearly was glad to get me out of the CIGS job," Dill observed. In his new position, the field-marshal was basically the British military ambassador to the United States and was at the center of allied strategic planning. This task required that Dill establish the administrative machinery of the Chiefs of Staff Committee and set the expectations for what this organization could and could not do. It helped that Dill developed a real friendship with General George C. Marshall, Chief of Staff of the U.S. Army. "His difficulties are immense," the field-marshal observed, "but he is straight, clear-headed and undoubtedly dominates the conferences on the American side." The two lunched regularly together and resolved troublesome issues before they came before the rather formal Combined Chiefs of Staff meetings. Dill also made sure that the U.S. Joint Chiefs of Staff were provided with as much information as possible. It was as if the Americans were on the distribution list for British documents. Candor was a vital ingredient in developing policies that served the interest of both nations. Dill was an honest broker between his friends Brooke and Marshall and helped them understand the political factors at work in each capital. Marshall also consulted him about internal U.S. debates. All in all, it was not particularly glamorous work. "I can make suggestions but I can decide nothing," Dill observed. "I have plenty of influence but not power." It was, however, work of exceptional importance to the alliance.[37]

In sending his cable, Churchill wanted to make sure Dill knew the policy of His Majesty's Government.

My war cabinet colleagues on the Defence Committee agree with me and urge strong political reasons against abandoning the Indian theatre. We all favour a direct attack across the Bay of Bengal, first on the islands and finally on the Malay Peninsula, and believe this can be delivered far sooner and with much stronger forces than could be deployed at the end of the communications encircling the whole of Australia.

His message would also help neutralize the Chiefs of Staff Committee's influence in Washington. "In my view the proposed shifting to the Pacific will divide our forces, particularly the Fleet, between two theatres, would lengthen enormously our communications and would put out of action a great number of bases and resources which we have gathered around the Bay of Bengal."[38]

The other cable that Churchill sent, the one that went to Roosevelt, basically got him the response he wanted. The president replied:

(a) There will be no specific operation in the Pacific during 1944 that would be adversely affected by the absence of a British Fleet detachment. (b) It is not at the present time possible to anticipate with sufficient accuracy future developments in the Pacific to be certain that a British Fleet detachment will not be needed there during the year of 1945, but it does not now appear that such a reinforcement will be needed before the summer of 1945.

Roosevelt also added a line in this message that could not have been better for Churchill even if he had written it himself. "In consideration of recent enemy dispositions it is my personal opinion that unless we have unexpected bad luck in the Pacific your naval forces will be of more value to our common effort by remaining in the Indian Ocean."[39]

Dill's response, however, was less to the prime minister's liking. The field-marshal reported that Roosevelt's qualification about 1945 was important. "Americans have considerable respect for Japan's strongest weapon, her Army. They learned their lessons at Guadalcanal and only wish to undertake a land campaign when some objective which is vital cannot otherwise be secured." The remaining battles required to defeat the Japanese were going to be difficult, and the United States might very well require assistance. "There are Americans who feel that British aid will be necessary to meet these inescapable commitments in the Pacific, but the whole problem has not been worked out in detail."[40]

"Dilly-Dally" need not have bothered. Churchill had the response from

Roosevelt that he wanted and he used it against the Chiefs in their meeting on March 17. At first, he threw out some new ideas, which the Chiefs rejected. He wanted to travel to Bermuda to confer with Roosevelt. The Chiefs were reluctant to make the trip—apparently they had never been to Bermuda. They pointed out that they had no agreement on strategic policy on the Far East with Churchill, and until then there was little they could discuss with their American counterparts on this matter. Another issue was the concern that Lord Moran expressed about the prime minister's health. Churchill was still recuperating from his bouts of pneumonia, and Moran feared he would find the trip seriously taxing. Roosevelt could not meet with him, however, and the Bermuda summit never took place. Thwarted in this effort, Churchill put forward another proposal. He suggested seizing Simeuluë, a small island near Sumatra. Portal and Cunningham explained that with a Japanese fleet stationed at Singapore, the enemy could easily defeat an extended Royal Navy and hit the island before the Royal Air Force had fields or aerodromes to sustain a British presence. Brooke's frustration had him ranting into his diary in overreaction: "I began to wonder weather I was Alice in Wonderland, or whether I was really fit for a lunatic asylum! I am honestly getting very doubtful about his balance of mind and it just gives me the cold shivers. I don't know where we are or where we are going as regards our strategy, and I just cannot get him to face the true facts!"[41]

Since Churchill had failed in his efforts to get the Chiefs to see reason, he decided to use Roosevelt's cable to end the debate on terms he dictated.

> My question and the President's reply . . . are directed not to whether it is in the interests of Britain not to intervene in American operations in the South-West Pacific, but solely to the point as to whether there is any obligation to the American authorities that we should do so or if their operations would be hampered if we stood out. We now know that there is no obligation and that their operations will not be hampered, also that they will not in any case require our assistance (barring some catastrophe) before the autumn of 1945. We are therefore free to consider the matter ourselves and from the point of view of British interests only.

In polite and proper language he suggested that this Chiefs were guilty of some sort of breech in their relationship. "Considering the intimacy and friendship with which we have worked for a long time in so many difficult situations, I never imagined that the Chiefs of Staff would get so deep into a great matter like this of long-term strategy into which so many political and other non-military considerations enter without trying to carry me along with them, so that we could have formed our opinions together." He then asserted civilian authority over the military. "The Ministers on the Defence Committee are convinced, and I am sure that the War Cabinet would agree if the matter were bought before them, that it is in the interest of Britain to pursue, what may be termed the 'Bay of Bengal Strategy,' at any rate for the next twelve months." Invoking his authority as Prime Minister and Minister of Defense, he gave five "rulings," the most important being the first two: "(a) Unless unforeseen events occur, the Indian theatre and the Bay of Bengal will remain, until the summer of 1945, the center of gravity for the British and Imperial war effort against Japan; (b) All preparations will be made for amphibious action across the Bay of Bengal against the Malay Peninsula and the various island outposts by which it is defended, the ultimate objective being the reconquest of Singapore." As a token gesture, he told the Chiefs he was still willing to send a mission to Australia to study available resources and facilities "should we at any time wish to adopt that policy."[42]

As far as Churchill was concerned, the matter was resolved.

> I should be very ready to discuss the above ruling with the Chiefs of Staff, in order that we may be clear in our minds as to the line we are going to take in discussions with our American friends. Meanwhile, with this difference on long term plans settled, we may bend ourselves to the tremendous and urgent tasks which are now so near, and in which we shall have need of all our old comradeship and mutual confidence.[43]

The paper infuriated Brooke. "We discussed at the COS how best to deal with Winston's last impossible document. It is full of false statements, false deductions and defective strategy. We cannot accept it as it stands, and it would be better if we all three resigned rather than accept his solution." The Chiefs planned to make their case to him verbally before putting it in writing and leaving a permanent record of their differences. "I don't know how tiresome he will insist in being. He may perhaps see some reason, otherwise we may well be faced with a most serious situation."[44]

In another indicator of the strength of the American-British alliance, Brooke had no problem seeking assistance from his allied counterparts in an effort to circumvent the "Bay of Bengal strategy." He sent a letter to Dill, explaining matters candidly. "I have just about reached the end of my tether and can see no way of clearing up the frightful tangle that our Pacific Strategy has got into." He quickly explained what the Chiefs of Staff Committee wanted to do strategically in the Pacific.

> From our examination up to date we consider that by adopting a line of advance parallel or similar to MacArthur's we should bring the war to an earlier conclusion than by operating from India through Sumatra and Malay Peninsula. In fact we feel that the Indian Ocean Policy will result in our walking round with the basket picking up the apples whilst the Americans climb up into the tree and shake the apples off by cutting their lines of communication.

Brooke thought that he, Portal, and Cunningham could have fought the issue out with Churchill, but there were several factors that made such an effort difficult. First, there was the problem of Mountbatten. "In South East Asia Command we have Dickie who is determined to do something to justify his supreme existence. He is therefore naturally doing all he can, and using all possible arguments and propaganda to bring about a Culverin Policy. His outlook fits in well with that of the P.M. and they encourage each other by periodic personal wires." Brooke figured he could have handled the Mountbatten factor were it not for "the fact that the P.M. after creating Dickie and his command is loath to see its wings clipped and reduced to a creature crawling about in Burma."[45]

A second problem, which was much more significant, was Australia. As Brooke told Dill,

> Reading between the lines it is pretty clear that neither MacArthur nor Blamey are very anxious for a British Force to arrive in Australia if it is likely to affect their present positions. I should think this applies to MacArthur mainly; he might accept the contribution of a few Divisions, Squadrons and Naval assistance provided these were closely integrated in his present forces. Any idea of a British or Imperial Force operating from Australia as a self contained whole, even under his orders, does not appear to attract him! Curtin seems to be

in MacArthur's pocket, and although there appears to be a great desire on the part of Australians generally for British cooperation, he appears to be framing his views more on MacArthur's wishes than what the Australians would like.

The Chief of the Imperial General Staff found the opposition of the Australian government disturbing. "It is a disappointing situation as I feel certain that from the bigger Imperial point of view it is quite essential that British forces, at sea, on land and in the air, should operate from Australia in the war against Japan." There were also good operational reasons for putting forth this proposal.

> I am quite clear in my own mind that strategically it is right for us to use all our forces in close cooperation from Australia across the Pacific directed in the General Direction of Formosa. By operating our forces alongside of MacArthur we can pool resources at sea and in the air for various closely connected steps. Whereas by retaining our forces in the Indian Ocean we operate independently, incapable of close cooperation, with the result that operations will be more protracted.

He finally came to the point of his letter. He told Dill that he wanted the support of the U.S. Joint Chiefs of Staff in this matter. It would help him in his efforts if they would oppose operations like CULVERIN.[46]

Dill would find that the Americans needed little prodding on the issue of Sumatra; they opposed the idea for their own reasons. Once MacArthur's command had liberated the Philippines, the strategic value of operations in and around Malaya would be rather minor. The U.S. Joint Chiefs knew why the British were interested in this region, but rebuilding the British Empire was not an American war aim. They wanted Mountbatten's South-East Asia Command to initiate operations not in Singapore but in Burma. Retaking control of that British colony would keep the land route to China open. The Joint Chiefs wanted to keep China active in the war, since it was containing the bulk of the Imperial Japanese Army. Otherwise Americans might have a tough road to victory, a very tough road, if they encountered large Japanese Army detachments in places like the Philippines, Okinawa, Formosa, and Japan itself. Nine days before Brooke sent his letter, the American Joint Chiefs of Staff stated, "The requirements for a major amphibious operation in the South East Asia Theatre this year are not in sight. We cannot, therefore, at this time agree to support Operation 'Culverin' or any similar operation involving large amphibious commitments in the South East Asia Command."[47]

Churchill, though, was committed to the ultimate liberation of Singapore. From the middle of March until the middle of April, he held regular meetings with the planners on Operation: CULVERIN. It was only in these meetings that he began to accept what Brooke, Portal, and Cunningham had been telling him all along—that the United Kingdom simply lacked the resources to initiate an amphibious assault in Southeast Asia in 1944.[48]

Brooke's frustration was spreading to staff officers and the subordinates of the Chiefs. "The P.M., up till now, has been obsessed with the Indian Ocean strategy and he believes that, politically, it is inevitable for us," Major-General Sir John Kennedy, Brooke's Director of Military Operations, observed. "But it would be a thousand times easier to make some headway in arriving at a decision if the P.M. would accept military advice and back his advisers." The problem was that Whitehall had little to show for all the debate. Kennedy noted: "In the meantime, vast energy had been expended fruitlessly here, and tempers frayed without any result which helps the war. The Chiefs of Staff have been in a state of desperation time after time. If we could only get on in a rational matter here, we could at least arrive at some basis of discussion with the Americans."[49]

Sumatra, though, was only a means to an end. The ultimate goal was the liberation of Singapore. In mid-April, the planners came up with what amounted to a compromise between the Chiefs of Staff Committee and the prime minister. They proposed what became known as the "middle strategy." All throughout the debate with Churchill, the Chiefs had always planned on basing a British drive through the Pacific from northeastern Australia. In this new plan, the King's forces would be based in northwestern Australia, and such a force could liberate Singapore, and then pivot and strike Saigon or even Hong Kong. Debate quickly pointed out that the problem with this suggestion was that the advance would make no direct contribution to the final defeat of Japan. After this proposal bounced around Whitehall, the planners adjusted their ideas and came up with what would become known as the "modified middle strategy." In this scenario the base for British forces would be eastern Australia, but the target area would be North Borneo. This strategic plan would allow the British to support the main U.S. advance into the heart of the Japanese Empire with landings of their own in Formosa or even in the home islands.[50]

At the beginning of May, there were four strategic proposals floating about Whitehall: the Pacific strategy, CULVERIN, and the two versions of the middle strategy. There would be no immediate resolution of the matter. The date for the invasion of Normandy was approaching, and it began absorbing more and more British attention. There was also a summit meeting in London between the prime ministers of the King's self-governing Dominions. This gathering threw numerous diplomatic and political factors into the already complicated effort to develop a British strategy for the Pacific war. The interests of Canada, New Zealand, and, most of all, Australia were different in ways large and small from those of the United Kingdom, but also from one another. Men who spoke English with different accents from those of Brooke, Portal, Cunningham, and Churchill entered into the debate, and for better or worse would have their say.

◼

THREE

The King's Men in the Loyal Dominions

Each major European power used its colonial empire to different ends. For some it was about economic exploitation; for others it was about securing markets for their finished goods. Still others found they needed land for military and naval bases in order to protect their interests, and for yet others it was about finding largely vacant lands to relieve overcrowding at home. In the case of the British, it was all four. Britons—be they Welsh, Irish, Scots, or English—left their homes and settled North America, New Zealand, Australia, and South Africa in the eighteenth and nineteenth centuries. Most of these settlements slowly developed into countries that were extensions of the United Kingdom. There were exceptions, though. The colonies on the eastern coast of North America rebelled and became the United States, while South Africa was a land heavily populated with several African ethnic groups as well as the Afrikaners, descendents of Dutch settlers, who hardly welcomed British rule. Overall, though, His Majesty's self-governing Dominions of Australia, Canada, and New Zealand had interests as British nations in the conduct of the war with Japan. In 1944, this issue was one of the major topics of discussion at a conference in London of the prime ministers of these Dominions along with those of South Africa, Rhodesia, and the government of India. Churchill had to at least listen to and brief his Dominion opposites about the British role in the Pacific.

The first of these men was William Mackenzie King of Canada. The leader of His Majesty's Canadian Government was no fan of his British counterpart. "I would be terrifly [*sic*] afraid of consequences of taking Churchill and Eden in the Government as is being urged just now," he observed in April of 1939 as war clouds gathered in Europe. Later in the year, King George VI told his Canadian prime minister he would never agree to Churchill's becoming prime minister of Great Britain. "I confess I was glad to hear him say that because I think Churchill is one of the most dangerous men I have ever known." Churchill, however, had been right on the moral issue of opposing Hitler's Nazi movement long before others saw the danger. His inspirational resistance to the German war machine earned him respect and admiration around the planet, and many, including Mackenzie King, changed their views about him. More importantly, the Canadian prime minister agreed with Churchill about standing up to the Americans.[1]

Overweight and with thinning hair, the 69-year-old Mackenzie King was to Canada what Churchill and Roosevelt were to their two countries: the dominant political figure of his era. Born in what is now Kitchener, Ontario, he earned the nickname "Rex" while a student at the University of Toronto, where he earned three degrees in the 1890s. After a brief stint at the University of Chicago, he earned another graduate degree at Harvard University.[2]

During this time, Mackenzie King, at the request of a family friend who also happened to be a member of the Cabinet, wrote a report on sweatshops. The finished product impressed people and he quickly received an offer to serve as the editor of a Labour Ministry publication. In 1900 he moved to Ottawa and shortly thereafter became deputy minister of the new Labour and Post Office Department. He decided to make politics his life and set out to become prime minister. After eight years as a civil servant, he won election to Parliament from the constituency of North Waterloo. He also got the prime minister, Sir Wilfrid Laurier, to make him the Minister for an independent Department of Labour. He was 35 years old at the time.[3]

He suffered a major professional setback when the Liberal Party lost the 1911 election. In the process Mackenzie King lost his seat in Parliament. Before this electoral defeat, he had decided that his political future required that he find a wife. Sir Wilfrid and his wife had tried introducing him to some ladies before, but nothing had come of these early efforts. Now Mackenzie King became extremely determined to find himself a wife. "I know that if I can find the right one to share my life with, & can be freed from dependence on others, I can be the Leader of the Liberal Party & ultimately Premier of Canada," he wrote in his diary. As this entry shows, he was looking for a wealthy woman. Yet, he intended to marry for love as well. He was more than willing to look for a wealthy woman south of the border even though Laurier warned him it would hurt him at the ballot box if he married an American. In the end, he was unable to find the ideal woman, refused to compromise, and remained a bachelor his entire life.[4]

When World War I came to Canada, Mackenzie King was in the United States working for John D. Rockefeller, Jr. As the director of the Department of Industrial Relations at the Rockefeller Foundation, the Canadian's job was to oversee management-labor relations in Rockefeller-owned mining operations in Colorado. He established good industrial relations between the unions and companies, keeping the mines operational throughout the war. He stayed active in Canadian politics, though. In the 1917 election, he stood with Laurier and refused to join a national coalition government. The issue in dispute was conscription. There was support for this program in English-speaking Canada, but French-speaking Quebec had little love for their British king, and little more for the France that abandoned them to this foreign rule centuries ago. The Conservatives won the polarizing election, but Quebec remained in the Liberal camp. Mackenzie King failed to regain a seat in Parliament, but he was in a good position to claim leadership of the Liberal Party after the ailing Sir Wilfrid died in 1919. The votes from Quebec were decisive in the intraparty contest that followed. Mackenzie King won the contest and two years later, the Liberals retook control of the House of Commons and made their pudgy leader the prime minister of British North America. It was the first of his three separate administrations in office.[5]

Mackenzie King lived a double life that one writer has used the term "Jekyll and Hyde" to describe. In public, he was rather bland and dour. His poor skill as a public speaker added to this reputation. He spoke in a flat voice and his rhetoric was confusing rather than inspiring. At private dinners, though, he could be witty. Despite a lifelong pursuit of a spouse that bordered on the pathetic, he could charm women of all ages. When the wife of a member of Parliament asked him why he had never married, the prime minister replied, "My dear, if I'd met a girl like you forty years ago, I would be married." A workaholic, he had no reservations about calling on his staff during weekends and holidays. Yet he also managed to present himself as a man of the people. "While King commanded an army of supporters, his admirers wouldn't have made up a platoon," Brian Nolan observed in his study of Mackenzie King's political leadership during the war.[6]

In 1926, ruling with a minority government and with a corruption scandal in the Customs Department, Mackenzie King asked the governor-general, Viscount Byng of Vimy, to dissolve Parliament. When Lord Byng refused, Mackenzie King resigned. The Conservatives took control of the Cabinet and quickly suffered an electoral setback. The governor-general dissolved Parliament, and another election took place in which Mackenzie King made complex constitutional issues and the intervention of the foreign governor-general campaign issues. He won and gained a renewed lease on life.[7]

The Great Depression, though, cost the Liberals the election of 1930. For five years Mackenzie King waited, watching the power that had once been his until the economy did in the Conservatives the way it had done in the Liberals. He regained control of the Cabinet in 1935. When he arrived in London, he had been prime minister for nine consecutive years. During the war he gave up alcohol, but found other ways to cope emotionally with the stress of war. Like many elderly individuals, he developed a close relationship with his pet dog that was overly emotional and even a bit repulsive in its intensity.[8]

Joining Mackenzie King in London was Peter Fraser, prime minister of New Zealand. A stooped, balding man who wore steel-rimmed glasses that gave him an intellectual appearance, Fraser came across as a serious and slightly self-righteous man. He was neither a smoker nor a drinker and was a bit uptight about issues involving sex. "It is a terrible confession for a Scotsman to make, but I get as much exhilaration out of a cup of tea as some people get out of champagne or whisky." He paid little attention to religion until late in his life. He was a fan of the sport that most people on the planet call football, but that New Zealanders call soccer. As a good politician, he projected well. His speeches, though, were known for their authority rather than their eloquence.[9]

Fraser was born in Scotland in 1884 and spoke English for the rest of his life with a Scottish burr. Attracted to the politics of socialism and New Zealand's reputation as a "social laboratory," he decided to emigrate and become a Kiwi in 1910 at the age of twenty-five.[10] Fraser became active in politics soon after arriving in New Zealand. In 1914, like many socialists around the British Empire, he opposed his Dominion's participation in the

Great War. Thinking the conflict was the product of imperialism, he worked against conscription. He soon found himself under arrest for his politics. His incarceration was, in reality, an effort on the part of the government to eliminate the leadership of the Labour Party. Despite his stay in prison, he ran for a seat in Parliament. Conscription was the issue of the day. An opponent said a vote for Fraser was a vote for the Kaiser. When asked if he was loyal to New Zealand, he gave an evasive reply until the issue was put to him bluntly. His response was to the point. "I think I am." Applause and electoral victory followed. At 34, he was the youngest member of the legislature.[11]

In 1919, he married Janet Kemp. A committed Socialist in her own right, Janet Fraser's main interest was in advancing her husband's career. The couple was devoted to one another and preferred to spend the evening together alone rather than going out. They were the best of friends and were the type of couple that would most likely have resented children for taking time away from each other. She was a much more gregarious and outgoing individual and clearly played a role in turning her husband into what two of his biographers call the "best all-round politician" in the New Zealand Labour Party. One official who worked closely with Fraser when he was prime minister recalled, "She was a delightful lady and a good influence on Peter."[12]

When the Labour Party formed its first Cabinet in 1935, Fraser became the minister responsible for education, health, the marine, mental hospitals, police, and machinery inspection. He was 51 years old, a young man in a government in which the average age was 57.[13] The Labour Party would retain control of the Cabinet for over a decade, and Fraser was a major reason. In 1938, Prime Minister Michael Joseph Savage began suffering from major health problems but delayed having surgery for a full year until August of 1939. Savage went months without attending sessions of Parliament and found it difficult to put in more than half a day in his office. As a result, Fraser became the acting leader of the House of Representatives and as the deputy prime minister was the head of the government in everything but name. He followed the diplomatic cable traffic on a regular basis as a crisis developed between Great Britain and Nazi Germany over the status of Poland. When war did come, it was Fraser who addressed the nation via radio to explain what had happened. There was never any doubt that the Dominion would support the United Kingdom in a European war. Even though he had opposed conscription during the first con-

His Majesty King George VI entertains the Dominion Prime Ministers at Buckingham Palace. Left to right: Peter Fraser of New Zealand, John Curtin of Australia, Winston Churchill of the United Kingdom, His Majesty the King, William Mackenzie King of Canada, and Field-Marshal Jan Christian Smuts of South Africa. Courtesy of Australian National Archives

flict with Germany, Fraser was to be an early architect of the Kiwi military effort in this second outbreak of hostilities. Since it was clear that the Nazis were a danger far greater than the Kaiser's imperial minions, Fraser supported this war without reservation. In 1939, he traveled to London for a series of meetings. After receiving briefings from British officials, he recommended that the New Zealand Cabinet send an expeditionary force to Europe. He also selected Major-General Sir Bernard Freyberg, a Kiwi serving in the British Army, to serve as the General Officer Commanding, 2nd New Zealand Expeditionary Force. It was during this time that Fraser first met Winston Churchill. The two men developed a good working relationship. Despite the differences in their political views, Churchill told the War Cabinet that Fraser was a reasonable man.[14]

When Savage died on March 27, 1940, Fraser became prime minister. "For many months he has borne the responsibility. Now he also wields the power. That is the supreme test of any man," the editors of the *New Zealand Herald* declared.[15] Fraser carried a heavy load as prime minister. In addition to leading the Cabinet, he at various times during the war held eight other ministerial positions. Some of these positions required little work, but others, such as External Affairs or Finance, were extremely demanding. Needless to say, he worked long hours. He ate poorly and at irregular hours. It was no surprise that he began to put on weight, his stoop grew more pronounced, and his eyesight became weaker.[16]

Foreign policy was a topic that he found intriguing and worthy of his attention. As the leader of a small nation, Fraser was attracted to the ideas that Woodrow Wilson had advocated during World War I. He would call the League of Nations "one of the noblest conceptions in the history of mankind." He supported the creation of another international organization that would allow its members to practice collective security. Because of its remote location and the limits of weapons technology in the 1940s, New Zealand was probably the most secure nation on the planet from foreign invasion. The Dominion, though, wanted a voice in world affairs. Fraser realized that what the great powers could do to Czechoslovakia they could, in time, do to New Zealand. An organization of nations, large and small, would give the Kiwis a say in world affairs.[17]

While Churchill thought Fraser was a reasonable man, he was less certain about the delegation from Australia. The group from this Dominion was deeply interested in the strategic direction of the Pacific war, probably more than Canada and New Zealand combined, but they would have little influence in the mother country. The Australians were at war with themselves on both personal and professional grounds. In fact, personal differences among the delegation's three key members had grown during the trip to London and would shape their views about the Pacific war.

The most important figure involved in shaping Australian foreign and defense policy was the prime minister, John Curtin. He had a high nasal voice that he delivered in rapid speech that accentuated his Australian accent. A bespectacled man with a round face, Curtin possessed a strong sense of humility—which is rare in successful politicians in most countries—and a sense of his own destiny, which gave him a tranquil personality. Curtin was the son of Irish Catholic immigrants of the Fenian nationalist movement. Although his father found employment in the service of the crown as a police officer, the political legacy of his parents was one of left-wing politics with little love for the English.[18]

Curtin made his living as an activist in the Australian labor movement and then in politics. Early in his career he was a committed Socialist. When World War I started, Curtin—like Fraser—opposed conscription for a conflict that he considered imperialistic. He soon found himself incarcerated in a small cell with limited access to exercise. He responded poorly to life as an inmate and was fortunate that the Australian Labor Party got him released after only three days.[19]

His brief prison stint only inflamed his growing abuse of alcohol. He turned to the bottle to deal with the stress of politics, and despite his progress up the ranks of the party, many of his colleagues found him unreliable. During his first election, he showed up at campaign appearances "in an alcoholic haze." He was up-front in speaking about his problem. In an effort to quell growing gossip, he said it was an issue that was now in the past. Despite a pledge he gave when he became party leader to give up drinking, he continued. Like many alcoholics he went to great lengths to hide his habit and often drank alone. His most recent biographer, David Day, shows that his drinking continued until just before taking office as prime minister. After getting sober, Curtin replaced liquor with another addictive habit, tobacco. At one time, he was smoking forty cigarettes a day.[20]

Curtin became prime minister in 1941 before the hostilities with Japan started. Curtin was an Australian nationalist but was also a good British Imperialist despite his Irish Fenian heritage. He wanted officials of His Majesty's Government in London to recognize that the British nation of Australia was now the political equal to the United Kingdom in setting the strategy and policy of the empire that King George VI ruled.[21]

A key element in defining Australian nationalist sentiment was the issue of race. The Australians stressed their British identity as a countermeasure to the fact that nonwhite nations surrounded their island continent. Australian law limited immigration to applicants from Caucasian nations. As Australia grew from a collection of British crown colonies into a nation that was fully sovereign in its own right, the great fear of many Australians was that the hordes of nearby Asia would invade and overwhelm the small British population. Japan, however, was the only country of Asia that had the industrial, economic, and military resources to project its power beyond its boarders. Australians feared the Japanese would turn on them and lead an Asian invasion into their homes. The coming of war to the Pacific in 1941 represented, then, the greatest fear of many in the Dominion, including John Curtin.[22]

In late December 1941, Curtin attempted to redirect the attention of the Great Powers to the Pacific. The Melbourne *Herald* asked him to provide a New Year's message to the people of Australia. What followed was a famous statement in which he declared, "Without any inhibitions of any kind, I make it quite clear that Australia looks to America, free of any pangs as to our traditional links or kinship with the United Kingdom." Although many Australian nationalists have looked at this statement as the breaking of Australia's dependent colonial relationship with the mother country, such was hardly the case. Curtin hoped the Soviet Union would declare war on Japan to take some pressure off Australia. Since the German advance had just crested beyond the reach of Moscow, such a move was hardly in Soviet interests. Churchill did become angry about the statement, and many Australians objected to what they saw as an effort to abandon Great Britain. Roosevelt even described the message as reeking of "panic and disloyalty." Differences and disputes involving the return of the Australian Army from the Middle East to face the new enemy, the diversion of Australian units to Singapore, and then the collapse of that island fortress to the Japanese embittered relations between Curtin and Churchill. The British prime minister suspended direct cables between the two of them and would be slow at both forgiving and forgetting.[23]

The second key figure in the strategic direction of Australia's war was Sir Frederick Shedden, the secretary of both the Defence Department and the War Cabinet. He was influential because he controlled what might seem relatively unimportant: the flow of official documentation. Shedden subtly established his authority through minutes and memoranda that assumed the reader had a familiarity with the issue, which most of the politicians serving in the Cabinet did not possess. He summarized current issues, often referring to the immediate history of an issue that he had participated in without a direct reference to himself. If the Cabinet members asked questions, this would be the opening for him to offer his advice and knowledge without threatening the elected representatives. While Shedden was willing to forego media attention, he was an exceptionally uptight man with an arrogant sense of his self-importance. His biographer, David Horner, found only one photograph of the man in which he was not wearing a tie. He was sensitive about his status and the perks that went with his position. Shedden traveled by air when it was extremely uncommon for most civilians, and when he went by train, he demanded and usually got the cabins in the center of the car that would rock the least.[24]

CHAPTER THREE

The Warlords? Sir Frederick Shedden (left) and John Curtin (right) directed Australian strategy during World War II. The two abdicated much of their responsibility to Douglas MacArthur, allowing this foreign general a large say in Australian defense policies. Courtesy of the Australian National Archives

Shedden's life revolved around his career. He had no children and kept long hours at the office. His job came to dominate his life despite attempts on his part to establish some outside interests. "I have been trying to master golf for the past year, but my golfing life is more a matter of hours rather than of days," he admitted at the time. He was a distant figure to his staff. When his liaison with the headquarters of General Douglas MacArthur went months before meeting Shedden, the liaison quipped, "Dr. Livingston, I presume?" Shedden got the joke.[25]

Curtin told him he was "his right and left hand and head too."[26] There are additional ways to measure Shedden's influence in Australia. He had several nicknames. "Defence Czar" and "Defence Supremo" speak to his authority. One of the few regular hobbies Shedden had was bike riding, which he shared with his wife. Therefore, many younger bureaucrats, wishing to emulate him, took up riding to work, and eventually the sport became so popular in Canberra that the Australian government had to build bike shelters and racks at public buildings and shopping centers.

Educated in the United Kingdom—he attended the London School of Economics and the Imperial Defence College during the interwar period—Shedden viewed Australia as an extension of Great Britain and saw Australia's national security strategy as a component of overall imperial military policy. The fall of Singapore shocked him, souring him on the mother country. As Australia turned toward the United States, he worked to develop a relationship with General Douglas MacArthur. Working closely with the American seemed the only way that Australia would have any influence in the formation of allied strategy. In April 1942, the Australians also agreed to the creation of a joint allied command giving MacArthur authority over all Australian armed forces in the Pacific region. This arrangement effectively established the American general, rather than the Australian Chiefs of Staff, as Curtin's primary advisor on strategy. In the letter that Shedden drafted for Curtin to sign giving MacArthur formal authority over Australian units, the prime minister declared:

> You have come to Australia to lead a crusade, the result of which means everything to the future of the world and mankind. At the request of a sovereign State you are being placed in Supreme Command of its Navy, Army and Air Force, so that with those of your great nation, they may be welded into a homogeneous force and give that unified direction which is so vital for the achievement of victory.[27]

The command and advisory relationship that Curtin and Shedden established with MacArthur was a major abrogation of national sovereignty at a time when Australia was contributing not only the territory, but the bulk of the personnel for the Southwest Pacific Area Command. There were 38,000 Americans and 369,000 Australians taking orders from the general. Shedden and Curtin, in his role as Secretary of Defence, would be the main links between the Australian government and the American. Shedden was, or at least thought he was, at the center of strategic planning for the war against Japan in the first half of 1942. He and MacArthur both looked at Pacific strategy in much the same manner. "General MacArthur has a profound knowledge of military art and history, is a shrewd judge of men, and, what is essential for a successful Commander, great personal courage and leadership, as was exemplified during the campaign in the Philippines," Shedden wrote of the American. He believed "Australia is very fortunate to have such an officer responsible for operations in the Southwest Pacific Area."[28]

Before the Australian delegation left for the gathering of prime ministers, Curtin and Shedden consulted MacArthur. He briefed them on how to deal with Roosevelt and the U.S. Chiefs of Staff during their stop in Washington, D.C. Shedden showed him the statement that the Australians would give the British on the role of the Dominion in the war. "I regard your paper as a very able and brilliant analysis of the Australian situation," the general told Sir Frederick.[29]

The third major figure in shaping Australia's war effort was General Sir Thomas Blamey. He was making the trip to London as well and was probably the most important Australian ever to wear his country's uniform. More significantly, both Shedden and MacArthur saw him as a rival to their position. Sir Thomas had an Australian-bred physical toughness about him. He did not let physical pain deter him. Once, in order to get rid of a kidney stone, he went horseback riding. "I thought the best thing to do was go for a ride and shake the thing down," he explained. Despite this hard approach to life, he had a particular fondness for animals. His rugged exterior also masked immense emotional pain. His eldest son was killed in a flying accident in 1932, and three years later his wife died following a long illness.[30]

Blamey was born in 1884 in the southern region of New South Wales, Australia. A short and stocky man, he grew up enjoying the outdoor life. He was considering a career in the clergy when World War I intervened and turned him into a professional soldier. He had a talent for the military life. He started as a 30-year-old Major and when the conflict ended, he was a Brigadier-General. He was at Gallipoli on the first day and helped plan the withdrawal from the beaches months later, which was the only part of that campaign that went according to plan. He was also the Chief of Staff for the Australian Corps during its operations in France in the climactic days of 1918. After the war, Sir John Monash, General Officer Commanding of the Corps, praised Blamey. "He possessed a mind cultured far above the average, widely informed, alert and prehensile." His Chief of Staff had stood up to the intense physical and psychological demands of combat. "Blamey was a man of inexhaustible industry, and accepted every task with placid readiness." Monash also believed that the operational orders and reports that his Chief of Staff had written would become perfect examples that military staff colleges could use in their courses. "They were accurate, lucid in language, perfect in detail, and always an exact interpretation of my intention." The war cost Blamey dearly, though. He lost his faith in Christianity and returned home to Australia to meet a 9-year-old son who barely remembered him and a younger son whom he had never seen before.[31]

Australia, like the United States and the other British nations of the Commonwealth, had little interest in keeping a large standing army in a time of peace, and Blamey had to find other employment. He became chief commissioner of the Victoria police. He enjoyed the different challenges the job entailed. "It is less of a routine job than anything else I know." Very early on in his tenure, though, he became involved in what was popularly referred to as the "Badge 80 Incident." On October 21, 1925, police raided a brothel they suspected of selling liquor without a license. The three constables conducting the raid did indeed find that people were serving alcohol, but they also found a man in the process of using the services of a prostitute. He told them he was a police officer himself and produced badge number 80. This badge belonged to Blamey. Shortly thereafter, the badge ended up in Blamey's mailbox at his club. An official investigation found that the badge was "in some way removed from the possession of the Chief Commissioner of Police." This explanation sounded lame to many, so another investigation followed. The detectives at the brothel that night reported that the man in question bore no resemblance to the new police commissioner. The second report said it would have been possible for someone to enter Blamey's office and remove his badge. In private, the commissioner said he had loaned his key ring, which included his badge, to

Australian Knight. General Sir Thomas Blamey was a strategic and administrative genius when it came to military systems. He, however, had major shortcomings in his character, which made many question his leadership ability. Courtesy of the U.S. National Archives

an old army buddy, thinking he was going to get liquor from Blamey's locker at his club. The incident would haunt him for years. Despite this stain on his reputation, he did a good job of building a modern and professional police force, which was particularly difficult during the Great Depression. In recognition of his work, the government of Australia knighted him in 1935. A year later, in a dispute with the Cabinet, he offered his resignation. Its acceptance stunned him: "My resignation has been accepted," he remarked to others with him at his club when he learned of the news. "Let's have a drink." Later in life, Blamey would say that his resignation "was probably a good thing for my character." It taught him resilience and enabled him to stand the stress and shock of combat.[32]

Hitler's actions soon resolved Blamey's employment issues, bringing him back into the military. After the Dominion declared war against Germany, Blamey became the General Officer Commanding of the second Australian Imperial Force and then held two posts in the Pacific war: Commander, Allied Land Forces, in MacArthur's theater and Commander-in-Chief, Australian Military Forces. In these three positions, he showed an interest in his own well-being that was at various times either indulgent or ruthless. He had no concern about his public reputation: "I think above all I am one of those who do not care much what others think so long as I know what I think." While this is a healthy attitude in general, he never showed any interest in leading by example. His desire to be judged by what he accomplished ignores the fact that leadership is part of generalship. He had numerous extramarital affairs. In December of 1940, he arranged for his wife to get a passport to visit him in Palestine when average soldiers had to endure separations from their families much as Blamey had done in the Great War. The presence of Lady Olga Blamey was the subject of considerable negative commentary back in Australia, and the Cabinet asked that she return home. Blamey refused, noting his wife had obtained a passport legally. After the disastrous British campaign in Greece in which Australian and New Zealand units participated, Blamey received orders to depart Greece immediately and establish a headquarters in North Africa. Obeying this order was the proper response. His decision to include his son, Major Thomas Blamey, among the staff that accompanied him, though, damaged his standing with many of his colleagues. When he announced his decision at a nighttime formation, one officer remarked in the dark, "He *would* take his bloody son."[33]

In the war against Japan, Blamey was the only significant foreigner on MacArthur's staff. He, however, never became a trusted subordinate. Early on in the Pacific campaigns, MacArthur needed Australian manpower—the U.S. Army was then still small—but he also needed a political lever to use against his superiors in Washington to ensure that adequate American resources went to his command in the Pacific rather than to Europe or the Hawaii-based command of Admiral Chester Nimitz. He tolerated Blamey as a necessary intrusion, but came to have deep reservations about his Australian lieutenant.[34]

Although his moral values were an extremely significant shortcoming in his character as a leader, Blamey molded the Australian Army into a professional force that played a significant role in defending the Dominion and the empire. The Australian soldiers obeyed him because of his rank and professional competence, but there was little admiration for him among the troops. His personal behavior made such popularity extremely difficult. He also had no rapport with them or interest in learning about the experiences of the frontline soldiers and officers.[35]

Blamey's relationship with Curtin was similar to the one he had with his men. They were wartime mates, but no personal friendship ever developed between the two. The prime minister tolerated Blamey's indiscretions because he needed him. "Gentlemen, I want a commander of the Australian Army, not a Sunday school superintendent," Curtin told a group of Labor politicians seeking the general's removal on personal grounds. Blamey reciprocated this support. On hearing a negative comment about Curtin in his officer's mess, he turned on the individual, saying, "Do you realize you are speaking of the Prime Minister? I won't have any criticism of the Prime Minister whatever his politics may be."[36]

His relationship with Shedden, though, was uneasy. They were rivals for influence with Curtin. After Blamey left the Victoria Police, Shedden was responsible for getting him a critical promotion. This action came before the government had named a General Officer Commanding of the Australian Imperial Force and helped bolster Blamey's claim to that position. Still, Shedden was uncomfortable with the general and once climbed out of his office window to avoid meeting with an angry Blamey. More importantly, the command arrangement that Shedden had established with Curtin and MacArthur limited the influence Blamey had as Commander-in-Chief of the Australian Military Forces.[37]

Needless to say, the trip that Curtin, Shedden, and Blamey took to London was an unpleasant one. The Australian delegation went to England via North America and left Australia aboard the USS *Lurline*. In violation of U.S. naval regulations, Blamey smuggled whisky, gin, and wine aboard. He held a big party in his cabin, and it showed the next morning. "Gen B had obviously too much to drink last night. He was very jolly and very talkative and the PM commented on it," Shedden noted. Sir Frederick was uptight on matters of drink, and as a recovering alcoholic, Curtin had no interest in being around excessive consumption. After arriving in North America and transiting the United States by train, Curtin met with Secretary of State Cordell Hull and President Franklin Roosevelt. These meetings did not go well, with disputes arising about postwar planning. After seeing Roosevelt, Curtin had some sort of nerve-related illness that produced intense pain in his head and back. He spent two days of the conference in bed before the Australian delegation had to leave for London. They took a flying boat that encountered strong headwinds and almost had to turn back. Blamey, showing the same selfish interest in his own creature comforts, took a bed that had been put on the boat for Curtin. The prime minister hated flying and was racked with nerves as he sat "tight lipped," anxiously waiting to see if they would get across the Atlantic. Despite the pain in his spine, Curtin managed to fall asleep in a sitting position.[38]

Relations among the three principal members of the Australian delegation were even worse on the return trip to Australia. Shedden recorded petty comments about not only Blamey, but also Curtin. Shedden's accommodations were apparently less luxurious than those of the others in the delegation, and he thought they were not appropriate for an individual of his importance. Blamey's indulgent behavior continued on the return trip home. In New York, the Australian general had female companionship every night during his stay in the American city. Blamey was equally frustrated with the slow pace of the return trip and came up with an excuse to leave the prime minister's party and return home ahead of them by air. Curtin and his wife were glad to see him go. Shedden fostered his own resentments and noted in his diary with contempt that the prime minister was extremely worried about knowing the correct procedure for abandoning ship while they were in the Pacific.[39]

This trip and Blamey's behavior on it damaged his relations with Shedden and, more importantly, Curtin. The immediate manifestations of the decline in these relationships would begin in London even before the group returned to Australia. The uneven and conflicting views of the Australians made them unwelcome guests. This would also reduce their influence at a time when it could have been authoritative.

■

FOUR

A Gathering of Prime Ministers

A number of matters needed to be discussed at this summit meeting, but British and Commonwealth strategy in the war against Japan was the most important. Australia and New Zealand had obvious interests in what the United Kingdom decided, but so did Canada, with a western coast that ran alongside the northern Pacific. The King's other prime ministers were willing to support some version of the middle strategy, but a number of issues minimized much of their influence. Despite it all, the British seemed to be on the verge of a resolution of this troublesome policy dispute. The major problem was that this issue still remained unresolved in Whitehall.

Cunningham noted as much in his diary. "Not easy to find out what is required from the COS as no one knows or can find out what the P.M. will say," he wrote just before the start of the conference.[1]

The summit began on May 1. The Australians arrived on April 29, and had only one full day to get adjusted to the new time zone and prepare for the gathering. Curtin spent most the day taking a tour of bombed-out sections of London and visiting the English countryside. When the conference started with a reception at 10 Downing Street, he made sure he was the first to arrive. From the start, he wanted to make sure that both Whitehall and the British public appreciated his views about Australia's relationship to the United Kingdom: "I should like it understood that I speak for seven million Britishers." Curtin went on to note that Australia was proud to be part of the United Kingdom and wanted His Majesty's armed forces in the war against Japan. The government in London, however, had to respect Australia and accord it a voice in the formulation of policy for the empire and Commonwealth. When praised for his comment, he privately explained, "it's what I genuinely felt; I felt it to be the truth."[2]

Fraser, on the other hand, had done little work to prepare for the conference, preferring to operate on instinct and analytical skills. He was sometimes sharp in the proceedings that followed. "Fraser put searching questions to CIGS about the Italian operation," Cunningham recorded. Since the Kiwi prime minister had done little preparation for the meeting, he was largely silent on matters involving the Pacific war. Despite the silent prime minister from New Zealand, Cunningham found the assembled politicians "rather talkative," which made the meetings rather lengthy and "drawn out."[3]

It was not until May 3 that the prime ministers had a full discussion about the fight against the Japanese. There were actually two meetings devoted to this subject. The first started just before noon, and Japan was the topic of discussion in the second half of that session. Field-Marshal Jan Smuts, the prime minister of South Africa, dominated the initial conversation with comments about the Italian campaign. He said the world was weary of war and that it was necessary to defeat Germany quickly because Japan still remained. Churchill made some remarks about the strategic direction of the war in Europe, and then Fraser began discussing New Zealand's role in the Mediterranean theater and the use of Kiwi troops there without proper consultation of the government in Wellington. "Fraser (NZ) made somewhat of an ass of himself and got ticked off by Winston," Brooke observed.[4]

After lengthy discussion on these topics, Churchill initiated a conversation on the struggle against the Japanese. He reported that the Royal Navy was in the process of putting together a fleet that would be the equal of the Japanese Combined Fleet. He said the Commonwealth and empire should do battle with the enemy where they could deliver the most firepower. The British prime minister also noted that the Americans had failed to honor their agreement to concentrate their air and naval strength in the Pacific. In this presentation, Churchill was honest, admitting that the United Kingdom had no firm plans for this region. He then summarized the various ideas that had been debated in London during the first half of the year. Churchill explained in frank fashion several times during his talk that regardless of what was decided in London, the British would be the junior partner to the Americans in the fight against the Japanese.[5]

Curtin raised the issue of command and control, bluntly asking if British forces would serve under MacArthur. Churchill was forthcoming and said the Combined Chiefs of Staff had yet to address the subject, but that the Americans would have the largest voice in determining the course of the war against Japan. Fraser noted that any command arrangement could be reconsidered and renegotiated. That comment provoked Curtin. He pointed out that the majority of troops in MacArthur's command were from his Dominion. He then stressed that the general had always handled himself properly, consulting regularly with the government in Canberra. Curtin also expected that future advances would move much faster than the British thought possible. Churchill said he remained skeptical, but Curtin said the advance toward Japan would place great demands on the logistical infrastructure of Australia, which would be difficult for it to handle, particularly if more forces arrived down under. He added that he had made these points in a cable that he sent back in October to which the British had never responded. Cunningham observed in his diary, "The Australians have evidently swallowed the American programme lock stock + barrel + firmly believe the dates can be achieved. I am not so sure. The Americans have not yet come up against the hard core of Japanese resistance. Curtin looks as if he is in MacArthur's pocket. Blamey certainly is. Curtin rather rude + gave the impression that he did not want UK forces in Australia."[6]

At this rather fractious point, the prime ministers decided to adjourn and reconvene at 5:30 that afternoon. That second meeting went much differently. Curtin started off the meeting, speaking from a nine-page prepared statement. Mackenzie King said he read it "emphatically." The Australian prime minister summarized his nation's war effort and focused particular attention on defense at the start of the conflict with Japan. "No country faced a greater danger with less resources than Australia." He noted that 72 percent of Australian manpower was devoted to the war effort, which compared favorably to Great Britain's 75 percent. Curtin did not explain, though, that the existing command structures determined the relationship of service and support operations for new armed forces in relation to Australia's job of exporting food to the United Kingdom and the U.S. military. Curtin recommended that Blamey and representatives of the Australian Air Force and Navy meet with British officials and begin discussing the technical requirements of a British deployment based in the Dominion.[7]

The discussion that followed was far less combative than that of the first meeting. Viscount Cranborne, secretary of state for Dominion Affairs, said the reason that there had never been any reply to Curtin's cable of October 1943 was that the British government had not yet decided on a strategy for the fight against the Japanese. Churchill quickly added that there was no question that the United Kingdom would play a role in the war against the Japanese. Curtin said it was important that Australia balance its war effort. He and MacArthur had a good relationship, but the partnership with the United States should in no way be taken as an act of disloyalty to His Majesty the King or "Australians' deep sense of oneness with the United Kingdom." He wanted to see the prestige of the empire restored in the Far East. It was a "civilizing agent" that the region needed. Curtin said delaying action until Germany was defeated might make it impossible for the British to use Australia as a base. He knew in the blunt reality of world affairs that the amount of influence Australia would have in shaping the peace would be a function not of the amount of logistical support that the Dominion provided, but the contribution Australians made in combat operations.[8]

The meeting then moved into a discussion of technical military matters. Blamey gave a lengthy presentation on Australian operations. "It was really very deeply moving," the Canadian prime minister noted. Curtin worried that MacArthur's advance would leave the British in South and Southeast Asia in bypassed regions. He also discussed the tides and port facilities available in western Australia. Churchill said that British forces would be engaging the Japanese somewhere in the summer of 1945 with the idea of either taking territory from them or wearing Japanese forces down. He added that until that moment he had little appreciation for the demands on Australian resources. Fraser added that New Zealand had faced similar demands, and that Curtin was being rather humble in discussing the expansion and growth of Australian industry during the conflict. After both Cunningham and Portal discussed naval and air issues, Churchill adopted Curtin's proposal to have Blamey meet with British officials.[9]

The Australian prime minister gave a much better account of himself in this meeting. "Curtin led off with an excellent statement which quite did away with the impression he had given in the morning," Cunningham wrote in his diary. "They are anxious for UK forces but do not know how many they can support + are most anxious not to have to be relegated to producers only but to keep force in the field commensurate with the importance at the peace table of their views on the Pacific being taken into account. A very laudable point of view. New Zealand much the same."[10]

Mackenzie King was also taken with the performance of his opposites. "Curtin did not spare anyone's feelings. I confess I admired his straightforward direct statements. I equally admire Churchill's restraint in listening to the presentation as Curtin made it."[11]

British Foreign Minister Anthony Eden was also impressed with the dialogue that was taking place in London. "It soon became apparent that they were whole-heartedly in approval of our Empire policy. This was not in a passive sense of acceptance but with rigorous, active approval. Fraser + Curtin both made this very clear."[12]

There were several other meetings related to the war against the Japanese. On May 5, the prime ministers reviewed world affairs, spending a good deal of time talking about their individual and collective relations with the United States. Mackenzie King explained that American public opinion shaped that of his nation to some degree. He went on to add that Canada was a Pacific power, had a stake in the region, and would do its part to defeat the emperor's forces. Smuts said the British-American alliance was one of "happy co-operation," adding that the good working relationship between the empire and the United States was one of the greatest achievements of the war. Given the close relationship between the two great English-speaking powers, he was optimistic about the future regardless of what might come. A close relationship with the United States should be the "sheet anchor" of every British nation.[13]

On May 12, manpower was the major issue of discussion. Ernest Bevin, the British minister in charge of manpower, discussed postwar employment. Given economic pressures and simple numbers, he expected that the principal British contribution in the Pacific would come in the form of air and naval forces. He added that a general demobilization would have to wait until Japan had been defeated. Bevin did admit, though, that there would be "some" reorientation of industry when combat operations ended in Europe. He wanted the government to be careful in the language it used to avoid disillusionment among the public when a full-fledged demobilization did not occur. Curtin claimed that Australia's whole war effort was focused on the conflict with Japan. Clement Attlee, the deputy prime minister, said that until the requirements of the war were known, it was impossible to determine at what level the government would maintain the armed services, but that there was no way that Britain was going to ship an army of three million to the Pacific.[14]

One of the major initiatives that Curtin wanted to implement was the creation of an imperial war cabinet or council with a permanent secretariat. Australians had been advocating the creation of such an organization even before World War I, which reflected their desire to have British officials recognize that Australia was the constitutional equal of the United Kingdom. The idea might have had strong support in Australia, but it had little elsewhere. Churchill had opposed such proposals before and decided to avoid the meeting when it was discussed—in his defense, he was attending a planning meeting for the D-Day invasion, which was far more important. Smuts was also absent, attending the same meeting with Churchill. Mackenzie King had opposed earlier attempts along these lines and made it clear that he would never concur, because it would reduce his influence and might require that Canada make a bigger military contribution to the war than it desired to make.[15]

The formal end of the Prime Ministers' Conference came the next day on May 16. Each prime minister made statements of resolution. "I repeat and renew solemnly," Fraser declared, "but with great pride, the pledge given by our late Prime Minister, Mr. Savage, in 1939—where Britain goes, we go; where she stands, we stand." Curtin's statement was also bold in its rhetoric. "I give you the pledge of my country and I am sure any other Government of the Commonwealth would give the same pledge of inflexible determination to be with you until the victory is won."[16]

Cunningham listened to these declarations with reservations. "P.M. had passed a statement rather high flown + with some statements of doubtful accuracy in it particularly as regarded future plans." Churchill delivered a poor performance in the admiral's opinion. "Winston for him rather halting + appeared to have difficulty in finding suitable phrases. Perhaps the doubt of how it would appear in the press was influencing him." Cunningham had more substantive reasons to look on these statements skeptically. "The desirability of getting agreement on *some* strategy for the war against Japan stressed + realized by all. We are quite hung up for want of decision."[17]

Many public events accompanied the conference. The prime ministers attended a number of dinners, award presentations, and various other social engagements while they were in the London area. They also visited units from their armed services. The purpose of these various functions was to keep the imperial bonds among the various British nations strong, bolster the spirit of those involved in the fighting, and recognize individuals for their efforts in the war. The King and the Royal Family dined with his various first ministers several times. On May 8, Cunningham noted of one dinner: "First Lord made quite a good speech followed by Curtin quite good + Fraser very emotional + nearly in tears when he spoke of the Navy's evacuation of the New Zealanders at Crete. My ears burned badly. Smuts made a fine speech + was loudly cheered."[18]

Curtin and Fraser were quite busy in making various public appearances. Both received honorary degrees from Cambridge. Early on in the conference, the King swore Curtin in as a Privy Councillor, and both Curtin and Fraser received the Freedom of the City of London. In his speech accepting his Freedom, a ceremonial honor similar in nature to an honorary degree from a university, Curtin backed away from his strident stands with Churchill, telling his audience, "Australia is a British people, Australia is a British land, and 7 000 000 Australians are 7 000 000 Britishers." Hugh Dalton, the British Labour politician serving as the President of the Board of Trade, was in the audience and noted in his diary:

Attend ceremony at the Guildhall of Presentation of the Freedom of the City to Curtin and Fraser. The former makes an excellent speech without a single note. This performance, I think, puts the latter off his balance. He had prepared careful notes, but now feels he must not use them. He therefore goes on a good deal too long and seems to find it impossible to finish his speech, though what he says is quite good.

Fraser also received the Freedom of the City of Edinburgh and an honorary degree from the University of Cambridge. "Judging by the general atmosphere the Imperial bonds seem at present to be strong," Brooke informed his diary after one of these many functions.[19]

After zigging and zagging, Curtin zigged again. He dined privately with Dalton one night. The British Labour politician arrived expecting a private meal with Shedden, a former student of his at the London School of Economics, and found Curtin there as well. Dalton recorded the evening in his diary: "After some general talk, J.C. begins to criticise the P.M. and, still more, his entourage. 'That old boy's no friend of yours,' he says, (he means of the Labour Party generally), 'and the people round him are even worse.'" The popular idea at the time in Australia was that Curtin and Churchill got along well together. Curtin certainly used that idea to his advantage politically back at home. In London, though, he said Dalton was the best candidate British Labour had for taking 10 Downing Street. The President of the Board of Trade dismissed this comment, saying he had other offices in mind.

> He persisted, however, in his view, and added "If I were you, I should seriously consider the question of coming out of the Government if some good reason presents itself. Of course you can't and shouldn't do it until the big operation has been launched and is well under way. But there would be a lot to be said for your crossing over to the other side of the House before the Government breaks up and before there is a general election."

Dalton said he would think about what Curtin had said, and noted that the Australian was "an impressive person."[20]

He was less impressed with his former student. Sir Frederick was diligently advocating the policies that Curtin wanted to see enacted. Dalton recalled the last time he saw Shedden when he was part of the delegation traveling with then–Australian Prime Minister Robert Menzies:

> Shedden, who last time he was here with Menzies was advocating an Australian National Government under the latter's premiership, and asked me to tell him the inside story of how we formed ours, to whom I replied that I thought Menzies should be prepared to serve under Curtin, since the Labour Party was the largest single party in Australia, is now the most devoted servant of Curtin. He praises him highly and says that Menzies has completely fallen out. Civil Servants, I suppose, must be time-servers. But this, I thought, was faintly indecent.[21]

Churchill was no fool. It was no accident that he had sat in Parliament for forty years. He invited Curtin to spend a day at Chequers, the weekend retreat of the British prime minister. Curtin would later explain that he arrived under the impression that Churchill was going to introduce him to his daughters. Given the context of the times, this claim sounds weak. Instead, he found a number of British officials present wanting to discuss strategy. None of his host's daughters were present. In the "ambush" meeting that followed, Churchill agreed to return Australian ships, planes, and men then serving in Europe to the Dominion. During an after-dinner drink session, the British prime minister started questioning Curtin about his appeal in 1941 to the United States for aid and military assistance. This action violated imperial principles. According to Shedden the following exchange took place:

CURTIN: "If the British Commonwealth had been at war with Japan, and war with Germany arose later, what would you have done? Would you have appealed to the United States?"

CHURCHILL: "Yes, most certainly."

CURTIN: "Well, that was just what I did, when we were at war with Germany and Japan came in."

Shedden would later write, "The discussion of this subject ended at that."[22]

These personal disputes complicated the efforts to use the conference as a mechanism for reaching a decision about British policy for the Japanese war, but this process started nevertheless. On May 4, planning officers for the Chiefs of Staff Committee put together a study on the various options that the British had. "Our primary consideration should be to play a vigorous part in the war to the utmost of our capacity, with a view to bringing about the defeat of Japan at the earliest possible moment. This is as much a political as a strategical objective." After discussing the advantages of placing the British center of gravity in either Southeast Asia or the Pacific, the planners noted, "Finally, not only our influence at the peace conference but our position and prestige in the Far East for many years to come will be determined by the extent and effectiveness of the contribution which we now make (and are generally recognised as making) towards the total defeat of Japan."[23]

Four days later, Churchill had another late night meeting with Portal, Brooke, and Cunningham to discuss strategy in the fight against Japan. The Chiefs had to leave early from one of the dinners honoring the visiting prime ministers. Cunningham noted: "The Sumatra project trotted out + at last I had to say quite plainly that I did not agree with it. P.M. took it well but moaned about there being apparently nothing for British forces to do against the Japanese this year. I agreed with him on this + suggested to Brooke that the whole thing should be reexamined."[24]

Two days after the end of the Prime Ministers' Conference, Cunningham thought they were getting close to reaching an agreement. He noted in his diary: "Generally agreed in order to reach agreement to plump for Central Strategy."[25] Brooke was far less optimistic, and the corrosive frustration he was feeling is readily apparent in a diary entry where he lashed out at everyone, including his friends:

> The problem is full of difficulties, although the strategy is quite clear. Unfortunately the right course to follow is troubled by personalities, questions of command, vested interests, inter-allied jealousies, etc. etc. Curtin and MacArthur are determined to stand together, support each other and allow no operation to carry out, Andrew Cunningham is equally determined that Mountbatten should not control the Eastern Fleet. Americans wish to gather all laurels connected with Pacific fighting, Winston is equally determined that we should not be tied to the apron strings of the Americans!! How on earth are we to steer a straight course between all these snags and difficulties.[26]

With time, Brooke joined Cunningham in his optimism. Both thought Churchill was slowly backing away from the Sumatra proposal. On May 24, Sir Andrew noted in his diary, "A quiet afternoon and a meeting in the map room with the P.M. at 2200. Discussion on the Middle Strategy i.e., attack on Amboina from North Australia. P.M. seemed favourable so perhaps we may get agreement." Brooke ate with Churchill alone before the meeting, and after the conference was cautiously upbeat. "I think we have at last got him swung up to an Australian based strategy as opposed to his old love of the 'Sumatra tip.'"[27]

The Australians appeared to be supportive. Blamey, attending several Chiefs of Staff Committee meetings, said Australia wanted to keep six divisions, seventy air force squadrons, and current naval forces in the field. The maximum contribution that Great Britain would be making would be six divisions, sixty air force squadrons, four battleships, and five fleet carriers with appropriate cruisers and destroyers. "We had a good discussion on Australia as a base assuming that the Pacific strategy was adopted," Cunningham observed.[28]

CHAPTER FOUR

Despite the quality of these talks, the British, Brooke in particular, had reservations about the Australian general. "Blamey is not an impressive specimen," the field-marshal noted in the safety of his diary. "He looks entirely drink sodden and somewhat repulsive." The Australian improved a bit with further acquaintance. After another meeting, Brooke observed, "I found him easy to get on with, but not inspiring." Blamey undercut his standing two days later when he showed up at another Chiefs of Staff meeting. "Blamey looked as if he had the most frightful 'hangover' from a debauched night. His eyes were swimming in alcohol!" Brooke noted, with a mixture of disgust and wonder.[29]

Brooke had good reason for being skeptical of the Australian general. Blamey was supporting Curtin's proposals publicly, but privately liked the idea of a separate imperial command that the various versions of the middle strategy offered. His motivation was easy to understand. There was a good possibility that Sir Thomas Blamey would be one of the leading candidates for that command, which might even result in his promotion to the rank of Field-Marshal. "Blamey in complete agreement, so much so that we shall now be accused by Winston of settling things without his agreement and behind his back!" Brooke wrote, with clear exasperation.[30]

The only problem was that the prime minister of Australia had reservations and was determined to protect his relationship with MacArthur. There was much to the argument that he was in the pocket of the American general. Shortly after the end of the Prime Ministers' Conference, he informed Churchill that the command structure in the Pacific could only be altered by the Combined Chiefs of Staff—which is to say, the United States. On May 26, Churchill had the Chiefs brief Curtin about the middle strategy. Churchill, according to the minutes, declared that it was important for the empire to stand together: "It was, in his view, essential that the British Empire as a whole should play an important part in the overthrow of Japan, so that the slur on our reputation that the earlier Japanese successes had inflicted should be wiped out."[31]

Curtin reacted to these ideas with a healthy dose of caution. Having just seen the paper, he had not had any time to study the Pacific strategy or consult with his cabinet. He then listed the various command arrangements that Australia had been a party to, noting that only the arrangement with MacArthur had given Australia a real voice in allied strategy. As the minutes of the meeting document, "He feared that there was a danger of the gravest misunderstanding with the United States if the Australian forces were taken away from General MacArthur's direct command and placed under a new Commander." Churchill replied that there was no firm proposal on the table. The British had not even discussed these matters with the U.S. Joint Chiefs of Staff, but it was important that they consult Curtin so that he knew what proposals His Majesty's Government was considering. Churchill said he wanted Australian help in determining the required base structure. Curtin accepted none of this explanation. His government had to make decisions about issues of fundamental importance, including the balance of forces and the production of supplies. To make informed decisions, his cabinet needed to know if the British were going to send troops to Australia. Oliver Lyttelton, the Minister of Production, said the United Kingdom could provide relief in the production of munitions, so the Australians could focus on other items. Brooke made some effort to answer the Australian prime minister's questions. He argued that there was no possibility of shifting all the troops in Europe to the Pacific.[32]

Cunningham thought Curtin was reluctant to make any commitment. In his memoirs he wrote, "He seemed rather shy of coming to grips on naval matters." That evening in his diary, he observed,

> Several discussions on Middle Strategy. Curtin not wishful to commit himself but inclined to relate everything to what was required of Australia in the way of maintenance. He made the statement that the Admiralty were asking him to man more ships, and asked for a reply to his query made last October to the effect that he wanted back the men manning RN ships. I put him right on the first question by pointing out it had been the Australian authorities who had raised the question of manning more ships + told him that the Admiralty would welcome an offer from Australia to man an a/c + one or two cruisers + would gladly provide the ships!

The conversation cleared up a lot of matters. Cunningham later called Curtin's views "very sound." As he observed in his diary, "The meeting closed with a good address by the P.M. + we all parted great friends."[33]

Anthony Eden was more pessimistic. In a handwritten notation for his subordinates in the Foreign Office, he observed, "As minutes show we got nowhere in discussion with W. Curtain [sic]; naturally enough for the poor man had only just seen C.O.S. paper before meeting, and he was clearly disturbed by some questions of command which it raised."[34]

CHAPTER FOUR

Curtin, no doubt, had some strong feelings of a similar color the next day when he received a message from Churchill. The British prime minister expressed an interest in developing Freemantle and Darwin as bases for a British advance. That part of the message probably had little impact on the Australian, but the next bit of information probably reduced his confidence in Churchill. The British prime minister went back on the statement he had made only a week before, telling Curtin that releasing RAAF personnel was impossible, because they were intermixed within British units. Their loss would only weaken these formations and undermine the war effort against Germany. It was also difficult to release Royal Australian Navy personnel. These officers and men were serving on twenty-six ships mainly in the Indian Ocean, and their release would shut down minesweeping operations in the area.[35]

Another document that would have been of even greater interest to Curtin was a paper the Chiefs sent to Churchill nine days later. "We propose," they wrote, "that British and Imperial Forces should be formed into a task force under General MacArthur's Command for the capture of Amboina. We believe that, with United States co-operation, particularly in the allocation of landing craft, this operation could be carried out during late 1944 and early 1945. Such an operation would clearly have to be related to other operations being undertaken at the time." Putting this paper together had been difficult for the Chiefs given all the various political and diplomatic factors they had to consider. "My God how difficult it is to run a war and to keep military considerations clear of all the vested interests and political foolery attached to it!!" Brooke wrote in a moment of deep despair. "I am tired to death of our whole method of running war, it is just futile and heart breaking."[36]

In the Foreign Office, British diplomats were telling Eden that a decision needed to be made. Ashley Clark, who would later become the British ambassador in Washington, observed: "I venture to submit that a decision on Far Eastern strategy is long overdue and cannot be postponed until after the outcome of OVERLORD is clear. Any further delay is likely to be seriously detrimental to our power to participate effectively in the Far Eastern war and therefore to the long-term interests of the Empire." As a result, Eden informed Churchill, "Our broad political objectives in the Far East are (a) the complete defeat of Japan; (b) the re-establishment of British prestige, especially in our own territories and in China; and (c) the promotion of long-term collaboration with the United States and eventually the Soviet

Union." With these goals in mind, Eden supported the Chiefs' proposal, but he noted it was

> only a beginning. But it has the double merit of being a distinctively British effort and of placing us in a position, if strategical and political considerations so demand, to contribute in a more direct manner to the main assault on Japan when the next phase opens. Naturally, if at that time it appears necessary and desirable to proceed to attack the Japanese in British territory, that also is not precluded.[37]

Little came of this initiative. The fight against the Japanese and the return of Australian personnel were minor issues at this point in the war. "When history comes to be written," Ismay wrote, "I believe that the waffling that there has been for nearly nine months over the basic question of our strategy in the Far East will be one of the black spots in the record of the British Higher Direction of War, which has, on the whole, been pretty good."[38]

Perhaps Ismay was right, but Churchill had far bigger concerns on his mind. D-Day was about to happen. In fact, the invasion was originally scheduled to take place the same day the Chiefs submitted their paper. Churchill had been looking forward to this undertaking for some time and had been an early proponent of an amphibious assault into France. The famous disputes between the Americans and the British about the second front focused on the timing of the operation rather than its merits. Churchill had wanted to strike around the periphery of Europe a bit longer for two reasons. First, he wanted to secure for Great Britain a dominant role in the postwar Mediterranean. This sea had been a British lake for the last century and a half and was a vital pathway connecting the United Kingdom with its empire. His second reason for dancing on the edges of Nazi territory had far more operational merit than the Americans were willing to admit. The Allies needed time to build up their armies. Operations in and around the Mediterranean allowed the British Army, which had been humiliated in 1940, to rebuild, and an American army that had little, if any, combat experience to get some. These peripheral operations did indeed slowly inflict losses on the Axis powers that they had difficulty in regaining. The day that Churchill had foreseen was approaching. Even if it was a bit earlier than he thought wise, the prime minister looked toward the day with a complex mixture of dread and anticipation. Japan could and would wait.[39]

The leaders of the American war were also deeply concerned about the outcome of Operation: OVERLORD. The Joint Chiefs of Staff traveled together to London to observe directly what they had spent two and a half years preparing. It is at this point that they enter into this story, and it is appropriate to take a moment in this account to consider these four men.

■

The Road to Quebec

With the end of the Prime Ministers' Conference, the British government examined the matter of Pacific strategy once again. Yet, the discussion that took place in the summer of 1944 proceeded almost as if there had been no conference or any compromise. The old battle lines and positions remained almost identical to those that the Chiefs and the prime minister had taken earlier in the year. Churchill almost single-handedly reverted the discussion back to the beginning.

Before His Majesty's Government reached this dangerous terrain, the U.S. Joint Chiefs of Staff intervened in the debate. The leader of the Joint Chiefs of Staff—at least on paper—was Admiral William D. Leahy. He turned 69 in 1944 and was a skilled and influential bureaucrat. Physically, his looks were less than impressive. He had a weak chin, which, added to his bald scalp, made his head look like an egg. He was a traditionalist in outlook and thinking, which might explain his success within the confines of the bureaucracy. It was a bit ironic that Leahy was the Chairman of the Joint Chiefs of Staff and Chief of Staff to the Commander-in-Chief; Roosevelt had created these two positions just for him.[1]

Leahy started his career at the U.S. Naval Academy at Annapolis, Maryland, graduating with the Class of 1897. He served on the battleship USS *Oregon* during the war with Spain. "I participated in some very mild bom-

The JCS. The U.S. Joint Chiefs of Staff at one of their regular meetings. From left to right: General Henry "Hap" Arnold, Commanding General, U.S. Army Air Forces; Admiral William D. Leahy, Chairman of the Joint Chiefs of Staff and Chief of Staff to the Commander-in-Chief; Admiral Ernest J. King, Chief of Naval Operations and Commander-in-Chief, U.S. Fleet; and George C. Marshall, Chief of Staff, U.S. Army. Courtesy of the Naval Historical Center

bardments; one at Guantánamo, Cuba. I did not like it then. We probably killed some women and children. Maybe we killed some of the enemy."[2]

As a naval officer on the rise, he preferred proven methods, but could do some inventive work within established boundaries. He realized that the navy needed more commissioned officers than Annapolis could provide, so he helped establish the Naval Reserve Officer Training Course (NROTC) that would allow students at civilian universities to receive a commission. He was also aware of the importance of naval airpower. He believed that the United States had the most combat-effective carrier force, because the U.S. Navy had retained control of the aircraft and pilots that flew off these ships, unlike the Royal Navy.[3]

When Roosevelt selected him to become the Chief of Naval Operations, it should have been the culmination of his professional career. Roosevelt liked having Leahy around and invited him to take cruises on the presidential yacht and attend Washington Senators baseball games with him. Before his retirement from the navy, Roosevelt told him, "Bill, if war breaks out in Europe, I'll want you right back here advising me."[4]

After retiring from the U.S. Navy, Leahy continued to serve the public. He was Governor of Puerto Rico for two terms before becoming the U.S. Ambassador to the Vichy French regime. Leahy found his work in France frustrating, since the United States and the Nazi puppet government of Marshal Philippe Pétain had conflicting policies. In his memoirs, he would call his stay in France "difficult but interesting" and a "long and sometimes weary mission." He often corresponded directly with Roosevelt, ignoring Secretary of State Cordell Hull. Just before his departure, his wife, Louise Leahy, died from an embolism right in front of him. The loss of his wife "has left me not only crushed with sorrow, but permanently less than half efficient for any more work the future may have in store for me and completely uninterested in the remaining future."[5]

Leahy returned to Washington and active duty, becoming both the Chairman of the Joint Chiefs of Staff and Chief of Staff to the Commander-in-Chief. In 1942, the idea to create a new position for Leahy came from Army Chief of Staff George C. Marshall. At the time, there were two representatives of the army on the Joint Chiefs but only one naval officer. Leahy had a reputation, in Marshall's words, for being "entirely impersonal and a man of good judgment," and he could be a regular liaison between the Joint Chiefs and the president. Even though he liked Leahy, Roosevelt had reservations about this idea, but Marshall's constant lobbying eventually carried the day.[6]

In his new job, Leahy met daily with the president. He also chaired the weekly meetings of the Joint Chiefs. As Chairman, his job was to resolve confrontations between the army and navy. He was the unifier. His main duties, though, were overseeing the White House Map Room. His influence came from his relationship with Roosevelt, which was friendly, but the two could hardly be called friends. Their relationship was professional rather than personal in nature.[7]

Leahy was soon giving political and diplomatic advice. His preference for proven, traditional methods made him an isolationist at heart. In late 1944, he recorded in his journal that he hoped the United States would issue a statement "that we do not intend to sacrifice American soldiers and sailors in order to impose any government on any people, or to adjust political differences in Europe or Asia, except to act against an aggressor with the purpose of preventing an international war." He was particularly suspicious of the British.[8]

The real leader of the Joint Chiefs of Staff was General George C. Marshall, Chief of Staff of the U.S. Army. Marshall was the only Chief on either side of the Atlantic who attended all the U.S.-British summits. In 1944, he was 63 and an exceptionally talented administrator. Born in Pennsylvania, Marshall came from a well-known Virginia family (John Marshall, the former Chief Justice of the Supreme Court and author of the concept of judicial review, was the most famous member of the family). He later remarked, "I thought that the continual harping on the name of John Marshall was kind of poor business. It was about time for somebody else to swim for the family."[9]

In choosing a military career, he followed a family tradition of attending the Virginia Military Institute. While in Lexington, he met Elizabeth Carter Coles. Marshall wanted to marry her and provide for his wife. To do this, he decided he needed to obtain a commission in the active duty army. Only West Pointers got automatic commissions at the time, but the service was taking a few hundred more that passed an examination. Marshall went to Washington and took his case directly to the White House. He slipped into President William McKinley's office with a group that had an appointment. When they left he had a chance to meet privately with the president of the United States. "Mr. McKinley in a very nice manner asked what I wanted and I stated my case. I don't recall what he said, but from that I think flowed my appointment or rather my authority to appear for examination." He passed and received his commission. Shortly thereafter, he and Lilly Coles married in a quick wedding.[10]

It was World War I that opened up professional opportunities for Marshall. As a Major in Europe, he became Acting Chief of Staff of his division, a position usually reserved for a Colonel or a Brigadier General. During an inspection trip, General John Pershing, head of the American Expeditionary Force, lost his temper with the division's commanding general and berated him and his staff. Angry at what he saw as unjust criticism, Marshall blurted out, "General Pershing, there's something to be said here and I think I should say it because I've been here longest." Pershing turned back and Marshall started throwing out facts at a rapid pace: lack of uniform, gear, quarters, and vehicles, and men too dispersed among the countryside to do any good. Pershing respected and indeed wanted officers that would tell him the truth rather than trying to avoid unpleasant facts. He quickly added Marshall to his staff.[11]

Tragedy entered Marshall's life after the war when his wife died. General Charles P. Summerall, Chief of Staff, offered Marshall several new jobs in an attempt to help him deal with his grief. Marshall accepted the offer to serve as the assistant commander of the Infantry School at Fort Benning, Georgia. Long hours of work helped to relieve the loneliness. His new position put him in control of curriculum, and over the course of the next five years he would train scores of junior officers in new infantry tactics and techniques. He wanted the lessons the students learned to be practical and encouraged student initiative. Of the students and instructors at the Infantry School during Marshall's tenure, a total of 150 earned general's stars in the next war. He also married a second time, becoming a stepfather in the process.[12]

As the Chief of Staff of the U.S. Army, Marshall was the person most responsible for converting the service from a sleepy peacetime garrison force into a force that could fight war on a global scale. Having learned that overworking himself could be counterproductive, he attempted to follow a routine and discipline his use of time. He insisted that officers reporting to him be succinct both in person and on paper. Time was a precious commodity in this conflict. He normally took his lunch in his quarters. If he had no guests, he tried to take a brief nap. He once remarked, "Nobody had an original thought after 3 P.M.," and while he worked long hours when necessary, he tried to leave the office around 4 P.M. He and his second wife would relax with walks through Arlington Cemetery or with canoe trips on the Potomac.[13]

Marshall realized that war was a young man's game. There were many officers in the middle ranks, but senior in age. They were awaiting promotion before retiring. Many were no longer physically up to the task of leading in the field or had become too conditioned to the routine of garrison work to provide the dynamic leadership that war would demand. He had to find new men to take these positions. "I have been absolutely cold-blooded in this business," he declared. Soldiers had to believe in the officers leading them. "It is morale that wins the victory," he stated. "It is steadfastness and courage and hope. It is confidence and zeal and loyalty. It is élan, *esprit de corps*, and determination. It is staying power, spirit which endures to the end."[14]

Like Pershing, he wanted to hear from dissenters. "Whenever I find these fellows who seem to have ability and a certain amount of disagreement with what we are doing, I am always interested in seeing them, and getting first hand impressions," he explained.[15]

Marshall's counterpart in the U.S. Navy was Admiral Ernest J. King, an exceptionally able and supremely arrogant man. He had a temper that even the slightest of events could trigger. "King was the only naval officer I ever knew who would actually curse his subordinates," one observer remarked.[16]

King respected men who stood their ground with him, though. While he and Pound were able to call each other friends, that was not the case with Cunningham. "Marshall was as charming as ever, and King as saturnine," the British admiral once told his diary. "I cannot bring myself to like that man." The Scotsman did, though, give him respect: "On the whole I think Ernest King was the right man in the right place, though one could hardly call him a good co-operator."[17]

Like most officers of his era, King started his career at the Naval Academy at Annapolis. He made a conscious decision to avoid graduating first in his class; it would make him too conspicuous in the navy. It would be best if he graduated third or fourth, which would be impressive enough. His final year at Annapolis he served as the battalion commander and graduated fourth in his class. He was also a combat veteran. When the United States went to war with Spain in 1898, the U.S. Navy needed junior officers. King managed to get orders to serve on the USS *San Francisco*, a cruiser that took part in the blockade of Cuba and came under fire from Spanish forts in Havana. "I must say I had a fine time on that leave," he remarked. "I had been to sea and I had been shot at!"[18]

King had a good career until it stalled after World War I. He then turned to naval aviation. Congress mandated that command of the new aircraft carriers and naval air bases go to qualified naval aviators or naval aviation observers. Even though he was 48 years old, King decided to go to flight school, where all the instructors were junior to him. King took this awkward situation in stride. "Although I was a captain," he remarked later, "I was merely a student aviator and nothing more." He did the bare minimum to earn his wings, but it was enough to get him command of the USS *Lexington*.[19]

The U.S. Navy was for all practical purposes King's life. His marriage was a hollow shell. His methods for coping with the stress of his job were limited. He was a religious man, but he rarely found the time to attend Episcopalian church services. He found temporary satisfaction in bed with various women and played some golf here and there. He was addicted to cigarettes, which did nothing to improve his health or disposition. Despite several attempts, he could never break free of the habit.[20]

His career stalled a second time and he was actually reduced in rank, going from Vice Admiral to Rear Admiral, but with the onslaught of the U-boats that came as war engulfed Europe, the U.S. Navy needed proven commanders. Then, in the days immediately following Pearl Harbor, Secretary of the Navy Frank Knox and Roosevelt made King the Commander in Chief, U.S. Fleet, and then later the Chief of Naval Operations.[21]

Throughout the war, King followed a fixed schedule. He would get up at 7 A.M. and do some stretching exercises before breakfast at 7:30. He usually had a daily conference with the Secretary of the Navy and dined with his staff in a late lunch. Conversation was usually only between King and his two flag lieutenants. The rest of the staff limited their conversations to asking people to pass condiments or responding when directly asked a question. At roughly 4 P.M., the admiral would slip away from his office and visit the Maryland farm of family friends, where he tried to escape the stress of his job for a few hours.[22]

Given his authority and personality, it would be easy to misunderstand King's actions during the war and see him as an Anglophobe. It was in the sapphire-colored waters of the Pacific where the U.S. Navy would win or lose the war against the Japanese. Nowhere else. No one else. He was, as a result, the foremost defender of the institutional interests of the U.S. Navy. He was more than willing to oppose the Royal Navy or the U.S. Army if either challenged the interests of his service, because his navy, and only his navy, could defeat the Japanese. Anything that challenged the well-being of the service put the national security of the United States at risk. King realized that the United States had important political and diplomatic reasons for having the United Kingdom play a role in the Pacific, but he wanted to make sure it was clear who the junior partner was in the coalition—particularly in the Pacific theater.[23]

The fourth member of the Joint Chiefs of Staff was not really a chief of staff. General Henry "Hap" Arnold was the Commanding General, U.S. Army Air Forces. He was also Deputy Chief of Staff for Air. In 1944,

Arnold was a pudgy 58-year-old man with thinning and receding white hair. His nickname "Hap" was short for "Happy," because he had a cheerful disposition. He was deeply in love with his wife, Eleanor, whom he called Bee. "He was an intensely likable person was Hap Arnold, transparently honest, terrifically energetic, given to unorthodox methods, and though shrewd and without many illusions, always with something of a schoolboy naïveté about him," Marshal of the Royal Air Force Sir John Slessor would later recall. "In spite of his white hair and benignly patriarchal appearance, he was a bit of a Peter Pan."[24]

Arnold's military career was almost entirely unplanned and went through a series of peaks and valleys. His father pressured him into attending West Point and becoming an army officer only after his older brother refused to apply. He was one of the first airpower pioneers in the United States. He learned to fly from the Wright brothers themselves, and earned the second pilot license in the U.S. Army. He helped William "Billy" Mitchell during the influential American airpower theorist's court-martial, but a few months later came close to getting himself put on trial for misusing government funds. Exiled, he slowly shed his pariah status through solid work and good networking skills. His efforts paid off when he was promoted from Lieutenant Colonel to Brigadier General and became the Assistant Chief of the Air Corps. He became Chief after the accidental death of his predecessor.[25]

Arnold wanted innovation within the service. He hated being told something could not be done. Something that the Wright brothers told Arnold deeply affected his thinking: "Nothing is impossible." He respected arguments that something should not be done and was unwise, but saying it was not possible seemed like a dodge to him and tended to get him angry. During the war, he had a placard on his desk that declared: "The Difficult We Do Today; The Impossible Takes a Little Longer."[26]

In the application of airpower, Arnold believed that the U.S. Air Forces had to do three things. The first was daylight strategic bombing in mass formations to destroy the elements of the enemy's society that supported its military forces. The B-17 bomber was the first plane that would actually allow airmen to put this idea into action. The plane, he declared, represented "not just brilliant prophecies, good coastal defense airplanes, or promising techniques; but, for the first time in American history, Air Power that you could put your hand on."[27]

He also realized that combat in the skies would turn on factors other than the number of planes available to sortie. "Air power is not made up of airplanes alone. Air power is a composite of airplanes, air crews, maintenance crews, air bases, air supply, and sufficient replacements in both planes and crews to maintain a constant fighting strength regardless of what losses may be inflicted by the enemy."[28]

The final element in applying airpower was having the right men in command positions. A key consideration in making command selections, according to Arnold, was "personal integrity: This covers a very wide field. To touch upon one or two—it means, for example, maintaining the courage of one's convictions. By no means should this be confused with stubborn thinking." This confidence could motivate and inspire others, particularly in combat. "Personal integrity also means moral integrity. Regardless of what appear to be some superficial ideas of present-day conduct, fundamentally, today as always, the man who is genuinely respected is the man who keeps his moral integrity sound; who is trustworthy in every respect. To be successful, a man must trust others; and a man cannot trust others, who does not trust himself."[29]

It was during his time as a member of the Joint Chiefs of Staff that Arnold had real influence on military affairs in the United States. One of the keys to his success was to never make a policy argument personal. Just as important was his relationship with George C. Marshall. The two generals first met years earlier in the Philippines when Arnold and his wife, Eleanor, were next-door neighbors to the Marshalls. During a field training exercise, Arnold was leading a company of infantry and stopped to give his men some rest. Years later, he described what he saw: "Under the shade of a bamboo clump lay a young lieutenant with a map spread before him. It developed he was dictating the order for the attack that was to break through the defender's line. This youthful officer was our side's chief of staff for the maneuvers, a job any lieutenant colonel or major in the outfit would have given his eyeteeth to have." The respect he had for Marshall never wavered. "If George Marshall ever took a position contrary to mine," he said as a Joint Chief, "I would know I was wrong."[30]

These four men traveled to London and met their British counterparts on June 14 in the War Cabinet Office. Collectively the seven became the Combined Chiefs of Staff. This summit was not the first one between these groups. Brooke and Marshall first met on April 9, 1942, and it was a mixed beginning. "I liked what I saw of Marshall, a pleasant and easy man to get on with, rather over-filled with his own importance. But I should not put him down as a great man," Brooke informed his diary. Four days later, he added, "The more I see of him the more I like him." The British general was busy trying to size up his American counterpart and conceded that the man had talent. "He is, I should think, a good general at raising armies and providing the necessary links between the military and political worlds. But his strategical ability does not impress me at all!!" Brooke never changed his opinion of Marshall on these matters. The more he learned of U.S. politics and civil-military relations, the more he came to understand the problems Marshall faced, but his general assessment of him never changed much. That is not to say that he had no respect for the man. After the war, in additions he made to his diary, he elaborated: "There was a great charm and dignity about Marshall which could not fail to appeal to one. A big man and a very great gentleman, who inspired trust, but did not impress me by the ability of his brain." In another addition, he explained, "I have seldom met a straighter or more reliable man in my life and thank heaven for these qualities of his. It was only in his lack of strategic vision that my patience with him used to become frayed."[31]

The views of the U.S. Chiefs were more complex. Marshall observed that the British "always present a solid front," which was more than he could say about his own delegation. In an interesting if ironic twist, Marshall had almost the same view of Brooke that he had of him. "While he may be a good fighting man, he hasn't got Dill's brains." It was unfortunate that the two generals never got along, but it was nothing more than unfortunate. They were professionals, put their personal feelings aside, and focused on the task of winning the war.[32]

With the establishment of a beachhead in France the Chiefs were in an upbeat mood, and the early part of their talks focused on operations in Normandy. Admiral King made a brief presentation on the course of the war in the Pacific and then the conversation turned to the role the British would play in the fight against the Japanese. The American admiral expressed a concern about logistical complications but also told the British that the U.S. Navy had no need for port facilities in Australia, which the British would probably use. With Cunningham in the lead, the British Chiefs then explained the middle strategy to the Americans and said their main target would be Amboina. Marshall stated that the Americans had been thinking of an attack on the island of Formosa. Brooke thought that seizing the entire island would take a long time. The minutes of the meeting indicate that discussion soon turned to bypassing Formosa and invading Kyushu, the most southern of the Japanese home islands. During this discussion, Portal repeatedly mentioned concerns about maintaining long communication lines in the Pacific. Both King and Marshall explained that it was important to avoid engaging the Japanese in large land areas, with the admiral specifically mentioning China. After further discussion, Marshall said the Americans would like to see specifics from the British. Brooke replied that the British Chiefs would draw up a concrete proposal for an advance on MacArthur's left flank using British naval forces and Australian and New Zealand air and ground forces. Portal and Brooke were careful to add that they would first need to get the views of the Australians and Churchill.[33]

Eight days later, on June 22, the British Chiefs sent a paper to the War Cabinet. "We propose that the British and Imperial forces should be formed into a task force under General MacArthur's supreme command to undertake operations of which the general object would be:—(a) To secure oil installations and air bases in North Borneo. (b) To co-operate on the left flank of General MacArthur's advance."[34]

Churchill quickly objected to the paper:

The political importance of our making some effort to recover British territory must not be underrated. Rangoon and Singapore are great names in the British eastern world, and it will be an ill day for Britain if the War ends without our having made a stroke to regain these places and having let the whole Malay Peninsula down until it is eventually evacuated as the result of an American-dictated peace at Tokio, even though there is a very small British force in the American Armies.[35]

Suddenly, the debate was back to where it had been in February.

John Curtin and Douglas MacArthur then reentered at this point. When Curtin returned to Australia, he promptly met with MacArthur and informed him of what had transpired in London. Shedden also informed the American that Curtin wanted to talk without Blamey present. Shedden also wanted to meet with the general alone. In both meetings MacArthur made it clear that he opposed any change in the boundaries of his command. In an example of the American general's paranoia, he ranted on about Blamey. He told Shedden that he considered Blamey's support for an imperial force operating from the western coast of Australia as an act of disloyalty to him, and since Curtin supported the current command arrangements, an act of disloyalty to the prime minister as well. Although the meeting with MacArthur was a private one, Shedden was not going to turn down a chance to undercut Blamey and made sure that Curtin got a copy of the minutes he made of this conversation.[36]

MacArthur had no problem with the British contributing forces to the war against the Japanese. A naval force would be particularly welcome in his command. Whatever type of combat units the United Kingdom sent to the Pacific, though, the general insisted that they "should come under the present setup." MacArthur tended to see his own career and U.S. policy interests as one. In one example, he told George C. Marshall,

> A British Commander would be completely destructive of American prestige in the Far East and would have the most serious repercussions. It is my belief that such a line of action would not receive the approval of the American people and that if consummated, would give rise to a condition that would be prejudicial to the maintenance of cordial relations between the United States and Great Britain during the post-war period.[37]

Curtin wanted a British presence in the Pacific, but he advocated only what he knew MacArthur wanted. On July 4, he cabled Churchill, "As British land and air forces will not become available for some time, I have reached the conclusion that the best manner of ensuring the earliest and most effective association of British forces with those of the United States and Australia in the war against Japan would be to assign to the Commander-in-Chief, South West Pacific Area, the Naval forces becoming available this year." Curtin believed sending a British force would enhance the influence of the empire and Commonwealth, and by extension that of Australia.

> This presents an ideal opportunity for the employment of the British Naval Task Force. It not only would contribute in great measure to the acceleration of the operations, but would be the Naval spearhead in a large portion of this campaign. It is the only effective means for placing the Union Jack in the Pacific alongside the Australian and American flags. It would evoke great public enthusiasm in Australia and would contribute greatly to the restoration of Empire prestige in

the Ear East. The opportunity that presents itself is very real, but the pace of events here demands immediate action.[38]

The requirement of a timely decision was real enough—it was also the main snag. Even though Curtin's July 4 cable worked against their specific proposal, the Chiefs quickly seconded the Australian's main idea. "Mr. Curtin's proposal is in general accord with our present view of the most effective initial contribution we could make. The latest information received from Australia on a staff level confirms Mr. Curtin's opinion that the necessary base facilities would be available in Australia." The Chiefs added: "These proposals bring to a head the question of command." They believed that they had to persuade the U.S. Joint Chiefs of Staff to bring MacArthur's command under the purview of the Combined Chiefs, giving the British some say on strategy in the Pacific.[39]

Late on the evening of July 6 in a meeting with the Chiefs of Staff, Churchill made it clear that he was still attached to his ideas about where the British should engage with the Japanese. In his diary, Eden noted: "After dinner a really ghastly Defce Cttee (Defense Committee) nominally on Far Eastern strategy." He called the discussion "meaningless when it was not explosive." Cunningham recorded that Churchill dominated the discussions and the assembled officials had spent nearly four hours "listening to him talking mostly nonsense + got nowhere." Churchill began the meeting on a bad note when he echoed American criticisms of General Sir Bernard Montgomery. A polarizing figure even within the British Army, Montgomery was a protégé of Brooke's, and the Chief of the Imperial General Staff defended his subordinate in blunt terms, accusing Churchill of subterfuge. Brooke took what was probably one of the worst approaches possible with the prime minister. Eden noted in his diary, "W protesting vehemently. He was clearly deeply hurt on his most sensitive spot, his knowledge of strategy + his relationship with his generals." Cunningham saw that Churchill was hurt, but joined in. "I had a couple of blows with him about the Far East." After returning home, Brooke wrote: "He was very tired as a result of his speech in the House concerning the flying bombs, he had tried to recuperate with drink. As a result he was in a maudlin, bad tempered, drunken mood, ready to take offence at anything, suspicious of everybody, and in a highly vindictive mood against the Americans." Eden and Cunningham made similar points in their diaries. "W hadn't read the papers and was perhaps

vas in a pleasant mood. We wandered like a swarm of bees from
er to flower, but never remained long enough at any flower to
it of any honey being produced. It was a blank evening as far as
ulating plans went. However he was less vindictive towards the
ricans, and more easy to manage. But what a waste of time it all
le does not know the situation, has a false picture of the distribu-
of forces and of their capabilities. A complete amateur of strat-
he swamps himself in details he should never look at and as a
lt fails ever to see a strategic problem in its true perspective.[45]

e conference on July 14 was better at least in the sense that the differ-
were aired, but no decision came even after Attlee, Eden, Lyttelton,
ie Chiefs spent two and a half hours discussing the issue with Chur-
During the meeting, Attlee handed a note to Eden: "Two hours of
ul thinking." In his diary, Eden observed that "he was not far wrong."
te was even harsher. The talks "settled absolutely nothing!!"[46]
urchill was the chair of the meeting and declared that he thought lit-
the Chiefs' proposal. He did, though, suggest splitting the difference.
British could contribute a fleet to the drive through the Pacific and still
k Sumatra. If British forces failed to retake British territory, there
d be little hope that a peace conference would return them to the
ed Kingdom. He wanted to take forces from Burma and use them in an
hibious landing. Brooke responded, stating it was impossible to re-
e units and still hold on to current positions in Burma. Eden argued
CULVERIN was the better plan, but there were two small problems: the
sh lacked the landing craft and men. His sarcastic analysis of Chur-
's proposal comes through decades later even in the fairly understated
ord of the meeting. In his diary, Eden explained his views more fully:
ie Far Eastern war is going to be a problem for our people and what I
about Chiefs of Staff plan is that it give us the nucleus of an Imperial
te at an early date and upon this we can build." Brooke bore the main
den of arguing with Churchill, but well into the conversation, Portal in-
med Churchill that early contacts with the Australian and New Zealand
itary staffs indicated that both Dominions supported the "Middle
urse Strategy" because it would put their forces in the "forefront" of the
sade against the Japanese. Portal made it extremely clear in his remarks
it these early contacts were informal and in no way committed the

rather light," the foreign minister observed. I
tering that resources were available, but prod
by accusing us all of trying to corner the Prir
him or some such phrase." The admiral noted,
was in no state to discuss anything. Very tired ·

Eden tried to smooth the matter over, but t
evening had been set. Brooke explained a prop
would send a "substantial" British naval forc
serve under MacArthur's command. Land and
ter the defeat of Germany. Eden added that bec
ble, this proposal was the best force the United k
field at the moment.[41]

Churchill objected, noting that the British wc
nor contribution. The minutes read: "The sham
pore could, in his opinion, only be wiped out
fortress." He also noted that the British Indian A
would be unforgivable not to make use of it in th
be humiliated if the United States defeated Japan l

The Chiefs responded, disputing this analysis.
that MacArthur had plans that were solid and ti
vancing their own cause and pursuing a strategy th
tribution to the defeat of Japan. He added that a
would not make use of British naval forces, whi
Brooke also noted that Curtin's telegram made it cle
about to initiate an advance that would move rapidl
to play the biggest factor in the defeat of Japan. Por
United Kingdom had strength in the water, but not
mained skeptical and apparently inebriated. The mee
tively.[43]

The Defense Committee met again only four days
egy on the Far East. "Now we are faced with another
pm meetings!! I only hope I shall not lose my temper
Brooke wrote.[44]

The meeting was a superficial affair that failed to pr
sion. The meeting went marginally better than Brc
though. In a diary entry that is as condescending as
field-marshal noted:

United Kingdom to any course of action. Lyttelton said another strength of CULVERIN was that it would prevent the development of a rubber shortage in British industry. Churchill ended the meeting by saying nothing he had heard had convinced him of anything.[47]

Brooke was frustrated. "Both Attlee and Eden were against him, and yet on and on we meandered." As the conversation continued, the Chief of the Imperial General Staff decided to try to force the prime minister to make some type of decision.

> In the end I said to him: "We have examined the two alternatives [an attack on Japan based mainly on India or Australia] in great detail, we have repeatedly examined them for you, we have provided you with all possible information, and we are unanimous on our advice to you as to which course to select. They both have certain advantages, but in our minds we are quite clear as to which course we should select. However, we are even clearer still that one or other course must be selected at once, and that we cannot go on with this indecision. If the Government does not wish to accept our advice let them say so, but for heaven's sake let us have a decision!" He then stated that he must go on thinking about it and would give us a decision within a week! I doubt it!![48]

Cunningham was aggravated as well. "We had hoped to get some decision on Far Eastern strategy but we were treated to the same old monologue of how much better it was to take the tip of Sumatra + then the Malay Peninsula + finally Singapore than it was to join with the Americans + fight Japan close at home in the Pacific." The admiral had a difficult time understanding why the issue remained unresolved and was outraged at Lyttelton's comment about forestalling a rubber shortage.

> The attitude of much of the politicians about this question is astonishing. They are obviously frightened of the Americans laying down the law as to what is to happen when Japan is defeated to the various islands, forts + other territories. This appears to be quite likely if the Americans are left to fight Japan by themselves. But they will not lift a finger to get a force into the Pacific they prefer to hang about the outside + recapture our own rubber trees.[49]

The admiral's condemnation of the Cabinet was understandable, but unfair. Many ministers found the never-ending dispute maddening. The minutes of the meeting show that Attlee and Eden argued against holding out for CULVERIN. Although Eden preferred some type of attack on Sumatra, he realized the idea was unrealistic. "Moreover, since it is remote from the centre of conflict with Japan, if we cannot see it through we shall be regarded by Americans as having played virtually no part in defeat of Japan."[50]

As Brooke had suspected, the matter took longer than a week to resolve. On July 20, he vented into his diary:

> We then considered Winston's minute stating that he had decided that he could not give a decision on the Pacific strategy without discussing matters once more with Dickie Mountbatten!! We had sent him a minute stating that Supreme Commanders were not the people to decide world strategy, that these decisions must rest with the Combined Chiefs of Staff and governments concerned. However he cannot understand strategy and argues the relative advantages of an attack on North Sumatra as opposed to one on Amboina, instead of discussing relative merits of an attack on Japan based on India as opposed to one based on Australia.[51]

Another three weeks passed before Churchill met with the Chiefs again on this subject. The battle continued without pause in a marathon series of meetings on August 8. That evening Eden wrote in his diary: "Three meetings during day on Far Eastern strategy and at the end we were further off than at the beginning. W. harks back to 'Culverin' always and generally seemed very tired and unwilling to address himself to the arguments. As a consequence Brookie became snappy at times which didn't help much."[52]

The first meeting took place in the small confines of the Map Room at 11 A.M. Brooke started off the meeting discussing the campaign in Burma and also said a decision was needed on strategic priorities in the war against Japan. The campaigns that Mountbatten planned would leave much of the Royal Navy without a mission, and the Chiefs thought that a British fleet, along with Australian ground troops, could help the American drives through the Pacific. Units of the Royal Air Force and British Army would join this advance after the war in Europe ended. Churchill disagreed, saying that the main British goal should be to liberate Japanese-occupied colonies. With the late arrival of Attlee, Eden, and Mountbatten, the conversation returned to the topic of Burma. Instead of the prime minister and the Chiefs concentrating on the real issue—their fundamental differences over British strategy and foreign policy—they spent much of the time talking about details like the number of men and types of units required to protect the air route into China and to retake Rangoon. The conference agreed to meet again later that day and examine British strategy against Japan.[53]

Churchill and the Chiefs met again in the Map Room at 6 P.M. The bulk of the argument took place between the prime minister and the Chief of the Imperial General Staff. Brooke repeated the proposal he made at earlier meetings. Eden complained that it was unlikely that the British would play much of a role under MacArthur's command and suggested that British naval and Australian military forces consolidate in Burma. In response, Brooke believed the Australians already had missions that would preclude them from being reassigned and that the biggest contribution the British could make to the campaign against Japan would be through the deployment of the Royal Navy in a drive that would take them to the home islands. Cunningham added that MacArthur would most likely object to a proposal that gave him additional naval forces but took away Australian ground troops from him. Churchill then turned the conversation to how they should broach the subject with the Americans. He proposed that he contact Roosevelt, as he had earlier in the year, and see what British resources the United States required in the Pacific. Brooke disagreed, saying the government had to decide what Great Britain wanted to do in the Pacific, and then the British could make proposals to the Americans. The sooner they reached a decision the better, since logistical work required a lot of advance planning. Cunningham supported Brooke, explaining some of the technical requirements that the Royal Navy needed to resolve. The minutes of the conversation indicate that the conversation lost focus, meandering among a number of minor topics, which probably reflected the prime minister's problems in concentrating. Churchill then brought up the topic of CULVERIN again. With a rambling conversation and no decision likely, the meeting adjourned to meet again at 10:30 P.M.[54]

In the confines of his diary, Brooke unleashed the fury of his pen:

Up to the present we have settled absolutely nothing and as far as I can see we are unlikely to settle anything tonight. We have been discussing the Pacific strategy, recommending the capture of Burma by a landing at Rangoon combined with a Pacific strategy of naval, air and Dominion forces operating from Australia. Winston still hovers back to his tip of Sumatra and refuses to look at anything else.[55]

When the third meeting started, the assembled ministers dominated the initial discussion. Attlee noted that it was important the government decide on a strategy for the Far East. He personally favored the Chiefs' proposal to have the Royal Navy operate under MacArthur's command. Eden suggested that an attack on Rangoon made the best sense since it gave the British options on what to do afterward. Cunningham and Portal both argued for sending a naval task force to the Southwest Pacific. Lyttelton agreed. Brooke argued that an attack on Rangoon would allow the British to pursue either a Bay of Bengal strategy, which is what Churchill wanted, or a Pacific strategy, which is what the Chiefs had been recommending.[56]

Many people were wanting a decision, any sort of decision. The government had been debating the issue for eight months. The prime minister observed that the debate on the Pacific had had no impact on any military operations. Other factors yet to be determined, like the defeat of Germany and the pace of the American advance toward the Japanese home islands, had to be considered in making strategic decisions. He supported an invasion of Rangoon. The conversation then veered into a discussion of the Italian campaign, which no doubt infuriated and exasperated the taunt Brooke. Toward the end of the meeting, the prime minister declared he had no problem sending the Royal Navy to the Pacific to serve under an American and hoped that it would take part in an attack on Japan itself. Even though Portal and Cunningham quickly voiced support for this view, Churchill had resolved nothing. He said strategy for the Far East required more thought to avoid coming to a wrong decision and recommended that the group meet again the next day.[57]

At 1 A.M., a weary Brooke made an addition to his diary about the last meeting:

It was if anything worse than any of the conferences of the day. I believe he has lost the power of giving a decision. He finds every possible excuse to avoid giving one. His arguments are becoming puerile, for instance he upheld this evening that an attack on the tip of Sumatra would force a withdrawal of Japanese forces in northern Burma and would liquidate our commitment in this area. We have conferred for 7 hours!!! with him today to settle absolutely nothing. Nor has he produced a single argument during the whole of that period that was worth listening to. I am at my wits' end and can't go on much longer![58]

Cunningham, as always, thought much the same as Brooke. His view of Churchill was more negative in nature, but more controlled in tone: "No decisions were reached in fact a thoroughly wasted day. What a drag on the wheel of war this man is. Everything is centralized in him with consequent indecision + waste of time before anything can be done."[59]

On August 9, the next day, Churchill met again with the Chiefs three times. Brooke, Portal, and Cunningham met together as a group first, and as they compared their recent paper and the one that Churchill had produced they were surprised at what they saw. "Curiously they were not very different," Cunningham observed. The core of each paper recommended that the British offer a fleet to serve under either Nimitz's command, which was the preferred option, or that of MacArthur. During the discussion that followed, Churchill said he wanted to get a British effort on record in case Americans tried to accuse the United Kingdom of placing the burden for defeating Japan solely on the United States. Cunningham, thanks to his service in Washington, knew that the officers serving at U.S. Navy headquarters had an extremely proprietary view of the Pacific war, and that there was wisdom in this position. "One good political point he wishes to make. He wants to be able to have on record that the US refused the assistance of the British Fleet in the Pacific. He will be bitterly disappointed if they don't refuse!!" The conference charged Ismay with the job of merging the two documents into one. Everyone would then meet again at 10:30 P.M. to discuss this combined paper. The general finished the task at 4 P.M., but Churchill had him wait until the start of the meeting before circulating the paper to the Chiefs, putting them at a disadvantage in the discussions that followed. Cunningham was appalled at this duplicity. "Thus we are governed!! I presume he himself has such a crooked mind that he is suspicious of the COS."[60]

Brooke wanted time to study the paper. Cunningham looked at the document and noticed that the first four paragraphs discussed how to approach the U.S. Chiefs, while the fifth paragraph explained how to "doublecross them." This memo did nothing to improve his view of Churchill. "I often wonder how we expect the USCOS to have any respect for us. We allow our opinions to be over ridden + ourselves persuaded against our own commonsense at every turn." The group agreed on the main strategic elements, but the language in the telegram that the British would send to the U.S. Joint Chiefs of Staff was another battle the Chiefs would fight with Churchill.[61]

Upset with this version, the Chiefs once again thought about initiating a confrontation that could have destroyed them all. "Message to US COS drafted this morning came back after dinner as amended by the P.M.," Cunningham recorded in his diary on August 10. "As usual full of inaccuracies, hot air + political points. Not the sort of business like message we should send to our opposite numbers." On the morning of August 11, the committee met with Ismay to discuss how to handle the situation. No other staff officers were present. Cunningham recorded:

> In a closed session Ismay told us that he was just raving last night + absolutely unbalanced. He cannot get over having not had his own way over Anvil. To my surprise it was Portal that suggested we should have to have a show down with him before long if he went on as he is now. I have long thought it. He tries now to dictate to the COS what they shall say to the US C.O.S. We decided to alter the message to some extent to meet his views + hold it up for 24 hours to let him recover his balance a bit.[62]

This pause worked and no confrontation ever occurred. At the end of the day, Eden wrote in his diary: "We are, I think, 'home' as far as our plans are concerned + I don't think we could devise better. But we are very late."[63]

The Chiefs of Staff sent their American counterparts a telegram on August 18 that represented the official British position. The British noted that they were "building up a strong fleet." The British Chiefs explained, "It is our desire in accordance with H.M. Government's policy that this fleet should play its full part at the earliest possible moment in the main operations against Japan wherever the greatest naval strength is required." The British Chiefs reported that the fleet would comprise six King George V class battleships, another twenty-five aircraft carriers of different classes, twenty cruisers, forty to fifty fleet destroyers, a hundred escorts, and a large fleet train. "If for any reason United States Chiefs of Staff are unable to accept the support of the British fleet in the main operations (which is our distinct preference) we should be willing to discuss an alternative." The alternative they suggested was a task force of British imperial units serving under MacArthur.[64]

When the British telegram arrived in Washington, the planning officers working for the Joint Chiefs of Staff started studying the proposal. Only three weeks separated them from the meeting in Quebec, and speed was important in this effort. The note arrived, though, after the Americans had made some important strategic decisions. After much consideration, planning officers working for the Joint Chiefs of Staff had decided that the ultimate objective in the Pacific war would be an invasion of the main Japanese islands. Earlier in the summer, while Churchill and the Chiefs worked to establish a strategy for the Far East, officers on the British Joint Staff Mission in Washington had informally given their American colleagues a paper proposing a British force of eight divisions. As a result, U.S. planners were already thinking about what role their ally would play in the fight with Japan. General Douglas MacArthur, however, remained suspicious of the British. In the first half of the year, he had been letting officers in the Royal Navy know that they and their ships would be welcome in his command. A British naval task force would have given him a fleet and would have freed him from his obligations of working with the U.S. Navy, which he saw as a threat to his place in history. In July, after receiving a letter from King, he became antagonistic toward the Royal Navy. King made a smart bureaucratic ploy, telling MacArthur that staff talks in London had raised the possibility of assigning some of the territory in his theater to Mountbatten's South-East Asia Command. The general was going to sacrifice nothing to the British.[65]

Staff officers in Washington suggested to the Joint Chiefs that before they agree to this proposal, they get logistical information and details from the British on how they planned to support this force. At a Joint Chiefs of Staff meeting on September 8, Leahy observed that the type of detailed questions the staff officers wanted to put to the British was less than welcoming. He believed the United States should accept that the United Kingdom would make an honest effort to provide the largest force that was possible when they were able to do so. Discussion on issues of implementation would follow, but the details could, and should, be worked out later. For now, the main thing was to get both the offer and an acceptance on the record. Marshall agreed and informed MacArthur: "In considering the proposal of the British Chiefs of Staff, the U.S. Chiefs of Staff felt that they had no action but to accept the British proposal. For our government to put itself on record as having refused agreement to the use of additional British and Dominion resources in the Pacific or Southwest Pacific Area was unthinkable."[66]

While the Americans worked out their response, the British delegation was in transit aboard the RMS *Queen Mary*. American servicemen traveling on the ship had lost a week of their leave waiting for the prime minister and his party to board. Churchill made it up to them, asking Roosevelt that they receive an extension. The president agreed and Churchill informed the Americans of as much before the ship reached port. Needless to say, these soldiers were happy at this good news. Even though the British did much work on the trip, they also had time to rest and relax. They saw films, which were usually standing-room-only affairs. Churchill also got to indulge himself in steering the *Queen Mary* during the trip, much to Cunningham's disapproval.[67]

What made this voyage to the New World particularly significant were the unresolved differences between Churchill and the Chiefs on Pacific strategy. Brooke pondered this issue as he stood on the bridge with Portal and Cunningham while the ship pulled out from its dock. He was in a particularly morose mood as he explained a little later that day: "I am not looking forward to this journey and conference. Winston is still always set on capturing the tip of Sumatra." The war was also taking its toll on the field-marshal. "Added to it all that I am feeling frightfully mentally tired and disinclined for a difficult conference!"[68]

After the war, Brooke decided to add another section to this diary entry:

> It was probably just as well that I was not able to look into the future and see what was facing me. I was in for a series of the most difficult conferences with Winston on this journey. Conferences where he repudiated everything he had agreed to up to date. I do not think that he had thoroughly recovered from his go of pneumonia and he was still suffering from the after effects of the heavy doses of M and B [May and Baker, a sulphonamide] which he had been given. He was quite impossible to argue with.[69]

While Churchill was infuriating Brooke, the prime minister was having his own problems with the ever troublesome Curtin. The British sent the

Australians a routine telegram informing them of the proposal they had sent to the Americans. This message initiated a meeting in Canberra of the Australian Advisory War Council. Curtin made two strong points in this meeting. The first, which he also made in a cable to Churchill, was that the command arrangement for operations in the Pacific could only be changed if Australia had a voice in the decision and a say in determining strategy. His government had no intention of removing troops from MacArthur's command with operations in the Philippines about to begin in full.[70]

His second position, which he made with more force in the meeting than in the cable, was that he and his Cabinet supported the restoration of the United Kingdom in the region. In the minutes of this meeting, Shedden wrote: "The Prime Minister said that the British Government and the Australian Government were fully aware of the necessity for maintaining British prestige in the Pacific, and were aware also that British prestige could only be restored by the presence of British forces in the war against Japan."[71]

These two views might seem contradictory. Was Curtin an Australian nationalist or a royalist? The answer is: both. Australia was a British nation, and it was the equal of the United Kingdom. Canberra should and would have as much voice in determining the fate of the empire and Commonwealth as London.

After receiving Curtin's message, which made its main point in exceptionally polite language, Churchill responded. He attempted to explain that "the proposal that we put to the U.S. Chiefs of Staff appears to have been completely misunderstood." He continued on, though, saying that the Combined Chiefs of Staff would make the decisions "without previous reference to the various Governments whose forces are included in the plans. Any other system would lead to almost innumerable people being brought into consultation before any plan could be settled." Curtin answered: "I feel we have not misunderstood your proposal." This discussion might have continued, but the Australian's health soon collapsed, leaving matters unresolved between the two British capitals.[72]

Curtin was, however, a less than immediate concern for Churchill. His disputes with Brooke, Portal, and Cunningham were ever present. These differences worried Brooke immensely. A meeting the Chiefs had with Leathers on September 6 about shipping did nothing to shake the field-marshal's concerns. "The call on shipping will be enormous, what with move of forces to the Japanese war, Canadians to Canada, New Zealanders to their homes and South Africans to South Africa, and on top of it all certain civilian requirements which will have to be provided for. It is going to be a difficult problem to lay down priorities for all these moves." Brooke found Churchill failing during the trip. "He was not looking at all well and was most desperately flat." Cunningham agreed with this assessment: "The P.M. still very flat, not much sparkle about him." After another meeting, Brooke recorded: "He looked unwell and depressed. Evidently found it hard to concentrate and kept holding his head between his hands. He was quite impossible to work with, began by accusing us of framing up against him and of opposing him in his wishes." The field-marshal's feelings for the prime minister were complicated, as he readily admitted. "It was hard to keep one's temper with him but I could not help feeling frightfully sorry for him. He gave me the feeling of a man who is finished, can no longer keep a grip of things, and is beginning to realize it."[73]

On September 8, the Chiefs met with Churchill just after noon. After the war, Brooke recalled,

> He got into his head that we were going to "frame up" (he used those actual words to me) with the American Chiefs against him. As he knew that the American Chiefs could handle the President fairly easily, he feared that he would be faced with a military block of Chiefs of Staff plus the President against him. As matters stood we were very far from "framing up" with our American colleagues even if we had wished to, which was unlikely as we were about to have a most difficult time to get any agreement at all with them. I could not get Winston to appreciate this, all his suspicions were aroused. Kept on sending for me to find out what we were settling, and trying to alter every decision. It was a ghastly time from which I carried away the bitterest of memories.[74]

The Chief of the Imperial General Staff was using his diary as a way of coping with the stress of the war, which accounts for some of the shrill, exasperated tone and explains why Brooke refused to concede some of the legitimate points Churchill had made. The field-marshal was on the mark, though. Cunningham's diary entry for September 8 only confirms Brooke's recollections: "He was in his worst mood. Accusing the COS of ganging up against him + keeping papers from him + so on." Churchill was determined to preserve the empire and believed the very future of the United Kingdom was at stake. Cunningham resented Churchill's behavior as much as Brooke but recorded that the prime minister unleashed a diatribe against his allies: "The worst of it is his feeling against the Americans whom he accuses of doing the most awful things against the British. There is no question he is not feeling well + is feeling this hot sticky weather." Ismay took much of the brunt of the prime minister's temper. His restrained recollection: "Although the sea was calm, some of us had rough passage."[75]

Both Brooke and Cunningham were right in their observations. Churchill's health was affecting his ability to do his job, which explains a good deal of the intensity of the various confrontations between him and the Chiefs of Staff Committee. Lord Moran in his book—which was a massive violation of doctor-patient confidentiality—reports that in late August, the prime minister had come down with another case of pneumonia. It was, however, milder than what he had suffered from earlier in the year. He had a shadow on his lung and his temperature was high during the trip, which made him ill-tempered. John Colville of Churchill's staff told Moran: "The P.M. is very tired. He insists on everything being boiled down to half a sheet of notepaper. It simply can't be done. He misses half the argument."[76]

The Chiefs had another meeting on September 9 with Churchill, and Brooke prepared for that session with little enthusiasm. "Spent the afternoon working up notes for tomorrow's meeting with him. In the evening went to see a film. I am feeling *very very* depressed at the thought of this meeting, unless Winston changes radically we shall be in hopeless situation."[77]

Brooke had good reason for feeling such despair. Commanders at lower levels needed direction. "I hope that, at long last, we here shall get some clear guidance and help," Lieutenant-General Sir Henry Pownall, the Chief of Staff in the South-East Asia Command, observed. "Little enough has come our way so far." He had heard fairly accurate gossip about the debate in Whitehall.

Winston, at one meeting, made an astonishing remark—it is recorded that he said "at the next meeting with the Americans we should *ask them what they would like us to do in the war against Japan*." This, mark you, one whole year after this command was set up! There could be no more illuminating remark, it shows the negation of all policy-direction and is proof positive of the feeble way the whole problem has been tackled in *our* quarters.[78]

The response from the U.S. Joint Chiefs of Staff only complicated matters. The document stated: "The United States Chiefs of Staff accept the British proposal in C.C.S. 452/18 for the formation of a British Empire task force under a British commander, consisting of British, Australian, and New Zealand land, sea, and air forces to operate in the Southwest Pacific Theater under General MacArthur's supreme command. It is noted that this will enable the British fleet to be well placed to reinforce the U.S. Pacific Fleet if this should later be desired." The Americans had intended to accept the British offer, making provision for logistical considerations, but to the British on the *Queen Mary* the reply seemed to reject their first preference for operating in the Central Pacific, which became a troubling issue that Brooke, Portal, and Cunningham would have to discuss with their American counterparts.[79]

Then, in a routine procedure, Ismay sent Churchill a memo in which he simply repeated the findings of the August 9 conference in the Map Room. The Chiefs wanted to discuss the matter with Churchill to make sure that Churchill understood what they would be talking about with their American counterparts. In the document, Ismay reported that the British would initiate an offensive in Burma and would propose to contribute a fleet to operate under U.S. command in the Pacific. If the United States rejected this offer, which seemed a possibility, the British would form a task force of British, Australian, and New Zealand units that would operate under the command of MacArthur. Churchill, forgetting that he had approved such a proposal a month earlier, sent Ismay a short memo. He had no problem with the Royal Navy operating in the Pacific, but the imperial task force was a different matter altogether. "I do not agree," he stated bluntly. "As is known, I consider that all United Kingdom forces should operate across the Indian Ocean and not in the South-West Pacific."[80]

Suddenly, just hours before the start of a British-American summit, Churchill had renounced a policy proposal that had taken nine months to put together. Brooke was stunned.

He now repudiates an agreement which we secured with him weeks ago, and which we submitted to the Americans with his approval! Namely the possible formation of a British task force under MacArthur, a subject repeatedly thrashed out in the War Cabinet, is now repudiated, and disapproved as a matter of discussion with the

Americans. The situation becomes quite impossible and I am at my wits' end as to what we are to do.

He attributed Churchill's bad behavior not to a difference in opinion on strategy, but to the prime minister's health. "I am afraid that he is very definitely ill and doubtful how much longer he will last. The tragedy is that in his present condition he may well do untold harm!!"[81]

The Ulsterman was beside himself with rage and responded by making one of the harshest assessments that he made during the war of his prime minister.

He knows no details, has only got half the picture in his mind, talks absurdities and makes my blood boil to listen to his nonsense. I find it hard to remain civil. And the wonderful thing is that 3/4 of the population of the world imagine that Winston Churchill is one of the Strategists of History, a second Marlborough, and the other 1/4 have no conception of what a public menace he is and has been throughout this war! It is far better that the world should never know, and never suspect the feet of clay of that otherwise superhuman being. Without him England was lost for a certainty, with him England has been on the verge of disaster time and again. And with it all no recognition hardly at all for those who help him except the occasional crumb intended to prevent the dog from straying too far from the table. Never have I admired and despised a man simultaneously to the same extent. Never have such opposite extremes been combined in the same human being.

When Lord Alanbrooke had portions of his diary published in 1959, this passage never made it into print.[82]

It was left to Ismay to attempt a resolution. "The Chiefs of Staff have asked me to invite your attention to the following conclusions," he wrote in polite language. He quoted the previously agreed findings, and reminded him that a telegram to the U.S. Joint Chiefs of Staff had been sent "which was submitted to, and approved by, you."[83]

Even after arriving in Quebec, Churchill continued to advance the arguments he had made earlier in the year. On the first full day of the conference, he explained that his objection was to "the great diminution of the forces engaged with the enemy which results from lengthening the communications. A gush has to be poured into the pipeline at one end to produce only a trickle at the other, so great is the leakage as the route lengthens." The United Kingdom could make the greatest contribution to the defeat of Japan where it could engage with the most Japanese soldiers, and that would only come in Southeast Asia. Here and only here is where the British could project real force and power. One can only imagine what Brooke thought when he read Churchill's memoirs about their trip to the New World: "As a result of our lengthy talks on the voyage we reached agreement about what we should say to our great Ally."[84]

With Churchill behaving so unpredictably, it is easy to understand and sympathize with Brooke's frustration and concern about the disaster pending in Canada. In bad health, Churchill had ignored the agreements fashioned in Whitehall. Brooke was only human to wonder what would follow in Quebec. The prime minister's previous behavior also makes what followed all the more surprising.

SIX

■

Codename: OCTAGON

Brooke was in a full panic, but soon events proved that the field-marshal had inflated his fears out of proportion. The meeting in Quebec brought about half a decision, but this partial decision came only when the sick Churchill pushed the even sicker Roosevelt into a corner.

It was the close relationship among the seven Chiefs of Staff that set the stage for the conversations between prime minister and president. Field-Marshal Sir John Dill was of exceptional importance in maintaining a good relationship between the sets of chiefs, particularly the two army Chiefs. As the head of the British Military Mission, he was basically the military ambassador to the United States. The fact that both Brooke and Marshall respected him and considered him a friend in the true sense of that word helped him enormously. Dill explained to the Americans the relationship between the Chiefs of Staff Committee and Churchill, which was always strained, and to his countryman, he described the internal relations among the U.S. Joint Chiefs of Staff, which were always uneven. "He knew Americans, and their way of doing things," Arnold wrote in his memoirs. Brooke recalled, "Marshall had the highest respect for him and I was devoted to him, consequently he was in a unique position to reduce difficulties between us."[1]

Churchill became suspicious, though, that Dill was too sympathetic to the Americans. Concerned that the prime minister might remove his friend,

Marshall decided to arrange an honorary degree from either Harvard or Yale University for his friend in the hope that it would impress Churchill. Providing such a distinction on short notice proved impossible, but Yale President Charles Seymour proposed instead to give Dill the first Charles P. Howland Award for contributions to world affairs.[2] The presentation was a full-blown media event and Marshall attended to introduce his friend. Although specifically focusing on the campaign in Europe, Marshall's views are relevant to the efforts being made in all theaters of the war:

> In my opinion the triumph over Germany in the coming months de-
> pends more on a complete accord between the British and American
> forces than it does on any other single factor, air power, ground power
> or naval power . . . The harmful possibilities of . . . discord have been
> serious in the past and will continue to be so in the future because of
> the necessity in the European Theater of combined operations, even
> involving on occasions the complete intermingling of troops . . . That
> we have been able to master these very human difficulties, that in fact
> we have triumphed over them to the disaster of the enemy, is in my
> opinion the greatest single Allied achievement of the war.[3]

The friendship between Arnold and Portal epitomized Marshall's views on the alliance. Reflecting in retirement on the relationship between the Chiefs, Arnold observed that postwar relations should have been put in the hands of those wearing uniforms, since "the military people would get along much better at the conference table than the diplomats ever had in the past." The leaders of the two air forces were very close in both a professional and personal sense. Arnold thought Portal was the "most brilliant" member of the British delegation. "He had a remarkably agile and logical mind. He was far-sighted in his military planning, and on the many problems we had in common we worked extremely well together." One of the few hobbies that Arnold indulged in during the war was fishing, and both he and Portal got to cast lines together. Portal provided assistance in helping the U.S. Army Air Forces establish themselves in Great Britain and was willing to provide discreet advice, when sought, on the creation of the air force as an independent service. Arnold appreciated Portal's courtesy, intelligence, and integrity. "The R.A.F. was able to teach our own Eighth Air Force a great deal, especially about radar, radio, and navigational aids," he recalled.[4]

King was an exception—of sorts. He respected the British as individuals and as a group, but he also harbored a degree of suspicion toward his allies. He thought Portal was the smartest of the Chiefs. Brooke seemed to be too inflexible. "He talked so damned fast," the admiral commented, "that it was hard to understand what he was saying." He did have respect for Cunningham. "Then they got a *man*. A fighter. He would fight like hell. When I had something to say against the British he would stand up and say, 'I don't like that.'"[5]

The OCTAGON conference started on September 11 with much media attention. It was wartime and those of the high command enjoyed the celebrity status that normally goes to film stars. The Canadians treated their guests well. "The Conference has opened in a blaze of friendship," Churchill telegraphed back to Attlee. It says something about the rationing on the British home front that several of the British chiefs took enough note of the provisions to make record of it in their diaries. The cabins on the train that the British delegation took to Quebec had a double bed. "Very good food + most comfortable," Cunningham recorded. Crowds cheered as the Chiefs arrived at the train stations. Canada was a British nation, and Churchill wanted to underline that fact by arriving first at Quebec so he could be a good host and greet his guests when they arrived from the south. When he reached the train station, though, Roosevelt was waiting for him.[6]

The Chiefs stayed at the luxurious Hotel Frontenac, while Churchill, Roosevelt, and Leahy were at the Quebec Citadel. The British Chiefs had a good view of the St. Lawrence River below and a light breeze coming off the water helped with the heat. Brooke noted in his diary: "excellent accommodation." Brooke complained about the drive between his hotel and the Citadel when Churchill wanted to meet with the Chiefs, which reflected his exasperation with his political master since the ride takes all of a minute. The Canadian government sponsored a luncheon and a dinner that were huge functions with large crowds of people in uniform. The Royal Mounted Police of Canada in their crimson tunics provided security and were on guard at the various functions. A Canadian staff officer who had been present at the first Quebec conference observed that the allied "military situation infused a note of confidence into the Conference which was lacking in 1943." He recalled that there was a "scent of victory in the air."[7]

As the conference started, Churchill made a dramatic change in his stand about the British role in the Pacific. His new policy was nearly 180 degrees opposite of the arguments he had been making since the beginning of the year. In the late afternoon of September 12, the Chiefs of Staff Committee met to consider his latest minute on Pacific strategy. "He is gradually coming round to sane strategy, but by heaven what labour we have had for it," the Chief of the Imperial General Staff noted in his diary. The Chiefs had less than two hours to discuss the new document before meeting with the prime minister. "He was all smiles and friendliness for a change," Brooke observed. "How quickly he changes. An April day's moods would be put to shame by him."[8] Cunningham was equally bemused, noting that he "found him in a mood of sweet reasonableness."[9]

That evening involved another banquet. Brooke and Cunningham found themselves sitting next to the Roosevelts. The two British officers had very different experiences. Brooke noted, "I sat on President's right and found him very pleasant and easy to talk to." Cunningham recorded in his diary, "I sat next Mrs. Roosevelt. Pretty hard going until we started to exchange remarks on wounded men + hospitals."[10]

Already in failing health at the time of OCTAGON, Roosevelt would play a pivotal, but brief, role in Canada. Born in 1882 into a prominent New York family of Dutch descent that had been in the state since it had been called New Holland, Franklin Roosevelt and his mother attempted to reproduce the career of his distant cousin Theodore Roosevelt in ways large and small. The first Roosevelt had gone to Harvard University, been a member of the state legislature, assistant secretary of the navy, governor of New York, and vice president of the United States before he occupied the White House. Franklin Roosevelt would hold these same positions except vice president, although he was a candidate for that office in 1920. When he entered politics it was as a Democrat, but he did so only after making sure this move would not alienate his famous relative. The elder Roosevelt was largely supportive of his young and distant cousin's move into politics, even if it was in the wrong party.[11]

The younger Roosevelt learned much from "Uncle Ted" and Woodrow Wilson, whom he served as assistant secretary of the navy: "Theodore Roosevelt lacked Woodrow Wilson's appeal to the fundamental and failed to stir, as Wilson did, the truly profound moral and social convictions. Wilson, on the other hand, failed where Theodore Roosevelt succeeded in stirring people to enthusiasm over specific individual events." He realized from the experience of Wilson that he only had so long to make his mark in office. He quoted the former president as saying, "It is only once in a generation that a people can be lifted above material things. That is why conservative government is in the saddle two-thirds of the time." In a letter to a biographer of Woodrow Wilson, Roosevelt advised him to "be sympathetic to the view that the public psychology and, for that matter, individual psychology, cannot, because of human weakness, be attuned for long periods of time to a constant repetition of the highest note in the scale." Roosevelt saw himself perfectly suited for such work. He once described himself: "I am like a cat. I make a quick stroke, and then I relax."[12]

In the White House, Roosevelt proved to be a master of synthesizing and analyzing the mass of information that came to him. He was a fast reader and paid attention to what appeared in the newspapers. He read both those that were favorable and those hostile toward his administration, usually in the morning while in bed. Roosevelt often conducted interviews in his bedroom while still in his pajamas, which was less cumbersome than being in the Oval Office in his braces he wore as a result of his bout with polio. He rarely bothered to immerse himself in the details or history of an issue, but he could get to the heart of a matter and understand the political and administrative consequences of various policy options.[13]

Although domestic politics had tempered his actions, Roosevelt pursued a fairly consistent policy toward the European war. The British were fighting for objectives that were basically those of the United States. If the British could defeat Germany without any American intervention, that result would serve U.S. interests better than any other possible outcome. Under Roosevelt, the United States would support the British as much as possible without becoming a belligerent in the conflict. The ultimate manifestation of Roosevelt's approach was the Lend-Lease program. This policy underwrote the British with equipment that was on "loan" during the war. Churchill's response to Lend-Lease was ecstatic: "I would like to get them hooked a little firmer, but they are pretty on now."[14]

Roosevelt was particularly gifted at having a political vision for U.S. involvement in world affairs. He understood that national spirit was exceptionally important in sustaining a country through the conflict, even when it was going well. In his 1939 State of the Union address, he declared, "We have learned that God-fearing democracies of the world which observe the sanctity of treaties and good faith in their dealings with other nations cannot safely be indifferent to international lawlessness anywhere."[15]

It is clear in hindsight that Roosevelt was in declining health at Quebec. It was also apparent at the time. One just had to look at him. After not seeing his father for months, Elliot Roosevelt was stunned at his appearance. "Well, what did you expect," the president snapped.[16]

Even if the president decided to ignore the indicators, others worried, including the British delegation. "I wonder how far Roosevelt's health impaired his judgment and sapped his resolve to get to the bottom of each problem before it came up for discussion," Lord Moran wondered years later. "At Quebec he seemed to me to have but a couple of stone in weight—you could have put your fist between his neck and his collar—and I said to myself then that men at his time of life do not go thin all of a sudden just for nothing." Ismay noticed as well. "He seemed to have shrunk." His collar was too big for his neck and his coat looked several sizes too big. Churchill asked Roosevelt's physician about his health. The navy doctor assured him that the president was fine. At one of the many evening social events that accompanied this conference, the principals watched the film *Wilson*, a biographical account of Woodrow Wilson. The similarities between the collapsing health of the fictional president and that of Roosevelt made Churchill uneasy, so he got up and left. "By God, that's not going to happen to me," Roosevelt declared, unnerved at the prime minister's action.[17]

On September 13, at the first plenary meeting of the conference when the Combined Chiefs of Staff met with Churchill and Roosevelt, the prime minister forcefully advocated the very policies he had fought for most of the year. He started off the session complimenting his allies on the effort they were making in the war and reminding the Americans that Britain had been fighting it longer and had a smaller population on which to draw. Much of the conversation focused on the campaign in Italy and then Southeast Asia, before Churchill broached the subject of the Pacific. He explicitly offered the services of the Royal Navy to the ongoing crusade against Japan, noting that there were factions in the United States hostile to Great Britain and that he wanted to make sure that the Americans knew that the British were willing to help defeat the Japanese.[18]

If Churchill was just making the offer as a formality to have an American objection on record as Cunningham thought might be the case, then Churchill had vastly misjudged the situation. There really was only one response Roosevelt could give once the matter was out in the open. If he had said no, he would have been allowing Americans to die in Japan on a larger scale than if he had said yes, and that would have been an issue on which he would have been vulnerable to much-deserved political criticism.

The U.S. minutes of this meeting read, "The President said that the offer was accepted on the largest scale." The British version comes closer to capturing the actual words the two used. Churchill said his empire was "ardent to play the greatest possible part." Roosevelt responded by saying "the British fleet was no sooner offered than accepted."[19]

Churchill then explained that he wanted a bomber force of 1,500 planes to take part in strikes against Japan. The conversation meandered back to the war with Germany, but a little later in that same meeting, Portal suggested a more modest force of 600 to 800 planes for deployment in the Pacific theater. The talk then turned to the details about the transit of the Royal Navy. The response of Roosevelt in the two documents varies, but it is clear that he was trying to avoid specifics. Churchill detected this ambiguity and asked Roosevelt point blank if his offer had been accepted. The language of both documents is identical: "The President replied in the affirmative." Cunningham was ecstatic: "And now the die was cast. Mr. Churchill had offered our fleet, and the offer had been accepted!"[20]

The prime minister turned next to the matter of the Royal Air Force. Portal and Marshall clarified that the offer was not to dispatch British air units against the Japanese just anywhere, but to specific areas where they could strike at the home islands.[21]

This British document also contains a statement not in the U.S. version of statements the prime minister made toward the end of the meeting. The document reads:

> The Prime Minister remarked that for the future good relations of the two countries, on which so much depended, it was of vital importance that the British should be given their fair share in the main operations against Japan. The United States had given the most handsome assistance to the British Empire, in the fight against Germany. It could only be expected that the British Empire in return should give the United States all assistance in their power towards the defeat of Japan.[22]

Explaining this dramatic about-face is difficult. It was, according to Cunningham, "somewhat to the surprise of Brooke, Portal, and myself."[23] General Sir David Fraser, Brooke's biographer, credits the ill-mannered opposition of Admiral King to any British role in the Pacific for restoring unity among the U.K. delegates. Portal of the RAF was of the opinion that

King seemed to want to make the crippling of the British Empire a U.S. war aim. As Fraser put it, "Even a suspicion of this was, of course, sufficient to bring Churchill charging to his Chiefs of Staff's support."[24] While there is truth in this observation, it is inadequate. King's outburst was yet to come. More importantly, Churchill raised the matter on the first day of the conference.[25]

The explanation lies in the fact that Churchill essentially saw airpower as a solution to both his dispute with the Chiefs of Staff and the efforts of the United Kingdom to reassert its colonial authority. He had always been an airpower enthusiast and told the Canadian War Cabinet that there was a good possibility that Japan would fall to a bombing campaign alone. He repeated this view to Roosevelt and the Combined Chiefs toward the end of the conference. These views represented more than wishful thinking on Churchill's part. Portal and Brooke had also entertained thoughts along those lines. Churchill also suspected that the war might come to an end if the Soviet Union entered the conflict.[26]

At first glance, it seemed that Churchill had little leverage with his allies. The large ocean area in the Pacific required the use of very long-range bombers, of which the RAF had none, and which the United States had only in the B-29. The British, however, told the Americans that they could improve the range of their Lancasters with in-flight refueling. One plane with a little modification could serve as a tanker and the other as a bomber. These aircraft would be available for service in the early summer of 1945. In the paper the British Chiefs of Staff Committee sent to their American cousins, they offered 40 squadrons—half of which would be tankers.[27]

A Canadian initiative also worked to the prime minister's advantage. At the conference, the Ottawa government informed the British that it intended to contribute an army division to the invasion of Japan. Churchill actually welcomed this development. It appeared to solve several of his problems, since most Americans looked at Canada as a North American extension of the United Kingdom. In 1945 the British Union Jack was part of the Canadian national flag, just as was the case with Australia and New Zealand. Although a separate service, the Canadian Army was for all practical purposes an appendage of the British Army, wearing matching uniforms, using the same equipment, employing identical tactics and doctrine, and exchanging officers on a large scale. The Canadians would do just fine as representatives of the British Empire and Commonwealth in the invasion of Japan. Churchill could have his cake and eat it, too, and told the Canadians the British Army would be deployed—for the most part—to Southeast Asia.[28]

Churchill's presentation made it clear to the U.S. Joint Chiefs that this issue was larger than a simple enhancement of operational performance. Two of the U.S. Chiefs were keeping diaries at the time of the gathering at Quebec, and each recorded that finding a role for the British was a political and diplomatic issue. Leahy noted, "Mr. Churchill expressed strongly his desire that British ships and troops take part in the war against Japan in order to do Britain's part and to share in the credit."[29] Arnold observed, "there was no doubt as to the Prime Minister desiring for political reasons to be there with his main Fleet and some 500 to 1000 H.B.s. There was also no doubt as to the President's being in accord." The air general also recorded a comment Churchill directed to him personally: "The British could not hold up their heads if such was not done. With all your wealth of airdromes you would not deny me a mere pittance of a few."[30] Years later, Marshall was succinct when discussing this episode: "Churchill was very anxious."[31]

Roosevelt's political motivation was clearer. He had little choice but to accept Churchill's offer once it was made. The American people would wonder why they were battling the Japanese alone. The public would have been infuriated if they discovered that U.S. officials had turned down a British offer of help. He had to accept. Even before the conference in Quebec, U.S. diplomats were warning President Roosevelt and his advisors that the administration would come to regret excluding the British from the Pacific. "The really gallant people of Great Britain are as anxious to join us in the fight against Japan as we are ourselves to defeat Japan," John Winant, the U.S. ambassador in London, argued in a letter he sent to presidential advisor Harry Hopkins. The ambassador worried that the American generals and admirals might do severe damage to bilateral relations if they prevented an allied contribution to this last great effort.

If we allow the British to limit their active participation to recapture areas that are to their selfish interests alone and not participate in smashing the war machine of Japan, if British soldiers don't cross the Atlantic to our ports and entrain for our Pacific ports, and if we shuck the British air force in order to prove our own dominance in the air, we will create in the United States a hatred for Great Britain that will make for schisms in the postwar years that will defeat every-thing that men have died for in this war. Repetition of the tragedy of 1918 will be unforgivable.

The ambassador closed his letter asking Hopkins if the president were aware of this concern.[32]

Hopkins wrote back immediately and assured Winant that Roosevelt understood the issue. Indeed, he had personally discussed the matter with the president two weeks earlier. In a letter addressed to "Gil"—short for Winant's middle name of Gilbert, the presidential advisor agreed with the argument the ambassador had made. "We simply must find a way to have Great Britain take her full and proper place in the war against Japan. This, with the best goodwill in the world is full of many difficulties—transportation, supply, etc."[33]

Four days after Hopkins sent his response, Secretary of State Cordell Hull expressed these concerns to Roosevelt in political terms. "It is clear that one of the most important objectives of United States policy must be to bring the British into war operations in the Far East to the greatest possible extent," he declared. The advantages were "obvious." British partici-pation would end the war more quickly than would otherwise be the case, which would in turn save lives and expenses. "The disadvantages of the failure of the British to participate to the full in the war in the Far East de-serve special emphasis." If no British forces fought in Japan, the American public would react in a hostile manner, and the United Kingdom might also have an opportunity to expand their share of the export markets in the Pa-cific while the United States was busy fighting. The relevant sections of the business community would be angry at this development. A British absence would also expose Lend-Lease as a failure, at least to some degree. "All of these factors will combine to produce the most difficult of circumstances in which to attempt to build Anglo-American and general political and eco-nomic collaboration to face the problems of the post-war world."[34]

In confronting these issues, Roosevelt thought it might all be moot. The day Hopkins wrote Winant, he met with the president. Roosevelt, accord-ing to Hopkins's account, told him that he thought Japan might surrender once Germany was defeated. When the Soviet Union was free to focus on Asia, it might compel a Japanese surrender. In short, Roosevelt had no problem accepting whatever offer Churchill made.[35]

The only mar to the smooth working of this meeting of coalition leaders came on the fourth day of the gathering during a Combined Chiefs of Staff meeting when Ernest J. King exploded in a rage. The British Chiefs of Staff Committee was a much more unified group than the U.S. Joint Chiefs. Marshall understood that rejecting a British offer of help was, as he put it to MacArthur, "unthinkable." King, however, had different ideas and was more than willing to expose the internal differences of the Joint Chiefs in order to protect the interests of the U.S. Navy. Prior to the conference, the Americans thought British forces would serve in MacArthur's theater of operations. The Joint Chiefs had a paper that their staff had produced before the plenary meeting, welcoming British participation in operations against the Japanese along the western flank of the Southwest Pacific Area Command. Brooke, Portal, and Cunningham received this document after the exchange between Roosevelt and Churchill. Such an arrangement was fine with King, but including the Royal Navy in Nimitz's theater was an entirely different matter. The Combined Chiefs of Staff meeting on September 14 started out with Brooke trying to clarify matters. He wanted to make sure that events had outpaced the memo. "Not much excitement," Arnold wrote in his diary. "Everything normal until British participation in the Pacific came up. Then Hell broke loose."[36]

King, angry at what he saw as unnecessary concessions made the night before to the British, first insisted that the Royal Navy had to be "self-supporting." He then rejected any significant role for the British in the final operations against Japan, saying the deployment was an issue for another day. Cunningham, then Brooke, and then Portal disagreed, reminding the admiral that Churchill and Roosevelt had reached agreement on this matter. King fought the three of them single-handedly, denying that the president and prime minister had agreed to anything specific. The U.S. Navy could handle the Japanese on their own, had no interest in sharing the glory and fame awaiting it, and wanted to avoid having to support and supply a British fleet. In what was according to most accounts a harsh tone and strong language, King said the use of British ships was unacceptable solely for political reasons, particularly if it required the displacement of U.S. resources. Cunningham and Portal working in tandem reminded him that Churchill and Roosevelt believed it was important that the British be in the Pacific for political reasons.[37]

King overplayed his hand. When Marshall appeared to make a concession to the British, King turned on him. Leahy stopped the angry exchange, commenting, "I don't think we should wash our linen in public." Arnold also sided against King. Recalling the actions of the Chief of Naval Operations in his retirement, Marshall said, "He made it quite embarrassing." Cunningham was more blunt: "King made an ass of himself." The other American Chiefs overruled the admiral and agreed to British naval participation in the defeat of Japan. Cunningham noted that King "gave way" at that point, "but with such bad grace."[38]

Previous writers trying to explain King's behavior focused on his Anglophobia and argued that the historical rivalry between the U.S. Navy and Royal Navy was still strong in his mind. While this explanation has merit, it obscures the fact that logistics was a legitimate issue of concern.[39] For the last century, the British had never had to operate at sea beyond a few days and had no experience or quartermaster system able to keep a fleet at sea for a month.[40] Before the summit, Leahy admitted in meetings of the Joint Chiefs of Staff that logistics was a reasonable concern, but these were details that could be worked out later. It was vital that the United States get a British commitment to fight the Japanese.[41] The next day, Cunningham thought King had accepted that he would have to live with the Royal Navy. "A quiet day until a meeting with Admiral King + his staff at 1630. But things went smoothly + we had a very useful exchange of ideas. He seems more or less resigned to having the British fleet in the Pacific." He repeated his stipulation that the British had to be self-supporting and should expect no supplies from the U.S. Navy at all. "From this rather unhelpful attitude he never budged," Cunningham remarked.[42]

King was vague in his memoirs on the OCTAGON meeting, but he did offer an explanation to a historian writing an official history of the Joint Chiefs of Staff:

> I was not reluctant to use the British Fleet in the Pacific. I was, however, opposed to combining the two fleets operationally because the British had plenty of use for their own fleet in Southeast Asia recovering their losses to the Japanese. When the President accepted Churchill's offer of British fleet units for the U.S. Pacific Fleet I told Nimitz to set up the British units as a separate Task Force and assign them their own jobs.[43]

The British and American chiefs found reaching an agreement on the Royal Air Force a much easier task. Arnold supported the British effort to play a role in the defeat of Japan. The RAF really was an institutional ally of the army air forces in the effort to prove the significance of airpower in military affairs and the ultimate goal of establishing an independent U.S. Air Force. He made this position quite clear in a letter he wrote to MacArthur a year later: "The Royal Air Force, when the situation was reversed and we were beginning to arrive in 1942 in England, did everything possible to facilitate our buildup. I feel we now have an opportunity to reciprocate now that the position is reversed."[44]

Bringing in British planes raised two sets of logistical issues. The United States faced acute supply and support problems in the Pacific. Unlike the campaign in Europe, where there was plenty of ground on which to build airfields, the army air forces had limited space on a few small islands to construct the bases it needed. "We had no place where we could use either the R.A.F. or our own B-17's or B-24's to any extent," Arnold explained. "As a matter of fact, if we could use 1500 of the 3500 we had in the E.T.O., we would be very, very lucky. Certainly, we would much rather have the B-29's with their longer range and their heavier bomb load than we would the B-17, the B-24, the Lancaster, or the Halifax."[45] The Royal Canadian Air Force also wanted to participate in missions over Japan. On September 14, Air Marshal Robert Leckie, the Chief of the Canadian Air Staff, told Arnold that his service wanted to provide forty-seven squadrons. "Just where we were to base them, I did not know," the American stated later.[46]

A second logistical issue was inventory. The American air campaign against Japan was at the end of an extremely long supply line and adding a contingent from the RAF to these operations would only complicate matters. British planes would require different spare parts than American ones, taking up valuable cargo space.[47]

Arnold was convinced—with good reason—that the allied militaries had worked well together throughout the long conflict. As he would later explain in his memoirs, "Despite conflicting national aims and interservice rivalries, the Combined Chiefs of Staff, for all their arguing, had achieved both compromise and cooperative action." In his diary, he was sympathetic on the issue of British participation in the Pacific theater, but he was also honestly concerned about logistical issues that limited the usefulness of RAF planes. In a memo he wrote in response to the initial British proposal, he suggested that the United States should welcome the participation of their allies in the Pacific theater, but only if they could secure territory on the eastern coast of China on their own in order to avoid complicated administrative problems. This suggestion died a quick death, and Arnold clearly expected political factors to come into play. "Where can we use the R.A.F. heavies? Who knows—National pride is a very strong stimulant and may be a compellant if used in the highest levels."[48]

The Combined Chiefs also pushed back their target date for the surrender of Japan. For planning purposes, U.S. staff officers had always estimated that the end of the war in the Pacific would come one year after the defeat of the Nazis. The British thought it would be easier to schedule redeployment of their services and allocate manpower if the end were set at two years. Since this process really was educated guesswork, the Chiefs compromised at a year and a half.[49]

OCTAGON had gone well for the British Chiefs. Their American colleagues had agreed to almost every policy initiative they had put forward—yet concerns remained. King's behavior indicated that his commitment to implementing these understandings was suspect. Brooke, Portal, and Cunningham held a brief meeting immediately afterward to discuss what they should do about the American admiral. They decided to ask Churchill to confirm explicitly with Roosevelt at the final plenary meeting that the U.S. Navy would deploy the King's ships to the waters surrounding the Japanese home islands.[50]

It was a wise plan, but Churchill had other ideas. Relations between the Chiefs and the prime minister had once again deteriorated. The Chiefs decided to resign. Ismay thought such a move would have been a disaster. "The troops were in hard battle at the time and the resignation of these great figures at that particular junction would have spelt disunity at home and started people looking over their shoulders," he explained after the war. "I therefore stepped into the breach by saying that I would resign and that even if Winston accepted my resignation no one had heard of Ismay and it wouldn't matter very much." A verbal tirade by Churchill was the last insult he could endure and made the general almost eager to offer himself up as a sacrifice—but he soon hesitated. Ismay met privately with Churchill and handed him not a letter of resignation, but an offer to resign.

> He dealt with it in typical fashion; handed it back to me saying: "don't write me this sort of rubbish, dear Pug: we are going to the end—together—you and I. I'm sorry if I get angry, but you must admit I have cause." I replied that he had abundant cause, but why vent it all on me! He denied this: said he had every confidence in me, and

was much dependent on my industry, tact and judgment. So that is that! He was really rather sweet.[51]

This mood was brief. In a meeting with his Chiefs on September 15, Churchill exploded over the final report of the Combined Chiefs of Staff. "A satisfactory day in everything except our contacts with the Prime Minister!" Brooke in wry exasperation told his diary. At a 6 P.M. meeting with the three Chiefs, Churchill raised numerous complaints about the agreement. "He was just at his worst + Brooke was very patient with him," Cunningham recorded. Brooke called it "a frightful interview!!" He added, "Winston was in one of his worst tempers." The draft of the instructions that Mountbatten would receive after the conference had enraged the prime minister. Now it was the turn of the Chiefs to suffer Churchill's wrath. Cunningham wrote, he "was quite impossible + looked likely to wreck all the good that had been done."[52]

There was no exaggeration in this comment. Brooke went to bed unsure of what would happen the next day. As was so often the case in Churchill's relations with the Chiefs, the prime minister had been prodding, pushing, and testing the advice he was getting from the three. The plenary session was rather uneventful. Leahy read the report aloud, so Churchill and Roosevelt could make any alterations they saw fit. Churchill did manage to get a provision added on about the participation of the Royal Canadian Air Force in the Pacific. The record of this meeting indicates that the prime minister did almost all the talking. "The President looked very frail + hardly to be taking in what was going on," Cunningham observed.[53]

After the session came to an end, Churchill and Roosevelt held a press conference with Mackenzie King on the promenade of the Citadel some 300 feet above the water of the St. Lawrence. A reporter for the *Chicago Daily Tribune* noted that Roosevelt looked "gaunt." The White House staff banned direct quotes of Roosevelt—a normal practice at the time—so Churchill's comments got prominent play. "The enemy," he remarked, "will learn soon all we did here." When the topic of the Pacific war came up, Churchill put the United Kingdom's desire on the public record, saying, "we felt the United States meant to keep too much of it to itself." He also added in lighthearted fashion, "You can't have all the good things to yourselves. You must share them. We will be in on the death with forces proportionate to the national strength."[54]

During lulls in the conference, the flag officers of these two Atlantic powers took opportunities to relax. There were band concerts during the day, allowing the principals and the vast contingent of staff officers, secretaries, and typists that accompanied them a chance to unwind from the stress of their duties. Arnold and Marshall took walks along the banks of the river. Portal and Arnold also played cards in between meetings.[55] Sometime during the conference, King announced that he wanted to take the Combined Chiefs on a tour of the site where the Battle of Quebec had been fought on the Plains of Abraham. It was something of a bonding experience and all the Chiefs, except Leahy, went. The group leader turned out to be a regular tourist guide, offering no more information than one could get from the markers and monument signs. Most of these flag officers had visited the site before and were disappointed. Marshall and Arnold walked off from the main group and met a Catholic priest. The good father only spoke French, but he was also quite informed about the battle and began discussing the engagement. He gave what Arnold called "a very absorbing critique." The others began drifting over to listen to the priest's lecture. He went on and on in French—most of the Chiefs had some ability in the language—and was entirely unaware of his audience's identity.[56]

When the conference finally ended, the British Chiefs and Leckie of the Royal Canadian Air Force traveled to Orinskany Lake for a fishing expedition. This type of joint break from the press of the war shows how close the British Chiefs had become. Churchill nearly ruined their plans when he sent a note telling them he wanted a meeting. "He really is a most selfish + impossible man to work with," Cunningham scribbled into his diary. Portal told the prime minister that he was wrecking their vacation and Churchill cancelled his request. On their brief holiday, the Chiefs stayed in a log cabin compound with electrical power and would portage their canoes to the lakes, where they reeled in some fish. After two days Cunningham left, and the rest of the group moved on to Lac des Neiges. When they returned to Quebec, a telegram awaited them. "It was from Winston and very typical of his better side," Brooke recalled. The message read:

GUNFIRE (305)
Following for CIGS and CAS from Prime Minister.
Please let me know how many captives were taken by land and air forces respectively in Battle of Snow Lake.

Portal responded for the both of them:

CORDITE (420)
Following for Prime Minister from CIGS and CAS.
Your gunfire 305 only just received. Battle of Snow Lake began at dawn 19th and finished 2.30 pm on 20th. Enemy forces were aggressive throughout and put up fierce resistance at all familiar strong points particularly Churchill Bay and Brook Bay. Casualties inflicted by our land and air forces were approximately equal and totaled about 250 dead including the enemy general who surrendered to Land forces on Tuesday afternoon. In a short rearguard action at Cabane de Montmorency our air forces accounted for the largest submarine yet seen in these waters. We trust that you had a comfortable journey.[57]

Cunningham returned to the United Kingdom with Churchill. Accounts of the atmosphere on the *Queen Mary* on the voyage home vary significantly. Lord Moran found Churchill moody and suffering from an emotional letdown. "What is this conference?" he asked his physician. "Two talks with the Chiefs of Staff; the rest was waiting for the chance to put in a word with the President. One has to seize the occasion." He also told Moran, "I don't think I shall live long."

Moran refuted this contention: "You haven't lost your grip on things."

"Oh, my head's all right," Churchill replied. "But I'm very tired. Can't you give me something to pick me up?"[58]

Cunningham's diary entries for these days show a different man. "Lunched with the P.M. who seemed well + pleased with himself. The usual heavy lunch," the admiral recorded in his diary. Their meal was soft shelled crabs and large steaks. "I found the former a much over rated dish." Stocked up with provisions from North America, the passengers on the ship ate well throughout their passage. The topic of conversation over one meal was the supply requirement for the British Pacific Fleet and they talked until 4 P.M. Churchill was determined to follow through on securing a British role in the Pacific. "He told Leathers that the fleet train must be done on a handsome scale + that if we wanted 30–40 more ships we must have them!!" In his memoirs, Cunningham recalled, "Lord Leathers became somewhat pensive." Since he was the only member of the Chiefs of

Staff Committee on board, Cunningham saw a lot of Churchill during that voyage. "The Prime Minster was always most interesting, but particularly so when he was able to relax during meals." Cunningham records that the conversations usually lingered on into the early hours of the morning. The trip was at best a working vacation, and Churchill invested much time in dictating a speech that he was to give to Parliament and had Cunningham proof it for him. The admiral objected to the focus on the army and added a few comments on what the Royal Navy had accomplished. Moran does note that Churchill made an upbeat comment about the First Sea Lord. "I like Cunningham very much. I'm lucky to get such a successor to dear old Pound."[59]

Such sentiment would have surprised the admiral. The debate on Pacific strategy had on three occasions come close to bringing about a break between the military and the prime minister, and the matter was far from over. It is now time to examine how the various nations involved implemented this agreement, and this story moves next not to Scapa Flow, Washington, or even Honolulu, but rather Ottawa.

CHAPTER SIX

SEVEN

■

Canada

Without exception, all the British nations would contribute to the victory over Japan. The Canadians were loyal British subjects, but controlled their armed forces independent of the government in London and had their own reasons for wanting to do battle with the Japanese. The process that led to the Canadian decision to take battle to the Japanese—one that Mackenzie King dominated—was less than orderly.

Various motivating forces lay behind Canadian diplomacy. The first was the realization that Canada was one of only four powers in the North Pacific. The others were the United States, the Soviet Union, and, of course, Japan. Mackenzie King made a statement to his colleagues at the conference of prime ministers that the note takers summarized as: "Canada realized full well that she was a Pacific power on the west, as she was an Atlantic power to the East, Canada intended to do her full part in the Pacific struggle." Canadians had a keen interest in what happened in the region.[1]

Another factor at work was Canada's close relationship with both the United States and the other Dominions. Mackenzie King explained to the other Commonwealth prime ministers that the views of the U.S. public shaped those Canadians had of world affairs. The foreign policy of Canada was different from that of the United States, but his government had to take into account this influence, wedged as the nation was between the forty-eight states to the south and Alaska to the north. Canada always desired close relations with "her sister dominions." Australia and New Zealand could count on Canada to be in the fight with them.[2]

A number of Canadian officials, mainly those holding sub-Cabinet rank, also believed that participating in the Pacific war generally, and the final operations in and around Japan specifically, was critical for their nation's postwar future. The only way Canada would have a say in the occupation of Japan was if it participated in the invasion. Being part of the victorious coalition would also open up trade opportunities in China and mainland Asia, which would foster the development of northern and western Canada.[3]

A final consideration was the strong desire in the Canadian Army to avenge the defeat of Hong Kong. In the first major engagement of the war for Canadian soldiers, they surrendered the crown colony during the Japanese advances of 1941–1942.[4]

There were also factors working against any Canadian role in the Pacific theater. Inside the Dominion, many people were reluctant to engage in world affairs if it required large military appropriations. Mackenzie King had profited politically from the "never again" sentiment that infused Canadian politics after World War I. Even before that conflict there was little militarism in Canadian culture. With those points having been made, Canada had already done a good deal to fight this war. In his diary, Mackenzie King pointed out, "Our men have fought for 2 1/2 years before the Americans were in the war at all. There is no reason on earth why we should be sending large additional numbers to the Pacific."[5] Canadians, as far as he was concerned, had already done their part.

On top of this sentiment, it seemed to the prime minister that Canadian soldiers had no legitimate mission to fulfill. Before the second Quebec Conference, he wrote in his diary: "Were the troops needed against Japan or even wanted, the situation would be different but there is no justification for incurring, for reasons of prestige or above all to suit the army's pleasure and desire to increase its own importance, further sacrifices of life and enormous unnecessary expenditures." Mackenzie King's view that pride was the main factor pushing Canada in this direction was one from which he never wavered for the rest of the war. In between VE Day and VJ Day, the prime minister met with many influential figures who wanted Canada to play a larger role in the Pacific theater. He disagreed with them and, according to his own account, told them: "We had no possessions overseas. Spoke also of the difficulties the British had had in getting into the Pacific War. Having to take second place to the Americans in so doing. It is amazing how ready men are to sacrifice human lives, if need be, just to make a 'show' though there is nothing to be gained therefrom."[6]

The prime minister was deeply suspicious of the armed services. He thought—with good reason—that his admirals had tricked him in 1943 when he agreed to an expansion of the Royal Canadian Navy. There was a widespread sentiment within the naval planning staff that "it was vital for the maintenance of Canadian prestige that the Canadian Navy takes a direct and important part in the war against Japan." Knowing that the prime minister would reject their suggestions for an expansion of the service, Canadian naval officers decided to have their British counterparts ask Churchill to make the request personally. He had much more influence with Mackenzie King than any Canadian admiral. British admirals, for their part, were more than willing to help in this regard, since the Royal Navy was falling behind in its ability to meet its operational obligations. After complex and quiet negotiations, in which the Canadians stated that they were trying to ensure the Royal Canadian Navy survived in the postwar era, they managed to have the British persuade Churchill to make this request of Mackenzie King at the first Quebec Conference. The Canadian prime minister agreed that his navy would expand to include big ships. Two months later he realized what naval officers were trying to do: "it was our department rather than the British that really occasioned the cruisers being forced upon us by Churchill and Dudley Pound." He believed the ministers overseeing the armed forces had tricked "the rest of the Cabinet in the way they have forced the pace for their services."[7]

Even with all these qualifications and concerns, Mackenzie King recognized that Canada would have to make some type of contribution. "It may be necessary for Canada to participate if she is to maintain her position vis-à-vis the US and Britain, though I am sure she will get little credit from either for what she does." If Canada had to make a contribution, the prime minister was determined it be where it would make a real difference.[8]

The general sentiment among other members of the Cabinet was a wary, qualified willingness to contribute to the Pacific theater. During the two weeks before the OCTAGON conference, the Cabinet and the Cabinet War Committee debated what role Canadians should play in the fight against the Japanese. C. D. Howe, the munitions and supply minister, opposed any Canadian involvement, unless the United States really required the assistance. There was, in his opinion, "no purpose in operating against Japan in combination with the United Kingdom." In the end, the politicians decided that Canada should take part in operations against Japan. Their reasoning, though, had little to do with the United Kingdom. A week before the second Quebec Conference, the entire Cabinet declared, "Canadian military forces should participate in the war against Japan in operational theatres of direct interest to Canada as a North American nation, for example in the North or Central Pacific."[9]

Bureaucratic politics also played a role in Canadian decision making. Put into simple terms, the Canadian Army had an organizational interest in wanting to survive the war as an institution. Although it was a separate organization, the Canadian Army was essentially an appendage of the British Army. John A. English, the military historian, makes this point strongly in a specialized study of the First Canadian Army during the campaign in Normandy: "Though no formal alliance existed between Britain and Canada, the forces of both nations were more closely integrated than those of the NATO allies today. Canadian and British formations were completely interchangeable and their artillery and staff systems perfectly gloved."[10]

While some modern Canadian nationalists might find this description degrading, the Canadian Army in 1944 had a history within the larger context of the British Empire and Commonwealth in which it could take pride. The Canadian Expeditionary Force of World War I had been quite good. Deployed in combat as the Canadian Corps, this force developed a strong sense of esprit de corps. The men and units trained and fought together regularly. In short, the composition of the Corps remained consistent. The Canadians pioneered new machine gun tactics, developing ways to mass their fire in support of offensive operations. Canadian soldiers also helped pioneer the use of combined arms—the joining of artillery, infantry, and cavalry/armor units—in operations. Brigades, and then battalions, of armored cars proved their worth in delivering indirect machine gun fire on the enemy during the mobile phase of the war in 1918. The Canadians mastered and then refined British artillery tactics. During the allied offensives of 1918, the Canadian Corps fired about one-fourth of all the shells the British Expeditionary Force discharged. One of the reasons this unit excelled in its use of the big guns was it had highly talented British officers seconded to them. Three of these men, including Brooke, went on to become Chief of the Imperial General Staff. The Canadian Corps was the most professional military force that the Dominion had ever fielded in combat.[11]

The interwar period, however, was unkind to Canadian military professionals, and it was this fate that the current leadership in the Canadian Army feared reliving. With the merger of Canadian Expeditionary Force units into the militia, Canada quickly reverted to the prewar status quo. The national myth of loyalist part-time soldiers driving out the invading hordes of Americans in 1812 had a strong hold on Canada in military affairs. The militia units were more social organizations than fighting forces, and political patronage determined much of their focus. As an institution, the armed forces of Canada soon forgot about the role of combined arms, tanks, machine guns, mechanization, and how to run a large field army during this period.[12]

Confusion gripped both Canada and the United Kingdom about the mission of the British Army and what role the Dominion would play in relation to the mother country. British officers, acknowledging political sentiments in the United Kingdom, basically refused to plan on fighting another continental war and instead focused on policing the empire. The Canadians, at first, thought that it might be necessary to send another expeditionary force to fight with the British, but they soon reverted to tradition and prepared to do battle with their neighbors to the south. In the 1930s, this mission changed subtly. The major perceived threat in the Canadian defense community during this time was that a war between the United States and Japan would result in the Americans violating Canadian neutrality. According to planning documents, a U.S. intervention into British Columbia in an effort to strike at Japan was the biggest threat the Dominion faced. Lieutenant-General Maurice A. Pope was a staff officer at the time, and in his memoirs he calls the plans "the height of absurdity." There was, though, some legitimate basis for these concerns in Ottawa. Roosevelt had made statements about threatening Canada in a war against Japan that had unnerved Mackenzie King and other members of the Cabinet. The army embraced this scenario mainly to increase appropriations. Most of the equipment it actually acquired was poorly suited for the terrain of western Canada but would operate well in western Europe.[13]

Military professionalism in Canada did survive in a small way. The Canadian military establishment was part of the British imperial system. Canadian officers often did detached duty with the British Army, and the General Staff in Ottawa received documents and journals from the various commands and headquarters spread throughout the empire. As a result, there was a professional backbone to the Canadian Army when the Dominion declared war on Germany in 1939. Canada, though, faced enormous difficulties of its own making. The army had grown fifty-fold over its prewar strength. In comparison, the British Army expanded only fifteen times over its original size. The quality and professional expertise were wafer thin, and the service had to learn on the battlefield—never an easy or painless process.[14]

With these facts in mind, members of the Canadian General Staff wanted to avoid having history repeat itself. The ultimate mission of peacetime military is to prepare against the day when it might be called upon to engage with the enemy. The Canadian Army never had the chance to ready itself and had to pay a high cost for it on the battlefield. If it could survive as an institution after the war, it might be able to preserve some of the expertise it had developed.

This position mimicked the one the Royal Canadian Air Force and the Royal Canadian Navy took. The proposal for forty-seven RCAF squadrons in the Pacific was a means to this end. Hap Arnold had good reason to wonder about what he would do with a force of this size. There were forty-eight RCAF squadrons in Europe.[15]

The goal of Canadian naval officers was to have a large and balanced fleet after the war. In the Atlantic, the battle against the U-boats required small frigates and corvettes. These small ships, however, would be of little use in the Pacific. Participation in the war against Japan would require the destroyers, cruisers, and carriers that these officers hoped to have in their postwar navy. This ideal was the reason that Canadian admirals in 1943 convinced Churchill to request an increase in the size of the RCN. The problem that thwarted these efforts was the vagueness of naval staff officers on the location where Canadian sailors would fight the Japanese; would it be with the Royal Navy in the Indian Ocean or in the North Pacific?[16]

The key difference among these three proposals was that the army put forward a plan that was much more modest than either those of the RCAF or RCN. Only one Canadian division would take part in the Pacific theater instead of the entire service, which the Cabinet was far more likely to approve.[17] The army also concentrated its proposal on doing battle in the most significant area of the region: Japan itself. "It is considered most important that, should a major war effort be inaugurated against Japan by way of the North Pacific, either through Hawaii or the Aleutians, Canada be represented in the final assault on the Japanese homeland," the Canadian Chiefs of Staff informed their ministers. "The North Pacific area is one of particular importance to Canada both geographically and politically."[18]

All these factors came to a head just before OCTAGON. Mackenzie King was suspicious of the bureaucratic agenda of his armed services when the Cabinet War Committee convened on August 31. The prime minister made it clear that with a coming election, the members of the government would have to explain honestly to the public what the Dominion was going to do in the Pacific conflict. As a result, he said Canada should send forces to the Pacific, but only to areas north of the Equator.[19]

A week later, on September 6, Mackenzie King met with his entire Cabinet. The calling together of the full Cabinet was rare, but the prime minister had a good reason. He wanted to show the defense ministers that there was little support for a Canadian role in the fight against the Japanese, or at least not on the scale they advocated. The conversation focused on the need for Canada to establish an identity for itself separate from that of the United Kingdom. The government committed the Canadian nation to fight the Japanese, but only if it took place north of the Equator. This requirement ensured that Canadians would be part of the invasion of Japan proper. This proposal also helped Mackenzie King avoid a political firestorm that seemed to be in the offing if Canadian soldiers were perceived in the Dominion to be helping the British reclaim their lost colonies. The Canadian effort would be made on a small scale, though. The politicians cut both the air and naval proposals. The Cabinet did, however, approve the army's request without making any change to the original suggestion. "The Equator theory seems to me fantastic," Minister for National Defence for Naval Services Angus Macdonald told his diary. "In air and naval operations it is impossible to draw lines arbitrarily and say that you will not go beyond them."[20]

A week later, during the second Quebec Conference, the War Committee had a three-and-a-half-hour meeting. Mackenzie King said the Canadian people had already contributed much to the war. Their taxes were high. How much more would they be willing to take? Macdonald challenged the prime minister directly, saying he was turning what had been a deployment preference into a requirement. Mackenzie threatened to resign, and that threat carried the day. The War Committee ratified the position of the Cabinet: "Canadian military forces should participate, as a matter of preference in the war against Japan in operational theatres of direct interest as a North American nation, for example in the North or Central Pacific, rather than in more remote areas such as Southeast Asia."[21]

Mackenzie King then sealed his victory the next day when he met separately with Churchill and Roosevelt. In doing so, he was basically reversing what had been done to him at the first Quebec Conference. With Roosevelt's and Churchill's support, it would be impossible for the armed services to argue that the Allies required a larger commitment from Canada. Mackenzie King saw Churchill as part of a meeting that the Canadian Cabinet War Committee had with the British prime minister and the British Chiefs. As the head of the host government, he started the meeting by telling his guests that the Cabinet believed that its men should be sent to areas where Canada had distinct interests. He faced a significant problem, because the Americans had made no firm plans for their final operations against Japan. Churchill said he understood the Canadian situation and he would talk to Roosevelt about the matter. He added that he only had that morning received approval to have the Royal Navy and Air Force participate in operations against Japan. Churchill said it was his hope that Canada would contribute men, ships, and planes to these two formations. Having the Canadian Army prepare for duty in Japan itself, he said, made sense, but he cautioned that it might be unnecessary. He thought that Japan might surrender without an invasion.[22] After this meeting, Mackenzie King talked to Roosevelt at one of the evening banquets that took place at the conference. He told the American that Canada would make a small contribution to the Pacific war, but that this effort should be concentrated either in the Central or Northern Pacific areas. Roosevelt took a sympathetic attitude and told his host amidst their meal that the Canadian force need not be large.[23]

In between these two meetings, the British and Canadian Chiefs of Staff gathered to discuss the details about the deployment of Canadian forces after the war in Europe ended. After covering troop requirements for the occupation of Germany and the Middle East and shipping shortages, Brooke turned to the war with Japan. He explained that the preliminary use of British land forces would be in Southeast Asia. Although this statement was vague, he was referring to an offensive that Mountbatten eventually launched designed to retake Burma. After that operation, Brooke said it was possible the British Army could do battle in several different regions.

In making these comments, he knew the matter had yet to be resolved with Churchill. Then, Portal and Cunningham made brief presentations and both said Canadian air and sea forces could be integrated into the British units that were scheduled to fight in the final and decisive operations.[24]

The Canadians also talked with the U.S. Chiefs. After meeting with both Churchill and Roosevelt, Mackenzie King authorized Lieutenant-General John Murchie, Chief of the General Staff, to meet with George C. Marshall. On September 16, Murchie informed Marshall that Canada would like to contribute troops to the invasion of Japan. He clearly communicated the geographical areas in which the Cabinet would allow deployment. Murchie added a condition of his own, saying that duty in the Kurile Island chain between Japan and the Aleutians, which a Canadian general had proposed earlier in the war, was unacceptable. "It was the Canadian desire to share in the final assault on Japan proper," according to an aide-mémoire that the Canadian gave Marshall. The American responded, saying the issue of "making room" for allies was an issue that was getting a lot of attention at the conference. He said there were good "psychological" and "political" reasons to include the Canadians in the invasion. A division would be the right type of unit to include. The only constraint would be equipment and spare parts, but that was a detail that could be worked out at a later date. He added that there was no real problem in including the Canadians.[25]

This answer was encouraging, but it was also less than firm. On December 9, Major-General H. F. G. Letson, the Chief of the Canadian Joint Staff in Washington, wrote Marshall asking if the United States was going to accept the Canadian offer. Major General J. E. Hull, Assistant Chief of Staff, in a memo to Marshall, observed, "Canadian participation as proposed by General Letson would be helpful." Leahy wrote back a week and a half later. "The Joint Chiefs of Staff accept the proposal that a Canadian Army Force of one division with such ancillary troops as may be required will participate in the war against Japan under the higher command of United States force." Leahy did add one requirement: that the Canadians be "available for use in any of the operations mounted in the Pacific."[26]

This reaction from the United States boded ill for the rest of the Canadian military. In the months after OCTAGON, Mackenzie King asserted his authority. In Cabinet War Committee meetings that followed the conference, he relentlessly forced the air force and navy to reduce the size of their forces for the Pacific. Since the United States and the United Kingdom already had more than enough forces to do the job of vanquishing the enemy, the Canadian contribution would be token in nature and nothing more. There was little the two services could do to challenge this position.[27]

The prime minister had his reasons for this pruning. Within a few days, he faced what was easily the biggest challenge of his tenure. Mackenzie King and his party drew significant electoral strength from Quebec. Canada might be a British nation, but the people of the French-speaking province had never taken to any of their foreign kings. France had little claim, either, to the loyalties of French-speaking Canada. The mother country had abandoned the French of North America nine generations earlier. While most of Canada was prepared to rally to the British imperial standard in World War I, Quebec refused. When the Canadian government attempted to introduce conscription, it divided the nation, provoked rioting in the streets, and led to the downfall of the Liberals. Mackenzie King was determined to keep from repeating history. Canada went to war with an all-volunteer military.[28]

The leaders and ministers of Canada's three armed services understood political realities and designed the force structure within the boundaries of a volunteer service, but this policy started falling apart in August. The casualty rate in the army mounted as the Allies broke out of Normandy and zipped across northern France. Replacements were few in number, so units became smaller as combat consumed Canadian fighting effectiveness. Smaller units were stretched thin and took losses at higher rates. The situation was particularly bad in the infantry, and the wounded often returned to the front lines before they had finished their convalescences. Minister of National Defence James Ralston received a report on manpower problems, but apparently under the press of his duties, he initialed the document and turned to other matters. It was only when he went on an inspection trip to Europe that he fully grasped the nature of the problem. He returned to Ottawa and reported to Mackenzie King.[29]

Over the course of the war, the prime minister had worked out a number of compromises to avoid another confrontation over initiating a draft. He had always known that the day might come when he might have no other choice. His standard slogan: "Conscription if necessary, but not necessarily conscription." The generals believed that the time had come. Mackenzie King did not. He believed a draft would tear the country apart. If the fate of the war was at stake, he would do the right thing and implement conscription. The scenario he had in mind, though, involved something like the D-Day landings failing, or the Germans driving the Allies back into the sea in a second Dunkirk. Higher casualty rates, whatever the impact the operational ineffectiveness of ground forces had on alliance cohesion, failed to meet this criterion.[30]

Army staff officers had put together the one division proposal for the Pacific aware of the manpower problems in Europe. The public announcement of this deployment, however, was hostage to the contest between Ralston and Mackenzie King. Before it was over, this confrontation would destroy two army ministers.

Ralston reported his findings to the prime minister on October 18. The news of that day hit him hard. "To me it is about as heavy a task as could be given to a man to bear for whatever decision is made I shall be the one that is pilloried," he observed.[31]

Ralston's return from Europe instigated a series of War Committee meetings. During the second half of October, the prime minister played for time. The strain of his position was wearing Mackenzie King down. He had been suffering from ringing in his ears for months and it got even worse. He realized almost from the beginning that Ralston would feel obliged to resign. He had to contain the political damage. The first committee came one day later. Ralston explained what he wanted. As part of earlier compromises worked out on conscription, Canada had initiated a draft between 1940 and 1942, but the service of these soldiers was limited to Canada itself. Ralston proposed to send these trained soldiers to Europe immediately. Mackenzie King explained that the issue was too serious to decide in haste. The committee met again one day later, and Ralston challenged Mackenzie King directly, reminding him of his promise to institute conscription without qualifications on deployment.[32]

The War Committee and Cabinet considered the issue over the course of the next week. Ralston was never in a position to carry the entire Cabinet, but several conscriptionists believed the prime minister would never honor his word and were willing to align themselves with the minister for National Defence. Mackenzie King feared he would lose as many as eight of his twenty-one ministers, and they were eight of the best. The prime minister, in these meetings, argued that conscription might bring down the Cabinet or initiate a civil war. It was, he said, the most crucial political issue in Canadian history since confederation. The contentious debate also had the potential to cripple the war effort against Japan.[33]

The debate continued into a third week. At a Cabinet meeting on October 31, in an effort to make the conscriptionists face their lack of political support, he asked his army, navy, and air force ministers if they were prepared to form a government if he resigned. The climax came on November 1. After spending two stressful weeks in trying to get Ralston to back down, Mackenzie King asked him at a Cabinet meeting for his resignation. "This was not a personal matter," the prime minister told his diary. Ralston agreed and after making a few comments, he left. The entire group stood and shook his hand. "I then went back to my seat," Mackenzie King wrote later, "and repeated to Council that it was one of the hardest things I had to do in my life."[34]

At the same meeting, the prime minister announced that General Andrew McNaughton would replace Ralston. Mackenzie King had actually informed the Cabinet of this selection before the general had agreed to resign. The selection was a shrewd move on the prime minister's part. Until December of 1943, McNaughton had been the commanding officer of Canadian soldiers stationed in Europe. He had insisted that soldiers enter combat under their own command and fight as a formation that was distinctly Canadian in the most decisive theater of the war—which is to say, northwestern Europe. He refused to allow the British Army to use individual regiments or divisions in peripheral operations like North Africa or Italy. As a result, Canadian soldiers sat in England and watched the war go by. Ralston overruled him and sent Canadian units to Italy. When McNaughton-led training exercises went poorly, Ralston removed him, citing McNaughton's poor health as the reason—the man did indeed have pneumonia. Stripped of his command six months before D-Day, an operation he had been preparing for many, many years, McNaughton eagerly seized the opportunity to have his revenge against the man who had removed him. Mackenzie King had started talking to the deposed general about joining the Cabinet when the crisis started. Still immensely popular with the public, McNaughton could help limit the political turmoil that would follow Ralston's resignation. McNaughton assured the prime minister that he believed that an all-volunteer force was still feasible—other options remained—and blamed Ralston in part for the crisis for overextending Canadian resources with deployments to Italy. Mackenzie King slowly shared the news with other members of the Cabinet, bolstering their resolve as the debate continued. When he announced McNaughton's selection, he even quoted written statements Ralston had made about the general's fitness for command. Since Ralston had used health as a pretext in removing McNaughton, there was little he could say about his successor.[35]

The issue went public as McNaughton and Mackenzie King attempted to convince drafted soldiers to volunteer for oversees duty. McNaughton squandered much of his public standing in this effort. Veterans and the families of servicemen in Europe were angry at the coddling of Quebec. Britain and the United States had conscript soldiers in combat. Why not Canada? In a speech he gave, intending to persuade draftees to volunteers, Mackenzie King only made things worse: "In this world conflict Canada has produced a race of noble warriors. The light in their eyes is the light of liberty, and the fire in their hearts is the fire of spirits dedicated to the service of their fellow man." He added: "You will be helping to remove a source of misunderstanding, bitterness and division in our own country and to preserve its strength through years to come." If their cause was so great, why was military service a source of discontent? Did the prime minister even have a plan? After three weeks of effort, it was clear that the volunteer system had reached its limits, and on November 23, the prime minister made public an order-in-council that would send the draftees to Europe. The crisis was over.[36]

Many have criticized Mackenzie King for his handling of the whole conscription issue, and with good reason. He ultimately failed both English- and French-speaking Canada on this issue. He failed the English in taking so long to institute conscription, and he failed the French in not honoring his original pledge of no conscription. His procrastination and insistence on voluntary enlistments for foreign duty continued long after this approach became counterproductive. To his credit, though, he eventually instituted conscription without serious social unrest. The three weeks between Ralston's resignation and the order-in-council were necessary to show Quebec that all other options had been exhausted.[37]

With that point made, Mackenzie King's lukewarm stand and duplicity hurt him politically. As a result, he used the Canadian contribution to the Pacific campaign to rebuild some of his credentials as a war leader. In April 1945, just as Parliament began debating military appropriations, he suggested in Cabinet that he make a general statement about the role the Dominion would play in these last campaigns. According to the minutes of the Cabinet meeting, there was "considerable discussion." In the end, the other ministers agreed.[38]

The prime minister's timing was good. The next day, as he readied to address the House of Commons, the *Gazette* of Montreal declared in an editorial: "Canada cannot forget the fact that her western sea coast is washed by the Pacific ocean, and she cannot avoid making commitments in cooperation with the United States to protect her interests on the Pacific coast." The editors of the paper also added: "The United States will expect from Canada a contribution towards the Japanese war at least in proportion to her own. For the future relationship between Americans and Canadians, there should not be cause given for censure on that point."[39]

In a fifteen-minute presentation, the prime minister stood before the other members of the House and talked in what he admitted were vague terms. "Canada's effort to maintain her just part in the further prosecution of the war against Japan will, as measured in numbers, necessarily be very much less than has been the case in the war in Europe. These considerations are most important in respect of the contribution of the Canadian army, but they also apply to the Canadian navy and to the Canadian air force." These forces would be in either the northern or central region of the Pacific. The force would train in Canada before going to the Pacific and would be composed of volunteers. Those who had served in Europe would get a chance to take leave. After the conscription crisis, those two points were most necessary.[40]

It was a statement that few could find much with which to dispute. The prime minister was delighted:

It was received with pretty much of a dead silence and an attentiveness I have seldom witnessed, or which I have witnessed only at time of great expectancy. I could feel that the House was receiving it well and that there was a tendency to applaud the latter portion of it but I saw equally clearly that the Conservatives were in a quandary as to what they should say when I had concluded.

In his diary, he added: "I think today's statement is perhaps the most effective thing that has been said this year and will go further than all else to win us the next general election."[41] He was right. The speech drew heavy and generally favorable press coverage.[42]

There were exceptions, though. The editorial board of the *Gazette* was less than impressed: "It would appear from the Prime Minister's words that Canada's interest in maintaining and safeguarding the peace of the world is such that totalitarian aggression in the Pacific is of less concern to this country than totalitarian aggression in Europe."[43]

In a sign of how strong the prime minister was politically, he bested the paper in this dispute. The authors of this editorial were in error when they referred to a quota system for the retention of Canadian troops in Germany as the mechanism for selecting those that would fight the Japanese. The next day Mackenzie King got up on the floor of the House of Commons and blasted the paper for a "deliberately misleading" opinion piece. He went on in his diary to discuss the political advantages of sending troops to Japan. None of the Conservatives had found grounds on which to attack or challenge his policy. "The Tories however were very quiet, their numbers in the House pretty thin. The truth is they see they are completely outmanoeuvered." The newspaper ran an editorial the next day admitting error, even if it continued to attack the wisdom of the limited Canadian role in the defeat of Japan.[44]

The Royal Navy, the Royal Air Force, and the Canadian Army were committed to partaking in the defeat of Japan. The process had been messy. It seemed as if there would be no role for the British Army and that Churchill would get his way in the dispute with Portal, Brooke, and Cunningham. War is, however, an untidy business. A series of events on both sides of the Pacific would change the balance of power calculations, if not in the war itself, at least within the alliance between the United States and Great Britain, making British forces a welcome addition in the righteous fight against the Japanese. The first of these factors that came into play was the heart of Henry "Hap" Arnold. Literally.

EIGHT

■

Rain of Fire

While the Canadians resolved their policy and political differences, work continued without pause for the U.S. Chiefs. Work as a Chief of Staff is always demanding, more so in a time of war. All four of the Americans found their duties stressful, but Hap Arnold had the most difficulty in coping with the demands of his job. While he had a good strategic vision for what the U.S. Army Air Forces required to develop as an armed service, his skills as an administrator fell apart when it came to managing his own office and time. These shortcomings might seem trivial, but Arnold's failure in these areas had a serious impact on his health and marriage. Those problems, in turn, incapacitated him in early 1945 and created a power vacuum in the army air forces. Even though the United States was about to start striking at Japan itself, the U.S. Army Air Forces had yet to make a significant contribution to the war in the Pacific. This factor, and the void in the leadership of the army air forces that developed as Arnold lay in a hospital bed, would have enormous consequences in the spring and early summer as U.S. airpower hammered Japan proper.

In January of 1945, four months after OCTAGON, Arnold suffered a heart attack. This coronary was his fourth in less than two years and was by far the worst. Arnold was what Americans would in later decades call a workaholic. He normally arrived at his office at 7 A.M., an hour before his staff, and usually stayed until 8 P.M. As the war progressed, he began his day at 6:30 A.M. and stayed until nine in the evening. He and his staff were on the job seven days a week. "We worked 10, 12, 14 hours a day," one officer on Arnold's staff recalled. "In the wintertime, we would arrive at the Pentagon before day light and leave after dark. And many a man never saw the light of day from one day to the other."[1]

What made the demands of his job more taxing than what the other members of the Joint Chiefs of Staff faced was that Arnold had no method for dealing with the stress that accompanied his position. He was the only one of the Chiefs who did not smoke. He almost never touched hard liquor and mixed drinks. He had few hobbies. He did like to hunt and fish, but after the United States entered the war, he rarely had the time. When he did get to spend the time in the out-of-doors, it was almost always in the company of other Chiefs of Staff, either American or British, and these usually amounted to working vacations. The result was that Arnold gained a significant amount of weight, which taxed his heart.[2]

A little over a year into the war, Arnold had his first heart attack. After a meeting at the White House, Arnold returned to his quarters and soon began complaining of chest pains. The airman was initially reluctant to seek medical treatment at first because U.S. Army regulations at the time required retirement following a heart attack. Arnold was lucky, though. Neither Secretary of War Henry Stimson nor Marshall wanted to lose him. Lee B. Martin, the physician treating Arnold, reported that his patient could still perform his duties, but legally the only person who could override the regulations was the commander-in-chief. Roosevelt decided to keep Arnold. The general then suffered another heart attack three months later.[3]

Arnold improved his behavior, but the lull in his frantic life was only temporary. As 1943 turned into 1944, he reverted to his intense work habits. In May, the demands became too much for his body, and he suffered a third heart attack.[4]

Eight months later, just before Arnold was to host a quiet dinner at his quarters with a few select guests, he felt a sudden and sharp pain. He barely made it to his bed. Arnold's wife, Bee, was in California, and he left word with his orderlies not to let anyone disturb him. Brigadier General Gene Beebe, Arnold's former personal pilot, forced his way past the orderly on duty. Martin, the doctor who had treated the general after his first heart attack, was working that evening and quickly decided his patient needed to be in the hospital and out of the Washington, D.C., area. Within a day, Beebe had him on a plane and was flying him down to Florida, where he was soon under twenty-four-hour-a-day care.[5]

It took Bee Arnold nine days to make her way from California, and her arrival at the hospital set the stage for a massive confrontation. When she arrived in Florida, Bee occupied the room next to her husband's, but Colonel Gilbert Marquardt, the doctor attending to the general, quickly noticed that the Arnolds were having problems in their marriage. She started a fight with Arnold about his "ambitious career" and how it had ruined his health. Marquardt wanted nothing agitating his patient that raised his blood pressure. Since Bee Arnold fit that description, the doctor decided she should have no contact with her husband. Following his doctor's instructions, Arnold asked his wife to leave and go back to Washington.[6]

Bee Arnold was crushed. After all they had been through—the travels to the Philippines, the death of an infant son, the frequent moves of a career army family—he had rejected her. She had also been under considerable stress herself. Her work with the Air Forces Aid Society had been draining her emotionally as she interacted again and again with the widows of men killed in action. It was more than she could handle. "I had no control of myself at all," she observed in later years. Not being welcome in her husband's hospital room crushed her. She returned to Washington and suffered a nervous breakdown in February and March of 1945.[7]

At least for the time being, Arnold knew little of what his wife was going through. He was more worried about how Marshall would respond to his heart problems. Making an exception for a heart attack was one thing; but four in less than two years was an entirely different matter. As he recovered, Arnold promised Marshall that his treatments were making him stronger and that he would be in a position to provide "far better service than I have been able to during the last two years."[8]

Arnold was being honest. Even though he was a five-star general, the third-ranking officer in the entire U.S. Army, and the commanding general of the army air forces, he had about as much influence on the war as the other convalescents at the Biltmore. He spent most of his days in Florida confined to his bed, undergoing regular blood tests and cardiographs. His diet became extremely bland and his weight dropped from 210 pounds to 193. The medical staff of the hospital told him that his heart blockage was clearing and that a natural bypass was forming. To avoid boredom, he read books, including Douglas Southall Freeman's three-volume study of the

Confederate Army's command, *Lee's Lieutenants*, and wrote long letters to his family. "Apparently one of my cylinders blew a gasket and I had to get down here to have an overhaul job done," he wrote lightheartedly to his daughter Lois. "While I was here they checked my lubrication, ignition and gasoline system and they said they were working alright."[9]

The letters he sent to his wife were of a far different nature. He worried about her health. "I am not sure that you are in A-1 shape now by any means." The more he reflected on the argument that led to Bee being banned from his hospital room, the more he realized her concerns had merit. "What you said has caused me to do a lot of thinking—you are right—right as you can be. I have been driving—driving myself to the point where I broke—driving others in the office just as hard until they broke— All for a purpose—to build up the finest—the most powerful Air Force this country can produce—All toward bringing this war to an end as soon as possible."[10]

In early March, after Arnold had been in the hospital for nearly six weeks and just after he resumed receiving regular reports from his staff, Bee Arnold wrote her husband and told him their marriage was over. She wanted some type of separation or a divorce. Her letter does not survive, but his responses make it clear what had transpired. Arnold was still deeply in love with his wife despite all their troubles, and the danger of losing Bee moved to the forefront of his concerns. "We have come down a long road together—we have had our pleasures—our disappointments—our hardships and the satisfaction of having four wonderful children. I can not conceive of traveling the last stretch without you." The next day he added, "I still have hopes that we can get together again."[11]

Soon Bee reconsidered, which was wonderful news to Arnold. "Let me tell you again that I love you," he wrote to her, "and you are the only woman I ever have loved. I regret that I have caused you so much trouble—so many disappointments—so much grief. I am sorry that I have not measured up to your requirements—especially when you needed me so much. I am sorry that I have been so inconsiderate." In closing he added, "Please have faith in me."[12]

Serious health or marital problems have a conspicuous, negative impact on job performance, and Arnold was no different. For half of his two-month stay in Florida, he received no memos or other papers from his staff, received no briefings, and took part in no conferences with the Joint Chiefs of Staff or the Combined Chiefs of Staff. Dik Alan Daso, an Arnold biographer, observes, "Arnold's heart troubles effectively removed him from the Commanding General's chair throughout his rehabilitation period; in effect, his command would never again be as total as it had been before the attack." In short, a power vacuum developed within his command due to his health and marital problems. In addition to his Washington positions as U.S. Army Deputy Chief of Staff for Air and Commanding General of the U.S. Army Air Forces, Arnold was also the Commanding General of the Twentieth U.S. Air Force based on Saipan. Since Saipan was at that time a four-day trip from San Francisco, Arnold's authority under the best of circumstances would have been extremely weak. With him incapacitated in the hospital, his command authority was nonexistent.[13]

When Arnold's fourth heart attack struck, the army air forces were attempting to hit Japan. Arnold gave this mission to the XX and XXI Bomber Commands, which were part of the Twentieth Air Force of which Arnold was the commanding general—at least on paper. Both of the bomber commands were equipped with the new long-range B-29 bomber. It soon became apparent that the XX Bomber Command, based in India, was too far from Japan to do much strategic damage to the enemy's industrial foundation. The task of hitting Japan proper, therefore, was exclusively that of the XXI Bomber Command, under Brigadier General Haywood "Possum" Hansell, Jr. This unit seemed better positioned for success. Hansell's bases were in the Marianas Islands, which were beyond the reach of the Japanese and had better supply lines, neither of which was the case for the XX Bomber Command. Hansell was a proven staff officer who was finally getting a chance at command. He was also one of the principal authors of AWPD/1, the main army air forces document setting forth the doctrine of precision strategic bombing during daylight hours.[14]

Despite promise and potential, Hansell and the XXI Bomber Command failed to produce any meaningful results. The general and his flyers faced a number of problems in trying to initiate a bombing campaign. The B-29 still had a number of design flaws limiting its utility. The most important was that the engines tended to fail under severe stress, which resulted in a high abort-mission rate and many accidents. The planes should have been able to bomb by radar, but the crews had received little training in the United States due to equipment shortages. To complicate matters even more, the targets the XXI Bomber Command had were inappropriate for radar targeting.[15]

The Americans also faced unexpected weather problems. The B-29 could fly at 30,000 feet, higher than other U.S. bombers, but crews at this altitude had to deal with the jet stream. These winds often exceeded 230 knots. Bombardiers supposedly had the ability to compensate for air currents, but these speeds exceeded the maximum limits of their bombsights. Clouds were another problem, creating difficult flying conditions and forcing bomber formations to disperse.[16]

Hansell was too committed to the doctrine that he had developed to consider other ways of using the B-29. Arnold was not. Despite Hansell's significant role in developing doctrine and establishing a mission for the army air forces, which would continue in the U.S. Air Force, he was not getting results. The United States had invested much in the development of the B-29, second only to the atomic bomb. Arnold needed to have results to show for this investment.[17] Just before his heart attack he decided to replace Hansell with Major General Curtis LeMay.

The new commander of the XXI Bomber Command was a tough man in a mean, hard business. LeMay was 38 years old when he went to the Pacific. The general was a husky, heavyset man with full-faced jowls and dark hair. Since early in the war he had suffered from Bell's palsy—an infection of the nerves—on the right side of his face, which made the muscles around his mouth sag—and he used pipes and cigars to hide the droop. He tended to thrust his jaw out, which, combined with his piercing stare and reluctance to smile—because of his mouth—gave him a fierce and intimidating look.[18]

LeMay's personality seemed to match. He had no real sense of humor and was not a talkative man. In fact, he was so shy, reticent, and socially awkward that he came across as rude and made others feel uneasy. He preferred to spend his time with his family and was never one to socialize at the officers' club. He knew he had little natural grace and decided to make no effort to polish his personality. He was blunt and direct in his speech, earning him the ironic nickname of "the diplomat."[19]

LeMay had an early interest in aviation, which combined with a vague inclination he had toward the military. "I had that yearning for airplanes right from the start. With me it was flying first and being in the Service second." At Ohio State University he majored in engineering and was a cadet in the Buckeye ROTC program. He also worked full-time while in school, which resulted in a couple of failing grades. As a result, he received a commission in the army reserves before he finished his degree. LeMay quickly learned that National Guard officers had a higher priority in getting flight

Airpower Genius. Major General Curtis LeMay was 38 years old when he took command of the XXI Bomber Command. Despite a reputation for being a hard man, he was never callous about war. He always remembered the human cost of military operations. Courtesy of the U.S. National Archives

school assignments than reservists. Proving himself adept at manipulating military red tape, he resigned his commission to take another one in the National Guard only to resign to attend flight school and then accept a regular slot in the army. Despite the confusing nature of the military bureaucratic process, LeMay succeeded.[20]

While on active duty he met his wife. Their marriage was an example of opposites attracting. Helen Maitland was a student at the University of Michigan. They had mutual friends who were engaged, and this couple decided to introduce their friends to one another. "I was attracted to her from the start. I liked her wild blue eyes and her hair," LeMay recalled. "She talked plenty, couldn't seem to stop. And it was all in a bubbling effusion which I found myself rather enjoying. She'd skip from one topic to another, like a dancer hitting the high points. Often you couldn't get a word in edgewise."[21]

The first years after the wedding were "wretched times," to use LeMay's own words, for the newlyweds. The two wanted to have children, but Helen LeMay miscarried twice. Religion offered little comfort to LeMay. In essence, his personal religious beliefs were like his commitment to air-power: strong in a general sense, but vague on the details. He said he "wasn't quite settled" on a specific faith. "I believe in a Supreme Being, but I don't feel that I need some other character to advise me how to conduct myself to please this Supreme Being." He threw himself into his work to deal with his own pain and loss. The LeMays were overjoyed when they eventually had a daughter, Janie, in 1939. "There were a lot of wonderful years ahead, and maybe a greater happiness with my daughter than I ever deserved," the general reflected in his memoirs.[22]

LeMay was something of an outsider in the army air corps/army air forces of the prewar years. He was an Ohio State Buckeye, while most of his contemporaries, the early pioneers of airpower, were graduates of West Point. He advanced rapidly in rank as the army air corps expanded during the first few years of the war when the United States was neutral. This rapid advancement was typical of a service with few experienced officers even at the start of the air campaigns against Germany.[23]

As a commander, LeMay believed in leadership by example and flew air missions himself. He had a reputation for being tough, but fair and even-handed. His men called him "Iron Ass," but not to his face. He knew war was an ugly business but never flinched. He had enormous respect for the men under his command and hated to lose any of them. Throughout his memoir, the general makes it clear he was alive to the human cost of war. Still, he was more than prepared to make decisions that would cost some of his men their lives. "If you are going to fight you're going to have some people killed," he commented. "But if you have done everything humanly possible to prepare for that mission and plan it properly, and you have re-sults which you wished to attain—Then you can think, and feel in your heart, 'The losses were paid for.'"[24]

When LeMay took command of the XXI Bomber Command, he knew

what was at stake. Arnold had informed him both in person and in writing. "As I told you before you went out to India, the B-29 project is important to me because I am convinced that it is vital to the future of the Army Air Forces." Arnold knew there were going to be all sorts of complications in deploying these new weapons, but these difficulties simply had to be overcome. "We will have problems of logistics, of material, of organization, and we will always continue to have problems of one kind or another. None of them, however, are insurmountable and we must not let ourselves use them as an excuse for doing anything less than the best possible under the circumstances."[25]

LeMay also had an incredible amount of operational freedom. For all practical purposes, he answered to no one—at least for the time being. The general was, as his record in Europe showed, an "operator." He was willing to experiment with different applications of airpower and had no dogmatic commitment to one doctrine over another. Whatever got results was good enough for him.[26]

Despite this flexibility, LeMay knew precision bombing was the focus of the army air forces. At first, he attempted to pursue daylight missions over Japan, but cloud cover obscured the targets. The planes dropped their ordnance using radar, but the personnel manning the scopes lacked training and experience. The bombs fell on targets of chance and had little impact on Japanese industrial production.[27]

LeMay began rethinking the tactics and target criteria his command was using. There had been talk and studies on the vulnerability of Japanese cities to firebombing. An army air forces report in January 1945 called the possibility of striking the urban areas of Japan with incendiaries "a tempting point for argument." Both Hansell and LeMay conducted high-altitude bombing missions over Japan using incendiaries, but neither had gotten much as far as results were concerned. "I had to do something, and I had to do something fast," LeMay explained.[28]

Do something he did. LeMay decided to gamble on a wholesale basis. He implemented a broad number of new tactics and methods. The first and probably the most significant change was the altitude at which the B-29s would fly. One of the biggest problems the XXI Bomber Command faced was the complications of flying at high altitudes. The jet stream and cloud cover made bombing difficult. "Weather continues to be our worst operational enemy. During my first six weeks here we had one visual shot at a target. This was primarily the reason I lowered the altitude for our incendiary attacks," he informed Arnold weeks later.[29] He decided to have the B-29s fly between 5,000 and 10,000 feet instead of the 20,000 to 30,000 feet of the previous missions. "With those overheating engines, it began to seem that this high altitude stuff was strictly for the birds," he joked. These lower altitudes would put less strain on the engines and require less fuel, which would increase bomb loads. Radar at lower altitudes would have better scope definition and would be more accurate. "I expected," LeMay stated years later, "that we would have less trouble with the airplane flying at low altitude—it wouldn't be such a strain on the engines and we would probably have less mechanical trouble."[30]

The main reason planes flew at high altitudes was to stay out of the range of antiaircraft fire. The general, however, had studied surveillance photos and deduced that the Japanese had limited defensive resources. The 20- and 40-millimeter flak guns stationed in Tokyo only had a range of 4,500 feet. While 25-millimeter guns could hit targets 8,000 feet up, they lacked the necessary speed to traverse and track the B-29s. "All of the studies we'd made on the defense of Japan indicated an absence of light flak or certainly not in the numbers that we found in Europe. I expected that if we went in at night at low altitude, say five thousand feet and up, we would surprise them and we would be able to get away with it, at least for a short period of time," LeMay explained. "In Europe we couldn't have adopted these tactics at all, but in Japan, yes, I thought they would work."[31]

Most of his staff opposed this move, predicting high losses. LeMay knew the nature of the risk he was taking. "I could never be certain just how good my Intelligence really was. We had pictures; we couldn't find any low-altitude defense; but that didn't mean it wasn't there."[32]

Next, he decided the planes would fly at night. This idea had been bouncing around the army air forces for a while, but LeMay was the first to implement the change. Flying at night reduced the danger of flak. Japanese antiaircraft gunners would need searchlights and radar to track the planes. Fighters were also less of a danger due to limited visibility, and the Japanese only had two units of night fighters in the home islands.[33]

Since there was less danger from Japanese countermeasures, LeMay made another decision, but one that was much riskier. He decided to strip the B-29s of all their defensive armaments, except for the tail guns. This move eliminated 2,700 pounds and would allow the planes to carry more bombs. This change also significantly reduced the possibility of the bombers hitting one another with friendly fire.[34]

There was no reason for the planes to fly in group formations if they no longer had guns, and LeMay ordered that the B-29s fly alone. This move reduced the rate of fuel consumption, but required greater piloting and navigational skills. The planes that took off first, however, would fly at slower speeds than those leaving later. The idea was to have the planes arrive over Tokyo, which would be the target, and drop their bombs in as short a time as possible. The faster they hit their targets, the more difficult it would be for the Japanese to respond.[35]

Another major change that LeMay made was the decision to use incendiaries against Japanese cities. The urban areas of Japan were densely populated. The industrial infrastructure, however, was the opposite. Japanese firms used many widely distributed feeder factories to construct small machine parts. These production facilities were often intermixed with major residential areas, making it particularly difficult for the army air forces to select specific strategic targets. Since the primary construction material in Japanese cities was wood, Americans had long known the home islands were exceptionally vulnerable to fire. Arnold, in his open-minded way on things related to airpower, had ordered some studies and exercises of vulnerability in an incendiary campaign, but had never made any effort to redirect the attention and focus of his commanders in the field. The initiative instead came from LeMay. He decided to have the XXI Bomber Command use fire against the enemy in area attacks. A good number of noncombatants would die, but the flames would also destroy the dispersed industrial system of Japan.[36]

Finally, LeMay initiated a rigorous radar training program. Flying at night, the crews could use either celestial methods with clear skies or the LORAN navigational device to guide them to their targets, but radar would still be exceptionally important once the planes reached the Tokyo area. Navigation at night would depend on the ability of radar operators to find geographic landmarks, and the men operating these devices desperately needed to improve their skills. LeMay knew the crew members assigned to operate these machines had little instruction on how to use the equipment. "Their training consisted of (about): 'This is a radar set. This is the way you turn it on.'" The general sent one of his radar specialists to Saipan, and told him: "Look. You go up there and pick out a couple of the stupidest radar operators they have, and Lord knows that's pretty stupid." He wanted the bomb wing stationed on the island to practice finding the tip of Saipan from 5,000 feet. The XXI Bomber Command would use a similar point near Tokyo Bay as a checkpoint. After the practice, the outcomes of the Saipan test were in the low range of what was acceptable, but LeMay decided those results were adequate enough to move on with his plan.[37]

The combination of incendiaries and radar navigation was a clear sign the army air forces had intentionally decided to pursue area bombing. Officially, though, the service made no change in tactics. The mission report for the first strike against Tokyo, using LeMay's new methods, declares, "The object of these attacks was *not* to indiscriminately bomb civilian populations. The object was to destroy the *industrial and strategic targets* concentrated in the urban areas." Aviation historian Kenneth P. Werrell disagrees in *Blankets of Fire*, his highly readable study of the strategic bombing of Japan. In rather simple and direct words, he states: "nighttime incendiary bombing was a weapon of area destruction, not precision bombing."[38]

The first test of this new approach came on the night of March 9–10, 1945. Many of the crews went into the mission afraid of these new tactics, thinking that a low-altitude approach without guns amounted to nothing more than suicide. Despite these concerns, a total of 325 planes took part in Operation: MEETINGHOUSE. It took almost two hours for all the B-29s to take off, and each one would be in the air for fifteen hours. On Guam, LeMay went to the runway and watched the 314th Wing take off. "I'll admit I was nervous about it," he stated later. "I made the decision. I had weighed the odds. I knew the odds were in my favor. But still, it was something new. I could have lost a lot of people, appeared to be an idiot."[39]

LeMay had initiated these changes on his own authority. He did technically send a report to the Commanding General, Twentieth Air Force—that is to say General of the Army Henry H. Arnold—but LeMay sent the document less than twenty-four hours before the first plane took off. In his memoirs, he explained that he was trying to spare Arnold for the good of the service. "He's on the hook, in order to get some results out of the B-29's. But if I set up *this* deal, and Arnold O.K.'s it beforehand, then he would have to assume some of the responsibility. And if I don't tell him, and it's all a failure, and I don't produce any results, then he can fire me. And he can put another commander in here, and still have a chance to make something out of the 29's."[40]

The general spent the evening waiting for reports from his planes. Colonel St. Clair McKelway, LeMay's public information officer, visited the operation control room at 2 A.M. and found him there with the overnight staff. LeMay smiled at the colonel, asked what he was doing there, and then said, "I'm sweating this one out myself. A lot could go wrong. I can't sleep. I usually can, but not tonight."[41]

The colonel and the general whiled away the evening talking as they sat on a bench under the mission control boards. LeMay had a lot of nervous agitation to work off. According to McKelway, the general declared,

> If this raid works the way I think it will, we can shorten this war. In a war, you've got to try to keep at least one punch ahead of the other guy all the time. A war is a very tough kind of proposition. If you don't get the enemy, he gets you. I think we've figured out a punch he's not expecting this time. I don't think he's got the right flak to combat this kind of raid and I don't think he can keep his cities from being burned down—wiped right off the map."

LeMay was chomping on a cigar while he talked. He had taken to cigars exclusively after arriving on Guam, because the humidity quickly ruined pipes and their tobacco. The general continued, "He hasn't moved his industries to Manchuria yet, although he's starting to move them, and if we can destroy them before he can move them, we've got him. I never think anything is going to work until I've seen the pictures after the raid, but if this one works, we will shorten this damned war out here."[42]

The bombing began at 1 A.M. and continued for three hours, but 81 percent of the B-29s released their payload in the first two hours. The airmen dropped 500-pound firebomb clusters that night, which deployed thirty-eight M-69 incendiary bombs. Each M-69 contained a flammable gel that eventually became known as napalm. A 3-foot streamer followed the cylinder and stabilized its descent. When the ordnance made contact with the surface, a device would eject and ignite the napalm. The crews set these clusters to spread on the ground 50 feet apart. As a result, the load of each plane could cover a 350 by 2,000–foot area, or roughly 16 acres.[43]

The B-29s turned Tokyo into a version of Hell. From a distance, the bombs looked beautiful as they floated down. From the vantage point that Sophia University offered, Father Gustav Bruno Maria Bitter watched "a silver curtain falling, like the *lametta*, the silver tinsel that we hung from Christmas trees in Germany." Lars Tillitse, a Danish diplomat, recalled that the incendiaries "did not fall; they descended rather slowly, like a cascade of silvery water. One single bomb covered quite a big area, and what they covered they devoured."[44]

The flames were devastating. Bitter and Tillitse were in the western and northern parts of Tokyo, but the eastern region was the focal point of the American effort. As the incendiaries hit the ground, they engulfed the area in flame. The wind then helped spread the destruction, pushing fires to the northwest with rapid speed. The breeze also picked up burning debris that would then drift down on nearby areas, bringing ruin to parts of the city that had escaped the initial blasts. Within an hour a firestorm had engulfed eastern Tokyo. The heat became so intense it turned glass into liquid. Those who tried to fight the flames died where they stood. The best way to survive was to run.[45]

Many residents of the burning city sought shelter in large bodies of water. People thronged to swimming pools, rivers, canals, and ponds. Individuals choked the banks of the Sumida River, and the later arrivals hovered on the edge of the water and crushed those that had been the first to arrive. Schools, Western-style buildings, and large open areas like parks were other popular destinations.[46]

The fire killed in many ways, and the locations where people hid did little to protect them. As the inferno grew it sucked up oxygen. One of the biggest causes of death that night was suffocation. Those individuals were the fortunate ones. They died quickly. Many others died slowly as they burned to death. Waves of flame swept through parks as trees went up in flames and became kindling to the blaze. The heat turned many sanctuaries into killing grounds. One Tokyo resident, Tsuchikura Hidezo, took his family to a nearby school known for its large swimming pools. Many other people in the neighborhood had the same idea, so Tsuchikura took his family to the roof rather than endure the crowds in the school. The Tsuchikuras suffered through the bombings as flames surrounded the school. Burning pieces of paper and wood showered them. They doused themselves with water from tanks on the roof when their clothes caught fire. The heat was so intense, though, that steam escaped from their garments. After the bombing ended, Tsuchikura discovered that of the thousands that had sought refuge at the school only his family and twelve others that had been on the roof had survived. "The entire building had become a huge oven three stories high," he remarked. "Every human being inside the school was literally baked or boiled alive in the heat."[47]

Captain Kubota Shigenori, an instructor at the Imperial Japanese Army Medical School, took twenty-four men to Tokyo that evening to treat survivors and found much the same thing as Tsuchikura. When he reached the Sumida River, he discovered, "The entire river surface was black as far as the eye could see, black with burned corpses, logs, and who knew what else." From a distance it was impossible to tell the human remains from wooden poles, or the differences between men and women. "All that remained were pieces of charred meat. Bodies and parts of bodies were carbonized and absolutely black." He estimated that the dead in the river numbered in the tens of thousands.[48]

A mile up in the air, the foul smell of burning flesh forced bomber crews to wear oxygen masks to keep from vomiting. The planes were flying at staggered altitudes between 5,000 and 7,800 feet, which was a blind spot in what little Japanese antiaircraft fire existed in the Tokyo area. The intense heat created updrafts that flipped B-29s on their backs, pushed some as high as 15,000 feet, and were the factor most responsible for destroying the planes the Americans lost that evening. When the B-29s returned to their bases, their underbellies were black from soot.[49]

The firebombing of Tokyo on the night of March 9–10, 1945, is one of the most destructive air raid missions ever. It was more deadly than Hamburg, Dresden, and even Nagasaki. In one night, the aircrews of the XXI Bomber Command destroyed 16 square miles of Tokyo, which amounted to about 8 percent of the urban area of the Japanese capital. That number, however, fails to tell the full story. The Americans burned down one-fourth of all the buildings in the city. To be even more specific, the bombers (combined with those on earlier missions) eliminated 18 percent of the industrial area and 63 percent of the commercial area of Tokyo. Roughly 80,000 to 100,000 people died, and another 1 million were left homeless. The inferno would claim even those who had survived that evening as smoke inhalation, shock, and infections did their work. All told, it would take Japanese authorities twenty days to remove and bury the remains of the dead.[50]

More was to come, although none of these missions would equal the destructive power unleashed on Tokyo. On the night of March 11–12, the XXI Bomber Command hit Nagoya, a city with 1.5 million people, third largest in Japan at the time. The bomb crews set the intervalometers, the devices controlling the distribution of the incendiaries, to distribute at 100 feet instead of the 50 feet used on Tokyo. The thinking among crews and staff planners was that it was a waste to drop bombs into areas already on fire, and a wider setting would spread the fire further. The strike force hit Nagoya in two waves in an effort to reduce congestion over the target. These changes were tactical mistakes. Only 54 percent of the B-29s got over the target in the first two hours. Although the attack did much damage, the Japanese on the ground had enough time and distance to fight the fires and keep them from combining the way they had in Tokyo.[51]

One day later, it was Osaka's turn to suffer. The U.S. airmen returned to the tactics they had used over Tokyo. The B-29s destroyed 8 square miles of the second largest Japanese city. There were 3,000 Japanese deaths, but roughly 500,000 people became homeless.[52]

Kobe was the target of the XXI Bomber Command's fourth major firebombing operation, but the aircrews were beginning to run afoul of supply shortages. The bombers were dropping munitions faster than the U.S. Army logistical system could supply them. The M-69s were basically gone. The Americans used M-47, M-50, and M-76 incendiaries instead, as well as fragmentation bombs to wound those trying to fight the fires. The Kobe mission was the first time the Americans got 300 bombers over the target, and 96 percent dropped their ordnance in the first two hours. The B-29s did much damage to the city, burning down 3 square miles of urban area, or 21 percent of the city. A total of 8,000 people died in this strike, and 650,000 lost their homes.[53]

The B-29s returned to Nagoya on March 18 for the last firebombing mission of that spring. The airmen of the XXI Bomber Command did a better job of concentrating their B-29s over their targets than they did during the first trip to Nagoya. This time 88 percent of the bombers got over target in the first two hours and dropped a denser pattern of bombs (.45 ton per acre of city versus .145 the first time). Militating against the creation of a firestorm was the fact that the Americans had very few M-69 incendiaries and used high explosives, which hurt people and buildings, but had little potential to spread their destruction on the ground. Nonetheless the results, 3 square miles of Nagoya burned out, were striking. Perhaps most astonishing of all, not a single American died on this mission.[54]

By any measure, the results of these five firebombing missions were terrifyingly impressive. When discussing strategic bombing there is a danger of getting lost in the statistics of it all. The most remarkable thing about these five missions was not the number of sorties that the XXI Bomber Command flew, the tonnage of bombs dropped, or even the square mileage destroyed, but rather the efficiency of the XXI Bomber Command in destroying Japanese cities. In ten days, using only 1 percent of the tonnage dropped on Germany during the whole war, LeMay and his aircrews had equaled 41 percent of the destruction that airpower had visited upon the Nazis. With a simple change in doctrine, and the process of bombing, the XXI Bomber Command was getting much more bang for far fewer bucks.[55]

The person most responsible for this development was Major General Curtis LeMay. His decisions to lower bombing altitudes, strip the B-29s of their gun crews, fly at night, use incendiaries, and target industrial areas were the key elements that led to success in these missions. Compression of time and space was another significant factor. It took American airmen some time, however, to discover the importance of these last two elements to the outcome of their operations.[56]

Arnold was not one to quibble with success. As he recovered his health and put his marital problems behind him, he focused more attention on his command of the Twentieth Air Force. He was pleased with LeMay's results. "I have followed closely the progress of the XXI Bomber Command and I want you and your people to understand fully my admiration for your fine work." Arnold knew that there was a lot more to these missions than the work of the commanding general, the pilots, and even the crews of the planes. "Your recent incendiary missions were brilliantly planned and executed, but I appreciate that behind these successful missions there are thousands of men who do not participate actively as combat crews. The individual abilities of all of these men, welded into a well organized and ably led team, account for the success of the XXI Bomber Command."[57]

The only major figure who questioned these new tactics was Secretary of War Henry Stimson. He had some moral misgivings about the operations and voiced his concerns to Arnold. In his reply, the general explained that the widely spread nature of the Japanese industrial system made it "practically impossible to destroy the war output of Japan without doing more damage to civilians connected with the output than in Europe." He did reassure the secretary that "they were trying to keep it down as far as possible." These statements were apparently enough to satisfy Stimson.[58]

The firebombing missions did come to a halt for a time, but the pause had nothing to do with moral qualms about LeMay's new tactics. The reasons instead were operational in nature. The biggest problem was logistics. In ten days, the XXI Bomber Command had consumed its entire supply of incendiary devices. Spare parts for the B-29 became another problem. The

Bombs Away. These B-29s of the XXI Bomber Command are dropping their payload over Yokohama during a daylight raid. Courtesy of the U.S. National Archives

tempo of operations had picked up so much speed that the flyers went through their supplies faster than support personnel could get them across the vast waters of the Pacific. Another factor bringing about this temporary halt was the exhaustion of the B-29 crews. The flight time of each mission was fourteen and a half hours. In addition, there was the stress of being in combat. All these missions occurred in a concentrated, ten-day period.[59]

LeMay and his unit did stay busy, though. In late March and early April, the 313th Bomb Wing dropped mines in the waters between the Japanese home islands. The wing flew seven missions—two of which saw 100 planes take part. In the other five operations, the numbers were 20 or lower. The Shimonoseki Strait became the main target of these runs, and the Americans put 1,800 weapons into the water, which closed this passageway for two weeks. The mines reduced monthly imports by half and sank or damaged 35 ships. In May, the Americans initiated a new phase in their mining operations in an effort to seed the entire Inland Sea with explosives and blockade the ports of Tokyo, Kobe, Nagoya, and Osaka. Two bombing missions dropped 1,422 mines. In the second half of the month another eight missions deployed an additional 1,313. The destruction that followed was extraordinary. The Japanese actually lost more ships to mines than submarines in May.[60]

The XXI Bomber Command, however, spent most of its efforts between the beginning of April and mid-May flying suppression missions against airfields in southern Kyushu. These bases were home to most of the kamikaze units attacking U.S. forces in and around Okinawa. The B-29 crews resented such missions, seeing them as unproductive diversions from operations that could bring the war to an end. "All we were doing at last was plowing the fields," LeMay argued.[61]

Starting in mid-April, once the XXI Bomber Command replenished their stocks of munitions, the American airmen worked in some strategic bombing missions in between their other obligations. LeMay had his crews try a number of tactics, including daylight and nighttime precision raids on aircraft factories, and low- and high-elevation flights. After getting modest results with precision strikes, LeMay had his aircrews focus more on city busting. There were five area bombing missions in the second half of May. Two took place against Nagoya, which, combined with the previous attacks, had one-fourth of that city in ruins. There were two attacks against Tokyo. The second one, on the night of May 25–26, burned down 19 square miles of the Japanese capital, which was more than the mission of March 9–10. The Japanese, however, put up a strong defense. A total of 464 planes dropped bombs on the city, but 26 were lost, and 110 returned with damage. Most of the Japanese success came from flak. The fifth raid came on May 29 during the day in the skies over Yokohama. In this daylight mission 454 bombers burned out 6.9 square miles of the city.[62]

In July, the Americans began turning their attention to medium-sized Japanese cities. The Twentieth Air Force hit a total of thirty-five municipalities, starting early in the month with those that had populations of over 100,000, and then worked its way down through smaller cities in systematic fashion.[63]

In his retirement, LeMay remained proud of the operations he had overseen. "It was my decision and my order which sent the B-29's to the task in the manner described. I was glad that I had not consulted General Arnold. I'd talked to subordinates, and some had gone along with me in the notion, and others had disapproved, sincerely and almost heartbrokenly. But again—*My* decision and *my* order. There has to be a commander." His only regret was the price that the U.S. Army Air Forces had paid: "Seemed to me that if I had done a better job we might have saved a few more crews."[64]

Even though the air strikes brought the war home to the Japanese in a way that nothing else could, the Imperial Army and Navy still had fight in them. The war in the Pacific was no chess game that ended when the out-

CHAPTER EIGHT

come was clear. The air raids did nothing to undermine the determination of the Japanese military to resist the enemy. In fact, as events would soon show, the destruction that the operations wrought encouraged the Emperor's soldiers and sailors to continue the fight. They believed they were fighting an American enemy who was using the most barbaric of tactics to defeat Japan. It was no accident that Americans would encounter the toughest opposition they had faced in the Pacific on and around a small island called Okinawa. And they would soon be glad to have their British friends with them.

■

Okinawa: Sea Battle

While Tokyo smoldered, the invasion of Japan started. This campaign started on Okinawa, the largest of the Ryukyu Islands. Okinawa was a prefecture of Japan, part of the nation itself, not a Japanese colony. The fight for control of the island began at sea, and became the single bloodiest battle in the entire history of the U.S. Navy. Working in combination, Okinawa and LeMay's tactics fostered intense Japanese resistance in the waters around the small prefecture. This intense battle would see the arrival of the British Pacific Fleet and set in motion factors that altered politics and diplomacy in Washington.

Why was Okinawa the bloodiest battle in U.S. Navy history? The answer can be found in two words: the kamikazes. As Fleet Admiral Chester W. Nimitz explained, "This was not a battle by vast opposing forces, but an unending series of small fights."[1]

The person responsible for commanding the kamikazes was Vice Admiral Ugaki Matome, Commanding Officer, Fifth Air Fleet. Born in Setomachino in the Okayama Prefecture, he graduated from Etajima in 1912. As a young officer, he had many duty assignments at sea. He visited Australia, and during the Great War his ship sailed on a training cruise to North America. As a lieutenant, he became a gunnery officer, serving in that function on a destroyer and battleship. After he attended the Imperial Japanese Navy's war college, he began serving in a series of staff jobs.

These positions included duty as a naval attaché in Germany, staff work at the Second Fleet, and a return to the war college as an instructor. A well-rounded professional, he returned to the Combined Fleet as a captain and served as the commanding officer of the training cruiser *Yagumo*, and then the battleship *Hyuga*. In 1941, Rear Admiral Ugaki became Chief of Staff of the Combined Fleet when Admiral Yamamoto Isoroku was the Commander-in-Chief. He played a key role in planning the attack on Pearl Harbor. Ugaki was also shot down with Yamamoto in April 1943. Unlike Yamamoto, he survived. After recuperating from the injuries he suffered in the crash, he commanded the First Battleship Division and took part in the Battle of Leyte Gulf, where the Imperial Japanese Navy came close to defeating American naval forces before being destroyed as an effective fighting force. In February of 1945, he took command of the Fifth Air Fleet, which attempted to destroy the naval forces supporting the invasion of Okinawa. This position gave him operational authority over the Third and Tenth Air Fleets. In addition, the Imperial Japanese Army attached the Sixth Air Army to the command of the Combined Fleet for operations in the area of the Ryukyu Islands, including Okinawa.[2]

At the beginning of the war, when Japan was seizing territory, Ugaki was as arrogant as any officer in the navy. During war games testing the planned invasion of Midway, he ruled the sinking of the carrier *Akagi* inadmissible. In actual battle, however, the Americans failed to play by his rules and sank that ship and three other aircraft carriers. Following that defeat, Ugaki was smart enough to understand that the bravery and courage of his men were of limited value against the doctrine, tactics, organization, and firepower of the enemy. He escaped from the gloomy turn of the war with excursions into the outdoors. Horseback riding, hunting, fishing, and outdoor walks allowed him to escape from the grim nature of his job. Ugaki found that when he did not take a daily ride, he usually felt ill—most likely from stress. Flowers and grassy fields also made him philosophical. "Nature's great progress in a few days' time seemed to laugh pityingly at the silly little human world, where we were making a fuss about war and enemy task forces and so on." A strong-willed man, but also sentimental and emotional, he worried about what he called his "weak mind" getting the better of him. Men with iron resolve often worry about their weakness, and constantly work on their tenacity, making it one of their most dominant personality traits. Ugaki was no different. He knew that his young pilots, men with lives full of promise and potential ahead of them, would die in kamikaze operations. He regretted their loss profoundly, but in the cold, hard calculus of war where the lives of some are spent as the cost of operational success, it was a price he was prepared to pay. Writing on what he considered a successful operation, he observed, "I couldn't be pleased because of the young boys." That remorse was difficult to live with, so he decided "to follow the example of those young boys some day."[3]

His Chief of Staff, Rear Admiral Yokoi Toshiyuki, thought the suicide effort was idiotic. The expenditure of men and material was huge with no opportunity to employ either a second time. He doubted that the striking velocity of a plane would be sufficient to sink a ship. Yokoi also realized that measuring the effectiveness of these operations would be extremely difficult, since the pilots would not return to base and make reports. He reflected that a "surge of enthusiasm that overrode all defects of the kamikaze attacks" dominated Japanese thinking in both the military and the public.[4]

Americans at the time had—and still have—a hard time understanding the motivation of the kamikaze pilots, seeing them as some unique and twisted manifestation of Japanese culture. Attributing these suicide flights to cultural differences, be it a different value on human life or the nobility of failure, exaggerates differences far more than it explains and clarifies.[5] Death before dishonor was an old concept in the Western world and respected in the United States of the 1940s.[6] More to the point, there are many examples in Western military history of soldiers fighting to the last man long after victory is no longer possible in order to accomplish a military mission. This list is long: the Spartans at Thermopylae, the Imperial Guard at Waterloo, the Texians at the Alamo, the Argylls at Le Cateau, and the British 30th Brigade at Calais during the Dunkirk evacuation, to name just a few.[7]

From a Japanese perspective, their situation in 1945 looked more than dire. In the aftermath of LeMay's firebombing tactics, propaganda claiming that the Americans wanted to exterminate the Japanese and destroy the Japanese nation and its culture were fairly easy to believe. Racism had been a major factor in the Pacific war. The strategic bombing stunned the nation to its very core. "This savage raid shocked the nation beyond anything that had gone before," Nagatsuka Ryuji, a pilot in kamikaze training, observed. These views were hardly the emotion of a fanatic. Lieutenant Colonel Fujiwara Iwaichi, the author of a history of Japanese defensive efforts, noted, "The damage caused by these operations was almost incalculable." Nagatsuka believed that "exceptional means were needed to salvage the situation." The ultimate mission of any armed service is to protect a nation, government, and society, and in 1945 the basic future of Japan seemed at stake. "The security, the very existence of our families was threatened," Nagatsuka explained. "Women, children and old men had already been among the innumerable and pathetic victims of bombing and machine gun fire. It was therefore natural that we should go to any lengths, regardless of our own safety, to protect our families." As Hosokawa Hachiro, who, like Nagatsuka, survived the war, explained, "I do not believe this so-called suicide mentality is unique to the Japanese. The spirit of self-sacrifice exists in all countries among all peoples, particularly among the young, who are innocent and free of cynicism when they are in a life-or-death situation. World history, in fact, is filled with similar examples."[8]

The firebombing attacks on Japanese cities did not create the kamikazes—the Japanese had turned to this tactic in October 1944—but they made it much easier for the Japanese military to find volunteers for these one-way sorties. Ugaki told a group of pilots that their country needed their devotion with "B-29s raiding our homeland every day." While in Tokyo, a woman approached Nagatsuka, who was in uniform, and told him, "For us, you are one of the guardian angels. I wanted to express my gratitude, in the name of all people." Her statement, he says, set "my spirit on fire."[9]

The men who flew these planes were not suicidal in the sense that they had no regard for their own lives and futures. "I say this quite frankly: I am not dying voluntarily," Otsuka Akio wrote before his death. "I am not going to my death without regrets." Nagatsuka believed that sinking a U.S. ship was a rational transaction for his life and would give his sacrifice meaning. Miyagi Yoshi, who died in an attack, explained, "This suicide is a form of sacrifice which can be understood only in Japan, the country of idealism."[10]

The theater commander who had to deal with the kamikaze threat was Chester W. Nimitz, in his capacity as Commander-in-Chief of the Pacific Fleet and the Pacific Ocean areas. He came from a family that had a long history that reached back into the Saxony of the thirteenth century and immigrated to the United States in the 1840s. Chester William Nimitz was born on February 24, 1885, in the German colony of Fredericksburg, Texas. Interested in leaving the small-town life of the central Texas hill country, Nimitz took an appointment to Annapolis after learning that his first choice, West Point, no longer had any openings. Nimitz accepted this consolation prize and did well in Maryland, graduating seventh out of 114 in the class of 1905.[11]

Nimitz's naval career showed a steady upward progression despite a couple of disappointing dips. He received good evaluations and during a trip to Japan met and shared a drink with Admiral Togo Heihachiro, the victorious commander who had destroyed the Russian Baltic Fleet at the Battle of the Tsushima. He was a 22-year-old ensign when he got the command of his first ship, the destroyer *Decatur*. Then as now, officers of such junior rank and inexperience rarely got the chance to command such a large ship. Nimitz quickly proved why. He ran the *Decatur* aground, which resulted in a court-martial that found him guilty of "neglect of duty." The judicial proceeding could have easily destroyed his career, but mitigating circumstances such as the lack of adequate charts for the area and the fact he was operating in a role so far above his rank saved him.[12]

His next assignment came in submarines, which was a professional disappointment, but was good to him in a personal sense. While stationed in Massachusetts, a friend from his Naval Academy days introduced Nimitz to a neighborhood family. The Freemans took a liking to the young naval officer and Nimitz soon found himself growing romantically interested in Catherine Freeman. She shared these feelings, and they married after a courtship of a year and a half. Despite the frequent separations that went along with the life of a naval officer, the Nimitzes had a healthy marriage. They had four children over the span of eighteen years.[13]

Submarine duty was mostly good to Nimitz in a professional sense. He became a Lieutenant less than two years after his court-martial, and what is even more impressive is that he skipped the rank of Lieutenant (junior grade). Nimitz played an important role in developing and designing diesel engines. During this time, his duties required him to give tours of the New York Navy Yard to visiting engineers. At one point during his standard walk through the facilities, Nimitz would point to the gears of a diesel engine as he explained different aspects of their performance. He had given this tour a number of times, but on this occasion he was wearing canvas gloves to keep his hands from getting dirty. The tip of the glove got caught in the machinery and pulled his left hand into the gears. The wheels ground up his ring finger, and would have amputated his left hand had it not been for his Naval Academy class ring. In the years that followed, he was self-conscious about his missing finger and would often try to cover or hide his hand in photographs. With World War I, he received another promotion but missed seeing combat. After the war, he had the assignment of building a submarine base at Pearl Harbor, which he did with material he often had to "appropriate" in creative fashion.[14]

After studying at the Naval War College, Nimitz helped pioneer the use of a circular formation for daylight carrier operations, which would become commonplace during World War II. Nimitz then became a teacher and trainer of midshipmen. He established one of the first six naval ROTC units at the University of California. He successfully established the unit and came to enjoy Berkeley so much that he made the San Francisco Bay area his home after he retired.[15]

In 1938, after nearly ten years as a Captain, Nimitz was promoted to Rear Admiral. Within two days of the Japanese attack on Pearl Harbor, he received command of what remained of the Pacific Fleet. He brought with him a number of managerial, administrative, and personal habits that served him well in the years to come. Nimitz was a simple and direct man skilled at making complicated matters clear and understandable. He also had a good understanding of and empathy for people, which made him adept at getting the most out of the individuals in his headquarters and selecting good officers for command. The admiral devoted an hour of every day to meeting the commanding officers of all the ships and vessels in the Pacific Fleet, which gave him a feel for the operational readiness of his crews. "Some of the best help and advice I've had," he remarked, "comes from junior officers and enlisted men." He also had an exceptional talent for remembering names and faces, which bolstered morale among his officers. Nimitz worked seven days a week, but regularly took time off to play a game of tennis, horseshoes, or do some target practice with a pistol, all of which were ways for him to combat the stress of his position.[16]

The U.S. Fifth Fleet was the naval formation that Nimitz sent to take the brunt of the kamikaze assault. The admiral commanding this formation was his former Chief of Staff, Raymond A. Spruance. Spruance was 58 at the start of the battle. He had a reputation for calm poise, quiet dignity, and a powerful intellect. Ernest J. King believed Spruance was the most intelligent flag officer in the service. A hypochondriac who exercised on a regular basis, he had the ability to inspire others to greater heights and was the last admiral in the U.S. Navy that Ugaki would have wanted his kamikazes to face.[17]

Fourteen Stars. Although Ernest J. King (center) was violently opposed to having the Royal Navy make any contribution to combat operations in and around Japan itself, Chester Nimitz (left) and Raymond Spruance (right) came to see real advantage to having the British in the fight against the kamikaze during the battle for Okinawa. All three are pictured on Spruance's flagship, the USS *Indianapolis*, in 1944. Courtesy of the Naval Historical Center

Five feet and nine and a half inches tall, Spruance sailed on Theodore Roosevelt's Great White Fleet and loved the experience. In 1913, as a Lieutenant (junior grade), he assumed his first command, the destroyer *Bainbridge*. During this time, he found that he could not handle alcohol, and swore off drink, making him something of an exception in the navy. After a year on the *Bainbridge*, Spruance went to Indianapolis where he proposed marriage to Margaret Dean, a woman whom he had met when they were children and had dated for a few weeks two years before. As Spruance's biographer Thomas B. Buell notes, the marriage was a gamble for both of the Spruances. Neither knew much about the other.[18]

Spruance's career advanced in a steady but slow fashion. He commanded five other ships. He attended the Naval War College in 1926 and thrived in its applied intellectual atmosphere. "I believe that making war is a game that requires cold and careful calculation," he stated years later. "Each operation is different and has to be analyzed and studied in order to prepare the most suitable plans for it. That is what makes the planning of operations in war such an interesting job." Promotion to Captain and then, to his surprise, Rear Admiral, followed.[19]

Spruance was at sea when the Japanese attacked Pearl Harbor, which let him escape the recriminations that followed. Spruance made a name for himself at the Battle of Midway. At the start of the battle, he was junior to Rear Admiral Frank Jack Fletcher. The engagement started when Midway-based spotter planes found two of the enemy's carriers. Fletcher's decision was something of a gamble since the admiral knew the Japanese strike force had four or five flattops, and there was a real possibility he could have exposed his ships to a superior response. As it was, American planes ravaged three Japanese carriers with almost no protection and their decks loaded with fuel and ordnance. There was a Japanese attack in response, which damaged the USS *Yorktown*, Fletcher's carrier flagship. Fletcher was forced to transfer his flag to a cruiser, without any offensive firepower and limited command and control ability, and thus his influence on the course of the battle came to an end. American carrier doctrine gave Spruance, as the commander of a carrier group, a good deal of independence even before events marginalized Fletcher, and planes from his flagship, the carrier *Enterprise*, played a key role in hitting the first three carriers. After a search found the fourth carrier, Spruance ordered another attack, which destroyed the ship. At that point, Spruance broke off from the enemy, which was a wise move. Admiral Yamamoto Isoroku was bringing up the rear with the battleships of the Combined Fleet, which could have destroyed the U.S. ships in a night engagement.[20]

The action north of Midway Island made Spruance a war hero. He, however, had little interest in the praise that came from the media. "A man's judgment is best when he can forget himself and any reputation he may have acquired, and can concentrate wholly on making the right decisions."[21]

After a year as Nimitz's Chief of Staff in which he introduced many staff officers to exotic coffee blends, Spruance returned to sea as the Commander of the Fifth Fleet and the third star of a Vice Admiral. In this position he initiated the long-planned drive through the Central Pacific toward both the Philippines and Japan itself. Facing enemy forces, he always asked himself, "Now what would I do if I were a Japanese with these capabilities in this position?" He received his fourth star only eight months later, making him the youngest Admiral in the history of the U.S. Navy. After the United States began its assault on Saipan in June 1945 Spruance fought the Battle of the Philippine Sea, another carrier engagement. Spruance achieved a victory based on the strength of the forces he commanded rather than on his decisions. The slaughter of Japanese aviators was enormous. In what became known as "The Marianas Turkey Shoot," the Combined Fleet lost 383 planes to American losses of 25. Most of the Japanese carriers, however, survived, and Spruance would always let this outcome bother him, but it hardly mattered. Without skilled pilots, the carriers were impotent.[22]

Spruance had no illusions about the war he was facing. After the U.S. seizure of Iwo Jima, he wrote his wife,

> I understand some of our sob fraternity back home have been raising the devil about our casualties on Iwo. I would have thought by this time they would have learned that you can't make war on a tough fanatical enemy like the Japs without our people getting hurt and killed. I recommended both Iwo and our next operation, and I have never had any doubt as to how tough the next one is going to be. It is going to be very expensive to us, but the results should be of the greatest value in pushing the war along.[23]

Because of the kamikazes, his predictions were largely correct. The Japanese codename for the attacks at Okinawa was Operation: TEN-GO. Ugaki would deploy his suicide pilots in massive assault waves aimed at U.S. ships. The designation for these assaults was *kikusui* (floating chrysanthemum). Individual kamikaze attacks and conventional dive-bomber and torpedo plane missions also struck U.S. ships. Planes from the Imperial Japanese Navy made about 3,700 sorties, while army planes made about half as many.[24]

The Americans used a number of weapons to defend against these attacks. The best way to limit the damage these suicide planes caused was to keep them from reaching the fleet. Spruance, as a result, assigned destroyers to radar picket duty around Okinawa. There were fifteen stations at various distances that radiated off the northern tip of the Hagushi Beaches, a spot the Americans designated as Point Bolo. These destroyers provided a radar screen that gave early warning of impending attacks. Fighters on combat air patrol would then shoot down the kamikazes before they reached their targets. Since these ships were often the first ones the inexperienced suicide pilots encountered, they often became targets of opportunity. Land-based radar on some smaller islands off Okinawa allowed the navy to reduce the number of pickets to five after May 16. If the Japanese planes got through, then it was the job of the antiaircraft gun crews on ships to shoot them down before they slammed into their targets. The guns five inches in caliber and above used shells with variable time fuses. Rather than requiring a direct hit on a target, this ordinance exploded at a preset altitude or when it came within proximity of an object of a certain density. As a result, this ammunition increased the effectiveness of antiaircraft guns. Lieutenant Robert F. Wallace, in a memoir of his experiences as a gunnery officer on the USS *Idaho*, observed that the only time his men cheered the downing of any enemy plane was their first victory. "Almost immediately the scene became too grim for such shallow emotions." Even with variable time fuse ordnance, the crews threw up so many shells that smoke from their guns could easily obscure a ship. The shells that missed the planes would splash into the water, creating geysers putting mist into the air. The jets of water also had the added benefit of disorienting enemy pilots. "I would venture to say that the antiaircraft personnel did not experience fear during action. We were too highly drilled and too confident of our skill for that. When we saw a plane approaching, we never doubted for a moment that we would shoot it down," Wallace observed. "Yet after it was all over, it felt definitely scary. The general atmosphere was one of high-strung alertness."[25]

The attacks that would make Okinawa such a costly battle started before the actual invasion of the island. The fast carriers of the Fifth Fleet were hitting targets in Japan when Ugaki had several small groups of pilots retaliate. Just after sunrise on March 19, a Japanese plane found the carrier *Wasp* and dropped a bomb that penetrated to the number three deck before exploding. The casualties were high: 101 killed and 269 wounded, but damage control parties had the fires out in fifteen minutes. The ship continued with operations for several more days before retiring for repairs. The damage to another carrier, though, was much worse. Two Japanese bombs hit the USS *Franklin*, the fifth ship of the U.S. Navy to carry that name. The first bomb detonated in the hangar deck. The second one proved more deadly. It sent fire across the ship and initiated a series of secondary explosions as fuel and munitions went up. Admiral Marc Mitscher, the commander of the fast carriers, was below the horizon from the *Franklin* in the *Bunker Hill* and heard six detonations. The ship went dead in the water as fires raged across her decks. The loss of life was heavy: 724 killed and missing with another 265 wounded. A total of 1,700 members of the *Franklin* crew were pulled out of the water by cruisers and destroyers that came to the carrier's assistance. The damage warranted an abandon ship order, but the captain thought he could save his ship and held off for the time being. The carrier did regain power in the wee hours of the next morning and was eventually able to make its way to New York for repair.[26]

Small kamikaze sorties would follow in the days ahead. On March 31, one plane hit the USS *Indianapolis*, the flagship of the Fifth Fleet. Due to the damage, Spruance eventually had to transfer his flag to the battleship *New Mexico*.[27]

The first *kikusui* attack came in the early morning hours of April 6. The destroyer *Bush* was on duty at Radar Picket Station 1 to the north of Okinawa. Just before 3 P.M., forty to fifty planes arrived at this spot and stacked themselves at various altitudes in orbit above the ship, while some of their comrades went in for the kill. The *Bush* downed two planes and drove another two away, before a fifth plane slammed into the ship in between its two stacks. The bomb the plane had been carrying exploded in the forward engine room, killing everyone inside. The *Calhoun* was at Station 2 and made its way to render assistance. An hour later this destroyer arrived to find *Bush* dead in the water and in the process of sinking. Then the *Calhoun* came under attack. A series of heavy volleys knocked down three planes, but a kamikaze hit the ship in the port bow. Good damage control work prevented a significant loss of speed. Within fifteen minutes the ship came under attack again. Gun crews from either the *Bush*, the *Calhoun*, or a landing ship that was also at the station downed two planes, but a third slammed into the *Calhoun* with a bomb that exploded and tore a 4 by 20–foot hole below the waterline. The destroyer went dead in the water. Less than ten minutes later three more suicide pilots attacked the *Calhoun* and *Bush*. Antiaircraft fire downed only one of these attackers. One of the planes that survived clipped one of the *Calhoun*'s stacks, which spun into one of the gun turrets and then bounced off the deck into the sea. The bomb detonated in the water, and the pressure from the explosion punched a hole 3 feet square below the ship's waterline. The pilot of the third plane missed the *Calhoun*, but turned his attention on the *Bush*, driving his machine straight into the area between the two stacks. The explosion came close to severing the destroyer in two. Within fifteen minutes the *Bush* was under attack again. Another kamikaze crashed into the port side of the ship, staring a fire that caused ammunition to start exploding. Another fifteen minutes passed before another Japanese plane came upon these two wounded ships. The pilot decided to focus his energies on the *Calhoun* and slammed into her port side.[28]

As the light failed, the rough sea did in the *Bush*. That night was cold, with a strong wind making the ocean swells 10 to 12 feet high and white-capped. Strong waves made the ship start caving inward until she sank. The captain of the *Calhoun* decided that his ship was lost, too, but waited until rescue ships had an opportunity to search for the survivors from the *Bush*. This effort had to take place in the dark, since Japanese planes were still about. Exhaustion drowned many sailors in the rough waters. Many who tried to swim to rescue ships became tired and drowned or found themselves broken against the hulls. Most of the crew of the *Calhoun* transferred to USS *Cassin Young* and a landing ship. A skeleton crew stayed on board until fires got out of control and they abandoned ship. The *Cassin Young* then sank the *Calhoun* with gunfire.[29]

That evening the attacks continued to the west of Okinawa. In this action, Japanese pilots flew so low over the water that lookouts spotted the planes before onboard radar. In less than ten minutes three kamikazes attacked the *Newcomb*. The first one crashed into one of the ship's stacks. Gun crews splashed the second plane just before the third crashed amidships and initiated a huge explosion in the lower decks. Another suicide plane hit *Newcomb* in her forward stack and sprayed gasoline over the deck, producing a huge fire that reached 100 feet into the air. The crews of other nearby ships assumed the *Newcomb* had been fatally wounded. The destroyer *Leutze* came alongside to rescue survivors and, discovering the ship was not going down, helped fight the fires instead. While these two ships were alongside one another, a fifth kamikaze attacked the *Newcomb*. Gunfire deflected the plane slightly and it flew over its intended target and slammed into the fantail of the *Leutze*. This ship started taking on water and settling before the efforts of the crew saved her. Both *Newcomb* and *Leutze* survived but had to leave the combat zone under tow.[30]

The Combined Fleet attempted a surface action at Okinawa during the second day of the *kikusui* operation. In 1945, the HIJMS *Yamato*, along with her sister ship, the *Musashi*, was one of the two biggest battleships ever built. Her 18.1-inch guns could outfire and outrange any U.S. ship. The Combined Fleet sent the *Yamato* as part of the Surface Special Attack Force with the mission of arriving at the Hagushi roadstead to the west of Okinawa, where it would attack U.S. naval forces supporting the invasion. The ship and her escorts would also serve as a diversion. Japanese commanders hoped the *Yamato* would pull U.S. planes away from the Fifth Fleet and allow the kamikazes to hit the ships. This plan began to unravel when a U.S. submarine spotted the ship. Spruance ordered an aerial assault on the monster battleship but also had his own officers plan to engage the ship in a surface action should the pilots fail in their efforts. The engagement that followed lasted almost four hours. Plane after plane struck at the supersized ship, which took five bombs and ten torpedo hits before she sank. Of the 2,767 officers and men on board, only 269 survived.[31]

Ugaki had served on the *Yamato* and mourned her loss, but over the next few days he also found encouragement from reports about the results of this operation. By April 9, he believed that Japanese planes, most under his command, had sunk sixty-nine U.S. ships. "The great success of *Kikusui* No. 1 Operation was thus clarified." Sorties smaller in size followed. Radio reports led Ugaki to believe the kamikazes had incapacitated all U.S. carriers. "In the light of so many reports of crashing on enemy carriers, there can't be so many undamaged carriers still operating, even if they were decoys," he told his diary. These erroneous and inflated reports stemmed from the poor ship identification skills of his pilots. Despite his enthusiastic belief in the misleading information, Ugaki could tell something was wrong. "Every day we try to finish the enemy task force, and yet they can't be finished." He refused, however, to believe the reports were totally in error.[32]

The next FLOATING CHRYSANTHEMUM operation started the day after Ugaki vented his frustration in his diary. Thursday, April 12, was a clear and cool day, and approximately 150 fighters and 45 torpedo planes escorted 185 kamikazes to the Okinawa area. American planes and fighters shot down 298 of these aircraft. Picket Station Number 1 to the north of Bolo Point saw a good deal of action that day. The *Cassin Young* took slight damage but soon had to retire from the area. The Japanese sank one landing craft and damaged another. The gun crews of the *Purdy* shot down an attacking plane only to watch it crash 20 feet away and ricochet into the side of the ship. The explosion killed thirteen and wounded twenty-seven others. The ship lost steering control and had to leave her station. At another picket position, a kamikaze hit the *Mannert L. Abele* and the ship went dead in the water. Then, about a minute later, one of what the Americans called a *baka* bomb—a manned missile that a bomber released with a suicide pilot on board who guided it to its final target with rocket boosters—hit the ship on its starboard side beneath the forward stack. The explosion tore apart the *Mannert L. Abele* with her midships evaporating in the blast. The two parts of the ship sank in only five minutes, giving it the less than enviable distinction of being the first vessel lost to what the Japanese called an *Oka* plane.[33]

At Fifth Air Fleet headquarters, the staff and the fleet's commander were listening to radio reports the bombers were sending back. Ugaki recorded, "Those in the operation room were thrilled as reports of 'Stand by for release of *Oka*,' 'Release—hit a battleship,' and 'One battleship sunk' came in."[34]

There were so many Japanese planes that day that two ships traveling to Picket Station 1 to replace the *Cassin Young* came under attack while in transit. A Japanese dive-bomber crashed into the starboard bow of the destroyer *Stanly* and went straight through to the port side. The explosion that followed tore a huge slice out of both sides of the bow. The officers and men of the *Jeffers* had luck on their side while on a mission to rescue survivors of the *Mannert L. Abele*. A *baka* dove on the ship and missed, crashing fifty yards away. Another destroyer, the USS *Rall*, was on antisubmarine duty when it came under attack. A Japanese Army fighter slammed into her starboard side amidships, killing twenty-one, wounding another thirty-eight, and doing extensive internal damage to the ship.[35]

A number of the kamikazes got past these pickets and attacked ships supporting the ground invasion of Okinawa. Radar let the American sailors know the attack was coming. In an action that lasted only ten minutes, Japanese planes hit two ships south of Okinawa. Flying only 15 feet off the smooth water, three planes attacked the destroyer *Zellars*. The gun crews shot down two of the planes and they splashed into the water at safe distances, but the third crashed into the port side. The damage was severe, but damage control parties had the fires under control in 10 minutes. The *Zellars* was traveling alongside the battleship *Tennessee*, which came under attack immediately afterward. Five planes attacked and gun crews downed one at 4,000 yards. Two others splashed into the water at 100 and 500 yards. The fourth caught on fire and flew across the bow of the ship before crashing into the ocean. These four, however, distracted the crew of the ship from the fifth, which was detected just 2,500 yards away. This range was too close to give the gun crews enough time to down the plane, but they did deflect the kamikaze. The plane crashed into one of the 40-millimeter gun stations, slid across the deck, and came to a stop against one of the 14-inch turrets. The bomb the plane was carrying went through the deck, exploded, and killed many sailors but did little structural damage to the ship.[36]

The *Idaho* was the target of another four Japanese planes. "The air was electric," Wallace recalled of the sentiment on the *Idaho*. The gun crews were ready and the first two planes that attacked the ship were shot down in two short bursts of twenty-five and thirty seconds. A lone gunner took down a third plane as it tried to pass the ship and attack from a different angle. The fourth plane got in close. The kamikaze was only twenty-five feet away when he and his plane disintegrated from antiaircraft fire. Wallace was bracing for impact. "A bomb exploding so close to you does not make a booming sound, as heard in the movies," he explained. "It makes a crackling sound, like lightning." Debris from the explosion rained down on the deck, and Wallace found ball bearings that had "MADE IN USA" stamped on them.[37]

Back in the headquarters of the Fifth Air Fleet, Ugaki was receiving erroneous reports suggesting this *kikusui* was inflicting much greater damage on the Americans than was actually the case. He believed his planes had gained control of the air. He also made optimistic assumptions that once planes charged on a ship, they scored a hit. According to his information, the *kikusui* assault resulted in the sinking of one carrier, two cruisers, and two unidentified ships. He also had one battleship on fire and another battleship torpedoed. "The general offensive of today also was successful. We must further attack the enemy task force so as to wipe it out, taking this chance."[38]

Kikusui number three started on April 15. Ugaki believed he was on the verge of destroying Spruance's fleet. "According to observations of military experts, the United States Navy's losses were extremely heavy, so if it continues like this it will result in a tragic end within two weeks," he brushed into his diary. He ordered the third assault to push his advantage. The effort proved to be costly. Just before 8:30 A.M., the *Laffey* became the first ship to come under attack in this wave. At one time radar operators counted fifty planes on their screens. The attackers came in from every direction. Over the course of eighty minutes, Japanese pilots made twenty-two runs on the ship. Strafing fire, six kamikazes, and four bombs hit the *Laffey*. Damage control parties kept fires under control, only to have another hit undo their work.[39]

Later in the day a kamikaze hit the flight deck of the carrier *Intrepid*, incapacitating the ship. The biggest success kamikaze pilots enjoyed in this assault, though, was the sinking of the *Pringle*, a destroyer on picket duty at station fourteen. Her destruction only took one hit. The explosion buckled the keel, breaking the ship in two. What was left of the *Pringle* sank in roughly five minutes. The *Hobson*, a destroyer minesweeper also at this radar station, came under attack immediately afterward. The crews of the two ships shot down one plane, but it was so close that its forward momentum carried it into the minesweeper, killing four and starting a fire in the forward engine room. The *Hobson* thwarted two other planes and then went to the rescue of *Pringle* survivors. The *Bowers* and *Harding* also suffered heavy damage that day. In fact, the damage to the *Harding* was so extensive the navy decommissioned the ship rather than attempt repairs.[40]

As costly as these attacks had been, Ugaki thought they had been even worse. "All considered, two battleships or cruisers seem to have been almost surely sunk," he noted in his diary. "According to a reconnaissance report, one battleship, one cruiser, and four transports were seen sunk off Kadena." The day after *kikusui* three, he stated, "I think we need one more push to wipe out the enemy task force, but I regret that our fighting strength can't be maintained any longer."[41]

Ugaki was right. It took him almost two weeks before he could launch another assault. Rainy weather interfered, and, according to Yokoi, the command was exhausted. The Japanese Army also was keeping most of its planes in reserve for an invasion of Japan. The navy withdrew the Tenth Air Fleet from Ugaki's command, limiting the assets with which he had to work. "The Combined Fleet issued its policy for subsequent air operations," Ugaki wrote.

In the end, it means that from now on our strength doesn't permit us to carry out more than air guerrilla warfare in both name and reality. Now we have come to the stage that we have expected to reach for some time. We can't do anything at all, with little money remaining in our pocket when it's most needed. Most regrettably, our past operations have always taken the same course. And that's the very reason why we have been following the road to defeat.

While Ugaki put together the next massed assault, small sorties had some significant success. On April 22, a kamikaze hit a landing craft, sinking the ship in three minutes. Half an hour later, another plane hit the *Swallow*, and this minesweeper sank in seven minutes. In contrast, when *kikusui* number four came on April 27–28, it did mostly minor damage. The only significant U.S. loss was a cargo ship full of ammunition. A kamikaze hit the stern of the *Canada Victory* and the ship went down with twelve hands, with another twenty-seven wounded. Given the cargo, the loss of life could have been much worse. Despite this impressive victory, the assault overall was ineffective. Even Ugaki admitted as much: "The special attacks seem to have become less effective lately," he commented in the safety of his diary. "I'm afraid that the explosive power of our planes might not be big enough."[42]

There were isolated attacks, but April had seen the last of the *kikusui* assault waves. A plane crashed into the hospital ship *Comfort*, despite proper illumination as the Geneva Convention required. The plane hit the superstructure, did significant damage to the upper works, killed thirty-six, and injured or reinjured thirty-eight. This attack could have been due to malice or, more likely, the pilot's lack of skill in ship recognition. As Rear Admiral Samuel Eliot Morison, a Pulitzer Prize–winning historian in civilian life and author of the semi-official United States Naval Operations in World War II series, notes about the attacks of April, "For the Navy it was one of the toughest months in the entire Pacific War." Morison was, of course, correct, but more, much more, was to come.[43]

The fifth assault wave of Operation: TEN-GO started on May 3 in conjunction with an offensive the Japanese 32nd Army launched on Okinawa. In the waters to the west of Okinawa, the attackers hit four of the six ships at Picket Station Number 10. The *Aaron Ward*, named after an admiral in Theodore Roosevelt's Great White Fleet, shot down a number of attacking kamikazes. She suffered only from the debris of one that splashed into the water, doing no serious damage to the ship and inflicting no casualties. A navy Mitsubishi Zero-3 fighter, however, dropped a bomb that hit the engine room and set the ship on fire. A half hour later another kamikaze released its bomb before hitting amidships. The explosion of that bomb tore a hole in the side of the ship, flooding the forward fire room, and the de-

Bloodied but Unbent. The *Aaron Ward* after a kamikaze hit. The ship never sank but the damage was so severe that the navy decommissioned her. Courtesy of the Naval Historical Center

stroyer lost propulsion. Within roughly two minutes two more kamikazes struck the *Aaron Ward* and caused fires that spread quickly. With the ship dead in the water, another plane slammed into the base of the number two stack. For an hour the crew fought the fires before they had them under control. The *Aaron Ward* refused to sink, but was beyond repair, and the navy decommissioned the ship.[44]

The *Little* came under attack at the same time as the *Aaron Ward*. In just twelve minutes, a total of four kamikazes hit this ship. She sank with six dead and another twenty-four missing. Kamikazes also sank a landing ship and damaged another at Station 10.[45]

The onslaught continued the next day. Early that morning, just after 8 A.M., Radar Picket Station 12 came under attack. A kamikaze dove on the *Luce*, but fire from the gun crews turned it just before it hit the destroyer. The explosion, however, knocked out power, forcing the gun crews to manually adjust their sights as another plane attacked. This kamikaze moved too fast for the crews to track, and it hit the *Luce*. The ship began to take on water, and the captain ordered his men over the side. The injuries and deaths on board were extensive. Of the 335 officers and men, only 93 escaped unharmed. The engagement was also fast. All of six minutes passed between the first attack and when the ship sank. The Japanese sank a landing ship in that attack as well.[46]

The attacks of that day continued at Station 1. A small Japanese air fleet attacked the *Morrison*. The combat air patrol managed to knock most of them down, but two Mitsubishi navy fighters got through, making vertical dives on the ship. The damage was acute, but the *Morrison* might have survived had not two vintage biplanes then attacked. Although slow, the planes lacked the density to trigger the proximity shells the gun crews were firing at them. The planes crashed into the ship with bombs that detonated and started rapid flooding. The captain ordered the crew to abandon ship. In less than ten minutes the ship went down, aft first, with heavy loss of life.[47]

The sixth FLOATING CHRYSANTHEMUM operation started on the evening of May 10 and continued on into May 11 at radar Picket Station Number 15 northwest of Okinawa. Starting a little before 8 A.M., the ships at this station endured an attack lasting a little over an hour and a half. Fighters covering this picket station downed about fifty Japanese planes, but another fifty attacked the destroyers. The *Evans* shot down fifteen kamikazes but parts of four others hit the ship. At one point, the *Evans* came under attack from ten planes. The damage they inflicted was extensive and Commander Baron J. Mullaney, the commanding officer, ordered most of his crew to abandon ship. While the *Evans* was fighting for her life, the crew of another destroyer, the *Hugh W. Hadley*, shot down twelve aircraft. In this desperate fight the American pilots on patrol above the ships had so many targets they ran out of ammunition. They were using their better flying skills to constrain the inexperienced Japanese from gaining altitude or forcing them into the water. Both ships survived, but were eventually scrapped as beyond repair.[48]

The most significant action of the assault came late that morning when a fighter dived on the aircraft carrier *Bunker Hill*. The plane made a shallow dive from the starboard quarter. It crashed on the flight deck, skidding across through parked planes and setting them on fire before it went over the side. The bomb the plane had been carrying punched through the flight deck and exploded. Just as this fighter made contact with the ship, crewmen aboard spotted a dive bomber astern of the ship coming in from a high angle. This plane slammed into the *Bunker Hill*'s flight deck at the

On Fire. The *Bunker Hill* after it was hit by a kamikaze. The damage was severe and the crew came close to abandoning ship. Courtesy of the U.S. National Archives

base of the island. At the moment of impact the plane came in at a nearly vertical angle, and the explosion started a raging inferno three decks below. Captain G. A. Seitz put his ship through a sharp seventy-degree angle turn, an action forcing flaming wreckage into the sea. A cruiser and a number of destroyers came alongside to help fight the fire. Even with assistance from these ships it took five and a half hours to put out the flames. The loss of life was heavy, mostly due to smoke inhalation: 396 dead and missing, and another 264 wounded. The only carrier to take a tougher beating and survive was the *Franklin*. Late in the afternoon Vice Admiral Marc A. Mitscher, commanding officer of the fast carrier task force, transferred his staff to the *Enterprise*.[49]

A week and a half would pass before Ugaki ordered another *kikusui* assault. Bad weather was the main reason for the delay. There were, however, a number of smaller kamikaze sorties. On May 12, two suicide pilots attacked the battleship *New Mexico*. "I was scared of course—one always is scared," recalled Commander Michael Le Fanu, the British liaison officer on Spruance's staff, "but it was very exciting, even though you think the thing is coming at *you*." Gun crews hit the first plane with a five-inch shell burst that forced it up over the masthead of the ship and detonated the bomb it carried. From other nearby vessels the *New Mexico*'s stack resembled a giant blowtorch. The second plane took a number of hits, but continued on its run, slamming into the stack, which resulted in heavy casualties: 54 dead or missing and 119 wounded. For a moment, Spruance was missing and his staff feared he had become a casualty. When they found him, he was working a fire hose in the damaged area. The admiral had been headed to that area of the ship when the attack forced him to take cover. He was almost killed.

Two days later, twenty-six kamikazes attacked the USS *Enterprise*. The combat air patrol cover shot nineteen of them, and antiaircraft fire knocked down another six, but the one that survived hit the carrier, tearing a hole in the flight deck. The plane's bomb exploded inside the ship, blowing parts of an elevator 400 feet into the air. The damage was extensive and repairs kept the carrier from returning to combat before the war ended. Mitscher transferred his command to another ship for the second time in four days.[50]

The day before the seventh *kikusui* started, Ugaki fumed about another B-29 attack, "They were pretty many and powerful. The enemy now is attempting to reduce our fighting strength and also frustrate our fighting spirit by launching coordinated attacks against us from the east and west. But we can't be beaten this way. We shall take our revenge upon them for this from tonight until tomorrow."[51]

The revenge started on May 25. Just after 12:30 A.M., the destroyer transport *Barry* came under attack. A Japanese plane strafed the ship and then crashed into the starboard side, starting fires below deck. Although thirty members of the crew were injured, the only person who died from this attack was the Japanese pilot. Unable to flood the magazines and fearing an explosion would kill the *Barry*, the crew abandoned ship for a time. With the help from the *Sims*, though, the crew returned and put the fires out just before 4 A.M. The injuries to the ship were widespread. The *Barry* was a total loss. The navy decommissioned her during the battle and used her hulk as a kamikaze decoy.[52]

Later, after daybreak, Japanese pilots found more ships. One kamikaze hit the *Spectacle*, a minesweeper, and the fire was so extensive the crew abandoned ship. A landing craft picked up a number of survivors, only to be hit by another plane half an hour later. The crew beached the vessel, and the survivors from the *Spectacle* had to abandon ship a second time. Two hours later two planes crashed the *Bates*. Damage control parties were unable to gain control of the fires, and the crew abandoned ship. For a while it looked as though the ship might be saved after all. Then that evening, while it was under tow, *Bates* capsized and sank. On May 25, Ugaki brushed into his diary: "It is regrettable indeed that *Kikusui* No. 7 Operation ended in failure." His information on the attack was again incorrect, but this time he was underestimating the results his pilots had achieved. The next day, he realized that "they achieved a good deal of success" after all.[53]

The experiences of Lieutenant Sakamoto Takashige explain why the Japanese were receiving information that was often incorrect. He flew fighter escort for four kamikazes during a nighttime attack on the American fleet. After reaching Okinawa, antiaircraft fire quickly turned two of the kamikazes into fireballs. He lost visual contact with the other two suicide pilots, but the fire from the U.S. ships indicated the pair had started an attack. In the dark, he saw one explode into the side of a ship that was "quite big" and then saw the other strike a target. He was unable to identify either type of ship. Sakamoto reported the kamikazes had hit two medium-sized cruisers. "This was not accurate, but I had to say something."[54]

The assault of *kikusui* eight started on May 27 and lasted until May 29. It was also the last attack in which the Japanese used over 100 planes. Bad weather forced U.S. land-based fighters to return to their home airfields. In these conditions, the kamikazes had to worry only about antiaircraft fire coming from their intended targets when they came out of the clouds that morning. American sailors on destroyers at Picket Station Number 5 saw three or four dive on them. One plane took fire from the *Braine* and *Anthony* and crashed into the water. Another plane was on fire when it crossed over the *Anthony* and then crashed into the side of the *Braine*. While the attention of this ship's crew focused on the immediate threat to their lives, another kamikaze came in on an attack run. The *Anthony* gun crews shot the plane down 50 feet from the ship. The attack failed, but the pilot eventually reached his target. The plane exploded on impact when it hit the water, which created a geyser that shot his body up into the air. The corpse landed on the deck of the *Anthony* along with bits and pieces of the plane. During this attack, another Japanese plane crashed into the *Braine* with a bomb that detonated on impact. The ship went dead in the water and fires quickly split her into three. This division complicated firefighting efforts, and it took about four hours before the crew managed to extinguish the flames. The *Anthony* came alongside to help and later towed her from the area.[55]

The action continued the next day at Radar Picket 15 to the northwest of Okinawa. The kamikaze pilots in this assault were apparently of above-average skill, since they were able to make complicated turns. Several planes attacked the USS *Lowry* and *Drexler*. Fighters shot down the first plane trying to attack the ships. A second Japanese attacker then appeared to be diving on the starboard bow of the *Lowry*. The *Drexler* started firing on the aircraft when it was over the *Lowry*. The pilot recovered just enough from his dive and the antiaircraft fire to hit the topside of the *Drexler*. Less than a minute later, another plane dove on the *Lowry*, but gun crews shot it into the water. A fourth suicide pilot tried to hit the *Drexler*, but U.S. Corsair fighters on his tail made him miss. Just as it seemed he was going to splash astern of the ship, the pilot recovered from the dive, made another pass, and slammed into the superstructure from ahead, which caused the two bombs he was carrying to explode. Flames shot several hundred feet into the air, and ship parts flew in several directions. The *Drexler* rolled over and sank in less than a minute. All told, this entire action lasted less than fifteen minutes.[56]

Back at Fifth Air Fleet headquarters, Ugaki believed the attacks had been even more successful. His reading of intercepted U.S. radio traffic indicated the loss of eleven ships. He had overruled his staff officers in ordering the attack and was proud of its results: "I thought its success could be attributed to the full moon and to the divine help of our predecessors on the occasion of Navy Day."[57]

That evening just before midnight a kamikaze spotted the USS *Shubrick* as the ship was in transit to Picket Station 16. The plane flew into the destroyer and the ensuing explosion put a large hole in the deck and tore out the aft starboard side of the ship. The engine room flooded, and the captain ordered most of his men to abandon ship. For a while it seemed the *Shubrick* would sink, but the situation soon stabilized and a tug took her in tow.[58]

Typhoons forced the Japanese to spread Operation: FLOATING CHRYSAN-THEMUM 9 out over five days. Since the planes never concentrated their power against any specific U.S. naval forces, the attack failed, as even

Ugaki conceded. Three days after this operation ended, a lone aircraft attacked the destroyer *William D. Porter*. The plane dove out of an overcast sky from 1,500 feet, but missed the ship, splashing into the water. The detonation of its bomb, however, created a mining effect that opened the seams of the ship. The *Porter* quickly started to flood and the crew abandoned ship. What is amazing about this attack is that not one crewman was lost when the ship went down.[59]

On June 22, the Japanese launched what would be the tenth and last *kikusui* operation. The attack attempted to come down on the destroyers at Radar Picket Station 15. Two combat air patrol groups intercepted these aircraft and downed about three-fourths of them. The ships in Station 15 never fired a shot in their own defense. Two landing ships that were not part of this group were hit, but neither sank. Ugaki, however, was getting reports of a different nature. He thought his pilots had attacked three carriers with one confirmed hit, another struck a destroyer, and one last plane crashed into an unidentified ship. "As a whole," he wrote, "this time *Kikusui* No. 10 Operation, made at a break in the rainy season, is considered to have achieved considerable results."[60]

Ugaki believed the kamikazes were having a significant impact on the battle at Okinawa. His diary is full of references like "they achieved a good deal of success" and "it was quite a success, and I felt keen delight after a long time," making it plain that he thought the suicide operations were working. At the end of May, Japanese naval officers estimated the kamikazes had sunk or severely damaged 358–360 ships. As is clear from Ugaki's diary, these figures were the product of more than wishful thinking. The Japanese thought they had confirmed these numbers through radio intercepts or multiple sightings. History, of course, shows that these reports were in error. With the faulty information Ugaki had, it is easy to understand how he could write, "Enemy losses on land and at sea were extremely heavy, and enemy communications indicating its hardship were seen occasionally. This can be said to have shown the necessity for a decisive battle. We should attack the enemy more consistently and tenaciously." Yet, he also recognized what Operation: TEN-GO had cost Japan. In a poem, he lamented:

> Flowers of the special attack are falling,
> When the spring is leaving.
> Gone with the spring

Are you boys like cherry blossoms.
Gone are the blossoms,
Leaving cherry trees only with leaves.[61]

On the other side of the battle, Spruance worried about his own losses, recognizing that he was in a deadly battle of attrition. After the war he observed, "None of us, however, foresaw the suicide plane threat while we were making our plans for Okinawa." At the time, he told his former Chief of Staff, "The suicide plane is a very effective weapon, which we must not underestimate." He added, "I do not believe any one who has not been around within its area of operations can realize its potentialities against ships."[62]

With the nature of their opponent, it is hardly surprising the U.S. Navy was badly bloodied at Okinawa. Although resilient, moving forward, and meeting their strategic objectives, it is understandable that American sailors would appreciate having some friends in this fight. Allies did arrive and they appeared early during the kamikaze onslaught flying the White Ensign of the Royal Navy.

The Forgotten Fleet at Okinawa

While the U.S. Navy endured the kamikaze assaults, they received help from an ancient foe that had turned into a staunch ally. Although the British had long been the masters of naval warfare, they would be confronting issues and problems off Okinawa that they had never before had to face. The Royal Navy would prove itself a competent and professional force in the way it handled logistical and operational complications. The British Pacific Fleet was also the only force from the United Kingdom that saw combat in and around Japan proper. Despite the resistance Ernest J. King had shown in having the Royal Navy in the Pacific, the British soon became in American eyes a welcome addition to the war against Japan and showed there had been much merit in the arguments that Brooke, Portal, and Cunningham had made in their battles with Churchill.

For much of its early existence, the British Pacific Fleet was an organization that existed mainly on paper, but once expansion began it actually continued until after the surrender of Japan. The BPF was an imperial force. His Majesty's Australian, Canadian, and New Zealand Ships sailed in formation with those from the Royal Navy. The crews of these ships were also transnational in composition. Officers from the South African Maritime Defence Force served alongside those from the Royal Australian Navy on British ships. Ships from the Dominions also had British officers serving on board. There were also personnel from the Dominions serving in the Royal Navy itself.[1]

The fleet train supporting the warships was even more diverse. This mixture caused numerous logistical problems. Since the British merchant marine had suffered significant losses at the hands of the U-boats, the Royal Navy depended on Belgian, Chinese, Danish, Dutch, and Norwegian crews for its supplies. Problems in differing customs, diets, religions, and articles of agreement for service with the fleet complicated efforts to keep the force supplied. As a result, logistical problems would plague the British Pacific Fleet for its entire existence.[2]

The Commander-in-Chief of this growing fleet was Admiral Sir Bruce Fraser and he served British interests well. A portly man who liked to smoke a pipe, he took command on November 22, 1944. Born the second son of a British Army general, Fraser joined the Royal Navy in 1902 and became a specialist in gunnery. He joined the Grand Fleet only after the Battle of Jutland, but was present to take part in the surrender of the German High Seas Fleet. When the Germans scuttled their fleet to prevent it from being taken as a prize in a peace settlement, Fraser led a party aboard SMS *Baden* to stop the effort. He recalled he found it "a bit worrying" to patrol a ship that could still suddenly collapse under the waves and take him with it.[3]

During the interwar period, the navy was in the midst of a massive downsizing, but Fraser's career prospered during this period. Staff duty was punctuated with service afloat. After three years as captain of HMS *Effingham*, a heavy cruiser, Fraser went to the Admiralty to serve as Director of Naval Ordnance. There he oversaw the development of quadruple 14-inch gun turrets for the King George V class battleships. These ships gave the British both speed and the heavy firepower that could answer 16-inch gunfire, but kept the Royal Navy within treaty limitations on tonnage. After commanding the carrier *Glorious*, he received a promotion to the rank of Rear-Admiral. Just before the war started, he returned to the Admiralty, where he worked as Third Sea Lord and Controller and oversaw shipbuilding and repair. Fraser worked closely with Churchill during this period, so it often fell to the admiral to oppose some of the prime minister's less than practical ideas. The two got into an argument over statistics indicating how many men were working on merchant vessel versus naval repairs. "When Churchill looked at the figures he said 'You've disobeyed my orders.' I couldn't stand that," Fraser recalled. "So I spoke out. I said 'Sir, you are being most unfair and unjust. We're carrying out your orders, but you can't take a cruiser out of dock with its bottom out. It's impossible to change over as quickly as that.' And Churchill never said a word: he turned to some other subject."[4]

Promotion, a knighthood, and command of the Home Fleet followed. Fraser always embodied the true meaning of the word "gentleman" to those who served with him. He respected the dignity of others. Early in his career, while visiting port in India, he wrote, "I think some people were quite shocked when I danced with an Indian at our dance, but I said that I didn't mind—what was good enough for the Viceroy was sufficient for me! & then they shut up."[5]

Churchill respected Fraser. When Pound resigned, the prime minister offered him the job of First Sea Lord. Still, not having taken his fleet into combat, Fraser declined and the post went instead to Cunningham.[6]

As the Commander-in-Chief of the Home Fleet, he led the last battleship action the Royal Navy fought and would later take the title Baron Fraser of North Cape in recognition of this victory. The Battle of North Cape was an engagement fought off the Norwegian coast in December 1943. The German battle cruiser *Scharnhorst* and an accompanying screen of five destroyers set out to intercept and sink the ships of convoy JW55B. In a long-range duel, the *Duke of York*, a King George V class battleship, and the *Scharnhorst* scored hits on one another. The damage to the German ship was more significant. It lost speed, allowing British destroyers to close on the *Scharnhorst*. Fraser, though, had no way of knowing the damage his flagship had done. An hour before the battle ended in victory, he signaled the commander of his other attack force, "I see little hope of catching *Scharnhorst* and am proceeding to support convoy." Five minutes later, his destroyers indicated they were in position to use their torpedoes. Only four of twenty-eight torpedoes scored hits, but they slowed the German ship down even further as it took on water. The *Duke of York* and the cruiser *Belfast* closed and delivered a devastating barrage that killed the *Scharnhorst*.[7]

The British Pacific Fleet was Fraser's second fleet command and he realized that he had both operational and diplomatic missions. A quiet man with a tendency toward understatement and an impish sense of humor, he also had a sense of ethical pragmatism. He would need all these skills in the job that lay ahead. In a report to the Admiralty after the war, he declared, "I am entirely convinced that no better employment could have been found for the major British combat fleet." He explained his reasoning to the Admiralty: "On purely strategic grounds it is clearly the best policy to employ the largest forces possible against the centre of the enemy's power, and it would be uneconomical to dissipate one's total forces in areas away from the centre."[8]

The admiral also believed it was in the institutional interests of the Royal Navy to pursue the type of fighting in the Pacific the United States had mastered. "From a national point of view, it was of the utmost importance that the British Fleet should engage in the most modern type of naval warfare yet evolved, and to do so by fighting in company with its originators and prime exponents. In no other way could we have learned the technical lessons which this type of warfare teaches." The war against the *Kriegsmarine* in the Atlantic and the Mediterranean was one in which the British operated from shore bases. The distances in the Pacific were much greater and required more logistical support and endurance from crews of the ships since they would be at sea for longer periods of time. Writing after the war, he noted, "The Navy has already obtained combat lessons of incalculable worth in the large scale strategic deployment of big naval forces at long distances from their home bases, and in the tactical operation of these forces at previously unheard of distances from their most advanced bases."[9]

Fraser realized the deployment of the fleet served larger political and diplomatic interests.

> Finally, from a point of view of national prestige, it has been of the utmost importance that our Dominions should see the British navy engaged, if not in equal numbers, at least on an equal footing, with the American forces in the Pacific, and it would have been disastrous from this point of view if the British Pacific Fleet, after being sent to the Pacific, had been relegated, as the Australians consider their own forces to have been relegated to a "back area."[10]

Far more important than the perceptions found in this Dominion were those of the Americans, the U.S. Navy in particular. Fully aware that Ernest King looked on British participation in the Pacific theater with little enthusiasm, Fraser decided to travel to Hawaii to meet directly with Nimitz. The commander-in-chief of the Pacific Fleet would largely determine how significant a role the British played in operations against the Japanese homeland. Fraser and his staff spent the week and a half before Christmas of 1944 in Honolulu and received a reception that was at odds with the attitude that King had displayed toward the Royal Navy in Canada. "There was no doubt," Lieutenant-Commander Charles Sheppard, Fraser's intelligence officer, observed, "that the US command in the Pacific wanted the B.P.F., and from the moment of the arrival of the party at Pearl Harbor we had the maximum co-operation from Admiral Nimitz down to individual staff officers."[11]

If there was any question about what the American attitude would be, Nimitz resolved all lingering concern when the Fraser party arrived. He assigned each member of the British delegation a guide of equal rank from the U.S. Navy and had these individuals waiting at the jetty when the flying boat landed. Since Fraser held the rank of Admiral and was the Commander-in-Chief of a fleet, Nimitz himself served as his host. "My main memory of the Pearl Harbor visit," Sheppard recalled, "is that it was like a family party, rather than an Admiral and Staff visiting little-known relations and finding them friendly and likable, and returning with a feeling that it had been a most successful visit in every way."[12]

The tangible product of this visit was N/F1, commonly referred to as the "Pearl Harbor Agreement." In this document, Fraser agreed to have the British Pacific Fleet report to King and accept assignment under either Nimitz or MacArthur with the same status as a U.S. task force, which entailed accepting orders from American officers. Nimitz offered little in return, at least formally. He had to abide by the limits King had placed on the British. The American admiral, however, made it clear that he would be much more welcoming. "When I saw him at Pearl Harbour, Fleet Admiral Nimitz was most cordial," Fraser informed the Admiralty.

In his mind there was clearly no political objection to the participation of the B.P.F. in Pacific operations, and in fact he was delighted at the prospect of our co-operation. His only anxiety was that the B.P.F. might find it necessary to make demands on American resources, and I am sure that in this his reason was realistic and not political. Although his resources in the Pacific are vast they are not lavish and are carefully planned to meet the full requirements of his operating Fleet and no more.[13]

Fraser was determined to integrate His Majesty's Ships into the U.S. Pacific Fleet with as few complications as possible. The Americans had mastered a form of naval warfare in the Pacific different from any the Royal Navy had ever fought, and he wanted his allies to understand that the British were prepared and willing to study and gain from their experiences. He was attentive to both matters of substance and symbolism in this regard. Fraser proposed that the British Pacific Fleet adopt khaki uniforms while operating in the Pacific rather than donning tropical whites. Sticking to the whites would signal to the Americans that the British intended to fight the war a new way. "Cunningham was very insistent that we should stick to whites," Fraser later recalled, "but I told him we might have to change to khaki in the end. Which we did."[14]

A far more substantial issue was communication. Although both the United States and the United Kingdom were and continue to be English-speaking countries, their navies maintained contact with their ships in vastly different ways. Fraser realized early on that the British would have to adopt American methods. There was historical precedent on this matter. In the Atlantic during World War I and World War II, squadrons from the U.S. Navy had served under British command and had used the codes and techniques of the Royal Navy. Fraser and his communications officer, Richard Courage, realized that it was now their turn to adopt a different system. "They won't accept us unless we use their signal books; it won't work," Courage told Fraser. The admiral concurred and in the N/F1 agreement, Fraser committed his fleet to using the American system. Nimitz distributed U.S. codebooks to the British and provided a liaison team to each of His Majesty's Ships to help their signal personnel adopt to this different form of exchange. Courage traveled to Pearl Harbor just after Fraser departed to work out the technical details on matters like call signs, radio frequencies, recognition signals, and equipping each ship in the British Pacific Fleet with U.S. ciphering machines. "The welcome I received from Admiral Nimitz's Signal Officer could not have been more encouraging," he recalled.[15]

The admiral was also determined to learn from the American experience even on subjects that were more internal to the operation of his command. In early January, he boarded the USS *New Mexico* and observed the U.S. Navy in action during the invasion of Luzon. The Americans had kept their ships in the Pacific at sea for months at a time. One of the ways that the U.S. Navy reduced the strain and fatigue of such long service was having a number of shipboard amenities for the sailors, such as soft drink ma-

CHAPTER TEN

chines, ice, regular mail deliveries, ice cream, and films. Cunningham was having nothing to do with such ideas. "I hope our people will not get too blinded by American lavishness. We cannot compete with them in either personnel or material, nor do I think we should train our men to expect the same waste as is practiced in the American Navy." Cunningham believed mightily in the power of tradition in the Royal Navy and was an often demanding superior, which made it difficult for him to see the merit in Fraser's ideas. "I am sure that soda fountains, etc., are very good things in the right place, but we have done without them for some hundreds of years and I daresay can for another year or two."[16] Despite this opposition, a number of other key figures in the Royal Navy were alert to the fact that the war in the Pacific was different from the type of operations the British had previously conducted. The huge distances required sea duty of a duration not seen in the Royal Navy since the days of Lord Nelson. "I feel that A.B.C. was inclined to think your demands were too Rolls Royce," Admiral James Somerville, head of the British Naval Mission in Washington, informed Fraser, "but my personal view is that he is rather judging your situation by what happened in the Eastern Mediterranean when ships were never away from their base for more than a few days and certainly not longer than a week."[17]

Fraser also studied how the U.S. Navy responded to the attack of the kamikazes. He was on the *New Mexico* on January 6, 1944, when a suicide plane hit the port side of the bridge. The battleship, with its heavy armor, withstood the blast without major structural damage, but the explosion killed Lieutenant-General Sir Herbert Lumsden and a lieutenant on Fraser's staff who were near the point of impact. Others only 15 feet away were unharmed, although thoroughly shaken. In his report to the Admiralty, Fraser attempted to draw lessons from this experience, including the effective use of saturation antiaircraft fire, the need to have a minimal number of fighter planes in the air to direct this gun work, the necessity of having alternative bridges manned at all times so the commanding officer could maintain control of a ship, and the essential requirement of having crews frequently practice firefighting techniques. Although these were important observations, Fraser's biographer, Richard Humble, believes that the main purpose of the trip was so that the admiral could face the danger of the kamikazes himself. He planned to exercise his command from shore, but he was not about to send his men and ships off to fight without having experienced the same type of threat. The only way he was going to face the kamikazes was on this trip. Feeling guilty for putting his lieutenant and Lumsden into a situation that resulted in their deaths, he never talked about this incident again.[18]

While early signs indicated that Nimitz and the bulk of the U.S. Navy in the Pacific were willing and perhaps even eager to incorporate the British into the fight against the Japanese, the reaction Fraser got from the Australians, or to be more accurate from the Australian Cabinet, was one of indifference. The Admiralty's initial plan was to base the British Pacific Fleet in Sydney. There were several problems complicating this effort. Despite the desire of the Australian government to play a role in the defeat of Japan and have a voice in the peace settlement, the Cabinet also expected that the end of the war in Europe would reduce the amount of economic mobilization that Australia had to endure. Having the Royal Navy based in Sydney would require the Australians to focus manpower on building new or expanding existing airfields, storage facilities, and ports rather than on beginning the conversion to a peacetime economy and civilian consumption. In addition, John Curtin was quite ill. In fact, he would soon be dead, but he still held on to the power of his post with a firm hand. Acting Prime Minister Ben Chifley was a caretaker with authority that was less than certain in meeting labor protests on the dockyards from workers who were understandably tired of the demands that wartime mobilization had put on them. After the war, Shedden attempted to write a history of Australian defense policy. He never finished the project, but he summarizes Australian views with the title of the chapter covering this period: "The United Kingdom Government's Demands for the British Pacific Fleet Ignore the Australian Limits to Possible Aid." Fraser looked at the problem in a different light. "It is doubtful if they had any idea of the implications behind the basing of a Fleet." To be blunt, these problems continued throughout the spring, because the government lacked the political will to pay the price for a policy it desired.[19]

Soon Fraser had a serious problem: dock strikes were beginning to affect the operational performance of the British Pacific Fleet. He had to send several ships out into combat without their having undergone repairs. The admiral responded by threatening to take his command to Auckland, New Zealand. He also made some discreet, but public, remarks about the problems he faced. He reported to the Admiralty that he said he "had to send ships forward improperly maintained for the causes stated, and that I did not think that people in Australia could realize that this was happen-

CHAPTER TEN

ing, since in every other way they had been so co-operative." The Cabinet bitterly resented what they saw as an intrusion into Australian politics. On May 15, Fraser met with Chifley and several other ministers. The subject of discussion was the various logistical and manpower support needs of the fleet. In another meeting with Shedden, he called the government's attitude toward his needs "deplorable." In his report to the Admiralty, Fraser noted, "Since the meeting a large number have gone back to work." In private, Shedden thought the admiral was all wrong and compared him unfavorably to MacArthur.[20]

The Cabinet had good reason to finally exert its influence. The mood among the Australian public was extremely enthusiastic about the arrival of the British Pacific Fleet. In a report about public sentiment in the Dominion that made it to the desks of Cunningham and Brooke, the chief of the intelligence staff of the Eastern Fleet observed,

> Australia as a whole is still grateful to the Americans but tired of them and apprehensive. As a result, the feeling in all classes is preponderantly in favour of Great Britain. There is a general longing— the word is no exaggeration—for the presence of H.M. ships, the R.A.F. and the British Army. This feeling is so strong that it has affected even the Labour Cabinet, in spite of the fact that Mr. Curtin is still spoken of by his opponents as "MacArthur's man."[21]

Fraser made similar observations in his report to the Admiralty: "There is little doubt that both the people and the Government of Australia genuinely wanted the B.P.F. to be based in Australia and were delighted at the return of British prestige to this theatre."[22]

There is much evidence that supports these assessments. When the fleet arrived in Freemantle on February 4, three months after Fraser took command of a nonexistent force, the welcome the Australians extended stunned the arriving crews. "The bluffs were like antheaps, they were packed with people," one officer recalled. Six days later as the fleet steamed into Sydney harbor, thousands of people were gathered at various areas waving and cheering the return of the Royal Navy and, according to one historian, "the city went mad."[23]

In port, members of the fleet received an extremely warm welcome. "The hospitality of the Australian families, with their own sons still overseas or POWs and with a far higher percentage of their population in the forces than ourselves, had to be seen to be believed," a pilot from the HMS *Implacable* observed years later. Another officer noted, "The people were exceptionally kind to us, and Sydney soon proved to be the sailor's paradise." Officers going into restaurants rarely saw their bills, because local residents insisted on paying for them.[24]

The sailors of the fleet were as happy to be in Australia as the Australians were to have them. Many officers and men had gone months without meeting basic needs during the long trip to Australia and were interested in making up for lost time. Good food was one of these items. "A pint of milk at the door every morning is the most trivial of the day's events," Norman Hanson, a pilot serving on board the HMS *Illustrious*, explained. "But when you have subsisted for months on the powdered variety, the sight of a jug of the real stuff is a matter for universal rejoicing. Throw in some fresh eggs, lettuce, vegetables, fruit and meat—and you have firmly laid at least one of the foundations of a very happy ship!" The men, however, had to do some adjusting to the variances in Australian cuisine from their normal fare. "Steak and salad never tasted so good. We'd never had pineapple, orange and banana with a salad before and it was excellent," Lieutenant Stuart Eadon of the *Indomitable* declared. Knowing that the luxury of fresh food was something they would be able to enjoy for a limited time, the sailors indulged themselves. "We made up for lost time ashore with green salads, fresh fruit, milk and ice cream."[25]

Sailors being sailors, sexual gratification was another need that many of these young men sought to satisfy. "There appeared to be more than enough females to provide escorts for all those who felt lost," Eadon discreetly observed.[26]

Fraser's work as a diplomat in uniform paid enormous dividends in operational matters as the fleet grew and prepared for combat. The closer the Royal Navy came to engaging the enemy, the more the British saw an "us versus them" mentality among the Americans and the more supportive the U.S. Navy became of their allies. This attitude started at the top and worked its way down. The British Pacific Fleet needed an intermediate base closer to Japan than Australia. Nimitz offered to share U.S. facilities at Manus. Since the island was actually a British crown colony, there was a certain amount of awkwardness to an arrangement that required the Royal Navy to receive American permission to use territory over which the King was sovereign. Fraser and Nimitz, however, made the situation work. "Despite their doubts, the Americans put their trust in us unstintedly, and the generosity and help of all were invaluable to our success, a result which I know is most satisfactory to them," Fraser reported to the Admiralty.[27]

Many American naval officers did their best to ignore King's requirement on supply matters. The requirement had to be heeded, though, at least on paper. The Americans were more than willing to provide the British with any surplus items they had available. Commanders and supply officers, however, had to turn down requests that had to go to Washington, at least officially. The doctrine of self-sufficiency was always the rationale for this response. Fraser saw this policy at work firsthand when Nimitz rejected a routine request for the temporary loan of three Avenger aircraft. Fraser asked his U.S. liaison officer if he could explain this negative response. "He couldn't understand this at first," Lord Fraser would later recall. "And then he said, 'Ah, it has to go through Washington! I think you'll find that they'll provide you with some.' Sure enough, when we got up to Manus, the American CO there said, 'I'm sorry, but we don't issue less than six—and if you've got a bottle of whisky you can have a dozen!'" American officers told Rear-Admiral Douglas Fisher, commander of the British Fleet Train, that he could have anything and everything "that could be given without Admiral King's knowledge."[28]

Another area in which the Allies worked together was sea rescue. The Americans had developed a system of submarines, flying-boats, and destroyers designed to rescue the crews of crashed and shot-down planes. The British contributed resources to this network as well, but it was primarily an American operation and they rescued all pilots, making no reference to any self-sufficiency requirement. Admiral Sir Philip Vian observed, "The knowledge that there was every chance of being picked up if they were forced down in the sea was a vital element in the upkeep of the aircrews' morale."[29]

The U.S. Navy, like any larger organization, had personnel who deviated from the norm and were upset at seeing the British in the Pacific. Courage informed Fraser that several British officers suspected that the Americans viewed them as unwelcome guests, and he postulated that "the people who have formed the 'unwanted' impression have only come into contact with those desk-ridden Staff officers who have had to amend their plans because of our arrival. I personally am more than ever convinced that the Americans of the Fleet and a large part of those ashore are damn glad we are with them and rather admire us for it."[30]

Despite American assistance, the British faced a huge problem that there was no getting around. The architects of His Majesty's Ships had designed them for duty in European waters, not the Pacific. Since the English Channel, western approaches, North Sea, and the Mediterranean were smaller bodies of water, these ships lacked the fuel storage capacity to cruise and operate under fire in the Pacific. "The distances were staggering, to those of us accustomed to the conditions of the European War," Vian stated.[31]

As an institution, the Royal Navy had little experience in resupplying ships while underway. The British transferred fuel while at sea using hoses that trailed astern of the tankers since they lacked catamarans to keep ships apart and the appropriate block and tackles to sail side by side while fueling. Vian called this method "an awkward, unseaman-like business." This approach was dangerous and caused incidents like the one on May 3, when His Majesty's Canadian Ship *Uganda* fouled one of its propellers on a hose. It should be no surprise that it took the British twice as long as the Americans to replenish their ships. As the British learned the techniques that the U.S. Pacific Fleet had mastered, like having ships refuel abeam of their tanker, the time required decreased.[32]

Since the original purpose of these ships was to operate primarily in climates that had brief and temperate summers, they had no air conditioning. In the tropical areas of the Pacific the heat belowdecks quickly became quite intense—127 degrees Fahrenheit, in one case—and made physical labor exhausting. The temperature also made officers and men drowsy while doing their paperwork. The crews took lots of showers and drank as much water as possible, quickly overwhelming the evaporators and forcing water rationing.[33]

There was also little standardization in Royal Navy equipment. "The aircraft which constitute the Fleet's main offensive weapon, leave much to be desired," Fraser informed the Admiralty. He believed the Royal Navy had too many types, which made logistics difficult, and recommended standardization of the machines and designing a plane specifically for carrier warfare. The Royal Navy was using the Seafire, which was basically the Spitfire. Although a good plane in the air, the Seafire had problems withstanding the stress of the sudden stops of carrier landings. Many of the planes in the fleet were of U.S. design, but the British had modified them for service on British ships, which made it impossible for them to obtain spare parts from the Americans. The British were also using British bombs that would not fit aboard their aircraft carriers and had to be stored aboard other ships. This use of a middleman in the storage process made supplying the ships at sea an even more time-consuming task than otherwise would have been the case.[34]

Ship design also created a number of logistical problems that the British survived rather than resolved. Keeping the fleet equipped with enough fuel, food, water, and ammunition was an ever-present concern for Fraser, his staff, subordinate commanders, and the Admiralty. "Since I think we cannot hope to compete with American standards we must at any rate be sure that we do not fall too far short of these," Somerville argued. "In my opinion it would be disastrous if a British Task Force has to leave a scene of active operations because they cannot maintain themselves for anything like the same period as the Americans."[35]

Fraser noticed that his supply problems actually became worse after V-E Day.

> Now that the war with Germany is over, the situation seems to be worse than before, and the resources necessary for rehabilitation at home leave less for the Pacific than was the case earlier in the year. Expected reinforcements of ships and personnel are not forthcoming and resources are even tighter than before. Furthermore there is an unpleasant feeling that the landslide towards rehabilitation at home, once having been started may easily sweep everything before it, Japanese War and all.[36]

The Royal Navy never really overcame these problems. "Our Fleet Train was still far from adequate," Vian honestly noted in his memoirs. These supply ships were small and slow, and, as a result, they carried less and took longer to replenish the fleet than their American counterparts. There were also acute shortages in aircraft, radar, and radio spare parts. "We had left Sydney lacking quantities of such items. The lack had never been made good."[37]

It was only the assistance of the U.S. Navy that prevented these problems from affecting the combat performance of the British Pacific Fleet. "I have found that the American logistical authorities in the Pacific have interpreted self sufficiency in a very liberal sense," Fraser commented.[38] This assessment was one with which Vian agreed: "Indeed, the Australian base never was able to supply and maintain us properly."[39] The base commander at Manus turned over many of his facilities, including a church, hospital, and film theater, to the British.[40] Eventually, even Ernest J. King backed away from his own hard line. Somerville recounted that "recently King has admitted that pooling of resources to some extent must obviously be necessary if we are to keep the maximum number of ships, both U.S. and British, ready for operations."[41]

Fraser ultimately believed his command had done a good job of responding to these operational and logistical problems. The U.S. Navy had taken years to build up to its current level, whereas the Royal Navy had to change quickly after doing battle against the U-boats. "The entry of a British Fleet into the Pacific operations has been an exacting test which the Navy can reasonably congratulate itself on having passed satisfactorily," he concluded.[42]

Despite all these complications, the British Pacific Fleet did see combat in the indigo-colored waters off Okinawa. There were two periods in which the British participated in this campaign. The first was from March 26 to April 20. The fleet steamed out of Sydney on February 28 under the seagoing command of Vice-Admiral Sir Bernard Rawlings. Since Fraser was a full Admiral, he decided to avoid complicated questions of seniority and rank when interacting with the Americans. He, like Nimitz, would be a shore-based commander, which was a wise move. Unlike the days of Nelson and Drake, a fleet commander had to worry about vastly more complicated supply, manpower, training, and diplomatic issues. Fraser had much work to do in Australia.[43]

In ordering his fleet to sail, the commander-in-chief was moving to prevent King from assigning the British to some peripheral area. Vice-Admiral Charles M. Cooke, Jr., King's chief planning officer, while returning from the Yalta Conference called on Admiral The Lord Louis Mountbatten, the Commander-in-Chief of the South-East Asia Command, and suggested that the British Pacific Fleet serve in his theater.[44]

There was operational and logistical merit in this idea, but the deployment of the Royal Navy was about diplomacy more than combat effectiveness. "It is impossible to avoid the conclusion that there is an element in the United States Navy Department, of which Admiral Cooke is the vocal exponent, which is attempting to delay or postpone the employment of the British Pacific Fleet in the main operations against Japan," the British Chiefs stated when they informed Churchill of this development. "It is not, however, believed that this feeling in any way extends to the United States

206   CHAPTER TEN

Fleet in the Pacific under Admiral Nimitz's command." On March 9, Somerville met with King to discuss this matter and told him that the British Chiefs were unhappy with Cooke's move. King told Somerville he had not approved of the idea. He assured his guest that he was making no effort to scuttle the OCTAGON agreements. He also said Nimitz wanted a decision on Okinawa, but he had to wait and see if MacArthur decided to attack or bypass Borneo. Only then could he assign the British to Operation: ICEBERG. Somerville replied that the British Chiefs wanted to avoid having the fleet involved in follow-up operations. As this last-minute maneuvering went on, the British Pacific Fleet was at anchor off Manus, having arrived on March 7. The ships had no orders and waited in the humidity and heat. Without air conditioning on British ships, mini-epidemics of boils, heat exhaustion, and prickly heat broke out. Faced with Fraser's move and Nimitz's interest in having the British under his command, King accepted defeat and on March 15 assigned the fleet to operations off Okinawa.[45]

Fraser's orders to Rawlings were simple: "In accordance with instructions received from Cominch you are to report TASK FORCE 113 together with TASK FORCE 112 to Cincpac forthwith for duty in operations connected with ICEBERG."[46] Rawlings quickly reported for duty to Nimitz. "I would add that it is with a feeling of great pride and pleasure that the BPF joins the US Naval forces under your command."[47]

Nimitz was equally glad to have the British in the current undertaking. "The British Carrier Task Force and attached units will greatly increase our striking power and demonstrate our unity of purpose against Japan. The U.S. Pacific Fleet welcomes you." Captain Harold Hopkins, the British liaison officer on Nimitz's staff, noted that the British and American navies worked in complete unison. "From the moment that the British Fleet was reported to Admiral Nimitz as ready for duty, until the end of the war, there was a complete understanding and perfect harmony between the two allies."[48]

The British ships became Task Force 57 and operated as part of the U.S. Fifth Fleet under the command of Admiral Raymond Spruance. The Americans assigned the British to the southwestern flank of the fleet. Their mission was to neutralize Japanese airfields in the Sakishima Islands, located between Okinawa and Formosa. "Our routine, during the twenty-six days during which we remained in the combat area on this occasion, was usually two or three days of strike operation, followed by a withdrawal for re-

Sailor-Diplomats. Admiral Raymond Spruance (left), Admiral Sir Bruce Fraser (center), and Admiral Chester W. Nimitz (right) at a reception during Fraser's visit to Hawaii in December of 1945. Fraser showed a good deal of professional flexibility in converting the Royal Navy to the type of long-range warfare that the U.S. Navy was using in the Pacific. His position required that he be a diplomat as much as he was a commander. Courtesy of the U.S. National Archives

fueling, which might take anything from one to three days," Vian explained.[49]

The first day of combat came on March 26. Carrier planes carried out sweeps of ground targets. Losses of men and machines were light and were mainly due to ground fire. Strikes that cratered airfields were fairly routine but extremely dangerous. "Flak was the great leveler," Hanson of the *Illustrious* observed. "It could send to a sudden, flashing death the experienced and the sprog alike."[50]

The first kamikaze attack on Task Force 57 came on April 1. The British adopted the American tactic of deploying destroyers in advance of the main body so that they could use their radar to detect incoming Japanese planes. Since destroyers operating in these exposed positions often came under attack, and because the British versions of these ships were poorly equipped to defend themselves against aircraft, cruisers accompanied them on picket duty. A few planes evaded the fighter patrol covering the fleet and one crashed into the HMS *Indefatigable*, a carrier, at the base of the ship's superstructure, making it impossible for it to launch or recover any planes. Lieutenant-Commander Pat Chambers, the Flight Deck Officer, wounded in the incident, later described what he saw: "The picture I retain of the scene is quite vivid; the starboard wing of the Japanese plane burning on the island abaft the funnel and a great gap from there to the flight-deck where the whole lot had blown up, leaving a hole about eight feet long in the island sickbay." Within an hour, though, the carrier was back in operation.[51]

Task Force 57 was already proving itself a worthwhile commodity to the U.S. Pacific Fleet. British and American officers soon learned that the carriers of the Royal Navy stood up to the suicide attacks better than their American counterparts. Designed to take a beating from enemy aviation, the British carriers had more defensive plating. "The armoured decks of our C.V.s have caused a great sensation among the Americans and have certainly proved their worth against suicide aircraft with their comparatively small penetrating power," Fraser observed. The resilience of the *Indefatigable* impressed the ship's U.S. liaison officer. "When a kamikaze hits a U.S carrier it means six months of repair at Pearl. When a kamikaze hits a Limey carrier it's just a case of: 'Sweepers, man your brooms.'"[52]

Another kamikaze dived on the HMS *Victorious* later in the day. The ship turned hard under full helm. The plane brushed the flight deck with the tip of its wing and did several cartwheels into the water, where it exploded. A cascade of plane pieces and pilot body parts showered the *Victorious*, doing little damage.[53]

Shortly thereafter the British broke off patrol and met with the tankers from their fleet train. Refueling took two days. Even then, Rawlings had to take a calculated gamble. Some of the bigger ships had fuel tanks that were only half full. If he was to return to station at the time he had promised the Americans, Task Force 57 had to leave before the tankers had completed their mission. Rawlings decided to take the chance. He knew that delaying would only bolster the position of those in the U.S. Navy, like King, who saw the British as a liability.[54]

On April 6, the aircraft carrier HMS *Illustrious* suffered a kamikaze strike. Like the *Victorious*, the *Illustrious* turned quickly to dodge the plane. Antiaircraft crews acquired their target and their fire separated the tail assembly from the rest of the plane. Without a rudder the kamikaze veered from his target of the carrier's island. The wingtip of the plane did graze the structure, coming within about 9 feet of hitting the bridge. The grazing contact angled the plane into the water, where it exploded about 30 yards beyond the ship. The wind carried debris back onto the carrier, including the pilot's skull. This attack had little impact. The British strikes against Japanese airfields continued without interruption.[55]

After breaking off contact to refuel for two days, the Americans gave Rawlings orders to strike at airfields in northern Formosa. The kamikazes coming from this island were far better pilots than those who had struck the U.S. Pacific Fleet from bases in Kyushu. The Americans needed help and the British were eager to be of assistance. The British pilots were finding the unopposed strikes against airfields in the Sakishimas monotonous and the flak deadly. Fatigue can set in faster when people feel their assignments have little value. Going up against Japanese pilots above Formosa offered a challenge that would test their abilities. The resistance in these missions was light and no Japanese planes struck any British ships. As Task Force 57 was refueling, Rawlings received a request from Spruance to return. The Fifth Fleet was taking a beating from the kamikazes and needed help. The British had planned to leave the Okinawa area and dock in the Philippines for a week of rest and recreation. The American request changed everything, though. Vian was for going forward: "It seemed unthinkable to me that our own Task Force should retire at such a moment." Rawlings agreed: "I came to the conclusion during the evening that we must contrive to remain for a further period. Even if we could do little more than occasionally strike at Sakishima Gunto, we should anyhow provide an alternative target to take some of the weight."[56]

The air strikes that followed saw gallant action on the part of some extremely weary British aircrews. In his memoir, Hanson of the *Illustrious* recalls that he and many other pilots were having problems sleeping, so preoccupied were they with devising different ways to dodge flak. Breakfast, once a lively meal with plenty of conversation, was a time of silent exhaustion. Some pilots, in what Hanson calls "a fine 'Oh!-Sod-it!' spirit," arrived at their mess and flew missions in their pajamas. Lethargy bred carelessness, which produced in turn many sloppy landings that were dangerous to the entire ship. The aircraft maintenance crews were also showing strain. Since these detachments had fewer men than their American counterparts, they had to work longer into the night to keep up with the pace of events. Individuals from other parts of the ship often volunteered to assist in whatever way they could.[57]

On April 20, the battered but proud British ships left their stations and headed toward San Pedro Roads, Leyte, in the Philippines. The pounding the British had taken from the kamikazes had proven their worth to the Americans. Fraser reported to the Admiralty, "Doubt as to our ability to operate in the Pacific manner was somewhat naturally in American minds. This, however, was soon changed. The toll taken by the suicide bomber of the more lightly armoured American carriers led to an increase in the proportionate effort provided by our carriers, and the evidence of American eyes that we could support ourselves logistically, relieved their anxieties on that score." Vian pointed out that with fewer carriers, the British needed ships that could take a harder beating. Although the combat role of the British was of great consequence in and of itself, perhaps the biggest contribution they made was psychological and political: letting their American allies know that they had friends and were not alone.[58]

Fraser's comments might be easily dismissed as those of a proud commander, but Spruance praised Task Force 57 in even stronger terms.

I cannot speak too highly of the full and intelligent co-operation which Admiral Rawlings has been giving in support of this operation. The stout fighting qualities which history leads us to accept as normal in the Royal Navy are up to the usual high standard. Ever since Admiral Fraser came to Pearl last December, I have been most favorably impressed by the very high quality of all British officers I have seen and by their earnest desire to learn from our experience out here and to help with the war in every way they can. It has been a source of both satisfaction and pleasure to me to have the British Fleet associated with us.[59]

The second period of active combat duty for the British came between May 4 and 25. The British used the intervening time in the Philippines to recover from the mauling they took at the hands of the Japanese. The time was hardly relaxing. The task of resupplying the fleet was an around-the-clock operation. During this period, King attempted to pull the British out of the Okinawa operation and send them to Borneo, which was in

MacArthur's theater of operations. Nimitz, Spruance, and MacArthur all opposed this idea and forced King to back down. The admirals wanted the armored decks of the British carriers, while MacArthur, in a tenuous supply situation, wanted to avoid making it even more complicated with the addition of the British.

On May 1, His Majesty's Ships sailed back for Okinawa "rested, if not refreshed," to use Vian's words. Three days later, Task Force 57 was back on station and once again faced the kamikazes. The British had learned new ways to deal with these strikes. "The Japanese seem to have suddenly made up their minds to increase the attacks on us," Rawlings informed Fraser. "Their tactics are not too easy to deal with because we get such very short warnings due to their low approaches." Attacking Japanese aircraft tended to separate into several groups, which allowed them to draw off the fighter patrols protecting the fleet. One or two would get through. The gun crews were slow to open fire on planes, fearing that they might hit one of their own—which happened on occasion. "I have a suspicion also that we may have got into the habit of expecting the fighters to prevent attacks developing on us," Rawlings stated. If a plane got through the outer pickets, the antiaircraft fire of the carriers became their main line of defense. Vian explains, "It was essential to stop the suicide pilot before he entered his dive; once in the dive, neither the death of the pilot nor hits on the aircraft were likely to deflect it from its target." The only other option available at that point was for the aircraft carrier to turn as sharply as possible in the direction of the dive since the kamikazes tended to approach from the stern or quarter of a ship. If this move worked, the pilot would have to pull around to try another time, and this maneuver usually exposed the kamikaze to more antiaircraft fire. The Japanese had expected such a tactical response and a manual produced for kamikaze pilots advised them: "Your target may evade you. But always remain calm. Try again. Don't give up trying."[60]

On their first day back in combat, Rawlings decided to take his two battleships, the *King George V* and the *Howe,* along with a squadron of cruisers to strike the airfields on Miyako, one of the Sakishima Islands located to the south of Okinawa. He thought that bombs the carrier planes were dropping were insufficient and believed that a bombardment from his heavy guns might permanently incapacitate these bases. This move was a mistake. The deployment divided his fleet in two and denied his carriers the early warning that the radar equipment on these ships provided. Their absence

The Formidable *Formidable*. Repair crews scramble to contain and repair the damage to HMS *Formidable*. This effort was successful and the ship was operational again after only six hours. Courtesy of the Imperial War Museum

also reduced the antiaircraft firepower of Task Force 57. Vian admitted his error in not opposing this idea: "I was not sufficiently alive to the effect on our defensive system which would be caused by the temporary absence of the radar sets and anti-aircraft armaments of the battleships. The Japanese were." Rawlings also knew he had made a mistake. "It was rather bad luck that the Japanese should have chosen the time I was away bombarding Miyako on the 4th of May, for the attack on the Fleet."[61]

Vian described what followed as "the most serious Kamikaze attack we had yet suffered." Decoy planes drew off the combat air patrols and allowed some kamikazes to reach the carriers. Vian acknowledged that the Japanese pilots had bested his command: "The first knowledge we had of their presence was when one of them was seen diving from a height straight down on *Formidable*." The ship turned and forced the kamikaze to make a second run after flying over the full length of the flight deck at an elevation of 50 feet. The plane banked and returned to the starboard side, flying straight into the carrier's island. The explosion punched a hole in the flight deck and started a series of fires as the planes with the full fuel tanks caught fire.[62]

Through the smoke the captain of the ship signaled to Vian by lamp: "Little Yellow Bastard."

The admiral, with dry wit, replied: "Are you addressing me?"[63]

Three minutes later a kamikaze attacked the *Indomitable*, Vian's flagship. The plane continued in its attack despite taking numerous hits, but its angle was low enough that it skidded across the flight deck before slipping into the sea. The damage was so light that Vian had no idea the carrier had been hit until told. Gunfire tore a second plane apart that attacked minutes later and it crashed 30 feet short of the ship.[64]

The British quickly recovered from these attacks. The heavy armor minimized the structural damage. Using quick-drying cement and a steel plate, repair crews on the *Formidable* had the ship back in operation six hours later.[65]

Rawlings assured Fraser he had learned from his mistake. "I do not feel inclined yet to carry out a further bombardment because it means that I take away battleships and cruisers too far from the carriers. They cannot follow me in because the radar gets blanked by the land."[66]

The next few days were anticlimactic. Duty on station ended briefly for a refueling rendezvous with the fleet train. Afterward, on May 9, Task Force 57 once again did battle with the kamikazes. The first target was the HMS *Victorious*. One plane dived in on the carrier at an angle of 10 degrees. Antiaircraft fire ripped the plane to pieces, and it was on fire when it hit the ship near the forward lift. The explosion that followed holed the flight deck. While firefighting crews were putting out the blazing inferno, another kamikaze made a run on the carrier. The ship's guns shredded the plane and deflected its dive. The kamikaze was burning as it glided across the flight deck and went over the side into the water. The captain of the *Victorious* admitted the suicide attacks were tactically effective. He called them "a first class show from the enemy point of view." In both cases, shiphandling work reduced the effectiveness of the attack. "Our anti-aircraft fire was pretty effective and the *Victorious* was an immensely handy ship to handle, with a big rudder. I could spin her around quite rapidly and I managed to ruin both my Kamikaze attacks."[67]

Less than ten minutes later, two planes attacked the *Formidable*. Carriers are at their most vulnerable when they are either launching or recover-

Tough Ship. HMS *Victorious* after suffering a hit from a kamikaze on May 9, 1945. Despite the implication of the image, the damage was quite minimal and the ship stayed on station. Courtesy of the Imperial War Museum

ing their aircraft, and at this particular moment the deck park of the *Formidable* was full of planes readying for takeoff. The pilots strapped into their cockpits were helpless and could do nothing as they watched the kamikazes dive on their ship. One of the planes slammed into the deck park, killing many of the British pilots. Secondary explosions wracked the ship as the fuel tanks and bombs of the British planes detonated. Fire penetrated one hangar, but within an hour the crew had the blazes under control. The U.S. liaison officer on the *Formidable* said that a similar strike on an American carrier would have destroyed the ship.[68]

The British revised their tactics a bit. They put their radar picket ships out a little further from the main body of the task force and assigned four fighters to combat air patrols. Since the Japanese liked to attack carriers over their sterns, the British stationed a destroyer behind each one to provide concentrated fire. The task force also tightened up their formation into a 2,000-yard circle, which increased mutual gun support for all the ships.[69]

When the British departed Okinawa on May 25, they and their American allies could take pride in the operational work of Task Force 57 and the harmony in which the coalition partners functioned. The British Pacific Fleet had been at sea longer than any other Royal Navy unit since Nelson fought the Battle of Trafalgar in 1805. Task Force 57 has received less attention than it deserves, due in part to Rawlings's decision to ban journalists from his ships. Yet, the people who mattered knew what the Royal Navy had done in the waters surrounding Okinawa. As the British Pacific Fleet sailed to Australia, Spruance saluted his allies: "I would express to you, to your officers and to your men, after two months operating as a Fifth Fleet Task Force, my appreciation of your fine work and co-operative spirit. Task Force 57 has mirrored the great traditions of the Royal Navy to the American Task Forces." Rawlings had similar feelings about the U.S. Navy: "It will not, however, be out of place to remark on the helpfulness of the American authorities at Manus and Ulithi; I trust we did not ask for their assistance until we were faced with problems which frankly seemed beyond us, but whenever we did so appeal it was responded to with the utmost vigour." All the carriers the British had on station had suffered kamikaze hits and all of them had remained operational. Task Force 57 flew 5,335 sorties and dropped 958 tons of bombs. The Royal Navy had made a worthwhile contribution to the fight.[70]

The service of the British Pacific Fleet was far more important than just the number of bombs dropped. The Royal Navy had proven that the United Kingdom would stand with its American allies as the war reached Japan. The invasion of Okinawa was an extremely costly battle both ashore and afloat, and would soon make many in and out of the U.S. armed services pause. The British proved themselves a worthwhile asset in American eyes, and the performance of Task Force 57 bolstered the cause of those interested in seeing the British included in further operations.

CHAPTER TEN

■

ELEVEN

Okinawa: Land Battle

The resistance that the Japanese were offering at sea was also taking place on the small island of Okinawa. Now that the Americans were reaching the very edge of an ancient empire that had never known defeat, the soldiers of the Imperial Japanese Army were putting up a vicious resistance. In addition to resolve and determination, the defenders had plenty of supplies, firepower, and resources. The Americans, on the other hand, were beginning to face serious logistical problems that constrained their operational performance. It should be no surprise then that Okinawa became the bloodiest battle for Americans in the Pacific theater. The decisions made on how to fight this engagement, combined with the naval operations taking place in the waters off Okinawa, would have significant political and diplomatic ramifications.

As the theater commander, Nimitz was also responsible for the land battle to take control of Okinawa. In his office, the admiral had posted a sign that listed three questions that he routinely asked when assessing any undertaking:

1. Is the proposed operation likely to succeed?
2. What might be the consequences of failure?
3. Is it in the realm of practicability of materials and supplies?[1]

If Nimitz asked those questions about Okinawa, he would have liked the answers. Success was highly likely. Seizing the island would cut Japan off from the mineral-rich areas of Southeast Asia that it needed to keep its industrial economy running. Control of the island would also give Americans a staging area for the invasion of Japan. The Ryukyu Islands, of which Okinawa was the largest, were also home to a number of airfields that would prove useful in both the strategic bombing campaign—even though Nimitz thought burning civilians to a cinder had limited military utility—and in tactical support of an amphibious assault on the home islands. Failure—even in a worst-case scenario—would only have caused a small delay in the U.S. advance through the Pacific. Finally, Operation: ICE-BERG was within the range of what was practical, although U.S. armed forces would start encountering logistical problems that only would have grown had the advance continued.[2]

The seizure of Okinawa would require a force the size of a field army, and the admiral assigned the task to a little-known U.S. Army officer with a well-known name: Lieutenant General Simon Bolivar Buckner, Jr. A graduate of West Point—he received his appointment from President Theodore Roosevelt—Buckner was the son of his namesake, Simon Sr., who had earned the stars of a Lieutenant General in the Confederate States Army. The elder Buckner was one of the first Confederates to discover the military genius of his old friend, Ulysses S. Grant. After Grant had left the army and quickly ruined his finances, Buckner lent him money. In 1861, after Union forces had outmaneuvered the defenders of Ft. Pillow, Buckner found himself taking over after the political generals responsible for the disaster had fled. He expected something better than the "unconditional and immediate surrender" that his friend demanded of him but had no choice but to accept what he called "ungenerous and unchivalrous terms." After the war he entered politics and the people of Kentucky elected him governor. He was also the vice presidential nominee of a splinter group of Democrats in 1896. He married late in life and had a son when most men his age were becoming grandfathers.[3]

The younger Buckner followed his father in making a career in the military. He was an outdoorsman who loved to hunt and fish. During the Battle of Okinawa he would often make observations in his diary about the natural beauty of Okinawa. He missed combat duty in World War I and spent most of the interwar period in training assignments. He thrived in this environment, as much as it was possible to thrive in the U.S. Army of the interwar period. He was alert to developments in the military application of the airplane and the internal combustion engine that made the tank possible. He returned to West Point as Commandant of Cadets, a position roughly equal to dean of students, and developed a reputation for being harsh in his discipline. A handsome man except for a large nose, Buckner was in amazingly good physical shape for a man in his thirties, much less his sixties. He enjoyed socializing, but—also like his father—he married late in life. He still liked the company and comforts of other females. During the fighting on Okinawa, he complained: "My social news here may be briefly summarized as 'No women, no liquor.'" When the United States entered World War II, he found himself stationed in Alaska. He enjoyed the land and nature, but the upper reaches of North America were "stepping stones to nowhere."[4]

In Alaska, he had clashed with the local naval commander, which had the potential to destroy his career, but he learned from this experience. During the battle on Saipan, Lieutenant General Holland M. Smith, a marine and Commanding General of the V Amphibious Corps, relieved Major General Ralph Smith as Commanding General of the 27th Infantry Division, a substandard unit. The division occupied the middle of the American line and made the least amount of progress, creating a U-shaped salient that jeopardized the marine units on both sides. This incident initiated a fierce interservice dispute, since the two generals were from different services. Buckner was in charge of an army commission that investigated the relief of Ralph Smith. He was convinced that his handling of this situation was a key factor in his receiving the mission to take Okinawa. "Adm. Nimitz after sounding out my attitude on the Smith vs. Smith controversy and finding that I deplored the whole matter and harbored no inter-service ill feelings, announced that I would command the new joint project."[5]

The invasion of Okinawa looked to be the culmination of his professional career. He ended up the subject of a *Time* magazine cover story. His plan was simple. He was going to bring his material advantage in ammunition to bear against his enemy. "We're relying on our tremendous fire power and trying to crush them by weight of weapons," he told reporters.[6]

As U.S. ships cut across the smooth waters of the Pacific heading toward the small island, nervous tension was the order of the day. The day before the invasion started, Ernie Pyle, the syndicated newspaper columnist, captured the sentiment among those whom he would accompany on the assault who would establish the beachhead: "You feel weak and you try to think of things, but your mind stubbornly drifts back to the awful image of tomorrow. It drags on your soul and you have nightmares." The operation was an ever-present thought and concern regardless of rank. "Tomorrow is Easter Sunday, my father's birthday and the day of my first battle," Buckner recorded in his diary. "I hope that I shall be able to look back upon it with the same degree of enthusiasm with which I anticipate it." There were no illusions about what would come, as Pyle noted. "We will take Okinawa. Nobody has any doubt about that. But we know we will have to pay for it. Some on this ship will not be alive twenty-four hours from now." Many, many men escaped their concerns by sleeping as much as possible.[7]

The first day of ground combat was nothing like what the Americans had expected. The Commanding General of the Japanese Thirty-second Army, Lieutenant General Ushijima Mitsuru, had decided not to defend the beaches. The tall, thin general with a short mustache was a 1908 graduate of the Japanese Military Academy at Zama. He had served as the Vice Minister of War and had been stationed in Burma earlier in the war. He knew that defeating an invasion was simply beyond the capacity of his command. His goal was simple: inflict heavy casualties on the Americans. Ushijima would be defeated—this he knew—but he would make it an exceptionally costly victory for the Americans. As a result, the Japanese decided to meet the Americans on ground that worked to their advantage. There was no amphibious combat as the Americans landed on Okinawa on a sandy beach where the big guns of the U.S. ships could fire on the defenders. In his memoirs, William Manchester captured the confusion of that day as the troops approached the island. "Slowly we realized that something that we had anticipated wasn't happening. There were no splashes of Jap mortar shells, no roars of Jap coastal guns, no grazing Jap machine gun fire. The enemy wasn't shooting back because, when we hit the beach at 8:27 A.M., there wasn't any enemy there." Joy was a natural reaction, but confusion and tension were other reactions as well. Where was the enemy? Standing above them on Mt. Shuri, watching the invasion, Ushijima and his staff watched the landings and enjoyed a perverse laugh as they thought about the perplexed American reaction to the unopposed assault.[8]

Buckner at first failed to comprehend what his opponent was doing. "Opposition was light, the Japs evidently having expected us to land elsewhere on the island," he informed his wife that first day. "We gained more ground today than we had hoped to get within three days." He had company in his optimistic relief. "Don't ask me why we haven't had more opposition," Major General Roy S. Geiger, Commanding General of the III Amphibious Corps, said to a reporter. A day later, Buckner had a better idea of what his opponents were doing. "So far, the Jap's apparent misconception of our plan, his failure to oppose our landing have made things easy for us, but very hard fighting against a strong system of concrete and underground defenses is still ahead of us. However, we are here to stay."[9]

The mountainous northern half of Okinawa would make it impossible for the Americans to build runways and airfields in that region of the island, so Ushijima decided to make little effort to defend the area. The III Amphibious Corps had the mission of taking this region and with almost no opposition in the area, the marines advanced quickly. The Motobu peninsula was the only part of the north that the Japanese contested. The heights in the area overlooked Ie Shima, an island with airfields just off the northwestern coast of Okinawa. As long as the Japanese controlled the peninsula, they could deny the Americans the use of these bases. It took the corps just under two weeks to reach the northern tip of the island as it marched over uneven terrain. Motobu was fully under marine control on April 20. Eugene Sledge, a veteran of the 1st Marine Division, was standing on high ground and saw flickering light and heard rumbling coming from the south. "No one said much about it. I tried unsuccessfully to convince myself it was thunderstorms, but I knew better."[10]

Sledge was watching the angry snarl of battle. The XXIV Corps, the other half of the Tenth Army, had made full contact with their enemy. The Japanese soldiers defending Okinawa were prepared to sell their lives, but at an exceptionally high price. This determination is quite understandable when put into context. The Americans were on the doorstep of Japan. Okinawa was no Japanese colony like Saipan or Guam: it was a Japanese prefecture, part of Japan itself. The soldiers defending the island were now defending their homeland rather than some foreign conquest, and the Thirty-second Army had the resources to exact a heavy price for control of the island. The army had more artillery than any Japanese formation that the Americans had encountered in the Pacific war and a six-month supply of ammunition. The guns of the 5th Artillery Command were inside caves and well camouflaged. As effective as Japanese artillery was, there were limits to its utility. Communication was the biggest problem. Radios became inoperative inside the caves and combat cut telephone wires quickly, making it almost impossible for the Japanese heavy gun crews to respond quickly to tactical offensives.[11]

The Japanese were also well fortified. The defenders had established three lines of defense, using an interconnected system of tunnels, trenches, caves, blockhouses, pillboxes, and Okinawan tombs on both the reverse and forward slopes of hills. The Japanese also established positions to control important roadways. Coral makes up much of the terrain in southern Okinawa, making it easy for Japanese defensive trenches to neutralize American artillery and channel attacking units into prepared fire zones, which often overlapped with one another. The underground elements of this system also limited the advantage that air superiority gave the Tenth Army. The Americans had no idea of where the Japanese were until they made contact with their opponent. There were, however, two significant shortcomings to Japanese defenses. First, the system was well integrated only up to the battalion level. Far more significantly, the Thirty-second Army lost flexibility and mobility in these entrenched positions. Japanese soldiers had no ability to maneuver, even in retreat, and with no other options, they often held their positions to the last man. This inflexibility guaranteed that the Americans would win the battle if they could pay the high cost of the campaign.[12]

As much as Buckner tried to avoid interservice issues, the beating the navy was taking from the kamikazes put pressure on the Americans. "Adm. Spruance is trying to hurry us in the capture of Ie [Sh]ima," Buckner noted in his diary. The slow pace was the work of the Japanese. Combat on Ie Shima was savage. It took a U.S. Army infantry division three days to secure the island. The combat included street-to-street battles in the main town. "The last three days of this fighting were the bitterest I ever witnessed," Major General Andrew D. Bruce, Commanding General of the 77th Infantry Division, remarked. One of the deaths on this little island included Ernie Pyle. Pinned down with a number of others by a Japanese machine gun, he looked over the crest of a small mound and took a bullet in the head. He died instantly.[13]

Buckner refused to alter his plans for Ie Shima to satisfy Spruance. He knew what was about to come. "This would gain no time in completing the field and would use up the army reserves before the main fight starts." In a letter to an old friend, Spruance commented:

I doubt if the Army slow, methodical method of fighting really saves any lives in the long run. It merely spreads the casualties over a longer period. The longer period greatly increases the naval casualties when Jap air attacks on ships is a continuing factor. However, I do not think the Army is at all allergic to losses of naval ships and personnel. There are times when I get impatient for some of Holland Smith's drive, but there is nothing we can do about it.

Spruance's biographer, however, disagreed with the admiral's assessment, arguing that Okinawa was better suited for army units.[14]

In the south, the XXIV Corps had as happy an initial experience on Okinawa as their marine comrades. "We came ashore, got into columns of companies and moved inland as if it were a school exercise," one lieutenant recalled. On April 4, the Americans made contact with the Japanese defenders. "All units are doing splendidly but heavy resistance is developing in the south as I anticipated," Buckner wrote his wife. "We have a deep area of concrete and steel to break, but we can break it. Casualties so far have been light, but will be heavier from now on." The advance, though, was molasses-like, and the Japanese actually blunted the American advance on their lines even though they were outnumbered two to one. "The enemy in front of the XXIV Corps is superbly fortified and probably outnumbers our 2 attacking Divs," Buckner recorded in his diary. "Our 96th is receiving a considerable number of casualties. The 27th Div landed today but rains have bogged it down and held up arty ammunition which is now short on our southern front."[15]

As the battle progressed, the Tenth Army began using artillery shells at a faster pace than staff officers had planned, making supply an issue in the advance. The transportation network on Okinawa was unable to support the American advance. The narrow roads on the island only allowed one-way travel, and American vehicles kicked up thick clouds of dust that blinded those behind them. Heavy rains then turned these dirt paths to muddy truck traps. American vehicles sank into the ground down to their floorboards. Weather limited the capacity of the beaches to absorb the unloading of supplies, and the lack of experienced logistical personnel also slowed down the invasion. This situation never improved.[16]

Between April 14 and April 19 there was no change in the lines between XXIV Corps and the units of the Japanese Thirty-second Army. The Commanding General of the corps, Major General John Hodge, was waiting for artillery shells to reach his gun positions before launching an offensive. During the night of April 18–19 the corps finally had enough supplies to let loose a heavy artillery barrage, which did little damage to the fortified Japanese positions. Since Japanese fortifications were not connected, there were a number of gaps in the line where the Americans could infiltrate during artillery bombardments. The Japanese response was to launch immediate infantry counterattacks. In these close-quarter firefights it was too dangerous for the Americans to call in artillery strikes. Small arms fire usually determined the outcome of these engagements.[17]

The tank was highly effective against the Japanese fortifications, and the defenders made the destruction of these vehicles a priority. The Japanese had few antitank guns, but the ones they had were highly lethal to American tank crews. Artillery barrages were also good ways of killing the tanks, but Japanese infantry companies often had no radios to direct artillery strikes. The defenders would use mortar barrages, which posed no danger to the tanks but were highly lethal to the infantry that advanced alongside them, forcing both to retreat when conditions became too dangerous for the riflemen. Failing in these efforts, the Japanese would attempt to target the treads and wheels with satchel charges and grenades. While oftentimes successful, these attacks usually resulted in the death of the assaulting soldier. Sometimes these missions were intentionally suicidal, but many times they were not. Either way, to the Americans they looked like a ground version of the kamikazes. With tread or wheel damage, tanks became immobilized and vulnerable targets which their crews abandoned. The Japanese would then destroy the abandoned vehicles before their crews returned to retrieve them.[18]

The place of battle produced profound emotional reactions. "By sheer chance," Manchester noted, "I had chosen a spot from which the entire battlefield was visible. It was hideous, and it was also strangely familiar, resembling, I then realized, photographs of 1914–1918. This, I thought is what Verdun and Passchendaele must have looked like." Buckner had a slightly more upbeat response. "Yesterday I had the rare experience of finding an observation point that permitted me to observe the entire battle front," he informed his wife. "It was really a superb spectacle, plane strikes, artillery concentration, smoke screens, flame throwers, tanks and the steady determined advance of the infantry closing with the enemy. Along with this were the crash of bombs, the screech of projectiles, the whistle of shell fragments, the sputter of machine guns and the sharp crack

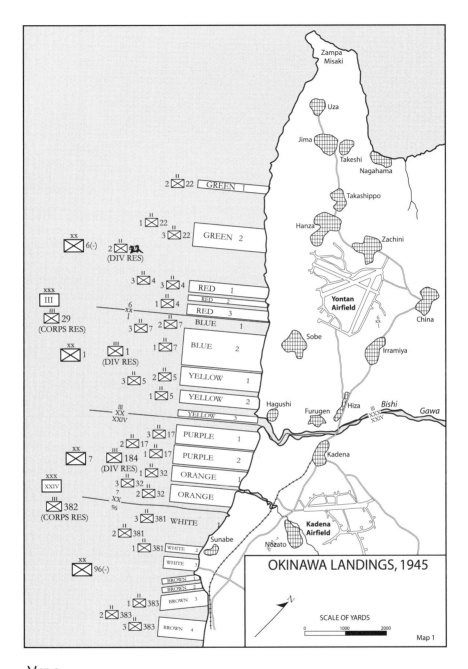

OKINAWA LANDINGS, 1945

SCALE OF YARDS

Map 1

Map 2

of rifles. I shall never forget it. It was really stirring." Such are the different perspectives of the rifleman and the general.[19]

The slow advance forced U.S. ships to stay on station, where they took a beating from the kamikazes. Buckner was well aware of what was happening at sea. It took him over a week to establish his headquarters on Okinawa and during that time he was aboard the USS *Eldorado* for the first FLOATING CHRYSANTHEMUM attack. "I have had thrills in duck blinds but none comparable to that of seeing an enemy plane shot down when it was heading directly at our ship," he observed. On April 22–24, Nimitz visited Okinawa. The admiral supposedly complained about the slow advance, which Buckner dismissed, informing him that a ground advance was army business. Nimitz's biographer has him responding, "Yes, but ground though it may be, I'm losing a ship and a half a day. So if this line isn't moving within five days, we'll get someone here to move it so we can all get out from under these stupid air attacks." The problem is that this account and quote are highly suspect. It would have been out of character for Buckner to be so dismissive of a superior officer. He also knew that Tenth Army was a joint force and that the effort to take Okinawa was an operation that required all the armed services to work together. Nimitz's biographer offers no explanation of his sources—which were probably members of the admiral's staff—who were most likely remembering general sentiment and attributing it to the admiral. Buckner, on the other hand, makes no mention of any confrontation in his diary or letters to his wife. His account implies that the sentiment in the conference room was almost an exact opposite of what the gossip suggests. "Adm. Nimitz left this morning, apparently well pleased."[20]

The day Nimitz left Okinawa the Tenth Army actually breached the first Japanese line of defense. The advance, however, was a success only because the defender retreated when it became clear that their position was untenable. The skill of American arms had little to do with the results.[21]

Despite this progress, Buckner cancelled the next stage of his battle plans to seize smaller islands lying off Okinawa. Shortages in the number of service personnel available to support this operation were a major factor in this decision. The Tenth Army needed more support personnel than planners had expected. Many logistical units were helping engineers build durable roads on Okinawa. Issues of supply and transportation are rarely exciting, but they were proving exceptionally crucial to the Tenth Army. Buckner was facing the ramifications of U.S. logistical shortcomings.[22]

Supply efforts became even more constrained following *kikusui* number four. Kamikazes sank the supply ship *Canada Victory* and damaged another one. At sea, this suicide assault had minimal impact. It did, though, have more significant repercussions on land.[23]

In the second half of April, several people put forward the idea of staging a second landing on the beaches of southern Okinawa as a way of getting around the Japanese defensive positions. The first person to put forward this idea was Major General Andrew D. Bruce, Commanding General of the 77th Infantry Division. Buckner respected Bruce's command ability and aggressiveness: "Bruce, as usual, is rarin' to go and is looking well ahead for action. I much prefer a bird dog that you have to whistle in to one that you have to urge out. He is of the former variety." He also appreciated Bruce's putting forward this idea. "As usual, he is rarin' to try a landing behind the Jap main position in southern Okinawa." Buckner, however, rejected this idea, concerned that it would complicate already difficult supply and logistical efforts. When the marines argued on behalf of this operation later in the month, he turned the proposal down a second time. He told the authors of the official U.S. Army history that a second landing would become "another Anzio but worse." Geiger of the III Amphibious Corps agreed with Buckner's decision. Given already existing supply problems, a second assault might have been beyond the capacity of the Tenth Army.[24]

The Japanese were waging a skillful battle of attrition that was inflicting painfully high losses on the American invaders. Buckner knew what he was facing. "The Japs here seem to have the strongest position yet encountered in the Pacific and it will be a slow tedious grind with flame throwers, explosives placed by hand and the closest of teamwork to dislodge them without very heavy losses," he wrote his wife. "In the meanwhile, however, we are making great headway with the part of the island we have and are developing splendid air facilities that we are already using."[25]

The next line of defense proved just as difficult for the Americans to breach as the first. Buckner deployed the marines in the south, taking up the western portion of the front lines. Ushijima then made a major mistake. His chief of staff, Lieutenant General Cho Isamu, and a number of the commanders of subordinate units were chafing at the defensive stance of the Thirty-second Army. They wanted to initiate a counteroffensive. Ushijima agreed. In the predawn hours of May 4, the Japanese unleashed heavy artillery fire and then attacked as light crept over the horizon. The effort

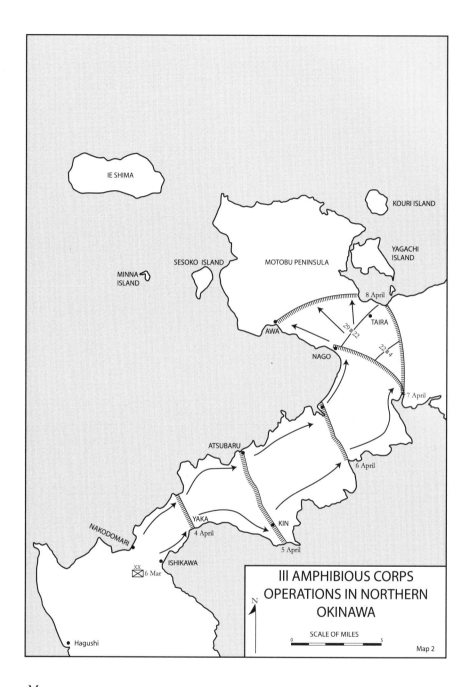

IE SHIMA

KOURI ISLAND

YAGACHI ISLAND

SESOKO ISLAND

MOTOBU PENINSULA

MINNA ISLAND

8 April

AWA

TAIRA

29–22

NAGO

22–4

7 April

ATSUBARU

6 April

YAKA

KIN

4 April

5 April

NAKODOMARI

ISHIKAWA

XX 6 Mar

Hagushi

III AMPHIBIOUS CORPS OPERATIONS IN NORTHERN OKINAWA

N

SCALE OF MILES

0   5

Map 2

Map 3

lasted for a day before Ushijima accepted defeat and ended the operation. His units suffered terrible casualties in attacks launched primarily against the XXIV Corps, which made no progress except for a small penetration into the sector of the 77th Infantry Division. Japanese soldiers were often caught out in the open, where U.S. artillery quickly demolished their ranks. Historians James and William Belote in their book on the battle describe May 4–5 as the "only serious Japanese mistake of the Okinawa campaign." The authors of the official U.S. Army history on Okinawa called the counteroffensive "a colossal blunder." Ushijima admitted as much to Colonel Yahara Hiromichi, the officer on his staff who was the architect of the battle of attrition that he had been waging up until then. The general told Yahara that he would follow his lead from that point forward. "I was not only frustrated, I was furious," the colonel wrote in his memoirs years later. The damage had already been done. The counteroffensive had consumed vast amounts of ammunition and, more importantly, lost many men who could have easily continued to inflict casualties on the Americans.[26]

Although futile, the counteroffensive had been an impressive and professional effort. Buckner had a begrudging respect for his opponent, calling the operation "one of the best coordinated attacks I have ever seen." He also added: "The enemy means business, but he had waited too long and he didn't have what it took."[27]

Still, the Japanese would hold the second line for an additional two weeks, and it required some exceptionally vicious fighting before this situation changed. "The Jap artillery was unbelievable," Manchester recalled. One of his friends, Wally Moon, was buried alive in a foxhole after a barrage caused a mudslide. Moon did not survive. Another member of his company, Bubba Yates, a former student at the University of Alabama, had, like many southerners, an inferiority complex about the Civil War. On one occasion, he was trying to convince Manchester that helmets were a needless piece of equipment. If the great and mighty Army of Northern Virginia had no need of them, why should they need them? As Yates was trying to indirectly redeem the South, a piece of shrapnel hit him in the helmet. He took off his headgear, looked at the dent, put it back on, and returned to his earlier argument. When the 1st Marine Division was at Sugar Loaf Hill, Yates spent a night firing off a Browning automatic rifle at the Japanese. He was finally dragged from the front lines, wounded four times, mumbling, "Vicksburg, Vicksburg." Shiloh Davidson III tried similar heroics with a raid to the crest of the hill. He was less lucky than Yates. A shell

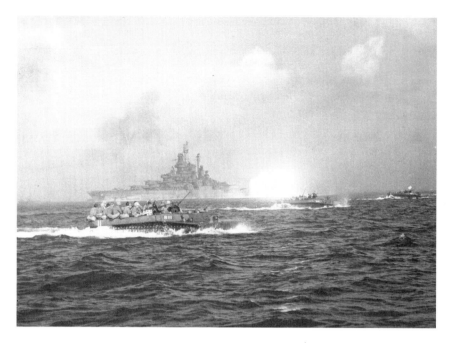

Purple in Action. The USS *Tennessee* hammers the Okinawan coast while U.S. Army and Marine Corps units land on the island. The invasion of Okinawa was a joint operation in that all the armed services contributed to the operation. The color of joint operations in the U.S. military is purple. Courtesy of the U.S. National Archives

hit him, cutting him to pieces and knocking him back into barbedwire. He died slowly, in the pale moonlight, calling for his mother. His friends could do nothing to help since he was in a well-lighted and exposed position. "My father had warned me that war is grisly beyond imagining," Manchester reflected in his memoirs. "I believed him."[28]

Torrential rainstorms worked to the advantage of the Japanese. "Heavy rain bogged down our tanks and slowed our advance," Buckner recorded in his diary. On May 21, the Japanese began withdrawing their forces from the line anchored around the city of Shuri using a plan that Colonel Yahara called "retreat and attack." Yahara drew up this plan, and he got his inspiration from Napoleon's actions at the Battle of Marengo and the French counterattack on the Marne. "Our general retreat policy . . . was aimed at a total retreat toward fortifications." He counted on the rain and the mud that would follow on slowing down the Americans.[29]

After hard-fought victories at Sugar Loaf Hill in the west and Conical Hill in the east, the anchors of the Japanese line were gone and it seemed possible that the Tenth Army would encircle the defenders. On May 27, Buckner issued an order to his corps commanders: "Indications point to possible enemy retirement to new defensive positions with possible counteroffensive against our forces threatening his flank. Initiate without delay strong and unrelenting pressure to ascertain probable intentions and keep him off balance. Enemy must not repeat not be permitted to establish himself securely on new position with only nominal interference."[30]

Yahara was working to do just that. His plan required an attack before U.S. troops went on the offensive. The weather helped him as he had hoped. The rainstorms made it impossible for aerial reconnaissance to provide the Americans with any information even though the Japanese were above ground. The successful withdrawal of the Thirty-second Army thwarted Buckner's plans to destroy the forces defending Shuri.[31]

Despite Buckner's order, the Japanese finished pulling out on May 29. A battalion of the 1st Marine Division captured Shuri Castle, which until recently had served as the headquarters of the Japanese Thirty-second Army. The marines took the castle with the authorization of their division commander, Major General Pedro A. Del Valle, even though the objective was in the operations zone of the 77th Infantry Division. Del Valle informed Bruce of his decision only minutes before the marines stormed into the castle. Bruce had a prearranged artillery and air strike scheduled to hit the fortress and had his staff work frantically to call off the barrage in time.[32]

Buckner knew that the enemy had gotten away.

Strong enemy resistance still confronts the 77th and 96th Divs and the right of the 7th. However, the 7th has now advanced 3,000 yds south of and 2,000 yds to the west of Yonabaru. The Naha and Shuri fronts have apparently been deserted permitting the 6th and 1st Mardivs to advance from 1,000 to 1,800 yds, giving most of Naha to the 6th and Shuri Castle to the 1st with almost no opposition.

He still hoped to destroy at least some of the defenders.

I ordered a rapid drive to the southeast by the III Phibcorps, changing the corps boundary so as to pinch out the 77th Div. The XXIV Corps was ordered to drive west with the 7th Div and meet the III Phibcorps, thus cutting off the Japs still holding the line. The 7th also to be prepared to make a turn later to the south so as to outflank the next fortified line to the south if the enemy gets back to it.[33]

The commanding general of the Tenth Army remained optimistic for several more days. "The entire enemy line appears to be crumbling," Buckner observed. The Japanese had actually withdrawn their forces in time to form a new defensive line on the Yaeju-Dake-Yuza-Dake escarpment, a giant coral wall on the southern tip of the island. They had, however, lost most of their artillery pieces in the move south. The Thirty-second Army was still a fighting force, but with much less capacity than it had at the beginning of the campaign. Despite waning Japanese strength, the battle still had another month before it reached its conclusion.[34]

The rain and mud complicated operations for the Tenth Army just as Yahara had hoped. "All movements during most of May and early June were physically exhausting and utterly exasperating because of the mud," Sledge recalled in his memoirs. Manchester explained that mud is different for the average rifleman than it is for a civilian: "There is one massive difference between peacetime mud and wartime mud. In peacetime it is usually avoidable. You can step around it, or take another route. In combat you fight in the mud, sleep in it, void in it, bleed in it, and sometimes die in it." Agreement came from the highest levels of the army. General Joseph W. Stilwell, Commanding General, U.S. Army Ground Forces, was on an inspection tour of the Pacific that took him to Okinawa, and he told soldiers of the 96th Infantry Division: "Mud is bad anyplace, but where caterpillars and bulldozers sink and spin their tracts, it's damn bad." There was so much precipitation that it was seeping through the limestone. When Manchester tried to take a nap in a cave, he discovered that dripping water made it difficult. "Now it was raining *indoors*."[35]

Ground conditions had a bigger impact beyond just draining the energy of the troops at the front. Airfield construction on Okinawa began within days of the American landing. Engineering and construction units began building or enhancing airfields that could support B-29 bombers, which could then strike Japan proper. The rains of May changed these priorities. "We have had about a foot of rain in one week," Buckner observed. "Some troops have been taken from airfield construction and put on roads. I shall probably be taken to task for this by higher HQ but it is the right thing to do." The rain that turned the roads into massive bogs of mud was a critical

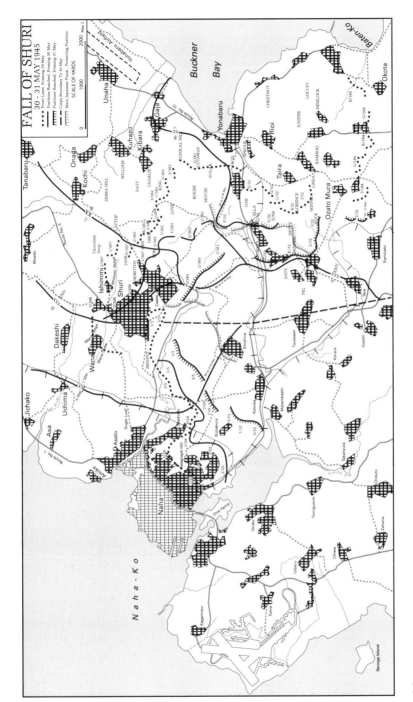

Map 4

factor in slowing down the American advance. Many routes simply broke down from heavy use or became impassable because of the rain, making maintenance work critical. In fact, road conditions were one of the first things Stilwell noticed after arriving. "Road layout is ambitious, but the muck is terrible." At the end of June, construction and engineering units were maintaining 340 miles' worth of roads on the island. The more important roads were expanded to carry two lanes of traffic. In addition to slowing down the construction of airfields, the 14.68 inches of rain that fell on the island slowed down unloading operations on the beaches.[36]

The advance on Japanese defensive positions continued, but with almost no artillery remaining it was much more difficult for the Thirty-second Army to resist. With only thirty-six hours of notice, elements of the 6th Marine Division made an early morning amphibious landing. The units crossed the open sea in front of the Naha harbor mouth and landed on the Oroku peninsula on the south side of the harbor across from Naha. "Sixth Mardiv made amphibious landing just south of Naha, met little resistance and advanced about 1,000 yds," Buckner noted. Japanese defenders on the peninsula slowed the marines, if ever so briefly. The marines took an island in the middle of Naha Harbor, which they planned to use as a supply depot. Japanese defenders on the peninsula operating heavy machine guns prevented the Americans from building a bridge to the island. Gunfire would puncture and sink the pontoons keeping the bridge afloat. It was only after these positions had been neutralized that the marines could use the island.[37]

Stilwell was less than impressed with the commanding general of the Tenth Army. "Tactics all frontal. Sixth Marine landing south of Naha only attempt to go by. No thought of repeating it. Buckner laughs at Bruce for having crazy ideas. 'Two out of 15 are O.K. The rest are impossible.' It might be a good thing to listen to him." After visiting frontline units, he tried to brief Buckner on what he had seen. "Buckner is tiresome. I tried to tell him what I had seen, but he knew it all. Keeps repeating his wisecracks. 'The Lord said let there be mud,' etc. etc.—Sat through number 53 again." Stilwell vented his anger in his diary. "Buckner is obviously playing the Navy. He recommended Geiger as army commander. Nimitz is perfect. His staff is perfectly balanced. Cooperation is magnificent. The Marine divisions are wonderful. In fact, everything is just dinky. His own staff is perfect—he picked them himself. It is all rather nauseating. There is NO tactical thinking on push."[38]

There is more than a little merit in what Stilwell wrote, but the implication that Buckner was unwilling to try new ideas is misleading. On June 9, he made an effort to bring the battle to an end. "Will drop offer of surrender to Japs tomorrow with little hope of results but largely at the behest of psychological 'experts,'" Buckner observed in his diary. A reporter for the *New York Journal-American* called the gesture "without precedent in the Pacific War." The message, addressed to Ushijima, read, "The forces under your command have fought bravely and well, and your infantry tactics have merited the respect of your opponents. Like myself, you are an infantry general long schooled and practiced in infantry warfare. I believe, therefore, that you understand as clearly as I, that the destruction of all Japanese resistance on the island is merely a matter of days." When Ushijima received the note, he said with a smile, "The enemy has made me an expert on infantry warfare." Surrender was out of the question, and the battle would go on.[39]

Just before he left Okinawa, Stilwell gave a press conference. According to newspaper accounts, Stilwell warned that Japanese soldiers were fighting with more intensity than the Germans and suggestions that the war would soon end were, at best, overly optimistic. "All that is slop. When they are so tenacious individually I don't see how we can expect a crack in morale in the mass." He dodged directly answering a question about the number of troops it would take to invade Japan. A reporter from the *New York Times* said he thought it would take half a million. "We'd be foolish to try to do it with less, don't you think," was how Stilwell replied. He added that if the Japanese armies in China and Manchuria fought on after the fall of the home islands, the war would continue for another two years. In an editorial, the *New York Sun* commented: "Everybody will hope, of course, that the general is overconservative, but none can deny that he is qualified to speak from experience."[40]

Buckner and the Tenth Army were on the verge of victory in the middle of June, but their battle, combined with developments in the United States, would create conditions that made a larger British presence in the final drive against Japan welcome. The death of the commander-in-chief and the concern that his successor had about the casualties on Okinawa were two of the most important factors in modifying American attitudes. The new commander-in-chief was, like Buckner, a son of the Confederate border. His name: Harry S. Truman.

■

In the Wake of ICEBERG

Franklin Delano Roosevelt was the president of the United States when the Battle of Okinawa started. Like so many others, he did not live to see the end of that engagement. After being inaugurated for an unprecedented fourth term, he decided to rest in Warm Springs, Georgia, for a few weeks. His death on that trip altered American history, bringing to the White House a failed haberdasher from Independence, Missouri. Harry S. Truman entered office in better spirits and health than what Roosevelt displayed during his last days. He would also look at developments in the Pacific war with an extremely large amount of well-founded concern. His worries about the casualties on Okinawa and what they signaled about an invasion of Japan became a new dynamic in coalition diplomacy. He quickly became Brooke's greatest asset, even if neither man knew of the other's efforts.

Roosevelt arrived in Warm Springs in late March and told his cousin Margaret Suckley that his goal was to "sleep and sleep and sleep." Almost genetically optimistic in temperament, even Roosevelt saw that his time was coming to an end. He talked with Suckley about seeing the war to the end and then resigning and retiring from politics. Those around him could tell that the end would be much more permanent. His complexion had little color and he was slow both physically and mentally. An aide noted: "He is slipping away from us, and no earthly power can keep him here."

When Morgenthau visited, Roosevelt's hands shook so much that he nearly knocked over the glasses while pouring drinks. The treasury secretary was "in agony watching him."[1]

Roosevelt at this point had long since renewed his acquaintance with his former mistress, Lucy Mercer Rutherfurd. She visited Warm Springs during those last few days. She was with him on April 12, while he was posing for a painting being done by one of her friends. Around 1 P.M., he rubbed the back of his head and in a low voice told his cousin: "I have a terrific pain in the back of my head." He then collapsed from what was a cerebral hemorrhage. Two and a half hours later he died.[2]

Honors and tributes started almost immediately. "A great and gallant wartime leader has died almost in the very hour of the victory to which he led the way. It is a cruel and bitter irony that Franklin D. Roosevelt should not have lived to see the Allied armies march into Berlin," the editorial board of the *New York Times* declared. Toward the end of their tribute, these journalists observed, "To the pages of history we may safely leave the appraisal of this man at his full measure, secure in our own knowledge that his greatest work was done. He had led the country through the valley of indecision to the high ground of certainty in its own purpose."[3] Off the waters of Okinawa the British Pacific Fleet flew their colors at half-mast in honor of the U.S. president.[4]

In Warm Springs, the day after he died, a thousand infantrymen slowly marched alongside the hearse carrying the president's coffin while a U.S. Army band kept beat with muffled drums. Black streamers were flying from their flags and tears were running down the faces of several soldiers. The procession took half an hour to reach the train station. A reporter from the *New York Times* traveling on the train taking Roosevelt's body back to Washington saw crowds of people gathering at "every" train station along the route even in the middle of the night. Many in the crowds wept openly.[5]

Late in the afternoon of April 14, there was a brief and simple service in the East Room of the White House, which was lined with flowers. The ceremony consisted of the funeral rites of the Episcopal Church, two hymns that Roosevelt liked, and a quotation from his first inaugural address: "All we have to fear is fear itself." Assistant Secretary of State Dean Acheson watched as "large crowds came and stood in front of the White House. There was nothing to see and I am sure that they did not expect to see anything. They merely stood in a lost sort of way. One felt as though the city

Mourning in America. After becoming president, Harry S. Truman led the nation in paying tribute to Franklin D. Roosevelt. Here he is at the FDR funeral in Hyde Park, New York, talking with the late president's daughter, Anna Roosevelt. Courtesy of the Truman Presidential Library

had vanished, leaving its inhabitants to wander about bewildered, looking for a familiar landmark."[6]

About 200,000 of them decided to line the route between the White House and Union Station. About 25,000 were in the plaza in front of the train station when the hearse bearing the president's casket arrived. Truman accompanied the Roosevelt family on the 17-car train that took them to Hyde Park.[7]

Roosevelt was laid to rest the next morning in New York. A 21-gun salute from artillery pieces greeted the president's body as the train arrived on a special spur that ended just below the Roosevelt estate on the banks of the Hudson River. Cadets from nearby West Point accompanied the body to the grave, moving at a slow funeral cadence of muted drums. Roosevelt was buried among 15-foot-high hedges. Truman, his wife, Bess, and their daughter, Margaret, stood with the Roosevelts. Mourners stood to the west, north, and east of the grave flanking it like a giant, upside-down, box-like U. King, Marshall, and Lieutenant General Barney Giles, representing the army air forces, were in front of the eastern phalanx, but were not in a position to see the graveside services. Leahy was with the members of the Cabinet a little further behind. The service itself was brief, taking less than twenty minutes. As the West Point cadets standing to the west fired off a three-gun volly, Roosevelt's dog, Fala, barked "ferociously" in response each time. As he had requested, the president had a gravestone that listed only his name and the dates of his birth and death.[8]

The man who replaced Roosevelt could not have been more different in background or personality, and it was now his job to decide policy and strategy for the end of the war. To any reasonable observer, the end of the war in the Pacific seemed to be far off in the future. Roosevelt had made no effort to keep Truman apprised about strategy or foreign policy, but Truman was far more capable of doing the job than even he realized.

Born in 1884, the new president was a man of the nineteenth century, rather than the twentieth. He never took to the typewriter and wrote plenty of letters by hand. He preferred traditional art such as Frederic Remington westerns to other modern forms of expression such as jazz. He read Mark Twain instead of F. Scott Fitzgerald. He disliked the idea of women smoking or having their hair bobbed. As a boy growing up in Independence, Missouri, he had always done well in history, and his family home always had books for him to read. "Reading history, to me, was far more than a romantic adventure. It was solid instruction and wise teaching which I somehow felt that I wanted and needed." He was a moderately observant Baptist. "I am by religion like everything else. I think there's more in acting than talking." Truman was loyal and fair-minded, willing to consider people on their merits. He was also prejudiced, at least on social issues, and had a flair for slurs that he directed toward almost every significant racial and ethnic group in America: blacks, Catholics, Hispanics, Italians, Irish, and Jews.[9]

He was tenacious and a romantic, two traits that he combined in his courtship of Bess Wallace. They had gone to school together and had been attracted to one another early on. He only seriously started trying to win her heart in 1910, nine years after they graduated from high school. She was clearly interested. Wallace was in her late twenties and was not getting any younger. In 1911, he asked for her hand in marriage in a letter. She turned him down, but kept seeing him romantically. After three years of dating, she told him that if she ever got married it would be to him. They agreed in 1913 to a secret engagement. Bess Wallace's mother thought little of Harry Truman. He had no education, and she thought her daughter could do better than him. An even bigger factor was that she refused to let go emotionally of Bess following her husband's suicide, which left her with feelings of shame. She worried about her family maintaining its leading status in Independence, Missouri. During this time, Truman worked the family farm with his father and brother. It was not the life he wanted to lead. When the United States entered World War I, he decided to enlist. Afraid of losing him, Wallace told him she wanted to get married. This time, he said no. "I don't think it would be right for me to ask you to tie yourself to a prospective cripple."[10]

Truman did a good job as a soldier and his regimental commander recommended him for a promotion to the rank of Major in the regular army. Truman, though, had no interest in a military career and returned to Missouri to marry Bess. He entered politics after his men's clothing store failed. After holding county-wide office, Truman decided to run for the U.S. Senate in 1934. The rural countryside was the key battlefield. "Fact is, I like roads," he remarked. "I like to move."[11]

He won and had his biggest impact in the Senate during his second term as chair of what was formally known as the Senate Special Committee to Investigate the National Defense Program, but more commonly as the Truman Committee. "I have had considerable experience in letting public contracts; and I have never yet found a contractor who, if not watched, would not leave the Government holding the bag," he told his colleagues. The Senate agreed and approved a resolution creating the committee. Composed of senators younger and junior to Truman, there was little doubt that the chairman would be the dominant force in committee proceedings. Truman led the committee well, making sure every member had some responsibility and an opportunity to stand out. A student of history, he knew that the Joint Committee on the Conduct of the War had been a major liability to Lincoln during the Civil War. Truman was determined to keep his commission from becoming counterproductive. He avoided matters of strategy, tactics, or the selection of unit commanders, issues that the Joint Committee took up in the Civil War. Still, Roosevelt would have preferred that the committee disband. Truman fumed about the issue to his wife: "It must be done or I'd tell him to go to hell. He's so damn afraid that he won't have all the power and glory that he won't let his friends help." Investigations tended to focus on large corporations rather than small and medium-sized businesses. In public, though, the committee was more than willing to be critical of both labor and management.[12]

Many observers of Washington saw that Truman was doing good work with the committee. Reporters from publications as diverse as the *New York Times*, the Washington *Evening Star*, the *St. Louis Post-Dispatch*, the *Nation, Look,* and *Business Week* wrote articles and editorials that praised Truman for making a constructive effort to combat price gouging, war profiteering, and bureaucratic incompetence. He was even the subject of a *Time* magazine cover story in 1943.[13]

Lightning struck in 1944 when Truman became the vice presidential nominee of the Democratic Party. His tenure as Vice President of the United States was brief. During his one month in office, he played no role in making policy or strategy, and in most cases no one had even bothered to inform him about current initiatives. Truman was, for all practical purposes, just another member of the general public when he walked into the family quarters of the White House on April 12 and heard Eleanor Roosevelt tell him: "Harry, the President is dead."[14]

Since Okinawa was the only major U.S. ground operation in the late spring and early summer of 1945, the costly nature of seizing control of the island surprised and shocked the American public. Truman was at one with the people on this matter. He had taken office during the battle on Okinawa and became deeply concerned that the conquest of the main Japanese islands would entail even larger losses given the larger number of personnel that were going to take part in this undertaking. The president's aversion to heavy losses was a new dynamic and changed American attitudes toward a British role in the Pacific.

On May 29, the *New York Herald Tribune* published an article critical of Buckner's refusal to launch a second landing. Homer Bigart, the author of the piece, correctly observed that the Japanese were fighting a battle of attrition in the southern half of the island. He also noted that the marines took the northern half of Okinawa quickly, because the Japanese made little effort to defend that section of the island. Once the III Amphibious Corps finished taking the north, Buckner deployed them in the south, using what Bigart called "ultra-conservative" tactics. "A landing on southern Okinawa would have hastened the encirclement of Shuri. Instead of an end run, we persisted in frontal attacks," he wrote. "It was hey-diddle-diddle straight down the middle." Syndicated columnist David Lawrence used this dispatch as the basis for two columns that harshly criticized Buckner's strategy and interservice leadership. In his first column, Lawrence insisted that an amphibious assault would have worked and saved American lives. He noted that Buckner had no combat experience and wondered why Nimitz had not ordered a second assault. A week later, he called the battle a "fiasco," and blamed Buckner. In a deliberate distortion of the facts, Lawrence wrote that the marines' rapid conquest of the north was ample proof of the soundness of their tactics. He demanded an immediate investigation into Buckner's decision.[15]

Buckner was not one to take criticism lightly, and he vigorously defended his approach in a press conference he held on Okinawa in which he discussed American strategy and progress on the island. The purpose of taking the island, Buckner said, was to use its airfields to bomb Japan and to build it up as a base for the invasion of the main Japanese islands. This mission and the geography of southern Okinawa worked against a second landing. Reefs would have made an amphibious assault difficult and the hilly terrain would have made it easy for the Japanese to contain American forces on the beach. "If we'd scattered our forces we might have got licked, or it might have unduly prolonged the campaign; or we might have been forced to call on additional troops, which we did not want to do."[16]

Buckner also had defenders in the navy. When Nimitz read the Lawrence columns, he responded with a statement that attacked the journalist and defended Buckner. "The article, which has been widely reprinted shows that the author has been badly misinformed, so badly as to give the impression that he has been made use of for purposes which are not in the best interest of the United States," the admiral charged. While the criticism might seem reasonable in the United States, he explained that the invasion of the island was planned and his staff had considered a number of options. "During the operation each service took losses and each service inflicted great damage to the enemy. Comparisons between services are out of place and ill-advised." A reporter for the Associated Press characterized the admiral's statement as "rare" in its bluntness, while Richard Kluger notes in his history of the *New York Herald Tribune* that Nimitz avoided criticizing any of Bigart's reporting.[17]

Buckner never lived to see Nimitz's statement. On June 18, he visited the 1st Marine Division. His inspection trips often provoked Japanese fire. He usually arrived in a jeep flying the three stars of his flag, accompanied by a large band of staff officers. Instead of wearing subdued insignia on these

CHAPTER TWELVE

visits, Buckner wore three silver stars displayed prominently on his helmet. These symbols of his rank were visible even from the distance of the Japanese positions, and a marine officer recalled that this showy display regularly got a response from Japanese artillery crews as they attempted to kill this high-ranking officer. In most cases, this shelling started just after the general left. Not this time. Climbing a hill to visit a forward observation post, the general expressed concern about the plight of Okinawan civilians. Marines at the post saw Buckner's helmet with three shiny stars, and asked him to remove it and wear one that was less conspicuous. Buckner said no, telling the marines he had no intention of hiding from the Japanese. Minutes later, a battalion command post on a nearby hill radioed a warning that Buckner's stars were clearly visible from a long distance away. The general finally removed his helmet, placed it on a rock to his left, and put another one on that had no rank insignia, but it was too late. A Japanese artillery unit had seen Buckner, and as he stood just beyond the crest of the hill with his hands akimbo looking in their direction, they fired a round. The shell exploded on the rock next to Buckner, tearing a hole in the left side of his chest.[18]

Officers standing 3 feet behind him got up unhurt, but saw Buckner lying on the ground, bloody, with mud splattered in his hair. "General Buckner has been hit!" a radio operator yelled into his equipment. The marines carried him off the hill on a poncho. Buckner asked if anyone else was hurt and seemed relieved when told no one else was harmed. He died a few minutes later at a battalion aid station, while a marine private held his hand and kept repeating, "You are going home, General; you are homeward bound." Silence gripped the small crowd surrounding the general, until someone began reciting the Twenty-third Psalm: "Yea, though I walk through the valley of the shadow of death, I will fear no evil: for thou art with me . . ."[19]

The reaction to his death in the United States showed that the newspaper controversy the week before had done little to discredit him. Buckner was the highest-ranking officer to die from enemy action in the war, and his death was front-page news across the country. The accounts that followed honored him without reservation. A *New York Times* reporter on the island gave him the titles "defender of Alaska, liberator of the Aleutians," and "conqueror of Okinawa." The article concluded with quotes from King, Nimitz, Secretary of War Henry Stimson, and Secretary of the Navy James Forrestal paying tribute to both Buckner's ability and leadership. No marines were quoted, although Forrestal observed that he was "held in high regard in the Navy and Marine Corps." The *New York Herald Tribune* ran an extremely flattering obituary, which included a section on the Battle of Okinawa.[20] Editorial writers commenting on his passing fell into either one of two groups. A number of journalists praised him as a tough, demanding warrior, but one who was considerate of his men's needs and interests. In Kentucky, the Louisville *Courier-Journal*, the modern incarnation of the paper that his father had once edited, noted: "General Buckner was a professional soldier" and that "he died as such a man would choose to die, in action with his men." The *Cleveland Plain Dealer* praised him simply as a "soldier's general," while the *Los Angeles Times* called him "a soldier's ideal of a fighting leader."[21] Other journalists chose to use their tributes to defend him against Bigart and Lawrence. The *Honolulu Star-Bulletin* and the Portland *Oregonian* argued that recent events, including Nimitz's defense and the impending defeat of the Japanese, had repudiated any criticism of the general. Admiral William V. Pratt, military affairs columnist for *Newsweek*, made similar comments. He rhetorically asked if Lawrence even had the expertise to comment on amphibious landings: "Does the source of the criticism, coming from an excellent reporter but one who, nevertheless, is not thoroughly versed in the art of war, insure its complete reliability?"[22]

It was Buckner's death that brought the controversy to an end—at least temporarily. With the general dead, questioning his ability was in bad taste. Lessons could be learned, but there was no profit in continuing to speak ill of the dead. If Buckner had made mistakes, there was nothing that could be done about it now.[23]

Concern about the casualty rate, however, remained simmering below the surface. There had been some momentary concern about the casualties at Iwo Jima, but the power of Joseph Rosenthal's Pulitzer Prize–winning photograph of marines raising the U.S. flag gave that battle a dramatic conclusion that wrapped the engagement in glory that was difficult to question. Okinawa never had such an end, nor was it a major turning point in the war like Midway. Just after the landings on Okinawa, George C. Marshall told a group of academics, "We are approaching one of the most difficult periods of the war." One of his concerns was "the possibility of a general letdown in this country."[24]

Truman, like any good politician, was alert to public sentiment, and despite the high position he held, he had about as much information on strat-

The New Commander-in-Chief. Harry S. Truman taking the oath of office as president of the United States on April 12, 1945. Courtesy of the Truman Presidential Library

egy and military operations as the average, attentive newspaper reader. The day before Bigart's article appeared in the *Herald Tribune*, former president Herbert Hoover met with the new occupant of the Oval Office and warned him that an invasion would entail losses of between 500,000 and 1,000,000 Americans. Hoover did not invent these numbers. Military officers were leaking information to the former president. These figures had their effect and worried Truman. As the controversy about Okinawa swirled in the press, the new president decided to take action. He informed the Joint Chiefs that he wanted to talk to them about the war in the Pacific. In a notation that Truman made in his diary the day before this meeting, he stated, "I have to decide Japanese strategy—shall we invade Japan proper or shall we bomb and blockade? That is my hardest decision to date. But I'll make it when I have all the facts."[25]

In a memo that Leahy sent to the other members of the Joint Chiefs of Staff about this meeting, he made Truman's concerns plain. The president wanted "an estimate of the time required and estimate of the losses in killed and wounded that will result from an invasion of Japan proper." He also explained that it was Truman's "intention to make his decision on the campaign with the purpose of economizing to the maximum extent possible in the loss of American lives. Economy in the use of time and in money cost is comparatively unimportant."[26]

The Chiefs walked into this meeting exceptionally divided in their views on how to end the war with Japan. They had little problem with the goal of forcing Japan to accept unconditional surrender. The question was what strategy best served the nation's interests in reaching that policy objective. The dispute pitted those who favored invasion against those who advocated a siege or blockade.[27] Marshall's dominant worry was about time. How much longer would the public tolerate and endure the sacrifices of war? Time was a resource of limited quantity. "A democracy cannot fight a Seven Years War," he told a biographer after the war. Marshall believed that the United States had to win the war quickly, before the public reached its limits. "War weariness in the United States may demand the return home of those who have fought long and well in the European war regardless of the effect of such a return on the prosecution of the Japanese war," he advised his Joint Chief colleagues in May. At the same time, military and political factors demanded that the United States maintain the pressure on Japan. Other operations, no matter their advantages, risked losing the public's resolution to see the war through to its conclusion.[28]

Arnold would miss the meeting with the president; he was on a tour of facilities in the Pacific. His views on this matter were simple. He thought that airpower alone could defeat the Japanese. The geography of the Pacific, however, was working against the army air forces. The Americans had access to only a few airfields and runways hundreds of miles from Japan. They needed more bases that were closer. Arnold favored an invasion, but only of Kyushu, the southernmost of the Japanese home islands, with the sole purpose of acquiring more airfields.[29]

The representatives of the navy, Leahy and King, both thought an invasion was unnecessary. Despite this view, King was concerned about the public: "The American people will weary of it quickly, and that pressure at home will force a negotiated peace, before the Japs are really licked." He worried about "a long, plodding, costly war that will stretch out for years to come." He thought, though, that a naval blockade of the home islands would be sufficient to force Japan to surrender. Despite this position, he believed planning for an invasion was a prudent move that "could be reversed if it seemed necessary." He did think that the United States would require bases and facilities on Kyushu and considered it "essential to a strategy of strangulation." There was a reason then behind his partial support for an invasion. Leahy was even stronger in his opinion. King, as Leahy admitted in his memoirs, "had never been as positively opposed to invasion as I had."

The war was basically over. "The Army did not appear to be able to understand that the Navy, with some Army air assistance, already had defeated Japan." He saw no political need to occupy Japan. The cost in lives and resources would far exceed the value of what could be gained. "It is my opinion at the present time that a surrender of Japan can be arranged with terms that can be accepted by Japan and that will make fully satisfactory provision for America's defense against future trans-Pacific aggression."[30]

Marshall had different ideas and he prepared carefully for this meeting. The British Pacific Fleet and the ongoing deployment of Royal Air Force squadrons became assets in his efforts to make sure that Truman approved Operation: OLYMPIC—the invasion of Kyushu. Marshall intended to use America's British allies as a lever against hesitation.[31] He also made sure he had casualty figures that would seem reasonable to Truman. The problem the general faced: there were a number of different estimates circulating on the rate of casualties. What might seem like a simple task becomes extremely complicated when individuals can be counted more than once: someone could get wounded, recover, go back into combat, and get wounded again. People would also be hurt or killed in noncombat operations: something heavy might fall on them while they were in transit to the combat zone. Others broke from the mental and psychological trauma of combat and became noncombat casualties. Would the losses in aircrews and naval personnel also be included in these calculations? What type of formula would staff officers use to come up with their figures? The math reflected different variables: length of the combat operation, strength of the defender, and pace of the advance were just a few of the factors that might be represented in a formula. Using different formulas, different officers in different commands came to different predictions. What is important to note is that all these calculations were nothing more than educated guesses. "The cost in casualties of the main operations against Japan are not subject to accurate estimates," an early draft of a paper by the Joint Staff planners stated.[32]

Such qualifications, complexity, and ambiguity were unlikely to impress the new president. Marshall needed some clean, simple, hard facts to give to Truman. As the theater commander, MacArthur's estimates would speak with powerful authority. After Marshall requested the information, MacArthur replied with the following figures for the first ninety days of the operation, which he stated in his message were "for planning purposes":

Time Period	Battle Casualties	Nonbattle Casualties
D-Day to D-Day plus 30	50,800	4,200
D-Day plus 30 to D-Day plus 60	27,150	4,200
D-Day plus 60 to D-Day plus 90	27,100	4,200

All told, these figures add up to 117,650 wounded or dead Americans. These figures were a bit light. Staff officers had deducted service personnel that could return to duty.[33]

Still, this cable troubled Marshall. Brigadier General George A. Lincoln, Chief of the Strategy and Policy Group, Operations Division of the War Department General Staff, was Marshall's main strategic planner, and he called this estimate "a conservative figure on the topside." Lincoln thought that this calculation represented worst-case scenario planning for managing evacuations and controlling the flow of replacements. Marshall, though, wanted some clarification. "The President is very much concerned as to the number of casualties we will receive in the OLYMPIC operation," he informed MacArthur. "Is the estimate given in your C-19571 of 50,800 for the period of D to D+30 based on plans for medical installations to be established or is it your best estimate of the casualties you anticipate from the operational viewpoint."[34]

MacArthur could easily read between the lines and understood Marshall's unstated subtext. He responded with a strong argument in favor of OLYMPIC. "Estimate of casualties contained in my C-19571 was a routine report submitted direct by a staff section without higher reference for medical and replacement planning purposes. The estimate was derived from the casualty rates in Normandy and Okinawa the highest our forces have sustained," he explained in his response.

The estimate is purely academic and routine and was made for planning purposes alone. It had not come to my prior attention. I do not anticipate such a high rate of loss. I believe the operation presents less hazards of excessive loss than any other that has been suggested and its decisive effect will eventually save lives by eliminating wasteful operations of a nondecisive character. I regard the operation as the most economical one in effort and lives that is possible.

CHAPTER TWELVE

His closing was strong: "I most earnestly recommend no change in OLYMPIC. Additional subsidiary attacks will simply build up our final total casualties." One thing was missing from his cable. He never provided Marshall with a lower estimate.[35]

The moment of decision came at 3:30 P.M. on Monday, June 18, when the Joint Chiefs of Staff met with Truman in the White House along with Stimson, Forrestal, and Assistant Secretary of War John McCloy. Lieutenant General Ira Eaker was present representing Arnold and the army air forces. Before the meeting was over, this group would discuss a wide range of issues, including race, domestic politics, Okinawa and Iwo Jima, the atomic bomb, casualty estimates, unconditional surrender, and command and control in the Pacific. Truman might have been new to the job, but he was the president and as such he set the agenda for the meeting. He started off by saying he wanted to get more information about the final operations against Japan. He asked each of the Chiefs, including Eaker, for their opinions.[36]

Marshall went first. The general began by reading a portion of the memo that had been prepared for Truman, but the president apparently never actually read the document. Marshall explained that the main Japanese islands were isolated from the rest of their empire and that the army air forces had delivered devastating damage to industrial targets in Japan. Taking control of Kyushu, he said, was the next operation that made the most sense. It would allow the United States to do two things: first, it would give the army air forces and the navy bases to tighten their blockade on Japan; and second, it would provide a staging area for the invasion of the Tokyo Plain. A statement in the minutes of the meeting easily summarizes Marshall's views but also the basic U.S. strategy in the summer of 1945: "We are bringing to bear against the Japanese every weapon and all the force we can employ and there is no reduction in our maximum possible application of bombardment and blockade, while at the same time we are pressing invasion preparations." On the subject of casualties, Marshall told Truman that American experiences in the Pacific war had been so diverse it was wrong to try to predict numbers for an invasion of Japan.[37]

Marshall went on, noting that MacArthur's command from March 1, 1944, to May 1, 1945, had a U.S. killed–to–Japanese killed ratio of 1 to 22. It is important to note that this ratio was incorrect. The campaign to retake the Philippines had been extremely costly, but the 1 to 22 ratio is what Marshall put before the president. He said the first thirty days in Kyushu would most likely be less than what it took to retake Luzon. If the Japanese defenders on Kyushu fought to the last man, this campaign could end up being extremely bloody. No one, particularly Truman, appears to have considered this fact. Marshall was providing Truman with honest and sobering information, but he took care to answer the issue of casualties indirectly. In his diary, Leahy claims that Marshall gave a direct answer of 63,000 casualties, which he might have done using Luzon as an analogy, but none of the other participants in the meeting who kept diaries at the time made similar assertions. The minutes of this meeting offer no verbatim quotes, but several lines that follow this presentation summarized well the general's thinking: "It is a grim fact that there is not an easy, bloodless way to victory in war and it is the thankless task of the leaders to maintain their firm outward front which holds the resolution of their subordinates. Any irresolution in the leaders may result in costly weakening and indecision in the subordinates."[38]

After briefly discussing command and control issues and Russian entry into the Pacific war, Marshall then read MacArthur's statement. Marshall concluded his presentation, explaining that airpower alone lacked the force to do the job. The combined power of two English-speaking air forces had failed to defeat Germany on their own. There was no reason to think they would do so against Japan.[39]

King then spoke. He took less time than Marshall and basically supported his army counterpart, but only to a degree. The admiral believed that taking control of Kyushu was necessary to conduct a siege and, as a result, he was direct in explaining that he would support OLYMPIC and OLYMPIC only. Planning for the operation was prudent; if this effort never started it would be impossible to launch an invasion at all, but his ambiguity was readily apparent when he said that it was an option that could cancel at a later date and one they needed to revisit in August and September.[40]

Leahy then spoke and tried to direct the group's attention to the issue that had brought the meeting about: casualties. He said the U.S. casualty rate on Okinawa had been 35 percent. He added that this percentage should be applied to the number of troops that would fight on Kyushu. King replied that Okinawa and Kyushu were geographically different. There had been little room to maneuver on Okinawa, and frontal assaults were the only option. Kyushu was bigger and offered more maneuver room. With this statement King had indirectly validated Buckner's campaign on Okinawa. The only wrinkle in this statement was that King was wrong. The island had limited terrain on which battlefield operations could take place. Marshall then informed the group that there would be 766,700 assault troops taking part in OLYMPIC. No one, including either Leahy or Truman, did the math to figure out that 35 percent of 766,700 was 268,345. Leahy did contest the geographical matter, explaining that the main value of taking Kyushu was that it would give the United States more air bases to strike the rest of Japan.[41]

Truman then asked for Eaker's views as an airman. The general explained that Arnold agreed with Marshall. Eaker also pointed out that the United States needed more space for airfields and airdromes. He noted that air forces suffered higher casualties when they faced the enemy on their own and that American crews over Japan were suffering losses of 2 percent per mission or 30 percent a month. Delay only worked to the enemy's advantage.[42]

Truman then asked the Joint Chiefs of Staff if they supported an invasion of Kyushu. All of them, according to the minutes, said yes.[43]

The conversation then moved into the political realm of unconditional surrender. Except for Leahy, the Joint Chiefs remained silent. Their job was to implement, not make, policy. Stimson said he suspected that there was a large group of influential figures in Japan who no longer supported the war. They were patriotic and would fight along with the rest of their countrymen if attacked, but the United States might do something to help this group come to power. Truman asked Stimson if being attacked by a white nation would unify Japanese resistance. The secretary said race could indeed play such a role. Forrestal made some brief remarks, before McCloy suggested that the United States should make an effort to help Japanese moderates come to power. Leahy then voiced his qualms about unconditional surrender. Japan was no longer a threat to the United States, and the U.S. insistence on these terms would only increase American casualties. Truman explained that he had been thinking on the same lines, but changing public opinion was a power beyond those he possessed. If Congress wanted to weigh in on the issue, that would be fine. As the meeting ended, the president made a remark that was captured in the minutes as: "He had hoped that there was a possibility of preventing an Okinawa from one end of Japan to the other." By this comment Truman meant a long and costly engagement. He expressed his satisfaction with the situation and told the Chiefs that they should go forward with the invasion of Kyushu. He would hold off judgment on other operations until a later date. The discussion then turned to the topic of the atomic bomb.[44]

What happened at the June 18 meeting is a highly contentious issue, but it was hardly the decisive turning point in history that Leahy and Truman had expected. Marshall was largely responsible for maintaining forward progress on OLYMPIC. He preserved the tenuous consensus on strategy for ending the war, and he answered Truman's questions, but only indirectly.[45]

Disputes about this meeting have produced numerous and detailed studies, some of them prize winners.[46] Varying interpretations of what happened at this meeting were part of the extremely intense and public dispute about the *Enola Gay* display at the National Air and Space Museum in 1995.[47] Much of this argument is based on an assumption of moral arithmetic: the more Americans that would have died in the invasion, the more acceptable the use of the atomic bombs. Stimson and Truman established the foundations of this ethical, moral, but ahistorical debate with the secretary of war's memoirs and the president's letter to the historian supervising the official U.S. Air Force history of World War II, claiming that the choice the U.S. faced in 1945 was invasion *or* atomic bombing.[48] This assertion is just plain wrong.

There never was any either-or decision. In the June 18 meeting, Truman, to his credit, was genuinely concerned about the likely casualty ratios. It should be noted, though, that there were a number of other military leaders who were also worried about these figures. This concern was no manufactured postwar myth. Truman and Stimson, however, mislead their readers, as politicians tend to do at times. Truman can be forgiven if he were confused on that day back in 1945, but only a bit. He had enough information to know that OLYMPIC would be costly, but the uniformed leaders of the military services that had just defeated Germany had offered him no alternative. When asked, all four of the Joint Chiefs, including Leahy, favored Operation: OLYMPIC, and Truman approved the invasion of Kyushu. At least for the time being, the United States would go forward with an invasion *and* a blockade *and* a bombing campaign that would target cities with conventional *and* atomic explosives.

King's support for the invasion was conditional and marked with ambiguity, and unlike Arnold, much less Eaker, he could and did openly and bluntly oppose Marshall. Two days after the meeting, King told the other Joint Chiefs that the briefing the president had received was "not satisfactory." The Chiefs had failed to answer Truman's basic question, and he wrote that "it appears to me that the Chiefs of Staff will have to give an estimate of casualties expected in the operation." Nimitz had different casualty estimates, and they included losses the navy would take. A "fair estimate" for the losses that a U.S. fleet would take assembled off the shores of Japan would be "at approximately the same rate" as those suffered at Okinawa. This document contradicts Leahy's claims in his diary that Marshall gave Truman a direct answer. Marshall responded to King a week later: "In view of the fact that casualties were discussed at the meeting on 18 June, it seems unnecessary and undesirable for the Joint Chiefs of Staff to make estimates, which at best can be only speculative." The differences between King and Marshall, the U.S. Navy and the U.S. Army, would continue to simmer for the rest of the summer.[49]

Still, the planned invasion left leaders within the U.S. Army unnerved and concerned. "We had just gone through a bitter experience at Okinawa. This had been preceded by a number of similar experiences in other Pacific islands down north of Australia," Marshall recalled in retirement. "With this knowledge, particularly of Okinawa, where I think we killed 120,000 Japanese without a surrender—I think there were several badly wounded that we picked up, but literally not a surrender—it was to be expected that the resistance in Japan, with their home ties, would be even more severe." Stimson had identical concerns. In this atmosphere, anything that reduced American casualties, be they foreign troops or new weapons, would be welcome.[50]

On Okinawa, General Joseph W. Stilwell, Buckner's successor as the Commanding General of the Tenth Army, shared similar worries. At the end of June, he inspected Shuri. "A mess," the veteran of World War I recorded in his diary. "Much like Verdun: *Japs held here nearly 2 months.*" In a memo he wrote to Marshall, he expressed his concerns. "The terrain in Japan is rugged and lends itself to defense; unless we are prepared for the conditions we are likely to meet not only a determined defense in well dug-in positions in depth, but the fanatical opposition of the entire population, who will resort to any extremity to oppose us." He offered several suggestions to Marshall based on what Americans had encountered on Okinawa. In order to have enough firepower, the army should provide adequate numbers of mortars, self-propelled artillery, and recoilless guns; the number of flamethrowers and tank-dozers should be increased for units that would have to reduce pillboxes; and individual infantrymen should be provided body armor. He also recommended that paratroopers be used to attack Japanese units in the rear.[51]

Stilwell saved his most controversial suggestion for last. "Consideration should be given to the use of gas. We are not bound in any way not to use it, and the stigma of using it on the civilian population can be avoided by restricting it to attack on military targets."[52] MacArthur was even stronger in his views. While Arnold was on an inspection of units in the Pacific at this time, and directly quotes MacArthur telling him he could "see no reason why we should not use gas right now against Japan proper. Any kind of gas."[53]

Marshall was thinking along the same lines as Stilwell. In late May, he ordered a series of tests to determine the tactical feasibility of using gas against Japanese units. The Chief of Staff knew that these weapons trials would have enormous political repercussions and rejected recommendations from officers in the Operations Division of the General Staff that the army also consider using gas against Japanese cities. In May, June, and July, personnel assigned to conduct Project: SPHINX attempted to determine the effectiveness of different types of gases and delivery systems using enemy rabbits and goats as test subjects in caves, tunnels, and mines. These experiments showed that gas was no magic wand and would have to be used in conjunction with other weapons.[54]

Marshall was willing to consider any of the resources he had available, including the tactical use of nuclear weapons. "We had to visualize very heavy casualties," he remarked later, "unless we had enough atomic bombs at the time to supplement the troop action, if the bomb proved satisfactory for that purpose." He was just developing his ideas on how to use the bomb tactically. The danger that radiation would pose to American ground forces moving in or near these bombed areas was unknown at this point in time and was never a factor in these early considerations. The early thinking about tactical use was that atomic bombs might destroy entire army divisions or Japanese communication centers.[55]

The Joint Chiefs also pondered the diplomatic and political factors that might allow Japan to surrender without an invasion. On July 16, while at the Potsdam Conference, Cunningham made an important entry in his diary about remarks the American Chiefs made during a session of the Combined Chiefs of Staff: "We questioned them as to whether it was proposed to define 'unconditional surrender' in the case of the Japanese war with a view to reassuring the Japs that the Emperor + their mode of life would be allowed to remain. We found them surprisingly willing to talk. Leahy most insistent that the President would like to have a memo from the P.M. suggesting some reduction in the terms." According to Cunningham, Marshall believed "that the moment the Russians come in was the psychological moment to let the Japs know what the term 'unconditional surrender' did not mean." Sir Andrew considered the significance of the comments as he wrote in his journal. "Thinking it over I am convinced that both the President + USCOS would like to find some way of bringing the war quickly to an end with[out] incurring the terrible casualties that may come with an invasion of the main islands of Japan. They are however frightened of the American public opinion + would like a proposal to come from us."[56]

Several negative factors were at work in the summer of 1945 that made these precautions seem wise. For the first time in the war, the United States was starting to encounter serious logistical problems. That summer, American military leaders faced three sets of problems, any one of which could easily be considered a crisis. Port facilities were proving to be inadequate to the task at hand in two different ways. The west coast of the United States simply could not handle the traffic that an invasion of Japan would require. Rail lines leading into the ports of Los Angeles, Seattle, San Francisco, and Portland were unable to handle the needed tonnage. Storage facilities and labor resources were another set of complications. In an effort to alleviate the looming crisis, army transportation officers were planning to ship out of Canadian cities, use facilities on the Gulf of Mexico and have ships transit the Panama Canal, and send supplies to India and Burma from east coast cities through the Suez Canal. In fact, the navy already was facing many of these problems. One navy storage facility had a backlog of a million tons. The navy had already started using cities on the east coast for low-priority items. An even bigger problem was the limited capacity of ports in the Pacific. The docks in the Philippines lacked storage facilities or were too damaged from combat operations to handle the traffic coming from the United States. Okinawa was no better. A significant backlog had already developed on that island due to its limited dock capacity. Other possibilities, including the use of facilities in Hawaii and Saipan and direct transit to ports in Kyushu once they were under U.S. control, simply failed to make up the difference.[57]

Another significant problem facing the Americans was that the number of cargo ships they had available for the Pacific war was inadequate to their needs. As the American advance reached Japan itself, the amount of supplies needed to reach the front lines was growing in kind. Supply requirements remained in Europe. The Allies needed to maintain their armies of occupation, return soldiers to their homes, and keep up civilian commerce. At this point, American shipyards were making the wrong type of vessels. There was no longer any need to produce more warships. The threat in the Atlantic had ended, and the U.S. Navy could easily handle what remained of the Imperial Japanese Navy with the current fleet. The lack of cargo ships was a problem. Factories across America were producing the supplies needed to fight the war, but getting this material to combat units was proving extremely difficult. Buckner had learned about the limited number of cargo ships when kamikazes sank two of them off Okinawa. In early May, a conference of army and navy logistical planners expected to use 25 million deadweight tons of shipping in both the Atlantic and Pacific per quarter. The United States had access to 32 million deadweight tons. That extra 7 million would serve commercial interests but would involve an actual reduction in civilian shipping. The logistical planners just assumed that military necessity would give the required number of ships and that the American people would have to endure further shortages on the home front. Given the public belief that victory in Europe would bring at least some relief from wartime rationing, this expectation seems unrealistic.[58]

Manpower resources were the third supply factor that presented a major problem to the U.S. armed services. Personnel shortages had been a concern for Stimson toward the end of 1944. He discussed the matter several times with Marshall and Roosevelt. Before leaving for Okinawa, Stilwell, during his tenure as Commanding General, Army Ground Forces, had warned that the U.S. military had basically incorporated all the young men in the country available for active duty into one of the armed services. The army was rapidly going through its infantrymen, and there were going to be shortages in the number of riflemen available for combat operations. The end of the war in Europe complicated manpower issues even more. The American public expected that there would be some relief with half the war won. The resulting demobilization of the army or at least part of it and a high rate of consumption were going to make it difficult to put an adequate number of men in uniform. The army air forces tried to resist a reduction at first—before political reality set in. Plans for downsizing the service were inadequate to the task at hand. According to one unit historian, the outcome of this effort to ignore the facts of life was "utter confusion, pervading all echelons of command." The navy also tried to ignore, or at least put off, demobilization. Nimitz recommended that the navy wait on reducing its size until after OLYMPIC. The admiral had a good argument. Most navy personnel were stationed in the Pacific, and it was only reasonable that the service delay any reduction until it had fulfilled its main mission. How such a position would have fared against public pressure is questionable.[59]

If these problems were not difficult enough for American planners to deal with, intelligence officers were seeing troubling indicators about enemy strength. In July, reconnaissance flights flew over all 243 known airfields in Japan and photo analysts counted 8,010 planes. Most of these machines would become kamikazes. The interception of signals intelligence from Kyushu produced an almost identical number. From enemy radio signals American intelligence officers could tell that the Japanese were fortifying the exact sites where MacArthur planned to stage OLYMPIC. The defenders were placing heavy artillery in caves to cover the beaches and were digging tunnels to connect field fortifications and concrete bunkers.[60]

This information had Major General Charles A. Willoughby, MacArthur's intelligence officer, extremely disturbed. A large man at 6 feet, 3 inches, who moved from brooding to fiery explosions of temper, Willoughby was utterly loyal to MacArthur, but a mediocre analyst of raw data. On July 29, he warned: "If this deployment is not checked it may grow to a point where we attack on a ratio of one (1) to one (1) which is not the recipe for victory." He also added that the growth of the defending force would most likely continue. "There is a strong likelihood that additional major units will enter the area before target date; we are engaged in a race against time by which the ratio attack-effort vis-à-vis defense capacity is perilously close." Military historian Edward J. Drea notes, "The one failing of which Willoughby was never guilty was overestimation of Japanese forces." His analysis was uneven: sometimes it was on the mark, and at other times it underestimated the forces the Japanese would put up against MacArthur's men.[61] If Willoughby was concerned, then there was good reason to be worried.

These concerns would lead military and naval planning officers in Washington to reconsider the then-current plans for OLYMPIC. This reassessment also included scrapping this operation altogether and looking for a new site. To some degree, this new evaluation was just the product of good staff work, but had officials in Washington known about the most closely guarded secret of the war, this effort would have been more than just a precaution.[62]

The best-guarded secret of the war was not the code-breaking efforts of American and British intelligence personnel, or even the development of the atomic bomb, but the fact that MacArthur's headquarters lost the plans for the invasion of Japan. Embarrassed intelligence officers did an exceptional job of covering up their failure, and it took military historian Alvin D. Coox fifteen years to piece together the story. Coox discovered that at some point that summer, Japanese agents acquired these plans. Security was strict in regard to U.S. personnel, but in an example of racial, social, and class bias, no one paid much attention to the Filipino custodial staff. After the war, when U.S. personnel were interviewing Japanese officers about the war, one of the things they were trying to learn was how the Imperial Japanese Army had placed their defending units in the perfect positions to defend against OLYMPIC. Had they some source of intelligence? Japanese officers said no. Their preparations had been the product of competent staff work. There were only a few places where the Americans might have staged an amphibious assault. In the end, the Japanese success in obtaining copies of the invasion plans had no impact on the war. The Japanese spies were never able to get the plans back to Tokyo. Had news of this security breach made its way back to Washington, though, it could easily have had a dramatic impact on decisions involving strategy and policy.[63]

Using allies was another possible way to deal with the expected surge in casualties. This idea was something that the American public was pushing. Truman's concern about casualties accelerated this inclination regardless of operational complications. Editorials in the *Chicago Daily Tribune*, the *San Francisco Examiner,* and the *Washington Post* faulted the British for making little contribution to the crusade against the Japanese.[64] Field-Marshal Sir Henry Wilson, the new head of the British Joint Staff Mission in Washington, wrote to Brooke in late April, "The belittling of what our forces are doing, as compared to the US Forces, is on the increase, and, in addition, there is continual sniping at our policy, intentions and administration in every theatre. This will, I fear, have a tendency to increase when the war changes completely to the Pacific."[65]

In the chambers of the House of Representatives, Leon H. Gavin of Pennsylvania, after noting that many allies had been in the war longer than

CHAPTER TWELVE

Jumbo. Churchill sent Wilson to Washington to serve as the head of the British Military Mission. In this position, he gave Brooke accurate information about sentiment in the Pentagon. In a sign of respect for their allies, the Joint Chiefs of Staff met him at the airport when he arrived in Washington. From left to right: Air Marshal Douglas Colyar, Lieutenant General Sir Gordon MacReady, Admiral Sir James Somerville, Wilson, Leahy, and Marshall. Courtesy of the U.S. National Archives

the United States and had made important contributions to the cause, declared, "When the European war ends all the manpower of the Allies and total resources and equipment should go into the South Pacific for a speedy and total victory." Other members of Congress were making similar comments to American generals and British diplomats, but in much harsher and hostile language. Average Americans were beginning to express this view in their own way. Sir Gerald Campbell, Director General of the British Information Service, reported on a trend at dance clubs where American girls refused to dance with sailors of the Royal Navy because the United Kingdom was absent from the fight in the Pacific. "We are definitely on the downward grade in the opinion of the average American," he stated succinctly.[66]

The British ambassador in Washington, the Earl of Halifax, made a similar report that focused on the opinions of influential Americans. "Problem of British participation, has of course been discussed intensively on and off since Pearl Harbour and despite reiterated statements to the contrary of Prime Minister and all other responsible British statesmen and newspapers, it is still generally assumed that we may not carry too much of the burden," he stated in the abbreviated language of diplomatic cables.

> We must naturally be prepared for criticism from some quarters whatever we do: if we prosecute Eastern War with might and main, we shall be told by some people that we are really fighting for our colonial possessions the better to exploit them and that ourselves and Dutch and French to perpetuate our unregenerate colonial Empires; while if we are judged not to have gone all out, that is because we are letting America fight her own war with little aid after having let her pull our chestnuts out of European fire.

Like many other British officials, he attributed much of this sentiment to Admiral King. "There are probably elements throughout Navy Department likely to be prey to both these lines of simultaneous thought, torn as they are by desires to make Pacific victory as purely and American victory as possible and not to let us off too great a share of heat and burden of the day."[67]

The end of the war in Europe required a fairly immediate decision on strategy in the Far East. The British could easily take the position that the allied strategy for the war had been to defeat Germany first and engage in holding operations against Japan, which is what they had done, but with the Nazis defeated the matter had to have a resolution. "We want if possible, to participate with all three services in the attacks against Japan," Brooke explained on the pages of his diary. "It is however not easy to make plans as the Americans seem unable to decide between a policy of invasion as opposed to one of encirclement."[68]

Brooke also knew the attitude of the prime minister would be another issue. The relationship between Churchill and the Chiefs was strained when victory arrived in Europe. The prime minister then made an effort to rectify the situation. When the Queen's father, the Earl of Strathmore, died,

it created an opening in the Order of the Thistle, one of the most prestigious orders of chivalry in the United Kingdom. Membership in the order
was limited to fewer than thirty members outside of the royal family, and
then only to Scots. Churchill suggested Cunningham to the King as the successor to Lord Strathmore. The admiral was touched: "It was so unexpected that I was rather at a loss for words." When the prime minister gave
a radio address to Great Britain on May 13, he included a passage praising
the work of the Chiefs.

> And here is the moment when I pay my personal tribute to the British
> Chiefs of Staff with whom I worked in the closest intimacy through-
> out these heavy, stormy years. There have been very few changes in
> this small powerful and capable body of men who, sinking all Service
> differences and judging the problems of the war as a whole, have
> worked together in perfect harmony with each other. In Field-Mar-
> shal Brooke, in Admiral Pound, succeeded after his death by Admiral
> Andrew Cunningham, and in Marshal of the Royal Air Force Portal,
> a team was formed who deserve the highest honour in direction of
> the whole British war strategy and in its relations with that of our al-
> lies.

It says much about the Chiefs' views toward Churchill that when he
toasted them at a small gathering at 10 Downing Street the day before the
war ended, not one of them replied in kind.[69]

Despite these hurt feelings, the time for decision had come. If there was
any doubt on this matter, Wilson made this point clear to Brooke in mid-
June as public concern and Truman's unease about battle casualties began
to percolate down into the U.S. military bureaucracy. On June 11, he
warned the Chief of the Imperial General Staff that the time for a British
proposal for ground forces to take part in the invasion of Japan was "fast
approaching."[70]

Dill died from a blood disorder in November of 1944. "His loss is quite
irreparable and he is irreplaceable in Washington," Brooke wrote after
hearing of his friend's death.[71] Dill's good personal relations with both the
U.S. Joint Chiefs of Staff and the British Chiefs of Staff were unique and
impossible to reproduce. Wilson was as worthy a successor as was possible. In fact, he was so good in his post that he would stay in Washington
until 1947. One of the major assets that he brought to the job was his close

relationship with Churchill. Born in 1881, Wilson graduated from the Royal Military College Sandhurst in 1900 and served in the Boer War immediately afterward. Over 6 feet tall, he quickly earned the nickname "Jumbo." He was primarily a staff officer in World War I. He held a number of troop commands during the interwar period and was also an instructor at the Staff College. In an evaluation of him as a lieutenant colonel, a superior officer noted, "Possibly his most outstanding characteristic is his gift of getting the best out of everyone, both juniors and seniors." He clearly had more impact on people in person than in writing, which explains his success as a troop commander. He was a good judge of character and was steadfast in his temperament, an exceptionally important characteristic in the chaos of war.[72]

Wilson spent most of the war in regions of peripheral importance. In 1944, he replaced Eisenhower as Supreme Allied Commander in the Mediterranean. The Italian campaign received much attention during the first half of 1944 until the focus of the allied war effort moved to the cross-channel invasion.[73]

In November, he received a cable from Churchill sending him to the United States: "I can find only one officer with the necessary credentials and qualities, namely yourself." The prime minister knew his man well. A biographer notes: "Wilson was at his best guiding meetings, cementing relationships, smoothing ruffled feathers, engineering acceptable compromises and persuading the reluctant." Wilson had mixed feelings about this assignment. "I accepted the appointment with regret; after five and a half years in the Mediterranean I would have liked to have seen the war through from that end, but at the same time I realized the importance of the appointment." In a sign of the significance they placed on the alliance with the British and the respect they had for the departed Dill, the U.S. Joint Chiefs of Staff were waiting to meet Wilson at the airport when he arrived in Washington. Wilson spent the next few weeks introducing himself to the people he would work with in the capital and trying to learn the structure of the U.S. government.[74]

The day after sending his first warning, Wilson sent another, longer message to Brooke. He told the Chief of the Imperial General Staff that the Americans were currently generating plans for the invasion of Japan. He learned from staff officers working in the Pentagon that a British proposal to contribute to the operation would be welcomed. He explained that this information "prompted me to telegraph you yesterday that the time was fast approaching when any suggestion of this nature, if it is to be made, should be presented." The Americans that Wilson had talked to also hoped that the British would take the Canadian division off their hands. "I have heard that they would welcome an excuse to be rid of it." American officers also thought a British force would be well received among the American public. "All this suggests an opening for the formation of an Imperial army, with Dominion contingents in it. I feel there is no time to lose, as already the plan for the main attack on the Japanese islands is beginning to take shape."[75]

Before Brooke, Portal, and Cunningham could send their proposal to the Americans, they had to get Churchill's approval, and they sent their final report to him at the end of June. "In framing these proposals, we have had very much in mind your anxious insistence that British forces should play their full part in the war against Japan and share, as far as limitations of resources allow the same labour and risks as American forces." The Chiefs were careful in the language they used, reminding the prime minister that British units were already committed to the fight in Japan. "We should therefore, now like to add to the British Pacific Fleet and the V.L.R. Bomber Force an offer of a British Commonwealth land force for participation in the operations against the main islands of Japan. This would be a further assurance to the Americans of our resolution to share with them the heavy cost which these main operations are bound to involve." The Chiefs also added a new argument about the ability of the United Kingdom to assert its influence in the Pacific after the end of the war. "Moreover, it is in our view essential that we should stake a claim to a share in the final occupation of Japan, and this it would be difficult to do if we had not taken part in the operation of invasion." There was also the advantage of asserting the authority of London in defense matters over Australia and Canada. This issue was vital in regard to a ground force, since the Americans had agreed to include a Canadian division in the operation. Brooke, Portal, and Cunningham were recommending the deployment of a corps of three to five divisions with a British commander. The issue that had been so divisive between Churchill and the Chiefs had reached another point of climax, and Brooke worried. "I have no idea how Winston will receive this proposal."[76]

The Chiefs needed to meet with Churchill before they could send the proposal to the Americans. Scheduling a meeting turned out to be difficult. The United Kingdom was in the middle of a general election to seat a new Parliament. Churchill had wanted to hold the coalition Cabinet together until the end of the Japanese war. The problem was, the date when the war would end was highly uncertain. The Labour Party wanted to hold an election in October. The Conservative Party, on the other hand, wanted to hold the election immediately or wait until after the war with Japan ended. Moving immediately allowed the Conservatives to take advantage of the prime minister's popularity. Delaying until the end of the campaign in the Pacific would give new Labour voters time to find jobs that would take them to other parts of the United Kingdom where they were not registered to vote. Conservative Party leaders expected that the new voter registration rolls of 1945 would be out-of-date by the time Japan surrendered and would favor them ever so slightly.[77]

Churchill honestly regretted the loss of the coalition. At a banquet he gave at 10 Downing Street for his departing Labour ministers, he told them: "The light of history will shine on all your helmets." Tears were running down his cheeks when he spoke. But politics is politics. A week later he gave the worst political speech of his life. Speaking over the radio, he said, "No Socialist government conducting the life and industry of the country could afford to allow free, sharp or violently worded expressions of public discontent. They would have to fall back on some sort of Gestapo, no doubt very humanely directed in the first instance." Not only were the words offensive in their own right, but the voice that had rallied the entire nation in its darkest hour was now voicing views that could only divide. The public shock that followed hurt Churchill.[78]

In May and June, the campaign took priority over matters of policy and strategy. On July 2, a frustrated Cunningham recorded: "The P.M. has put off the Staff meeting we were to have tonight till Wednesday at 2200. I hope he will not have indulged too much to be sensible. This electioneering is the devil."[79]

The meeting waited until noon on July 4, the day before the electorate cast their ballots. The conversation, in the words of Brooke, "rambled" for half an hour before they addressed the Far East. Churchill was exhausted from the heavy demands on him of the election and admitted he had not had a chance to read the paper the Chiefs had submitted. Brooke was more than a little perturbed. "And yet if the proposed strategy in the long run turns out successful, it will have originated in his futile brain! This has happened so frequently now!"[80]

Brooke decided to explain the proposal with a map, which Churchill liked. He told the prime minister that the Chiefs wanted to send five divisions (one New Zealand, one Australian, one British, one British-Indian, and one Canadian or another British-Indian) and that they thought U.S. plans for the amphibious assault on Japan were best described as optimistic. Churchill remarked that success in the Far East had come at a much faster tempo than expected, but that a campaign through the four main islands of Japan would be long, extensive, and bloody. The United Kingdom should be prepared to stand with their American allies for as long as it took to subdue the Japanese. He then agreed to propose to the Americans that the British contribute a ground force of three to five divisions that would take part in the invasion of Japan, suggesting only that two British divisions rather than just one be included in the Corps.[81]

When Brooke returned home that evening, he wondered about the meeting. "How much he understood and really understood in his exhausted state is hard to tell. However I got him to accept the plan in principle, to authorize our sending the paper to the Americans, and to pass the telegram on to the Dominion P.M.s for their co-operation! A great triumph." Cunningham, as always, was more succinct. "A good meeting with the P.M. who obviously was very tired after all his electioneering."[82]

With Churchill's approval, the British Chiefs of Staff sent a cable to the U.S. Joint Chiefs of Staff formally proposing a British ground force take part in ground operations in Japan itself. In what was officially classified as CCS 889, the British Chiefs proposed that a force of three to five divisions from the United Kingdom, India, and the Commonwealth serve under American command in Operation: CORONET, the invasion of Honshu, the biggest of the main Japanese islands. The size of the ground force would be a function of the combat role the Americans gave British units. If this force were in the actual assault phase, then it would be smaller; if the British divisions first saw combat as follow-on elements after the establishment of the initial beachhead, then the force would be bigger. The paper included three proposals dependent on supply matters, but the British Chiefs declared that their preference was to take part in the initial amphibious assault. Brook, Portal, and Cunningham said the British government could support this force with their own shipping and also proposed to include a tactical air force of fifteen squadrons.[83]

There was some opposition to this proposal still.

The Foreign Office has a rather thankless task in commenting on this paper. For drawing attention to certain realities we may be thought to be throwing cold water on the idea of contributing a land force to the final assault on Japan and to be faint-hearted towards a spectacular conception. Our position is that we believe the balance of advantage to lie in making a spontaneous offer of a contribution on land. But we feel that we ought not to be under the illusion that the result will necessarily be spectacular.[84]

The reaction from the British Embassy in Washington was supportive of the Chiefs' proposal. "I profoundly disagree (repeat disagree) with analysis of the probability of American reactions," Lord Halifax wrote. "These paragraphs in my opinion carry the meaning that it would make little real difference to United States opinion if we were not (repeat not) in on the assault on Japan." This assessment was wrong.

> The effect of our non-participation on American public opinion would be in the highest degree unfortunate for us. Apparent justification would be given to those who are already out to maintain that Britain will only participate in the Pacific war to the extent necessary to regain British Colonial possessions. Over and above this there would be a general feeling common to our friends as well as our critics that the British had quit when the boar was at bay whereas the United States had seen it through in Europe.

The United Kingdom had to make some kind of contribution. "Even if British participation were of necessity small or comparatively so, there would be an overwhelming difference between this and total absence."[85]

The Chiefs of Staff also sent the Americans another memo that bore the classification of CCS 890. This document addressed administrative and command issues in the Pacific. Throughout the war, the Pacific war had been under the exclusive oversight of the U.S. Joint Chiefs of Staff. The British Chiefs wanted that to change and proposed: "The Combined Chiefs of Staff will exercise general jurisdiction over strategic policy and the proper coordination of the Allied efforts in all theatres engaged against the Japanese."[86]

The Chiefs of Staff Committee explained their views to Wilson in Washington. "We feel that we are entitled to this now that a British Fleet is already operating in the Pacific and the V.L.R. bomber force is practically about to start for that theatre. Moreover, the gap between SEAC and the Pacific area is daily shrinking."[87]

Would the Americans welcome a contribution from the British allies? Would there be a confrontation in the Combined Chiefs of Staff over strategic command and control issues? The answer to those questions would come in Washington, D.C., but also in Manila.

■

MacArthur and Mountbatten

The future of the alliance between the United States and Great Britain was a concern in both Washington and London as leaders in both governments planned for a war aimed just at the Japanese. It is a bit odd, then, that much of the future of this partnership would be determined in neither of these cities, but rather in Manila.

On July 4—the same day that Brooke made his presentation to the prime minister—President Harry S. Truman celebrated Independence Day with a cruise aboard the presidential yacht *Potomac*, taking with him a group of aides, friends, and advisors. The main topic of conversation was the forthcoming conference with Churchill and Joseph Stalin. The consensus of the group—which was ironic given the historical origins of the holiday they were celebrating—was that Truman had to secure, among other things, the full participation of the United Kingdom in the Pacific war.[1]

There were some operational and obvious diplomatic reasons to have the British involved in the Japanese war, and the fact that France had already been allotted a role in the invasion only underscored the goal of getting the British in the fight. In the last days of spring and the early days of summer, the French had put together a proposal that they contribute a corps of infantry to the war against Japan. Marshall had been indifferent to the proposal, but Leahy had been more supportive. The big concern in the Pentagon was: would French officers comply with orders from Americans? There had been a major rift in relations between the French and U.S. Armies as they drove the Nazis back into Germany when a French commander refused to take orders from an American superior. On May 18, French Foreign Minister Georges Bidault met with President Truman and discussed this matter. Truman agreed in principle to include France in the invasion but said he would leave it up to General MacArthur to decide on the practicality of using the French soldiers. Marshall cabled MacArthur to seek his opinion. "The French have, when well led and where political considerations were not involved, fought well in this war," Marshall observed. MacArthur knew a thing or two about the French and their history and said he would welcome their corps. He wanted to use it as a follow-on unit. He thought, however, that the language barrier would create too many problems in using French air units and recommended that the United States decline that part of the offer.[2]

When the British proposal arrived in Washington, then, there was strong sentiment favoring acceptance. George C. Marshall believed allied participation in an invasion would have psychological and political importance in the United States. British participation would help reduce the number of U.S. casualties, but it would also bolster the resolve of the American public to see the war through to the end knowing that they had friends in the fight. It was also in the best interests of the English-speaking alliance, which Marshall valued so much. He made all these points subtly but clearly in the cable he sent to MacArthur informing him of the British proposal. At the end of the message, he explained: "It is evident that the use of these British Divisions should replace U.S. Divisions to the same number. Such a course would meet with wide public approval from the viewpoint of lessening the requirements for U.S. soldiers, especially on the part of the articulate who assail British and attack administration for non-participation of Allies in conquest of Japan, etc."[3]

The reaction of the commander in the field, though, was as important as anyone else's, and General of the Army Douglas MacArthur was a man quite different from George C. Marshall. MacArthur was West Point; Marshall was VMI. MacArthur was dramatic in his language; Marshall was terse and economical. MacArthur was the grandson of a Scottish immigrant and the son of a war hero; Marshall's family claimed one of the founding fathers as their own. In the future, one would become one of Truman's biggest foes; the other would become his biggest defender. That battle, though, lay in the future. In 1945, these two different men, both of whom wore five stars on their uniform, were united in the efforts to see that the invasion of Japan go forward and both would look at the British in the same way. Again, there were significant differences. For one the allied force represented a major change in attitude, for the other it was a continuation of views he had advanced throughout the war.

MacArthur's father, Arthur MacArthur, Jr., won the Medal of Honor during the U.S. Civil War. The senior MacArthur went on to a long career in the U.S. Army and retired with the three stars of a Lieutenant General, which was higher than the rank of Major General that senior officers usually left the service with during that age. He, however, was angry, nursing a grudge, believing that his rivalry with the Governor-General of the Philippines, William Howard Taft, had cost him the chance to serve as Chief of Staff of the U.S. Army. The slights the father felt would make the son suspicious of civilians and determined to redeem the family name.[4]

Both of the general's sons chose careers in the armed services of the United States. Arthur III was a little more than three years older than his famous brother. He decided to become a naval officer and attended Annapolis. The brothers were close and Arthur named a son after his younger brother. Arthur MacArthur III was well on his way to becoming a major star in the U.S. Navy when he died in 1923 of a ruptured appendix.[5]

The younger brother decided to follow his father into the army and attended the U.S. Military Academy. The fact that his mother decided to live at West Point and that his father was a general made life difficult for him. Still, he thrived at the academy. He earned an athletic letter as a member of the baseball team. His last year at the academy, he became the First Captain of the Corps of Cadets, the highest distinction possible for a cadet at West Point, and finished first in a class of 93.[6]

After an initial tour of duty of the Philippines, MacArthur received orders to attend the Engineering School in Washington. President Theodore Roosevelt also had him assigned to the White House as his military aide.[7] The Philippines would be an important part of MacArthur's life. He would serve there several times during his military career. Yet MacArthur's first claim at major military fame came during the U.S. intervention in Mexico in 1914. He took part in a small unit engagement and was nominated for the Medal of Honor. A review board rejected the nomination.[8]

World War I was a major boon to MacArthur's career. He spent most of the war in France with the 42nd Infantry Division. As the division's Chief of Staff, he played a large role in preparing what the Germans would con-

Khaki Giants. A mutual admiration society developed between Admiral The Lord
Louis Mountbatten and General of the Army Douglas MacArthur during
Mountbatten's trip to Manila in 1945. MacArthur rarely had dinner parties, but
he made an exception when the British admiral visited. Mountbatten, for his part,
was deeply impressed with MacArthur's strategic vision during the trip. Courtesy
of the Imperial War Museum

sider one of the best American units they faced. He became the youngest Brigadier General in the American Expeditionary Forces, a distinction that he would hold for four months. He was one of the more dashing figures in the army and was the subject of much coverage in the press. His mother started keeping a scrapbook of the newspaper clippings that mentioned him. He added to his fame with his command of the 84th Brigade and the seizure of the Côte-de-Châtillon. Charging over ground that the Germans overlooked, MacArthur and his men took the high points from the enemy. "Officers fell and sergeants leaped to the command. Companies dwindled to platoons and corporals took over," MacArthur later commented. Major General Charles P. Summerall, Commanding General of V Corps, nominated MacArthur for promotion and the Medal of Honor. MacArthur probably deserved the highest combat decoration the United States had to offer, but the AEF was particularly stingy when it came to awarding medals, which reflected General John J. Pershing's attitudes. He thought awarding such a prestigious combat decoration as the Medal of Honor to a general for showing decisive leadership under fire would debase the award. Needless to say, MacArthur was bitter at this rejection. His fame, though, was secure. Secretary of War Newton Baker declared, "He was the greatest American field commander produced by the war." There was more than a little truth behind this statement. When the war ended he had the star of a Brigadier General, two Distinguished Service Crosses, seven Silver Stars, two Purple Hearts, and the Distinguished Service Medal.[9]

After the war, the Chief of Staff of the U.S. Army made MacArthur the superintendent of the U.S. Military Academy, a position equivalent to president of a university. "I am not an educator. I am a field soldier," he said, protesting the assignment. The Chief of Staff ignored this objection and told MacArthur to modernize the academy. He was the youngest superintendent of West Point in over a century. The position was one of the most prestigious in the army and allowed him to keep his rank, instead of suffering a demotion like so many other career officers did after the war when the army shrank in size. The future officer that a new West Point had to produce would be, according to MacArthur, "a type possessing all of the cardinal military virtues as of yore, but possessing an intimate understanding of his fellows, a comprehensive grasp of world and national affairs, and a liberalization of conception which amounts to a change in his psychology of command." In order to train this type of officer, he believed he needed "to introduce a new atmosphere of liberalization" at the academy.[10]

MacArthur's career dominated his life. He had few outside interests. He was not one to socialize with his fellow officers and had little conversational skill. He had no interests in art or literature and his reading focused mainly on works of nonfiction that were relevant to the armed services. His only outside interests were football, and to a much lesser extent, baseball. He attended practices of the academy teams on a regular basis. While at West Point, he was not above designing plays for the football team, or showing cadets how to hit a curveball. One of the reforms he did successfully institute while at his alma mater was a mandatory system of intramural athletics. Even this interest had some military utility. "Over there," he explained, "I became convinced that the men who had taken part in organized sports made the best soldiers. They were the most dependable, hardy, courageous officers I had. Men who had contended physically against other human beings under rules of a game were the readiest to accept and enforce discipline. They were outstanding."[11]

After his stint at West Point, he made a major mistake and got married. The mistake was not marriage itself; MacArthur had the temperament to make a good spouse. The mistake was rather in his choice of a mate. Louise Cromwell Brooks was the child of money and, like many others who grow up with resources that wealth offers, she had a warped personality as an adult. The attraction between MacArthur and Brooks was instant. He invited her to an army football game. After the game ended, he proposed and she accepted. The two were convinced that fate was on their side. "Some great destiny is involved in our union," he told her. Such a rapid courtship, though, suggests lust rather than love.[12]

The marriage lasted only seven years, although the couple had stopped living together after five. MacArthur was losing his sexual interest in his wife as she gained weight. She, for her part, had little liking for the life that accompanied an army officer. On June 18, 1929, Louise MacArthur obtained a divorce in Reno, Nevada. "General MacArthur and I divorced because we were wholly incompatible to each other. I have the greatest respect and admiration for him and we part as friends," she told reporters. In later years she would make all sorts of derogatory statements about her former husband, including "It was an interfering mother-in-law who eventually succeeded in disrupting our married life." MacArthur took the wise course of saying nothing publicly on the matter. The former Mrs. MacArthur, though, apparently had many issues in her personal life that had little to do with her in-laws; all four of her marriages ended in divorce.[13]

With his combat record, it was hardly surprising that MacArthur became Chief of Staff of the U.S. Army in 1930. At 50, MacArthur was the youngest man to become Chief of Staff, and was the only man in the U.S. Army wearing the four stars of a General. The biggest mistake MacArthur made as Chief of Staff came not in the realm of military planning, but in politics. Only his confrontation with Truman during the Korean War would do more to damage his reputation than his actions in 1932 as veterans of World War I sought early payment of bonuses that they were due. In 1924, Congress issued certificates to veterans that could be redeemed for cash in 1945 or upon the death of the veteran by his survivors. Out of work, many of these veterans wanted to get paid then in 1932 rather than in thirteen years. About 10,000 formed the Bonus Expeditionary Force that gathered in Washington that spring to demand their payment. After Congress refused to pass legislation speeding up payment, many members of the Bonus Army went home. Still, 5,000 remained camped out in the Anacostia Flats. On July 28, the BEF seized several of the buildings and when the Washington, D.C., police tried to remove the veterans, violence ensued. Police officers, including the chief of police, were hit in the head with bricks. Another incident resulted in shootings and a death. President Herbert Hoover then authorized the use of the army. Soldiers forced the protestors out of the area at bayonet point. MacArthur insisted on making grandiose comments to the press: "That mob down there was a bad-looking mob. It was animated by the essence of revolution." He claimed that the forces under his control had saved the day. His comments damaged his reputation immensely.[14]

After his tenure as Chief of Staff came to an end, the new president, Franklin D. Roosevelt, exiled MacArthur to the Philippines. The general went to Manila with his mother and his sister-in-law. As their ship sailed across the indigo-colored waters of the Pacific, he struck up an acquaintance with Jean Marie Faircloth. He needed a friend. His mother's health was poor and she died a few months after they arrived in Manila. Faircloth was there for him in his time of need, which clearly made them close. Unlike his previous courtship, MacArthur took his time and after eighteen months the two got married during a return trip to the United States. Late in his life, he wrote that marrying Jean "was perhaps the smartest thing I have ever done. She has been my constant friend, sweetheart, and devoted supporter ever since." Ten months into their marriage, Jean MacArthur delivered a little boy that they named Arthur IV after an uncle, a grandfather, and a great-grandfather that he would never know.[15]

MacArthur was a legitimate hero of World War I and reached even greater fame in this second conflict. The irony in all this is that he was a better general in the first war than in the second. On the first day of the war, the Japanese destroyed a significant chunk of the air forces under his command while they were still on the ground. These losses included most of the bombers he had on Luzon, but only about a third of his fighters. What is most significant about the loss of these plans is not the number, but rather the strategic ramification of this attack. MacArthur lost his most important asset in opposing the Japanese advance into the South Pacific. MacArthur, his Chief of Staff, and his air commander all bear responsibility for this disaster. MacArthur also attempted to defend the entire island of Luzon. As a result, supplies were in the wrong positions as his men retreated into the Bataan peninsula. MacArthur had been thoroughly outfought by his Japanese opponent, Lieutenant General Homa Masaharu. Afraid that MacArthur's capture would be a major propaganda victory for the Japanese, Roosevelt ordered him to leave for Australia. MacArthur, like any good commander, found the order distasteful, and wept at the idea of abandoning his men. It was only with great reluctance and the delusional goal of building a rescue force in Australia to relieve the Philippines that he left. In order to thwart Japanese efforts to claim that MacArthur had deserted his men, Marshall had him awarded the Medal of Honor. It is a cruel twist of fate that an officer nominated for this award twice before on reasonable grounds would receive the decoration for fraudulent reasons.[16]

MacArthur's stay in Australia was important to him and the Dominion. He played a key role in reviving the morale of the nation after the disaster of Singapore. More significantly, he would use Australia to pressure London and Washington to keep his command from becoming a station of minor importance. While Australian troops would form the majority of his command until late 1943, he had no intention of entering into partnership with them. The Australians would be useful as long as they served his interests. "Shortly after I arrived in Australia, General MacArthur ordered me to pay my respects to the Australians and then have nothing further to do with them," Lieutenant General Robert L. Eichelberger, who would command a field army under MacArthur, remarked.[17]

MacArthur was a complication in U.S. Pacific strategy. The war was going to be a naval conflict, but MacArthur was senior to any admiral the navy could send to the region. There was no way King was going to allow an army officer to command in an area in which the navy would be doing most of the work. The two services agreed to divide the Pacific theater into two mutually competitive commands with two supply chains. MacArthur admitted this division weakened U.S. power: "Out here I am busy doing what I can with what I have, but resources have never been made available to me for a real stroke. Innumerable openings present themselves which because of the weakness of my forces I cannot seize." The result was that he adopted the strategy of island hopping to avoid strong areas of Japanese strength, hitting smaller targets, and leaving enemy garrisons isolated.[18]

MacArthur's advance started off poorly at Papau, mainly because the American attackers lacked heavy equipment to defeat the well-entrenched Japanese defenders. With battles and campaigns at Bismarck Sea, Bougainville, Admiralties, Hollandia, Biak, Leyte, and Luzon, MacArthur's command moved steadily forward. His air commander, Lieutenant General George C. Kenney, proved to be adept, willing to use planes as the tactical situation required rather than sticking to predetermined doctrine. During the CARTWHEEL operations that isolated Rabul on the island of New Britain, MacArthur also effectively limited the authority of his ground commander, Blamey, to Australian troops only. He refused to use any Australians in the Philippines and soon assigned them the thankless task of mopping up Japanese forces in bypassed areas.[19]

If members of the Joint Staff or the Joint Chiefs read MacArthur's response to Marshall carelessly, they might have become disillusioned if they supported the inclusion of the British in operations against Japan. MacArthur was using a favorite rhetorical tactic of his in citing false options. In this case it was a move as clever as it was legitimate. The general began his message explaining all the problems the British proposal entailed: "The scope of the British proposal for participation in CORONET presents problems not heretofore encountered when the Canadian and French contingents were considered." He continued, noting, "Acceptance of the British in the assault with the difference in organization, composition, equipment, training procedures, and doctrines will complicate command, operations, and logistic support."[20]

Then, MacArthur's language shifted in the middle of the message. "The following general plan is suggested as being one which will obviate the full impact of the objectionable features indicated above." If his requirements were met he could include a British ground force in the operation. He stipulated that he wanted just one corps composed of three divisions coming from the United Kingdom, Australia, and Canada. He wanted these units supplied with U.S. equipment to avoid complicating logistics. They also had to receive training in U.S. amphibious doctrine and had to be made available by December 1. The British corps would fight within a U.S. field army and would be used as a follow-up force once a beachhead was established.[21]

The question of race also came into play in his response. "Where homogeneity of language with the corps is required I doubt the advisability of employing troops of native origin. Likewise there is a question of the advisability of utilizing troops of tropical origin in a temperate zone without an extended acclimatization period. Hence, acceptance of Indian troops is not concurred in. British division should be Anglo-Saxon."[22]

MacArthur's ban on the British-Indian Army is suspect. The command and control language of this service was English. There were too many linguistic groups in the subcontinent to use any other language. The issue of climate is also dubious. The Indian Army had fought in a variety of environments from desert to jungle in Burma alone. Indian units had also fought in Italy, which is quite similar in its weather to Japan.

MacArthur had two real reasons for rejecting the British-Indian Army. First, it did not have a great reputation for combat effectiveness, particularly its units serving in India. Such a reputation was not entirely fair, since many units were assigned policing duties rather than being sent into combat situations for which they were trained. Another factor was race. MacArthur's invasion force would consist of armies from white nations. This force would teach the Japanese a lesson about challenging the West.

MacArthur explained his views most fully about foreign participation in the invasion of Japan in mid-July with his counterpart from the South-East Asia Command, Admiral The Lord Louis Mountbatten. MacArthur's military secretary, Brigadier General Bonner Fellers, was less than excited about this meeting: "He has no military reason for Conference." Fellers also recorded that "W.D. has instructed that certain operations will not be discussed with him." The British Chiefs of Staff apparently thought along similar lines. They informed Mountbatten about their proposal in a cable before his visit to see MacArthur: "You will be fully informed of the results of these discussions as soon as decisions have been reached. Meanwhile, any rumours which may come to your ears are clearly unfounded, and should be treated accordingly." The Chiefs instructed Mountbatten to avoid discussing the idea about British inclusion in the invasion with MacArthur. Fellers referred to Mountbatten as "Lord Plushbottom" in his frustration at being assigned the task of escorting the foreign guest.[23]

The man Fellers called "Lord Plushbottom" was born on June 25, 1900, in Frogmore House on the grounds of Windsor Castle, and his original name and titles were H.S.H. Prince Louis Francis Albert Victor Nicholas of Battenberg. He was the second son of Prince Louis and Princess Victoria of Battenberg. His mother was a granddaughter of Queen Victoria. Although both parents were German royalty (his mother was the eldest daughter of the Grand Duke of Hesse), they lived in England, and the elder Prince Louis was an officer in the Royal Navy. Despite his foreign accent and title, his career progressed smoothly and he eventually became First Sea Lord. Such things were possible before 1914, and both of his sons, Prince George and Prince Louis, followed him into the navy. The patriotic fervor that World War I unleashed took a toll on the English branch of the Battenbergs. All things German became suspect, and having a head of the Royal Navy who spoke with an enemy accent was too much for some people to take. At the same time, Battenberg's health began to fail him. Even though he had joined the service before the founding of the German Empire, public sentiment, combined with his collapsing health, forced him from his post. King George V decided to bend to the chauvinism of the day and decreed that the name of the royal family would be Windsor rather than Saxe-Coburg-Gotha. All British citizens who bore German titles of nobility and royalty had to surrender them and accept English titles. The Battenbergs became the Mountbattens and Prince Louis became the Marquess of Milford Haven. His elder son became the Earl of Medina and his younger son became Lord Louis Mountbatten.[24]

The insults, slights, and humiliations the Battenbergs suffered during the war were unwarranted and made Mountbatten an ambitious man determined to seek redemption. Although the Mountbattens were no longer royalty, they were still members of the Windsor family. When Mountbatten decided to marry Edwina Ashley, the King had to provide his consent. The Ashley-Mountbatten wedding was a major social function. The groom's second cousin, the Prince of Wales, served as the best man. There were 1,400 invited guests, a crowd of 8,000 gathered to watch the various titled dignitaries arrive at the church, and the service was the subject of much coverage in the major news dailies.[25]

The Mountbatten marriage was typical of the upper-class British. Ashley's grandfather was a German Jew who had immigrated to the United Kingdom and had acquired a multimillion-pound fortune. He acquired a knighthood and saw his daughter marry a member of Parliament. Ashley's family had much wealth and some social standing. Mountbatten, on the other hand, was a member of the royal family, had social standing to no end, but little income of his own. The newlyweds had a busy social life, were often at nightclubs, or were hosting dinner parties that mixed royalty and film stars. The Mounbattens had two children, but the attraction they had to one another began to fade. Their personalities meshed poorly. She wanted to go out, did not need or want to be close to her spouse, and wanted as little to do with child rearing as possible. Mountbatten, separated from his family at times due to his sea duty, wanted these very elements of domestic life. The traditional gender roles in their marriage became reversed. Their two daughters report that their father was most responsible for their upbringing and that their mother, often traveling in powerful social circles, was only briefly around. She sought out romantic and sexual partners outside the marriage but became possessive when her husband did the same. She was less than discreet on many occasions and gossip found its way into the society sections of American and British newspapers. The humiliation Mountbatten suffered at the hands of the woman he cared most about only drove him to succeed that much harder.[26]

Like MacArthur's, Mountbatten's career became all-consuming. He had little religious faith to see him through his pain. His only side interests were playing polo and his family, which really meant his two daughters. He had done well as a junior officer in World War I, and his career, with a specialization in communications, was progressing nicely in the 1920s and 1930s. He received a promotion to Captain when he was 37 years old. He formally took command of HMS *Kelly*, the lead ship of the 5th Destroyer Flotilla, on June 27, 1939. His initial speech to the crew later became immortalized in the film *In Which We Serve*: "In my experience, I have always found that you cannot have an efficient ship unless you have a happy ship, and you cannot have a happy ship unless you have an efficient ship. That is the way I intend to start this commission, and that is the way I intend to go on—with a happy and an efficient ship."[27]

Mountbatten was only adequate in his seamanship as captain of the *Kelly*. He often pushed this ship faster than conditions merited or were safe. He did, however, understand the sea well enough to question an order about rushing to the rescue of a tanker that he suspected had been hit by a mine rather than a torpedo. His superior officers rejected his challenge, the *Kelly* went as ordered, and it hit a mine that put the ship in dry docks for three months. Shortly after returning to the sea the *Kelly* collided with HMS *Gurkha*. When the *Kelly* made its second return to duty, it helped evacuate British and French forces from Norway. A week later, Mountbatten and the *Kelly* had a near-fatal encounter with a U-boat. Accompanying the HMS *Birmingham* on a hunt for German minelayers, Mountbatten ignored his orders and went looking for a German submarine that was reported to be nearby. Finding nothing, he returned to join up with the *Birmingham* and with a light signaled: "How are the muskets? Let battle commence." The bright signal made the *Kelly* highly visible and an E-boat that had been spotted nearby fired a torpedo that tore a 50-foot-wide hole in the ship's side. A cloud of smoke and steam rose high into the air and covered the *Kelly*. Observers on other ships thought it had gone down. After a third set of repairs, the navy transferred the *Kelly* and the 5th Destroyer Flotilla to the Mediterranean Fleet in 1941, which was under Andrew Cunningham's command at the time. On May 23, after a raid on Crete, the *Kelly* and HMS *Kashmir* were racing from the island when twenty-four Junker dive bombers attacked the ships. "Christ, look at that lot," Mountbatten remarked as half of the planes dove on each ship. Both sank in minutes with heavy loss of life. "I had lost more than half my officers and ship's company and was naturally feeling very sad," he remarked later. "Cunningham made me feel that their loss had been worthwhile, and that the Navy had never put up a finer show."[28]

Winston Churchill significantly advanced Mountbatten's career twice. When Louis of Battenberg had been First Sea Lord, Churchill had been the First Lord of the Admiralty. He had done nothing to protect the father in 1914 from hostile chauvinism, but in 1941 he would now make it up by advancing the son. During a mission to the United States following the loss of the *Kelly*, Mountbatten received a telegram from Churchill. "We want you home here at once for something which you will find of the highest interest," the prime minister declared. When Mountbatten returned, he was less than pleased. He had been designated as the next Captain of the aircraft carrier *Illustrious*, and he wanted command of the ship rather than some administrative position. "You fool!" the prime minister responded. "The best thing you can hope to do there is to repeat your last achievement and get yourself sunk." Churchill put Mountbatten in command of Combined Operations. He was to prepare all of the armed services—the British Army, the Royal Navy, the Royal Marines, and the Royal Air Force—for an invasion of France. There was no bigger job. Mountbatten accepted the position and a promotion to Commodore. Soon he was promoted to the acting rank of Vice-Admiral, making him the youngest man since Lord Nelson to hold that rank. Combined Operations initiated a number of raids along the French coast during Mountbatten's tenure. The biggest and most disastrous was the attack on the French port city of Dieppe in August of 1942. Mountbatten would assert for the rest of his life that the Allies learned many lessons about staging an amphibious assault during this attack that later bore fruit on D-Day. Eisenhower also advocated this view, but that claim is highly dubious. Any benefit from Dieppe was accidental at best.[29]

Churchill advanced Mountbatten's career a second time. When the Americans and British began investing resources in a cross-channel invasion, it became clear that Combined Operations would disappear as an organization. Mountbatten soon began looking for another assignment. During one of his free moments, the prime minister talked to the young vice-admiral about Southeast Asia. Thinking he was being asked to go on a temporary inspection mission, Mountbatten agreed, but indicated he wanted a naval command. The prime minister's response was similar to the first time he offered Mountbatten high command: "Go to sea! Don't you understand that I am proposing you should go out as a Supreme Commander?"[30]

The position of Supreme Commander of South-East Asia Command was an exceptionally trying one even though Mountbatten earned a promotion to the rank of Admiral. The goals of the three main allied powers—the United Kingdom, the United States, and China—were significantly different. The British wanted to preserve their empire and reclaim colonies lost to the Japanese in 1942; the Americans wanted to bolster Chinese resistance to the Japanese since the bulk of the Imperial Japanese Army was on the mainland of Asia, and they expected the British to help in keeping the supply lines open to China; the Chinese wanted to stake a postwar claim to the Japanese-occupied colony of Burma. The Nationalist regime was hording its Lend-Lease supplies, which its officials believed was their due as a major power. This materiel would be better used in the confrontation with the Chinese Communists that would come after the war rather than against the Japanese. Mountbatten also had to worry about imperial issues, as Nationalists in India and Burma were working for postwar independence rather than bolstering the colonial authority of a foreign King-Emperor.[31]

It was during his time in command that the British-Indian and Imperial Japanese Armies fought the Battle of Imphal. The town in the eastern part of British India was a gateway straight into the heart of the subcontinent. The British had to defeat the Japanese or lose India, which would have denied the British a number of vital commercial and industrial resources and would have come close to forcing the United Kingdom out of the war. The Japanese surrounded the town, but the British and Indian soldiers inside refused to surrender. The key to the siege was keeping the troops supplied through the air, and Mountbatten forcefully convinced the British Chiefs of Staff, Churchill, and, in turn, the U.S. high command to turn over U.S. cargo planes to operate in a unified command under a British commander. These planes were critical in keeping the garrison supplied while British-Indian divisions hammered at the Japanese. "It now became clear that we were going to require air supply on an unprecedented scale," Lord Louis recalled. "The whole of IV Corps was cut off in the Imphal Plain." When the Chiefs of Staff instructed Mountbatten to return the planes, he refused. With the fight still in doubt, Churchill informed the theater commander: "Let nothing go from the battle that you need for victory. I will not accept denial of this from any quarter, and will back you to the full." In the end, the British victory was the worst defeat the Imperial Japanese Army suffered in its history.[32]

The British then advanced into Burma. Mountbatten made another important but intangible contribution to the British war effort: building up the morale of those in his command, convincing them that they could defeat the Japanese. The British had used an air bridge out of desperation at Imphal to blunt the Japanese, but now they would use it in their advance. Mountbatten later estimated that the Fourteenth Army under General Sir William Slim got 96 percent of its supplies through the air. "We had only about half the aircraft that were really required, but we made up the other half by the expedient of flying almost double the number of hours allowed for sustained operations," he explained. "Normally this would be considered an extremely dangerous policy, but we had no alternative." The South-East Asia Command sustained these operations for months and then more months. "Although there was the gravest risk that the whole air transport arrangements might break down, they could see the results of their supplies

CHAPTER THIRTEEN

in the daily advance towards Rangoon and their morale was so high that they somehow managed to carry on." Lord Louis was also fond of the Chindits, which were the idea of Major-General Orde Wingate. A special operations force, the Chindits operated behind Japanese front lines and received their supplies through the air instead of supply lines from their rear. This approach was unconventional. Mountbatten disbanded this unit after Wingate died, but basically took their "nonlinear" approach to war and incorporated it into his entire command. The use of air bridges allowed the British to fight on even when small units were isolated by geography and the enemy. This approach to logistics was far better than anything the Japanese had and allowed the British to keep fighting during the unhealthy monsoon season. Mountbatten also used open-ended orders in which he explained his intent and gave the local commander flexibility in how they achieved these objectives. Two and a half months before his meeting with MacArthur, Mountbatten's command achieved a decisive victory when British Army units liberated Rangoon, the capital of Burma.[33]

The meeting in Manila went well and has been immortalized to a degree in James Webb's novel, *The Emperor's General*. One of the reasons it went so well was that both Mountbatten and MacArthur respected one another. A British officer assigned to MacArthur's staff once noted of the general: "He is shrewd, selfish, proud, remote, highly-strung, and vastly vain. He has imagination, self-confidence, and physical courage and charm, but no humour about himself, no regard for truth and is unaware of these defects. He mistakes his emotions and ambitions for principle. With moral depth he would be a great man: as it is he is a near-miss." Mountbatten's official biographer notes that this description is also a fairly accurate one of the admiral. In his diary, Mountbatten noted of his host: "I fully admit it I am under his spell he is one of the most charming and remarkable characters I have ever met, and so sympathetic and friendly towards the South-East Asia Command." MacArthur left no written comments about the British admiral, but his actions speak for themselves. He almost never entertained socially during the war or in Japan afterward. Mountbatten's stay in the Philippines was different. The general hosted a luncheon and a dinner for his guest. These two functions were major and noticeable exceptions to his Spartan social calendar. Mountbatten charmed even those that were suspicious of him. Fellers recorded in his diary: "He is tall dark Handsome—pleasant—a good Ambassador. But his 25 officers + 7 men upset GHQ no end."[34]

Despite the fact that both men had orders to be on guard with the other, they ignored their instructions. On July 12, after the luncheon, MacArthur raised the issue of British participation in CORONET. He wanted a corps from the United Kingdom to take part in the operation. Mountbatten asked him if this unit would come from his theater. In his memo documenting this conversation, Mountbatten directly quotes MacArthur's response: "Certainly not. You have had enough troubles to contend with and have had enough resources robbed, without your neighbouring Theatre adding to your troubles. Quiet apart from this, it would be logistically unacceptable." MacArthur added that he wanted British troops to come "straight from the United Kingdom through the United States, where I shall insist on their being re-equipped with American weapons and then straight from the United States into CORONET." Mountbatten then showed MacArthur his plans for retaking Singapore. The American was impressed at the plan and complimented his counterpart on his vision. Fellers was more caustic:

My reaction:
1. Did not make it clear
2. made it clear but I cannot understand it
3. have no plan at all.[35]

In his diary entry for that day, Mountbatten wrote: "I had a long and interesting conversation with MacArthur, or, to be more precise, I listened to a fascinating monologue, and found the same difficulty in trying to chip in as I have no doubt most people find in trying to chip into my conversations (a very useful object lesson for young Supreme Commanders!)"[36]

On the evening of July 14, MacArthur hosted a dinner in honor of Mountbatten. Here the conversation turned to the invasion of Japan. This time Mountbatten initiated the conversation, but MacArthur did most of the talking. The American host told his British guest that the casualties at Okinawa had been heavy because of the continued frontal assaults. If they had staged a second amphibious landing in the south, as he had done at Leyte, then the Tenth Army would probably have taken the island with lower losses. He also thought having the fleet hang around the island had been a mistake. The navy had not made good use of its air superiority at Okinawa, or Iwo Jima, either. Bombardments had not been sustained, because carriers had to leave constantly to refuel. There was little the fleet ended up doing, except taking heavy losses from the kamikazes. Fellers noted in his diary: "MacA also said: Japan went well initially because of balance air land + sea. Now off balance."[37]

There was nothing new about MacArthur's low opinion of Buckner, but his reasons had shifted. Even before the battle on Okinawa started, Lieutenant General Robert L. Eichelberger, Commanding General, Eighth Army, wrote his wife: "Big Chief says if Buck ever comes under him he would bust him because he has sold out to one of our sister services." Just before the landing on Okinawa, Colonel Weldon Rhoades, MacArthur's pilot, witnessed another conversation between MacArthur and Eichelberger. MacArthur was agitated about a field army serving under naval command but was also grateful that he would not be responsible for the operation. He expected the Japanese would fight to the last man and that American forces would suffer extremely heavy casualties. MacArthur apparently forgot that Okinawa would be a thankless task and was soon blaming the results on Buckner's leadership. The day Buckner died, Stilwell and MacArthur discussed replacing Buckner. Stilwell recorded in his diary the main points of their conversation:

He had asked about Okinawa and I told him. He has not a high opinion of Buckner. Agreed he [is] facetious. Told me he would rather have me as an army commander than anyone he knew, and if GCM was willing, he was. This is contingent on a change in the Tenth Army. He will welcome Buckner's relief and my transfer. Navy refused to give up Tenth Army. If they persist, he will just take the troops and let them keep the army, asking for another, which I am to command.[38]

At the Mountbatten dinner when MacArthur addressed his plans for OLYMPIC, he said he would avoid making the mistakes that had occurred at Okinawa. He would pour a quarter of a million tons of bombs into Kyushu to soften up the enemy. In one memo, Mountbatten has MacArthur saying he would keep casualties under 35,000. In another, he says OLYMPIC would end up resulting in 50,000 casualties. MacArthur, according to Mountbatten, said it was impossible to estimate the losses for CORONET. In his diary Fellers noted: "wants to destroy Emperor who is C in C of Japanese forces."[39]

Mountbatten deeply appreciated MacArthur's attitude toward unit assignments. After the war had ended, he sent the general a message on this matter: "I am most grateful to you for the way you handled the question of British Commonwealth participation in CORONET. Your solution would undoubtedly have been best from the point of view of S.E.A.C."[40]

Up until this point, MacArthur had been wary of all U.S. allies. Why, then, was he willing and even eager to have British and Commonwealth units take part in Operation: CORONET? The answers to this question show MacArthur at his best and his worst. He wanted to add more flags to his operation. He wanted the political force of an international coalition, but one in which he was the controlling authority. The invasion would be the largest amphibious operation ever conducted, putting his former aide Dwight Eisenhower in his proper, which is to say subordinate, position. Eisenhower had, of course, led the greatest amphibious assault in recorded history on June 6, 1944. The assault force that landed in Normandy was multinational. MacArthur would have the same. For a time, he had more Australians under his command than Americans. MacArthur stopped using them when Americans arrived in sufficient numbers. Now, in 1945, including the Australians again in his operations along with Canadians, New Zealanders, and the British would add momentum to plans. From his perspective, Truman's willingness to reconsider the invasion at the June 18 meeting had been too close for comfort. The general honestly believed that Operations: OLYMPIC and CORONET were the best military options available. From his exchanges with Marshall, he knew that casualty numbers were the concern of the day and that he had to keep them below a certain level. He was sure he could limit losses, but if allied units were taking part in combat operations, they would absorb some of the casualties, and it was unlikely that the American public would become concerned about the number of Australians killed on a Japanese beachhead. He also knew that the United States would soon be facing troop shortage problems, and having allies involved in the fight would mitigate this problem to some degree.[41]

After MacArthur's message arrived in Washington, the Joint Staff recommended that the Joint Chiefs of Staff accept the British proposal on MacArthur's terms. The recommendation was an extremely reluctant one. "From a military viewpoint, acceptance of the British offer of ground forces, as stated, is undesirable, because of derangement to world-wide redeployment plans, the additional logistic complications, the uncertainty as to availability of the troops offered or their probable impact upon further operations by the British in Southeast Asia, and other reasons expressed by

CINCAFPAC." These planning officers, though, realized that coalition warfare is a political and diplomatic exercise.

> Political considerations probably will require that the United States Chiefs of Staff accept in principle the offer of participation by a British Commonwealth land force. Acceptance would be in accord with previously established policies for the participation under U.S. command of Allied forces in the main operations against Japan. Some advantage might accrue in the reduction of U.S. casualties. Prior to final agreement, however, clarification of a number of factors is essential.[42]

The issue of British participation in the Pacific was near resolution. MacArthur was willing to accept a British ground force in the invasion of Japan. The issue of command and control remained unresolved and that issue would have to be decided by the Combined Chiefs of Staff. They would do so at their next conference, which would be held outside the smoldering ruins of Berlin. This international gathering in the suburb of Potsdam, where the Kings of Prussia and Kaisers of the Second Reich had once lived and ruled, had the appropriate codename of TERMINAL.

FOURTEEN

■

The British Pacific Fleet
Visits Japan

As Mountbatten and MacArthur were discussing future operations against the Japanese and as the U.S. delegation to the Potsdam Conference sailed across the North Atlantic with few safety precautions now that peace had come to those waters, the British Pacific Fleet was headed to the North Pacific where combat still reigned. Despite serious logistics problems, the Royal Navy was making a worthy contribution to operations against Japan, which their comrades in the U.S. Navy appreciated. Although this involvement was significant at a tactical level, the diplomatic and political impact had even more weight.

King remained skeptical. Notwithstanding the valuable performance of the Royal Navy at Okinawa, he tried to get rid of the fleet, recommending that it use Brunei rather than Manus as an intermediate base. Fraser, Nimitz, and Spruance all thought this was a bad idea. Brunei was too far away. Undaunted, King told his staff in late June that they were going to keep the British out of the Pacific. He would turn over as much of the Mariana Islands as possible to them and he would keep them out of the Philippines altogether. Although counterproductive in political and diplomatic terms, King's views on operational and tactical issues had some merit. Even British admirals admitted this point, privately. Operations against the main Japanese islands would move at a faster pace than at Okinawa, and Vian wondered to himself, "Could we make good?"[1]

The BPF first had to undergo refurbishing after its service in the Ryukyus. The fleet had new aircrews replacing the exhausted ones that had flown at Okinawa. With these new men, with good morale, the British could put 255 planes into the air. The idea that they would be attacking the home islands was invigorating. Many of the pilots were from the Dominions, New Zealand, primarily, with Australia and then Canada making up smaller contingents. With their homes much closer to Japan than Britain itself, they had a considerable amount of motivation to see the conflict through to the end. For them there was no possibility that the war would be over until the last Axis nation was defeated. Many of these pilots were young and inexperienced, but they were in better health than their colleagues from the four home countries of the United Kingdom.[2]

The Royal Navy provided the ships with new equipment, replacing many of the 20 mm guns with heavier 40 mm weapons. The British had also adopted new antiaircraft tactics. Problems remained nonetheless. Engineers on the carrier *Implacable* worked around the clock and even while the ship was underway in order to have it ready for combat. The air compressors on another carrier, *Indefatigable*, stopped working while it was at Manus, and the ship would miss three days of combat.[3]

The British had even mastered some of the skills of refueling at sea. On July 13, the *King George V* fuelled abeam of a tanker, the first time a British battleship had conducted this maneuver.[4]

The British rendezvoused with the Third Fleet on July 16. "Everywhere you looked there were ships. You felt we couldn't lose the war now," one sailor on the *Implacable* remarked. "In fact, we almost felt we were being big bullies."[5]

This time the British Pacific Fleet would come under the command of William F. Halsey, Jr., the admiral with the thick chest of the halfback he had once been when he played football at the U.S. Naval Academy. One of the most popular naval heroes of the war—he appeared on the cover of *Time* magazine twice—Halsey was an aggressive, offensive-minded commander who tended to exploit opportunities when they presented themselves, much like the meleeists of the eighteenth century. The Royal Navy's doctrine of "general chase" during the Age of Sail embodied his approach toward naval warfare even in his own era of complex fighting with submarines, aircraft, and logistical complications. He acknowledged this legacy: "If I have any principle of warfare burned within my brain, it is that the best defense is a strong offense. Lord Nelson expressed this very

Visiting Japan. The *King George V* sailing off the coast of Japan in August of 1945. Just beyond the British battleship is the USS *Missouri*, with a British destroyer alongside. An American Essex class aircraft carrier is visible in the distance. Courtesy of the Naval Historical Center

well: 'No captain can do very wrong if he places his ship alongside that of an enemy.'" This simple statement effectively summarizes Halsey's command style and also explains why he would get along so well with his British allies and, yet, test their resources even further.[6]

The son of a professional naval officer, Halsey had spent his youth growing up at the U.S. Naval Academy in Annapolis, Maryland. Halsey attended the University of Virginia at first, but soon received an appointment to the academy from none other than William McKinley, the then president of the United States. His mother had used a family friend to get an appointment to see McKinley and then she explained why her son was deserving of the appointment. On July 7, 1900, Halsey was sworn in as a naval cadet—as students at Annapolis were called at the time. He was an indifferent student and at times was in danger of flunking out of the academy. In an act of rebellion on his summer cruise in 1902 that also showed that he was a real salt, he got a tattoo on his shoulder of an anchor with "USNA" on the crown and a chain forming "04." This age was one when the only people who got tattoos were sailors and even then it was usually only the lower ranks. In his last year at the academy he received the Thompson Trophy Cup that went to the first-year classman who did the most to promote athletics at the school.[7]

Halsey's career progressed at a steady, upward pace. He sailed as a lieutenant in Theodore Roosevelt's Great White Fleet in 1908–1909. He received his first command immediately afterward, the torpedo boat *Du Pont*. Another followed with the destroyer *Flusser*. He made a strong and favorable impression on Assistant Secretary of the Navy Franklin D. Roosevelt, when he let the civilian take the conn of the ship. Command of the destroyer *Jarvis* followed, where he served as part of the Atlantic Destroyer Flotilla under Captain William S. Simms. Destined to lead U.S. naval forces during the Great War, Simms served as a patron for Halsey and many other naval leaders in World War II. During World War I, Halsey was the captain of the USS *Benham*, which was based out of Queenstown, Ireland. During this period, he briefly commanded a group of American and British ships. "My first experience in multiple command in the war," he noted. "I was as proud as a dog with two tails." In the 1930s, he attended both the Naval War College and then the Army War College, before he was offered the command of the aircraft carrier *Saratoga*. Federal law required that all carrier captains be qualified naval aviators. For thirty years most of his sea duty had been in destroyers, but Halsey also saw the potential of naval-based airpower. The *Saratoga*, along with the *Lexington*, were also the largest ships in the navy, and Halsey decided the opportunity was worth the challenge of mastering a new tactical skill. So, at age 51, Captain William F. Halsey, Jr., went to flight school. He was only to have earned aviation observer wings due to a failed eye exam required for pilots, but Halsey managed to get around this regulation and had his status changed from student observer to student pilot. He legitimately earned his pilot's wings, but he came to flying late in life and would never be a legitimate combat asset in the cockpit.[8]

Halsey's wings got him the *Saratoga* and facilitated his promotion to Rear Admiral—there was no rank of Commodore at the time—and then Vice Admiral. He was one of only five flag officers in the service with aviator's wings. Although a convert to airpower, he was no zealot. Developing carrier and air tactics for the coming war against Japan in the late 1930s and early 1940s, he became convinced that the quality of the planes was still inadequate and prevented the full application of naval airpower in the way theorists imagined.[9]

The gregarious and friendly Halsey was a man whom the reporters liked and became one of the first heroes of the war. In April 1942, he took the B-25s under the command of Lieutenant Colonel James H. Doolittle to the waters of Japan, where they launched the first attack on the Japanese home islands. Now, in 1945, he would be delivering the last strikes.[10]

In the years in between, Halsey had promoted his friend Raymond Spruance to take over his carriers for what became the Battle of Midway when he contracted a skin disease. Halsey returned as a theater commander when he took over the South Pacific Forces. Here he fought a series of tough naval engagements in which the Combined Fleet, the oceangoing element of the Imperial Japanese Navy, gave as good as it got. These battles ultimately gave the Americans control of Guadalcanal and Halsey his fourth star. A long campaign of attrition followed in the Solomons. The dual MacArthur-Nimitz/army-navy allied advance (Australians and New Zealanders were contributing, but mainly in supporting roles) turned Halsey's command into a rear area, and Nimitz responded by rotating command of U.S. naval forces in the Pacific between Halsey and Spruance. Under Halsey the ships were known as the Third Fleet and under Spruance they were the Fifth Fleet.[11]

In essence, Halsey's success in this new position came despite himself. When MacArthur invaded the Philippines in October 1944, Halsey had two missions: protecting the beachhead from a Japanese sortie and destroying the Combined Fleet. The orders he received from Nimitz stated, "In case opportunity for destruction of major portion of the enemy fleet is offered or can be created, such destruction becomes the primary task." Complicating matters was the fact that the amphibious force, the Seventh Fleet, was under the command of Vice Admiral Thomas Kinkaid. Halsey had no authority over this formation. The two admirals had to coordinate their actions, which sounds simple enough, but could easily fall by the wayside during the stress of combat. The Japanese decided to contest the landing with their naval and ground-based air forces. The ensuing Battle of Leyte Gulf, if measured by ship tonnage or by area covered, became the biggest naval battle ever. The Combined Fleet sortied with a three-pronged

Command Relationship. Vice-Admiral Sir Philip Vian and Admiral William F. Halsey, Jr., conferring about the deployment of the British Pacific Fleet. Halsey was at first reluctant to include the British in the Third Fleet, but admiration for the willingness of British admirals to work as part of a team changed his mind. Courtesy of the U.S. National Archives

advance. Fighters from Halsey's Third Fleet engaged the Center Force, and he believed had they had turned it back. Kinkaid's Seventh Fleet went after the Southern Force. Then, spotter planes found the Northern Force sailing down with Japan's remaining carriers. This force was a decoy, which the Japanese were hoping would draw off the American carriers. Believing he had the potential to destroy the remaining shreds of the Combined Fleet, Halsey took the bait. Kinkaid pursued the Southern Force, thinking Halsey had left a line of battleships guarding against the possibility of the Center Force turning back. Intending to destroy what remained of Japanese fighting power, Halsey instead took the battleships with him. When the Center Force did indeed turn back, there was no U.S. force between them and the beachheads. The Japanese had the potential to destroy the ships putting ground units ashore, but the valiant resistance of little destroyers and the incessant, near-desperate attacks of planes flying off small escort carriers convinced them that they were up against a much bigger U.S. force than was actually the case and they retreated. Leyte Gulf was an American victory on a stunningly large scale, but Halsey's aggressive inclination had come close to turning it into a major defeat.[12]

Halsey continued to make other mistakes. In December, his audacious manner resulted in the loss of three destroyers when he let his fleet sail into a typhoon in order to meet his strike schedule. The next month, in an effort to hunt down two carriers that had survived the destruction of the Northern Force, Halsey allowed a sizeable merchant convoy to sail past him without destruction. As it was, he never found the two Japanese carriers, which were virtually useless without any planes. In June, just before the British joined up with him, he led his fleet into another typhoon.[13]

In his memoirs, Halsey makes no effort to hide that he was less than eager to have the British alongside in the fight even though he had never met either Rawlings or Vian. He did admit, though, that they had impressive reputations. "Reluctantly I opened the conference. I say 'reluctantly' because I dreaded it." The source of Halsey's reservations was the issue of full operational control of the British fleet. He had no authority over the British ships, which in his way of thinking was the most essential part of war making. In his Naval War College thesis, he wrote: "Command is the nerve center that directs, controls, and coordinates the strategic and tactical. They are command's right and left hands. As command controls these hands, so command controls the war. Strategy, tactics, and command may be called the trinity of war; and the greatest of these is command."[14]

Halsey believed that the inclusion of the British in his fleet would complicate the command and control issues and he tried to rectify this matter. In a message to Nimitz, he proposed that he use the British Pacific Fleet on the flank of U.S. naval forces with a significant gap between the two fleets. "CTF 38 will prescribe point option and maneuvers for US groups and CTF 37 will confirm thereby contributing to and sharing the benefits of our force defense."[15]

Nimitz quickly rejected this proposal. His agreement with Fraser, and King's insistence on self-sufficiency, made it impossible to accept Halsey's idea. "Your 160007 is not approved. Operate TF 37 separately from TF 38 in fact as well as in name under arrangements which assign to Rawlings tasks to be performed but leave him free to decide upon his own move-ments and maneuvers." Nimitz was being a bit too legalistic in his view of his agreement with Fraser. "I myself did not mean this to preclude the pos-sibility of British task group operating in an American force," Fraser in-formed the Admiralty, "but the C.-in-C. Pacific appears to have taken it to mean that, and during the July operations he counterordered Com. Third Fleet's expressed intention to operate the British Task Force as a group, as part of his own Task Force."[16]

Halsey started the conference, explaining that he intended that the strikes against the home islands weaken enemy resources before the invasion started. Then, he gave Rawlings three options: (1) the British could operate as a component element of the fleet: Halsey would not give it orders, but would give "suggestions," which would allow the Allies to concentrate their power against the Japanese; (2) Rawlings could operate as a semi-indepen-dent force separated by 60–70 miles of ocean from U.S. ships; (3) the Royal Navy could operate totally on its own. Halsey recalls that Rawlings never hesitated in his response: "Of course, I'll accept Number 1."[17]

The British admiral had impressed Halsey. "My admiration for him be-gan at that moment. I saw him constantly thereafter, and a finer officer and firmer friend I have never known." Michael Le Fanu of the Royal Navy was still serving as the British liaison to the commander-in-chief of the American fleet, and he observed, "The day's conversation in the Third Fleet flagship could not have been more cordial and at their end the Fleet Commander sent for me to tell me how confident he felt about the prospects of co-operating with the British." The British felt the same way. "It was apparent at once that we had struck lucky; there appeared in Halsey all the attributes of mind and body which go to make up a great seaman, to which was added a wide humanity," Vian stated years later. "He showed himself fully aware of our difficulties, and from that moment onwards, by kindly word or deed, he availed himself of every possible op-portunity to offer encouragement and to smooth our path."[18] Some of these comments could be dismissed as graciousness in victory and the typi-cal rhetoric of coalition warfare. The respect the British and American ad-mirals had for one another, though, was genuine. When Halsey died, his family asked Rawlings to serve as one of the pallbearers. Much to his re-gret, Rawlings was in poor health and was unable to attend.[19]

The military mission of the U.S. Third and British Pacific Fleets was fourfold: to reduce enemy tactical air forces, attack strategic targets on the mainland, explore Japanese defenses in northern Honshu and Hokkaido, and destroy Japanese shipping. The British had a fifth mission that was political and diplomatic in nature: support the alliance with the United States. In essence, just taking part in military operations met this goal, but the public needed to know that the United Kingdom was taking part in these final blows against the home islands. Statements that Nimitz released to the press clearly announced the attack as a combined U.S.-British operation and clearly identified as many of the British ships taking part in these operations as was prudent to make public. Hanson W. Baldwin, a defense correspondent for the *New York Times*, saw the Royal Navy as making a significant contribution to the defeat of Japan: "The participation of the British Fleet in the great naval blows against the Japanese homeland represents a psychological, as well as a military blow to the enemy."[20]

Logistics continued to plague the British in the operations against Japan, and ultimately limited the utility of the Royal Navy. It is worthwhile to note, though, that limit and eliminate are two different things. Halsey was glad to have the British in the fight and was more than willing to help when possible. He actually found requiring two supply lines a redundant exercise that reduced combat effectiveness. If His Majesty's Ships fueled from U.S. tankers, they were able to deliver just as many combat strikes as the U.S. ships. "One of my most vivid war recollections is of a day when Bert's flagship, the battleship *King George V*, fueled from the tanker *Sabine* at the same time as the *Missouri*," Halsey states in his memoirs. "I went across to 'the Cagey Five,' as we called her, on an aerial trolley, just to drink a toast." The Royal Navy allowed alcohol aboard its ships, while the U.S. Navy did not. American officers were always eager to visit British ships for some reason. The British made Halsey an honorary member of the officers' messes of both the *Duke of York* and the *King George V*. Hard liquor was an asset that served Task Force 37—the new designation of the British now that they were Halsey's command—well. When the *King George V* was short of a spare part for its radar, it signaled a nearby American destroyer asking if they could exchange the needed equipment for a bottle of whisky. "Man, for a bottle of whisky you can have this whole goddamned ship," someone responded on the loudspeaker.[21]

The lack of spare parts, though, was a real danger to the operational effectiveness of the British. This equipment irregularity was another problem that complicated the life of the carrier crews. Different hangar sizes on each ship resulted in five types of planes that could be serviced only on their home carrier and none of the others. The British found ways to stay operational, but by small margins.[22]

Combat operations started on July 17, the day after the British joined up with the Third Fleet. The British formed the northern flank. Since it was the weakest formation under Halsey's command, it made sense to send them north where this vulnerability would put them in less jeopardy. The Japanese had fewer airfields in this region. The Americans encountered bad weather and canceled their attacks. Task Force 37, as the British Pacific Fleet was now designated, had better luck. Planes from the *Formidable* and *Implacable* bombed and strafed airfields and rail facilities on the east coast of Honshu, the biggest of the four main Japanese home islands. No Japanese fighters greeted these planes, but the antiaircraft fire from the ground was heavy. Three planes were lost in this operation, but all the pilots survived. British ships rescued two of them and the USS *John Rodgers* recovered the third pilot. Later in the morning, planes from the *Formidable* and *Victorious* found clouds and weather obscuring their primary targets, so the pilots flew across Honshu and strafed an airfield in the western coastal city of Niigata. That same day the *King George V*, along with two destroyers, joined American ships to bombard the eastern coast of Honshu. The shelling took place in rain and fog, which made it difficult for aircraft to provide spotting. The shelling went on for an hour using radar and loran navigation.[23]

These air missions troubled the British pilots. "The general sensation of being over Japan was one of foreboding, deep fear. We had heard tales of what the locals did to airmen who got hacked down. We got 'in and out' as quickly as we could," Commander R. M. Crosley, the Commanding Officer of the 880th Squadron flying off the *Implacable*, recalled. "We kept below the radar echo height as long as possible so that we did not give warning of our approach. Near the target we split up and climbed to about 8,000 feet and approached in a sort of 'scissors,' with aircraft attacking from different angles. Thus we gave the gunners no time at all to get their fingers out before we were gone—*not* to return." Crosley also worried that the antiaircraft gunners on U.S. ships might not recognize a Seafire or a Firefly as a British plane and would fire on them. With this concern in mind, British pilots flew over U.S. ships slowly in an effort to make sure that their American friends got a good look at their planes.[24]

The logistics services of the Royal Navy faced an amazing challenge in keeping up with the pace the Americans were setting. Many of the tankers the British were using had never refueled a ship at sea, and this inexperi-

Bombing to Win. Bomb plumes rise over Fuge, Japan, after aircraft from the 849th Squadron flying off HMS *Victorious* hit these port facilities on July 28, 1945. Courtesy of the Imperial War Museum

ence slowed down the effort. The difference between success and failure under these conditions was exceptionally thin. Task Force 37 would have missed a day of operations had the course it had taken during the refueling effort not been in the direction of the launching position. Still, Rawlings had to ask Halsey if American oilers would assist their effort. The commander of the Third Fleet agreed, and three cruisers, HMCS *Uganda*, HMNZS *Gambia*, and HMNZS *Achilles* refueled from American tankers. Fraser knew the strengths and liabilities of both his fleet and that of his allies. "The Commander 3rd Fleet is carrying out a series of operations which both strategically and tactically are designed on the most flexible plan. With easy grace he is striking here one day and there the next, replenishing at sea as the situation demands," he observed, nicely summarizing Halsey's approach to naval operations. "With dogged persistence the British Pacific Fleet is keeping up, and if anything is going to stretch its muscles, these operations will. But it is tied by a string to Australia and much handicapped by its few, small, slow tankers."[25]

During these attacks on Japan, one of the missions of the Third Fleet was to destroy what remained of the Combined Fleet. On July 18, U.S. planes attacked Yokosuka in an effort to sink HIJMS *Nagato*, one of the last Japanese battleships. The effort failed and resulted in twelve downed planes. The *Nagato* would survive the war and be a target at the atomic bomb tests at Bikini Atoll in 1946. Then on July 24, 25, and 28, U.S. planes attacked the Kure naval base. "Kure is the port where Jap warships went to die," Halsey enthusiastically declares in his memoirs. The Americans sank a carrier, three battleships, five cruisers, and a number of smaller ships. During the efforts to destroy the enemy, he gave the British secondary targets at Osaka. Task Force 37 performed well in this assignment, setting a record for flying the most sorties in one day, 416. These pilots sank two frigates, doing a good deal of damage to an escort carrier, and several smaller ships in the Inland Sea.[26]

In a passage in his memoirs that is quoted often, Halsey explains that his Chief of Staff, Rear Admiral Robert B. Carney, argued against including the British in the Yokosuka and Kure strikes.

> At Mick Carney's insistence, I assigned the British an alternate target, Osaka, which also offered warships, but none of prime importance. Mick's argument was that although this division of forces violated a fundamental military principle about the concentration of force, it was imperative that we forestall a possible postwar claim by Britain that she had delivered even a part of the final blow that demolished the Japanese Fleet. I hated to admit a political factor into a military equation—my respect for Bert Rawlings and his fine men made me hate it doubly—but Mick forced me to recognize that statesmen's objectives sometimes differ widely from combat objectives, and an exclusively American attack was therefore in American interests.[27]

Vian wrote his memoirs after Halsey and, in fact, quotes this passage. He thought the Japanese ships were not worth the effort. The ships were "immobilized for lack of fuel, heavily camouflaged, and no longer military units except as anti-aircraft batteries." Even with fuel, some of the ships sunk at Kure were targets of little value. Two were built at the turn of the century and used only as training facilities.[28]

In authorizing this attack Halsey acted stupidly—twice. First, in excluding the British from the operation, he clearly confused the institutional interests of the U.S. Navy with the national interests of the United States of America. There might have been an exceptionally important reason to have the British involved in this operation. More to the point, the operation itself was a mistake. What was left of the Combined Fleet no longer posed any offensive threat to U.S. forces. The destruction of the Japanese ships was gratuitous. Even if the war had continued for a number of months, the Americans who died in these missions spent their lives cheaply on targets of little importance.

Halsey discussed this issue in his memoirs. He noted that Vice Admiral John S. McCain opposed the attacks on Kure. Halsey said he had four main reasons for rejecting his advice: national morale demanded revenge for Pearl Harbor; the U.S. Navy had to have total control of the waters of the North Pacific if it was to have regular supply lines to the Soviet Union; and to eliminate the fleet as a bargaining point for the Japanese at a peace conference as the Germans had done after World War I. "There was also a fourth reason: CINCPAC had ordered the Fleet destroyed. If the other reasons had been invalid, that one alone would have been enough for me." Perhaps, but as Halsey's actions in establishing command arrangements with Rawlings showed, there were orders and then there were orders.[29]

Task Force 37 spent July 26 and 27 replenishing their ships. Changes in operations moved the assembly point where the warships would meet up with their tankers. "It was a scramble to get finished in the two days allotted," Vian observed. Rawlings once again had to ask if U.S. ships could help. Halsey quickly agreed. Due to the Canadian government's insistence that only volunteers fight in the Pacific war, the *Uganda* left the war zone and sailed back to North America. A majority of the crew (556 no votes to 345 yes votes) were unwilling to volunteer for duty against Japan. "I am very sorry you are leaving us," Rawlings signaled the ship before it left. "I look forward to your return." The Americans at Eniwetok and Pearl Harbor were less than hospitable to the crew when the ship arrived in port.[30]

On July 29 and 30, the *King George V* joined American ships for the bombardment of Japanese factories in Hamamatsu in southeastern Honshu. On the way to the target, two destroyers, the *Urania* and *Ulysses*, collided with another in a fog. The U.S. commanding officer, Rear Admiral J. F. Shafroth, offered to provide two of his destroyers to escort the damaged ships back to their rendezvous site, but both ships soon reported they were able to continue on with the operation. By the time the British reached their targets, the fog had dissipated. The spotter planes had excellent vision in bright moonlight under a clear night. The battleship took only twenty-seven minutes to fire its salvos and hit everything it was targeting. "Geezus—smack on the kisser," the American spotter pilot reported after the first salvo hit home. The ships never came under fire from shore batteries or planes. The spotter aircraft, however, gave the British incorrect targeting information. The salvos were tightly grouped, but the production facilities escaped serious damage. An official history done at the Admiralty notes, though, that the indirect effects of this operation, such as absent workers and disruption of service, caused a total halt to production.[31]

On July 30 the British flew 336 sorties. The planes stumbled on HIJMS *Okinawa*, a frigate, and sank it. They also damaged a number of other vessels. The weather was poor and there was significant fog. Wind patterns required that the *Implacable* steam west into the fog-covered opening of Tokyo Bay to recover all its planes. The rest of Task Force 37 had no choice but to stay with the carrier, while U.S. ships sailed east, creating a huge gap between the two fleets. A crash on the landing deck slowed down recovery operations. When all the planes were on board, Task Force 37 found itself in Tokyo Bay without any fighter cover above. Vian notes in his memoirs that the British liaison officer on the *Missouri*, in writing a report, stated the BPF became separated from the Americans due to the lack of experience on the part of the admiral commanding the carriers. "This hurt," Vian stated.[32]

The Third Fleet spent the first week in August refueling and trying to avoid typhoons. "Fuelling was carried on as best we could in the unpleasant, long swell coming from the storm centre," Vian recalled. There was a real danger that the sea might indeed roll over some of the smaller ships, particularly those in the fleet train. The bad weather forced Halsey to cancel all operations, while his ships tried to avoid being swamped. For a while it looked as if the British Pacific Fleet would run out of fuel, but another postponement of operations provided enough time for another refueling effort.[33]

On August 9, the planes of the British Pacific Fleet returned to the sky over Japan and suffered one of their heaviest days in losses. The main target was airfields. The British also came across a number of ships and attacked them as targets of opportunity. The results of this combat were good. Royal Navy planes sank three destroyers and damaged several others.[34]

The men who flew planes in British sorties showed exceptional skill and courage on a regular basis, none more so than Lieutenant Robert Hampton Gray of the Royal Canadian Navy Volunteer Reserve. He won the Victoria Cross for leading an attack on the HIJMS *Amakusa*, an *Etorofu* class destroyer escort. His plane came under fire from shore batteries and from five planes. He was hit and on fire, but flew in at a low altitude and scored a direct hit that sank the ship. "The Captain asked to 'take it easy' and not to take undesirable risks," his squadron commander recalled years later. The planes were on a simple strafing mission over an airfield when the destroyer started firing on the British planes. Gray had a 1,000-pound bomb and decided to use it on this unexpected target. Flames enveloped his plane and he crashed into the water. His body was never recovered. "It has always seemed such a terrible shame to me that this quite unexpected chance should have occurred when the war was virtually over," his commanding officer observed sadly.[35]

Despite the problems the British faced in operating in the Pacific, they were making a credible showing. The number of sorties launched per fighter on each strike day had increased. During the operations near Okinawa, the Royal Navy averaged 1.08 in March and April and 1.09 in May. In July and August, the number jumped to 1.54. "Thus fighter effort was some forty per cent greater in the British operations against Japan than in the operations against Sakishima Gunto," Fraser observed in his report to the Admiralty.[36]

While the British Pacific and U.S. Fleets were doing battle on the very shores of Japan, the political leaders of their two nations were meeting in the suburbs of Berlin. Here Truman, Churchill, and the Combined Chiefs of Staff would determine what further involvement, if any, the British would have in the final defeat of Japan.

FIFTEEN

Codename: TERMINAL

The last summit meeting of the Allies took place in Potsdam, Germany, a suburb of Berlin. Much of history has tended to look at this gathering in the context of the start of the Cold War rather than the way it was looked at at the time: a conference still confronting issues relevant to an ongoing war. The danger in doing history is that we know how the story ends. The figures gathering in the ruins of the Third Reich had no way of knowing that the war would end in a matter of days. They were planning for a conflict that they could easily foresee continuing for another year and a half. Such preparation was more than prudent—it was necessary. The planning was real, and this conference shows that the biggest barriers in making a place for the United Kingdom in the fight against the Japanese had been in London. The Americans would welcome the British contribution without reservation, despite whatever Ernest J. King might have wanted in his heart of hearts.

The Americans had an easy trip across the Atlantic. With Germany defeated, there was less need for security than on previous transits. Truman liked music and had concerts played on the deck of the USS *Augusta*. He was also an early riser and declared that breakfast would be served at 7 A.M. "The President said with a smile that that was not a command," Leahy notes in his memoirs. Nonetheless, most members of the U.S. delegation decided that it would be a wise thing if they ate at the same time.

Leahy, like most military professionals, was a morning person, but that was not the case for many in the American contingent. "Some of the others appeared at times as if they would have liked very much to have a couple more hours of sleep," the admiral recalled. You can almost hear him chuckling.[1]

The Americans were going to a hot and muggy city in Europe, Berlin. The British Chiefs of Staff Committee were staying in a villa on the edge of a lake, but the water was dirty and stagnant. Mosquitoes were ever present and, in the words of Cunningham, were "very lively at night." British officials slept under netting to protect themselves from the insects. "Fairly comfortable + the food situation rather good. Drink situation poor. We are apparently expected to do with one soda each per day," the admiral noted. He also had no misperceptions about their Russian allies. "It is said that the Russians just cleared the inhabitants out of the villa lock stock + barrel. One report says they were sent to Russia + an old lady who refused to go was shot + buried at the foot of her own garden. However true that may be the gardens have obviously been tended up to the last moment."[2]

Despite the transition from Roosevelt to Truman, there was a good deal of consistency at this gathering in the form of the Combined Chiefs of Staff. The American and British officers knew each other well. In his memoirs, Leahy gave a famous description of the tone at the summit. "The British throughout the days that followed did most of the proposing and the Americans did most of the disposing."[3] The problem with this statement is that it is misleading, suggesting that the conference was more hostile and confrontational than was actually the case.

The summit reflected a British-American alliance functioning at its best. The Chiefs discussed strategy in rooms that slowly filled with the smoke of tobacco as they used the ashtrays that were carefully aligned in front of them at the tidy tables where they sat. Their first meeting was on July 16, and Cunningham made a record of the day's events: "A cordial meeting with Americans. They agreed to our programme." A long discussion on "unconditional surrender" followed. Cunningham found the Americans willing to be quite candid. Marshall agreed that they should define the term for the Japanese, but only when the Soviet Union entered the war. The admiral realized his American colleagues were looking for a nonmilitary end to the war and asked the British Chiefs to have Churchill raise the issue with Truman. "They are however frightened of the American public opinion + would like a proposal to come from us. Whether in [concern] of

CHAPTER FIFTEEN

a rumpus in America they wish to put the responsibility on us I dont know. However the P.M. who is quite clever enough to see the pitfalls may decide it worth taking some of the opprobrium. If so I'm sure he is right."[4]

Churchill was indeed, as Cunningham noted, a clever man. He did raise the issue of defining "unconditional surrender" when he met Truman for the first time, but he did it verbally. This approach allowed him the option of committing himself later on paper, if he thought it appropriate. The prime minister left a detailed account of his meeting with Truman, which covered a number of issues before getting to the war in the Pacific. Churchill's multipage account is too long to quote fully, but the relevant part about surrender terms deserves to be read in full:

4. I said that the Japanese war might end much quicker than had been expected, and that the eighteen months period which we had taken as a working rule required to be reviewed. Also, Stage III. might be upon us in a few months, perhaps earlier.

I imparted to the President the disclosure, about the offer from the Mikado, made to me by Marshal Stalin the night before; and I told him he was quite free to talk it over with the Marshal, as I had informed him at the Marshal's express desire. (See my conversation recorded by Birse.)

The President also thought the war might come to a speedy end.

Here I explained that Marshal Stalin had not wished to transmit this information direct to him for fear he might think the Russians were trying to influence him towards peace. In the same way I would abstain from saying anything which would indicate that we were in any way reluctant to go on with the war against Japan as long as the United States thought fit. However I dwelt upon the tremendous cost in American life and, to a smaller extent, in British life which would be involved in enforcing "unconditional surrender" upon the Japanese. It was for him to consider whether this might not be expressed in some other way, so that we got all the essentials for future peace and security, and yet left the Japanese some show of saving their military honour and some assurances of their national existence, after they had complied with all safeguards necessary for the conqueror. The President countered by saying that he did not think the Japanese had any military honour left after Pearl Harbour. I contented myself with saying that at any rate they had something for which they were ready to face certain death in very large numbers, and this might not be so important to us as it was to them. He then became quite sympathetic, and spoke as Mr. Stimson had to me two days earlier, of the terrible responsibilities that rested upon him in regard to unlimited effusion of American blood.

My impression is that there is no question of a rigid insistence upon the phrase "unconditional surrender," apart from the essentials necessary for world peace and future security, and for the punishment of a guilty and treacherous nation.

It has been evident to me in my conversations with Mr. Stimson, General Marshal, and now with the President, that they are searching their hearts on this subject, and that we have no need to press it. We know of course that the Japanese are ready to give up all conquests made in this war.[5]

There was no need for Churchill to go further and put a proposal for changing surrender terms on paper.

The new president was still insecure in his position and was wary of being manipulated. The conference was the first meeting between Churchill and Truman. Both men found that they liked and appreciated the other. Churchill's daughter Mary wrote her mother: "He told me he liked the President immensely—they talk the same language." During the conference Truman and Churchill were able to eat together alone. The new president remarked that it had been "the most enjoyable luncheon that he had had for many years." Truman also left an account of their meeting, which goes a long way toward explaining why he made no effort to take advantage of the opening that Leahy had worked to create for him:

He is a most charming and a very clever person—meaning clever in the English not the Kentucky sense. He gave me a lot of hooey about how great my country is and how he loved Roosevelt and how he intended to love me, etc. etc. Well, I gave him as cordial a reception as I could—being naturally (I hope) a polite and agreeable person. I am sure we can get along if he doesn't try to give me too much soft soap.

By the time he departed the White House, Truman would be less reserved. Just after Truman left the office, Roy Jenkins, a junior member of Parliament, visited with him. Later as The Baron Jenkins of Hillhead, he wrote

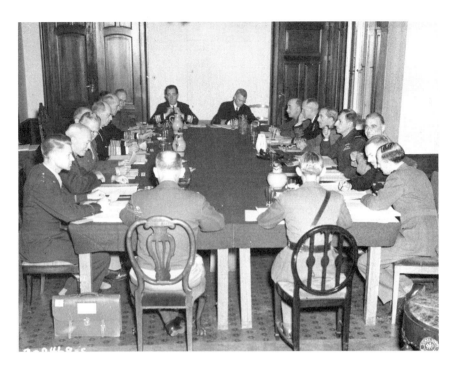

TERMINAL. Even though most people look at the Potsdam Conference as an early event in the Cold War, it was for those present a wartime meeting. The resolution of the war in the Pacific was a major issue for the Combined Chiefs of Staff. Courtesy of the Truman Presidential Library

about Truman and recalled that "all he wanted to do was talk about Churchill, and in a laudatory way." When the conference ended, Andrew Cunningham departed unimpressed with either man, but for different reasons. "Truman looked + talked like a successful small grocer. The P.M. was not at his best."[6]

The next day, July 17, at their 10 A.M. meeting, the U.S. Joint Chiefs of Staff took up the issue of what role their ally should play. In an observation for the record, Arnold noted that the Royal Air Force contribution would complicate logistics and would add little to the combat effectiveness of the bombers already striking Japan. Arnold, along with the other members of the Joint Chiefs, approved a paper accepting a British corps in the invasion of Japan. The next issue they took up was command and control in the Pacific war. This issue had been one fraught with enormous difficulties since the early days of the conflict. The MacArthur-Nimitz/army-navy rivalry had not gone away. Strategy in the Pacific had been the product of compromise, and nothing had changed. The British proposal to put the Pacific under the authority of the Combined Chiefs required that their American opposites do something for the final stages of the war that they had been unwilling to do previously: establish a central command structure and strategy. There was no way the U.S. Chiefs were going to resolve these matters for the British allies and they never even bothered to hold a vote on the proposal.[7]

The Joint Chiefs sent several papers to Brooke, Portal, and Cunningham. The most important one was CCS 889/1, the classification number for their response to the British. In it they first discussed the issue of a Royal Air Force bomber force to which they had already agreed. "In connection with the latter proposal it should be noted that there is little prospect that airfield space for more than ten squadrons of a British very long range (VLR) bomber force will become available at least before 1 December 1945." Marshall, King, Leahy, and Arnold then turned their attention to the question of ground troops. "The United States Chiefs of Staff agree in principle to the participation in the final phase of the war against Japan of a British Commonwealth land force, subject to satisfactory resolution of operational problems by Commander in Chief, U.S. Army Forces, Pacific, and Commander in Chief, U.S. Pacific Fleet." The Joint Chiefs sent a cable to the British a day later in which they listed MacArthur's qualifications, including the ban on the British-Indian Army, removing MacArthur's bluntest statements, but advancing the same reasoning nonetheless. They also forwarded MacArthur's entire memo in another document.[8]

The U.S. and British Chiefs met that afternoon to discuss the papers. Brooke started off the meeting saying he, Portal, and Cunningham were happy and satisfied that the Americans had accepted their offer. He hoped to have a corps composed of a British division, an Australian division, an Indian division, and the New Zealand division. He believed language would be no issue with the Indian division. It had served in Italy under the command of Mark Clark and had already undergone acclimation to a new environment. He also went on to add that he would like the Canadian division in the corps, but he wanted to avoid complicating MacArthur's plans. Portal said he hoped that the empire could contribute a tactical air force even though he knew the Americans had more than enough resources on their own. Arnold said he would look into the matter. Since the plan had been accepted on the contingency of working out operational problems with MacArthur, Brooke suggested that the British send the corps commander and his staff to meet with the field commander. Marshall said this idea was a good one. After some brief discussion about the Australians and New Zealanders, Brooke said he knew including the British in operations in the area of the home islands complicated planning for the Americans, and he deeply appreciated their acceptance of the proposal. Marshall said the United States was glad to have their ally in the last major campaign of the war.[9]

The British were extremely pleased with the views that their American allies had taken. "The reply was far better than we had hoped for, and the offer is accepted in principle," Brooke noted happily.[10]

The British Joint Planning Staff studied MacArthur's proposal and reported back on it in favorable terms.

> Since we have made an offer of a British force for participation in "Coronet" under American command, we consider that the views of the Supreme Commander concerned should be accepted wherever possible. Otherwise we feel there is a danger that the British force will be regarded by the Americans as a tiresome complication and that they will avoid using it if possible, as was the case with the Australian divisions in the Philippines operations.

These officers thought that these conditions were actually good. "From the purely British point of view there are considerable advantages in accepting General MacArthur's proposals in general." The British had a place in the invasion of Japan even though they would not be in on the initial assault on the beaches. "The Americans have offered to provide far more administrative assistance than we ever anticipated. We there by effect a great savings in engineers and problems are avoided."[11]

These issues included shipping and transit routes. There were also some incredible political advantages to having British soldiers, officers, and units train in America. "The passage of a British Division through the United States will have a good effect on United States public opinion." Lord Halifax, the British ambassador in Washington, had recommended such an action a year before:

> If it is at all militarily possible there would be great political advantages in sending through the United States, British land and air forces

destined to participate in operations against Japan. I can of course form no opinion on military difficulties where there may be but I would again urge these be weighed against political dividends, both short and long term, which would be likely to accrue to us provided forces were important enough.

He also suggested that the British military make efforts to facilitate the news coverage of their combat engagements by American reporters. Despite British appreciation for American generosity, staff officers strongly recommended that the British personnel continue to wear their own uniforms.[12]

The Joint Chiefs of Staff sent MacArthur a copy of a directive that the Combined Chiefs gave to Mountbatten—who was present at the conference. The document informed both of the decisions made in Germany that affected him. These matters included theater boundaries, base development, and operations in zones outside those of the Japanese home islands. In the first paragraph, the cable made it clear that the British force for the assault on Japan was the main objective of the empire and Commonwealth. In another section listed under the subheading "British Participation in Main Operations against Japan," the Combined Chiefs informed Mountbatten: "The requirements for the force taking part in the main operations against Japan must have priority over all the other tasks." In sending the cable to MacArthur, the Joint Chiefs were subtly endorsing the positions of their British colleagues and making sure the general understood the importance of having their allies involved in the fight with Japan.[13]

No one discussed the matter of command and control in the Pacific at the Combined Chiefs meeting on July 17. The issue, though, was on the mind of all the participants in the meeting. That same day the Joint Chiefs sent another document to their British counterparts on this topic. "Concerning the matter of higher strategic control in the war against Japan, the thought of the United States Chiefs of Staff is that the role of the Combined Chiefs of Staff in the European war cannot appropriately be applied to the Pacific war." The Americans offered a vague explanation why: "The Pacific area is devoted to the main effort, is organized under a command and control set-up peculiar to the United States, and has forces and resources overwhelmingly United States."[14]

The British Chiefs, in a speedy staff effort, responded that same day, making three points that they believed required their American colleagues

First Contact. Truman and Churchill met for the first time at Potsdam. With British and American advisors waiting in the background, this photograph is a stark documentation of power. Courtesy of the Truman Presidential Library "reconsider their attitude on this question." Great Power status drove the first point. "The United States and Great Britain are the two major powers allied against Japan, and thus jointly responsible for the prosecution of the war. It is most desirable that they should consult freely on all matters of major strategic importance relating to the conduct of the war." After making a weak second point about control over their own forces, the British made another strong argument. "Although the United States are of course providing the major share, the war against Japan, like that against Germany, is being fought with pooled United States and British resources, particularly shipping. It is right, therefore, that the British should have full understanding and knowledge of the proposed methods of applying these resources."[15]

On the afternoon of July 18, the Combined Chiefs met again. A number of minor issues on their agenda took only a few minutes at the beginning of the meeting. They then spent some time talking about moving the boundary lines between the theater commands of MacArthur and Mountbatten. The next major issue the group discussed was the strategic determination of the war in the Pacific. Marshall admitted that in the past the U.S. Joint Chiefs had failed to provide the British with information about the fight against the Japanese. They would correct this shortcoming in the future. The distances involved in this theater were immense and the U.S. Chiefs were unprepared to debate operations with their allies. The British would, of course, be free to withdraw their forces from any action to which they objected. At the meeting, Brooke said he and his colleagues did indeed feel excluded, but they supported the effort against Japan without reservation. Later that day in his diary, Brooke admitted that he and his colleagues "were on much thinner ice!" than they had been on the topic of getting troops involved in the invasion.

> We had asked for a quarter share in the control of operations in the Pacific, and the Americans showed every sign of reluctance to afford us such facilities. Marshall made a very nice speech pointing out the difficulties of control in the Pacific and the desirability to simplify the control + avoid delays. They would be prepared to discuss strategy but final decisions must rest with them. If the plan for the invasion of the Tokio Plain did not suit us we could withhold our forces but they would still carry on. On the whole I think that the discussion cleared the air a good deal.[16]

Cunningham took a similar view.

> At the latter we took the very thorny subject of control of strategy in the Pacific. We reached a friendly agreement which answered to us the right of being consulted but the final decision in case of disagreement must rest with USCOS. In view of the disparity in the size of the forces to be employed this is I think reasonable. King tried to be rude about it but nobody paid any attention to him. Marshal [*sic*] and Arnold going out of their way to be pleasant + friendly.[17]

The Combined Chiefs of Staff formalized these understandings on July 24 in their final report to the president and prime minister. The Chiefs reported: "The invasion of Japan and operations directly connected therewith are the supreme operations in the war against Japan; forces and resources will be allocated on the required scale to assure that invasion can be accomplished at the earliest practicable date. No other operations will be undertaken which hazard the success of, or delay, these main operations." The British Pacific Fleet would continue to operate with the U.S. Navy. The Royal Air Force would contribute ten squadrons of bombers to the strategic bombing of Japan. This force would increase to twenty squadrons when airfields became available sometime after December 1. There was also agreement in "principle" that a land force made of British and Commonwealth units would take part in the invasion of Japan, dependent on the resolution of operational issues. A small tactical air force might also take part in the invasion. The U.S. Joint Chiefs of staff would remain in control of operational strategy, but promised in the bureaucratic language of the report to give "full and timely information as to their future plans and intentions" to their British counterparts.[18]

In between their meetings and after they had discussed the various issues of strategy, the American and British Chiefs of Staff took time off to relax. Portal and Brooke tried to go fishing on the lake outside their villa, but Russian soldiers without much regard for their rank chased them off. During a lull in the conference, the two took a plane to Bavaria, where they fished in a German river. They caught only a few fish, and Brooke noted that German soldiers fishing with hand grenades and masses of American soldiers had "spoiled" local supplies. Still, staying in some of the finest accommodations that the U.S. Army managed to appropriate, Brooke found the area therapeutic and a refreshing break from the stress of planning a war. "The surroundings were most attractive, nice brown coloured cattle with lovely sounding bells, very fine pine forests, and a feeling of wilderness." Cunningham had no interest in relaxing and decided to spend his time inspecting German naval facilities.[19]

Visiting the various units stationed in and around the area of the conference was less a relaxation than a duty for the Combined Chiefs, but one that was a little less stressful than other parts of their jobs at the conference. The British flag officers accompanied their allies as they inspected the U.S. 2nd Armored Division on July 18. Three days later, the Americans reciprocated as British soldiers marched past the delegation from the United Kingdom in review. In a harbinger of things to come Deputy Prime Minister Clement Attlee, rather than Churchill, drew a huge cheer from the soldiers.[20]

Touring the German capital was another side activity. After one meeting, Marshall and Arnold had tea with their British colleagues, and then the group went into Berlin. The summit offered these officers the chance to see the destruction that war had brought to the German capital. The streets were clear, but the buildings were rubble. "Such a mess—hardly a house left standing," Cunningham noted. Arnold observed, "Twenty-five, fifty years to get Berlin back as a city—who knows?" The group went to the Reich Chancellery and in one room came across a mass of Iron Crosses and other medals that were strewn about the floor. As they were leaving, a boy about 10 years old put his head into Brooke's car and asked him for chocolate. Brooke replied in German, but there is no record if the boy got any chocolate. "He + I were in a car with Marshal [sic] who talked + talked + was most boring," Cunningham observed. In a reflective moment, Brooke found the experience a bit surreal. "The whole afternoon seemed like a dream, and I found it hard to believe that after all these years' struggles I was driving through Berlin!!" At other times, the British Chiefs were like almost any other group of foreign tourists and took in some of the sites in Potsdam with regular travel guides. Sans Souci, the palace of Frederick the Great, was in Cunningham's words "a rather foul place" that was overly ornate. He also observed, "No signs of a bathroom or lavatory." Brooke was more impressed. "Most interesting" was his comment. The Chiefs also got to visit Hitler's bunker. "A sordid and unromantic spot" in Brooke's words. "The more one sees of it the more one realizes how completely destroyed it is."[21]

As at other conferences, dinner meetings were part of this gathering. On

July 23, Churchill hosted a large banquet for all the Allies. "It was a good dinner with RAF band, rather spoilt by continuous speeches," Brooke commented. There was also much drinking. Cunningham recorded, "Leahy got very bottled + King very mellow fell on my neck + besought me to call him Ernie!!" After the meal, the guests began collecting each other's signatures on their menus. Cunningham got everyone present to sign his. Brooke made special note of his interaction with Stalin. "He turned round, looked at me, smiled very kindly and shook me warmly by the hand before signing." The playing of the various national anthems ended the evening.[22]

With the end of the war clearly in view, the Chiefs began thinking of their futures. In a sign of how close the American and British Chiefs had become, the idle talk over drinks was about personal plans. Marshall said he would retire in October. He was tired and Eisenhower would do well as the head of the U.S. Army. "I argued with him + told him I thought he should remain till the end of the Jap war," Cunningham noted. "Curiously sitting with Brooke over a whisky + soda he said he must retire at the end of the year." The field-marshal explained that he was tired and had been CIGS long enough. He thought it was time for another man to do the job.[23]

As Brooke prepared to leave Germany, he made an entry in his diary: "Thus finished our Combined Chiefs of Staff Meeting in Berlin!! where we had never hoped to meet in our wildest dreams in the early stages of this war. And now that we are here I feel too weary and cooked to even get a kick out of it. It all feels flat and empty. I am feeling very very tired and worn out." These comments could have applied to a lot of the victors in Berlin.[24]

In an ironic twist, the main British figure in Germany who still wanted to wield power was the one who would be stepping aside. The general election had ended and Churchill was awaiting the ballot count during the Potsdam conference. Some saw what was coming. While in Germany, Churchill had dinner with Mountbatten and they discussed the admiral's future. The prime minister was certain he would be shaping the postwar world. Mountbatten had been in India with troops who had already cast their ballots, and he had a different view of the future. "It was a mournful and eerie feeling to sit there talking plans with a man who seemed so confident that they would come off, and I felt equally confident that he would be out of office within 24 hours." It took forty-eight hours, but Mountbatten proved to be a better prognosticator. Labour won 393 seats to 213 for the Conservative Party. It was the first time in British history that the Labour Party had garnered more votes than the Conservatives. Churchill resigned on the evening of July 26 even though he could have waited until the seating of the new Parliament.[25]

Churchill handled the defeat as best as one could reasonably expect. He was philosophical about the results. "They are perfectly entitled to vote as they please. This is democracy. This is what we've been fighting for." When Lord Moran characterized the vote as "ingratitude," Churchill disagreed. "I wouldn't call it that. They have had a very hard time." He even showed some humor, black though it was. When Clementine Churchill said the defeat might be a blessing in disguise, Churchill replied, "At the moment it seems quite effectively disguised." His public farewell statement was proper and dignified: "It only remains for me to express to the British people, for whom I have acted in these perilous years, my profound gratitude for the unflinching, unswerving support which they have given me during my task, and for the many expressions of kindness which they have shown towards their servant."[26]

Brooke's diary entry reflected his complex feelings for Churchill. "It was a very sad and very moving little meeting at which I found myself unable to say much for fear of breaking down. He was standing the blow wonderfully well." In a postwar addition to his journal, Lord Alanbrooke continued: "The thought that my days of work with Winston had come to an end was a shattering one. There had been very difficult times, and times when I felt I could not stand a single more day with him, but running through all our difficulties a bond of steel had been formed uniting us together." He reflected on their relationship and its impact on the course of the war and explained why the Chiefs had never issued an ultimatum that could have resulted in mass resignations. "We had been so closely linked together in this vast struggle that it would have been impossible for us to go on striving together unless a deep bond of friendship had existed; had this not been the case there would have been only one alternative, that of parting." Alanbrooke knew, though, that at times the two had come close to their limits. "I marvel even now that as a result of some of our differences he did not replace me."[27]

When Churchill left office, he released his Farewell Honours List. He gave each of the Chiefs a title of nobility, making them Barons. Each of the new lords of the realm took titles representing their family homes. Brooke became Baron Alanbrooke of Brookeborough, County Fermanagh. Cunningham took the title of Baron Cunningham of Hyndhope of Kirhope in the County of Selkirk. Portal became Baron Portal of Hungerford, Hungerford, County Berks. Arnold wrote his friend and counterpart: "I have just received information that you are now to be known as Marshal of the Royal Air Lord Portal of Hungerford. God, what a handle! I don't know what it means so I don't know whether to congratulate or commiserate with you, but if it is something good I congratulate you." The new Lord Alanbrooke would have taken the offer of commiseration: "Apparently I can't get out of it under £200 which appals me."[28]

One of many ramifications of the election was that it would be the new Labour government and the new prime minister, Clement Attlee, who would oversee the policy that Churchill had so long fought against. On July 31, Attlee sent a cable to the prime ministers of the self-governing Dominions, informing them about the decisions reached on Japan in Germany. "Planning is premised on the belief that the defeat of enemy's armed forces in the Japanese homeland is a pre-requisite to unconditional surrender, and that such a defeat will establish the optimum prospect of capitulation by Japanese forces outside the main Japanese islands."[29]

Attlee had been elected on domestic issues. His job was to lead British society in recovering from the war, not to lead the United Kingdom in further conflict. It was clear in late July that the Allies were about to claim a victory over the Japanese. The problem was, the Japanese refused to concede the issue to their enemies. As a result, the leaders of the U.S.-British coalition had to confront the issue of how long it would take to defeat Imperial Japan. The answer to that question seemed anything but certain.

SIXTEEN

Australia and New Zealand

After Churchill made his decision and conceded to the Chiefs' views, it was necessary to consult with the Dominions. The force that Brooke, Portal, and Cunningham had proposed would be imperial in its composition. Units would come from all over the empire and Commonwealth. As such, the governments of the self-governing Dominions would have to agree to this proposal. Canada had already committed itself to contributing ground units to the invasion of Japan; Australia and New Zealand had not. Many casual observers tend to view Australia and New Zealand as a collective entity. Despite their common British heritage, each has some significant variations in its political, economic, and cultural composition. In 1945, these differences came into play and resulted in a situation where Australia, despite its intense interest in the defeat of Japan, was in danger of isolating itself, while New Zealand was moving to the center of events. Both outcomes were unexpected in London, and even in Canberra and Wellington.

On July 4, Churchill cabled both Curtin and Fraser informing them that the British were putting together plans to have an imperial force take part in the invasion of Japan. The only difference in each cable was the use of the words: "Australia" and "New Zealand." In the cable he sent to Curtin, Churchill stated, "I am well aware that the Australian Government wish to take part in the main operations against Japan and therefore it would be most welcome if the Australian Division, which I understand will be available, would join this force, the R.A.N. form part of the naval forces involved and the R.A.A.F. squadrons form part of the air component." There were critical political reasons for such a contribution. "I am sure you will agree with me that a joint Commonwealth Force of British, Australian, New Zealand, British-Indian and possibly Canadian divisions would form a striking demonstration of Commonwealth solidarity, and that it is important that we should share with the Americans the burden of the assault on Japan."[1]

With the war in Europe over, the Australian Cabinet was more interested in a reduction in the mobilization of the economy than in showing Commonwealth solidarity. Minister for War Organization of Industry John Dedman warned his colleagues in the War Cabinet that "very important issues are at stake from the viewpoint of the civil economy, and the progress of the Government's plans for an orderly re-diversion of resources from war to peacetime uses."[2]

One of the ways that the Cabinet hoped to start demobilizing the war economy was by cutting the size of the military, primarily the army and the air force. Even though the Advisory War Council and the War Cabinet made no conscious decision to have Australians do less fighting, that was the inevitable result of a move reducing the number of personnel in the armed services. Blamey realized what would happen and warned the government about the ramifications of their contemplated action. In September 1944, he told Curtin he had "grave misgivings" about the ability of the army to wage operations given the types of cuts that people in the government were discussing.[3]

The issue drifted for months in part because John Curtin was in extremely poor health. A colleague noted that after Curtin returned from London he "appeared to be listless, to have no energy, and to show a reluctance to face up to issues." The prime minister began having breathing problems, and on November 3, 1944, he had a heart attack while in Melbourne. The 60-year-old Curtin told his wife, "he felt his age."[4]

His health problems only increased. While in the hospital, he gave up smoking, and like many others found eliminating nicotine from his daily life an amazingly frustrating experience. His heart problems were severe and refused to go away. Colleagues found him under more stress and noticed that he became more irritable in dealing with reporters. Journalists also noted his declining health and wondered in print if he should resign.

Lung problems put him back in the hospital in April 1945. He spent a month in the hospital, but when he was released was too weak to climb the stairs to his bedroom. Curtin had access to no official papers, and told a friend he was "too tired to live."[5]

Few developments in the realm of policy took place during this time. The War Cabinet was unable to resolve manpower issues. In May 1945, the German surrender finally required that the Australian government make some sort of decision about its contribution to the crusade against the Japanese. Blamey brought the issue to a head. On May 16, he wrote a letter to the acting minister for the army, stating that with the defeat of the Nazis "the reallocation of the Australian Military Forces must therefore now be reconsidered." There were several options available, and it was up to the Cabinet to make the decision. "In any one of these cases it is not a strategical question as to where the Australian Military Forces should be employed, or as to what strength should be allotted. It is purely a political one for determination by the Australian Government." The Cabinet was going to have to be selective in the decisions it made about where its troops fought as it reduced its army, and Blamey said participating in the final defeat of Japan was the choice of the army itself. "It is probable that, if the Australian contribution is allotted to SWPA, it will ultimately be included in any organisation which reaches Japan proper. This would be most popular with a great many troops. The Americans would however endeavour to alter its organisation to American pattern."[6]

A series of War Cabinet meetings followed, all designed to resolve a number of issues related to the matters Blamey raised in his letter. On May 22, the general told the ministers that he was personally inclined toward participation in the attack on Japan itself, but he thought Australia would have to make some sort of token commitment to Mountbatten's command. On May 28, another meeting of the War Cabinet took place and most of the members were moving in the direction of Blamey's thinking. National prestige, influence at the peace conference, repaying the Americans for their assistance in Australia's darkest hour, and a desire to deliver retribution upon the Japanese were some of the reasons thrown about in these meetings for sending Australians to fight in the final and decisive operations. The efforts to retake Borneo, the Netherlands East Indies, and Malaya were nothing more than large-scale mop-up operations, which lacked the importance of the planned invasion of Japan. In rather bland language, the War Cabinet decided that it would commit itself to field:

"The main force, of a strength to be decided, but consisting of at least one Division and ancillary units, as recommended by General Blamey, to be assigned to General MacArthur for participation in his offensive against Japan."[7]

The question of manpower had yet to be decided. On May 31, the War Cabinet met again and decided to reduce the army and air force by at least 50,000 men. Those individuals with five years of service overseas would have the first opportunity to separate from the armed services. On June 5, the War Cabinet decided that they would also reduce the army to an operational force of three divisions. The Royal Australian Air Force would take a proportional reduction, but the Royal Australian Navy would take no cuts and would continue on at its current strength.[8]

These factors had an impact on the invasion of Balikpapan. This operation was to take place in July, but with Okinawa in American hands there was no reason for this assault, at least strategically. The seizure of the Ryukyus cut Japan off from its southern territories. Blamey realized, though, that the Cabinet's desire to reduce the numbers serving in the armed forces required downsizing the operation. In his letter of May 16, he wrote, "I would suggest that the United Kingdom Government be informed accordingly and that General MacArthur be informed that the 7th Division is not available for further operations until the overall plan is known." He also knew that all the local commanders believed the operation was short of "any real object."[9]

On May 20, Curtin's main deputy, Ben Chifley, asked MacArthur about Blamey's idea. The American responded that same day with a blunt and deceptive letter. "The Borneo Campaign in all its phases has been ordered by the Joint Chiefs of Staff who are charged by the Combined Chiefs of Staff with the responsibility for strategy in the Pacific," he stated. "The concentration is in progress and it is not now possible to substitute another division and execute the operation as scheduled. The attack will be made as projected unless the Australian Government withdraws the 7th Division from assignment to the Southwest Pacific Area." The ramifications of such a decision would be huge. "I am loath to believe that your Government contemplates such action at this time when the preliminary phases of the operation have been initiated and when withdrawal would disorganise completely not only the immediate campaign but also the strategic plan of the Joint Chiefs of Staff." If the Australians still persisted in such an action, he made it clear that he would take the matter up with the U.S. and British

Chiefs. Finally, there was no reason for the Curtin government to follow Blamey's suggestion, since there were "no specific plans as far as I know for employment of Australian troops after the Borneo campaign."[10]

This reply was dishonest, since the cancellation of the Balikpapan operation would hardly derail overall allied strategy in the Pacific. MacArthur had also convinced the U.S. Joint Chiefs of Staff to approve the operation since it represented a strong desire on the part of the Australian people and government. Now, he was telling the Australians that this operation represented a vital element in a larger strategic plan that the Joint Chiefs had set in motion.[11]

The comment about post-Borneo use of Australian combat troops should have been a warning to the Curtin government that MacArthur had no intention of using these units in the assault on Japan. Lieutenant-General Sir Charles Gairdner, Lumsden's replacement as the British political representative at MacArthur's headquarters, got the impression during this time that it was highly unlikely that Australians would see combat in Japan. No responsible official in Canberra took notice of these troubling indicators.[12]

Instead, Curtin bent to MacArthur's will. He replied, assuring the American that Australia had "no hesitation in agreeing to the use of the 7th Division as planned."[13]

The War Cabinet met two days later to formally ratify this decision. Blamey was in attendance and the main point of contention was Balikpapan and the use of the 7th Division. The conversation hardly does credit to the reputations of many of those present. Shedden tried to argue that Blamey had approved the operation before, but the general contested that point, saying he had approved other landings, but not Balikpapan. He then explained that if the 7th Division fought in this operation, then the Dominion would lose its "flexibility." Acting Defence Minister John Beasley said Australia wanted harmonious relations with MacArthur and suggested that at this late date it would be difficult to withdraw on the general. Chifley agreed. It was too late to do anything else, he said. Blamey warned that Balikpapan was a worthless target that the Allies could ignore. Shedden weighed in trying to protect the decision that Curtin had made and to which he contributed. He basically argued that MacArthur had never changed his plans on the Australians and that changing the commitment of the government to the operations at this late a date was wrong. In short, Australia had no other option but to go forward with current plans. While there was some truth to his argument, Shedden made no effort to argue the merits of the operation. Indeed, the idea of any government of any nation placing its relationship with a foreign general over its responsibility to make decisions in the best interests of its people is stunningly irresponsible.[14]

Curtin never read Churchill's July 4 cable. He died while the telegram was in transit. As a result, the indecision of the past few months continued as the official business of the Australian government was mourning the loss of its prime minister. The day after Curtin's death, His Royal Highness Prince Henry, the Duke of Gloucester, in his capacity as the Governor-General of Australia, commissioned Frank Forde to form a new government. That same day Curtin's body lay in state at Parliament House in King's Hall. A gun carriage took the body back to the airport for Curtin's final trip to Perth. A crowd of 100,000 people, about one-third the population of the city, lined the route the cortege took to the cemetery. Graveside services took place on a bright, sunny afternoon in the brisk temperatures of an Australian winter. Six servicemen then lowered the plain oak coffin into the ground.[15]

Forde's tenure as prime minister came to an end a week after it started, making his time in office the shortest in Australian history. On July 12, the MPs of the Labour Party elected Ben Chifley Prime Minister of Australia. A lanky man of Irish heritage, he had no real following with the public at the time. In 1912, he met Elizabeth McKenzie at a dance. She was a Presbyterian and he was a Catholic at a time when religious differences divided Australians socially, economically, and politically. Despite having little in common with one another, their relationship blossomed and in 1914, Chifley defied his parents and a papal decree prohibiting marriage outside of the church. "One of us has to take the knock," he told a friend. "It'd better be me." Neither set of parents attended the Presbyterian wedding service. Soon, the marriage foundered. She had a deformed spine that made it difficult for her to stand for long periods. Such a handicap also made having sexual relations a difficulty and this part of their marriage came to an end. This development hardly boded well, but divorce was out of the question. Instead, he sought sexual gratification with other women; with his secretary, Phyllis Donnelly, and occasionally her sister, Nell, an arrangement that had the apparent knowledge and consent of both women.[16]

Chifley worked on the railroads in New South Wales, becoming active in the union movement, and was instrumental in establishing the Australian Federated Union of Locomotive Enginemen. In 1922, he moved into politics trying to win a seat in the State Parliament of New South Wales. Failing in this attempt, it took him more tries to win a seat in the federal legislature as a member of the Labour Party in 1928. During his early days in Canberra, he developed a close relationship with John Curtin and quickly moved up in the political world, serving as Minister of Defense in 1931. Chifley lost his seat during the Great Depression, and tried twice to return to Parliament before finally enjoying success in 1939. During the war, he became Curtin's main deputy in fact, although not in name. In a sign of how little contact the Chifleys had with one another, Elizabeth Chifley learned from reporters that her husband had decided to run for prime minister.[17]

One of the first major policy matters Chifley examined was the role Australia would play in the final operations against Japan. He relied heavily on Shedden and had no love for Blamey, and the general had not cared for the new prime minister. "My experience of Chifley is that there is nothing he hates quite so much as a soldier," Blamey stated later. Curtin had protected the general from Cabinet colleagues that had no liking for him. Without his patron, Blamey's termination now was only a question of time.[18]

The new prime minister did, though, have concerns about the relationship that Sir Frederick had built for Australia with MacArthur. In April, members of the opposition began questioning the wisdom and merit of some military operations. Curtin had discussed the matter with Blamey, and the general said MacArthur had given the Australian First Army a strategic mission to contain bypassed Japanese units. He also explained that MacArthur had provided landing craft to the Australians, which suggested that the American approved of these operations. When Curtin died, Chifley took up the matter with the general. In his reply, MacArthur stated that in his last meeting with Curtin, he had told the prime minister, "I was in disapproval of the method suggested as being unnecessary and wasteful of lives and resources."[19]

This letter bothered Chifley to no end and it took him two months to formulate a response. "The Government has always worked on the assumption, in view of the powers vested in you as Commander-in-Chief, that, even within the limits of discretion allowed subordinate Commanders, their plans would be subject to your broad approval." Although polite, Chifley made it clear that he was unhappy with MacArthur's treatment of the Dominion. "In regard to the views expressed by you to the Prime Minister at your last interview in Canberra, it must not be overlooked, from the Australian Government's point of view, that it has not been fully and continuously in touch with all variations in your plans as was the case when your Headquarters were in Australia." In diplomatic language, he also made it clear that the exclusion of Australia from the forums of strategy and policy was no way for MacArthur to treat an ally. "I regret to say that the Government is greatly embarrassed by your reply."[20]

Shedden was worried about this exchange. In an effort to prevent a break in the relationship to which he owed so much of his own influence and importance, he wrote a cover letter to MacArthur attempting to minimize its impact. He informed the general that this was a letter that only Chifley and he had actually read. MacArthur never responded to the prime minister.[21]

The New Zealanders were far less troublesome and far more direct in dealing with their allies than the Australians. When Whitehall sent a cable to New Zealand, it was a gesture of courtesy more than a real effort to solicit troops. In 1945, the Dominion had a population smaller than that of either London or New York, yet it had an army, navy, and air force fighting in the war from almost the very beginning. With the bulk of its economy coming from agriculture, the New Zealanders also provided much of the foodstuffs that fed allied personnel. The Kiwis had done more than their fair share, so it was a pleasant surprise to officials in both London and Washington that they agreed to contribute troops. The factors most responsible for this surprising development were Fraser, the Labour Party, and the politics of New Zealand national interest and identity.

During World War II, New Zealand sent the bulk of its personnel to fight in North Africa, the Mediterranean, and Europe alongside other formations of the British Empire and Commonwealth. With the fight against Germany over, the Kiwis could be forgiven for thinking their war had ended, but that view belonged to a minority in Wellington. In 1940, the New Zealand House of Representatives declared "the unalterable determination of the Dominion to continue this struggle side by side with the United Kingdom and the other Members of the British Commonwealth until the final victory is attained." The legislature issued such resolutions on a yearly basis throughout the war and in 1944 declared on behalf of the New Zealand people its "determination to continue undiminished their efforts towards final victory against all our enemies."[22]

An extremely important factor in the thinking of many Kiwis was that they were a "British people" and that their country was one of the "British nations." Fraser wanted the United Kingdom to be a power in the Pacific region to counterbalance the growing power of the United States. "I emphasized the fact that New Zealand desired—and I was interpreting the mind of the Parliament of New Zealand—and was strongly of the opinion that the United Kingdom should continue to play her full part in the Pacific," he told Parliament about his talks in the United States during his travel to the Prime Ministers' Conference.[23]

While most New Zealanders thought of themselves as being British subjects, they were well aware that developments in the Pacific were of the utmost importance to them given the geographic location of their homes. "The Pacific is an area in which we are very much interested," Joseph Cotterill, a member of the House of Representatives from Wanganui, stated. Fraser's notes for a speech he gave state: "Probably more important to contribute land force aimed at the heart of Japan than maintain Air Forces engaged in mopping up back areas."[24]

The dictates of what is best described as New Zealand's national security strategy were another factor in motivating the Kiwis to send troops to fight in Japan. The country had a population that was so small that it lacked the simple numbers to physically protect itself. It had to have a larger patron and had to send some troops into combat in far-off places to keep threats far, far away. "In fighting in the Pacific we are fighting for our own security and for the security of future generations in this part of the world," Finance Minister Walter Nash declared. The New Zealanders were also aware that the United States was a new player in the Pacific on which it would rely more for security. "We are agreed in view of our position as a Pacific nation, the need for maintaining our relations with the United States of America on the friendliest terms and firmest basis," Nash stated in early 1945. At the time, officials in Wellington saw the Americans not as replacements to the British, but as a nice addition.[25]

The two-island nation as a whole was also an enthusiastic proponent of a liberal Wilsonian postwar world order in which the new United Nations organization was a key player. In such a system, small powers, like New Zealand, would have a voice and no longer suffer abuse from the likes of Germany and Japan. In this way, New Zealand would have influence in world affairs, but the price for this influence was that it had to make security contributions, even when it had no direct interests at stake. Support for such a view was broad and extensive among the Kiwi public, and the invasion of Japan was the acid test for such a commitment.[26]

New Zealand officials were earnest in their intentions and began making arrangements to send their soldiers to do battle with the Japanese long before the Americans and British had made final and firm plans. In late January, Churchill cabled Fraser about the deployment of New Zealand units after the war with Germany ended. The decision would be made in Wellington, but Churchill suggested that if the New Zealanders chose to operate with the United States, they would be assigned minor areas.[27]

One of the most important individuals in the decision-making process was a friend of Churchill's, Lieutenant-General Sir Bernard Freyberg, Commanding General of the 2nd New Zealand Expeditionary Force. A big, burly man who stood at six feet and one and a half inches with a square jaw, Freyberg was a good representative of the imperial or transnational nature of the British military. Born in England, he and the rest of his family moved to New Zealand when he was two. He grew up in Wellington and would always speak in his high-pitched voice with a New Zealand accent. In World War I, he joined the Royal Navy and later transferred to the British Army. As a Lieutenant-Colonel in command of a battalion, he won the Victoria Cross, the highest military decoration that Britain awards. A capable officer, he was promoted rapidly and at 28 became the youngest General in the British Army.[28]

After the war, he decided to make the army a career. He married the widow of an RAF pilot and raised her two sons as his own along with a third boy his wife delivered after their wedding. His career moved upward in steady fashion with Freyberg becoming a Major-General in 1933. In early 1935, he took a routine medical exam for a foreign posting and was stunned when the doctor found a heart murmur. This medical condition brought Freyberg's military career to an end in 1937—at least temporarily. When war returned to Europe in 1939, the British Army found itself facing a shortage of general officers. The service offered him the chance to return to active duty as the General Officer Commanding the Salisbury Plain Area, a training command. He accepted. One of the main activities that Freyberg oversaw was the administration of medical exams. He had his entire headquarters report for physicals, and the general stood in line with the cooks, privates, and junior officers. In this situation, the physicians were a little less diligent and a month after the United Kingdom went to war, an army doctor certified that "Major-General Freyberg has today been examined by me and is found fit for general service." Medical officials in the War Office were less than happy with this sleight of hand, but with a war on they were less stringent. Even though another medical board found the heart murmur again, it put fewer restrictions on his service.[29]

Just as this process concluded, Freyberg received a telegram from Fraser asking him to meet with him during a trip he was taking to London. The then–deputy prime minister of New Zealand was looking for an officer to command the expeditionary force that the Dominion was preparing. After consulting a number of other individuals and hearing nothing but praise for the man, Fraser offered him the position. Freyberg accepted on the spot.[30]

The English-born New Zealander serving in the British Army would now command the 2nd New Zealand Expeditionary Force and the 2nd New Zealand Division, which was the combat element of this detachment. The New Zealand Military Forces—which was the name of the army—like the Canadian Army, was basically an adjunct of the British Army in organization and doctrine.[31]

When it came to the New Zealand war effort after the defeat of Germany, Freyberg believed that participation in the Pacific war was an undertaking that was more diplomatic than military in nature. He believed Japanese soldiers and the Imperial Japanese Army were less effective than their German allies. "My personal opinion is that Japan may be defeated before end of 1946 in which case our participation in Japanese war would be very short."[32]

He thought, though, that New Zealand should concentrate its small resources in Japan, where it would have the most return for its efforts, and where New Zealand personnel could be most effective. "If employed in China and Japan NZ Division would be used not only at point of greatest military importance but in theatre where our heavy equipment could be used to advantage." Such a deployment would be in the interest of all concerned. "On facts as I know them it would seem that if suitable arrangements can be made to serve with AIF in China or Japan[,] New Zealand and Australia together could play part in decisive theatre thus serving national as well as allied interests."[33]

Lieutenant-General Edward Puttick, Chief of the General Staff, had different views on the matter. He thought New Zealand should focus on regions other than Japan. "Employment under South East Asia Command offers the most definite and important task for N.Z. forces so far as can be seen at present." In an argument that reflected the close orientation of

New Zealand to the mother country, Puttick said such a move would also be good for all His Majesty's Dominions. "From a British Commonwealth and Empire point of view, the employment of N.Z. troops in what would then be the most prominent British theatre of war should have an excellent morale effect on the British forces required to operate there." Working with their Americans allies was not such a good idea. "Owing to differences in organisation, ammunition and equipment it seems most unlikely that a N.Z. Division could participate fully with U.S. forces and would most likely be given garrison or other relatively unimportant work."[34]

In the wake of this military input, another English-born New Zealander played a major role in the War Cabinet debates that followed. Walter Nash was the Finance Minister and Deputy Prime Minister. While Fraser was in San Francisco for the conference that would create the United Nations, Nash served as Acting Prime Minister. He was 27 years old when he migrated to New Zealand in 1909 with his wife and son. Nash was something of a living contradiction. Prim and proper, he never used strong language and had a difficult time showing his feelings to anyone other than his wife. Despite this reserved personality, he was gregarious in public and was diligent about attending public events.[35]

Under Nash's leadership, the War Cabinet decided in early 1945 to send a division to Mountbatten's South-East Asia Command. The Royal New Zealand Air Force would most likely serve in that theater as well, although units and individuals might also be part of the strategic bombing force that would strike at Japan. The Royal New Zealand Navy, on the other hand, would send men and ships to serve in the British Pacific Fleet. Sending ground troops to fight in the South-East Asia Command seemed like the only option available to New Zealand. Fighting with U.S. forces appeared to be out of the question. Brooke informed Fraser: "It would not, however, be easy for her to operate with the Americans, by reason of the difference of equipment and of organisation, unless her Division formed part of a larger British Empire force." Nash agreed: "We have experience of operations with British units which have already been satisfactory." It was also clear to Fraser, who was on a trip to London at the time, that the British would welcome the Kiwis. "It seems clear that the United Kingdom Chiefs of Staff would welcome the idea of any such New Zealand force, particularly if it could be reorganized in the Middle East for immediate transfer to the concentration area, which would probably be South-East Asia Command," Fraser wrote to Nash.[36]

The main issue then became troop numbers. With the defeat of the Nazis, the government and War Cabinet expected some type of reduction in the mobilization of New Zealand society. "It is clear that we cannot maintain our present military commitments after the end of this year," Nash informed Fraser after one meeting.[37]

The politicians again turned to Freyberg. "Your cable of 8 April arrived eight hours before our offensive started here and, as you will realise, we are working under difficulties," he replied after his soldiers had started an assault across the Senio River in Italy. Told that the War Cabinet wanted to begin demobilization and could authorize a force of only 15,000 men, the general was a little disturbed. "I believe that this can be done by sacrificing the fighting efficiency and endurance as well as the welfare and eventual morale of the force." He thought a smaller force would be less effective since it would have less firepower. "I am strongly against a small division and strongly in favour of fighting the Japanese with heavy equipment rather than infantry." The fewer munitions New Zealanders threw at the enemy, the more likely they were to take a higher casualty rate. "Our policy should be to fight the Japanese with artillery and tanks as far as possible and avoid costly hand-to-hand fighting by infantry." He thought the defeat of the Japanese would be easier, so he was willing to consider using smaller reserves. Freyberg tinkered with the numbers a bit and found he could reduce the current size from 19,000 to 17,000, but he thought going below that figure was a sure way to take higher losses. The War Office in London had little enthusiasm for a light New Zealand division. "They appear, however, so anxious to have a New Zealand force that they will be grateful for any help," the general observed.[38]

There were several ways to make up the difference, and Freyberg cautioned against many of them. Although he saw the 2nd New Zealand Division as a formation of the British Army, the 2nd New Zealand Expeditionary Force was essentially a small national New Zealand army. Kiwi soldiers had more service and support facilities than their British counterparts, and as a result had more endurance on the battlefield. Attempts to have British tank units work closely with the New Zealanders failed early in the war, since these formations were foreign to the division and were unable to keep up with the rate of advance. Using British forces would also dilute the national character of the division. Freyberg realized one thing that the politicians back in Wellington were reluctant to face: "It seems, with the best will in the world, doubtful whether New Zealand's resources can produce the necessary men to meet all the demands made upon them."[39]

The War Cabinet met for two days and was unwilling to move much beyond 15,000 men. The politicians considered a number of options. They looked at reducing the size of the air force and the navy so that New Zealand could still have a division with a Kiwi identity. According to a series of studies done for the War Cabinet, the problem was that New Zealand had mobilized beyond its resources in 1943 and the navy and the air force had taken the lead in reducing their forces. The units that remained were filling "essential missions." There was no fat to cut. Since the War Cabinet was set on reducing the size of the armed services, it was clear the army had to bear the brunt of this force reduction. "It is quite beyond our available manpower resources to provide a full Division of say, 25,000 men."[40]

The War Cabinet also considered deploying the 2nd New Zealand Division with only two brigades, but staff officers warned that there were both operational and political dangers in this choice. "The force is tactically ill-balanced. If required to operate on a two brigade front it has not sufficient artillery support. It has no reserve no reconnaissance element no armour and no Anti Tank protection," Brigadier C. G. Goss, the Deputy Chief of the General Staff, stated in a study prepared for the ministers. He also noted that with fewer field hospitals, the division would have a more difficult time in caring for the wounded if there were heavy casualties in the fighting. Puttick also warned the unit might lose its distinctive characteristics and would have, as a result, problems living up to the impressive reputation that the 1st and 2nd New Zealand Expeditionary Forces had earned in two world wars.[41]

The domestic pressures at work were just too strong for the War Cabinet to ignore. Food rations actually became tighter after the war in Europe ended, as the devastated continent needed assistance to recover. Manpower restrictions had to be eased as a form of compensation. "After close consideration of all factors War Cabinet sees little prospect of being able to provide a force against Japan exceeding 15 or 16 thousand," Nash informed Freyberg. "We recognise the disadvantages of a force of less than a complete division and the difficulties that may arise if British or other troops are added to complete."[42]

This situation rankled everyone involved in the decision. Freyberg reworked his numbers and said he could put together a division of 16,000 men. The War Cabinet began rethinking the numbers, and a week later, accepted these figures. "The foregoing is provisional at this juncture and it will not be possible to give a final decision until after Parliament has met and discussed the matter," Nash advised the general. The War Cabinet also thought about adding units from Fiji to add strength to the New Zealand division. Sir Alexander Grantham, Governor of Fiji and High Commissioner for the Western Pacific, supported the idea. New Zealanders were already serving in the unit, and the proposal made sense.[43]

In July, though, the focus of debate changed dramatically with the arrival of Churchill's July 4 telegram. Up until that time New Zealand had been focusing on sending its division to fight in the South-East Asia Command. "I am fully seized of the value and importance of providing a British Commonwealth force such as you have in mind, and I have no hesitation in assuring you that the units of the Royal New Zealand Air Force and Royal New Zealand Navy will be fully available if required," Fraser replied back to Churchill. The 2nd New Zealand Division was a different story. He had to honor a promise he had made a year before and consult Parliament.[44]

This change in deployment had much operational merit. Freyberg, for one, liked the idea. "This proposal would appear to have much to recommend it from New Zealand's point of view. It enables us to get clear of jungle fighting and we will be used in our traditional role, together with all our guns and heavy equipment," he told Fraser.[45]

The only problem was New Zealand politics. When the war in Europe ended, it was only natural for New Zealanders to start wondering what role they would take in the remaining campaigns against Japan. With by-elections in May and then July and notice for another round of conscription, it was inevitable that the issue of repatriation would enter into the realm of politics. The return of the 2nd New Zealand Expeditionary Force was a vote winner for the National Party, which was in the opposition. They also had a reasonable argument that the Dominion should focus on agricultural production, serving as the breadbasket of the empire. Food shortages were likely to develop in Europe, and more focus on agricultural production would allow the country to eliminate some of the depravations of wartime mobilization that the people on the home front had endured.[46]

On May 25, Nash responded publicly. "We could have no influence in determining the peace settlement for the Pacific if we did not share in the fighting in this theatre," he said in some brief remarks. The issue drifted until June 19, when Nash gave a talk at the annual conference of the New

Zealand Returned Services' Association. He said Kiwi soldiers had fought well in the Mediterranean, but as long as Japan remained, the war would continue. Talk of "pulling out" was "nonsense." The time had come for New Zealand to show that it was a Pacific nation and that it had an interest in the outcome.[47]

The news media in New Zealand, most of which had an antagonistic relationship with the Labour Party, greeted these remarks with open hostility. "Such talk was just plain nonsense," the editorial board of the Wellington *Evening Post* declared. "So far as we are aware, no suggestion has been made from any responsible quarter that New Zealand 'should pull out of the war against Japan.'" The editors of the *Post* added: "So much power is now at the disposal of Britain and the United States that the numbers of men New Zealand could contribute to the war against Japan would make no difference to the result." That same day a writer for the Wellington *Dominion* took an even more explicit position. "Actually, all the available evidence seems to indicate that there is no particular military task awaiting the Division. Certainly there is none which promises to be greater or more urgent in the military sphere of the war against Japan, than is this Dominion's duty in respect to the supply of foodstuffs for the Allied nations and the freed peoples of Europe." The editors of the *Otago Daily Times* took a strong and negative view of the speech: "Nor is it 'just plain nonsense,' as Mr. Nash declares in one of his less penetrating moments, to argue against the provisions of foodstuffs as the greatest contribution New Zealand can now make to the war in the Pacific."[48]

Fraser returned from San Francisco to encounter an issue that was in danger of getting out of control. He quickly persuaded Sidney Holland of Christchurch and the leader of the National Party opposition to take the opportunity to read the relevant cable traffic and special studies. Holland and the National Party could hardly claim New Zealanders were unnecessary in the fight against Japan, when Churchill had explicitly requested their presence. This effort on Fraser's part was crucial because it kept manpower matters from becoming a divisive political issue.[49] The prime minister might have implemented New Zealand foreign policy, but he never made it on his own as some suggest.[50]

After the July by-election the stage was set for a dramatic parliamentary debate in Wellington. Despite the chill of the winter evening on August 2, the public galleries of the gray, half-built Edwardian building that sat on a gentle tilt were full of people.[51]

Fraser began the proceedings with a speech that lasted ninety minutes. He was well prepared. He had copies of facts, figures, and previous comments about New Zealand's war aims. He began his remarks by introducing a resolution that was vague but with which he meant to commit Kiwis to partake in the invasion of Japan. He then spent time quoting the various key passages of resolutions and statements that the New Zealand Parliament had made on the determination of the Dominion to fight the good fight. The question in front of the assembly that evening was the extent of the contribution that the nation would make. "We shall be unanimous in saying that if the Mother-country and our sister-dominions, and the British General Staff, ask us to do something we should endeavour to do it. If it is impossible, let us say so quite frankly. If it is possible, then our duty is clear." The key issue was the deployment of ground troops. In closing, he said the either/or question about choosing between maintaining a military role in the war and producing foodstuffs was misleading. "They are both part of our war effort, and both have had an all-important place in it up to now. It would be a false premise to say we must withdraw all our men who are fighting and concentrate entirely upon food."[52]

The long speech was on its own probably enough to kill most expectations of a dramatic exchange, but Holland's response made it clear that there were no major points in dispute. "Sir, I desire to claim the privilege of seconding the motion that was moved by the Prime Minister at the beginning of his speech," Holland said with his opening sentence. He explained that he supported the resolution because he was convinced it was what the United Kingdom required of New Zealand. "Three-quarters of the war is over but a great deal remains to be done; we still have to defeat Japan." Nash spoke after Holland finished, and the House then adjourned at 10:30 P.M.[53]

There is nothing worse than politicians with nothing meaningful to say. When the chamber met again, twelve hours later, that is basically what happened. The people that spoke were the lesser-ranking members of their parties and the Cabinet. Basically all said they were in agreement that the war with Japan had to be seen through to the very end. The speeches would go on until 4:33 P.M. The speakers meandered into a number of related but distinctly different areas, including the amount of foreign service required of individual soldiers, postwar employment, and enlistments. Only a few members talked on the issue of military service versus food production. Toward the end of the debate, Arnold Nordmeyer, the Minister of

Health, raised an issue that many others had ignored: the ability of New Zealand's economy to absorb returning veterans into the workforce. This was a subject worthy of full consideration at the time, but the worldwide shipping shortage eventually worked to New Zealand's advantage. The lack of ships delayed the return of Kiwi soldiers, giving the country time to absorb these new workers into a civilian economy. Ernest Corbett, a member of Parliament from Egmont, would have nothing to do with this view. In a nasty exchange, he said New Zealand had already made its contribution to the war. "Any suggestion that this country could not take a rightful place in those peace discussions, on account of it not taking part in the final phase of the war, to me, was an untenable argument." He also pointed out that the dairy industry had lost over 5,000 workers in the war and was just one of many places where veterans were needed and could find work. "So, how any responsible man in this House could make a statement of that nature beats me." Corbett went on to make a long statement on the problems facing agriculture in the postwar era. Although he had breeched the decorum that had governed most of the past two days, the representative from Egmont returned the conversation to real and substantial issues.[54]

At this point, the prime minister intervened and brought the debate to an end as the five o'clock hour neared. Corbett was unlikely to win over the bulk of his party, since there were cables from London requesting contributions from New Zealand, but he was a threat to the unity that Fraser wanted. "Sir," the prime minister stated, "I propose to say only a few words, because the weight of unanimity in the House renders it unnecessary to reply." Fraser was trying to explain away the problem. "There is still room for difference of opinion and there may be such a difference of opinion, not about the text, but rather about the implementing, of the resolution." Unlike the newspaper editorial writers, none of them were calling for an exclusive effort in agricultural production.

> I wish to thank the members of the House for the earnest way in which members have addressed themselves to this very important matter, for the unanimous feeling expressed, in regard to the fulfillment of our obligations, and the maintaining of the country's honour, and also for the practical way in which they have arrived at the conclusion that we can maintain our country's pledged word with a reasonable number of men in the Services.

And with that comment the discussion came to an end. The transcript of the debate simply reads: "Motion agreed to."[55]

The next day, Fraser sent a telegram to London informing the British government that New Zealand would contribute a division to the invasion of Japan. "The difficulties I referred to in my telegram of 14 July have now been surmounted and proposals have now been approved by Parliament for participation in the British Commonwealth Force in the forthcoming operations against Japan."[56]

The Dominion that was arguably the most English in its makeup would be part of the last great British cause of the war. There really never should have been any doubt on the matter. Now, the focus of the British nations turned to implementation, which proved to be a brief but difficult matter.

SEVENTEEN

Let This Day Be Done

The Americans and British had reached an agreement on the role the United Kingdom would play in the Pacific. If an invasion took place—and this seemed likely until the last two or three days of the war—the outcome of the conflict would be determined in this arena. Agreement is one thing, but implementation is another. Staff officers in Great Britain, each of the Dominions, and the United States were working hard to convert diplomatic agreements into military realities. Each nation was at a different stage in this process when the war ended. In addition, the British were attempting to reassert their authority over the Dominions. These efforts encountered a number of problems that were operational, political, and diplomatic in nature. Almost everyone involved in this work saw the war continuing for months and months. The plans for the invasion of Japan were hardly set when the war ended.

Of all the British nations, Canada was the one that had actually done the most work in preparing for the invasion of Japan. The problem with the agreement on Canadian participation was that it was vague and the Americans were unsure of what role they wanted their northern neighbors to play. In April, the Canadians proposed to offer an armored division, since it would be easier to supply and would be more representative of their ground forces. Planning officers in the Pentagon who had been working on the Pacific war greeted this idea with little enthusiasm. Keeping an armored division supplied would be more complicated, and there was more need for an infantry division.[1]

A month after the Americans indicated their preferences, the Canadians decided that the Canadian Army Pacific Force would take form as the Canadian 6th Division under the command of Major-General Bertram M. Hoffmeister, who had led the Canadian 5th Armoured Division in Italy and northwestern Europe. The unit would be organized along U.S. rather than British lines, and in order to get volunteers as the Cabinet had stipulated, the army distributed a pamphlet in mid-May titled *After Victory in Europe*. The volunteers would get a daily pay bonus for service in the Pacific and would have priority for transit back to Canada, where they would enjoy leave before preparing for their next mission.[2]

Manpower issues soon proved to be a problem. Over 78,000 officers and enlisted personnel volunteered to fight against the Japanese. Since the table of organization of a Canadian division required 15,848 individuals, it would seem that the Dominion had more than enough people to contribute to the Pacific war. Appearances, in this case, are deceiving. The Cabinet had also stipulated that all volunteers be single, a requirement that eliminated many individuals. A number also failed to meet the service's stringent health and age requirements for overseas deployment. Over 6,000 officers and enlisted personnel in the Canadian Women's Army Corps offered to serve in the Pacific, and while these individuals could make worthwhile administrative contributions, no one in Ottawa intended for them to see combat. As a result, the Canadians really only had about 39,000 eligible individuals to send into combat. This number, while much higher than the 15,848 that would make up the division, barely covered what the army needed. Units assigned to combat require replacement personnel for those that are wounded, killed, or become combat ineffective.[3]

In the middle of May, the U.S. War Department provided the Canadians with battle casualty projections that suggested their northern neighbors could make do with only 25,000 men at first. The issue of casualty estimates is a topic of intense debate among historians and the general public, as it is generally tied into a calculation about the morality of using the atomic bombs; the higher the number, the more legitimate the decision. These Canadian numbers are significant. These estimates were the ones that the headquarters of the U.S. Army believed their ally should use for manpower "planning purposes." There are several qualifications to keep in mind when discussing this issue. There were several sets of figures floating about various elements of the vast bureaucracies known as the U.S. Army and the U.S. Navy. The various numbers discussed in Truman's meeting with the Joint Chiefs of Staff and the MacArthur-Mountbatten summit make this point clear. These calculations were oftentimes nothing more than educated guesses. Many of them are vague in that they make no differentiation between individuals wounded and killed. Soldier, sailors, airmen, and marines could be injured on multiple occasions and count as more than one casualty. A unit could statistically absorb losses exceeding 100 percent and still continue to function, since replacements would take the place of the dead and incapacitated. The estimates show the Canadians suffering monthly losses from battle and nonbattle incidents of 2,195 individuals. This figure equals a monthly casualty rate of approximately 13.8 percent and a casualty rate for a ninety-day operation—the time for an invasion found in other estimates—of a painful but endurable 41.5 percent, although these losses would have probably mostly been in the form of infantry foot soldiers and that would have made the pain in that part of the division exceptionally painful. In examining these statistics, it is important to remember that the U.S. Army was an exceptionally large organization, and that these estimates only represented a general guess of an element of that organization—an exceptionally influential element to be sure. With that point made, these figures were the ones that the headquarters staff thought that their Canadian ally should use as a basis for planning its own manpower requirements. As a result, they have some real significance. On the other hand, MacArthur refused to make any assessment about the costs of CORONET at such an early stage, so there is a clear limit to the significance of these numbers as well. As it was, the Canadians figured that they had enough personnel for a combat deployment of approximately three months.[4]

Manpower was only one of the factors shaping Canadian preparations. The American-imposed requirements were a major factor affecting Canadian preparations. The stipulation that MacArthur made that British units use U.S. equipment and doctrine applied to the division from Canada as much as it did to the units from the United Kingdom. The Americans had imposed this requirement on the Canadians during the Aleutian campaign in 1943. The Canadian Army put up some understandable resistance to this idea. The Dominion had a proud military tradition as part of the British Empire and Commonwealth. Tradition is a significant part of a military organization's heritage, particularly in the development and maintenance of unit morale. In this particular case, adherence to the past was a luxury. The overall cohesion of the invasion force was the immediate consideration and required that the Canadian Army change its organizational structure and doctrine. The conversion from brigades to regiments, and the placement of Brigadiers in command in place of Colonels, began that summer. Canadian officers had also enrolled in U.S. Army training programs and were present in various U.S. schools when Japan surrendered in mid-August.[5] The Canadians rejected proposals to include their division within any larger British formation.[6] British and American records, however, show that planning went forward with expectations that the Canadians would be part of such a corps, indicating that more negotiations would have taken place had the war not ended when it did.

Reflecting the staggered nature of their agreements with their American allies, the British set about working to introduce their forces into the Pacific theater in two stages. The initial work concentrated on deploying the Royal Air Force (RAF) for operations in the strategic bombing of Japan. The planning staff in the Pentagon would be a key player in these technical discussions. While American staff officers understood and supported the diplomatic interests that required British participation, they focused more on operational concerns than their Chiefs, which militated against allied participation. Another problem was confusion on both sides of the Atlantic about the intentions of the other. On October 26, 1944, the Joint Chiefs of Staff approved a draft memo that was sent to their British colleagues, which stated, "The participation of Lancasters in the main air effort against Japan would be most welcome." A qualification followed: "Present plans are insufficiently firm to permit a worthwhile estimate of the location or numbers of bases which might be allocated to the RAF, but it appears that at the proper time some facilities can be made available within reach of Japan." Five days later, the U.S. Chiefs approved a staff study that noted that a British air contingent would disrupt the timing of coming operations and delay the defeat of Japan. This paper recommended that the Joint Chiefs wait until after the British gave a firm indication of determining when and where these additional forces would be used.[7] On February 1, 1945, Portal wrote Major General Laurence S. Kuter, the chief planner for the U.S. Army Air Force, and informed him that the RAF had found a way to add fuel tanks to the Lancaster and the Lincoln to increase their range. It now looked as if there would be no need to conduct midair refueling. He thought this force could become operational seven months after the war in Europe ended. "This RAF force will be thoroughly experienced in the technique of night bombing and in sea-mining, and will be capable of dropping the very effective 1,500 pound British mines." Kuter wrote back the same day and said his air force would welcome the presence of 36 Lancaster or Lincoln squadrons to operate under U.S. command.[8]

As the war came to an end in Europe that spring, the Americans offered the RAF the Cagayan Valley in northern Luzon for base development. This region in the Philippine Islands was hardly attractive, but Portal thought the British should accept since the undertaking was "more of a political than a military question."[9] MacArthur, however, objected strongly to putting the British, or anyone else for that matter, in the valley. "It would be impossible to provide logistical support in the area," he informed the War Department in a cable. He went on to explain that there was only one road of poor quality connecting this region to central Luzon, which could never sustain the traffic that would be necessary to support an air base. The existing ports in central Luzon were also unable to handle the necessary demands of such an installation. If this area were to be the site of a new military facility, it would require the building of a new port and road, in addition to the construction of the base itself, all of which would come during the rainy season in the Philippines. Finally, the weather in the valley made it likely that planes based there could fly only one day in five. MacArthur recommended that the planners drop the idea of developing the Cagayan Valley region.[10]

The Joint Staff Planners realized that political concerns required that they find some role for the British, so a week later they had a new study suggesting that the RAF deploy to the Ryukyu Islands, which included Okinawa. "It is considered that employment of British bombers from bases in the Ryukyus offers the greatest possibility for economical use of these aircraft." The Allies had two options. The United States could seize the island of Miyako. Having Lancasters based on this island would save the Americans some of the troubles of deploying eight groups of B-29s. Since the planners considered the B-29 a more economical weapon, this choice remained less than satisfactory. The other alternative was to put the RAF bombers on U.S. bases in southern Okinawa as the army air forces moved forward following the invasion of Japan. With this solution, there would no longer be any need for British engineers to build new bases, and it would also require that the RAF provide fewer support services, such as photo reconnaissance and rescue planes. The British, however, would have to wait until mid-January of 1946 before these bases became available. The RAF bombers would be ready before then, though, and would be waiting without any mission.[11]

The Planning Staff discussed the strengths and weaknesses of each plan. Colonel Curtis R. Low of the army air forces noted that the British had 10,000 engineers stationed in Canada and were prepared to send them and their equipment to the Pacific immediately. The British would be willing to help construct U.S. installations while they waited for an area to become available for the RAF. The British, however, wanted to get into the fray quickly. Brigadier-General George A. Lincoln questioned the undertaking. He was willing to consider a Royal Air Force contingent of very long-range bombers if it would save American lives and made sense militarily. Lincoln, however, thought the United States might need the available runways on Okinawa for tactical air forces to support the force invading Japan. If so, then giving the British bases might be counterproductive and cost lives. He suggested the planners study the issue some more and the staff agreed to defer action on the matter. A week later the planners considered the issue again, but decided to wait until they received an expected position paper from the British.[12]

The memorandum arrived on the desks of the planners on May 2 and the British made clear their desire to take part in operations against Japan as quickly as possible. Air Vice-Marshal Sir Hugh Lloyd, as the force commander designate, had visited Washington for some preliminary staff talks and learned of the liabilities of the Cagayan Valley area. He had also heard mention of Miyako and in the paper His Majesty's Chiefs of Staff suggested that this island would be much better for the RAF. The British wanted to have their first squadrons operational by December 1. "We are in the process of examining this alternative proposal but it is already evident that both from the operational point of view and from that of construction it is an incomparably better proposition." Miyako, however, was still in Japanese hands and the British Chiefs requested confirmation of U.S. intentions to seize the island. Buckner, who was still alive at this point in time, cancelled efforts to take this island when the fight on Okinawa became tougher than expected.[13]

As the planners read the British paper and debated its merits, they were in a difficult position. The Cagayan option was out, as was Miyako. Lincoln, Colonel Max Johnson, and Rear Admiral Donald B. Duncan all expressed unease about giving the British airfields, which the U.S. Army Air Forces might need. The Planning Staff decided to have the Joint War Plans Committee study the papers and issue a report in light of the new British paper.[14]

Over the course of the next week, the members of the committee, being talented military intellectuals and bureaucrats, produced a lengthy study along with a draft memo for the Joint Chiefs to send to their British colleagues that suggested a new option. Since the United States might need to use bases to provide air cover for the invasion of Japan, the committee recommended that the Joint Chiefs ask the RAF to provide a tactical air force of ten squadrons. These planes would be stationed on Okinawa alongside U.S. units. The committee suggested that the British could deploy these planes more quickly than the Lancasters, and the RAF would become operational at an earlier date and make a worthwhile contribution to the final campaign. The report stated that negotiations since Quebec had been on very long-range bombing because bombers were the only type of plane that had been capable of reaching Japan. In the not too distant future, this situation would change and it would be possible to employ other types of aircraft. The Royal Air Force had heavy and medium bombers that were as good as those in the U.S. air fleet and the use of these planes would reduce the deployment requirements of the U.S. Army Air Forces. Having the RAF contingent alongside U.S. units would reduce the British need for support service and would also put the British in territory that Americans dominated, reducing the chance that questions of command would develop. If, on the other hand, the Royal Air Force presence displaced B-29s, well, then that was another matter altogether. The Lancasters and Lincolns were inferior weapons to the B-9s in range and payload capacity and not needed.[15]

This paper was the subject of lengthy discussion at the Joint Planning Staff meeting on May 9. In fact, the issue of the RAF on Okinawa was the first matter on the agenda. Since World War I, airpower advocates had contended that an air force could bring about the defeat of an enemy if it was allowed to attack and destroy strategic targets. There was much debate in the international airmen community as to what was an appropriate target, but both air forces as institutions believed that airpower, when properly employed, had the potential to bring about victory on its own. Other missions, such as providing support for air and sea operations, while worthwhile, lacked this promise. It was also altogether likely that a small tactical air force would be unable to service the political and diplomatic needs of the British within the English-speaking coalition.[16]

These considerations dominated the discussion that followed. Johnson started the discussion with the circulation of a new proposed memo for the Joint Chiefs to give to the British. In this memo, the colonel stressed the shortage in airfield capacity. The United States could provide space for only ten Lancaster squadrons. These 220 planes would have a strategic bombing mission. If possible, the other ten squadrons could be added to the force if space became available. In his presentation, Johnson reminded his colleagues that the British had originally offered to make a contribution to the strategic bombing campaign against Japan and had always kept the negotiations focused on that topic. It would be inappropriate for the United States to change the nature of the discussion, but Duncan thought that circumstances had changed. Since U.S. forces were closer to Japan, it was possible to consider using planes in other missions. The only point on which all were in agreement, he noted, was that the British should have some sort of role in the air campaign. The admiral thought that at the very least, the British should have an opportunity to consider this proposal. Lincoln favored the tactical air force suggestion as well. Johnson's views won out, but the minutes of the meeting offer no explanation as to why. The planners forwarded the report to the Joint Chiefs, which they approved three weeks later.[17] In Germany the U.S. Chiefs told the British that they saw no possibility of the necessary airfields becoming available until at least December 1, 1945.[18]

The British accepted the offer and conditions a week after it was made. The first lines of the British memo read, "The British Chiefs of Staff gladly accept in principle the proposal of the United States Chiefs of Staff to base a British force of the order of ten squadrons of some 220 aircraft in the Ryukyus. This force to come under United States Command."[19]

Arnold sent a cable to MacArthur that was eventually forwarded to Nimitz and other commanders in the Pacific, informing them of the decision and asking for their comments on the immediate deployment of the British engineers. MacArthur had no difficulty including the British in forthcoming operations, but he worried about where to put them on Okinawa. He suggested either putting them in the southern portion of the island or delaying their introduction until November 1, when the U.S. units would have moved to bases in Japan itself and could make the facilities on Okinawa available to the British. Nimitz's reactions were extremely negative. Shipping considerations and the backlog at port facilities on Okinawa made MacArthur's first plan "extremely inadvisable." The second proposal was better, but he really did not want the British on Okinawa at all. The RAF units would create a mixed force with all the complications that such an organization entailed on a small and congested island.[20]

The reactions of allied commanders were also critical. Perhaps none more than Mountbatten. He believed the deployment of this force came at the cost of his command. "I hope you will agree," he cabled the Chiefs of Staff Committee, "that this theatre which is engaged in the only British land operations left and which has suffered many disappointments including not being allowed to retain light fleet carriers for a few more weeks for ZIPPER and is also committed to further campaigns, should be given priority over other British operations including the V.L.R. bomber project."[21]

The reactions of the U.S. commanders in the region were also in the negative and usually centered on the issue that had worried Arnold in Canada—the limited amount of usable terrain. General Barney M. Giles of the U.S. Army Air Forces, Pacific Ocean Areas, suggested that no British air units be used at all in the missions over Japan. Arnold quickly shot this idea down. While he might have recognized that Giles had an argument on operational grounds, Arnold knew that the United States was stronger politically with British participation than it was in trying to defeat Japan on its own. Shortly after he sent his initial cable, Arnold left for an inspection trip of army air forces bases in the Pacific. He met with MacArthur and Nimitz and got both to accept the immediate use of the engineers. The record is a bit unclear, but it appears that Arnold agreed to the second MacArthur proposal that Lancasters would not be stationed on Okinawa until December 1. The U.S. Joint Chiefs of Staff, however, had clearly implied at Potsdam that the first ten squadrons could be deployed before December 1.[22] The RAF also dispatched Lloyd to clarify matters. The squadrons under his command were on schedule to become operational in October.[23] There were obvious problems with these conflicting timetables. "These questions were never finally or firmly decided," Arnold explained in his memoirs.[24]

Work in preparing the Royal Air Force for the war against Japan was far more advanced than the preparations for the British Army. This effort started only in the summer of 1945. One of the consequences in the changeover in control of the Cabinet was that the new Labour government reconsidered the proposal to take part in the invasion of Japan. Both Prime Minister Clement Attlee and Foreign Minister Ernest Bevin supported the proposal and were blunt in describing it mainly as a diplomatic gesture in support of their American allies. One official in the South-East Asia Command warned that the military efforts in their theater would be

> effectively immobilized until the war with Japan is over (as it presumably must be after the final assault on Japan has taken place): if the Japanese continue to resist in outlying areas, as they probably will if the national structure is destroyed in Japan, it will mean that America will be free of the war while we European powers are left mopping up *ad infinitum*. We shall derive no benefit for taking part in the assault on Japan, while our idleness in South East Asia in the interim is liable to have the worst possible repercussions politically.

The discussion was a formality and the government approved the deployment.[25]

After six years of war, the British were beginning to hit the limits of their manpower resources. This pending shortage became an issue that the War Office had to confront. Churchill, while he had been in office, had hoped for an early end of the war to minimize such difficulties. "It may well be," he told Attlee, "that events will bring the Japanese war to an early close. Indeed I hope this may be so, for it means an immense lightening of the load we expected to carry."[26]

Consideration of military relations among the Commonwealth nations had been a secondary reason in Brooke's motivation for sending a British force to fight in the Pacific and had been centered mainly on Australia. The force as constituted had the added advantage of allowing the United Kingdom to reassert its authority over the wayward Canadians. The British were under the distinct impression that their American allies would just as soon be rid of the commitment to the Canadian division, and incorporating it into the British corps would solve a number of problems. Attlee sent a cable suggesting that the Dominion include its unit in the British formation, indicating such was the distinct preference of MacArthur.[27]

One of the tasks in deploying the corps would be to select the commander of the unit. The British decided that X Corps, then in Italy, would be sent to the Pacific under the command of Lieutenant-General Sir Charles Keightley. Vice-Admiral William Tennant would serve as the naval commander, and his main job would be getting the ground troops ashore. The hope in Whitehall was that the Australians would provide the commander for a tactical air force.[28]

With the British Army making such slow progress, the Americans began reconsidering their employment of ground forces from the old empire. Concerned about the amount of time it took to train the Canadians in U.S. amphibious doctrine and tactics, staff officers began to wonder if the British could field a force that could take part in the initial assault. The Joint Chiefs of Staff sent a memo across the Atlantic informing their colleagues that they "question very seriously the feasibility of utilizing any British forces requiring both U.S. equipment and amphibious training in an assault role." The Americans suggested that the British consider deploying their ground forces directly to Japan. The memo requested further information from London on this matter. This document was a request for technical information and hardly represented a major reversal in interalliance cooperation.[29]

The Australians also wondered about the technical ability of the British to field a ground force, and these reservations shaped the Dominion's response to Churchill's July 5 cable. Stanley Melbourne Bruce, the Australian High Commissioner in London, wrote Forde during his brief tenure as prime minister and informed him that the "operation against the main Japanese Islands in which a British Commonwealth Land Force may take part is not likely to begin before March, 1946." Blamey thought this delay was enough to make a British role in the operation unlikely. "I am quite convinced in my own mind that no British troops will be allowed to participate in the move to Japan," he told newspaper editors in an off-the-record press conference.[30]

The job of drafting a response fell to Blamey. He, however, saw no need to respond urgently, taking a long trip via car between Adelaide and Melbourne. The government was still in transition following Curtin's death, and Chifley had not yet taken office. Blamey's draft took an expected negative response: "Your proposal for a British Commonwealth Force with an Australian component for invading the main islands of Japan is most desirable, but under existing conditions appears to be unrealistic and impracticable." It was crucial that Australia take part in the main assault on Japan, and as he had told the journalists at the press conference, he thought the British would never get the resources in place to take part in the invasion.

In view of part played by Australian forces in this area it is desired that expeditionary division proposed should participate in main invasion operations against Japan. Public opinion has been restive under the allocation of our troops to secondary roles for so long and this has been cause of considerable discontent amongst forces. These considerations are emphasised by the allocation of a Canadian Division to the American main force, as at present understood to be the case.

The Defence Committee—the Australian Chiefs of Staff—approved the reply with some minor revisions the same day they received the document. Shedden also revised parts of the draft, softening the tone a little, but just a little.[31]

The Advisory War Council met to discuss the issue on July 19. The meeting started with many members congratulating Chifley on becoming prime minister. Then, the conversation turned to the issue at hand: responding to the British proposal. There was a near-consensus among the various officials. The Australians wanted the United Kingdom to be a power in the Pacific after the war ended and to that end it was crucial that it help subjugate the Japanese. All things being equal, the Chifley government would like to fight alongside the other Dominions. Time was of the essence, though. If it proved impossible for the British to constitute an invasion force, then Australia should participate with the United States. It was vital that Australia make some type of military contribution to the attack. The Advisory War Council then approved the message with the incorporation of these points.[32]

The cable that Chifley eventually sent to London was even more negative than Blamey's initial draft, if more polite in its language. One of the reasons it had such a tone is that the last section discussed the command and control relationship of Australian military units, although this matter had seen little discussion in the Advisory War Council meeting. Shedden added a section stating that MacArthur had given Australia a voice in policy formation in areas where its troops were used, and that the current Cabinet wanted as much from the British. "The Government would wish to be assured that any arrangements made for a change in the command set-up relating to the control of its Forces provided for this principle before expressing its agreement and assigning Forces under any new set-up." Shedden was deluding himself. MacArthur had used and abused the Australians. The civil servant, however, refused to acknowledge this fact, which would have required admitting that he had given some amazingly bad advice to the Cabinet. Nor were the British in any position to provide the Australians with what they were demanding. The Australians were having a hard time grasping that the power of the United Kingdom and the British Empire, their empire, a political entity in which they had so much invested, was fading. Chifley insisted on asking, "If Australian Forces were to be assigned to a British Commonwealth Command either in the South West Pacific Area or in the main operations against Japan, the Government would desire to know how this principle would be provided for." The British could not offer the Australians any input into policy formation, because they had none themselves.[33]

Less than a week later, Churchill's response basically ignored the Australian demand for a voice in policy formation.

> The Chiefs of Staff will proceed with the appointment of Force Commanders as early as possible and in order that Australia's views may be fully represented at the consultations with General MacArthur I suggest that you should appoint an Australian Officer to join the British Commanders at General MacArthur's Headquarters. This officer would then be able to return to Australia to explain in full detail all the arrangements proposed. I hope and believe that you will then find it possible to join with us in this enterprise.[34]

The reason that Churchill ignored the issue of an Australian voice on policy formation was that Chifley and Shedden were picking a fight with the wrong ally. The operations in Japan were going to be an American show in which the United Kingdom was welcome to participate, but in which they would have no real input. There was a subtle message in Churchill's reply, which the Australians were unable to grasp: events were moving forward. Australia could participate in the invasion of Japan on the terms offered, or it could sit the operation out. The British Joint Planning Staff had written the original draft of this message, and in a report to their Chiefs, officers in this organization informed their superiors that the issue of command and control was going to be difficult to solve. "We suggest that most of these difficulties will not be satisfactorily resolved by a series of telegrams between the Prime Ministers. We believe, however, that they are capable of solution by consultation and that the proper procedure, therefore, should be to ask the Prime Minister to send a reply on the lines of the telegram annexed." The British Chiefs approved the telegram, which Churchill sent out two days later.[35]

The language in Churchill's response infuriated Shedden. Years later when he was writing a history of Australian military policy, he commented, "It is to be observed that this was the traditional United Kingdom method, already note of roping a party into a commitment, which determined the pattern of the subsequent consultations on principles yet to be resolved." He also refused to accept that MacArthur had manipulated him and the Australian government. "This was in marked contrast with the principles which had operated in the South West Pacific Area under the American Commander-in-Chief." He was fostering a dispute with the British government using a standard that never existed.[36]

Chifley's response was to make a statement in the Australian House of Representatives on the future of the Dominion's role in the conflict.

> In regard to the strength of the Forces which should constitute the Australian war effort for the remainder of the war, the Government and the Council consider it to be a matter of vital importance to the future of Australia and her status at the peace table in regard to the settlement in the Pacific, that her military effort against Japan should be maintained on a scale which, with the Commonwealth's earlier record in the war, would guarantee her an effective voice in the peace settlement.

There would be no reduction in the size of the navy, the army would be reduced to three divisions, and the air force to thirty-six squadrons. "It is the view of the Government and the Advisory War Council that a war effort o[f] these dimensions will be worthy of the Commonwealth and will secure our status in the Pacific settlement."[37]

Chifley said the obvious when he pointed out that operations in the Pacific theater were critical to the Dominion. "In the view of the Government and the Advisory War Council, it is vital to Australia's future interests, as a Pacific Nation, that her Forces should participate in the main offensive against Japan."[38]

Then, the prime minister drew a line in the sand. "It has accordingly been proposed that Australia's contribution to the main offensive should be the R.A.N. Squadron under its own Commander, and Expeditionary Force components of the land and air forces which would operate under Australian Commanders in a similar manner to that of the A.I.F. in the Middle East." He was willing to provide three squadrons to participate in the very long-range bomber force that would be participating in the strategic bombing of Japan. "The Government and the Advisory War Council are of the opinion that any arrangements made for a change in the command set-up relating to the control of the Australian Forces should continue to provide for the Commonwealth having an effective voice in the policy governing the use of our Forces." Specifically, Australian commanders would have the right to refuse to take part in any operation if they had reservations about its wisdom and would also be able to communicate with the government in Canberra.[39]

Chifley explained that Australia had already informed the U.S. and British governments of these views.

> The proposals are now being considered by the Combined Chiefs of Staff, but the Government has been informed that finality will not be reached for some time. In view of the fact that the Commonwealth's views were formulated some time ago, it is considered to be in the public interest that an announcement of them should be no longer deferred. A further statement will be made by me when finality is reached.[40]

In going public with these policy initiatives, Chifley had lost much political flexibility. What would happen if the Americans or the British refused to accede to Australian views?

Despite this statement, Chifley decided to appoint an Australian to travel to MacArthur's headquarters. His choice was Blamey. In a conference he had with the general, and in his written instructions, Chifley made the limits of this mission clear in blunt fashion. The government had to approve any agreement he reached with MacArthur. He instructed Blamey to make sure that the agreement provided for giving Australia input into the strategic direction of the war and control over its own armed services.[41]

Blamey, for his part, was willing to take up this mission. If Australia agreed to contribute personnel to the British formation, there was a real possibility that the Dominion would find itself excluded altogether from combat operations in Japan. He believed Chifley firmly supported this position. While that might have been the case, his personal stock was declining.[42]

The Australians failed to appreciate that the Americans, rather than the British, were setting the conditions for their participation in the invasion of Japan. From London, Brigadier Henry Rourke told Shedden that Australia really only had one option.

There is wide sympathy here with the apparent Australian desire that the chance of Australian troops taking part in the assault on Japan should not be interfered with. If detailed examination shows that it is impracticable to stage a British force in time, the United Kingdom authorities would do everything in their power to help to ensure that the Australian division is included in the American plan. But they are quite sure that General MacArthur does not intend to include the Australian division in any operation before the one timed for March for which the British force is proposed. As far as I can see this will be the one chief operation.[43]

Chifley was getting the same information. High Commissioner Bruce forwarded to him a report that Major-General Charles Lloyd had completed about the talks he had been having in London with British officials. It was clear that plans were moving forward and that the United States was largely determining the nature of the agreements: "General British Policy will be conditioned by the view that having offered a British Commonwealth Force to serve under United States Command we should as far as possible comply with the United States requirements and General MacArthur's wishes." Toward the end of his report, Lloyd added, "The views of the Australian Government on command of the British Commonwealth Force and the maintenance of machinery to ensure adequate control over employment of Australian formations have been stressed and you will be fully consulted on both issues."[44]

The situation was rife for a miscue. On August 9, Clement Attlee, who was now the British prime minister, sent a cable to Chifley on the subject of the commanders of the Commonwealth contingent. He informed him about the designation of Tennant and Keightley. He then raised the issue of an air commander. "If a British Commonwealth Tactical Air Force is included in the British Commonwealth contingent it will consist mainly of Australian squadrons. We have therefore suggested that the Australian Government should nominate a commander of this force if it materialises."[45]

This response flabbergasted Shedden. "The comment about the Air Force Commander was presumptuous at that stage, for the Government had not taken any decision to participate in the British Commonwealth Force until it was re-assured on how the principles of control were to be provided for." There was no response on the issue of policy consultation. "This repetitive evasion was assuming the nature of unilateral dictation."[46]

Gavin Long observes in the official Australian history, "The Surrender of Japan a few days later terminated this discussion, but it is unlikely that the Australian Government would have concurred in the appointment of an army commander who had had no experience of fighting against the Japanese when so many tried commanders far senior to Keightley were available in the Australian Army and in Burma."[47] Long has a good point. It seems that the Australians were in danger of putting themselves into a position where they were faced with two unacceptable alternatives: accept the British commander and a role supportive of the British presence that MacArthur had allotted them without an appropriate voice in foreign policy and strategy, or find themselves excluded altogether from ground operations in Japan. Neither option was particularly good. The end of the war saved a number of officials in Canberra from a political humiliation of the first order.

New Zealand's agreement to send units to fight in Japan was unexpected. Planning had gone forward on the assumption that New Zealand would be unable to contribute a force, and MacArthur's response had only envisioned a corps of three divisions (one British, one Australian, and one Canadian). In London the Joint Planning Staff warned the Chiefs of Staff Committee that should New Zealand agree, the British should argue with the Americans for their inclusion. "We consider that, in view of previous proposals to them, we should, if they so desire press for its inclusion, if necessary in the build up." Given the lateness of the decision made in Wellington, efforts to include a New Zealand division within the British corps were still in their early stages. Despite the similarities in terrain and climate of Italy and Japan, the 2nd New Zealand Division would need to draw new supplies and undergo training in new tactical doctrine given MacArthur's requirement that a British imperial force use U.S. equipment. New Zealand officials had been thinking about where the division should be trained for some time. When it looked like Kiwi soldiers would be fighting in Southeast Asia, the assumption made in the army and the government was that the choice was between Egypt and New Zealand. Brigadier A. E. Conway, the Adjutant General of the New Zealand Army, favored keeping the force out of New Zealand. Otherwise "there would be great difficulty in preventing it from 'fading away.'"[48]

MacArthur's requirement solved what could have been a difficult political problem for the New Zealand Cabinet. Even though it would have made for good politics, it was no longer possible to even consider allowing

Kiwi soldiers to return to New Zealand. Freyberg was in London while the Parliament in Wellington was debating the future of its troops. He quickly realized that planning officers in London rather than in Italy were making the technical decisions about British deployment in the Pacific. The general reported that he had "had conferences with branches in the War Office to ensure that they appreciate our difficulties, which are considerable." In a diary entry, Brooke showed an almost 180-degree turn from the attitude he had toward Churchill on the matter of planning: "After lunch Freyberg came to see me, and I had a long discussion with him on the question of the New Zealand Div being made available for the Imperial Task Force destined for the invasion of Japan. It is hard to keep him on a high plane and he continually descends into detail."[49]

Preparation for the invasion of Japan continued until the very end of the war. On August 10, the same day that Japan indicated that it would surrender, New Zealand and British Army officers met in the War Office to resolve a number of logistical issues. The conference decided that the 2nd New Zealand Division should be transferred from Italy to the United Kingdom, starting on September 15, at a pace that would have the entire division relocated by early October. For morale reasons, Kiwi soldiers should get to take a leave, but it would be limited to the United Kingdom. They would not have time to travel back to New Zealand. The division would then start its relocation to the United States in November. If possible, the British Army would begin providing the New Zealanders with U.S.-issued equipment and small arms that it had in its supply depots. The British officers at the conference offered an important qualification, noting carefully that MacArthur had still not responded to the idea of including the New Zealanders in the British force, and that deployment was contingent on his approval.[50]

Freyberg also decided it was time for him to step aside. "I feel that after nearly six years constant service in Command of 2 NZEF that I should now give up my command and I am certain that a fully experienced successor could be selected by the War Cabinet." Although Freyberg thought it was time for someone else to take command, he still had some fight in him. On August 1, Brooke wrote in his diary: "Freyberg came to see me this evening to assure me that he was the one man to command the Corps for the invasion of Japan!"[51]

The Americans also had to do some implementation work in regard to British participation in the invasion of Japan. MacArthur, as he had told

Mountbatten, had decided that he would use the British and French as follow-up units in the assault on Honshu and that they would be integrated into a U.S. field army. Beyond those simple facts, he had made no other firm decisions on the matter. Even which American would have command over these foreign soldiers remained unresolved. Stilwell, sitting in his tent on Okinawa where he was preparing the island and the Tenth U.S. Army for the invasion, wrote in his diary: "British participation in CORONET. One corps of one Canadian, 1 Australian, and 1 Indian division to be under my command. Good God. This was brought up in war ministry and they *recommended* it. They said they knew where they stood with me. Mountbatten has to give up units for this operation! Ain't life funny?"[52]

The planning for the invasion of Japan was clearly in flux. At times Stilwell thought he would be participating in Operation: BLACKLIST, the occupation of Korea, and at others, that he would be in the invasion of Japan. MacArthur's planning staff decided to remove the Tenth Army from CORONET and assign the XXIV Corps and the III Marine Amphibious Corps to the First U.S. Army, which would be arriving from Europe. "Usual crap," Stilwell wrote in his diary on learning of this development.

Apparently, Tenth Army is cut out of any part in CORONET (First and Eighth to be used). Result of the Doug-Nimitz HATE. Nimitz has been trying to have Navy cut in on occupation forces, and wants Tenth Army, with III and XXIV Army Corps. This raises Doug's back, so, fearing it may come off, he plans with other units, leaving us to sit on our hands. Even in BLACKLIST, we get the hot spot to one side, instead of real participation. Maybe the Limmie pressure, plus the Navy will force Doug's hand. All I can do is wait it out.

Eichelberger wrote his wife: "Joe has been entirely eliminated as anything but a supply man according to the rumors."[53]

"What if" is a question that is beyond the power of history. No mortal can answer what would have happened had there been an invasion of Japan. What is clear is that the plans were undergoing revision when the war ended, and if there had been an assault on Japan it would have been different from what planners were imagining when the Japanese accepted their defeat and surrender. The efforts to prepare for this assault encountered a number of messy operational, political, and diplomatic problems. Such is the nature of war.

Conclusion:
Only the Dead

As this account winds down, it is important to make extremely clear one point that runs throughout the text: war is a means to an end. Fighting is usually not an objective in and of itself, but is usually a method to reach some objective. To be blunt: war serves politics.

What then determines political interests? Although many thinkers have debated this issue, seeing politics as the way a society makes decisions and expresses its interests will suffice for current purposes. Logically, then, war is a way that a society attempts to impose its will on others or protect what it values. When the bulk of a society is engaged and supportive of a war effort, you have a formidable war machine. Societies are rarely homogeneous and subgroups often have interests or objectives that are distinct from other groups or the society at large. As a result, the expression of a society's interests does not always make for the most effective of military operations. The mission of those responsible for overseeing the armed services is to ensure such interests do not degrade the military from being able to meet its ultimate missions.

So, what do these general themes have to do with the U.S. alliance with the British nations and the defeat of Imperial Japan? First, let us look at the events that transpired in the United Kingdom. Boiled down to its basic elements, the debate between the Chiefs of Staff Committee and Churchill was about the future. What role would the United Kingdom play in postwar world affairs in general, and, more specifically, in the Pacific? Each party had different ideas and their understanding of history shaped these views. Churchill believed that one of the main elements of British power in the past had been the empire. If the United Kingdom were to be a force in the future, the British had to redeem themselves in the eyes of their subject peoples. To the prime minister's way of thinking, this task required that the British liberate their colonies from Japanese occupation.

While Brooke, Cunningham, and Portal had no disagreement with efforts to rebuild the British Empire, they foresaw the alliance with the United States being the main element in the postwar foreign policy of their four-nation kingdom. The Chiefs of Staff Committee worried that the history of the two previous decades might repeat itself. After World War I, disputes between the United States and the United Kingdom ended their wartime collaboration and made the interwar period one of rivalry between the two Atlantic powers. If similar developments took place in the second half of the 1940s and into the 1950s, it would undo much of the hard work of the war years. Brooke, Cunningham, and Portal had good reason to hold such concerns given the long record of American hostility toward the mother country. Partnership had been the exception rather than the rule since 1776.

The debate between the Chiefs of Staff Committee and Churchill was intense. At one point Brooke, Cunningham, and Portal began talking about staging a mass resignation. Given what had happened to Churchill and the Cabinet in World War I after Admiral Lord Fisher's resignation, and that commentators would almost assuredly make mention of these similarities, this move had the potential to be extremely divisive. Although the issue of British participation in the final operations of the Pacific war might seem a minor issue, the matter seemed extremely important at the time to the participants. The reason: both sides thought the ideas of the other put the future of the United Kingdom at risk. Given what they saw to be at stake, it is hardly surprising that everyone involved was passionate on this particular issue.

Next, this investigation comes to the cases of the Commonwealth nations. Although there were major differences in the situations of Canada, Australia, and New Zealand, one should consider these three countries as a group for the immediate issue at hand. Although the political pressure to begin demobilization was strong in all three capitals, the leadership of these British nations wanted to contribute to the main defeat of Japan itself. Two of the three had committed themselves to participating in the invasion. The Australians, although the most vociferous on this matter, actually had given no word to London by the time the Japanese surrendered. Plans were going forward based on the belief that Australia would contribute troops to the operation, but the politicians in Canberra were raising issues based on a series of misunderstandings. Given the fact that the Australians participated in the occupation of Japan, it is highly likely that the leadership of the Dominion would have made participation in this operation the first of its priorities rather than getting political concessions from the British, which London was unable to make. Such a move would have required retreating from public statements that members of the Australian Cabinet had made in public; although such a move might have humbled some, politicians are generally good at reversing themselves. Despite the different accents in Ottawa, Canberra, and Wellington, the Canadians, Australians, and New Zealanders basically spoke with one voice when explaining their reasons for wanting to play a role in the defeat of Japan. The three governments had two reasons. First, they wanted to have a voice in shaping the future political settlement in the Pacific. Japan was a neighbor of sorts to all three and they all had an interest in the fate of that nation. A second reason was that all three wanted to bolster British power in the Pacific. The United Kingdom was a major influence in the lives of each of these countries. Many of their citizens thought of themselves as being British subjects and that Canada, Australia, and New Zealand were simply extensions of England, Scotland, Wales, and Ireland (north and south). The three Dominions also had long-standing military ties to the United Kingdom, which still had force despite the increased significance in their relationships with the United States. It was in their own interests to see that the United Kingdom remain a force in the Pacific region. If bolstering British influence also helped their relationship with the Americans, so much the better.

Finally, we must consider the perspective from Washington. There were a number of concerns floating about the U.S. capital in 1945. One set concerned the relationship the United States enjoyed with its British allies. The Joint Chiefs of Staff had concerns that were similar to those of their counterparts in London. Even though the armed forces of the United States had the resources to defeat Japan on their own, the uniformed military leaders knew that they served the larger interests of American society. They knew that they could have undone much of the work made in establishing a good working relationship with the British if they had insisted on an American-only effort in defeating and occupying Japan. Marshall, Arnold, Leahy, and—to some degree—even King worried about seeing the United States and the United Kingdom return to the state of affairs that dominated their relationship after World War I. The Joint Chiefs of Staff also had more mundane motives. Military operations in Japan, regardless of what estimates one believes were closest to the truth, were going to be costly, and many expected that the war would continue on for some time. These losses would hit at the same time that the United States was beginning to deal with manpower shortages. There should be little doubt that U.S. military leaders would have found solutions to these problems, nor is there any question that the American public would have wondered: "Where are our friends?" There was no way that U.S. military leaders wanted to explain that they had insisted that only Americans have the "privilege" of dying in Japan. In short, politics required that there be some sort of allied presence in the invasion of Japan and other operations designed to bring about victory.

Those journalists, historians, and filmmakers that have questioned the motivation of U.S. policy makers and military officials in the last days of the war were right to see politics shaping their decisions. The United States was acting in a way to protect its own political interests. These officials were not concerned about what was to them only a possible future in which there was a rivalry with the Soviet Union. No, instead they were more concerned with the rivalries of the past. It was fears about World War I that they had lived through rather than the concerns about some future Cold War that were motivating American leaders in the summer of 1945.

Having looked at the individual components of the United Nations coalition that defeated the Axis powers, it is appropriate that we look at the coalition as a whole. Policy makers and strategists in both Washington and London, particularly those in uniform, realized that the war was a cooperative effort that had to service many different interests, not just those found in their own capital. The British proposed and the United States agreed to their participation largely for political reasons. The considerations involved in these decisions were substantial and involved long-term interests rather than being petty or selfish, as the term "political" implies on occasion. To put it another way, the sum is greater than the whole of its parts. If expressed in mathematical terms, this point might be described as $1 + 1 = 3$, but as this story shows, the math is slightly more complex: $2 + 2 - 1 = 5$. The American-British coalition was an alliance that *worked*. Too many studies since the 1970s have focused on the disputes between the Allies. Given this emphasis, one might wonder how the Allies ever won the war.

These issues have a practical application. To bear witness to the sacrifices made in the past is to prepare against the day when war returns. As citizens, the readers of this account will in years to come make decisions about some future conflict. Perhaps in the role of a military commander, possibly as an opponent of war, or maybe as an average member of society influencing those around them as they wrestle with the issue of the day. No matter in what capacity, of the fact that people must address such issues in the future there can be little doubt. Plato was right: "Only the dead have seen the end of war."

Epilogue: In the Still of Peace

When the war ended, the individuals who had led the fighting continued on with life. Some, even those at the highest levels, never recovered from the war. Others went on to do more work of importance. In short, the fate that came to each one was as varied as the men they had been.

The Main Actors

Field-Marshal The Baron Alanbrooke of Brookeborough, County Fermanagh

Clement Attlee, believing that the three Chiefs of Staff deserved higher titles of nobility, had the King advance them each to the rank of Viscount on the New Year's Day Honours List of 1946. At the end of that year, the King made Viscount Alanbrooke a Knight of the Garter, the highest order of chivalry in the realm. Other honors large and small followed, but no remuneration. Field-Marshals never retire, but after he resigned as Chief of the Imperial General Staff, Alanbrooke received a yearly pay of only £300. He had to sell his home and his bird books to stay solvent. Service on the board of directors of a number of different corporations and banks helped ease the financial pressure. Hurt in a very powerful way at his almost total exclusion from Churchill's six-volume set of memoirs and needing income, the impoverished nobleman decided to publish portions of his diary. He allowed Sir Arthur Bryant to publish extracts in two volumes in 1957 and 1959. These works were best-sellers on both sides of the Atlantic, and made him a public figure for the first time. Brooke's words also represented the first major challenge of the heroic view of Churchill's wartime leadership. These books led to a break between the two men. As he neared 80, the viscount's health began to fail him and then on June 17, 1963, he died suddenly from a heart attack at his home.[1]

Admiral of the Fleet The Baron Cunningham of Hyndhope of Kirhope in the County of Selkirk

On January 1, 1946, Cunningham became Viscount Cunningham of Hyndhope. Admirals of the Fleet never retire, but on the second anniversary of the Normandy invasion Cunningham did leave the service in everything but name. The admiral had a long and active retirement, living outside Portsmouth. He spent his time collecting honors, commenting on current naval issues, and seeing to it that those who had served in the Royal Navy received just recognition for their efforts. He could not save the HMS *Warspite*, his flagship when he was Commander-in-Chief of the Mediterranean Fleet, from the scrap yard, but he hung its bell outside his front door.

His death was as unexpected as it was instant. On June 12, 1963, he was in London for an Admiralty meeting and a luncheon appointment. Sir Edward Appleton, the admiral's lunch companion, found him in great spirits and the "magnet of all eyes." Cunningham caught a taxi to take him to the Waterloo train station. He never reached his destination. Cunningham of Hyndhope, age 80, died en route. Six days later, in foul gale-force winds and rough waters, the Royal Navy buried its greatest admiral in over a century in the deep of the English Channel. One of the wreaths that followed him into the water included a cap ribbon from the *Warspite*.[2]

Marshal of the Royal Air Force The Baron Portal of Hungerford, Hungerford, County Berks

Like Alanbrooke and Cunningham, Lord Portal became a Viscount with the dawn of the new year in 1946. Later in the year he became a Knight of the Garter. Eleven days after stepping down as Chief of the Air Staff, Attlee asked him to oversee British production of an atomic bomb. He agreed and served in this post under various titles for five years. When Churchill became prime minister a second time, he asked Portal to serve as his Minister of Defence. Portal refused. During the 1950s, he, like Alanbrooke, served on the boards of several corporations. The highlight of his business career came in the early 1960s when he served as the Chairman of both the British Match Corporation and the British Aircraft Corporation. Reserved and almost stoic in the office, he became relaxed and talkative at home. He and his wife bought a small estate in West Ashling near Chichester Harbor. Rebuilding the fire-damaged main building and gardening became major recreations for him. In 1958, while he was doing some landscaping work, he lost control of the circular saw he was using and cut off his right index finger. Despite this injury, he continued to stay active in the out-of-doors. It was during a hunting trip in late 1970 that he fell ill. It was an advanced form of cancer. His doctors told him he only had six months. He made ready in the time he had left, and just as predicted, died on April 23, 1971. He was 77. The youngest of the Chiefs, he was also the last of them to go.[3]

Winston Churchill

Defeated in 1945, Churchill refused to go gentle into the good night of retirement. He became leader of the opposition, and six months later at Westminster College in Fulton, Missouri, following an introduction from President Truman, gave what was arguably his best-known speech:

> From Stettin in the Baltic to Trieste in the Adriatic, an iron curtain has descended across the Continent. Behind that line lie all the capitals of the ancient states of Central and Eastern Europe. Warsaw, Berlin, Prague, Vienna, Budapest, Belgrade, Bucharest and Sofia, all these famous cities and the populations around them lie in what I must call the Soviet sphere, and all are subject in one form or another, not only to Soviet influence but to a very high and in many cases, increasing measure of control from Moscow.

In 1948 he began publishing his six-volume memoir of the war in which he slighted the contributions the Chiefs of Staff made to strategy.

Churchill became Prime Minister a second time in 1951. He presided over the transition of sovereignty when Elizabeth II became Queen following the death of George VI. In 1953, Churchill received two exceptionally prestigious honors. The Queen made him a Knight of the Garter and he won the Nobel Prize for Literature. When he stepped down as prime minister in 1955, the Queen believed he deserved some title of nobility better than that offered to the average resident of 10 Downing Street, but she wanted to avoid inflating the highest ranks of the nobility and suggested making him a Duke only after learning he would turn it down. Still, as the grandson of a duke, he found the offer tempting and nearly accepted. He remained a member of the House of Commons until the end, but his wasting health in the early 1960s made it more and more difficult for him to attend to his duties. After a severe stroke, he died on January 24, 1965. The Queen arranged to have him lie in state at Westminster Hall, and attended the funeral service of her greatest subject at St. Paul's Cathedral. He was later buried next to his parents and brother.[4]

The Americans

General of the Army Henry H. Arnold

On February 9, 1946, Arnold resigned his position as Commanding General, U.S. Army Air Forces. He retired from the army later in the year for reasons of health. He and Bee moved to California and slowly repaired their marriage. "I'm going out to my ranch in the Valley of the Moon to sit under an oak tree," he said about his plans. "From there I'll look across the valley at the white-faced cattle. And if one of them even moves too fast, I'll look the other way." Arnold never really recovered his health and did indeed live the sedentary life he talked about. He kept his mind busy writing his memoirs, which did poorly in sales when published in 1949. That same year, Arnold transferred his rank to the now independent U.S. Air Force and took a new title to go with his five stars: General of the Air Force. Seven months later, in January of 1950, he died in his sleep. The only time he wore the blue uniform of the U.S. Air Force was in his coffin. He was the first of the U.S. Joint Chiefs to die.[5]

Fleet Admiral Ernest J. King

King left office in 1945, but he did not enjoy his retirement for long. He started a slow and painful collapse only two years later. He suffered the first of several strokes in 1947. He was an invalid when he died on June 25, 1956, in Portsmouth, New Hampshire. Four days later, on a cool, sunny afternoon, King traveled to the Naval Academy one last time. With carrier planes flying overhead and rifle volleys announcing the arrival of the funeral motorcade, a throng of white-clad midshipmen and officers watched a brief graveside service as the admiral came to rest on a tree-shaded hillside.[6]

Fleet Admiral William D. Leahy

Unlike the other U.S. Joint Chiefs of Staff, Leahy continued on in office, developing a relationship with Truman that was as good as the one he had with Roosevelt. "I want you in the White House. I have the utmost confidence in you. You tell me what you think," the president informed him. "You are my friend and I am yours come hell or high water." In JCS meetings, the admiral occasionally referred to the new Army Chief of Staff as "Mr. President." Dwight Eisenhower would respond, denying he had any political ambition. Leahy's initial inclination toward isolation faded quickly and he became one of the hardest of the Cold Warriors. After reading an early draft of Churchill's "Iron Curtain" speech, he observed, "I could find no fault with his proposed address." Health problems forced him to resign at the start of Truman's second term in office. Still, the president continued to consult him on issues of national security.

Leahy's public career essentially ended when Eisenhower came into office. His health problems grew as he crossed 80 and limited his retirement activities. He saw his son promoted to the rank of Rear Admiral and became a great-grandfather before he died on July 20, 1959.

Truman wrote to Leahy's son afterward: "There never was a finer man or an abler public servant. I could always depend on him to tell me the truth, whether I liked it or not, a quality too seldom found in men of his position."[7]

General of the Army George C. Marshall

On November 26, 1945, America's first five-star general left active duty. Or so he thought. Officers in his grade of rank never retire, and in Marshall's case it was true. Truman sent him to China as a special ambassador to attempt to negotiate a peace settlement that would prevent a Chinese civil war. This effort was probably doomed from the start, but Truman continued to value his advice, asking him in late 1946 to become Secretary of State. Coming into office in the early days of the Cold War, Marshall would have a profound influence on U.S. foreign policy. He established the Policy Planning Staff and made George Kennan its director. From this position, Kennan created the policy of "containment." At the 286th Harvard Commencement in 1947, knowing that Europe needed economic help to rebuild from the war, Marshall announced plans for the European Recovery Program—better known as the Marshall Plan. *Time* magazine made him its "Man of the Year" for 1947. After a brief retirement in which he served briefly as President of the American Red Cross, Truman asked him to become the Secretary of Defense. Since federal law prohibited military officers who had been on the active duty list in the last ten years from holding this position, Congress had to pass new legislation before he could be confirmed. He took office during the Korean War and oversaw efforts to rebuild the military for this conflict. He also backed Truman when the president decided to remove MacArthur from his command. After the congressional hearings that followed, he resigned, never to return to public service. In 1953, he received the Nobel Peace Prize for his effort in backing the European Recovery Program. Sick with the flu before he left for the ceremony in Oslo, Marshall never really enjoyed good health after returning from Norway. A steady decline in his health marked his seventies. After suffering two strokes, his heart stopped on October 16, 1959.[8]

Harry S. Truman

When the war ended, Truman still had over seven years left in office. The occupations of Germany and Japan, the onset of the Cold War, health care, the Marshall Plan, the Fair Deal, the Truman Doctrine, the Berlin blockade, the creation of the Central Intelligence Agency, the institution of a peacetime draft, the desegregation of the military, his narrow reelection, the creation of the North Atlantic Treaty Organization, appointment of a Chief Justice of the Supreme Court, McCarthyism, Korea, the veto of the McCarran Act, the seizure of steel companies, and his removal of MacArthur were all issues that awaited him in the future. He found seven years and eleven months in the White House enough, and declined to run for another term in 1952. In his farewell address, he told the public: "I want you to realize how big a job, how hard a job it is—not for my sake, because I am stepping out of it—but for the sake of my successor. . . . Regardless of your politics, whether you are Republican or Democrat, your fate is tied up with what is done here in this room." He also added, "In the long run the strength of our free society, and our ideals, will prevail over a system that has respect for neither God nor man."

In a sign of the admiration in which he held Truman, Churchill—back in office as prime minister—made a brief visit to Washington in January of 1953 to pay his respects one last time. Like any retired couple, Truman and his wife, Bess, traveled both in the United States and abroad. In 1956, a grand tour of Europe brought him to England, where he received an honorary degree from Oxford. The three-minute ovation he received reduced him to tears. Another major project was the building of his Presidential Library. A mile from his home, Truman moved his office to the new building and would often visit the research room, remarking to scholars, "I hope you find what you're looking for."

After he fell in his bathroom in October 1964, his health began to collapse. Still it took another eight years before his body failed him completely. He died on December 26, 1972.[9]

The British Supporting Actors

Admiral Sir Bruce Fraser

Fraser was on the deck of the USS *Missouri* when Japan formally surrendered, and he signed for Britain. Before he returned to England, the King made him a peer. The naval career of The Baron Fraser of North Cape, though, was far from over. He became Commander-in-Chief, Portsmouth, the senior shore command in the Royal Navy, and also served as the First and Principal Aide-de-Camp to King George VI. In these assignments, he was basically marking time until 1948, when he became the First Sea Lord, which included promotion to the rank of Admiral of the Fleet. Fraser's three years in this post were of exceptional importance to his service. During his tenure, the North Atlantic Treaty Organization came into existence, and he worked with his British and American colleagues to establish the command structure of the new alliance. The Korean War also broke out during this time. Once Britain committed itself to fight in this conflict, Fraser quickly sent the British Far Eastern Fleet to fight alongside the U.S. Navy. The Royal Navy played a significant role in the Inchon landing and later in the evacuation of United Nations forces from Pyongyang. It was under Fraser that veterans of the British Pacific Fleet began to dominate the Royal Navy as it moved into the Cold War. He left the Admiralty at the end of 1951. Without a family, he hosted holiday parties for local neighborhood tradesmen in East Molesey and enjoyed an extremely private retirement in which he refused to write memoirs. As a result, he received fewer honors than were his due, but when he died on February 12, 1981, a memorial service in Westminster Abbey honored his memory, which he deserved.[10]

Admiral The Lord Louis Mountbatten

The war was kind to the ambitious Mountbatten. He became a peer in his own right after the war first as a Viscount and then later as The Earl

Mountbatten of Burma. He then took up the thankless task of serving as the last Viceroy of India as the colony achieved its independence. Lord Mountbatten returned to the Royal Navy, was promoted to the rank of Admiral of the Fleet, and eventually became head of the navy as First Sea Lord. He had achieved all his youthful ambitions. He then became Chief of the Defence Staff, a new position that oversaw all the British armed services. The vindication of his family was complete. When Lady Mountbatten died in 1960, he increased his workload to compensate for the grief. After he retired in 1965, he regularly took a summer vacation in Ireland at a castle he had inherited through his wife. It was during a vacation in 1979 that the Irish Republican Army placed a bomb on his sailboat. The explosion killed Mountbatten, his grandson, a friend of his grandson's, and his son-in-law's mother.[11]

Field-Marshal Sir Henry Wilson
Wilson stayed in Washington until 1947. There was still a good deal of work to keep professional military officers busy. He contributed to efforts to dispose of equipment, the commissioning of official histories, and the translation of captured enemy documents in an effort to learn lessons that could be used in future years. Wilson observed, "I noticed a tendency for the willingness to collaborate, so alive during the period of hostilities, to cool off, especially on the non-service side; the attitude of Congress also showed a trend that way." While he was in the United States, the King awarded him a nobleman's title and he became The Baron Wilson of Libya and Stowlangtoft, County Suffolk. Returning to England, he wrote his memoir *Eight Years Overseas*, to which Eisenhower contributed the foreword. He became President of the Army Cadet Force Association and served as the Constable of the Tower of London for five years. He died at his home on the last day of 1964.[12]

The American Supporting Actors

Admiral William Halsey
Halsey was on the deck of the *Missouri*, his flagship, to witness the formal surrender ceremonies. With less than a year before reaching mandatory separation from the service, the admiral formally requested retirement before leaving Japan. A week after his retirement ceremony, Truman promoted him to the remaining open slot for a five-star admiral. Fleet Admiral

Halsey kept himself busy for a year writing his memoirs. After having commanded the largest fleet in the world, though, he found adjusting to life after the navy difficult. He was bored. He quickly took advantage of the opportunity to serve on several corporate boards. Soon, he was making more money than he ever had. His board work, however, required that he move to New York City. He was willing, but his wife refused. As a result, they separated. She moved to California, and he to New York. The couple never divorced, but lived separate lives from that point forward. On August 16, 1959, while vacationing, he died alone in a hotel room.[13]

Major General Curtis LeMay

Thirty-eight years old at the end of the war, LeMay would spend well over half his military career as a general officer. In 1948 he oversaw the Berlin airlift. After his success in Germany, LeMay became the Commanding General of the Strategic Air Command, a position he would hold for nine years. The command was responsible for conducting nuclear bomb strikes against the Soviet Union. During his command tenure, LeMay turned SAC into an organization that dominated Soviet airpower in every manner and was capable of waging an effective nuclear war. "We in SAC were not saber-rattlers. We were not yelling for war and action in order to 'flex the mighty muscles we had built.' No stupidity of that sort. We wanted peace as much as anyone else wanted it. But we knew for a fact that it would be possible to curtail enemy expansion if we challenged them in that way."

LeMay's career culminated with promotion to full General and an unhappy tenure as Chief of Staff of the U.S. Air Force, which was hardly surprising given his personality and blunt ways. After retirement, he wrote his memoirs, which contained a phrase, "bomb them back into the Stone Age," that many people mistakenly thought summarized a brutal man. In 1968, out of frustration with the conduct of the Vietnam War, he agreed to serve as the vice presidential running mate in Alabama Governor George Wallace's independent presidential campaign. LeMay would later admit that decision was a mistake. After living out a long retirement in Southern California, he died on October 1, 1990.[14]

General of the Army Douglas MacArthur

The most important period in MacArthur's life lay ahead of him when World War II ended. He became the Commander of the Allied Occupation of Japan. While he was in Japan, he oversaw reforms in a number of different areas with a number of different purposes. These included a new constitution that retained the monarchy but abolished titles of peerage. The document renounced war as a sovereign right, gave new rights to women, and instituted land reform. MacArthur would later call the document "probably the single most important accomplishment of the occupation."

He also had one more war in him. On June 25, 1950, North Korea attacked South Korea in an effort to unify the country through military means. The first few months were a military stalemate, but MacArthur reversed the situation in September with an amphibious assault at Inchon. The move destroyed the North Korean Army. The allies followed them into North Korea only to face a Chinese intervention in November. The longest retreat in U.S. Army history followed. After a series of disputes about strategy, Truman decided to relieve the general of his various commands. MacArthur returned home to a hero's welcome. The highlight of his return was the speech he gave to a Joint Session of Congress on April 19, 1951. His cadence, resonant voice, forceful delivery, and obvious sincerity gave the speech power beyond the mere words he used. He talked for thirty-seven minutes and was interrupted with applause over fifty times. He soon began his retirement in New York City. He died in 1964 after a series of operations failed to rectify his failing health. He was buried in the rotunda of the MacArthur Memorial in Norfolk, Virginia, wearing a simple tropical worsted uniform with only the U.S. and five-star insignias on his collar.[15]

Fleet Admiral Chester Nimitz

Secretary of the Navy James Forrestal needed to find a new Chief of Naval Operations when King stepped down. He did not want to give the office to Nimitz, but King fought for him, taking the matter directly to Truman. Forrestal made the appointment reluctantly, and as events transpired, he turned out to be more right than wrong. Nimitz did a poor job and had an unpleasant tenure in Washington, and Forrestal forced him out after only two years. Basically retired, he moved back to the San Francisco Bay area. Governor Earl Warren asked him to serve as a regent of the University of California. He accepted quickly, and was an active member of the board. He believed teaching should be a major consideration in faculty evaluations and opposed loyalty oath requirements. He also served briefly as an administrator for the United Nations to oversee a plebiscite to decide if the province of Kashmir should join India or Pakistan. When the willingness of these two nations to abide by the results collapsed, Nimitz resigned his position. He died in 1966, and was buried in Golden Gate National Cemetery on what would have been his 81st birthday. As the casket reached the grave, seventy navy jets flew over in formation.[16]

Admiral Raymond Spruance

After the war ended, Spruance replaced Nimitz as Commander-in-Chief, Pacific Fleet and Pacific Ocean Areas. He held this command for only ten weeks before he received orders to serve as the President of the Naval War College. "I tried to make the courses practical," he explained. "I can see no change in the future role of our Navy from what it has been for ages past for the Navy of a dominant sea power—to gain and exercise the control of the sea that its country requires to win the war, and prevent its opponent from using the sea for its purposes." When he retired in 1948, the U.S. Congress authorized that he receive full pay in retirement. In 1952 he became U.S. Ambassador to the Philippines. He held this post for three years, and then lived out his retirement in California. His memory began to fail with his health. When his son died in a car accident in 1969, he had trouble understanding what had happened. When he did, his grief was intense and accelerated his decline. He died in December of that year, and the navy buried him with full honors next to Nimitz.[17]

Supporting Actors from the Commonwealth

General Sir Thomas Blamey

Blamey represented Australia at the Japanese surrender ceremonies on the USS *Missouri*. He retired from the Australian Army in February 1946. The day after his formal discharge, he gave a speech critical of the Chifley government for its refusal to award knighthoods and other honors to deserving officers. His retirement was short, because his health failed in 1950. In an effort to make amends for the parsimonious attitude of the government under the Labor Party toward honors, the new Cabinet had Blamey promoted to Field-Marshal. On September 16, 1950, he became the first—and so far only—Australian to achieve this rank. A stroke had incapacitated him to such a degree that he sat through the ceremony in a wheelchair and was unable to deliver his acceptance speech. He died eight months later on May 27, 1951.[18]

Ben Chifley

A year after the war ended, Chifley led the Labor Party to a decisive victory that smashed the conservative opposition. It was the first time in Australian history that Labor had won two consecutive federal elections. He called on his party to work for "a great objective—the light on the hill—which we aim to reach by working for the betterment of mankind not only here but anywhere we may give a helping hand." He continued the policy of Australian assertiveness vis-à-vis the United Kingdom that Curtin's government had advanced, but the prime minister's main interest was giving Australia a greater voice within a British world. Proof of this comes in his insistence on having an Australian serve as the new Governor-General, while maintaining food rationing so that the Dominion could continue to ship agricultural products to Britain as it recovered from the war. Chifley was an exceptionally reluctant convert to the Cold War crusade. He believed the Soviet Union was too exhausted from the war to initiate another conflict, and saw the Americans aggressively trying to establish an international order that serviced their own economic interests. There was no denying, though, the brutal nature of the Soviet system, and after a trip to Europe, the prime minister had the Royal Australian Air Force contribute planes to the Berlin Airlift.

In 1949 the Australian electorate voted Labor out of office, worried in part about Chifley's Cold War policies. He was still a member of Parliament when he died from a heart attack on June 13, 1951. His wife and both his mistresses attended the funeral.[19]

Peter Fraser

With the death of his wife, Fraser devoted almost all of his time and energy to politics. While he had an inclination toward world affairs, domestic policy was what garnered him votes. The second half of the 1940s was a good time to be a New Zealander. Postwar Europe, including Britain, was rebuilding from the war and needed plenty of foodstuffs, which were the Dominion's major export. Spared physical damage during the war, New Zealand found itself enjoying full employment and a good standard of living for its citizens. Under Fraser's leadership, the government initiated a series of projects to support the arts in New Zealand, including the establishment of a national orchestra and a series of official histories on the war. In 1947 the Parliament in Wellington ratified the Statute of Westminster, which made New Zealand sovereign from the United Kingdom. In

1949 Fraser became Father of the House, the longest-serving member of Parliament, but the coalition supporting the Labour Party was coming apart as more people wanted rewards for wartime sacrifice and grew tired of excessive government regulation. Labour lost the general election at the end of the year. Fraser's long run as Prime Minister of New Zealand, the longest in the history of his party—then or since—was over. Shorn of power and exhausted in spirits, the 66-year-old politician died on December 12, 1950, a year minus a day after leaving office.[20]

Lieutenant-General Sir Bernard Freyberg

Even before the war ended, Freyberg was offered the post of Governor-General of New Zealand, in which capacity he would represent the crown in the Dominion. Although not a native-born resident, he became the first New Zealander to hold this position. According to his son and biographer, "The years that followed were the happiest of Bernard Freyberg's life." In 1951, on the recommendation of the prime ministers of both the United Kingdom and New Zealand, the King made Freyberg a peer. The new nobleman took a title that reflected his transnational life; he became The Baron Freyberg of Wellington, New Zealand, and of Munstead, County Surrey. He left New Zealand in 1952, returning to England, where he became Deputy Constable and Lieutenant-Governor of Windsor Castle. He kept busy serving on several boards like that of the National Bank of New Zealand, attending a number of ceremonies, and supporting the official New Zealand history of the war. Despite the battering Freyberg's body had taken earlier in life, he remained active until the very end. Then, on the afternoon of July 4, 1963, the stomach wound Lord Freyberg suffered at Gallipoli opened up, and he died later that evening. A transnational man to the end, his coffin was draped in the flags of Great Britain and New Zealand.[21]

William Mackenzie King

Recrimination from the conscription crisis lasted for years. The prime minister lost his seat in Parliament in the national election of June 11, 1945. The vote of servicemen was decisive. He quickly regained a seat in a by-election without having to hand over control of the Cabinet. When Ralston died, the prime minister attended the funeral, but the widow refused to receive him. When the war ended, the Canadian prime minister returned to a prewar practice of his and began attending séances. In 1947 he told Churchill that the dead Roosevelt had given him messages to give to the then-leader of Her Majesty's loyal opposition. Mackenzie King stayed in office until November 15, 1948, when poor health forced his resignation. His tenure in office was longer than any other individual's in Canadian history. He also broke Sir Robert Walpole's record of longevity for a first minister in any British nation. Politics had been his life and he soon found himself enjoying little of his retirement. He did discover, though, that he was much wealthier than he had imagined, having had no family on which to spend his holdings. He wanted to write memoirs about his long career, but nothing came of these efforts. After a year out of office, his health began to decline and absorbed most of his attention. He died on July 22, 1950.[22]

Walter Nash

Nash still had a long political career ahead of him in New Zealand when the war ended. He remained a Cabinet Minister in Fraser's government until the Labour Party was voted out of office in 1949. When Fraser died, Nash replaced him as leader of the party. In 1957, when Labour retook control of Parliament, Nash became Prime Minister. He was 75. He also served as Minister of External Affairs and was often absent on state visits to foreign countries. In 1960, Labour lost control of Parliament due to low voter turnout. He lost his post as leader of the party in 1963. In 1965 Queen Elizabeth II made him a Knight Grand Cross of St. Michael and St. George. He, however, turned down offers to become a Baron and assume a seat in the House of Lords. As a result, he remained a member of the New Zealand Parliament until the day he died. Sir Walter looked into writing his memoirs, but he died on June 4, 1968, having barely begun the project. The government of New Zealand gave him a state funeral, the first since that of Peter Fraser some two decades before.[23]

Sir Frederick Shedden

As the Secretary of the Defence Department, Shedden would dominate the formulation of Australian national security matters for the next decade. His authority was hollow, though. Chifley relied on the Department of External Affairs when it came to matters of international relations. The Soviets managed to recruit spies within the External Affairs Ministry that handed over secret American and British documents. The U.S. and British governments responded by cutting off all Australian access to their classified documents. Shedden was operating in a strategic vacuum. Under a new, Conservative government his influence slowly started to wane. He was not consulted about an Australian commitment to participate in the Korean War or the negotiation of a formal alliance treaty with the United States. Tired of constant bureaucratic battles with External Affairs, he began to put less energy into defense matters as the 1950s progressed, and the quality of his work declined. In an effort to rid himself of a tiresome civil servant, Prime Minister Sir Robert Menzies asked Shedden to leave office to write an official history of Australian defense policy. This project extended Shedden's official career for years, but his petty sense of self-importance suffered when the Defence Department refused to provide him with a car and driver during a visit to Canberra, or when he learned that his text would have to undergo vetting to see that there was no breach of security. Shedden proved unable to write a cohesive book and when he died from a heart attack on July 8, 1971, he was still at work on the project. It was never published.[24]

The Enemy

Vice Admiral Ugaki Matome

When Emperor Hirohito announced that Japan would surrender, Ugaki accepted responsibility for the disaster that had come to Japan. "As one of the officers the throne entrusted, I meet this sad day. I've never been so ashamed of myself." Having sent so many young men to their death, he decided he, too, should die "as a samurai, an admiral, a supreme commander. I renew a resolution today of entrusting my body to the throne and defending the Empire until death takes me away." On August 15, carrying a sword that Yamamoto had given him, he flew to Okinawa with a group of twenty-two other pilots and crewmen on one last suicide mission. American radar operators spotted the planes as they approached the island and U.S. fighters intercepted and downed all of the attacking kamikazes. None of the planes struck any ships. Ugaki's plane skimmed above a landing craft and crashed onto a small island just north of Okinawa.[25]

Notes

Abbreviations Used in the Notes

Alanbrooke Papers	Papers of the First Viscount Alanbrooke of Brookeborough, Liddell Hart Centre for Military Archives, King's College London
Arnold Papers	Papers of H. H. Arnold, Library of Congress, Washington, D.C.
Avon Papers	Papers of the First Earl of Avon, University of Birmingham
Berryman Papers	Papers of Sir Frank Berryman, Australian War Memorial, Canberra
Blamey Papers	Papers of Sir Thomas Blamey, Australian War Memorial, Canberra
BNA	British National Archives, Richmond, Surrey
AIR	Records of the Air Ministry
CAB	Records of the Cabinet Office
FO	Records of the Foreign Office
PREM	Records of the Prime Minister's Office
WO	Records of the War Office
Buckner Papers (Kans.)	Papers of Simon Bolivar Buckner, Jr., Dwight D. Eisenhower Presidential Library, Abilene, Kansas
Buckner Papers (Pa.)	Papers of Simon Bolivar Buckner, Jr., U.S. Army Military History Institute, Carlisle Barracks, Carlisle, Pennsylvania
CAC	Churchill Archives Centre, Churchill College, University of Cambridge

Chamberlin Papers	Papers of Stephan J. Chamberlin, U.S. Army Military History Institute, Carlisle Barracks, Carlisle, Pennsylvania
Cunningham Papers	Papers of Viscount Cunningham of Hyndhope, British Library, London
Dalton Papers	Papers of Baron Dalton of Forest and Firth, British Library of Political and Economic Science, London School of Economics and Political Science
Fraser Papers	Papers of Baron Fraser of North Cape, National Maritime Museum, Greenwich, London
Freyberg Papers	Papers of Baron Freyberg of Wellington, New Zealand, and Munstead, National Archives of New Zealand, Wellington
Ismay Papers	Papers of Baron Ismay of Wormington, Liddell Hart Centre for Military Archives, King's College London
Jacob Papers	Papers of Sir Ian Jacob, Churchill Archives Centre, Churchill College, University of Cambridge
King Papers	Papers of Ernest J. King, Library of Congress, Washington, D.C.
Leahy Papers	Papers of William D. Leahy, Library of Congress, Washington, D.C.
LeMay Papers	Papers of Curtis LeMay, Library of Congress, Washington, D.C.
Liddell Hart Papers	Papers of Sir Basil Liddell Hart, Liddell Hart Centre for Military Archives, King's College London
Lincoln Papers	Papers of George A. Lincoln, U.S. Military Academy, West Point, New York
Mackenzie King Papers	Papers of William Lyon Mackenzie King, National Archives of Canada, Ottawa, Ontario
MM	MacArthur Memorial, Norfolk, Virginia
Mountbatten Papers	Papers of the First Earl Mountbatten of Burma, University of Southampton, Hampshire
NAC	National Archives of Canada, Ottawa, Ontario
NANZ	National Archives of New Zealand, Wellington
Nimitz Papers	Papers of Chester W. Nimitz, Naval Historical Center, Washington Navy Yard, Washington, D.C.
Portal Papers	Papers of Viscount Portal of Hungerford, Christ Church Library, Christ Church College, University of Oxford
PREM	Records of the Prime Minister's Office, British National Archives, Richmond, Surrey
RDEAT	Records of the Department of External Affairs
Shedden Papers	Papers of Sir Frederick Shedden, National Archives of Australia, Canberra
Stilwell Papers	Papers of Joseph W. Stilwell, Hoover Institution, Stanford University, Stanford, California

Stimson Papers   Papers of Henry L. Stimson, Yale University Library, Yale University, New Haven, Connecticut
USNA   U.S. National Archives, College Park, Maryland

Introduction: Truman's Funeral

1. *Kansas City Times*, December 29, 1972; *Los Angeles Times*, December 29, 1972.

2. *Washington Post*, December 28, 1972; *Chicago Tribune*, December 28, 1972.

3. *Chicago Tribune*, December 28, 1972.

4. *Kansas City Star*, December 28, 1972.

5. *Christian Science Monitor*, December 27, 1972; *Philadelphia Inquirer*, December 27, 1972; *Atlanta Journal*, December 26, 1972; Baltimore *Sun*, December 27, 1972; *San Francisco Chronicle*, December 27, 1972; *Boston Globe*, December 27, 1972.

6. *Wall Street Journal*, December 27, 1972.

7. *Chicago Tribune*, December 27, 1972.

8. David McCullough, *Truman* (New York: Simon and Schuster, 1992), 826–831; *Washington Post*, December 27, 1972.

9. Baltimore *Sun*, December 29, 1972; *Kansas City Times*, December 29, 1972.

10. *Kansas City Times*, December 29, 1972; *Los Angeles Times*, December 29, 1972.

11. Ronald H. Spector, *Eagle against the Sun: The American War with Japan* (New York: Free Press, 1984), xiii.

12. Writing on the atomic bombs is extensive and there are three good historiographical essays on this topic: Barton J. Bernstein, "The Atomic Bomb and American Foreign Policy, 1941–1945: An Historiographical Controversy," *Peace & Change* 2, no. 1 (Spring 1974), 1–16; J. Samuel Walker, "The Decision to Use the Bomb: A Historiographical Update," *Diplomatic History* 14, no. 1 (Winter 1990), 97–114; the most recent is J. Samuel Walker, "Recent Literature on Truman's Atomic Bomb Decision: A Search for Middle Ground," *Diplomatic History* 29, no. 2 (April 2005), 311–344; Gar Alperovitz, *Atomic Diplomacy: Hiroshima and Potsdam: The Use of the Atomic Bomb and the American Confrontation with Soviet Power* (New York: Vintage, 1965); Gar Alperovitz, *The Decision to Use the Atomic Bomb and the Architecture of the American Myth* (New York: Alfred A. Knopf, 1995); Ronald Takaki, *Hiroshima: Why America Dropped the Atomic Bomb* (Boston: Little, Brown, 1995); Robert James Maddox, *Weapons for Victory: The Hiroshima Decision Fifty Years Later* (Columbia: University of Missouri Press, 1995); Barton J. Bernstein, "Roosevelt, Truman, and the Atomic Bomb, 1941–1945: A Reinterpretation," *Political Science Quarterly* 90, no. 1 (Spring 1975), 23–69; Martin J. Sherwin, *A World Destroyed: Hiroshima and the Origins of the Arms Race* (New York: Knopf, 1975); Robert Jay Lifton and Greg Mitchell, *Hiroshima in America: Fifty Years of Denial* (New York: G. P. Putnam's Sons, 1995); Herbert Feis, *Japan Subdued: The Atomic Bomb and the End of the War in the Pacific* (Princeton, N.J.: Princeton University Press, 1961); Herbert Feis, *The Atomic Bomb and the End of World War II* (Princeton, N.J.: Princeton University Press, 1966); J. Samuel Walker,

Prompt and Utter Destruction: Truman and the Use of the Atomic Bomb against Japan (Chapel Hill: University of North Carolina Press, 1997); Barton J. Bernstein, "Truman and the A-Bomb: Targeting Noncombatants, Using the Bomb, and His Defending the 'Decision,'" *Journal of Military History* 62 (July 1998), 547–570; Barton J. Bernstein, "Seizing the Contested Terrain of Early Nuclear History: Stimson, Conant, and Their Allies Explain the Decision to Use the Atomic Bomb," *Diplomatic History* 17, no. 1 (Winter 1993), 35–72; Barton J. Bernstein, "Writing, Righting, or Wronging the Historical Record: President Truman's Letter on His Atomic-Bomb Decision," *Diplomatic History* 16, no. 1 (Winter 1992), 163–173, and the essays that appeared in a special issue of *Diplomatic History* 19, no. 2 (Spring 1995) symposium and were later published in book form as Michael J. Hogan, ed., *Hiroshima in History and Memory* (New York: Cambridge University Press, 1996). The book contains one original chapter, and not all the articles from the symposium ended up in the book, so one must consult the two publications.

13. Charles F. Brower IV, "Sophisticated Strategist: General George A. Lincoln and the Defeat of Japan, 1944–1945," *Diplomatic History* 15, no. 3 (Summer 1991), 317–337; Charles F. Brower IV, "The Debate over Final Strategy for the Defeat of Japan," *Joint Perspectives* 2 (Spring 1982), 82–90.

14. John D. Chappell, *Before the Bomb: How America Approached the End of the Pacific War* (Lexington: University Press of Kentucky, 1997).

15. Edward J. Drea, *MacArthur's Ultra: Codebreaking and the War against Japan, 1942–1945* (Lawrence: University Press of Kansas, 1992); Douglas J. MacEachin, *The Final Months of the War with Japan: Signals Intelligence, U.S. Invasion Planning, and the A-Bomb Decision* (Washington, D.C.: Center for the Study of Intelligence, 1998).

16. Roger Dingman, *Ghost of War: The Sinking of the* Awa maru *and Japanese-American Relations, 1945–1995* (Annapolis, Md.: Naval Institute Press, 1997).

17. Kenneth P. Werrell, *Blankets of Fire: U.S. Bombers over Japan during World War II* (Washington, D.C.: Smithsonian Institution Press, 1996); Herman S. Wolk, "General Arnold, the Atomic Bomb, and the Surrender of Japan," in Günter Bischof and Robert L. Dupont, eds., *The Pacific War Revisited* (Baton Rouge: Louisiana State University Press, 1997), 163–178; Jim Smith and Malcolm McConnell, *The Last Mission: The Secret History of World War II's Final Battle* (New York: Broadway Books, 2002); Barton J. Bernstein, "Compelling Japan's Surrender without the A-Bomb, Soviet Entry, or Invasion: Reconsidering the US Bombing Survey's Early-Surrender Conclusions," *Journal of Strategic Studies* 18, no. 2 (June 1995), 101–148.

18. Thomas W. Zeiler, *Unconditional Defeat: Japan, America, and the End of World War II* (Wilmington, Del.: Scholarly Resources, 2004), is a study of the last two years of the war in which Zeiler argues that the Americans used their overwhelming resources at a tempo that exceeded the ability of the Japanese to respond; Wayne A. Silkett, "Downfall: The Invasion That Never Was," *Parameters* 24 (Autumn 1994), 111–120, is a very brief account; John Ellis van Courtland Moon, "Project SPHINX: The Question of the Use of Gas in the Planned Invasion of Japan," *Journal of Strategic Studies* 12 (September 1989), 303–323, is, as the title suggests, an examination of the use of gas in the invasion. Marc Gallicchio, "After Nagasaki: General Marshall's Plan for Tactical Nuclear

Weapons in Japan," *Prologue* 23 (Winter 1991), 396–404; and Barton J. Bernstein, "Eclipsed by Hiroshima and Nagasaki: Early Thinking about Tactical Nuclear Weapons," *International Security* 15 (Spring 1991), 149–173, are examinations of the use of nuclear weapons as tactical support weapons for the infantry landing on the beaches of Kyushu. A strong debate has developed over the expected casualties in such an operation. The dispute has been intense, because the findings have an impact on the exchange over the use of the atomic bomb. Part of this debate has involved the nature of the evidence one should use in writing history. Bernstein has argued in a series of articles that a reading of documents produced during the war shows that the argument that the invasion would have produced high casualties is suspect: Barton J. Bernstein, "The Myth of Lives Saved by A-Bomb," *Los Angeles Times*, July 28, 1985; Barton J. Bernstein, "A Postwar Myth: 500,000 U.S. Lives Saved," *Bulletin of the Atomic Scientists* (June/July 1986), 38–40; Bernstein, "Writing, Righting, or Wronging the Historical Record," 163–173; Barton J. Bernstein, "The Alarming Japanese Buildup on Southern Kyushu, Growing U.S. Fears, and Counterfactual Analysis: Would the Planned November 1945 Invasion of Southern Kyushu Have Occurred?" *Pacific Historical Review* 68 (November 1999), 561–591; Bernstein, "Truman and the A-Bomb," 547–570; Barton J. Bernstein, "Reconsidering Truman's Claim of 'Half a Million American Lives' Saved by the Atomic Bomb: The Construction and Deconstruction of a Myth," *Journal of Strategic Studies* 22 (March 1999), 54–95. For a similar view, see Rufus E. Miles, Jr., "Hiroshima: The Strange Myth of Half a Million American Lives Saved," *International Security* 10, no. 2 (Fall 1985), 121–140. Others have argued that other evidence, such as oral histories and low-level supply requisition documents, shows that there was indeed a great fear of a costly invasion that shaped policy. D. M. Giangreco, "Casualty Projections for the U.S. Invasions of Japan, 1945–1946: Planning and Policy Implications," *Journal of Military History* 61 (July 1997), 521–582; D. M. Giangreco, "Operation Downfall: The Devil Was in the Details," *Joint Forces Quarterly* 9 (Autumn 1995), 86–94; Norman Polmar and Thomas B. Allen, "Invasion Most Costly," U.S. Naval Institute *Proceedings* (August 1995), 51–56; Thomas B. Allen and Norman Polmar, *Code-Name* DOWNFALL: *The Secret Plan to Invade Japan — And Why Truman Dropped the Bomb* (New York: Simon & Schuster, 1995). Bernstein wrote an entire article that took apart the Allen-Polmar article and the evidence the two authors used: Barton J. Bernstein, "Reconsidering 'Invasion Most Costly': Popular-History Scholarship, Publishing Standards, and the Claim of High U.S. Casualty Estimates to Legitimize the Atomic Bombings," *Peace & Change* 24 (April 1999), 220–248. In addition to the Allen-Polmar book there is another on the invasion of Japan: John Ray Skates, *The Invasion of Japan: Alternative to the Bomb* (Columbia: University of South Carolina Press, 1994). Richard B. Frank, DOWNFALL: *The End of the Imperial Japanese Empire* (New York: Random House, 1999), and Max Hastings, *Retribution: The Battle for Japan, 1944–45* (New York: Knopf, 2008), provide broad studies of the many different factors at work that resulted in the defeat of Japan. All three works address matters other than the statistical estimates of dead and wounded. Skates and Frank come closer to supporting Bernstein rather than Giangreco and Allen and Polmar. Hastings comes to conclusions that are quite different from those of Skates and Frank. Another study: Alvin D. Coox, "Needless Fear: The Compromise of U.S. Plans to Invade Japan in 1945," *Journal of Military History* 64 (April 2000), 411–438, suggests that Japanese operatives were able to penetrate MacArthur's headquarters in Manila and steal the plans for the invasion, which they were unable to deliver to any Japanese commands.

19. Leon V. Sigal, *Fighting to a Finish: The Politics of War Termination in the United States and Japan, 1945* (Ithaca, N.Y.: Cornell University Press, 1988); Brian L. Villa, "The U.S. Army, Unconditional Surrender, and the Potsdam Proclamation," *Journal of American History* 63 (June 1976), 66–92; Barton J. Bernstein, "The Perils and Politics of Surrender: Ending the War with Japan and Avoiding the Third Atomic Bomb," *Pacific Historical Review* 46 (February 1977), 1–27.

20. Asada Sadao, "The Mushroom Cloud and National Psyches: Japanese and American Perceptions of the A-Bomb Decision, 1945–1995," *Journal of American–East Asian Relations* 4, no. 2 (Summer 1995), 95–116; Asada Sadao, "The Shock of the Atomic Bomb and Japan's Decision to Surrender—A Reconsideration," *Pacific Historical Review* 67 (November 1998), 477–512; Yukiko Koshiro, "Eurasian Eclipse: Japan's End Game in World War II," *American Historical Review* 109, no. 2 (April 2004), 417–444; Tsuyoshi Hasegawa, *Racing the Enemy: Stalin, Truman, and the Surrender of Japan* (Cambridge, Mass.: Harvard University Press, 2005). All of these works challenge a popular idea that Japan was looking for a way to surrender before the dropping of the atomic bombs. Hasegawa's study is particularly important because it is based on research in Soviet archives in addition to those in Japan.

21. Alfred Coppel, *The Burning Mountain: A Novel of the Invasion of Japan* (New York: Harcourt Brace Jovanovich, 1982); Yoshiaki Hiyama, *Nihon hondo kessen* [The decisive battle for Japan] (Tokyo: Kobunsha, 1981); David Westheimer, *Lighter Than a Feather* (Boston: Little, Brown, 1971); Robert Conroy, *1945: A Novel* (New York: Ballantine, 2007); Douglas Niles and Michael Dobson, *MacArthur's War: A Novel of the Invasion of Japan* (New York: Forge Books, 2008).

22. John E. Moser, *Twisting the Lion's Tail: American Anglophobia between the World Wars* (New York: New York University Press, 1999); Mark A. Stoler, *The Politics of the Second Front: American Military Planning and Diplomacy in Coalition Warfare* (Westport, Conn.: Greenwood Press, 1977); Mark A. Stoler, *Allies and Adversaries: The Joint Chiefs of Staff, the Grand Alliance, and U.S. Strategy in World War II* (Chapel Hill: University of North Carolina Press, 2000); Warren Kimball, *Swords or Ploughshares? The Morgenthau Plan for Defeated Nazi Germany* (Philadelphia: Lippincott, 1976); Warren Kimball, *Forged in War: Roosevelt, Churchill, and the Second World War* (New York: William Morrow, 1997); David Reynolds, *The Creation of the Anglo-American Alliance, 1937–1941* (Chapel Hill: University of North Carolina Press, 1982); Alex Danchev, *Very Special Relationship: Field Marshal Sir John Dill and the Anglo-American Alliance, 1941–44* (London: Brassey's, 1986); Fraser J. Harbutt, *The Iron Curtain: Churchill, America, and the Origins of the Cold War* (New York: Oxford University Press, 1986); Anne Orde, *The Eclipse of Great Britain: The United States and British Imperial Decline, 1895–1956* (New York: St. Martin's, 1996); David Reynolds, *Rich Relations: The American Occupation of Britain, 1942–1945* (New York: Random House, 1995).

23. Christopher Thorne, *Allies of a Kind: The United States, Britain and the War against Japan, 1941–1945* (New York: Oxford University Press, 1978); John J. Sbrega, *Anglo-American Relations and Colonialism in East Asia, 1941–1945* (New York: Garland, 1983); Merrill Bartlett and Robert William Love, Jr., "Anglo-American Naval Diplomacy and the British Pacific Fleet, 1942–1945," *American Neptune* 42 (1982), 203–216; H. P. Willmott, *Grave of a Dozen Schemes: British Naval Planning and the War against Japan, 1943–1945* (Annapolis, Md.: Naval Institute Press, 1996). There have been several articles on British strategy in the Pacific that have started the process of rectifying this lack of interest: Nicholas Evan Sarantakes, "The Royal Air Force on Okinawa: The Diplomacy of a Coalition on the Verge of Victory," *Diplomatic History*, 27, no. 4 (September 2003), 477–500; Christopher Baxter, "In Pursuit of a Pacific Strategy: British Planning for the Defeat of Japan," *Diplomacy & Statecraft* 15, no. 2 (June 2004), 253–278; Thomas Hall, "'Mere Drops in the Ocean': The Politics and Planning of the Contribution of the British Commonwealth to the Final Defeat of Japan, 1944–1945," *Diplomacy & Statecraft* 16, no. 1 (March 2005), 93–116; Nicholas Evan Sarantakes, "One Last Crusade: The US-British Alliance and the End of the War in the Pacific," *Royal United Services Institute Journal*, 149, no. 4 (August 2004), 62–67; Nicholas Evan Sarantakes, "One Last Crusade: The British Pacific Fleet and Its Impact on Anglo-American Relations," *English Historical Review* 121 (April 2006), 429–466; Nicholas Evan Sarantakes, "The Short but Brilliant Life of the British Pacific Fleet," *Joint Forces Quarterly*, no. 40 (1st Quarter, 2006), 85–91. Hall is dismissive of the British effort, while Baxter makes a similar argument to the Sarantakes articles, but attributes a change in the international balance of power allowing the British to make a political gesture. Australia is a bit of an inverted exception to this lack of interest. David Day and David Horner have written a series of attention-getting books. They both show that Australia was torn by personal and political rivalries within the government and a clash between Australian nationalist sentiment and British imperialism. David Day, *Reluctant Nation: Australia and the Allied Defeat of Japan, 1942–45* (New York: Oxford University Press, 1992), and D. M. Horner, *High Command: Australia and Allied Strategy, 1939–1945* (North Sydney, Australia: Allen & Unwin, 1982). Both fault the strategic leadership of the Australian government; Day, for failing to assert Australian nationalism in the country's relationship with the United Kingdom; Horner, in its relationship with the United States. These themes and the personality clashes are documented in a series of biographies both historians have authored: David Horner, *Blamey: The Commander-in-Chief* (St. Leonards, Australia: Allen & Unwin, 1998); David Horner, *Defence Supremo: Sir Frederick Shedden and the Making of Australian Defence Policy* (St. Leonards, Australia: Allen & Unwin, 2000); David Day, *John Curtin: A Life* (Sydney: HarperCollins, 1999); David Day, *Chifley* (Sydney: HarperCollins, 2001).

Chapter 1. ABC Comes to Whitehall

1. Viscount Cunningham of Hyndhope, *A Sailor's Odyssey: The Autobiography of Viscount Cunningham of Hyndhope K.T. G.C.B. O.M. D.S.O.* (London: Hutchinson, 1951), 203.

2. John Winton, *Cunningham* (London: John Murray, 1998), 2.

3. Winton, *Cunningham*, 1, 6, 19, 40; Eric J. Grove, "Andrew Browne Cunningham: The Best Man of the Lot," in Jack Sweetman, ed., *The Great Admirals: Command at Sea, 1587–1945* (Annapolis, Md.: Naval Institute Press, 1997), 420; John Winton, "Cunningham," in Stephen Howarth, ed., *Men of War: Great Naval Leaders of World War II* (New York: St. Martin's Press, 1993), 208.

4. Barbara Tuchman, *The Guns of August* (New York: Macmillan, 1962), 161–187; Winton, *Cunningham*, 16–32.

5. Winton, *Cunningham*, 33–34, 42–43, 50.

6. Winton, *Cunningham*, 46; Michael Simpson, *A Life of Admiral of the Fleet Andrew Cunningham: A Twentieth-Century Naval Leader* (London: Frank Cass, 2004), 25–26.

7. *Time*, February 17, 1941, and May 24, 1943; Philip Ziegler, *Mountbatten* (London: William Collins Sons, 1985), 91; Winton, *Cunningham*, 266.

8. Lord Cunningham, *Sailor's Odyssey*, 286; Winton, "Cunningham," 212–213.

9. Lord Cunningham, *Sailor's Odyssey*, 380, 387, 390; Winton, "Cunningham," *Men of War*, 214–217; Ziegler, *Mountbatten*, 143.

10. Winton, "Cunningham," 219–220; Simpson, *Life of Cunningham*, 128–129.

11. Simpson, *Life of Cunningham*, 150–152, 171.

12. David Fraser, *Alanbrooke* (London: HarperCollins, 1982), 183, 525; Viscount Alanbrooke of Brookeborough, *War Diaries 1939–1945*, ed. Alex Danchev and Daniel Todman (London: Weidenfield & Nicolson, 2001), 689; Baron Moran of Manton, *Churchill Taken from the Diaries of Lord Moran: The Struggle for Survival, 1940–1965* (Boston: Houghton Mifflin, 1966), 759.

13. Fraser, *Alanbrooke*, 8–15.

14. Ibid., 14, 27, 30.

15. Ibid., 34, 35, 47–48, 50–51.

16. Ibid., 64–65, 68–74.

17. Lord Alanbrooke, *War Diaries*, 81; Fraser, *Alanbrooke*, 100–101, 106–107, 123–135.

18. Lord Alanbrooke, *War Diaries*, 93.

19. Ibid., 199–200; Fraser, *Alanbrooke*, 174.

20. Lord Alanbrooke, *War Diaries*, 689; Fraser, *Alanbrooke*, 497.

21. Fraser, *Alanbrooke*, 175, 184–189.

22. Denis Richards, *Portal of Hungerford: The Life of Marshal of the Royal Air Force Viscount Portal of Hungerford KG, GCB, OM, DSO, MC* (New York: Holmes & Meier, 1977), 6–11, 35–47, 80.

23. Ibid., 72–73, 98, 354–355.

24. Ibid., 72–73, 98–99.

25. Ibid., 183, 202–203, 209, 214. There is a slightly different construction of the quote from the Jacob diary than in the Richards biography. The construction used here comes from the original diary: Diary of Ian Jacob, page 87, Jacob Papers.

26. John W. Huston, ed., *American Airpower Comes of Age: General Henry H. "Hap" Arnold's World War II Diaries*, vol. 1 (Maxwell Air Force Base, Ala.: Air University Press, 2002), 152; Richards, *Portal of Hungerford*, 215.

27. Lord Moran, *Churchill*, 720.

28. Richards, *Portal of Hungerford*, 185.

29. Ibid., 80, 184.

30. Ibid., 212.

31. Fraser, *Alanbrooke*, 501.

32. Richards, *Portal of Hungerford*, 203.

33. Lord Alanbrooke, *War Diaries*, 462.

34. Simpson, *Life of Cunningham*, 180; Lord Cunningham, *Sailor's Odyssey*, 661, 657.

35. Sir Martin Gilbert, *Churchill: A Life* (New York: Henry Holt, 1991), 3–7, 9, 15, 20, 21–23, 32–34, 53; Roy Jenkins, *Churchill: A Biography* (New York: Plume, 2002), 10, 20, 57.

36. Jenkins, *Churchill*, 17, 20–21, 23; Gilbert, *Churchill*, 48–49, 96–99.

37. Jenkins, *Churchill*, 49, 380; Gilbert, *Churchill*, 23, 92, 102, 104, 135, 139, 633.

38. Gilbert, *Churchill*, 173–174, 193–194.

39. Ibid., 200; Jenkins, *Churchill*, 140.

40. Jenkins, *Churchill*, 181; Gilbert, *Churchill*, 209.

41. Gilbert, *Churchill*, 268; Jenkins, *Churchill*, 240.

42. Jenkins, *Churchill*, 243, 245, 259.

43. Gilbert, *Churchill*, 290–291, 304, 310–311; Jenkins, *Churchill*, 261.

44. Jenkins, *Churchill*, 270–274, 276–277, 279; Gilbert, *Churchill*, 313–317, 431.

45. Gilbert, *Churchill*, 368–374.

46. Ibid., 453–457, 463–465.

47. Ibid., 522, 596, 590–599; Jenkins, *Churchill*, 528, 534, 542, 544.

48. Gilbert, *Churchill*, 624; Jenkins, *Churchill*, 543, 552, 553, 555.

49. Gilbert, *Churchill*, 638–639; Jenkins, *Churchill*, 576–582.

50. Gilbert, *Churchill*, 628, 642; Jenkins, *Churchill*, 588, 591.

51. Simpson, *Life of Cunningham*, 173–175, 180; Winton, "Cunningham," 221–225; Lord Cunningham, *Sailor's Odyssey*, 657, 661; David Reynolds, *In Command of History: Churchill Fighting and Writing the Second World War* (London: Allen Lane, 2004), 404–405; Stephen Roskill, *Churchill and the Admirals* (New York: William Morrow, 1978), 237.

Chapter 2. Churchill versus the Chiefs

1. John Ehrman, *History of the Second World War: Grand Strategy*, vol. 5, *August 1943–September 1944* (London: Her Majesty's Stationery Office, 1956), 422–424; Willmott, *Grave of a Dozen Schemes*, 47.

2. Lord Alanbrooke, *War Diaries*, 526.

3. Ehrman, *Grand Strategy*, vol. 5, 426; Gilbert, *Churchill*, 734; Willmott, *Grave of a Dozen Schemes*, 105.

4. Lord Alanbrooke, *War Diaries*, 515.

5. Jenkins, *Churchill*, 572, 732, 739; Gilbert, *Churchill*, 762–764, 770, 772; Lord Moran, *Churchill*, 194; David Dilks, ed., *The Diaries of Sir Alexander Cadogan O.M. 1938–1945* (London: Cassell, 1971), 612, 621.

6. Jenkins, *Churchill*, 572, 732, 739; Gilbert, *Churchill*, 762–764, 770, 772; Lord Moran, *Churchill*, 194; Dilks, *Diaries of Sir Alexander Cadogan*, 612, 621 (emphasis in the original).

7. Ehrman, *Grand Strategy*, vol. 5, 427, 433; David Day, "Promise and Performance: Britain's Pacific Pledge, 1943–5," *War & Society* 4 (September 1986), 77–79.

8. Lord Alanbrooke, *War Diaries*, 523.

9. Ibid., 521.

10. Ehrman, *Grand Strategy*, vol. 5, 440; Willmott, *Grave of a Dozen Schemes*, 61.

11. Lord Alanbrooke, *War Diaries*, 524–525.

12. Ibid.; Diary of Sir Anthony Eden, February 25, 1944, AP20/1/24, Avon Papers.

13. Ehrman, *Grand Strategy*, vol. 5, 439; Lord Alanbrooke, *War Diaries*, 524–525.

14. Lord Alanbrooke, *War Diaries*, 525.

15. Ibid., 525–528.

16. Ehrman, *Grand Strategy*, vol. 5, 441–444.

17. Ibid., 445–446.

18. Ibid., 446.

19. Ibid., 447.

20. Ibid., 447–448.

21. Jenkins, *Churchill*, 774; Lord Alanbrooke, *War Diaries*, 207.

22. Lord Alanbrooke, *War Diaries*, 647–648.

23. Ibid., 442.

24. Ibid., 566–567, 637.

25. Ibid., 712–713.

26. Richards, *Portal of Hungerford*, 185.

27. Lord Cunningham, *Sailor's Odyssey*, 647–648; Grove, "Andrew Browne Cunningham," 440.

28. Diary of Andrew Cunningham, September 16, 1944, ADD 52577, Cunningham Papers.

29. Lord Moran, *Churchill*, 761.

30. Gilbert, *Churchill*, 734, 758; Lord Moran, *Churchill*, 200, 720, 765.

31. John Colville, *The Fringes of Power: 10 Downing Street Diaries, 1939–1955* (New York: Norton, 1985), 489.

32. Lord Alanbrooke, *War Diaries*, 528.

33. Ehrman, *Grand Strategy*, vol. 5, 448–449; Baron Ismay of Wormington, *The Memoirs of General Lord Ismay* (New York: Viking Press, 1960), 399–400.

34. Lord Alanbrooke, *War Diaries*, 529.

35. Ibid., 530; Ehrman, *Grand Strategy*, vol. 5, 449–450.

36. Churchill to Roosevelt, March 10, 1944, PREM 3/164/6, BNA.

37. Alex Danchev, "Dill," in John Keegan, ed., *Churchill's Generals* (London: Weidenfeld & Nicolson, 1991), 51–69.

38. Churchill to Dill, March 10, 1944, PREM 3/164/6, BNA.

39. Roosevelt to Churchill, March 13, 1944, PREM 3/164/6, BNA.

40. Dill to Churchill, March 14, 1944, PREM 3/164/6, BNA.

41. Lord Alanbrooke, *War Diaries*, 531–534.

42. Churchill Minute, March 20, 1944, 6/3/8, Alanbrooke Papers.

43. Ibid.

44. Lord Alanbrooke, *War Diaries*, 533.

45. Brooke to Dill, March 30, 1944, 6/3/10, Alanbrooke Papers.

46. Ibid.

47. Ehrman, *Grand Strategy*, vol. 5, 452.

48. Ibid., 457.

49. Bernard Fergusson, ed., *The Business of War: The War Narrative of Major-General Sir John Kennedy G.C.M.G, K.C.V.O., K.B.E., C.B., M.C.* (London: Hutchinson, 1957), 323.

50. Ehrman, *Grand Strategy*, vol. 5, 458–462.

Chapter 3. The King's Men in the Loyal Dominions

1. William Lyon Mackenzie King Diary, April 27 and June 10, 1939, Mackenzie King Papers; Jenkins, *Churchill*, 740.

2. C. P. Stacey, *A Very Double Life: The Private World of Mackenzie King* (Toronto: Macmillan, 1976), 17–19, 40–42.

3. Ibid., 17–21.

4. Ibid., 21, 106–107, 110, 112, 115–117.

5. Ibid., 21–24.

6. Brian Nolan, *King's War: Mackenzie King and the Politics of War* (Toronto: Random House, 1988), 1–5, 8–9.

7. Stacey, *Very Double Life*, 21–35.

8. Ibid., 21–35, 139–144.

9. Michael Bassett and Michael King, *Tomorrow Comes the Song: A Life of Peter Fraser* (Auckland: Penguin Books, 2000), 75, 78, 95, 284, 350.

10. Ibid., 19, 33–34.

11. Ibid., 23, 72–73, 76–79, 83–84.

12. Ibid., 23, 77, 94–96, 170.

13. Ibid., 138, 140.

14. Ibid., 167, 169–170, 175.

15. Ibid., 182, 185.

16. Ibid., 234.

17. Ibid., 267–269, 290–296.

18. Day, *John Curtin*, 60, 131–132.

19. Ibid., 60–66, 180–184, 233.

20. Ibid., 180, 183–184, 332–333, 365–366, 396–397.

21. Ibid., 522, 539; Neville Meanney, "The Problem of Nationalism in Australian History and Historiography," *Australian Historical Studies* 32, no. 116 (October 2001), 79, 83.

22. Day, *John Curtin*, 474.

23. Ibid., 438–439, 540.

24. Horner, *Defence Supremo*, photo section, 1, 29, 74, 171, 179–180, 206, 211.

25. Ibid., 29, 59, 151.

26. Ibid., 160, 164–165, 179.

27. Ibid., 119, 145–150.

28. Ibid., 151, 162–164.

29. Ibid., 190.

30. John Hetherington, *Blamey: Controversial Soldier—A Biography of Field Marshal Sir Thomas Blamey, GBE, KCB, CMG, DSO, ED* (Canberra: Australian War Memorial and the Australian Government Publishing Service, 1973), 94–96; Horner, *Blamey*, 98–99

31. Horner, *Blamey*, xv–xvi, 49, 55, 56, 62.

32. Ibid., 80–83, 98, 99, 103.

33. Hetherington, *Blamey*, 116, 384; Horner, *Blamey*, 98, 159, 565, 203–205.

34. Horner, *Blamey*, 321, 324.

35. Ibid., 324, 352–353, 565–566.

36. Hetherington, *Blamey*, 208–209.

37. Horner, *Defence Supremo*, 145, 165.

38. Day, *John Curtin*, 535, 538–539; Horner, *Defence Supremo*, 192–193.

39. Horner, *Defence Supremo*, 193, 205–206.

Chapter 4. A Gathering of Prime Ministers

1. Diary of Sir Andrew Cunningham, April 26, 1944, ADD 52577, Cunningham Papers.

2. Day, *John Curtin*, 539–540, 543, 544–545.

3. Bassett and King, *Tomorrow Comes the Song*, 267; Diary of Sir Andrew Cunningham, May 2, 1944, ADD 52577, Cunningham Papers.

4. Lord Alanbrooke, *War Diaries*, 543; Meeting of Prime Ministers, P.M.M. (44) 4th Meeting, May 3, 1944, EA 153/20/6 pt. 1, RDEAT, NANZ.

5. Meeting of Prime Ministers, P.M.M. (44) 4th Meeting, May 3, 1944, EA 153/20/6 pt. 1, RDEAT, NANZ.

6. Ibid.; Diary of Sir Andrew Cunningham, May 3, 1944, ADD 52577, Cunningham Papers.

7. William Lyon Mackenzie King Diary, May 3, 1944, Mackenzie King Papers; Horner, *Defence Supremo*, 196; Conduct of the War against Japan: Summary of Observations by the Rt. Hon. John Curtin, M.P., Prime Minister of the Commonwealth of Australia, May 3, 1944, EA 153/20/6 pt. 1; Meeting of Prime Ministers, P.M.M. (44) 5th Meeting Confidential Annex, May 3, 1944, EA 153/20/6 pt. 1, RDEAT, NANZ.

8. Meeting of Prime Ministers, P.M.M. (44) 5th Meeting Confidential Annex, May 3, 1944, EA 153/20/6 pt. 1, RDEAT, NANZ.

9. William Lyon Mackenzie King Diary, May 3, 1944, Mackenzie King Papers; Meeting of Prime Ministers, P.M.M. (44) 5th Meeting Confidential Annex, May 3, 1944, EA 153/20/6 pt. 1, RDEAT, NANZ.

10. Diary of Sir Andrew Cunningham, May 3, 1944, ADD 52577, Cunningham Papers.

11. William Lyon Mackenzie King Diary, May 3, 1944, Mackenzie King Papers.

12. Diary of Sir Anthony Eden, May 4, 1944, AP20/1/24, Avon Papers.

13. Confidential Index Review of Foreign Affairs to Meeting of Prime Ministers, May 5, 1944, EA 153/20/6 pt. 1, RDEAT, NANZ.

14. Confidential Annex, Minute 1, May 12, 1944, EA 153/20/6 pt. 1, RDEAT, NANZ.

15. Horner, *Defence Supremo*, 199–201; Day, *John Curtin*, 543–545; Galen Roger Perras, "Hurry Up and Wait: Robert Menzies, Mackenzie King, and the Failed Attempt to Form an Imperial War Cabinet in 1941," *Working Papers in Contemporary Military and International History*, no. 3 (Salford, England, September 2004), 1–42.

16. Meeting of Prime Ministers, May 16, 1944, EA 153/20/6 pt. 1, RDEAT, NANZ.

17. Diary of Sir Andrew Cunningham, May 16, 1944, ADD 52577, Cunningham Papers.

18. Ibid., May 8, 1944.

19. Day, *John Curtin*, 541–543; Bassett and King, *Tomorrow Comes the Song*, 269–270; Lord Alanbrooke, *War Diaries*, 545; Diary of Hugh Dalton, May 10, 1944, pt. 1, vol. 30, Dalton Papers. This entry does not appear in the published version of Dalton's diary. Ben Pimlott, ed., *The Second World War Diary of Hugh Dalton, 1940–1945* (London: Jonathan Cape, 1986), 745.

20. Diary of Hugh Dalton, May 25, 1944, pt. 1, vol. 30, Dalton Papers.

21. Ibid., May 4, 1944. This entry does not appear in the published version of Dalton's diary. Pimlott, *Second World War Diary of Hugh Dalton*, 740.

22. Day, *John Curtin*, 541–547; Bassett and King, *Tomorrow Comes the Song*, 269–270; Shedden manuscript, Folder: Book (Original) Chapter 46—Planning for the Defeat of Japan, and the Deployment of United Kingdom Forces in the Pacific, A 5954/771/1, Shedden Papers.

23. "War against Japan—Summary of Various Courses," COS 44 396 (O) May 4, 1944, PREM 3/160/4, BNA.

24. Diary of Sir Andrew Cunningham, May 8, 1944, ADD 52577, Cunningham Papers.

25. Ibid., May 18, 1944.

26. Lord Alanbrooke, *War Diaries*, 547–548.

27. Lord Alanbrooke, *War Diaries*, 550; Diary of Sir Andrew Cunningham, May 24, 1944, ADD 52577, Cunningham Papers.

28. Diary of Sir Andrew Cunningham, May 5, 1944, ADD 52577, Cunningham Papers.

29. Lord Alanbrooke, *War Diaries*, 544–546.

30. Horner, *Defence Supremo*, 198; Lord Alanbrooke, *War Diaries*, 549.

31. Minutes of a Staff Conference held in the Prime Minister's Map Room, May 26, 1944, FE/44/66, Folios 87–176, vol. 7, Avon Papers.

32. Ibid.

33. Lord Cunningham, *Sailor's Odyssey*, 601; Diary of Sir Andrew Cunningham, May 26, 1944, ADD 52577, Cunningham Papers.

34. Eden notation: May 29, 1944, on Far Eastern Strategy Minute by Ashley Clarke, May 22, 1944, FE/44/62, Folios 87–176, vol. 7, Avon Papers.

35. Churchill to Curtin, May 27, 1944, PREM 3/160/4, BNA.

36. C.O.S. (44) 489 (O), June 5, 1944, PREM 3/160/4, BNA; Lord Alanbrooke, *War Diaries*, 552–553.

37. Far Eastern Strategy Minute by Ashley Clarke, May 22, 1944, FE/44/62, Folios 87–176, vol. 7, Avon Papers; Eden to Churchill, June 12, 1944, PREM 3/160/4, BNA.

38. Ismay to Pownall, May 27, 1944, 4/26/4/2a–2b, Ismay Papers.

39. Carlo D'Este, *Decision in Normandy* (New York: Dutton, 1983), 20–22.

Chapter 5. The Road to Quebec

1. Henry H. Adams, *Witness to Power: The Life of Admiral William D. Leahy* (Annapolis, Md.: Naval Institute Press, 1985), 97.

2. William D. Leahy, *I Was There: The Personal Story of the Chief of Staff to Presidents Roosevelt and Truman, Based on His Notes and Diaries Made at the Time* (New York: Whittlesey House, 1950), 461–462; Ed Cray, *General of the Army: George C. Marshall, Soldier and Statesman* (New York: Simon and Schuster, 1990), 278–280.

3. Adams, *Witness to Power*, 52, 88.

4. Ibid., 88, 96, 114.

5. Leahy, *I Was There*, 25, 117, 119; Adams, *Witness to Power*, 175.

6. Leahy, *I Was There*, 119; Cray, *General of the Army*, 278–280; Thomas B. Buell, *Master of Sea Power: A Biography of Admiral Ernest J. King* (Boston: Little, Brown, 1980), 184–185; Adams, *Witness to Power*, 178.

7. Adams, *Witness to Power*, 96, 184, 192, 223.

8. Ibid., 114, 266, 269.

9. Cray, *General of the Army*, 17.

10. Ibid., 28–30.

11. Ibid., 55–95.

12. Ibid., 102–106.

13. Ibid., 149–151.

14. Ibid., 173–177.

15. Ibid., 151.

16. Buell, *Master of Sea Power*, 36, 89, 106, 128, 274–275.

17. Winton, *Cunningham*, 355; Buell, *Master of Sea Power*, 427.

18. Buell, *Master of Sea Power*, 7, 9–12.

19. Ibid., 73–76, 95–97.

20. Ibid., 57, 65, 89.

21. Ibid., 117–119, 127, 132–133, 152–154.

22. Ibid., 302–308, 401–404, 409–410.

23. Thomas M. Coffey, *Hap: The Story of the U.S. Air Force and the Man Who Built It, General Henry "Hap" Arnold* (New York: Viking Press, 1982), 260; Donald G. F. W. Macintyre, *Fighting Admiral: The Life of Admiral of the Fleet Sir James Somerville, G.C.B., G.B.E., D.S.O.* (London: Evans Brothers, 1961), 256; Buell, *Master of Sea Power*, 274, 378–380; The Earl of Halifax, *Fulness of Days* (London: Collins, 1957), 259.

24. Dik Alan Daso, *Hap Arnold and the Evolution of American Airpower* (Washington, D.C.: Smithsonian Institute Press, 2000), 170, 181.

25. Coffey, *Hap*, 48, 63, 86–87; Richard G. Davis, *Hap: Henry H. Arnold, Military Aviator* (Washington, D.C.: Government Printing Office, 1997), 6–8, 13–17.

26. Coffey, *Hap*, 254–256; Daso, *Hap Arnold*, 228.

27. Daso, *Hap Arnold*, 155.

28. Ibid., 171–172.

29. Daso, *Hap Arnold*, 201, 229; Coffey, *Hap*, 255–257.

30. Daso, *Hap Arnold*, 70, 231; Coffey, *Hap*, 78, 80, 267, 346; Cray, *General of the Army*, 44.

31. Lord Alanbrooke, *War Diaries*, 246–249, 272–273, 490.

32. Cray, *General of the Army*, 309, 359; Alan F. Wilt, "Churchill and His Chiefs of Staff," page 10, paper presented at the 2001 Society for Military History Conference, University of Calgary, Alberta, Canada.

33. Informal Notes of the Combined Chiefs of Staff 165th Meeting, June 14, 1944, Microfilm Reel 4; Paul Kesaris, ed., *Records of the Joint Chiefs of Staff*, pt. 1, *The Pacific Theater* (Frederick, Md.: University Publications of America, 1981).

34. War against Japan—British Programme. Report by the British Chiefs of Staff, C.O.S. (44) 553 (O), June 22, 1944, PREM 3/160/5, BNA.

35. Churchill to Ismay, June 24, 1944, PREM 3/160/5, BNA.

36. Horner, *Defence Supremo*, 207.

37. D. Clayton James, *The Years of MacArthur*, vol. 2, *1941–1945* (Boston: Houghton Mifflin, 1975), 467; Lumsden to A.M.S.S.O., June 24, 1944, PREM 3/160/5, BNA.

38. Australia P.M. to P.M., July 4, 1944, PREM 3/160/5, BNA.

39. Chiefs of Staff to Churchill, July 8, 1944, PREM 3/160/5, BNA.

40. Diary of Sir Anthony Eden, July 6, 1944, AP20/1/24, Avon Papers; Lord Alanbrooke, *War Diaries*, 566–567; Diary of Sir Andrew Cunningham, July 6, 1944, ADD 52577, Cunningham Papers.

41. Earl of Avon, *The Memoirs of Anthony Eden, Earl of Avon: The Reckoning* (Boston: Houghton Mifflin, 1965), 536; Extract from C.O.S. (44) 225th Meeting (O) July 6, 1944, PREM 3/160/5, BNA.

42. Extract from C.O.S. (44) 225th Meeting (O) July 6, 1944, PREM 3/160/5, BNA.

43. Ibid.

44. Lord Alanbrooke, *War Diaries*, 568.

45. Ehrman, *Grand Strategy*, vol. 5, 485; Lord Alanbrooke, *War Diaries*, 568.

46. Diary of Sir Anthony Eden, July 14, 1944, AP20/1/24, Avon Papers; Lord Avon, *Memoirs*, 536–537; Lord Alanbrooke, *War Diaries*, 570.

47. Diary of Sir Anthony Eden, July 14, 1944, AP20/1/24, Avon Papers; Lord Avon, *Memoirs*, 536–537; Lord Alanbrooke, *War Diaries*, 570; Minutes of a Staff Conference, July 14, 1944, PREM 3/160/5, BNA.

48. Lord Alanbrooke, *War Diaries*, 570.

49. Diary of Sir Andrew Cunningham, July 14, 1944, ADD 52577, Cunningham Papers.

50. Minutes of a Staff Conference, July 14, 1944, PREM 3/160/5, BNA; Diary of Sir Anthony Eden, July 14, 1944, AP20/1/24, Avon Papers.

51. Lord Alanbrooke, *War Diaries*, 573.

52. Diary of Sir Anthony Eden, August 8, 1944, AP20/1/24, Avon Papers.

53. Minutes of a Staff Conference, August 8, 1944, PREM 3/160/6, BNA.

54. Ibid.

55. Lord Alanbrooke, *War Diaries*, 578.

56. Minutes of a Staff Conference, August 8, 1944, PREM 3/160/6, BNA.

57. Ibid.

58. Lord Alanbrooke, *War Diaries*, 579.

59. Diary of Sir Andrew Cunningham, August 8, 1944, ADD 52577, Cunningham Papers.

60. Diary of Sir Andrew Cunningham, August 9 and 10, 1944, ADD 52577, Cunningham Papers; Minutes of a Staff Conference, August 9, 1944, PREM 3/160/6, BNA.

61. Diary of Sir Andrew Cunningham, August 9, 1944, ADD 52577, Cunningham Papers; Minutes of a Staff Conference, August 9, 1944, PREM 3/160/6, BNA.

62. Diary of Sir Andrew Cunningham, August 10 and 11, 1944, ADD 52577, Cunningham Papers.

63. Diary of Sir Anthony Eden, August 10, 1944, AP20/1/24, Avon Papers.

64. Ehrman, *Grand Strategy*, vol. 5, 500–501.

65. Grace Pearson Hayes, *The History of the Joint Chiefs of Staff in World War II: The War against Japan* (Annapolis, Md.: Naval Institute Press, 1982), 627, 632–633; Michael Coles, "Ernest King and the British Pacific Fleet: The Conference at Quebec, 1944 ('Octagon')," *Journal of Military History* 65 (January 2001), 115–116; Diary of Sir James Somerville, April 13, June 27, 1944, ADD 52564, Cunningham Papers; Scale of British Army Effort in the Pacific after the Defeat of Germany, July 15, 1944, Folder: Great Britain (7-15-44) Sec. 1, Box 82, Geographic File, 1942–1945; W. A. Wood, Jr., to R. C. Moore, July 21, 1944, Folder: Great Britain (7-15-44) Sec. 1, Box 82, Geographic File, 1942–1945; Extract from the Minutes of the Joint Chiefs of Staff 170th Meeting, August 29, 1944, Folder: Great Britain (7-15-44) Sec. 1, Box 82, Geographic File, 1942–1945, Records of the U.S. Joint Chiefs of Staff, Record Group 218, USNA.

66. Hayes, *War against Japan*, 634–636; Minutes of the Joint Chiefs of Staff Meeting, September 9, 1944, Folder: Great Britain (7-15-44) Sec. 1, Box 82, Geographic File, 1942–1945, Records of the U.S. Joint Chiefs of Staff, Record Group 218; Marshall to MacArthur, September 12, 1944, Folder: Octagon, Box 31, ABC Files, Office of the Director of Plans and Operations, Records of the War Department General and Special Staffs, Record Group 165, USNA.

67. Gilbert, *Churchill*, 792; Diary of Sir Andrew Cunningham, September 6 and 8, 1944, ADD 52577, Cunningham Papers.

68. Lord Alanbrooke, *War Diaries*, 587–588.

69. Brackets in the original. Lord Alanbrooke, *War Diaries*, 588.

70. Minutes of Advisory War Council Meeting, September 7, 1944, Series: A 5954, Item 815/2, Minutes of Advisory War Council Meetings, vol. 5III, Shedden Papers; Dominions Office to Government of Australia and Government of New Zealand, August 23, 1944; Australia P.M. to P.M., September 1, 1944; Prime Minister to Prime Minister

of Australia, September 9, 1944, Curtin to Prime Minister, September 16, 1944, PREM 3/160/6, BNA.

71. Minutes of Advisory War Council Meeting, September 7, 1944, Series: A 5954, Item 815/2, Minutes of Advisory War Council Meetings, vol. 5III, Shedden Papers; Dominions Office to Government of Australia and Government of New Zealand, August 23, 1944; Australia P.M. to P.M., September 1, 1944; Prime Minister to Prime Minister of Australia, September 9, 1944, Curtin to Prime Minister, September 16, 1944, PREM 3/160/6, BNA.

72. Minutes of Advisory War Council Meeting, September 7, 1944, Series: A 5954, Item 815/2, Minutes of Advisory War Council Meetings, vol. 5III, Shedden Papers; Dominions Office to Government of Australia and Government of New Zealand, August 23, 1944; Australia P.M. to P.M., September 1, 1944; Prime Minister to Prime Minister of Australia, September 9, 1944, Curtin to Prime Minister, September 16, 1944, PREM 3/160/6, BNA.

73. Diary of Sir Andrew Cunningham, September 7, 1944, ADD 52577, Cunningham Papers; Lord Alanbrooke, *War Diaries*, 589.

74. Lord Alanbrooke, *War Diaries*, 588.

75. Diary of Sir Andrew Cunningham, September 8, 1944, ADD 52577, Cunningham Papers; Lord Ismay, *Memoirs*, 373.

76. Lord Moran, *Churchill*, 189, 194.

77. Emphasis in the original. Lord Alanbrooke, *War Diaries*, 589.

78. Brian Bond, ed., *Chief of Staff: The Diaries of Lieutenant-General Sir Henry Pownall*, vol. 2, 1940–1944 (London: Leo Cooper, 1974), 186.

79. Ehrman, *Grand Strategy*, vol. 5, 503–504; Minutes of the Joint Chiefs of Staff Meeting, September 9, 1944, Folder: Great Britain (7-15-44) Sec. 1, Box 82, Geographic File, 1942–1945, Records of the U.S. Joint Chiefs of Staff, Record Group 218, USNA.

80. Ismay to Prime Minister, September 8, 1944; Aide-Mémoire: War against Japan, [no date]; Churchill to Ismay for C.O.S. Committee, September 9, 1944, PREM 3/160/6, BNA.

81. Lord Alanbrooke, *War Diaries*, 590.

82. Ibid.

83. Ismay to Prime Minister, September 10, 1944, PREM 3/160/6, BNA.

84. Churchill to Ismay for C.O.S. Committee, September 12, 1944, PREM 3/160/6, BNA; Winston S. Churchill, *Second World War*, vol. 6, *Triumph and Tragedy* (Boston: Houghton Mifflin, 1953), 149.

Chapter 6. Codename: OCTAGON

1. Lord Alanbrooke, *War Diaries*, 273; H. H. Arnold, *Global Mission* (New York: Harper & Brothers, 1949), 228.

2. Cray, *General of the Army*, 447.

3. George C. Marshall, "Anglo-American Accord: Remarks on the Award of the Howland Memorial Prize to Field Marshal Sir John Dill of the British Army at Yale University, New Haven, Connecticut," February 14, 1944, in H. A. DeWeerd, ed., *Selected*

Speeches and Statements of General of the Army George C. Marshall Chief of Staff United States Army (Washington, D.C.: The Infantry Journal, 1945), 249.

4. Arnold, *Global Mission*, 568, 228, 262; Richards, *Portal of Hungerford*, 213, 215.

5. Winton, *Cunningham*, 355; Buell, *Master of Sea Power*, 274–275, 427.

6. Churchill, *Triumph and Tragedy*, 155; Maurice A. Pope, *Soldiers and Politicians: The Memoirs of Lt.-Gen. Maurice A. Pope C.B., M.C.* (Toronto: University of Toronto Press, 1962), 243; Conrad Black, *Franklin Delano Roosevelt: Champion of Freedom* (London: Weidenfeld & Nicolson, 2004), 991, 994; Lord Alanbrooke, *War Diaries*, 591–592; Diary of Sir Andrew Cunningham, September 10–11, 1944, ADD 52577, Cunningham Papers.

7. Churchill, *Triumph and Tragedy*, 155; Pope, *Soldiers and Politicians*, 243; Black, *Franklin Delano Roosevelt*, 991, 994; Lord Alanbrooke, *War Diaries*, 591–592; Diary of Sir Andrew Cunningham, September 10–11, 1944, ADD 52577, Cunningham Papers.

8. Lord Alanbrooke, *War Diaries*, 591.

9. Diary of Sir Andrew Cunningham, September 12, 1944, ADD 52577, Cunningham Papers.

10. Lord Alanbrooke, *War Diaries*, 591; Diary of Sir Andrew Cunningham, September 12, 1944, ADD 52577, Cunningham Papers.

11. Frank Freidel, *Franklin D. Roosevelt: A Rendezvous with Destiny* (Boston: Little, Brown, 1990), 6–7, 10, 11, 15, 17, 23; Black, *Franklin Delano Roosevelt*, 8, 17, 51–55.

12. Black, *Franklin Delano Roosevelt*, 96, 354, 1118; Freidel, *Franklin D. Roosevelt*, 23, 31.

13. Freidel, *Franklin D. Roosevelt*, 125, 185, 193.

14. Ibid., 358–362.

15. Black, *Franklin Delano Roosevelt*, 499.

16. Ibid., 932–933, 1039; Freidel, *Franklin D. Roosevelt*, 536–538, 544–545.

17. Black, *Franklin Delano Roosevelt*, 994; Lord Moran, *Churchill*, 192; Lord Ismay, *Memoirs*, 373.

18. David Day argues that Churchill made the offer just as a formality and was surprised when Roosevelt accepted. David A. Day, "Promise and Performance: Britain's Pacific Pledge, 1943–5," *War & Society* 4, no. 2 (September 1986), 81; Meeting of the Combined Chiefs of Staff with Roosevelt and Churchill, September 13, 1944, *Foreign Relations of the United States: The Conference at Quebec* (Washington, D.C.: Government Printing Office, 1972), 312–319 [hereafter *FRUS: Quebec*]; Ehrman, *Grand Strategy*, vol. 5, 518–519.

19. David Day argues that Churchill made the offer just as a formality and was surprised when Roosevelt accepted. David A. Day, "Promise and Performance: Britain's Pacific Pledge, 1943–5," *War & Society* 4, no. 2 (September 1986), 81; Meeting of the Combined Chiefs of Staff with Roosevelt and Churchill, September 13, 1944, *FRUS: Quebec*, 312–319; Ehrman, *Grand Strategy*, vol. 5, 518–519.

20. Meeting of the Combined Chiefs of Staff with Roosevelt and Churchill, Septem-

ber 13, 1944, *FRUS: Quebec*, 312–319; Ehrman, *Grand Strategy*, vol. 5, 518–519; Lord Cunningham, *Sailor's Odyssey*, 611.

21. Meeting of the Combined Chiefs of Staff with Roosevelt and Churchill, September 13, 1944, *FRUS: Quebec*, 312–319; Ehrman, *Grand Strategy*, vol. 5, 518–519.

22. Ehrman, *Grand Strategy*, vol. 5, 518–519.

23. Lord Cunningham, *Sailor's Odyssey*, 611.

24. Fraser, *Alanbrooke*, 445.

25. Ehrman, *Grand Strategy*, vol. 5, 517.

26. Richard Overy, *Why the Allies Won* (New York: Norton, 1995), 102–104, 110–111, 116–117; Extract from Minutes of Cabinet War Committee, September 14, 1944, Department of External Affairs. *Documents on Canadian External Relations*, vol. 10, pt. 1, *1944–1945* (Ottawa: Queen's Printer and Controller of Stationery, 1987), 413–415 [hereafter *DCER*]; Meeting of the Combined Chiefs of Staff with Roosevelt and Churchill, September 16, 1944, *FRUS: Quebec*, 379; Fraser, *Alanbrooke*, 491; Gilbert, *Churchill*, 795.

27. Memorandum by the British Chiefs of Staff, September 18, 1944, Folder CCS 373.11 Japan (9-18-44) Sec.1, Box 114, Geographic File, 1942–1945, Records of the U.S. Joint Chiefs of Staff, Record Group 218, USNA.

28. Extract from Minutes of Cabinet War Committee, September 14, 1944, *DCER*, 413–415; John A. English, *The Canadian Army and the Normandy Campaign: A Study of Failure in High Command* (New York: Praeger, 1991), 13–30, 159–160.

29. Diary of William D. Leahy, September 13, 1944, Box 4, Leahy Papers.

30. Diary of H. H. Arnold, September 14, 1944, Folder 3, Box 3, Arnold Papers.

31. George C. Marshall Interview, February 14, 1957, in Larry I. Bland, ed., and Joellen K. Bland, asst. ed., *George C. Marshall Interviews and Reminiscences for Forrest Pogue*, rev. ed. (Lexington, Va.: George C. Marshall Research Foundation, 1991), 427.

32. Winant to Hopkins, September 1, 1944, *FRUS: Quebec*, 255–256.

33. Memorandum of Conference with the President, August 18, 1944; Hopkins to Winant, September 4, 1944, *FRUS: Quebec*, 160–161, 257.

34. Secretary of State to the President, September 8, 1944, *FRUS: Quebec*, 178.

35. Memorandum of Conference with the President, August 18, 1944, *FRUS: Quebec*, 160–161.

36. Ehrman, *Grand Strategy*, vol. 5, 520–523; Diary of H. H. Arnold, September 14, 1944, Folder 3, Box 3, Arnold Papers; Marshall to MacArthur, September 12, 1944, Folder: Octagon, Box 31, ABC Files, Office of Director of Plans and Operations, Records of the War Department General and Special Staffs, Record Group 165, USNA.

37. Ehrman, *Grand Strategy*, vol. 5, 520–523; Ernest J. King and Walter Muir Whitehill, *Fleet Admiral King: A Naval Record* (New York: W. W. Norton, 1952), 569–570; Lord Alanbrooke, *War Diaries*, 592.

38. Ehrman, *Grand Strategy*, vol. 5, 520–523; Winton, *Cunningham*, 359; Lord Cunningham, *Sailor's Odyssey*, 612–613; Lord Alanbrooke, *War Diaries*, 592; George C. Marshall Interview, November 21, 1956, *George C. Marshall Interviews and Reminiscences*, 376; Diary of Sir Andrew Cunningham, September 14, 1944, ADD 52577, Cunningham Papers.

39. Coles, "Ernest King and the British Pacific Fleet," 105–129.

40. Richard Hough, *The Longest Battle: The War at Sea, 1939–45* (London: Weidenfeld & Nicolson, 1986), 337.

41. Minutes of Joint Chiefs of Staff Meeting, September 8, 1944; Minutes of Joint Chiefs of Staff Meeting, September 13, 1944, Folder: CCS 334 Joint Chiefs of Staff (7-4-44) Meetings 168th thru 185th, Box 198, Central Decimal File, Records of the U.S. Joint Chiefs of Staff, Record Group 218, USNA.

42. Lord Cunningham, *Sailor's Odyssey*, 612; Diary of Sir Andrew Cunningham, September 15, 1944, ADD 52577, Cunningham Papers.

43. King to Hayes, November 20, 1951, Folder: Comments by King Re: Official History of the J.C.S. 1950–1951, Box 35, King Papers; King and Whitehill, *Fleet Admiral King*, 569–570.

44. Arnold to MacArthur, July 4, 1945, Folder: Conference Reports October 1944–August 1945, Box 5, Chamberlin Papers.

45. Arnold, *Global Mission*, 526.

46. In his memoirs Arnold implies this meeting took place on September 13, but his diary indicates that it took place on September 14. Arnold, *Global Mission*, 527; Diary of H. H. Arnold, September 14, 1944, Folder 3, Box 3, Arnold Papers.

47. Memorandum by the Commanding General, Army Air Forces, September 26, 1944, Folder: Great Britain (7-15-44) Sec. 1, Box 82, Geographic File, 1942–1945, Records of the U.S. Joint Chiefs of Staff, Record Group 218, USNA.

48. Arnold, *Global Mission*, 568; Diary of H. H. Arnold, September 12, 1944, Folder 3, Box 3, Arnold Papers; Memorandum by the Commanding General, Army Air Forces, September 26, 1944, Folder: Great Britain (7-15-44) Sec. 1, Box 82, Geographic File, 1942–1945, Records of the U.S. Joint Chiefs of Staff, Record Group 218, USNA.

49. Hayes, *War against Japan*, 643.

50. Lord Alanbrooke, *War Diaries*, 592–593.

51. Sir Ronald Wingate, *Lord Ismay: A Biography* (London: Hutchinson, 1970), 112–113.

52. Lord Alanbrooke, *War Diaries*, 592–593; Diary of Sir Andrew Cunningham, September 15, 1944, ADD 52577, Cunningham Papers.

53. Meeting of the Combined Chiefs of Staff with Roosevelt and Churchill, September 16, 1944, *FRUS: Quebec*, 377–383; Diary of Sir Andrew Cunningham, September 16, 1944, ADD 52577, Cunningham Papers.

54. *Chicago Daily Tribune*, September 17, 1944.

55. Diary of H. H. Arnold, September 14, 1944, Folder 3, Box 3, Arnold Papers.

56. Arnold, *Global Mission*, 528.

57. Wilt, "Churchill and His Chiefs of Staff," page 7; Lord Alanbrooke, *War Diaries*, 593–596; Diary of Sir Andrew Cunningham, September 16, 1944, ADD 52577, Cunningham Papers.

58. Lord Moran, *Churchill*, 197.

59. Lord Moran, *Churchill*, 199–200; Lord Cunningham, *Sailor's Odyssey*, 612–613; Gilbert, *Churchill*, 794; Diary of Sir Andrew Cunningham, September 20, 1944, ADD 52577, Cunningham Papers.

Chapter 7. Canada

1. Galen Roger Perras, "Once Bitten, Twice Shy: The Origins of the Canadian Army Pacific Force, 1944–1945," in Greg Donaghy, ed., *Uncertain Horizons: Canadians and Their World in 1945* (Ottawa: Canadian Committee for the History of the Second World War, 1997), 82; Confidential Index Review of Foreign Affairs to Meeting of Prime Minister Minutes, May 5, 1944, page 5, EA 1 153/20/6/Pt.1, NANZ.

2. Perras, "Once Bitten, Twice Shy," 81; Confidential Index Review of Foreign Affairs to Meeting of Prime Minister Minutes, May 5, 1944, page 5, EA 1 153/20/6/Pt.1, NANZ.

3. Perras, "Once Bitten, Twice Shy," 78–82, 87.

4. Ibid., 78, 82; Philip Snow, *The Fall of Hong Kong: Britain, China and the Japanese Occupation* (New Haven, Conn.: Yale University Press, 2004).

5. J. W. Pickersgill and D. F. Forster, *The Mackenzie King Record*, vol. 2, *1944–1945* (Toronto: University of Toronto Press, 1968), 352.

6. Ibid., 447.

7. Roger Sarty, "The Ghosts of Fisher and Jellicoe: The Royal Canadian Navy and the Quebec Conferences," in David B. Woolner, ed., *The Second Quebec Conference Revisited — Waging War, Formulating Peace: Canada, Great Britain, and the United States in 1944–1945* (New York: St. Martin's Press, 1998), 150–154.

8. Sarty, "Ghosts of Fisher and Jellicoe," 156; Galen Roger Perras, "No Need to Send an Army across the Pacific: Mackenzie King and the Pacific Conflict, 1939–45," in John English, Kenneth McLaughlin, and P. Whitney Lackenbauer, eds., *Mackenzie King: Citizenship and Community — Essays Marking the 125th Anniversary of the Birth of William Lyon Mackenzie King* (Toronto: Robin Brass Studio, 2002), 124–150.

9. Perras, "Once Bitten, Twice Shy," 88; Cabinet Conclusion, September 6, 1944, *DCER*, 410.

10. English, *Canadian Army and the Normandy Campaign*, 159.

11. Ibid., 16–18.

12. Ibid., 19.

13. Ibid., 19–20; Pope, *Soldiers and Politicians*, 91; Galen Roger Perras, "Thirty Days or Thirty Hours? Canadian Interwar Plans for Armed Neutrality in an American-Japanese Conflict," pages 1, 18–21, paper presented at the 2001 Society for Military History Conference, University of Calgary, Alberta, Canada.

14. English, *Canadian Army and the Normandy Campaign*, 24, 310.

15. Perras, "Once Bitten, Twice Shy," 84–85, 89.

16. Sarty, "Ghosts of Fisher and Jellicoe," 150–152.

17. Perras, "Once Bitten, Twice Shy," 84–85, 89.

18. Chief of Staff to the Ministers, "Canadian Participation in the Pacific War and in Europe After the Defeat of Germany," September 6, 1944, Department of National Defence Records, Record Group 24, vol. 2921, File HOS 9131, NAC.

19. Perras, "Once Bitten, Twice Shy," 88–89; Sarty, "Ghosts of Fisher and Jellicoe," 160–161.

20. Perras, "Once Bitten, Twice Shy," 88–89; Sarty, "Ghosts of Fisher and Jellicoe," 160–161.

21. Extract from Minutes of Cabinet War Committee, September 13, 1944, *DCER*, 411–413; Sarty, "Ghosts of Fisher and Jellicoe," 161–163; Pickersgill and Forster, *Mackenzie King Record*, 352; Galen Perras, "'She Should Have Thought of Herself First': Canada and Military Aid to Australia, 1939–1945," in Margaret MacMillan and Francine McKenzie, eds., *Parties Long Estranged: Canada and Australia in the Twentieth Century* (Vancouver: University of British Columbia Press, 2003), 141.

22. Extract from Minutes of Cabinet War Committee, September 14, 1944, *DCER*, 413–415.

23. Perras, "Once Bitten, Twice Shy," 84–85, 91.

24. Memorandum by the Chiefs of Staff Committee, September 14, 1944, *DCER*, 416–419.

25. Galen Roger Perras, "Eyes on the Northern Route to Japan: Plans for Canadian Participation in an Invasion of the Kurile Islands—A Study in Coalition Warfare and Civil-Military Relations," *War and Society* 8, no. 1 (May 1990), 100–117; Memorandum by Minster of National Defence, September 16, 1944; Memorandum from Chief of the General Staff to Minister of National Defence, September 16, 1944; Aide-Mémoire from Chief of the General Staff to Chief of Staff, United States Army, September 16, 1944, *DCER*, 419–421; Aide-Mémoire for General Marshall, September 16, 1944, Folder: ABC 381 Canada (9-18-44), Box 407, ABC Files, Office of the Director of Plans and Operations, Record Group 165 Records of the War Department General and Special Staffs, USNA.

26. Leahy to Letson, December 21, 1944; Letson to Marshall, December 9, 1944, Folder: CCS 370 Canada (9-18-44), Box 24, Geographic File, 1942–1945, Record Group 218 Records of the U.S. Joint Chiefs of Staff; Hull to Chief of Staff, December 12, 1944, Folder: ABC 381 Canada (18 Sept. 44), Box 407, ABC Files, Office of the Director of Plans and Operations, Record Group 165 Records of the War Department General and Special Staffs, U.S. National Archives, College Park, Maryland.

27. Extract from Minutes of Cabinet War Committee, September 20, 1944; Extract from Minutes of Cabinet War Committee, September 22, 1944; Extract from Minutes of Cabinet War Committee, October 5, 1945, *DCER*, 421–424, 426–427.

28. R. MacGregor Dawson, *The Conscription Crisis of 1944* (Toronto: University of Toronto Press, 1961), 11–13, 19; Stacey, *Double Life*, 21–24.

29. Dawson, *Conscription Crisis*, 13–14; Nolan, *King's War*, 132–133.

30. Dawson, *Conscription Crisis*, 12, 18–19, 23–26, 31; Nolan, *King's War*, 133–134.

31. Dawson, *Conscription Crisis*, 18; Nolan, *King's War*, 133–135.

32. Nolan, *King's War*, 138–139, 141.

33. Dawson, *Conscription Crisis*, 19, 34–35; Nolan, *King's War*, 138.

34. Dawson, *Conscription Crisis*, 35, 37–38, 44–46.

35. Ibid., 42–46; Nolan, *King's War*, 136–138.

36. Nolan, *King's War*, 149–153.

37. Dawson, *Conscription Crisis*, 53–54; Nolan, *King's War*, 158.

38. Extract from Cabinet Conclusion, April 3, 1945, *DCER*, 453–454.

39. *Gazette* (Montreal), April 5, 1945.

40. Statement of W. L. Mackenzie King, April 4, 1945, House of Commons, *Debates* 19th Parliament, 6th Session, vol. 83, no. 11 (Ottawa: King's Printer, 1945), 446–449; *Gazette* (Montreal), April 5, 1945.

41. Pickersgill and Forster, *Mackenzie King Record*, 352.

42. *Ottawa Evening Citizen*, April 5, 1945; *Toronto Daily Star*, April 5, 1945; *Gazette* (Montreal), April 5, 1945.

43. *Gazette* (Montreal), April 5, 1945.

44. *Gazette* (Montreal), April 5–6, 1945; April 5, 1945, Statement of W. L. Mackenzie King, House of Commons, *Debates* 19th Parliament, 6th Session, vol. 83, no. 12 (Ottawa: King's Printer, 1945), 521–522; Pickersgill and Forster, *Mackenzie King Record*, 353.

Chapter 8. Rain of Fire

1. Coffey, *Hap*, 247, 265; Daso, *Hap Arnold*, 185.

2. Coffey, *Hap*, 249; Daso, *Hap Arnold*, 138, 170.

3. Coffey, *Hap*, 305–306, 308–309, 312.

4. Ibid., 312.

5. There are significant differences between Coffey and Daso in describing the events following the fourth heart attack. Coffey states that Arnold spent three days in his quarters without any contact from his staff or a physician. Daso, on the other hand, plainly states that Arnold was on a plane the next day. Since it is difficult to imagine Arnold going a day without contact with his office, much less three, the account of his heart attack closely follows that of Daso. Coffey, *Hap*, 358–359; Daso, *Hap Arnold*, 199.

6. Daso, *Hap Arnold*, 199; Coffey, *Hap*, 359.

7. Daso, *Hap Arnold*, 199–200.

8. Coffey, *Hap*, 359; Daso, *Hap Arnold*, 200.

9. Daso, *Hap Arnold*, 200–201.

10. Ibid., 201–202.

11. Ibid., 202.

12. Ibid., 202–203.

13. Ibid., 203.

14. Conrad C. Crane, *Bombs, Cities, and Civilians: American Airpower Strategy in World War II* (Lawrence: University Press of Kansas, 1993), 128.

15. Ibid., 128.

16. Ibid., 128–129.

17. Wolk, "General Arnold, the Atomic Bomb, and the Surrender of Japan," 163–178.

18. Thomas M. Coffey, *Iron Eagle: The Turbulent Life of General Curtis LeMay* (New York: Crown Publishers, 1986), 134; Curtis E. LeMay with MacKinlay Kantor, *Mission with LeMay: My Story* (Garden City: Doubleday, 1965), 220–224.

19. Coffey, *Iron Eagle*, 3, 135, 215, 244.

20. LeMay with Kantor, *Mission with LeMay*, 37–47.

21. Ibid., 79, 80–86, 99; Coffey, *Iron Eagle*, 216–217, 220, 226–227.

22. LeMay with Kantor, *Mission with LeMay*, 138–139, 174–175; Coffey, *Iron Eagle*, 227.

23. Coffey, *Iron Eagle*, 4, 244.

24. Ibid., 4, 153; Crane, *Bombs, Cities, and Civilians*, 126; LeMay with Kantor, *Mission with LeMay*, 313.

25. Arnold to LeMay, December 9, 1944, Folder: Arnold, Box 11, LeMay Papers.

26. Crane, *Bombs, Cities, and Civilians*, 124–126.

27. Werrell, *Blankets of Fire*, 152.

28. Ibid., 151, 157; Coffey, *Iron Eagle*, 147; LeMay with Kantor, *Mission with LeMay*, 347–348.

29. Arnold to LeMay, April 5, 1945, Folder: Arnold, Box 11, LeMay Papers.

30. Werrell, *Blankets of Fire*, 152–153; Crane, *Bombs, Cities, and Civilians*, 131; Coffey, *Iron Eagle*, 155; LeMay with Kantor, *Mission with LeMay*, 343.

31. Werrell, *Blankets of Fire*, 153; Coffey, *Iron Eagle*, 155.

32. Werrell, *Blankets of Fire*, 346–347.

33. Ibid., 155.

34. Ibid.; Crane, *Bombs, Cities, and Civilians*, 131.

35. Werrell, *Blankets of Fire*, 155; Coffey, *Iron Eagle*, 162.

36. Crane, *Bombs, Cities, and Civilians*, 126–127, 135; Werrell, *Blankets of Fire*, 159.

37. Werrell, *Blankets of Fire*, 155, 157; LeMay with Kantor, *Mission with LeMay*, 345–346.

38. Werrell, *Blankets of Fire*, 157–158.

39. Coffey, *Iron Eagle*, 162; Crane, *Bombs, Cities, and Civilians*, 132; Werrell, *Blankets of Fire*, 159–161.

40. Emphasis in the original. LeMay with Kantor, *Mission with LeMay*, 348; Frank, DOWNFALL, 64.

41. Frank, DOWNFALL, 65–66.

42. Coffey, *Iron Eagle*, 163.

43. Werrell, *Blankets of Fire*, 48–49, 160–161, 166; Frank, DOWNFALL, 55, 65.

44. Frank, DOWNFALL, 6–7.

45. Ibid., 7–9; Crane, *Bombs, Cities, and Civilians*, 132.

46. Frank, DOWNFALL, 10–11.

47. Ibid., 12–13.

48. Ibid., 14–15.

49. Werrell, *Blankets of Fire*, 161–163; Crane, *Bombs, Cities, and Civilians*, 132; LeMay with Kantor, *Mission with LeMay*, 352; Frank, DOWNFALL, 65.

50. Werrell, *Blankets of Fire*, 162–163; Frank, DOWNFALL, 16, 18.

51. Werrell, *Blankets of Fire*, 163–164.

52. Ibid., 164–165.

53. Ibid., 165.

54. Ibid., 165–166; Frank, DOWNFALL, 69.

55. Werrell, *Blankets of Fire*, 166–167.

56. Ibid.

57. Arnold to LeMay, March 21, 1945, Folder: Arnold, Box 11, LeMay Papers.

58. Crane, *Bombs Cities, and Civilians*, 134–136.

59. Werrell, *Blankets of Fire*, 166; Coffey, *Iron Eagle*, 153–154, 173–174.

60. Werrell, *Blankets of Fire*, 176–177, 188–189.

61. Ibid., 176–177; LeMay with Kantor, *Mission with LeMay*, 372.

62. Werrell, *Blankets of Fire*, 177–181, 187–189.

63. Ibid., 192–193, 201–202.

64. Emphasis in the original. LeMay with Kantor, *Mission with LeMay*, 355, 390.

Chapter 9. Okinawa: Sea Battle

1. Chester W. Nimitz, "Foreword," in Arnold S. Lott, *Brave Ship, Brave Men* (Indianapolis: Bobbs-Merrill, 1963), x.

2. Gordon W. Prange, Donald M. Goldstein, and Katherine V. Dillon, eds., *Fading Victory: The Diary of Admiral Matome Ugaki, 1941–1945*, Masatak Chihaya, trans. (Pittsburgh: University of Pittsburgh Press, 1991), xi–xiii, 561, 563, 591, 610, 620–621, 669–670; *Reports of General MacArthur*, vol. 2, pt. 2, *Japanese Operations in the Southwest Pacific Area* (Washington, D.C.: Government Printing Office, 1966), 626.

3. Prange, Goldstein, and Dillon, *Fading Victory*, 550, 552, 559–560, 584, 594, 613, 617–619, 621; Spector, *Eagle against the Sun*, 166.

4. Toshiyuki Yokoi, "Kamikazes in the Okinawa Campaign," Raymond O'Connor, ed., and David C. Evans, ed. and trans., *The Japanese Navy in World War II: In the Words of Former Japanese Naval Officers*, 2nd ed. (Annapolis, Md.: Naval Institute Press, 1986), 454–456.

5. Ivan Morris, *The Nobility of Failure: Tragic Heroes in the History of Japan* (New York: Rinehart and Winston, 1975), 276–334.

6. Two examples come from major motion pictures of that decade. The climax of *The Fighting 69th* (1940) comes when a misfit soldier redeems himself by jumping on top of a grenade and saving many others at the cost of his own life. In *Bataan* (1943) a small band of U.S. soldiers trapped on the Bataan peninsula during the Japanese invasion of the Philippines holds a critical location to the last man. See *The Fighting 69th*, directed by William Keighly, screenplay by Norman Reilly Raine, Fred Niblo, Jr., and Dean Franklin (Warner Brothers Pictures, 1940); and *Bataan*, directed by Tay Garnett, screenplay by Robert Hardy Andrews (MGM, 1943).

7. For more on these battles, see Ernle Bradford, *Thermopylae: The Battle for the West* (New York: McGraw-Hill, 1980), and for a well-researched fictional account, see Steven Pressfield, *Gates of Fire: An Epic Novel of the Battle of Thermopylae* (New York: Doubleday, 1998); William C. Davis, *Three Roads to the Alamo: The Lives and Fortunes of David Crockett, James Bowie, and William Barrett Travis* (New York: Harper-Collins, 1998); Randy Roberts and James S. Olson, *A Line in the Sand: The Alamo in Blood and Memory* (New York: Free Press, 2001); Tuchman, *Guns of August*; Robert Jackson, *Dunkirk: The British Evacuation 1940* (New York: St. Martin's Press, 1976), 49–55.

8. John W. Dower, *War without Mercy: Race and Power in the Pacific War* (New York: Pantheon Books, 1986), 203–206; Ryuji Nagatsuka, *I Was a Kamikaze*, Nina

Rootes, trans. (New York: Macmillan, 1972), 138, 139, 158; Hachiro Hosokawa, "Preface," in Hatsuho Naito, *Thunder Gods: The Kamikaze Pilots Tell Their Story* (New York: Kodansha, 1989), 16; Fujiwara cited in *Japanese Operations in the Southwest Pacific Area*, 613.

9. Prange, Goldstein, and Dillon, *Fading Victory*, 548; Nagatsuka, *I Was a Kamikaze*, 170.

10. Nagatsuka, *I Was a Kamikaze*, 169; Jean Lartéguy, ed., *The Sun Goes Down: Last Letters from Japanese Suicide-Pilots and Soldiers*, Nora Wydenbruck, trans. (London: William Kimber, 1956), 139, 143.

11. E. B. Potter, *Nimitz* (Annapolis, Md.: Naval Institute Press, 1976), 22–27, 30, 55.

12. Ibid., 59–62.

13. Ibid., 116–119, 125, 131, 150, 456.

14. Ibid., 62, 117, 122–124, 126, 132–134.

15. Ibid., 135–149.

16. Ibid., 4, 9, 19–21, 32, 165–167, 221–223, 225–227.

17. Thomas B. Buell, *The Quiet Warrior: A Biography of Admiral Raymond A. Spruance* (Boston: Little, Brown, 1974), xiii–xiv, 116, 155–156, 174, 246, 252.

18. Ibid., 8, 12, 14, 16, 19–21, 24–33, 36–37, 54–56.

19. Ibid., xvii, 33, 41–42, 53, 66–67, 73, 82.

20. Ibid., 96–98, 120–124, 132–150; Jonathan Parshall and Anthony Tully, *Shattered Sword: The Untold Story of the Battle of Midway* (Washington, D.C.: Potomac, 2005), 134–135, 174–175.

21. Buell, *Quiet Warrior*, 336.

22. Ibid., 151–166, 171, 227, 270, 275–280.

23. Ibid., 341.

24. Samuel Eliot Morison, *History of United States Naval Operations in World War II*, vol. 14, *Victory in the Pacific, 1945* (Boston: Little, Brown, 1960), 233–235.

25. Morison, *Victory in the Pacific*, 233–235; Robert F. Wallace, *From Dam Neck to Okinawa: A Memoir of Antiaircraft Training in World War II*, Jeffery G. Barlow, ed. (Washington, D.C.: Naval Historical Center, 2001), 24–25, 27, 29, 49; "Forgotten Islands," *News of the Day* 19, no. 207, Hearst Newsreel Collection, Film and Television Library, University of California at Los Angeles, Los Angeles, California; Nagatsuka, *I Was a Kamikaze*, 163–164.

26. Morison, *Victory in the Pacific*, 94–99, 138.

27. Ibid.; Buell, *Quiet Warrior*, 349.

28. Morison, *Victory in the Pacific*, 186–191.

29. Ibid.

30. Ibid., 182–186.

31. Ibid., 199–208; Russell Spur, *A Glorious Way to Die: The Kamikaze Mission of the Battleship Yamato, April 1945* (New York: Newmarket Press, 1981), 308, gives slightly different numbers of those that died on the *Yamato*.

32. Prange, Goldstein, and Dillon, *Fading Victory*, 578, 580.

33. Morison, *Victory in the Pacific*, 223–334.

34. Prange, Goldstein, and Dillon, *Fading Victory*, 582.

35. Morison, *Victory in the Pacific*, 225.

36. Ibid., 227–230.

37. Wallace, *From Dam Neck to Okinawa*, 39–42.

38. Prange, Goldstein, and Dillon, *Fading Victory*, 583.

39. Ibid.; Morison, *Victory in the Pacific*, 235–237.

40. Morison, *Victory in the Pacific*, 237–238.

41. Prange, Goldstein, and Dillon, *Fading Victory*, 588–589.

42. Prange, Goldstein, Dillon, and Chihaya, *Fading Victory*, 244, 595, 599; Yokoi, "Kamikazes in the Okinawa Campaign"; Morison, *Victory in the Pacific*, 238–239.

43. Morison, *Victory in the Pacific*, 250.

44. Lott, *Brave Men, Brave Ship*, 12–13, 159–211; Morison, *Victory in the Pacific*, 251–253.

45. Lott, *Brave Men, Brave Ship*, 12–13, 159–211; Morison, *Victory in the Pacific*, 251–253.

46. Morison, *Victory in the Pacific*, 253–254.

47. Ibid., 254–255.

48. Ibid., 256–258.

49. Ibid., 262–263.

50. Richard Baker, *Dry Ginger: The Biography of Admiral of the Fleet Sir Michael Le Fanu, GCB, DSC* (London: W. H. Allen, 1977), 74; Morison, *Victory in the Pacific*, 263–264, 269–270; Prange, Goldstein, and Dillon, *Fading Victory*, 614; Buell, *Quiet Warrior*, 358–359.

51. Prange, Goldstein, and Dillon, *Fading Victory*, 616.

52. Morison, *Victory in the Pacific*, 271.

53. Ibid., 271–272; Prange, Goldstein, and Dillon, *Fading Victory*, 617, 618.

54. Albert Axell and Hideaki Kase, *Kamikaze: Japan's Suicide Gods* (New York: Pearson Education, 2002), 161.

55. Morison, *Victory in the Pacific*, 259–260.

56. Ibid., 261.

57. Prange, Goldstein, and Dillon, *Fading Victory*, 620.

58. Morison, *Victory in the Pacific*, 261–262.

59. Ibid., 274; Prange, Goldstein, and Dillon, *Fading Victory*, 626–631.

60. Morison, *Victory in the Pacific*, 279; Prange, Goldstein, and Dillon, *Fading Victory*, 636–637.

61. Prange, Goldstein, and Dillon, *Fading Victory*, 599, 610, 620, 622.

62. Buell, *Quiet Warrior*, 356, 358.

Chapter 10. The Forgotten Fleet at Okinawa

1. Andre Wessels, "South Africa and the War against Japan 1941–1945," *Military History Journal* 10 (June 1996), located at: http://rapidttp.com/milhist/vol103aw.html (*Military History Journal* is now published online); Willmott, *Grave of a Dozen Schemes*, 207.

2. Richard Humble, *Fraser of North Cape: The Life of Admiral of the Fleet Lord Fraser [1888–1981]* (London: Routledge & Kegan Paul, 1983), 268.

3. Ibid., 3–9, 41–50, 55–63.

4. Ibid., 68–75, 87, 90, 99–106, 110, 115, 127–139, 142, 149, 161, 168–169, 176–177.

5. Ibid., 90, 149, 161, 168–169, 176–177.

6. Ibid., 68–75, 87, 90, 99–106, 110, 115, 127–139, 142, 149, 161, 168–169, 176–177.

7. Ibid., 187–224.

8. "Commander-in-Chief's Dispatches—November 1944 to July 1945," November 23, 1945, ADM 199/118, BNA.

9. Ibid.

10. Ibid.

11. Humble, *Fraser*, 251–252.

12. Ibid., 252.

13. Edwyn Gray, *Operation Pacific: The Royal Navy's War against Japan, 1941–1945* (Annapolis, Md.: Naval Institute Press, 1990), 177; "Commander-in-Chief's Dispatches—November 1944 to July 1945," November 23, 1945, ADM 199/118, BNA.

14. Humble, *Fraser*, 249.

15. Ibid., 249–250, 253; Gray, *Operation Pacific*, 177.

16. Humble, *Fraser*, 259–260.

17. Somerville to Fraser, February 27, 1945, FRS 23/6/3, Fraser Papers.

18. Humble, *Fraser*, 254–257.

19. Humble, *Fraser*, 272–274; Hough, *Longest Battle*, 340; "The United Kingdom Government's Demands for the British Pacific Fleet Ignore the Australian Limits to Possible Aid," A5954/771/8, Shedden Papers; Horner, *Defence Supremo*, 221; "Commander-in-Chief's Dispatches—November 1944 to July 1945," November 23, 1945, ADM 199/118, BNA.

20. Humble, *Fraser*, 272–274; Hough, *Longest Battle*, 340; "The United Kingdom Government's Demands for the British Pacific Fleet Ignore the Australian Limits to Possible Aid," A5954/771/8, Shedden Papers; Horner, *Defence Supremo*, 221–222; "Commander-in-Chief's Dispatches—November 1944 to July 1945," November 23, 1945, ADM 199/118, BNA.

21. Cunningham to Brooke, May 16, 1944, 6/3/11, Alanbrooke Papers.

22. "Commander-in-Chief's Dispatches—November 1944 to July 1945," November 23, 1945, ADM 199/118, BNA.

23. Stuart Eadon, *Sakishima and Back: "Where Men with Splendid Hearts May Go"* (Manchester, UK: Crecy Books, 1995), 159; Humble, *Fraser*, 261; Hough, *Longest Battle*, 340.

24. R. M. Crosley, *They Gave Me a Seafire* (Shrewsbury, UK: Airlife Publishing, 1986), 156; Eadon, *Sakishima*, 160.

25. Norman Hanson, *Carrier Pilot: An Unforgettable True Story of Wartime Flying* (Cambridge, UK: Patrick Stephens, 1979), 208; Eadon, *Sakishima*, 160–161.

26. Eadon, *Sakishima*, 160–161.

27. Sir Bruce Fraser, "The Contribution of the British Pacific Fleet to the Assault on

Okinawa, 1945," Supplement to the *London Gazette*, June 2, 1948, Liddell 15/4/238, Liddell Hart Papers. The Fraser report is also available in CAB 106/95, BNA.

28. Gray, *Operation Pacific*, 205; Hough, *Longest Battle*, 340; "Commander-in-Chief's Dispatches—November 1944 to July 1945," November 23, 1945, ADM 199/118, BNA.

29. Sir Philip Vian, *Action This Day: A War Memoir* (London: Frederick Muller Limited, 1960), 202.

30. Humble, *Fraser*, 270.

31. Vian, *Action This Day*, 170.

32. Peter C. Smith, *Task Force 57: The British Pacific Fleet, 1944–1945* (London: Kimber, 1969), 137; Gray, *Operation Pacific*, 243, 246; Vian, *Action This Day*, 170, 175; Fraser, "Contribution of the British Pacific Fleet," Supplement to the *London Gazette*, June 2, 1948, Liddell 15/4/238, Liddell Hart Papers.

33. Hanson, *Carrier Pilot*, 214–215; Gray, *Operation Pacific*, 206; Fraser, "Contribution of the British Pacific Fleet," Supplement to the *London Gazette*, June 2, 1948, Liddell 15/4/238, Liddell Hart Papers.

34. "Commander-in-Chief's Dispatches—November 1944 to July 1945," November 23, 1945, ADM 199/118, BNA; Fraser, "Contribution of the British Pacific Fleet," Supplement to the *London Gazette*, June 2, 1948, Liddell 15/4/238, Liddell Hart Papers; Smith, *Task Force 57*, 116; Gray, *Operation Pacific*, 208.

35. Somerville to Fraser, February 27, 1945, FRS 23/6/3, Fraser Papers.

36. "Commander-in-Chief's Dispatches—November 1944 to July 1945," November 23, 1945, ADM 199/118, BNA.

37. Vian, *Action This Day*, 188; Smith, *Task Force 57*, 117.

38. "Commander-in-Chief's Dispatches—November 1944 to July 1945," November 23, 1945, ADM 199/118, BNA.

39. Vian, *Action This Day*, 188.

40. Gray, *Operation Pacific*, 206.

41. Somerville to Fraser, February 27, 1945, FRS 23/6/3, Fraser Papers.

42. "Commander-in-Chief's Dispatches—November 1944 to July 1945," November 23, 1945, ADM 199/118, BNA.

43. Humble, *Fraser*, 256; "Commander-in-Chief's Dispatches—November 1944 to July 1945," 23 November 1945, ADM 199/118, BNA.

44. Gray, *Operation Pacific*, 206; "British Pacific Fleet" Memorandum by the British Chiefs of Staff attached to Ismay to Churchill, March 8, 1945; British Admiralty Delegation to Admiralty, March 9, 1945; British Admiralty Delegation to Admiralty, March 15, 1945, PREM 3/164/6, BNA; Fraser, "Contribution of the British Pacific Fleet," Supplement to the *London Gazette*, June 2, 1948, Liddell 15/4/238, Liddell Hart Papers.

45. Gray, *Operation Pacific*, 206; "British Pacific Fleet" Memorandum by the British Chiefs of Staff attached to Ismay to Churchill, March 8, 1945; British Admiralty Delegation to Admiralty, March 9, 1945; British Admiralty Delegation to Admiralty, March 15, 1945, PREM 3/164/6, BNA; Fraser, "Contribution of the British Pacific Fleet," Supplement to the *London Gazette*, June 2, 1948, Liddell 15/4/238, Liddell Hart Papers.

46. CINCBPF to CTF 113, March 14, 1945, Folder: 2939–3075, vol. 1 Command Summary, book 6, vol. 3, Nimitz Papers.

47. Rawlings to Nimitz, March 15, 1945, Folder: 2939–3075, vol. 1 Command Summary, Book 6, vol. 3, Nimitz Papers.

48. Nimitz to Fraser, March 16, 1945, in Fraser, "Contribution of the British Pacific Fleet," Supplement to the *London Gazette*, June 2, 1948, Liddell 15/4/238, Liddell Hart Papers; Harold Hopkins, *Nice to Have You Aboard* (London: George Allen & Unwin, 1964), 208–209.

49. Vian, *Action This Day*, 177; Gray, *Operation Pacific*, 207.

50. Smith, *Task Force 57*, 118; Gray, *Operation Pacific*, 208–210; Hanson, *Carrier Pilot*, 222.

51. Smith, *Task Force 57*, 118, 125; Gray, *Operation Pacific*, 210; Vian, *Action This Day*, 177.

52. Gray, *Operation Pacific*, 211; "Commander-in-Chief's Dispatches—November 1944 to July 1945," November 23, 1945, ADM 199/118, BNA.

53. Smith, *Task Force 57*, 126; Gray, *Operation Pacific*, 211.

54. Smith, *Task Force 57*, 127.

55. Ibid., 128; Hanson, *Carrier Pilot*, 236.

56. Vian, *Action This Day*, 179–181; Gray, *Operation Pacific*, 213.

57. Hanson, *Carrier Pilot*, 218, 220; Vian, *Action This Day*, 183–184.

58. Fraser, "Contribution of the British Pacific Fleet," Supplement to the *London Gazette*, June 2, 1948, Liddell 15/4/238, Liddell Hart Papers; Vian, *Action This Day*, 178; Willmott, *Grave of a Dozen Schemes*, 144.

59. Spruance to Stark, April 29, 1945, ADM 205/53; Spruance to Stark, April 29, 1945, PREM 3/164/6, British National Archives, Richmond, Surrey.

60. Axell and Kase, *Kamikaze*, 82; Vian, *Action This Day*, 184–187; Smith, *Task Force 57*, 144; Rawlings to Fraser, May 11, 1945, FRS 23/2/14, Fraser Papers.

61. Vian, *Action This Day*, 184–187; Gray, *Operation Pacific*, 218; Rawlings to Fraser, May 11, 1945, FRS 23/2/14, Fraser Papers.

62. Vian, *Action This Day*, 185; Gray, *Operation Pacific*, 219; Smith, *Task Force 57*, 138.

63. Vian, *Action This Day*, 185.

64. Ibid., 185; Gray, *Operation Pacific*, 220.

65. Vian, *Action This Day*, 185; Smith, *Task Force 57*, 138.

66. Rawlings to Fraser, May 11, 1945, FRS 23/2/14, Fraser Papers.

67. Smith, *Task Force 57*, 144–145.

68. Ibid., 146–147.

69. Ibid., 148.

70. Gray, *Operation Pacific*, 224; Crosley, *Seafire*, 156; Rawlings report, May 9, 1945, and Spruance to Rawlings, May 25, 1945, in Fraser, "Contribution of the British Pacific Fleet," Supplement to the *London Gazette*, June 2, 1948, Liddell 15/4/238, Liddell Hart Papers.

Chapter 11. Okinawa: Land Battle

1. Potter, *Nimitz*, 4, 9, 19–21, 32, 165–167, 221–223, 225–227.

2. Ibid., 372.

3. Lloyd G. Graybar, "The Buckners of Kentucky," *Filson Club Quarterly* 58, no. 2 (April 1984), 202–214; Shelby Foote, *The Civil War: A Narrative*, vol. 1, *Fort Sumter to Perryville* (New York: Random House, 1958), 210–213.

4. Graybar, "Buckners of Kentucky," 202–214; Galen Perras, *Stepping Stones to Nowhere: The Aleutian Islands, Alaska, and American Military Strategy, 1867–1945* (Vancouver: University of British Columbia Press, 2003); Buckner to Buckner, April 27, 1945, Box 1, Buckner Papers (Kans.).

5. Spector, *Eagle against the Sun*, 314–316; Harry A. Gailey, *"Howlin' Mad" vs the Army: Conflict in Command, Saipan 1944* (Novato, Calif.: Presidio Press, 1986); Diary of Simon Bolivar Buckner, Jr., October 7, 1944, Box 1, Buckner Papers (Kans.).

6. *New York Herald Tribune*, May 2, 1945; *Time*, April 16, 1945.

7. David Nichols, ed., *Ernie's War: The Best of Ernie Pyle's World War II Dispatches* (New York: Random House, 1986), 402; Diary of Simon Bolivar Buckner, Jr., March 31, 1945, Box 1, Buckner Papers (Kans.).

8. William Manchester, *Goodbye, Darkness: A Memoir of the Pacific War* (Boston: Little, Brown, 1980), 354; Hiromichi Yahara, *Battle for Okinawa* (New York: J. Wiley, 1995), xi–xii; Thomas M. Huber, *Japan's Battle for Okinawa, April–June, 1945*; Leavenworth Papers No. 18 (Fort Leavenworth, Kans.: Combat Studies Institute, U.S. Army Command and Staff College, 1990), 21–22, 27.

9. Buckner to Buckner, April 1, 2, 1945, Box 1, Buckner Papers (Pa.); James H. Belote and William Belote, *Typhoon of Steel: The Battle for Okinawa* (New York: Harper and Row, 1970), 72–74, 159–161, 172–183.

10. E. B. Sledge, *With the Old Breed at Peleiu and Okinawa* (Novato, Calif.: Presidio Press, 1981), 201; Diary of Simon Bolivar Buckner, Jr., April 10, 1945, Box 1, Buckner Papers (Kans.).

11. Benis M. Frank and Henry I. Shaw, Jr., *History of U.S. Marine Corps Operations in World War II*, vol. 5, *Victory and Occupation* (Washington, D.C.: Government Printing Office, 1968), 45, 48, 51; Huber, *Japan's Battle for Okinawa*, 75–79.

12. Huber, *Japan's Battle for Okinawa*, 1–3, 6–8, 59–60, 63, 65.

13. Roy E. Appleman, James M. Burns, Russell A. Gugeler, and John Stevens, *U.S. Army in World War II: The War in the Pacific: The Last Battle* (Washington, D.C.: Government Printing Office, 1948), 181; Diary of Simon Bolivar Buckner, Jr., April 2, 1945, Box 1, Buckner Papers (Kans.).

14. Buell, *Quiet Warrior*, 387.

15. Gerald Astor, *Operation Iceberg: The Invasion and Conquest of Okinawa in World War II, An Oral History* (New York: D. I. Fine, 1995), 129; Diary of Simon Bolivar Buckner, Jr., April 10, 1945, Box 1, Buckner Papers (Kans.).

16. Frank and Shaw, *Victory and Occupation*, 71–72, 192, 240–241; Appleman, Burns, Gugeler, and Stevens, *Last Battle*, 184–194.

17. Appleman, Burns, Gugeler, and Stevens, *Last Battle*, 184–194; Huber, *Japan's Battle for Okinawa*, 60, 63, 65–66.

18. Huber, *Japan's Battle for Okinawa*, 60, 63, 66–71.

19. Manchester, *Goodbye, Darkness*, 359; Buckner to Buckner, April 27, 1945, Box 1, Buckner Papers (Pa.).

20. Potter, *Nimitz*, 375; Diary of Simon Bolivar Buckner, Jr., April 8, 22–24, 1945, Box 1, Buckner Papers (Kans.); Buckner to Buckner, April 22, 27, 1945, Box 1, Buckner Papers (Pa.).

21. Appleman, Burns, Gugeler, and Stevens, *Last Battle*, 248, 265.

22. Frank and Shaw, *Victory and Occupation*, 241; Robert W. Coakley and Richard M. Leighton, *United States Army in World War II: The War Department: Global Logistics and Strategy, 1943–1945* (Washington, D.C.: Government Printing Office, 1961), 573; Diary of Simon Bolivar Buckner, Jr., April 25, 1945, Box 1, Buckner Papers (Kans.).

23. Morison, *Victory in the Pacific*, 391.

24. Belote and Belote, *Typhoon of Steel*, 212–214; Appleman, Burns, Gugeler, and Stevens, *Last Battle*, 259; Diary of Simon Bolivar Buckner, Jr., March 20, April 11, 1945, Box 1, Buckner Papers (Kans.).

25. Buckner to Buckner, April 22, 1945, Box 1, Buckner Papers (Pa.).

26. Appleman, Burns, Gugeler, and Stevens, *Last Battle*, 282–302; Belote and Belote, *Typhoon of Steel*, 218–226, 230–234; Yahara, *Battle for Okinawa*, 41, 207–216.

27. *New York Times*, May 11, 1945.

28. Manchester, *Goodbye, Darkness*, 366, 374, 376, 377, 381.

29. Yahara, *Battle for Okinawa*, 81–83; Diary of Simon Bolivar Buckner, Jr., May 8, 1945, Box 1, Buckner Papers (Kans.).

30. Frank and Shaw, *Victory and Occupation*, 278; Huber, *Japan's Battle for Okinawa*, 97–100.

31. Yahara, *Battle for Okinawa*, 81–83.

32. Frank and Shaw, *Victory and Occupation*, 286; Appleman, Burns, Gugeler, and Stevens, *Last Battle*, 396–397.

33. Diary of Simon Bolivar Buckner, Jr., May 29, 1945, Box 1, Buckner Papers (Kans.).

34. Appleman, Burns, Gugeler, and Stevens, *Last Battle*, 422–425; Diary of Simon Bolivar Buckner, Jr., May 31, 1945, Box 1, Buckner Papers (Kans.).

35. Sledge, *With the Old Breed*, 233; Manchester, *Goodbye, Darkness*, 361, 367; "The Deadeye Dispatch," June 8, 1945, Folder: Clippings 1945, Box 37, Stilwell Papers.

36. Karl C. Dod, *U.S. Army in World War II: The Corps of Engineers: The War against Japan* (Washington, D.C.: Government Printing Office, 1966), 648–649, 658–659; Frank and Shaw, *Victory and Occupation*, 241; Nicholas Evan Sarantakes, ed., *Seven Stars: The Okinawa Battle Diaries of Simon Bolivar Buckner, Jr. and Joseph Stilwell* (College Station: Texas A&M University Press, 2004), 72; Diary of Simon Bolivar Buckner, Jr., May 30, 1945, Box 1, Buckner Papers (Kans.)

37. Frank and Shaw, *Victory and Occupation*, 299, 304–308; Diary of Simon Bolivar Buckner, Jr., June 4, 1945, Box 1, Buckner Papers (Kans.).

38. Sarantakes, *Seven Stars*, 75.

39. Appleman, Burns, Gugeler, and Stevens, *Last Battle*, 463; *New York Journal-American*, June 12, 1945; Yahara, *Battle for Okinawa*, 136; Diary of Simon Bolivar Buckner, Jr., June 9, 1945, Box 1, Buckner Papers (Kans.).

40. *New York Herald Tribune*, June 12, 1945; *New York Times*, June 12, 1945; *New York Sun*, June 12, 1945.

Chapter 12. In the Wake of ICEBERG

1. Black, *Franklin Delano Roosevelt*, 1102, 1107–1109.

2. Ibid., 1108–1111.

3. *New York Times*, April 13, 1945.

4. Sir Bruce Fraser, "The Contribution of the British Pacific Fleet to the Assault on Okinawa, 1945," Supplement to the *London Gazette*, June 2, 1948, Liddell 15/4/238 Liddell Hart Papers of Sir Basil Liddell Hart, Liddell Hart Centre for Military Archives, King's College London, The Strand, London.

5. *New York Times*, April 14, 1945.

6. *Washington (D.C.) Evening Star*, April 15, 1945; Dean Acheson, *Present at the Creation: My Years in the State Department* (New York: W. W. Norton, 1969), 103.

7. *Washington (D.C.) Evening Star*, April 15, 1945.

8. Black, *Franklin Delano Roosevelt*, 1116; *New York Times*, April 16, 1945.

9. McCullough, *Truman*, 43–44, 58, 83, 141–142, 247–248.

10. Ibid., 80–82, 90–92, 103; Alonzo L. Hamby, *Man of the People: A Life of Harry S. Truman* (New York: Oxford University Press, 1995), 25–45, 58.

11. McCullough, *Truman*, 210; Hamby, *Man of the People*, 78–81, 94–100, 189, 192, 195–196.

12. Hamby, *Man of the People*, 249–260; McCullough, *Truman*, 258–259. Bruce Tap, *Over Lincoln's Shoulder: The Committee on the Conduct of the War* (Lawrence: University Press of Kansas, 1998).

13. McCullough, *Truman*, 285; Hamby, *Man of the People*, 260; *Time*, March 8, 1943, p. 14; *Business Week*, June 26, 1943, p. 19; *Nation*, January 24, 1942, pp. 80–81.

14. Hamby, *Man of the People*, 290.

15. *New York Herald Tribune*, May 29, 1945. Lawrence's syndicated column can be found in either the *New York Sun*, May 30, 1945; June 4, 1945, or the *Washington (D.C.) Evening Star*, May 30, 1945; June 4, 1945; *Washington (D.C.) Sunday Star*, June 17, 1945.

16. *New York Herald Tribune*, June 18, 1945.

17. For Nimitz's comments see *New York Times*, June 17, 1945; *Washington Post*, June 4, 1945; Richard Kluger, *The Paper: The Life and Death of the New York Herald Tribune* (New York: Knopf, 1986), 373; *New York Herald Tribune*, June 17, 1945, June 18, 1945; Clifton La Bree, *The Gentle Warrior: Oliver Price Smith, USMC* (Kent, Ohio: Kent State University Press, 2001), 89.

18. Astor, *Operation Iceberg*, 407; Fred Beans oral history, 90, 93, U.S. Marine Corps Historical Center, Washington Navy Yard, Washington, D.C.; J. Fred Haley, "The Death of Gen. Simon Bolivar Buckner," *Marine Corps Gazette* (November 1982), 100–105.

19. Buckner's aide, who was wounded in the artillery fire, offered a different version. He told reporters that Buckner never regained consciousness, *New York Journal-American*, June 19, 1945. Several other sources make it clear that this officer suffered some light wounds, and these along with Buckner's death traumatized him, making it difficult to accept his account. Astor, *Operation Iceberg*, 407; Haley, "Death of Gen. Simon Bolivar Buckner," 100–105.

20. *Baltimore Evening Sun*, June 19, 1945; *Baltimore Sun*, June 19, 1945; *Honolulu Star-Bulletin*, June 19, 1945; *Portland Oregonian*, June 19, 1945; *Los Angeles Times*, June 19, 1945; *New York Times*, June 19, 1945; *Washington Post*, June 19, 1945; *Seattle Post-Intelligencer*; June 19, 1945; *Cleveland Plain Dealer*, June 19, 1945; *Boston Daily Globe*, June 19, 1945; *New York Herald Tribune*, June 19, 1945; *Louisville Times*, June 19, 1945; *Louisville Courier-Journal*, June 19, 1945.

21. *Louisville Courier-Journal*, June 20, 1945; *Los Angeles Times*, June 20, 1945; *Cleveland Plain Dealer*, June 20, 1945. Other papers that lauded Buckner with similar tributes include *Anchorage Times*, June 19, 1945; *Boston Daily Globe*, evening edition, June 19, 1945; *Honolulu Star-Bulletin*, June 20, 1945; *Baltimore Evening Sun*, June 19, 1945; *Washington Post*, June 21, 1945; and *Louisville Times*, June 19, 1945.

22. *Portland Oregonian*, June 20, 1945; *Honolulu Star-Bulletin*, June 20, 1945; *Washington (D.C.) Evening Star*, June 20, 1945; *Newsweek*, July 2, 1945, 36.

23. Lawrence was an exception. He continued to urge an official investigation for months. *Washington (D.C.) Evening Star*, July 5, 7, 23, 1945; January 10, 1946.

24. Charles F. Brower IV, "The Joint Chiefs of Staff and National Policy: American Strategy and the War with Japan, 1943–1945" (Ph.D. diss., Department of History, University of Pennsylvania, 1987), 272–274; John D. Chappell, *Before the Bomb*, 82–84.

25. Robert H. Ferrell, ed., *Off the Record: The Private Papers of Harry S. Truman* (New York: Penguin Books, 1982), 47; D. M. Giangreco, "'A Score of Bloody Okinawas and Iwo Jimas': President Truman and Casualty Estimates for the Invasion of Japan," *Pacific Historical Review* 72 (February 2003), 93–132; Hoover Notes of Meeting with Truman, May 28, 1945, in Timothy Walch and Dwight M. Miller, ed., *Herbert Hoover and Harry Truman: A Documentary History* (Worland, Wyo.: High Plains Publishing, 1992), 37–43.

26. Frank, DOWNFALL, 132.

27. Charles F. Brower IV, "Assault versus Siege: The Debate over Final Strategy for the Defeat of Japan, 1943–1945," *Joint Perspectives* 2 (Spring 1982), 72–80.

28. Brower, "Sophisticated Strategist," 321; Brower, "Joint Chiefs," 272–274, 298.

29. Arnold, *Global Mission*, 567.

30. Brower, "Sophisticated Strategist," 321–322; King and Whitehall, *Fleet Admiral King*, 605–606; Leahy, *I Was There*, 305, 449; Diary of William Leahy, June 18, 1945, Box 4, Leahy Papers.

31. Memorandum for the President, no date, Folder: CCS 381 Japan (6-14-45) S.1, Box 118, Geographic File, 1942–1945, Record Group 218, Records of the U.S. Joint Chiefs of Staff, USNA.

32. Frank, DOWNFALL, 136–139.

33. CINCAFPAC to WARCOS, June 17, 1945, Folder 4, Box 17, Series 2, Record Group 4, MM.

34. Brower, "Sophisticated Strategist," 350, fn. 37; Marshall to MacArthur, June 19, 1945, Folder 4, Box 17, Series 2, Record Group 4, MM.

35. MacArthur to Marshall, June 19, 1945, Folder 4, Box 17, Series 2, Record Group 4, MM.

36. Minutes of Meeting Held at the White House, June 18, 1945, *Foreign Relations of the United States: The Conference of Berlin (The Potsdam Conference), 1945*, vol. 1 (Washington, D.C.: Government Printing Office, 1960), 903–909 [hereafter *FRUS: Berlin*].

37. Ibid.

38. Ibid.; Frank, DOWNFALL, 140–141; Diary of William Leahy, June 18, 1945, Box 4, Leahy Papers. The other three people keeping diaries were Stimson, Forrestal, and McCloy. For the information about their diaries, see Bernstein, "Alarming Japanese Buildup on Southern Kyushu," 574, fn. 23.

39. Minutes of Meeting Held at the White House, June 18, 1945, *FRUS: Berlin*, vol. 1, 903–909.

40. Ibid; Frank, DOWNFALL, 140–141.

41. Ibid.; Frank, DOWNFALL, 141, note.

42. Minutes of Meeting Held at the White House, June 18, 1945, *FRUS: Berlin*, vol. 1, 903–909.

43. Ibid.

44. Ibid.

45. Richard B. Frank and Admiral King would disagree with this assessment. Frank, DOWNFALL, 144.

46. Giangreco, "Operation Downfall," 86–94; Giangreco, "Casualty Projections for the U.S. Invasions of Japan, 1945–1946," 521–582; Polmar and Allen, "Invasion Most Costly," 51–56; Giangreco, "'Score of Bloody Okinawas and Iwo Jimas,'" 93–132. Barton J. Bernstein offers a different view in Bernstein, "Reconsidering 'Invasion Most Costly,'" 220–248; Bernstein, "Truman and the A-Bomb,'" 547–570. Also see his comments in Bernstein, "Reconsidering 'Invasion Most Costly,'" 244, fn. 23, and in Bernstein, "Alarming Japanese Buildup on Southern Kyushu," 572, fn. 16.

47. Martin Harwit, *An Exhibit Denied: Lobbying the History of the Enola Gay* (New York: Springer Verlag, 1997); Hogan, *Hiroshima in History and Memory*; Philip Nobile, ed., *Judgment at the Smithsonian* (New York: Marlowe, 1995); Edward T. Linenthal and Tom Engelhardt, *History Wars: The Enola Gay and Other Battles for the American Past* (New York: Metropolitan Books, 1995); "History and the Public: What Can We Handle? A Round Table about History after the *Enola Gay* Controversy," *Journal of American History* 82 (December 1995), 1029–1144.

48. Harry S. Truman, *Memoirs*, vol. 1, *Year of Decisions* (Garden City, N.Y.: Doubleday, 1955), 417–422; Henry L. Stimson, "The Decision to Use the Atomic Bomb," *Harper's Magazine* 194 (February 1947), 97–107; Truman to James L. Cate, January 12, 1953, in James L. Cate and Wesley F. Craven, eds., *The Army Air Forces in World*

War II, vol. 5, *The Pacific: Matterhorn to Nagasaki, June 1944 to August 1945* (Chicago: University of Chicago Press, 1953), between 712 and 713; Bernstein, "Writing, Righting, or Wronging the Historical Record," 163–173; Bernstein, "Seizing the Contested Terrain of Early Nuclear History," 35–72.

49. Frank, DOWNFALL, 144.

50. George C. Marshall Interview, February 11, 1957, *George C. Marshall Interviews and Reminiscences*, 423; Diary of Henry L. Stimson, July 2, 1945, Stimson Papers.

51. In Stilwell's diary he underlined his text. Sarantakes, *Seven Stars*, 90; Stilwell to Marshall, no date, Folder: 1945 A-27, Box 28A, Stilwell Papers.

52. Stilwell to Marshall, no date, Folder: 1945 A-27, Box 28A, Stilwell Papers.

53. Ibid.; Huston, *American Airpower Comes of Age*, vol. 2, 335.

54. Moon, "Project SPHINX," 303–323.

55. Gallicchio, "After Nagasaki," 396–404; Bernstein, "Eclipsed by Hiroshima and Nagasaki," 149–173.

56. Diary of Sir Andrew Cunningham, July 16, 1945, ADD 52578, Cunningham Papers.

57. Coakley and Leighton, *Global Logistics and Strategy*, 597–599; Lincoln to Wedemyer, July 10, 1945, Folder 7, Box 5, Lincoln Papers.

58. Coakley and Leighton, *Global Logistics and Strategy*, 599–601; Joel R. Davidson, *The Unsinkable Fleet: The Politics of U.S. Navy Expansion in World War II* (Annapolis, Md.: Naval Institute Press, 1996), 105, 110, 111, 133, 180–181. Chappell, *Before the Bomb*, 6–22, 39–71, makes it clear that the public saw material prosperity as a reward for winning the war.

59. Frank, DOWNFALL, 122–129; Diary of Henry L. Stimson, December 27, 1944; January 4, 11, 15, 21, 1945; February 15, 1945, Stimson Papers.

60. Drea, *MacArthur's Ultra*, 209, 212–213.

61. "Amendment No. 1," July 29, 1945, to "G-2 Estimate of the Enemy Situation on Southern Kyushu," April 25, 1945, Folder: Intelligence Situations, Box 6, Chamberlin Papers; Drea, *MacArthur's Ultra*, 223.

62. Bernstein, "Alarming Japanese Buildup on Southern Kyushu," 509–561.

63. Coox, "Needless Fear," 411–438.

64. *Chicago Daily Tribune* and *San Francisco Examiner* cited in Thorne, *Allies of a Kind*, 544, n.69; *Washington Post*, July 15, 1945.

65. Fraser, *Alanbrooke*, 465.

66. Remarks of Leon H. Gavin, April 23, 1945, *Congressional Record*, 79th Congress, 1st Session, 1945, vol. 91, pt. 11 (Washington, D.C.: Government Printing Office, 1945), A1847. Also see the remarks of other members of the lower house in the *Congressional Record*, pt. 2, 2501; pt. 11, A2246; and pt. 6, 7485–7486; Memorandum for General Persons, June 23, 1945; Memo for Record, June 27, 1945, Folder: OPD 336.2 GR Brit (Section II) (Cases 29–), Box 973, Office of the Director of Plans and Operations, General Records—Correspondence, Records of the War Department General and Special Staffs, Record Group 165, USNA; Report of Sir Gerald Campbell, April 6, 1945, 6/2/51, Alanbrooke Papers; Nicholas John Cull, *Selling War: The British Propaganda*

Campaign against American "Neutrality" in World War II (New York: Oxford University Press, 1995), 131.

67. Halifax to Foreign Office, May 13, 1945, FO 371/46439, BNA.

68. Diary of Sir Alan Brooke, May 24, 1945, 5/1/11, Alanbrooke Papers.

69. Gilbert, *Churchill*, 840; Winton, *Cunningham*, 365; "Forward, Till the Whole Task Is Done," May 13, 1945, in Robert Rhodes James, ed., *Winston S. Churchill: His Complete Speeches, 1897–1963*, vol. 7, 1943–1949 (London: Chelsea House Publishers, 1974), 7161; Diary of Sir Alan Brooke, May 24, 1945, 5/1/11, Papers of the First Viscount Alanbrooke of Brookeborough, Liddell Hart Centre for Military Archives, King's College London, The Strand, London.

70. Wilson to Brooke, June 11, 1945, 6/2/51, Alanbrooke Papers.

71. Lord Alanbrooke, *War Diaries*, 617.

72. Michael Dewar, "Wilson," in Keegan, *Churchill's Generals*, 166–167.

73. Dewar, "Wilson," 173–177.

74. Dewar, "Wilson," 178–179; Baron Wilson of Libya and Stowlangtoft, *Eight Years Overseas, 1939–1947* (London: Hutchinson, 1950), 244–247.

75. Wilson to Brooke, June 12, 1945, 6/2/51, Alanbrooke Papers.

76. British Participation in the War against Japan, June 30, 1945, PREM 8 29, BNA; Diary of Sir Alan Brooke, June 28, 1945, 5/1/11, Alanbrooke Papers.

77. Jenkins, *Churchill*, 789–792.

78. Ibid.

79. Churchill, *Triumph and Tragedy*, 585–598; Diary of Sir Andrew Cunningham, July 2, 1945, ADD 52578, Cunningham Papers.

80. Diary of Sir Alan Brooke, July 4, 1945, 5/1/11, Alanbrooke Papers.

81. Extract from C.O.S. (45) 169th Meeting Staff Conference, July 4, 1945, 5/1/11, Alanbrooke Papers.

82. Extract from C.O.S. (45) 169th Meeting Staff Conference, July 4, 1945; Diary of Sir Alan Brooke, July 4, 1945, 5/1/11, Alanbrooke Papers; Diary of Sir Andrew Cunningham, July 4, 1945, ADD 52578, Cunningham Papers.

83. CCS 889, "British Contribution to the Final Phase of the War against Japan," July 6, 1945, TERMINAL Conference Volume, pp. 136–138, Box 3, Combined Chiefs of Staff Proceedings, Eisenhower Presidential Library, Abilene, Kansas.

84. Foreign Office Comment on C.O.S. 45 423 (O), July 3, 1945, FO 371 46440, BNA.

85. Halifax to Foreign Office, July 5, 1945, FO 371 46440, BNA.

86. CCS 890, "Control and Command in the War against Japan," July 9, 1945, TERMINAL Conference Volume, pp. 149–151, Box 3, Combined Chiefs of Staff Proceedings, Eisenhower Presidential Library, Abilene, Kansas.

87. Chiefs of Staff to Field-Marshal Wilson, WO 193 304, BNA.

Chapter 13. MacArthur and Mountbatten

1. Memorandum for the President, July 6, 1945, *FRUS: Berlin*, vol. 1, 228.

2. Marcel Vigneras, *United States Army in World War II: Special Studies: Rearming the French* (Washington, D.C.: Government Printing Office, 1957), 396–399.

3. Marshall to MacArthur, July 7, 1945, Folder: CCS 370 Great Britain (7-15-44)

S. 1, Box 82, Geographic File, 1942–1945, Records of the Joint Chiefs of Staff, Record Group 218, USNA.

4. D. Clayton James, *The Years of MacArthur*, vol. 1, *1880–1941* (Boston: Houghton Mifflin, 1970), 14–15, 44, 96; Kenneth Ray Young, *The General's General: The Life and Times of Arthur MacArthur* (Boulder, Colo.: Westview Press, 1994).

5. James, *Years of MacArthur*, vol. 1, 44–46; Geoffrey Perret, *Old Soldiers Never Die: The Life of Douglas MacArthur* (New York: Random House, 1996), 145.

6. Perret, *Old Soldiers Never Die*, 37–39, 44–45.

7. Ibid., 54–55; James, *Years of MacArthur*, vol. 1, 96–97.

8. Perret, *Old Soldiers Never Die*, 70–73; James, *Years of MacArthur*, vol. 1, 118–125.

9. Perret, *Old Soldiers Never Die*, 92–95, 108–110; James, *Years of MacArthur*, vol. 1, 217–223, 238–239.

10. James, *Years of MacArthur*, vol. 1, 263–265.

11. Perret, *Old Soldiers Never Die*, 121–124.

12. Ibid., 125–127, 136–137.

13. Ibid., 125–127, 136–139; James, *Years of MacArthur*, vol. 1, 322–324.

14. Perret, *Old Soldiers Never Die*, 154–161; James, *Years of MacArthur*, vol. 1, 343–344, 358, 402–404.

15. Perret, *Old Soldiers Never Die*, 192–193; James, *Years of MacArthur*, vol. 1, 494–495, 554–555.

16. James, *Years of MacArthur*, vol. 2, 1–15, 100–103, 130–132; Perret, *Old Soldiers Never Die*, 226–229, 248–252, 272–273; Spector, *Eagle against the Sun*, 107–119; William H. Bartsch, *December 8, 1941: MacArthur's Pearl Harbor* (College Station: Texas A&M University Press, 2003), 409–410.

17. James, *Years of MacArthur*, vol. 2, 115, 171–173, 256, 375; Perret, *Old Soldiers Never Die*, 285.

18. James, *Years of MacArthur*, vol. 2, 349–353, 464–465; Spector, *Eagle against the Sun*, 142–147.

19. James, *Years of MacArthur*, vol. 2, 464–465; Spector, *Eagle against the Sun*, 227–229, 232–233, 242–247, 282–287, 291–294, 417–442; Thomas E. Griffith, Jr., *MacArthur's Airman: General George C. Kenney and the War in the Southwest Pacific* (Lawrence: University Press of Kansas, 1998), 92–96.

20. Memorandum by the United States Chiefs of Staff, July 18, 1945, *FRUS: Berlin*, vol. 2, 1336.

21. Ibid.

22. Ibid.

23. Chiefs of Staff to Mountbatten, July 5, 1945, PREM 8 29, PRO; Bonner Fellers Office Diary, July 11, 1945, Folder 27, Box 5, Office of the Military Secretary Diary, Record Group 44, MM.

24. Ziegler, *Mountbatten*, 22–24, 29–30, 44, 36; Robert K. Massie, *Castles of Steel: Britain, Germany, and the Winning of the Great War at Sea* (New York: Random House, 2003), 163–178.

25. Ziegler, *Mountbatten*, 67–70.

26. Ibid., 106–117, 483–484.

27. Ibid., 92, 98, 122; Sir Ian McGeoch, *The Princely Sailor: Mountbatten of Burma* (London: Brassey's, 1996), 19–21.

28. Ziegler, *Mountbatten*, 126, 128–131, 143–146; Christopher Langtree, *The Kelly's: British J, K and N Class Destroyers of World War II* (Annapolis, Md.: Naval Institute Press, 2002), 71.

29. Ziegler, *Mountbatten*, 2; Ronald Atkin, *Dieppe, 1942: The Jubilee Disaster* (London: Macmillan, 1980); T. Murray Hunter, *Canada at Dieppe* (Toronto: Balmur, 1982); Brian Loring Villa, *Unauthorized Action: Mountbatten and the Dieppe Raid* (New York: Oxford University Press, 1989).

30. Ziegler, *Mountbatten*, 217.

31. Ibid., 227–249; Louis Allen, *Burma: The Longest War, 1941–45* (London: J. M. Dent, 1984), 1–21.

32. Allen, *Burma*, 191–315; Ziegler, *Mountbatten*, 268–277; McGeoch, *Princely Sailor*, 111–112, 115, 121, 125.

33. McGeoch, *Princely Sailor*, 113, 116–117, 122, 126, 132, 135; John Atkins, *A Model for Modern Nonlinear Noncontiguous Operations: The War in Burma, 1943 to 1945*, School of Advanced Military Studies Monograph Series (Fort Leavenworth, Kans.: School of Advanced Military Studies, 2003), 22, 28–29.

34. James Webb, *The Emperor's General* (New York: Bantam Books, 2000); Ziegler, *Mountbatten*, 297; Philip Ziegler, ed., *Personal Diary of Admiral The Lord Louis Mountbatten Supreme Allied Commander, South-East Asia, 1943–1946* (London: Collins, 1988), 225; James, *Years of MacArthur*, vol. 2, 662; Bonner Fellers Office Diary, July 14, 1945, Folder 27, Box 5, Office of the Military Secretary Diary, Record Group 44, MM.

35. Mountbatten wrote two memos documenting this trip. Both basically cover the same events and repeat the same information. Except for this initial exchange it is difficult to tell from Mountbatten's accounts what was discussed on July 12 and on July 14. His narrative runs together in both memos, which is understandable since he was writing after his stay in the Philippines and not immediately after each event. Using Fellers's diary as an additional source, it appears that the luncheon focused mainly on Singapore and that the conversation at dinner was about OLYMPIC and CORONET. The topic of conversation of each meal would be an exceptionally minor point except for the fact that in Mountbatten's two accounts, he has MacArthur giving two different figures for Operation: OLYMPIC. Mountbatten might have been mistaken when he wrote one of his memos, or MacArthur might have mentioned two different numbers. Mountbatten provides no explanation as to why there are two different figures in these two memos. Bonner Fellers Office Diary, July 14, 1945, Folder 27, Box 5, Office of the Military Secretary Diary, Record Group 44, MM; "Record of Conversations with General of the Army Douglas MacArthur (Commander-in-Chief, U.S. Army Forces Pacific) at His Headquarters in Manila on 12th, 13th and 14th July," and "Notes of Statements made by General MacArthur at Luncheon on the 12th July and at a Dinner on 14th July," MB1/C213, Mountbatten Papers.

36. Ziegler, *Personal Diary of Admiral The Lord Louis Mountbatten*, 222.

37. Bonner Fellers Office Diary, July 14, 1945, Folder 27, Box 5, Office of the Military Secretary Diary, Record Group 44, MM; "Record of Conversations with General of the Army Douglas MacArthur (Commander-in-Chief, U.S. Army Forces Pacific) at His Headquarters in Manila on 12th, 13th and 14th July," and "Notes of Statements made by General MacArthur at Luncheon on the 12th July and at a Dinner on 14th July," MB1/C213, Mountbatten Papers.

38. Letter, Eichelberger to Eichelberger, March 4, 1945, Robert L. Eichelberger, *Dear Miss Em: General Eichelberger's War in the Pacific, 1942–1945*, Jay Luvaas, ed. (Westport, Conn.: Greenwood Press, 1972), 230; Diary entry, March 31, 1945, Weldon Rhoads, *Flying MacArthur to Victory* (College Station: Texas A&M University Press, 1987), 372.

39. Bonner Fellers Office Diary, July 14, 1945, Folder 27, Box 5, Office of the Military Secretary Diary, Record Group 44, MM; "Record of Conversations with General of the Army Douglas MacArthur (Commander-in-Chief, U.S. Army Forces Pacific) at His Headquarters in Manila on 12th, 13th and 14th July," and "Notes of Statements made by General MacArthur at Luncheon on the 12th July and at a Dinner on 14th July," MB1/C213, Mountbatten Papers.

40. Mountbatten to MacArthur, August 16, 1945, MB1/C169, Mountbatten Papers.

41. James, *Years of MacArthur*, vol. 2, 765, 774.

42. "British Contribution to the Final Phase of the War against Japan Report by the Joint Staff Planners," no date, Folder: CCS 370 Great Britain (7–15–44) S. 1, Box 82, Geographic File, 1942–1945, Records of the Joint Chiefs of Staff, Record Group 218, USNA.

Chapter 14. The British Pacific Fleet Visits Japan

1. Gray, *Operation Pacific*, 236–237; Vian, *Action This Day*, 197; Notes, June 30, 1945, Folder: Conferences 1944–1945, Box 20, King Papers.

2. Vian, *Action This Day*, 197; John Winton, *The Forgotten Fleet* (London: Michael Joseph, 1969), 308–309, 333.

3. Winton, *Forgotten Fleet*, 308–309.

4. Ibid., 310.

5. Ibid.

6. Clark G. Reynolds, "William F. Halsey, Jr.: The Bull," in Sweetman, *Great Admirals*, 483; *Time*, November 30, 1942, and July 23, 1945; E. B. Potter, *Bull Halsey* (Annapolis, Md.: Naval Institute Press, 1985), 175.

7. Potter, *Halsey*, 25–32.

8. Potter, *Halsey*, 87–101, 110–111, 125–132; Reynolds, "Halsey," 484.

9. Reynolds, "Halsey," 485.

10. Ibid., 483, 485, 486.

11. Ibid., 487–488.

12. Ibid., 489–497; Potter, *Halsey*, 288.

13. Reynolds, "Halsey," 499–500; Buckner F. Melton, Jr., *Sea Cobra: Admiral Halsey's Task Force and the Great Pacific Typhoon* (Guilford, Conn.: Lyons Press,

2007); Bob Drury and Tom Clavin, *Halsey's Typhoon: The True Story of a Fighting Admiral, an Epic Storm, and an Untold Rescue* (New York: Atlantic Monthly Press, 2007).

14. William F. Halsey, *Admiral Halsey's Story* (New York: McGraw-Hill, 1947), 261–262; Reynolds, "Halsey," 484.

15. Halsey, *Admiral Halsey's Story*, 261–262; Vian, *Action This Day*, 193; COM3RDFLT to CINCPAC ADV, June 16, 1945, vol. 1 Command Summary, book 6, vol. 3, p. 3177, Folder: 3076–3194, Nimitz Papers.

16. CINCPAC ADV to COM3RDFLT, June 17, 1945, vol. 1 Command Summary, book 6, vol. 3, p. 3178, Folder: 3076–3194, Nimitz Papers; Ministry of Defence (Navy), *War with Japan*, vol. 6, *The Advance to Japan* (London: Her Majesty's Stationery Office, 1995), 213.

17. Halsey, *Admiral Halsey's Story*, 261–262; Vian, *Action This Day*, 193.

18. Halsey, *Admiral Halsey's Story*, 262; Vian, *Action This Day*, 193; Winton, *Forgotten Fleet*, 313.

19. Winton, *Forgotten Fleet*, 385, fn. 1.

20. Ibid.; *New York Times*, July 17, 23, 1945.

21. Baker, *Dry Ginger*, 77–78, 82, Halsey, *Admiral Halsey's Story*, 262; Winton, *Forgotten Fleet*, 282–283, fn. 1.

22. Willmott, *Grave of a Dozen Schemes*, 142–143.

23. Smith, *Task Force 57*, 172–175; Winton, *Forgotten Fleet*, 316; Vian, *Action This Day*, 203; Ministry of Defence (Navy), *Advance to Japan*, 220–221.

24. Emphasis in original quotation in Winton, *Forgotten Fleet*, 322; Crosley, *Seafire*, 167.

25. Ministry of Defence (Navy), *Advance to Japan*, 222; Winton, *Forgotten Fleet*, 319–320; Vian, *Action This Day*, 208.

26. Halsey, *Admiral Halsey's Story*, 264; S. W. Roskill, *History of the Second World War: The War at Sea, 1939–1945*, vol. 3, pt. 2, *The Offensive, 1st June 1944–14th August 1945* (London: Her Majesty's Stationery Office, 1961), 374–375; Ministry of Defence (Navy), *Advance to Japan*, 222–224; Gray, *Operation Pacific*, 244–245.

27. Halsey, *Admiral Halsey's Story*, 265.

28. Vian, *Action This Day*, 205; Roskill, *War at Sea*, vol. 3, pt. 2, 375.

29. Halsey, *Admiral Halsey's Story*, 265. McCain was the founder of a dynasty within the U.S. Navy. His son also became a four-star admiral, making the McCains one of only two father-son teams to earn the four stars of an admiral in U.S. naval history. The younger McCain's son, John, is the best-known McCain of all, having run for president of the United States in 2000 and 2008.

30. Winton, *Forgotten Fleet*, 325–326; Vian, *Action This Day*, 208; Stephen Conrad Geneja, *The Cruiser Uganda* (Ontario: Tyendinaga, 1994), 229.

31. Ministry of Defence (Navy), *Advance to Japan*, 224–225; Winton, *Forgotten Fleet*, 327–329.

32. Winton, *Forgotten Fleet*, 329–330; Vian, *Action This Day*, 204.

33. Vian, *Action This Day*, 211–212; Ministry of Defence (Navy), *Advance to Japan*, 225–226.

34. Winton, *Forgotten Fleet*, 335–338.

35. Ibid., 337–338; Gray, *Operation Pacific*, 250.

36. "Commander-in-Chief's Dispatches—November 1944 to July 1945," November 23, 1945, ADM 199/118, BNA.

Chapter 15. Codename: TERMINAL

1. Leahy, *I Was There*, 451–452.

2. Diary of Sir Andrew Cunningham, July 15, 16, 17, 1945, ADD 52578, Cunningham Papers.

3. Leahy, *I Was There*, 409.

4. Diary of Sir Andrew Cunningham, July 16, 1945, ADD 52578, Cunningham Papers.

5. "Note of the Prime Minister's Conversation with President Truman," July 18, 1945, PREM 3/430/8, BNA.

6. Ferrell, *Off the Record*, 51; Jenkins, *Churchill*, 785; Diary of Sir Andrew Cunningham, July 23, 1945, ADD 52578, Cunningham Papers.

7. Meeting of the Joint Chiefs of Staff, July 17, 1945, *FRUS: Berlin,* vol. 2, 39–41.

8. Memorandum by the United States Chiefs of Staff, July 17, 1945; Memorandum by the United States Chiefs of Staff, July 17, 1945, *FRUS: Berlin,* vol. 2, 1313–1314, 1334–1337.

9. Combined Chiefs of Staff Minutes, July 17, 1945, *FRUS: Berlin,* vol. 2, 48–51.

10. Lord Alanbrooke, *War Diaries*, 706.

11. Joint Planning Staff, "British Participation in the War against Japan," July 31, 1945, WO 107/118, BNA; Halifax to Churchill and Eden, August 26, 1944, FE/44/114, Folios 177–263, vol. 7, Avon Papers.

12. Joint Planning Staff, "British Participation in the War against Japan," July 31, 1945, WO 107/118, BNA; Halifax to Churchill and Eden, August 26, 1944, FE/44/114, Folios 177–263, vol. 7, Avon Papers.

13. Joint Chiefs of Staff to MacArthur, July 22, 1945, Folder 4, Box 17, Series 2, Record Group 4, MM.

14. Memorandum by the United States Chiefs of Staff, July 17, 1945, Memorandum by the United States Chiefs of Staff, July 18, 1945, *FRUS: Berlin,* vol. 2, 1313–1314, 1334–1337.

15. Memorandum by the British Chiefs of Staff, July 18, 1945, *FRUS: Berlin,* vol. 2, 1315–1316.

16. Diary of Sir Alan Brooke, July 18, 1945, 5/1/11 Alanbrooke Papers; Combined Chiefs of Staff Minutes, 195th Meeting, July 18, 1945, Combined Chiefs of Staff Conference Proceedings, Terminal Conference Volume, pages 279–284, Box 3, Eisenhower Presidential Library, Abilene, Kansas.

17. Diary of Sir Andrew Cunningham, July 18, 1945, ADD 52578, Cunningham Papers.

18. Report to the President and Prime Minister of the Agreed Summary of the Conclusions Reached by the Combined Chiefs of Staff at the "Terminal" Conference, July 24, 1945, *FRUS: Berlin*, vol. 2, 1462–1464.

19. Lord Alanbrooke, *War Diaries*, 708–709; Winton, *Cunningham*, 375–376.

20. Diary of Sir Andrew Cunningham, July 18, 1945, ADD 52578, Cunningham Papers; Gilbert, *Churchill*, 852.

21. Arnold, *Global Mission*, 582–584; Lord Alanbrooke, *War Diaries*, 705–707, 710; Diary of Sir Andrew Cunningham, July 16–17, 1945, ADD 52578, Cunningham Papers.

22. Lord Alanbrooke, *War Diaries*, 710; Diary of Sir Andrew Cunningham, July 23, 1945, ADD 52578, Cunningham Papers.

23. Diary of Sir Andrew Cunningham, July 24, 1945, ADD 52578, Cunningham Papers.

24. Lord Alanbrooke, *War Diaries*, 711.

25. Gilbert, *Churchill*, 852–855.

26. Jenkins, *Churchill*, 799; Gilbert, *Churchill*, 855–856.

27. Lord Alanbrooke, *War Diaries*, 712.

28. Lord Alanbrooke, *War Diaries*, 720; Arnold to Portal, November 14, 1945, Box A, File IV, Portal Papers.

29. Prime Minister to Prime Ministers of Canada, Australia, New Zealand, and South Africa, July 31, 1945, PREM 8/29, BNA.

Chapter 16. Australia and New Zealand

1. Churchill to Curtin, July 4, 1945, *Documents on Australian Foreign Policy, 1937–49*, vol. 3, *1945* (Canberra: Australian Government Publishing Service, 1989), 236–238 [hereafter *DAFP*].

2. Paul Hasluck, *Australia in the War of 1939–1945*, Series 4 (Civil), vol. 2, *The Government and the People, 1942–1945* (Canberra: Australian War Memorial, 1970), 562.

3. Hasluck, *Government and the People*, 566–567.

4. Day, *John Curtin*, 555, 559, 560; Horner, *Defence Supremo*, 216.

5. Day, *John Curtin*, 556–557, 559, 560, 565, 567–568, 570–571, 573–574.

6. Blamey to Acting Minister for the Army, May 16, 1945, John Robertson and John McCarthy, *Australian War Strategy, 1939–1945: A Documentary History* (St. Lucia: University of Queensland Press, 1985), 422; Blamey to Acting Minister for the Army, May 16, 1945, Series A5954, Item 570/7, Shedden Papers.

7. Minutes of the War Cabinet Meeting, May 22, 1945; Minutes of the War Cabinet Meeting, May 28, 1945, Series A5954, Item 811/1, Shedden Papers.

8. War Cabinet Minute (4220) "Review of the Direct War Effort. The Service Manpower Position," May 31, 1945; War Cabinet Minute (4237) "Review of the Direct War Effort—The Service Manpower Position," June 5, 1945, 3DRL/6643, Series 2/18, Blamey Papers.

9. Blamey to Acting Minister for the Army, May 16, 1945, Robertson and McCarthy, *Australian War Strategy*, 423–424; Horner, *Defence Supremo*, 227; David Horner, *Inside the War Cabinet: Directing Australia's War Effort, 1939–45* (St. Leonards, Australia: Allen & Unwin, 1996), 182.

10. Horner, *Defence Supremo*, 228.

11. Ibid.

12. Ibid.

13. Ibid., 229; Shedden to MacArthur, July 21, 1945, Folder: Australian Govt., 25 April–1 August 45, Box 4, Record Group 4, MM.

14. Horner, *Defence Supremo*, 229–230.

15. *Sydney Morning Herald*, July 9, 1945; Day, *John Curtin*, 575–576; Hasluck, *Government and the People*, 588.

16. David Day, *Chifley* (Sydney: HarperCollins, 2001), 86, 92–94, 104, 155–157, 212, 239, 240, 259–260, 296–297, 415.

17. Ibid., 1–3, 86, 88–94, 104, 155–157, 160–162, 173–176, 204–208, 212, 233, 239, 240, 258–260, 278–279, 296–297, 326, 351–353, 370–376, 386–388, 411, 415, 533.

18. Horner, *Defence Supremo*, 231; Hetherington, *Blamey*, 367–368, 372–373; Horner, *Blamey*, 543, 546, 548–549.

19. Horner, *Blamey*, 548; Day, *Chifley*, 546–551; MacArthur to Chifley, May 20, 1945; Chifley to MacArthur, July 21, 1945; Shedden to MacArthur, July 21, 1945, Folder: Australian Govt., 25 April–1 August 45, Box 4, Record Group 4, MM.

20. Horner, *Blamey*, 548; Day, *Chifley*, 546–551; MacArthur to Chifley, May 20, 1945; Chifley to MacArthur, July 21, 1945; Shedden to MacArthur, July 21, 1945, Folder: Australian Govt., 25 April–1 August 45, Box 4, Record Group 4, MM.

21. Horner, *Blamey*, 548; Day, *Chifley*, 546–551; MacArthur to Chifley, May 20, 1945; Chifley to MacArthur, July 21, 1945; Shedden to MacArthur, July 21, 1945, Folder: Australian Govt., 25 April–1 August 45, Box 4, Record Group 4, MM.

22. "Extract from the Journals of the H. of R.," July 9, 1940; "Extract from the Journals of the H. of R.," August 24, 1944, EA1 87/25/1, Records of the Department of External Affairs and Trade, NANZ.

23. Ian Wards, "Peter Fraser—Warrior Prime Minister," in Margaret Clark, ed., *Peter Fraser: Master Politician* (Palmerston North, New Zealand: Dunmore Press, 1998), 154; Bassett and King, *Tomorrow Comes the Song*, 306; "Outbreak of War," September 4, 1939; "Speech Delivered by Rt. Hon. M. J. Savage," September 5, 1939, EA1 87/25/1, Records of the Department of External Affairs and Trade, NANZ.

24. *New Zealand Parliamentary Debates*, vol. 268, 2nd Session, 27th Parliament (Wellington: E. V. Paul, 1946), 425; Speech notes, August 2, 1945, EA1 87/25/1, Records of the Department of External Affairs and Trade, NANZ.

25. Wards, "Peter Fraser," 152, 154; *New Zealand Parliamentary Debates*, 847; Speech notes, August 2, 1945, EA1 87/25/1; Nash to Prime Minister, April 7, 1945, EA1 83/1/13, Records of the Department of External Affairs and Trade, NANZ.

26. James Thorn, *Peter Fraser: New Zealand's Wartime Prime Minister* (London: Odhams Press, 1952), 141; Michael Ashby, "Fraser's Foreign Policy," in Clark, *Peter Fraser: Master Politician*, 178, 185; Bassett and King, *Tomorrow Comes the Song*, 297.

27. Prime Minister of the United Kingdom to the Prime Minister of New Zealand, January 27, 1945, *Documents Relating to New Zealand's Participation in the Second World War, 1939–45*, vol. 3 (Wellington: War History Branch, Department of Internal Affairs, 1963), 462–463 [hereafter *DRNZPSWW*].

28. Paul Freyberg, *Bernard Freyberg, VC: Soldier of Two Nations* (London: Hodder & Stoughton, 1991), 7–10, 14, 64, 94–95, 102, 132, 147.

29. Ibid., 175–176, 180–190, 197–199.

30. Ibid., 200–202; Bassett and King, *Tomorrow Comes the Song*, 175–177.

31. Paul Freyberg, *Bernard Freyberg, VC*, 201–203, 216–217; Bassett and King, *Tomorrow Comes the Song*, 179.

32. Freyberg to Prime Minister, February 17, 1945, WAII 8/78, Freyberg Papers.

33. Freyberg to Prime Minister, February 19, 1945, WAII 8/78, Freyberg Papers.

34. Appreciation of the Chief of the General Staff, January 31, 1945, EA1 87/25/1, Records of the Department of External Affairs and Trade, NANZ.

35. Keith Sinclair, *Walter Nash* (Auckland: Auckland University Press, 1976), 14–16, 70–71, 85, 89.

36. Prime Minister of the United Kingdom to the Prime Minister of New Zealand, January 27, 1945; Nash to Fraser, April 7, 1945, New Zealand Military Liaison Officer to the Prime Minister, May 21, 1945, Prime Minister to Nash, April 20, 1945, *DRNZPSWW*, 463–466, 471–472, 475.

37. Nash to Fraser, April 7, 1945; Nash to Fraser, April 7, 1945, *DRNZPSWW*, 464–468.

38. Freyberg to the Acting Prime Minister, April 11, 1945; Freyberg to the Minister of Defence, May 15, 1945; Freyberg to the Acting Prime Minister, May 27, 1945, *DRNZPSWW*, 468–470, 473–474, 477–480.

39. Freyberg to the Acting Prime Minister, April 11, 1945; Freyberg to the Minister of Defence, May 15, 1945; Freyberg to the Acting Prime Minister, May 27, 1945, *DRNZPSWW*, 468–470, 473–474, 477–480.

40. Manpower Position in Relation to the War against Japan, no date; General Officer Commanding, First Australian Army to Isitt, June 30, 1945; Kenney to Commander, Royal New Zealand Air Force, June 26, 1945; Military Effort in the War against Japan, June 6, 1945; Nash to Fraser, June 9, 1945, EA 1 87/25/1, Records of the Department of External Affairs and Trade, NANZ.

41. Edward Puttick, "Appreciation of Situation by the Chief of the General Staff Regarding Future Participation on N.Z. Army Forces in the War against Japan," June 1, 1945; C. G. Goss, "Considerations and Estimated Manpower Required for Expediting Forces of Varying Sizes," June 4, 1945, EA 1 87/25/1, Records of the Department of External Affairs and Trade, NANZ.

42. Nancy M. Taylor, *Official History of New Zealand in the Second World War, 1939–45: The New Zealand People at War: The Home Front*, vol. 2 (Wellington: V. R. Ward, Government Printer, 1986), 1260; Nash to Fraser, June 9, 1945; Acting Prime Minister to Freyberg, June 9, 1945, EA1 87/25/1, Records of the Department of External Affairs and Trade, NANZ.

43. Acting Prime Minister to Freyberg, June 9, 1945; Freyberg to the Acting Prime Minister, June 14, 1945; Acting Prime Minister to Freyberg, June 21, 1945; Acting Prime Minister to the Secretary of State for Dominion Affairs, June 21, 1945; Acting Prime Minister to Freyberg, July 4, 1945, *DRNZPSWW*, 480–487.

44. Prime Minister of the United Kingdom to the Prime Minister of New Zealand, July 5, 1945; Prime Minister of New Zealand to the Prime Minister of the United Kingdom, July 14, 1945, *DRNZPSWW*, 488–489; Prime Minister's Report to the House of Representatives on His Visit Overseas, August 7, 1944, EA1 153/20/11, Records of the Department of External Affairs and Trade, NANZ.

45. Freyberg to the Prime Minister, August 7, 1945, *DRNZPSWW*, 494.

46. Nash to Fraser, May 30, 1945, EA1 87/25/1, Records of the Department of External Affairs and Trade, NANZ.

47. Wellington *Dominion*, June 20, 1945; Nash to Fraser, May 30, 1945, EA1 87/25/1, Records of the Department of External Affairs and Trade, NANZ.

48. *New Zealand Herald*, June 19, 1945; *Dominion* (Wellington), June 19, 1945; *Evening Post* (Wellington), June 20, 1945; *Otago Daily Times*, June 21, 1945.

49. Bassett and King, *Tomorrow Comes the Song*, 306.

50. Thorn, *Peter Fraser*, 141; Ashby, "Fraser's Foreign Policy," 178, 185; Bassett and King, *Tomorrow Comes the Song*, 297.

51. *Dominion* (Wellington), August 3, 1945; *New Zealand Parliamentary Debates*, 823.

52. *New Zealand Parliamentary Debates*, 823–834.

53. Ibid., 834–846.

54. Ibid., 846–877; Bassett and King, *Tomorrow Comes the Song*, 297.

55. *New Zealand Parliamentary Debates*, 877–879.

56. Prime Minister to the Secretary of State for Dominion Affairs, August 4, 1945, *DRNZPSWW*, 491.

Chapter 17. Let This Day Be Done

1. Wood to Lincoln, April 24, 1945; JCS 1198/1: "Canadian Army Participation in the War against Japan," no date, Folder: ABC 381 Canada (18 Sept 44), Box 407, ABC Files, Office of the Director of Plans and Operations, Records of the War Department General and Special Staffs, Record Group 165, USNA.

2. C. P. Stacey, *Official History of the Canadian Army in the Second World War*, vol. 1, *Six Years of War: The Army in Canada, Britain and the Pacific* (Ottawa: Cloutier, Queen's Printer, 1957), 516–517.

3. Stacey, *Six Years of War*, 517; C. P. Stacey, *The Canadian Army, 1939–1945: An Official Historical Summary* (Ottawa: Cloutier, King's Printer, 1948), 291.

4. "Proposed Basis for Planning Canadian Participation in the War against Japan" attached to McFarland to Letson, May 16, 1945, Folder: ABC 381 Canada (18 Sept 44), Box 407, ABC Files, Office of the Director of Plans and Operations, Records of the War Department General and Special Staffs, Record Group 165, USNA.

5. Stacey, *Six Years of War*, 515–516; Stanley W. Dziuban, *United States Army in World War II: Special Studies: Military Relations between the United States and Canada* (Washington, D.C.: Government Printing Office, 1959), 270. For more on the Aleutian campaign, see Galen Perras, *Stepping Stones to Nowhere: The Aleutian Islands, Alaska, and American Military Strategy, 1867–1945* (Vancouver: University of British Columbia Press, 2003).

6. Perras, "No Need to Send an Army across the Pacific," 147.

7. Memorandum by the United States Chiefs of Staff (CCS 691/1); Note on JCS 1120 British Participation in V.L.R. Bombing of Japan, October 26, 1944, Folder: CCS 373.11 Japan (9-18-44) Sec. 1, Box 114, Geographic File, 1942–1945, Records of the U.S. Joint Chiefs of Staff, Record Group 218, USNA.

8. Kuter to Arnold, February 1, 1945, Folder: CCS 373.11 Japan (9-18-44) Sec. 1, Box 114, Geographic File, 1942–1945, Records of the U.S. Joint Chiefs of Staff, Record Group 218, USNA.

9. Thorne, *Allies of a Kind*, 524.

10. MacArthur to War Department, April 10, 1944, Folder: CCS 373.11 Japan (9-18-44) Sec. 1, Box 114, Geographic File, 1942–1945, Records of the U.S. Joint Chiefs of Staff, Record Group 218, USNA.

11. British Participation in V.L.R. Bombing of Japan: Report by the Joint Staff Planners, April 17, 1945, Folder CCS 373.11 Japan (9-18-44) Sec.1, Box 114, Geographic File, 1942–1945, Records of the U.S. Joint Chiefs of Staff, Record Group 218, USNA.

12. Joint Planning Staff Minutes, April 18, 25, 1945, Folder CCS 373.11 Japan (9-18-44) Sec.1, Box 114, Geographic File, 1942–1945, Records of the U.S. Joint Chiefs of Staff, Record Group 218, USNA.

13. Message from the British Chiefs of Staff to the United States Chiefs of Staff, May 2, 1945, Folder CCS 373.11 Japan (9-18-44) Sec.1, Box 114, Geographic File, 1942–1945, Records of the U.S. Joint Chiefs of Staff, Record Group 218, USNA; Diary of Simon Bolivar Buckner, Jr., April 27, 1945, Box 1, Buckner Papers (Kans.).

14. Joint Planning Staff Minutes, May 2, 1945, Folder CCS 373.11 Japan (9-18-44) Sec.1, Box 114, Geographic File, 1942–1945, Records of the U.S. Joint Chiefs of Staff, Record Group 218, USNA.

15. British Participation in V.L.R. Bombing of Japan: Report by the Joint Staff Planners, no date, Folder CCS 373.11 Japan (9-18-44) Sec.1, Box 114, Geographic File, 1942–1945, Records of the U.S. Joint Chiefs of Staff, Record Group 218, USNA.

16. Joint Planning Staff Minutes, May 9, 1945; Memorandum by the United States Chiefs of Staff, May 29, 1945; British Participation in V.L.R. Bombing of Japan: Note by the Secretaries, May 30, 1945, Folder CCS 373.11 Japan (9-18-44) Sec.1, Box 114, Geographic File, 1942–1945, Records of the U.S. Joint Chiefs of Staff, Record Group 218, USNA.

17. Ibid.

18. Memorandum by the United States Chiefs of Staff, July 17, 1945, *FRUS: Berlin*, vol. 2, 1335.

19. Memorandum by the Representatives of the British Chiefs of Staff, June 5, 1945, Folder CCS 373.11 Japan (9-18-44) Sec.1, Box 114, Geographic File, 1942–1945, Records of the U.S. Joint Chiefs of Staff, Record Group 218, USNA.

20. Arnold to MacArthur and Richardson, June 2, 1945; MacArthur to War Department, June 6, 1945; CINCPOA (Nimitz) to COMINCH (King), June 7, 1945, Folder CCS 373.11 Japan (9-18-44) Sec.1, Box 114, Geographic File, 1942–1945, Records of the U.S. Joint Chiefs of Staff, Record Group 218, USNA.

21. Mountbatten to British Chiefs of Staff, June 6 1945, AIR 8/1278, BNA.

22. Memorandum by the United States Chiefs of Staff, July 17, 1945, *FRUS: Berlin*, vol. 2, 1335; Commanding General, Pacific Ocean Areas, Guam to Arnold, June 16, 1945; Arnold to War Department, June 17, 1945, Folder CCS 373.11 Japan (9-18-44) Sec.1, Box 114, Geographic File, 1942–1945, Records of the U.S. Joint Chiefs of Staff, Record Group 218, USNA.

23. John Ehrman, *Grand Strategy*, vol. 6, *October 1944–August 1945*, 235, 263; Arnold, *Global Mission*, 573.

24. Arnold, *Global Mission*, 527.

25. "British Participation in the War against Japan Memorandum by the Foreign Secretary," August 8, 1945, PREM 8 29; indecipherable to Sterndale-Bennett, August 3, 1945 (emphasis in the original); "British Participation in the War against Japan," August 8, 1945, FO 371 46440, BNA.

26. Gilbert, *Churchill*, 857.

27. Wilson to Brooke, June 12, 1945, 6/2/51, Alanbrooke Papers; Chiefs of Staff Committee, "British Participation in the War against Japan," June 30, 1945; Prime Minister to Prime Minister, August 4, 1945, PREM 8 29, BNA.

28. Allen and Polmar, *Code-Name* DOWNFALL, 303; Prime Minister to Prime Minister, August 9, 1945, Air1 130/34/1, Records of the Air Department, NANZ.

29. "British Participation in the War against Japan," August 9, 1945, Folder: CCS 370 Great Britain (7-15-44) S.2, Box 82, Geographic File, Records of the U.S. Joint Chiefs of Staff, 1942–1945, Record Group 218, USNA.

30. Bruce to Forde, July 7, 1945, *DAFP*, 242–243; Horner, *Blamey*, 546.

31. Horner, *Blamey*, 546; Proposed Draft Signal attached to C-in-C, AMF to CGS, July 13, 1945; Minute by the Defence Committee, July 13, 1945, 3DRL/6643, Series 2/17, Blamey Papers.

32. Minutes of Advisory War Council Meeting, July 19, 1945, Minutes of Advisory War Council Meetings, vol. 8, series A5954, item 815/2, Shedden Papers.

33. Prime Minister to the Prime Minister, July 20, 1945, CHAR 20/222/48–49, CAC.

34. Prime Minister to the Prime Minister of Australia, July 26, 1945, CHAR 20/222/53, CAC.

35. Report by the British Joint Planning Staff, July 23, 1945; Minutes of a Meeting of the British Chiefs of Staff Committee, July 24, 1945, Rohan Butler, M. E. Pelly, and H. J. Yasamee; *Documents on British Policy Overseas*, series 1, vol. 1, *The Conference at Potsdam, July–August 1945* (London: Her Majesty's Stationery Office, 1984), 610–613.

36. Sir Frederick Shedden, *The History of Australian Defence Policy* manuscript, pages 5 and 10, Folder: Book (Original) Chapter 54—A British Commonwealth Force to Share the Assault on Japan and Changes in the South West Pacific Area, A5954/77/1/9, Shedden Papers.

37. "The Future Strength and Role of the Australian Forces and their Operational Control Statement by Prime Minister in House of Representatives," July 27, 1945, 3DRL/6643/2/17, Blamey Papers.

38. Ibid.

39. Ibid.

40. Ibid.

41. Notes of Discussions with Commander-in-Chief, Australian Military Forces, July 31, 1945, A5954/4/4, Shedden Papers.

42. Horner, *Defence Supremo*, 232; Diary of Sir F. H. Berryman, PR 84/370, Berryman Papers.

43. Rourke to Shedden, August 1, 1945, A5954/1615/1, Shedden Papers.

44. Bruce to Chifley, August 10, 1945, 3DRL/6643/2/17, Blamey Papers.

45. Prime Minister to Prime Minister, August 9, 1945, Air1 130/34/1, Records of the Air Department, NANZ.

46. Sir Frederick Shedden, *The History of Australian Defence Policy* manuscript, pages 8 and 9, Folder: Book (Original) Chapter 54—A British Commonwealth Force to Share the Assault on Japan and Changes in the South West Pacific Area, A5954/77/1/9, Shedden Papers.

47. Gavin Long, *Australia in the War of 1939–1945*, Series 1 (Army), vol. 7, *The Final Campaigns* (Canberra: Australian War Memorial, 1963), 549.

48. Joint Planning Staff, "British Participation in the War against Japan," July 31, 1945, WO 107/118, BNA; Conway to Minister of Defence, March 21, 1945, EA1 87/25/1, Records of the Department of External Affairs and Trade, NANZ.

49. Freyberg to Prime Minister, August 3, 1945, *DRNZPSWW*, 490; Lord Alanbrooke, *War Diaries*, 714.

50. "Minutes of a Meeting Held in the War Office (Room 220) at 1130 Hrs Friday 10 Aug 45 to Discuss Problems Arising from the New Zealand Government's Offer of a Two Brigade Division to Take Part in Operation 'Coronet,'" WAII 8/79, Freyberg Papers.

51. Freyberg to Prime Minister, August 9, 1945, WAII 8/79, Freyberg Papers; Lord Alanbrooke, *War Diaries*, 714.

52. Sarantakes, *Seven Stars*, 99.

53. Letter, Eichelberger to Eichelberger, August 15, 1945, Eichelberger, *Dear Miss Em*, 300; Skates, *Invasion of Japan*, 202–203, 227–232; Sarantakes, *Seven Stars*, 102.

Epilogue: In the Still of Peace

1. Fraser, *Alanbrooke*, 512, 514–515, 520, 524, 540–562; Reynolds, *In Command of History*, 406, 514–519.

2. Winton, *Cunningham*, xiii, 384–397.

3. Richards, *Portal of Hungerford*, 341, 349–353, 357, 371–381, 401–402.

4. Gilbert, *Churchill*, 866, 897, 903, 911, 919, 939, 958; Jenkins, *Churchill*, 896.

5. Coffey, *Hap*, 376–388; Davis, *Hap*, 33.

6. Buell, *Master of Sea Power*, 509–512.

7. Adams, *Witness to Power*, 309, 314, 332, 334, 338, 340–341, 345, 346.

8. Cray, *General of the Army*, 553, 585–586, 607–617, 643, 672–673, 706–725, 730–734.

9. Hamby, *Man of the People*, 617, 626–627, 629–630, 633–634.

10. Humble, *Fraser of North Cape*, 278, 290, 301, 304–305, 309, 317–322, 325–327, 330–333, 339; Stanley Sandler, *The Korean War: No Victors, No Vanquished* (Lexington: University Press of Kentucky, 1999), 157–158.

11. Ziegler, *Mountbatten*, 311, 524, 544, 548, 575, 578, 699–700.

12. Dewar, "Wilson," 181–182; Wilson, *Eight Years Overseas*, ix–x, 262–266.

13. Potter, *Bull Halsey*, 365–381.

14. Coffey, *Iron Eagle*, 3, 269, 331–332, 357–359, 438–439, 444–448.

15. D. Clayton James, *The Years of MacArthur*, vol. 3, *Triumph and Disaster, 1945–1964* (Boston: Houghton Mifflin, 1985), 109, 126–131, 476–479, 612–616, 676–679, 686–689.

16. Potter, *Nimitz*, 409, 428, 432, 434, 438, 447–448, 451–452, 454, 472.

17. Buell, *Quiet Warrior*, 379, 386, 394, 401, 422, 428.

18. Horner, *Blamey*, 573, 580–581.

19. Day, *Chifley*, 446–449, 474–475, 488, 497–501, 526, 528.

20. Bassett and King, *Tomorrow Comes the Song*, 300–301, 308–309, 321–325, 334–335, 340–341, 352.

21. Freyberg, *Freyberg, VC*, 462, 507–508, 518, 535–536, 545–546, 559, 563, 572–574.

22. Stacey, *Double Life*, 31, 212, 214, 216, 224; Nolan, *King's War*, 156–157.

23. Sinclair, *Nash*, 278, 281, 302, 304, 320–336, 350, 357, 365–367.

24. Horner, *Defence Supremo*, 264–267, 276–284, 288, 303, 306–307, 326, 334–341, 351–353.

25. Edwin P. Hoyt, *The Last Kamikaze: The Story of Admiral Matome Ugaki* (Westport, Conn.: Praeger, 1993), 203, 207–210; Axell and Kase, *Kamikaze*, 174–178.

Bibliography

Archives

Australia
    Australian War Memorial, Canberra
        Papers of Sir Frank Berryman
        Papers of Sir Thomas Blamey
    National Archives of Australia, Canberra
        Papers of Sir Frederick Shedden

Canada
    National Archives of Canada, Ottawa, Ontario
        Papers of William Lyon Mackenzie King
        Record Group 24: Department of National Defence Records

New Zealand
    National Archives of New Zealand, Wellington
        Records of the Department of External Affairs and Trade
        Papers of the First Baron Freyberg of Wellington, New Zealand, and of Munstead, County Surrey

United Kingdom
    British Library, London
        Papers of Viscount Cunningham of Hyndhope
    British National Archives, Richmond, Surrey
        AIR   Records of the Air Ministry

CAB   Records of the Cabinet Office
FO   Records of the Foreign Office
PREM   Records of the Prime Minister's Office
WO   Records of the War Office
King's College London
    Liddell Hart Centre for Military Archives
        Papers of the First Viscount Alanbrooke of Brookeborough
        Papers of Sir Basil Liddell Hart
        Papers of Baron Ismay of Wormington
London School of Economics and Political Science
    British Library of Political and Economic Science
        Papers of Baron Dalton of Forest and Firth
National Maritime Museum, Greenwich, London
    Papers of Baron Fraser of North Cape
University of Birmingham
    Papers of the First Earl of Avon
University of Cambridge
    Churchill College, Churchill Archives Centre
        Papers of Sir Winston Churchill
        Papers of Sir Ian Jacob
University of Oxford
    Christ Church College, Christ Church Library
        Papers of Viscount Portal of Hungerford
University of Southampton
    Papers of the First Earl Mountbatten of Burma
University of York
    Borthwick Institute
        Papers of the First Earl of Halifax

United States
    Dwight D. Eisenhower Presidential Library, Abilene, Kansas
        Combined Chiefs of Staff Conference Proceedings
            Papers of Simon Bolivar Buckner, Jr.
            Walter Bedell Smith World War II Documents Collection
    Harry S. Truman Presidential Library, Independence, Missouri
        Papers of Charles G. Ross
        Papers of Harry S. Truman
        Naval Aide Files
        White House Confidential File
        White House Official File
    Hoover Institution, Stanford University, Stanford, California
        Papers of Joseph W. Stilwell
    Library of Congress, Washington, D.C.
        Papers of H. H. Arnold

Papers of Ernest King
Papers of William D. Leahy
Papers of Curtis LeMay
MacArthur Memorial, Norfolk, Virginia
Record Group 4: Records from General Headquarters, United States Army Forces, Pacific
Record Group 44: Papers of General Bonner Fellers
U.S. Army Military History Institute, Carlisle Barracks, Carlisle, Pennsylvania
Papers of Simon Bolivar Buckner, Jr.
Papers of Stephan J. Chamberlin
U.S. Military Academy, West Point, New York
Papers of George A. Lincoln
U.S. National Archives, College Park, Maryland
Record Group 165: Records of the War Department General and Special Staffs
Record Group 218: Records of the U.S. Joint Chiefs of Staff
U.S. Naval Historical Center, Washington, D.C.
Papers of Chester Nimitz
University of California at Los Angeles, Film and Television Library
Hearst Newsreel Collection
Virginia Military Institute, Lexington
Marshall Library
Papers of George C. Marshall
Yale University, New Haven, Connecticut
Yale University Library
Papers of Henry L. Stimson

Government Documents

Australia

Department of Foreign Affairs and Trade. *Documents on Australian Foreign Policy, 1937–49,* vol. 8, *1945.* Canberra: Australian Government Publishing Service, 1989.

Canada

Department of External Affairs. *Documents on Canadian External Relations,* vol. 10, pt. 1, *1944–1945.* Ottawa: Queen's Printer and Controller of Stationery, 1987.
Parliament. House of Commons. *Debates,* 19th Parliament, 6th Session, vol. 83. Ottawa: King's Printer, 1945.

New Zealand

Department of Internal Affairs. *Documents Relating to New Zealand's Participation in the Second World War, 1939–45,* vol. 3. Wellington: Government Printer, 1963.
House of Representatives. *New Zealand Parliamentary Debates,* vol. 268, 2nd Session, 27th Parliament. Wellington: E. V. Paul, 1946.

United Kingdom

Butler, Rohan, M. E. Pelly, and H. J. Yasamee. *Documents on British Policy Overseas*, series 1, vol. 1, *The Conference at Potsdam, July–August 1945*. London: Her Majesty's Stationery Office, 1984.

United States

U.S. Army. *Reports of General MacArthur*, vol. 2, pt. 2, *Japanese Operations in the Southwest Pacific Area*. Washington, D.C.: Government Printing Office, 1966.

U.S. Congress. *Congressional Record*, 79th Congress, 1st Session, 1945, vol. 91. Washington, D.C.: Government Printing Office, 1945.

U.S. Department of State. *Foreign Relations of the United States: The Conference at Quebec, 1944*. Washington, D.C.: Government Printing Office, 1972.

———. *Foreign Relations of the United States: The Conference of Berlin (The Potsdam Conference), 1945*, vols. 1 and 2. Washington, D.C.: Government Printing Office, 1960.

Official Histories

Australia

AUSTRALIA IN THE WAR OF 1939–1945

Hasluck, Paul. *Australia in the War of 1939–1945*, Series 4 (Civil), vol. 2, *The Government and the People, 1942–1945*. Canberra: Australian War Memorial, 1970.

Long, Gavin. *Australia in the War of 1939–1945*, Series 1 (Army), vol. 7, *The Final Campaigns*. Canberra: Australian War Memorial, 1970.

Canada

Stacey, C. P. *The Canadian Army, 1939–1945: An Official Historical Summary*. Ottawa: King's Printer, 1948.

———. *Official History of the Canadian Army in the Second World War*, vol. 1, *Six Years of War: The Army in Canada, Britain and the Pacific*. Ottawa: Cloutier, Queen's Printer, 1957.

New Zealand

OFFICIAL HISTORY OF NEW ZEALAND IN THE SECOND WORLD WAR, 1939–45

Taylor, Nancy M. *Official History of New Zealand in the Second World War, 1939–45: The New Zealand People at War: The Home Front*, vol. 2. Wellington: V. R. Ward, Government Printer, 1986.

United Kingdom

HISTORY OF THE SECOND WORLD WAR

Ehrman, John. *History of the Second World War: Grand Strategy*, vol. 5, *August 1943–September 1944*. London: Her Majesty's Stationery Office, 1956.

———. *History of the Second World War: Grand Strategy*, vol. 6, *October 1944–August 1945*. London: Her Majesty's Stationery Office, 1956.

Ministry of Defence (Navy). *War with Japan*, vol. 6, *The Advance to Japan*. London: Her Majesty's Stationery Office, 1995.

Roskill, S. W. *History of the Second World War: The War at Sea, 1939–1945*, vol. 3, pt. 2: *The Offensive, 1st June 1944–14th August 1945*. London: Her Majesty's Stationery Office, 1961.

United States

Atkins, John. *A Model for Modern Nonlinear Noncontiguous Operations: The War in Burma, 1943 to 1945*, School of Advanced Military Studies Monograph Series. Fort Leavenworth, Kans.: School of Advanced Military Studies, 2003.

Cate, James L., and Wesley F. Craven, eds. *The Army Air Forces in World War II*, vol. 5, *The Pacific: Matterhorn to Nagasaki, June 1944 to August 1945*. Chicago: University of Chicago Press, 1953.

Davis, Richard G. *Hap: Henry H. Arnold, Military Aviator*. Washington, D.C.: Government Printing Office, 1997.

Huber, Thomas M. *Japan's Battle for Okinawa, April–June, 1945*. Leavenworth Papers No. 18. Fort Leavenworth, Kans.: Combat Studies Institute, U.S. Army Command and Staff College, 1990.

MacEachin, Douglas J. *The Final Months of the War with Japan: Signals Intelligence, U.S. Invasion Planning, and the A-Bomb Decision*. Washington, D.C.: Center for the Study of Intelligence, 1998.

U.S. ARMY IN WORLD WAR II

The Corps of Engineers

Dod, Karl C. *U.S. Army in World War II: The Corps of Engineers: The War against Japan*. Washington, D.C.: Government Printing Office, 1966.

Special Studies

Dziuban, Stanley W. *U.S. Army in World War II: Special Studies: Military Relations between the United States and Canada, 1939–1945*. Washington, D.C.: Government Printing Office, 1959.

Vigneras, Marcel. *U.S. Army in World War II: Special Studies: Rearming the French*. Washington, D.C.: Government Printing Office, 1957.

The War Department

Cline, Ray. *U.S. Army in World War II: The War Department: Washington Command Post: The Operations Division*. Washington, D.C.: Government Printing Office, 1951.

Coakley, Robert W., and Richard M. Leighton. *U.S Army in World War II: The War Department: Global Logistics and Strategy, 1943–1945*. Washington, D.C.: Government Printing Office, 1961.

The War in the Pacific

Appleman, Roy E., James M. Burns, Russell A. Gugeler, and John Stevens. *U.S. Army in World War II: The War in the Pacific: The Last Battle*. Washington, D.C.: Government Printing Office, 1948.

HISTORY OF U.S. MARINE CORPS OPERATIONS IN WORLD WAR II

Frank, Benis M., and Henry I. Shaw, Jr. *History of U.S. Marine Corps Operations in World War II*, vol. 5, *Victory and Occupation*. Washington, D.C.: Government Printing Office, 1968.

Oral Histories

U.S. Marine Corps Historical Center, Washington Navy Yard, Washington, D.C.
Fred Beans oral history

Other Unpublished Sources

Brower, Charles F., IV. "The Joint Chiefs of Staff and National Policy: American Strategy and the War with Japan, 1943–1945." Ph.D. diss., Department of History, University of Pennsylvania, 1987.

Perras, Galen Roger. "Thirty Days or Thirty Hours? Canadian Interwar Plans for Armed Neutrality in an American-Japanese Conflict," paper presented at the 2001 Society for Military History Conference, University of Calgary, Alberta, Canada.

Wilt, Alan F. "Churchill and His Chiefs of Staff," paper presented at the 2001 Society for Military History Conference, University of Calgary, Alberta, Canada.

Newspapers and Magazines

Anchorage Times
Atlanta Journal
Baltimore Evening Sun
Baltimore Sun
Boston Daily Globe
Boston Globe
Business Week
Chicago Tribune
Christian Science Monitor
Cleveland Plain Dealer
Dominion (Wellington)
Evening Post (Wellington)
Gazette (Montreal)
Honolulu Star-Bulletin
Kansas City Star
Kansas City Times
Louisville Courier-Journal
Louisville Times
Los Angeles Times

New York Herald Tribune
New York Journal-American
New York Sun
New York Times
New Zealand Herald
Newsweek
Otago Daily Times
Ottawa Evening Citizen
Philadelphia Inquirer
Portland Oregonian
San Francisco Chronicle
Seattle Post-Intelligencer
Sydney Morning Herald
Time
Toronto Daily Star
Wall Street Journal
Washington (D.C.) Evening Star
Washington (D.C.) Sunday Star
Washington Post

Films and Novels

Bataan. Directed by Tay Garnett. Screenplay by Robert Hardy Andrews. MGM, 1943.

Conroy, Robert. *1945: A Novel.* New York: Ballantine, 2007.

Coppel, Alfred. *The Burning Mountain: A Novel of the Invasion of Japan.* New York: Harcourt Brace Jovanovich, 1983.

The Fighting 69th. Directed by William Keighly. Screenplay by Norman Reilly Raine, Fred Niblo, Jr., and Dean Franklin. Warner Brothers Pictures, 1940.

Hiyama, Yoshiaki. *Nihon hondo kessen* [The decisive battle for Japan]. Tokyo: Kobun-sha, 1981.

Niles, Douglas, and Michael Dobson. *MacArthur's War: A Novel of the Invasion of Japan*. New York: Forge Books, 2008.

Pressfield, Steven. *Gates of Fire: An Epic Novel of the Battle of Thermopylae*. New York: Doubleday, 1998.

Webb, James. *The Emperor's General*. New York: Bantam Books, 2000.

Westheimer, David. *Lighter Than a Feather*. Boston: Little, Brown, 1971.

Diaries, Memoirs, and Published Papers

Acheson, Dean. *Present at the Creation: My Years in the State Department*. New York: W. W. Norton, 1969.

Alanbrooke of Brookeborough, Sir Alan Francis Brooke, Viscount. *War Diaries 1939–1945*. Alex Danchev and Daniel Todman, eds. London: Weidenfield & Nicolson, 2001.

Arnold, H. H. *Global Mission*. New York: Harper & Brothers, 1949.

Astor, Gerald. *Operation Iceberg: The Invasion and Conquest of Okinawa in World War II, An Oral History*. New York: D. I. Fine, 1995.

Avon, Sir Anthony Eden, Earl of. *The Memoirs of Anthony Eden, Earl of Avon: The Reckoning*. Boston: Houghton Mifflin, 1965.

Bland, Larry I., ed., and Joellen K. Bland, asst. ed. *George C. Marshall: Interviews and Reminiscences for Forrest C. Pogue*, rev. ed. Lexington, Va.: George C. Marshall Research Foundation, 1991.

Bond, Brian, ed. *Chief of Staff: The Diaries of Lieutenant-General Sir Henry Pownall*, vol. 2, *1940–1944*. London: Leo Cooper, 1974.

Churchill, Winston S. *Second World War*, vol. 6, *Triumph and Tragedy*. Boston: Houghton Mifflin, 1953.

Colville, John. *The Fringes of Power: 10 Downing Street Diaries, 1939–1955*. New York: Norton, 1985.

Crosley, R. M. *They Gave Me a Seafire*. Shrewsbury, UK: Airlife Publishing, 1986.

Cunningham of Hyndhope, Sir Andrew Browne Cunningham, Viscount. *A Sailor's Odyssey: The Autobiography of Viscount Cunningham of Hyndhope K.T. G.C.B. O.M. D.S.O.* London: Hutchinson, 1951.

DeWeerd, H. A., ed. *Selected Speeches and Statements of General of the Army George C. Marshall Chief of Staff United States Army*. Washington, D.C.: The Infantry Journal, 1945.

Dilks, David, ed. *The Diaries of Sir Alexander Cadogan O.M. 1938–1945*. London: Cassell, 1971.

Eadon, Stuart. *Sakishima and Back: "Where Men with Splendid Hearts May Go."* Manchester, UK: Crecy Books, 1995.

Eichelberger, Robert L. *Dear Miss Em: General Eichelberger's War in the Pacific, 1942–1945*. Jay Luvaas, ed. Westport, Conn.: Greenwood Press, 1972.

Fergusson, Bernard, ed. *The Business of War: The War Narrative of Major-General Sir John Kennedy G.C.M.G, K.C.V.O., K.B.E., C.B., M.C.* London: Hutchinson, 1957.

Ferrell, Robert H., ed. *Off the Record: The Private Papers of Harry S. Truman.* New York: Penguin Books, 1982.

Halifax, Edward Frederick Lindley Wood, Earl of. *Fulness of Days.* London: Collins, 1957.

Halsey, William F. *Admiral Halsey's Story.* New York: McGraw-Hill, 1947.

Hanson, Norman. *Carrier Pilot: An Unforgettable True Story of Wartime Flying.* Cambridge, UK: Patrick Stephens, 1979.

Harwit, Martin. *An Exhibit Denied: Lobbying the History of the Enola Gay.* New York: Springer Verlag, 1997.

Hopkins, Harold. *Nice to Have You Aboard.* London: Allen & Unwin, 1964.

Hosokawa, Hachiro. "Preface," in Hatsuho Naito, *Thunder Gods: The Kamikaze Pilots Tell Their Story.* New York: Kodansha, 1989.

Huston, John W., ed. *American Airpower Comes of Age: General Henry H. "Hap" Arnold's World War II Diaries,* vols. 1 and 2. Maxwell Air Force Base, Ala.: Air University Press, 2002.

Ismay of Wormington, Sir Hastings Lionel Ismay, Baron. *The Memoirs of General Lord Ismay.* New York: Viking Press, 1960.

James, Robert Rhodes, ed. *Winston S. Churchill: His Complete Speeches, 1897–1963,* vol. 7, *1943–1949.* London: Chelsea House Publishers, 1974.

Kesaris, Paul, ed. *Records of the Joint Chiefs of Staff,* pt. 1, *The Pacific Theater.* Frederick, Md.: University Publications of America, 1981.

King, Ernest J., and Walter Muir Whitehill. *Fleet Admiral King: A Naval Record.* New York: W. W. Norton, 1952.

Lartéguy, Jean, ed. *The Sun Goes Down: Last Letters from Japanese Suicide-Pilots and Soldiers.* Nora Wydenbruck, trans. London: William Kimber, 1956.

Leahy, William D. *I Was There: The Personal Story of the Chief of Staff to Presidents Roosevelt and Truman Based on His Notes and Diaries Made at the Time.* New York: Whittlesey House, 1950.

LeMay, Curtis E., and MacKinlay Kantor. *Mission with LeMay: My Story.* Garden City, N.Y.: Doubleday, 1965.

Linenthal, Edward T., and Tom Engelhardt. *History Wars: The Enola Gay and Other Battles for the American Past.* New York: Metropolitan Books, 1995.

Manchester, William. *Goodbye, Darkness: A Memoir of the Pacific War.* Boston: Little, Brown, 1980.

Moran of Manton, Charles McMoran Wilson, Baron. *Churchill Taken from the Diaries of Lord Moran: The Struggle for Survival, 1940–1965.* Boston: Houghton Mifflin, 1966.

Nagatsuka, Ryuji. *I Was a Kamikaze.* Nina Rootes, trans. New York: Macmillan, 1972.

Nichols, David, ed. *Ernie's War: The Best of Ernie Pyle's World War II Dispatches.* New York: Random House, 1986.

Nobile, Philip, ed. *Judgment at the Smithsonian.* New York: Marlowe, 1995.

Pickersgill, J. W., and D. F. Forster, eds. *The Mackenzie King Record,* vol. 2, *1944–1945.* Toronto: University of Toronto Press, 1968.

Pimlott, Ben, ed. *The Second World War Diary of Hugh Dalton, 1940–1945.* London: Jonathan Cape, 1986.

Pope, Maurice A. *Soldiers and Politicians: The Memoirs of Lt.-Gen. Maurice A. Pope, C.B., M.C.* Toronto: University of Toronto Press, 1962.

Prange, Gordon W., Donald M. Goldstein, and Katherine V. Dillon, eds. *Fading Victory: The Diary of Admiral Matome Ugaki, 1941–1945.* Masatak Chihaya, trans. Pittsburgh: University of Pittsburgh Press, 1991.

Rhoads, Weldon. *Flying MacArthur to Victory.* College Station: Texas A&M University Press, 1987.

Sarantakes, Nicholas Evan, ed. *Seven Stars: The Okinawa Battle Diaries of Simon Bolivar Buckner, Jr. and Joseph Stilwell.* College Station: Texas A&M University Press, 2004.

Sledge, E. B. *With the Old Breed at Peleiu and Okinawa.* Novato, Calif.: Presidio Press, 1981.

Stimson, Henry L. "The Decision to Use the Atomic Bomb." *Harper's Magazine* 194 (February 1947), 97–107.

Truman, Harry S. *Memoirs,* vol. 1, *Year of Decisions.* Garden City, N.Y.: Doubleday, 1955.

Vian, Sir Philip. *Action This Day: A War Memoir.* London: Frederick Muller Limited, 1960.

Walch, Timothy, and Dwight M. Miller, eds. *Herbert Hoover and Harry Truman: A Documentary History.* Worland, Wyo.: High Plains Publishing, 1992.

Wallace, Robert F. *From Dam Neck to Okinawa: A Memoir of Antiaircraft Training in World War II.* Jeffery G. Barlow, ed. Washington, D.C.: Naval Historical Center, 2001.

Wilson of Libya and Stowlangtoft, Sir Henry Maitland Wilson, Baron. *Eight Years Overseas, 1939–1947.* London: Hutchinson, 1950.

Yahara, Hiromichi. *Battle for Okinawa.* New York: J. Wiley, 1995.

Yokoi, Toshiyuki. "Kamikazes in the Okinawa Campaign." In Raymond O'Connor, ed., and David C. Evans, ed. and trans., *The Japanese Navy in World War II: In the Words of Former Japanese Naval Officers,* 2nd ed. Annapolis, Md.: Naval Institute Press, 1986.

Ziegler, Philip, ed. *Personal Diary of Admiral The Lord Louis Mountbatten Supreme Allied Commander, South-East Asia, 1943–1946.* London: Collins, 1988.

Books

Adams, Henry H. *Witness to Power: The Life of Admiral William D. Leahy.* Annapolis, Md.: Naval Institute Press, 1985.

Allen, Louis. *Burma: The Longest War, 1941–45.* London: J. M. Dent, 1984.

Allen, Thomas B., and Norman Polmar. *Code-Name DOWNFALL: The Secret Plan to Invade Japan—And Why Truman Dropped the Bomb.* New York: Simon & Schuster, 1995.

Alperovitz, Gar. *Atomic Diplomacy: Hiroshima and Potsdam: The Use of the Atomic*

Bomb and the American Confrontation with Soviet Power. New York: Vintage, 1965.

———. *The Decision to Use the Atomic Bomb and the Architecture of an American Myth.* New York: Knopf, 1995.

Atkin, Ronald. *Dieppe, 1942: The Jubilee Disaster.* London: Macmillan, 1980.

Axell, Albert, and Hideaki Kase. *Kamikaze: Japan's Suicide Gods.* New York: Pearson Education, 2002.

Baker, Richard. *Dry Ginger: The Biography of Admiral of the Fleet Sir Michael Le Fanu, GCB, DSC.* London: W. H. Allen, 1977.

Bartsch, William H. *December 8, 1941: MacArthur's Pearl Harbor.* College Station: Texas A&M University Press, 2003.

Bassett, Michael, and Michael King. *Tomorrow Comes the Song: A Life of Peter Fraser.* Auckland: Penguin Books, 2000.

Belote, James H., and William Belote. *Typhoon of Steel: The Battle for Okinawa.* New York: Harper and Row, 1970.

Black, Conrad. *Franklin Delano Roosevelt: Champion of Freedom.* London: Weidenfeld & Nicolson, 2004.

Bradford, Ernle. *Thermopylae: The Battle for the West.* New York: McGraw-Hill, 1980.

Buell, Thomas B. *The Quiet Warrior: A Biography of Admiral Raymond A. Spruance.* Boston: Little, Brown, 1974.

———. *Master of Sea Power: A Biography of Admiral Ernest J. King.* Boston: Little, Brown, 1980.

Chappell, John D. *Before the Bomb: How America Approached the End of the Pacific War.* Lexington: University Press of Kentucky, 1997.

Coffey, Thomas M. *Hap: The Story of the U.S. Air Force and the Man Who Built It, General Henry "Hap" Arnold.* New York: Viking Press, 1982.

———. *Iron Eagle: The Turbulent Life of General Curtis LeMay.* New York: Crown Publishers, 1986.

Crane, Conrad C. *Bombs, Cities, and Civilians: American Airpower Strategy in World War II.* Lawrence: University Press of Kansas, 1993.

Cray, Ed. *General of the Army: George C. Marshall, Soldier and Statesman.* New York: Simon and Schuster, 1990.

Cull, Nicholas John. *Selling War: The British Propaganda Campaign against American "Neutrality" in World War II.* New York: Oxford University Press, 1995.

Danchev, Alex. *Very Special Relationship: Field Marshal Sir John Dill and the Anglo-American Alliance, 1941–44.* London: Brassey's, 1986.

Daso, Dik Alan. *Hap Arnold and the Evolution of American Airpower.* Washington, D.C.: Smithsonian Institute Press, 2000.

Davidson, Joel R. *The Unsinkable Fleet: The Politics of U.S. Navy Expansion in World War II.* Annapolis, Md.: Naval Institute Press, 1996.

Davis, William C. *Three Roads to the Alamo: The Lives and Fortunes of David Crockett, James Bowie, and William Barrett Travis.* New York: HarperCollins, 1998.

Dawson, R. MacGregor. *The Conscription Crisis of 1944.* Toronto: University of Toronto Press, 1961.

Day, David. *Reluctant Nation: Australia and the Allied Defeat of Japan, 1942–45*. New York: Oxford University Press, 1992.

———. *John Curtin: A Life*. Sydney: HarperCollins, 1999.

———. *Chifley*. Sydney: HarperCollins, 2001.

D'Este, Carlo. *Decision in Normandy*. New York: Dutton, 1983.

———. *Eisenhower: A Soldier's Life*. New York: Henry Holt, 2002.

Dingman, Roger. *Ghost of War: The Sinking of the* Awa maru *and Japanese-American Relations, 1945–1995*. Annapolis, Md.: Naval Institute Press, 1997.

Dower, John W. *War without Mercy: Race and Power in the Pacific War*. New York: Pantheon Books, 1986.

Drea, Edward J. *MacArthur's Ultra: Codebreaking and the War against Japan, 1942–1945*. Lawrence: University Press of Kansas, 1992.

Drury, Bob, and Tom Clavin. *Halsey's Typhoon: The True Story of a Fighting Admiral, an Epic Storm, and an Untold Rescue*. New York: Atlantic Monthly Press, 2007.

English, John A. *The Canadian Army and the Normandy Campaign: A Study of Failure in High Command*. New York: Praeger, 1991.

Feis, Herbert. *Japan Subdued: The Atomic Bomb and the End of the War in the Pacific*. Princeton, N.J.: Princeton University Press, 1961.

———. *The Atomic Bomb and the End of World War II*. Princeton, N.J.: Princeton University Press, 1966.

Foote, Shelby. *The Civil War: A Narrative*, vol. 1, *Fort Sumter to Perryville*. New York: Random House, 1958.

Frank, Richard B. DOWNFALL: *The End of the Imperial Japanese Empire*. New York: Random House, 1999.

Fraser, David. *Alanbrooke*. London: HarperCollins, 1982.

Freidel, Frank. *Franklin D. Roosevelt: A Rendezvous with Destiny*. Boston: Little, Brown, 1990.

Freyberg, Paul. *Bernard Freyberg, VC: Soldier of Two Nations*. London: Hodder & Stoughton, 1991.

Gailey, Harry A. *"Howlin' Mad" vs the Army: Conflict in Command, Saipan 1944*. Novato, Calif.: Presidio Press, 1986.

Geneja, Stephen Conrad. *The Cruiser Uganda*. Corbyville, Ontario: Tyendinaga, 1994.

Gilbert, Sir Martin. *Churchill: A Life*. New York: Henry Holt, 1991.

Gray, Edwyn. *Operation Pacific: The Royal Navy's War against Japan, 1941–1945*. Annapolis, Md.: Naval Institute Press, 1990.

Griffith, Thomas E., Jr. *MacArthur's Airman: General George C. Kenney and the War in the Southwest Pacific*. Lawerence: University Press of Kansas, 1998.

Hamby, Alonzo L. *Man of the People: A Life of Harry S. Truman*. New York: Oxford University Press, 1995.

Harbutt, Fraser J. *The Iron Curtain: Churchill, America, and the Origins of the Cold War*. New York: Oxford University Press, 1986.

Hasegawa, Tsuyoshi. *Racing the Enemy: Stalin, Truman, and the Surrender of Japan*. Cambridge, Mass.: Harvard University Press, 2005.

Hastings, Max. *Retribution: The Battle for Japan, 1944–45*. New York: Knopf, 2008.

Hayes, Grace Pearson. *The History of the Joint Chiefs of Staff in World War II: The War against Japan*. Annapolis, Md.: Naval Institute Press, 1982.

Hetherington, John. *Blamey: Controversial Soldier—A Biography of Field Marshal Sir Thomas Blamey, GBE, KCB, CMG, DSO, ED*. Canberra: Australian War Memorial and the Australian Government Publishing Service, 1973.

Hogan, Michael J., ed. *Hiroshima in History and Memory*. New York: Cambridge University Press, 1996.

Horner, D. M. *High Command: Australia and Allied Strategy, 1939–1945*. North Sydney, Australia: Allen & Unwin, 1982.

Horner, David. *Inside the War Cabinet: Directing Australia's War Effort, 1939–45*. St. Leonards, Australia: Allen & Unwin, 1996.

——. *Blamey: The Commander-in-Chief*. St. Leonards, Australia: Allen & Unwin, 1998.

——. *Defence Supremo: Sir Frederick Shedden and the Making of Australian Defence Policy*. St. Leonards, Australia: Allen & Unwin, 2000.

Hough, Richard. *The Longest Battle: The War at Sea, 1939–45*. London: Weidenfeld & Nicolson, 1986.

Hoyt, Edwin P. *The Last Kamikaze: The Story of Admiral Matome Ugaki*. Westport, Conn.: Praeger, 1993.

Humble, Richard. *Fraser of North Cape: The Life of Admiral of the Fleet Lord Fraser [1888–1981]*. London: Routledge & Kegan Paul, 1983.

Hunter, T. Murray. *Canada at Dieppe*. Toronto: Balmur, 1982.

Jackson, Robert. *Dunkirk: The British Evacuation 1940*. New York: St. Martin's Press, 1976.

James, D. Clayton. *The Years of MacArthur*, vol. 1, *1880–1941*. Boston: Houghton Mifflin, 1970.

——. *The Years of MacArthur*, vol. 2, *1941–1945*. Boston: Houghton Mifflin, 1975.

——. *The Years of MacArthur*, vol. 3, *Triumph and Disaster, 1945–1964*. Boston: Houghton Mifflin, 1985.

Jenkins, Roy. *Churchill: A Biography*. New York: Plume, 2002.

Kimball, Warren. *Swords or Ploughshares? The Morgenthau Plan for Defeated Nazi Germany*. Philadelphia: Lippincott, 1976.

——. *Forged in War: Roosevelt, Churchill, and the Second World War*. New York: William Morrow, 1997.

Kluger, Richard. *The Paper: The Life and Death of the New York Herald Tribune*. New York: Knopf, 1986.

La Bree, Clifton. *The Gentle Warrior: Oliver Price Smith, USMC*. Kent, Ohio: Kent State University Press, 2001.

Langtree, Christopher. *The Kelly's: British J, K and N Class Destroyers of World War II*. Annapolis, Md.: Naval Institute Press, 2002.

Lifton Robert Jay, and Greg Mitchell. *Hiroshima in America: Fifty Years of Denial*. New York: G. P. Putnam's Sons, 1995.

Lott, Arnold S. *Brave Ship, Brave Men*. Indianapolis: Bobbs-Merrill, 1963.

Maddox, Robert James. *Weapons for Victory: The Hiroshima Decision Fifty Years Later*. Columbia: University of Missouri Press, 1995.

Massie, Robert K. *Castles of Steel: Britain, Germany, and the Winning of the Great War at Sea*. New York: Random House, 2003.

McCullough, David. *Truman*. New York: Simon and Schuster, 1992.

McGeoch, Sir Ian. *The Princely Sailor: Mountbatten of Burma*. London: Brassey's, 1996.

Macintyre, Donald G. F. W. *Fighting Admiral: The Life of Admiral of the Fleet Sir James Somerville, G.C.B., G.B.E., D.S.O.* London: Evans Brothers, 1961.

Melton, Buckner F., Jr. *Sea Cobra: Admiral Halsey's Task Force and the Great Pacific Typhoon*. Guilford, Conn.: Lyons Press, 2007.

Morris, Ivan. *The Nobility of Failure: Tragic Heroes in the History of Japan*. New York: Rinehart and Winston, 1975.

Morison, Samuel Eliot. *History of United States Naval Operations in World War II*, vol. 14, *Victory in the Pacific, 1945*. Boston: Little, Brown, 1960.

Moser, John E. *Twisting the Lion's Tail: American Anglophobia between the World Wars*. New York: New York University Press, 1999.

Nolan, Brian. *King's War: Mackenzie King and the Politics of War*. Toronto: Random House, 1988.

Orde, Anne. *The Eclipse of Great Britain: The United States and British Imperial Decline, 1895–1956*. New York: St. Martin's, 1996.

Overy, Richard. *Why the Allies Won*. New York: Norton, 1995.

Parshall, Jonathan, and Anthony Tully. *Shattered Sword: The Untold Story of the Battle of Midway*. Washington, D.C.: Potomac, 2005.

Perras, Galen. *Stepping Stones to Nowhere: The Aleutian Islands, Alaska, and American Military Strategy, 1867–1945*. Vancouver: University of British Columbia Press, 2003.

Perret, Geoffrey. *Old Soldiers Never Die: The Life of Douglas MacArthur*. New York: Random House, 1996.

Potter, E. B. *Nimitz*. Annapolis, Md.: Naval Institute Press, 1976.

——. *Bull Halsey*. Annapolis, Md.: Naval Institute Press, 1985.

Reynolds, David. *The Creation of the Anglo-American Alliance, 1937–1941*. Chapel Hill: University of North Carolina Press, 1982.

——. *Rich Relations: The American Occupation of Britain, 1942–1945*. New York: Random House, 1995.

——. *In Command of History: Churchill Fighting and Writing the Second World War*. London: Allen Lane, 2004.

Richards, Denis. *Portal of Hungerford: The Life of Marshal of the Royal Air Force Viscount Portal of Hungerford, KG, GCB, OM, DSO, MC*. New York: Holmes & Meier, 1977.

Roberts, Randy, and James S. Olson. *A Line in the Sand: The Alamo in Blood and Memory*. New York: Free Press, 2001.

Robertson, John, and John McCarthy. *Australian War Strategy, 1939–1945: A Documentary History*. St. Lucia, Australia: University of Queensland Press, 1985.

Roskill, Stephen. *Churchill and the Admirals*. New York: William Morrow, 1978.

Sandler, Stanley. *The Korean War: No Victors, No Vanquished*. Lexington: University Press of Kentucky, 1999.

Sbrega, John J. *Anglo-American Relations and Colonialism in East Asia, 1941–1945*. New York: Garland, 1983.

Sherwin, Martin J. *A World Destroyed: Hiroshima and the Origins of the Arms Race*. New York: Knopf, 1975.

Sigal, Leon V. *Fighting to a Finish: The Politics of War Termination in the United States and Japan, 1945*. Ithaca, N.Y.: Cornell University Press, 1988.

Simpson, Michael. *A Life of Admiral of the Fleet Andrew Cunningham: A Twentieth-Century Naval Leader*. London: Frank Cass, 2004.

Sinclair, Keith. *Walter Nash*. Auckland: Auckland University Press, 1976.

Skates, John Ray. *The Invasion of Japan: Alternative to the Bomb*. Columbia: University of South Carolina Press, 1994.

Smith, Jim, and Malcolm McConnell. *The Last Mission: The Secret History of World War II's Final Battle*. New York: Broadway Books, 2002.

Smith, Peter C. *Task Force 57: The British Pacific Fleet, 1944–1945*. London: Kimber, 1969.

Snow, Philip. *The Fall of Hong Kong: Britain, China and the Japanese Occupation*. New Haven, Conn.: Yale University Press, 2004.

Spector, Ronald H. *Eagle against the Sun: The American War with Japan*. New York: Free Press, 1984.

Spur, Russell. *A Glorious Way to Die: The Kamikaze Mission of the Battleship Yamato, April 1945*. New York: Newmarket Press, 1981.

Stacey, C. P. *A Very Double Life: The Private World of Mackenzie King*. Toronto: Macmillan, 1976.

Stoler, Mark A. *The Politics of the Second Front: American Military Planning and Diplomacy in Coalition Warfare*. Westport, Conn.: Greenwood Press, 1977.

———. *Allies and Adversaries: The Joint Chiefs of Staff, the Grand Alliance, and U.S. Strategy in World War II*. Chapel Hill: University of North Carolina Press, 2000.

Takaki, Ronald. *Hiroshima: Why America Dropped the Atomic Bomb*. Boston: Little, Brown, 1995.

Tap, Bruce. *Over Lincoln's Shoulder: The Committee on the Conduct of the War*. Lawrence: University Press of Kansas, 1998.

Thorn, James. *Peter Fraser: New Zealand's Wartime Prime Minister*. London: Odhams Press, 1952.

Thorne, Christopher. *Allies of a Kind: The United States, Britain and the War against Japan, 1941–1945*. New York: Oxford University Press, 1978.

Tuchman, Barbara. *The Guns of August*. New York: Macmillan, 1962.

Walker, J. Samuel. *Prompt and Utter Destruction: Truman and the Use of the Atomic Bomb against Japan*. Chapel Hill: University of North Carolina Press, 1997.

Werrell, Kenneth P. *Blankets of Fire: U.S. Bombers over Japan during World War II*. Washington, D.C.: Smithsonian Institution Press, 1996.

Willmott, H. P. *Grave of a Dozen Schemes: British Naval Planning and the War against Japan, 1943–1945*. Annapolis, Md.: Naval Institute Press, 1996.

Wingate, Sir Ronald. *Lord Ismay: A Biography*. London: Hutchinson, 1970.

Winton, John. *The Forgotten Fleet*. London: Michael Joseph, 1969.

———. *Cunningham*. London: John Murray, 1998.

Villa, Brian Loring. *Unauthorized Action: Mountbatten and the Dieppe Raid*. New York: Oxford University Press, 1989.

Young, Kenneth Ray. *The General's General: The Life and Times of Arthur MacArthur*. Boulder, Colo.: Westview Press, 1994.

Zeiler, Thomas W. *Unconditional Defeat: Japan, America, and the End of World War II*. Wilmington, Del.: Scholarly Resources, 2004.

Ziegler, Philip. *Mountbatten*. London: William Collins Sons, 1985.

Articles and Chapters

Asada, Sadao. "The Mushroom Cloud and National Psyches: Japanese and American Perceptions of the A-Bomb Decision, 1945–1995," *Journal of American–East Asian Relations* 4, no. 2 (Summer 1995), 99–115.

———. "The Shock of the Atomic Bomb and Japan's Decision to Surrender—A Reconsideration," *Pacific Historical Review* 67 (November 1998), 477–512.

Ashby, Michael. "Fraser's Foreign Policy," in Margaret Clark, ed., *Peter Fraser: Master Politician*. Palmerston North: The Dunmore Press, 1998.

Bartlett, Merrill, and Robert William Love, Jr. "Anglo American Naval Diplomacy and the British Pacific Fleet, 1942–1945," *American Neptune* 42 (1982), 203–216.

Baxter, Christopher. "In Pursuit of a Pacific Strategy: British Planning for the Defeat of Japan," *Diplomacy & Statecraft* 15, no. 2 (June 2004), 253–278.

Bernstein, Barton J. "The Atomic Bomb and American Foreign Policy, 1941–1945: An Historiographical Controversy," *Peace & Change* 2, no. 1 (Spring 1974), 1–16.

———. "Roosevelt, Truman, and the Atomic Bomb, 1941–1945: A Reinterpretation," *Political Science Quarterly* 90, no. 1 (Spring 1975), 23–69.

———. "The Perils and Politics of Surrender: Ending the War with Japan and Avoiding the Third Atomic Bomb," *Pacific Historical Review* 46 (February 1977), 1–27.

———. "The Myth of Lives Saved by A-Bomb," *Los Angeles Times*, July 28, 1985.

———. "A Postwar Myth: 500,000 U.S. Lives Saved," *Bulletin of the Atomic Scientists* (June/July 1986), 38–40.

———. "Eclipsed by Hiroshima and Nagasaki: Early Thinking about Tactical Nuclear Weapons," *International Security* 15 (Spring 1991), 149–173.

———. "Writing, Righting, or Wronging the Historical Record," *Diplomatic History* 16, no. 1 (Winter 1992), 163–173.

———. "Seizing the Contested Terrain of Early Nuclear History: Stimson, Conant, and Their Allies Explain the Decision to Use the Atomic Bomb," *Diplomatic History* 17, no. 1 (Winter 1993), 35–72.

———. "Compelling Japan's Surrender without the A-bomb, Soviet Entry, or Invasion: Reconsidering the US Bombing Survey's Early-Surrender Conclusions," *Journal of Strategic Studies* 18, no. 2 (June 1995), 101–148.

———. "Truman and the A-Bomb: Targeting Noncombatants, Using the Bomb, and His Defending the 'Decision,'" *Journal of Military History* 62 (July 1998), 547–570.

————. "Reconsidering Truman's Claim of 'Half a Million American Lives' Saved by the Atomic Bomb: The Construction and Deconstruction of a Myth," *Journal of Strategic Studies* 22 (March 1999), 54–95.

————. "Reconsidering 'Invasion Most Costly': Popular-History Scholarship, Publishing Standards, and the Claim of High U.S. Casualty Estimates to Legitimize the Atomic Bombings," *Peace & Change* 24 (April 1999), 220–248.

————. "The Alarming Japanese Buildup on Southern Kyushu, Growing U.S. Fears, and Counterfactual Analysis: Would the Planned November 1945 Invasion of Southern Kyushu Have Occurred?" *Pacific Historical Review* 68 (November 1999), 561–509.

Brower, Charles F., IV. "Assault Versus Siege: The Debate over Final Strategy for the Defeat of Japan," *Joint Perspectives* 2 (Spring 1982), 72–80.

————. "Sophisticated Strategist: General George A. Lincoln and the Defeat of Japan, 1944–1945," *Diplomatic History* 15, no. 3 (Summer 1991), 317–337.

Coles, Michael. "Ernest King and the British Pacific Fleet: The Conference at Quebec, 1944 ('Octagon')," *Journal of Military History* 65 (January 2001), 105–129.

Coox, Alvin D. "Needless Fear: The Compromise of U.S. Plans to Invade Japan in 1945," *Journal of Military History* 64 (April 2000), 411–438.

Danchev, Alex. "Dill," in John Keegan, ed., *Churchill's Generals*. London: Weidenfeld & Nicolson, 1991, 51–69.

Day, David. "Promise and Performance: Britain's Pacific Pledge, 1943–5," *War & Society* 4, no. 2 (September 1986), 71–93.

Dewar, Michael. "Wilson," in John Keegan, ed., *Churchill's Generals*. London: Weidenfeld & Nicolson, 1991, 166–182.

Gallicchio, Marc. "After Nagasaki: General Marshall's Plan for Tactical Nuclear Weapons in Japan," *Prologue* 23 (Winter 1991), 396–404.

Giangreco, D. M. "Operation Downfall: The Devil Was in the Details," *Joint Forces Quarterly* 9 (Autumn 1995), 86–94.

————. "Casualty Projections for the U.S. Invasions of Japan, 1945–1946: Planning and Policy Implications," *Journal of Military History* 61 (July 1997), 521–582.

————. "'A Score of Bloody Okinawas and Iwo Jimas': President Truman and Casualty Estimates for the Invasion of Japan," *Pacific Historical Review* 72 (February 2003), 93–132.

Graybar, Lloyd G. "The Buckners of Kentucky," *Filson Club Quarterly* 58, no. 2 (April 1984), 202–214.

Grove, Eric J. "Andrew Browne Cunningham: The Best Man of the Lot," in Jack Sweetman, ed., *The Great Admirals: Command at Sea, 1587–1945*. Annapolis, Md.: Naval Institute Press, 1997, 418–441.

Haley, J. Fred. "The Death of Gen. Simon Bolivar Buckner," *Marine Corps Gazette* (November 1982), 100–105.

Hall, Thomas. "'Mere Drops in the Ocean': The Politics and Planning of the Contribution of the British Commonwealth to the Final Defeat of Japan, 1944–1945," *Diplomacy & Statecraft* 16, no. 1 (March 2005), 93–116.

"History and the Public: What Can We Handle? A Round Table about History after the

Enola Gay Controversy," *Journal of American History* 82 (December 1995), 1029–1144.

Koshiro, Yukiko. "Eurasian Eclipse: Japan's End Game in World War II," *American Historical Review* 109, no. 2 (April 2004), 417–444.

Meanney, Neville. "The Problem of Nationalism in Australian History and Historiography," *Australian Historical Studies* 32, no. 116 (October 2001), 76–90.

Miles, Rufus E., Jr. "Hiroshima: The Strange Myth of Half a Million American Lives Saved," *International Security* 10 (Fall 1995), 121–140.

Moon, John Ellis van Courtland. "Project SPHINX: The Question of the Use of Gas in the Planned Invasion of Japan," *Journal of Strategic Studies* 12 (September 1989), 303–323.

Perras, Galen. "'She Should Have Thought of Herself First': Canada and Military Aid to Australia, 1939–1945," in Margaret MacMillan and Francine McKenzie, eds., *Parties Long Estranged: Canada and Australia in the Twentieth Century*. Vancouver: University of British Columbia Press, 2003, 124–150.

Perras, Galen Roger. "Eyes on the Northern Route to Japan: Plans for Canadian Participation in an Invasion of the Kurile Islands—A Study in Coalition Warfare and Civil-Military Relations," *War and Society* 8, no. 1 (May 1990), 100–117.

———. "Once Bitten, Twice Shy: The Origins of the Canadian Army Pacific Force," in Greg Donaghy, ed., *Uncertain Horizons: Canadians and Their World in 1945*. Ottawa: Canadian Committee for the History of the Second World War, 1997, 77–99.

———. "No Need to Send an Army across the Pacific: Mackenzie King and the Pacific Conflict, 1939–45," in John English, Kenneth McLaughlin, and P. Whitney Lackenbauer, eds., *Mackenzie King: Citizenship and Community—Essays Marking the 125th Anniversary of the Birth of William Lyon Mackenzie King*. Toronto: Robin Brass Studio, 2002, 124–150.

———. "Hurry Up and Wait: Robert Menzies, Mackenzie King, and the Failed Attempt to Form an Imperial War Cabinet in 1941," *Working Papers in Contemporary Military and International History*, no. 3 (Salford, England, September 2004), 1–42.

Polmar, Norman, and Thomas B. Allen. "Invasion Most Costly," U.S. Naval Institute *Proceedings* (August 1995), 51–56.

Reynolds, Clark G. "William F. Halsey, Jr.: The Bull," in Jack Sweetman, ed., *The Great Admirals: Command at Sea, 1587–1945*. Annapolis, Md.: Naval Institute Press, 1997, 482–506.

Sarantakes, Nicholas Evan. "The Royal Air Force on Okinawa: The Diplomacy of a Coalition on the Verge of Victory," *Diplomatic History* 27, no. 4 (September 2003), 477–500.

———. "One Last Crusade: The US-British Alliance and the End of the War in the Pacific," *Royal United Services Institute Journal* 149, no. 4 (August 2004), 62–67.

———. "One Last Crusade: The British Pacific Fleet and Its Impact on Anglo-American Relations," *English Historical Review* 121 (April 2006), 429–466.

———. "The Short but Brilliant Life of the British Pacific Fleet," *Joint Forces Quarterly*, no. 40 (1st Quarter, 2006), 85–91.

Sarty, Roger. "The Ghosts of Fisher and Jellicoe: The Royal Canadian Navy and the Quebec Conferences," in David Woolner, ed., *The Second Quebec Conference Revisited: Waging War, Formulating Peace: Canada, Great Britain, and the United States in 1944–1945*. New York: St. Martin's Press, 1998, 143–170.

Silkett, Wayne A. "Downfall: The Invasion That Never Was," *Parameters* 24 (Autumn 1994), 111–120.

Villa, Brian L. "The U.S. Army, Unconditional Surrender, and the Potsdam Proclamation," *Journal of American History* 63 (June 1976), 66–92.

Walker, J. Samuel. "The Decision to Use the Bomb: A Historiographical Update," *Diplomatic History* 14, no. 1 (Winter 1990), 97–114.

——. "Recent Literature on Truman's Atomic Bomb Decision: A Search for Middle Ground," *Diplomatic History* 29, no. 2 (April 2005), 311–344.

Wards, Ian. "Peter Fraser—Warrior Prime Minister," in Margaret Clark, ed., *Peter Fraser: Master Politician*. Palmerston North: Dunmore Press, 1998.

Wessels, Andre. "South Africa and the War against Japan 1941–1945," *Military History Journal* 10 (June 1996), located at http://rapidttp.com/milhist/vol103aw.html.

Winton, John. "Cunningham," in Stephen Howarth, ed., *Men of War: Great Naval Leaders of World War II*. New York: St. Martin's Press, 1993, 207–226.

Wolk, Herman S. "General Arnold, the Atomic Bomb, and the Surrender of Japan," in Günter Bischof and Robert L. Dupont, eds., *The Pacific War Revisited*. Baton Rouge: Louisiana State University Press, 1997, 163–178.

Index

Australian Army, 62
  7th Division, 322

Baker, Newton, 272
Baltimore *Sun,* 4
Beasley, John, 322
Berlin Blockade, 6
Berlin conference. *See* Potsdam
    conference
Bevin, Ernest, 75, 345
Bidault, Georges, 269
Bigart, Homer, 241–242, 245
Blamey, Lady Olga, 68
Blamey, Sir Thomas, 50, 74, 80, 81
  background of, 65–68
  Brooke on, 81
  Chifley and, 324, 351
  Cunningham on, 73
  Curtin and, 69–70, 73, 96–97, 324
  drafts response to Churchill's cable,
    347–349
  forces War Cabinet to resolve issue,
    320
  postwar life of, 371
  Shedden and, 69–70, 96–97
  support for Imperial task force, 80, 81
  warns against Balikpapan, 322
  warns against force reduction, 319
Blamey, Thomas (the younger), 68
Boston Globe, 4
British Army
  deployment to the Pacific, 345–347
  command of, 346, 352–353, 354
  Fifteenth Army, 282
    IV Corps, 282
    X Corps, 346
British Pacific Fleet (BPF), 9, 30, 313
  adopts khaki uniform, 198
  adopts U.S. communication methods
    and codes, 198
  anti-kamikaze tactics used by, 212–216
  Australian reaction to arrival of,
    200–202
  combat effectiveness of, 302
  as Imperial force, 193–194, 289, 302
  journalists banned from, 216
  kamikaze attacks on, 208–209,
    212–216
  at Manus, 202–203, 205–206, 207

proposed creation, 106–108
resiliency against kamikaze attacks,
    209–211, 214–215
ship design inappropriate for Pacific,
    203–204, 207
Spruance on, 211, 216
Spruance opposes redeployment of,
    212
strategic mission of, 72, 195–196,
    295–296
supply problems faced by, 194,
    200–201, 203, 204–206, 212, 288,
    296–299, 301
as Task Force 37, 296–297, 300–301
as Task Force 57, 207, 208, 211, 216
as Task Force 112, 207
as Task Force 113, 207
See also Pacific theatre strategy
Brooke, Sir Alan (Viscount Alanbrooke),
    1, 8, 53, 79, 83, 96, 99, 112, 125,
    136, 193, 201, 236, 261, 263, 265,
    268, 308, 318
  on Anglo-American alliance, 357
  background of, 15–18
  on Blamey, 81
  Churchill and, 17, 32, 34, 35–36,
    39–40, 48, 52, 101, 102, 103, 111,
    130–131
  on Churchill, 80, 81, 98, 99–100, 102,
    104–106, 108, 110, 112–113, 118,
    121, 129, 316
  on Churchill's indecision, 103–104
  on Churchill's reversal on Pacific
    strategy, 121
  on command authority in Pacific, 312
  compares to Duke of Marlborough,
    113
  and Cunningham, 22, 44, 80, 121
  on Curtin, 80
  on Dill, 115, 261
  Eden on, 102
  fishing and, 21, 130–131, 313–314
  on Fraser, Peter, 72
  on Freyberg, 354
  King, Ernest on, 117
  on MacArthur, 80
  on Marshall, 94–95
  on Mountbatten, 50, 80
  on nature of war, 17, 39

Churchill, Winston, *continued*
anti-Americanism of, 37, 80, 101,
105–106, 111
approves Chiefs of Staff proposal on
Pacific strategy, 263–265
Arnold on, 123
background of, 22–28
Brooke and, 17, 18, 41
Brooke on, 80, 81, 98, 99–100, 102,
103, 104–106, 108, 110, 112–113,
118, 121, 129, 316
cable to Australian and New Zealand
prime ministers, 318–319, 323, 325,
327, 333
Canada and, 138, 140
on Chiefs of Staff Committee, 41,
48–49, 110, 114, 261
compares to Duke of Marlborough, 113
Cunningham and, 28, 41, 132,
260–261
Cunningham on, 41, 71, 76, 98–99,
101, 105, 106, 108, 118, 121,
129, 130, 131–132, 307
Curtin and, 78–79
Dill and, 45–46, 115–116
dukedom declined, 363–364
Eden on, 98–99
on Fraser, Peter, 60, 195
general election of 1945 and, 263–265,
315–317
health of, 32–33, 48, 108, 110–111,
113, 131
ignores Australian demands, 349–350
on Imperial unity, 78–79, 81
Ismay on, 106, 128–130
King, William Mackenzie on, 55, 75
knighthood of, 363
Leahy on, 123
memoirs of, 361, 363
on Montgomery, 98
Mountbatten and, 280–281
Nobel Prize in Literature received,
363
on Pacific strategy, 30, 33, 34–35,
36–37, 44–49, 74, 96, 102–103,
112, 113–114, 140, 346
and Portal, 21, 40–41
postwar life of, 363–364
on Pound, 41, 132

repudiates agreement on Pacific
strategy, 112–113
reverses position on Pacific strategy at
Quebec, 117–118, 120–123
on second Quebec Conference, 117,
129, 131
Truman, first meeting with, 305–307
Truman on, 306–307
on Wilson, 262
See also under Brooke, Sir Alan;
Cunningham, Sir Andrew; Pacific
theater strategy
Clark, Ashley, 83
Clark, Mark, 308
Cleveland Plain Dealer, 244
Colvill, John, 42, 111
Combined Chiefs of Staff, 125, 151
tours battlefield at Quebec together, 130
See also Chiefs of Staff Committee;
Joint Chiefs of Staff; *and individual
members*
Cooke, Charles M., Jr., 206–207
Coox, Alvin D., 258
Corbett, Ernest, 335
Cotterill, Joseph, 326
Cranborne, Viscount (Robert Gascoyne-
Cecil), 74
Crosley, R. M., 297
Cunningham, Sir Andrew (Viscount
Cunningham), 2, 50, 53, 74, 99,
103, 104, 108, 112, 125, 193, 201,
254–255, 261, 263, 265, 304–305,
308, 318
on airpower, 20
on Anglo-American alliance, 357
on Arnold, 313
background of, 11–15
on Blamey, 73
on Brooke, 22
Brooke on, 22, 44, 80, 121
Churchill and, 28, 41, 132
on Churchill, 41, 76, 98–99, 101, 105,
106, 108, 110, 118, 129, 130,
131–132, 307
on Churchill's indecision, 71, 76, 105
on Churchill's reversal on Pacific
strategy, 121
on Curtin, 73, 74–75, 82
fishing and, 21, 130

Ugaki, Matome
    background of, 168–170
    beliefs kamikazes an effective tactic,
        180, 181, 182, 183–184, 189,
        191–192
    death of, 375
    on kamikaze attacks, 170
Uganda, HMCS, 204, 298
    crew votes to leave Pacific, 300
unconditional surrender
    Churchill recommends revision,
        305–306
    Joint Chiefs of Staff ask British Chiefs
        to recommend revision, 254–255,
        304–305
    Leahy recommends revision of, 251
U.S. Army
    First Army, 355
        2nd Armored Division, 314
        7th Infantry Division, 231–232
        77th Infantry Division, 222, 227,
            229, 231
        96th Infantry Division, 223, 231
    Fifth Army, 2, 6
        5th Artillery Command, 221
    Tenth Army, 221, 226, 232, 235,
        284
        in invasion of Japan, 355
        logistical shortages of, 226–227,
            233–234
    Twentieth Air Force, 152, 159, 166
    XX Bomber Command, 152
    XXI Bomber Command, 152, 162,
        163–164, 165–166
    XXIV Corps, 221, 223, 229, 231,
        355
    27th Infantry Division, 219
    313th Bomb Wing, 165
    314th Wing, 159
U.S. Marine Corps
    III Amphibious Corps, 221, 227,
        231–232, 241, 355
    V Amphibious Corps, 219
    1st Marine Division, 221, 229, 242
    6th Marine Division, 234
U.S. Military Academy (West Point), 270,
    272–273

U.S. Navy
    Third Fleet, 289, 292, 295–296, 301
    Fifth Fleet, 178, 292
    Seventh Fleet, 292–293
Ushijima, Mitsuru, 220
    admits error in ordering, 229
    orders offensive, 227–229
    reaction to Buckner's surrender offer, 235

Vian, Sir Philip, 203, 204, 208
    on Halsey, 295
    on kamikaze attacks, 213–214
    on Kure raid, 299
    worries about viability of BPF, 288
Victoria Cross, 302, 327

Wall Street Journal, The, 4
Walpole, Sir Robert, 374
Washington *Evening Star,* 241
Washington Post, The, 4–5
    critical of British contributions to
        Pacific, 258
Waterloo, Battle of, 170
Webb, James, 283
Wellington *Dominion,* 333
Wellington *Evening Post,* 333
Werrell, Kenneth, 159
Willoughby, Charles A., 257
Wilson (film), 120
Wilson, Sir Henry
    on American criticisms of British in
        Pacific, 258, 261
    background of, 261–262
    Churchill on, 262
    postwar life of, 368
    recommendations on British in Pacific,
        263
Wilson, Woodrow, 118, 119, 120
Winat, John, 123–124
    warns Roosevelt to include British in
        Pacific, 123–124
Wingate, Orde, 283

Yahara, Hiromichi, 229, 230, 231, 232
Yale University, 116
Yamamoto, Isoroku, 169, 175
Yokoi, Toshiyuki, 170